THE ROUTLEDGE COMPANION TO CRITICAL MARKETING

The Routledge Companion to Critical Marketing brings together the latest research in Critical Marketing Studies in one authoritative and convenient volume. The world's leading scholars and rising stars collaborate here to provide a survey of this lively subdiscipline. In doing so they demonstrate how a critical approach yields an enriched understanding of marketing theory and practice, its role in society, and its relationship with consumers themselves.

It is the first attempt to capture the state of Critical Marketing research in many years. As such, this seminal work is unmissable for scholars and students of marketing and consumer research as well as those exploring sociology, media studies, anthropology, and consumption scholarship more generally.

Mark Tadajewski is Honorary Visiting Professor of Marketing at the University of York, UK.

Matthew Higgins is a Senior Lecturer in Marketing and Consumption at the University of Leicester, UK.

Janice Denegri-Knott is Principal Academic of Interactive Marketing at Bournemouth University, UK.

Rohit Varman is Professor of Marketing at the Indian Institute of Management, India.

"This edited volume on Critical Marketing Studies is essential reading for all constituencies, including academics, marketing practitioners, consumers, and advocacy groups, that wish to fully understand the good, bad, and ugly of how exchange relationships manifest in most economies. Well-written, timely, and documented to the finest detail, the various authors put forth an excellent analysis and critique of a system that impacts all of humanity and its quality of life. Read it or face the consequences of continued ignorance!"

Ronald Paul Hill (Ph.D. in Business Administration from the University of Maryland), Visiting Professor of Marketing and holds a Dean's Excellence Faculty Fellowship at the Kogod School of Business, American University, USA

"This book offers a foundational resource for critical work in marketing that goes beyond criticism to generate compelling new ideas, productive insights, and transformational paradigms. Close attention will cause readers to rethink their fundamental understanding of marketing."

Jonathan Schroeder, William A. Kern Professor in Communications, Rochester Institute of Technology, New York, USA

"There is a great need for more Critical Marketing Studies and this book brings together a thorough review of what has been done thus far. Inspiration abounds in these chapters and they will open the imagination and conscience to new problems that cry out for critical attention."

Russell Belk, Distinguished Research Professor and Kraft Foods Canada Chair of Marketing, York University, Canada

"Drawing on their vast collective knowledge, Tadajewski, Higgins, Denegri-Knott, and Varman skilfully help students and scholars understand the importance, trajectory, and scope of Critical Marketing Studies. This is the kind of companion I wish I'd had when I began my career. I can't recommend it highly enough."

Anthony Patterson, Professor of Marketing, University of Liverpool, UK

THE ROUTLEDGE COMPANION TO CRITICAL MARKETING

Edited by Mark Tadajewski, Matthew Higgins, Janice Denegri-Knott, and Rohit Varman

Routledge
Taylor & Francis Group
LONDON AND NEW YORK

First published 2019
by Routledge
2 Park Square, Milton Park, Abingdon, Oxon OX14 4RN

and by Routledge
711 Third Avenue, New York, NY 10017

Routledge is an imprint of the Taylor & Francis Group, an informa business

© 2019 selection and editorial matter, Mark Tadajewski, Matthew Higgins, Janice Denegri-Knott, and Rohit Varman; individual chapters, the contributors

The right of Mark Tadajewski, Matthew Higgins, Janice Denegri-Knott, and Rohit Varman to be identified as the authors of the editorial material, and of the authors for their individual chapters, has been asserted in accordance with sections 77 and 78 of the Copyright, Designs and Patents Act 1988.

All rights reserved. No part of this book may be reprinted or reproduced or utilized in any form or by any electronic, mechanical, or other means, now known or hereafter invented, including photocopying and recording, or in any information storage or retrieval system, without permission in writing from the publishers.

Trademark notice: Product or corporate names may be trademarks or registered trademarks, and are used only for identification and explanation without intent to infringe.

British Library Cataloguing-in-Publication Data
A catalogue record for this book is available from the British Library

Library of Congress Cataloging-in-Publication Data
Names: Tadajewski, Mark, editor.
Title: The Routledge companion to critical marketing / edited by Mark Tadajewski [and three others].
Description: Abingdon, Oxon ; New York, NY : Routledge, 2019. | Includes bibliographical references and index.
Identifiers: LCCN 2018020828 (print) | LCCN 2018021747 (ebook) | ISBN 9781315630526 (ebook) | ISBN 9781138641402 (hardback : alk. paper)
Subjects: LCSH: Marketing.
Classification: LCC HF5415 (ebook) | LCC HF5415 .R6425 2019 (print) | DDC 658.8—dc23
LC record available at https://lccn.loc.gov/2018020828

ISBN: 978-1-138-64140-2 (hbk)
ISBN: 978-1-315-63052-6 (ebk)

Typeset in Bembo
by Swales & Willis Ltd, Exeter, Devon, UK

CONTENTS

List of illustrations	*viii*
Notes on contributors	*ix*

1	Introducing and advancing Critical Marketing Studies *Mark Tadajewski, Matthew Higgins, Janice Denegri-Knott, and Rohit Varman*	1

PART I
Exploring the terrain of Critical Marketing Studies   35

2	Postmodernism and critical marketing *Nikhilesh Dholakia and A. Fuat Fırat*	37
3	Postcolonialism, subalternity, and critical marketing *Rohit Varman*	49
4	Feminist perspectives in marketing: past, present, and future *Pauline Maclaran and Olga Kravets*	64
5	Critical social marketing: reflections, introspections, and future directions *Ross Gordon*	83
6	Critical macromarketing, sustainable marketing, and globalization *William E. Kilbourne*	98

7	Critical perspectives on place marketing *Massimo Giovanardi, Mihalis Kavaratzis, and Maria Lichrou*	115
8	Critical arts marketing *Gretchen Larsen and Finola Kerrigan*	135

PART II
Critical Marketing: marketing practices in focus — 153

9	Critical studies of marketing work *Peter Svensson*	155
10	The cultural turn in lifestyle research: overview and reflections *Gokcen Coskuner-Balli*	172
11	Advertising practice and critical marketing *Chris Hackley*	185
12	Critical reflections on the marketing concept and consumer sovereignty *Mark Tadajewski*	196
13	Service-Dominant logic: the evolution of a universal marketing rhetoric *Chris Miles*	225
14	Metaphor and Relationship Marketing discourse *Lisa O'Malley*	243
15	Critical perspectives on ethical consumption *Michal Carrington and Andreas Chatzidakis*	256
16	Religious critiques of the market *Aliakbar Jafari*	271

PART III
Rethinking consumers and markets: critiques of markets — 285

17	Re-mapping power for critical marketing and consumer research *Janice Denegri-Knott*	287
18	Ideology and Critical Marketing Studies *Giana M. Eckhardt, Rohit Varman, and Nikhilesh Dholakia*	306

19	Non-Western cultures and Critical Marketing Özlem Sandıkcı Türkdoğan	319
20	Choice and choicelessness in consumer practice Ruby Roy Dholakia, A. Fuat Fırat, and Nikhilesh Dholakia	337
21	Managing racial stigma in consumer culture David Crockett	353
22	Consumer vulnerability: critical insights from stories, action research and visual culture Susan Dunnett, Kathy Hamilton, and Maria Piacentini	366
23	The embodied consumer Maurice Patterson	383

PART IV
Critical marketing: marketing practices in focus — 401

24	Critical perspectives on brand management Adam Arvidsson and Alex Giordano	403
25	Gender, marketing, and emotions: a critical, feminist exploration of the ideological helix that defines our working worlds Lorna Stevens	415
26	Biopolitical marketing and the commodification of social contexts Detlev Zwick and Alan Bradshaw	430
27	Exploitation and emancipation Bernard Cova and Bernard Paranque	439
28	Political economy approaches to transnational commodity markets: an application to the case of the global palm oil market Martin Fougère	453
29	Social media, big data, and critical marketing Christian Fuchs	467
30	Marketing and the production of consumers' objective violence Eduardo André Teixeira Ayrosa and Renata Couto de Azevedo de Oliveira	482

Index — *500*

ILLUSTRATIONS

Figures

17.1	Conceptual map of power	289
30.1	Improvised memorial to violence victims in Lagoa Rodrigo de Freitas, Rio de Janeiro	483

Tables

2.1	The binaries of modernity	39
2.2	The discursive domains of modernity	40
2.3	The practical domains of modernity	41
2.4	Concepts of transforming modernity that surround postmodernity	42
4.1	Types of feminism and their key emphases	65
10.1	Cultural research programs on lifestyle	176
15.1	Logics of growth in consumption	261
20.1	Ontological positions on choice	347
20.2	Ideological stances on choice	347
29.1	The matrix of digital alienation	478

CONTRIBUTORS

Adam Arvidsson is Professor of Sociology at the University of Naples, Federico II. In the past he has written on brands and the history of consumer culture. His present research looks at the economic sociology of the digital society, investigating emerging economic institutions and forms of organization. He is the author of *The Ethical Economy* (Columbia University Press, 2013, with Nicolai Peitersen) and *Brands, Meaning and Value in Media Culture* published by Routledge in 2006. Email: adamerik.arvidsson@unina.it

Eduardo André Teixeira Ayrosa is Professor of Consumer Studies, Qualitative Research Methods and Epistemology at the Universidade do Grande Rio (UNIGRANRIO). He is interested in the impact(s) of consumer culture on societies and subjectivities in consumer cultures. He is currently working on the interplay between violence and consumption; the impact of violent discursive objects on voting behavior; and mediation of religious beliefs in consumer narratives and practices. Email: eayrosa@gmail.com

Alan Bradshaw teaches and learns at Royal Holloway, University of London. Email: alan.bradshaw@rhul.ac.uk

Michal Carrington is Senior Lecturer in Marketing at the University of Melbourne, Australia. She teaches and researches in the areas of consumption and marketing ethics, retail, consumer culture, consumer and marketer behavior. Her research has appeared in a range of international journals such as the *European Journal of Marketing*, *Marketing Theory*, *Journal of Business Ethics*, *Journal of Business Research* and *Higher Education Research and Development*. Michal has recently published a co-edited multidisciplinary book with Deirdre Shaw and Andreas Chatzidakis titled *Ethics in Consumption: Interdisciplinary Perspectives*. Michal holds a BEng in Mechanical Engineering from the University of Melbourne and a Ph.D. also from the University of Melbourne. Prior to entering academia, Michal spent almost a decade working for Unilever in Australia and the UK. Email: michal.carrington@unimelb.edu.au

Andreas Chatzidakis is Senior Lecturer in Marketing at the School of Management, Royal Holloway, University of London. He received his Ph.D. from Nottingham Business School in 2007, focusing on consumer accounts and justifications for not supporting the Fair Trade movement. Since then he has been more broadly interested in the intersection of consumption with ethics and politics, working on projects such as consumer-oriented activism in post-2008 Athens, and the role of care and relationality in everyday consumption. His work also explores identity-based and spatial politics in contemporary consumer culture, drawing on disciplines such as human geography and psychoanalysis. He is co-editor of *Marketing Theory*, senior editor of *CITY*, and member of the editorial boards of *Journal of Macromarketing* and the newly formed *Journal of Consumer Ethics*. Email: Andreas.Chatzidakis@rhul.ac.uk

Gokcen Coskuner-Balli is an Associate Professor of Marketing at Argyros School of Business and Economics, Chapman University. Her research explores the cultural and political shaping of consumer–market interactions and offers theorizations for the politics of consumption, institutional legitimacy, market creation, and evolution. Her work has been published in the *Journal of Marketing, Journal of Consumer Research, Marketing Theory, Journal of Consumer Culture,* and *Journal of Consumer Behaviour*. Email: balli@chapman.edu

Bernard Cova is Professor of Marketing at Kedge Business School. He acts as Visiting Professor at Bocconi University, Milan. A pioneer in the Consumer Tribes field since the early 1990s, his work on this topic has been published – among others – in the *Journal of Consumer Research*, the *European Journal of Marketing*, the *Journal of Business Ethics, Marketing Theory,* and *Organization*. Email: bernard.cova@kedgebs.com

David Crockett is Associate Professor of Marketing at the Moore School of Business, University of South Carolina. His primary research interests are in the sociological aspects of consumer behavior and marketing. His research investigates social inequality in the marketplace and addresses public policy and social movement initiatives designed to alleviate it. It has appeared in leading marketing journals including the *Journal of Consumer Research*, the *Journal of Public Policy & Marketing*, and *Consumption, Markets & Culture*, as well as journals in sociology and public health. Email: dcrockett17@gmail.com

Janice Denegri-Knott is Director of the Promotional Cultures and Communication Centre at Bournemouth University's Faculty of Media and Communication. She specializes in the study of digital consumption and critical marketing. Her research interests span conceptualizing and documenting digital virtual consumption and its practices, the emergence of media technology, the socio-historic patterning of consumption, and, more generally, the subject of power in consumer and marketing research. She is also associate editor for *Marketing Theory* and co-editor of the *Journal of Promotional Communications*. Email: jdknott@bournemouth.ac.uk

Nikhilesh Dholakia is Professor Emeritus, University of Rhode Island (URI), and founding co-editor of *Markets, Globalization & Development Review*, the interdisciplinary journal of the International Society of Markets & Development. His research deals with globalization, technology, innovation, market processes, and consumer culture. His current work focuses on the critical examination of global and post-global aspects of new technologies such as robotics, artificial intelligence, autonomous vehicles, and extra-terrestrial venturing. Email: nikdholakia@gmail.com

Ruby Roy Dholakia is a Professor at the University of Rhode Island. Email: rrdholakia@uri.edu

Notes on contributors

Susan Dunnett is a Senior Lecturer in Marketing at the University of Edinburgh Business School. Her research is focused on consumer vulnerability and coping, consumer identity, collective practices, and interpretivist research methods. She has a longstanding interest in the experience of illness and the consumption of healthcare and her current work explores healthcare consumerism and obesity stigma. Susan was Principle-Investigator for an ESRC Seminar Series focusing on Vulnerable Consumers, with Dr Kathy Hamilton, University of Strathclyde and Dr Maria Piacentini, University of Lancaster, 2012–2015. Her work can be read in *Advances in Consumer Research*, *Journal of Consumer Behaviour*, *Journal of Marketing Management*, and *Journal of Public Policy and Marketing*. She is also co-editor of the book *Consumer Vulnerability: Conditions, Contexts and Characteristics* (2015), part of the Routledge Studies in Critical Marketing series. Email: susan.dunnett@ed.ac.uk

Giana M. Eckhardt is Professor of Marketing and Director of the Centre for Research in Sustainability at Royal Holloway, University of London. Her research is located in the field of Consumer Culture Theory, and currently focuses on the sharing economy, liquid consumption, consumer deceleration, and global branding. Giana is an author of *The Myth of the Ethical Consumer*, and an editor of the forthcoming *Handbook of the Sharing Economy*. Email: Giana.Eckhardt@rhul.ac.uk

Martin Fougère is Associate Professor in Management and Politics at the Hanken School of Economics, Helsinki, Finland. His research interests include business and society, corporate responsibility, critical management education, critical marketing, discourse theory, governmentality, political economy, and postcolonialism. His works have been published in numerous international journals, including the *Journal of Business Ethics*, *Journal of Macromarketing*, *Management Learning*, and *Organization*. Focusing specifically on Critical Marketing, his main contribution to date has been the book, *Marketing Discourse: A Critical Perspective*, co-authored with Per Skålén and Markus Fellesson. Email: martin.fougere@hanken.fi

A. Fuat Fırat is Professor of Marketing at the University of Texas Rio Grande Valley. Email: fuat.firat@utrgv.edu

Christian Fuchs is a Professor at the University of Westminster. His field of research is the critical theory and political economy of communication and digital media. He is co-editor of the journal *tripleC: Communication, Capitalism & Critique*: www.triple-c.at. Email: c.fuchs@westminster.ac.uk

Alex Giordano teaches Marketing, Communication and Advertising at the Social Sciences Department of University of Naples, Federico II. A pioneer of digital culture and the anthropology of innovation, he is considered among the leading experts on social innovation, the sharing economy, and social and technological innovation as applied to food and agriculture. He was the founder of Ninjamarketing.it, a digital strategist consultant for several Italian companies, and a member of the International Academy of Arts and Science of New York. As Professor of Social Innovation and Network Society at the IULM in Milan and also at the Federico II Social Sciences Department of the University of Naples, he studies the issue of complexity applied to the relationship between the infosphere and local communities by dealing with the issues of cultural interaction (small communities/migrants), inter-generational relations (young/old), and the relationships between centers and peripheries. Email: alex@etnografiadigitale.it

Massimo Giovanardi, who joined the School of Business at the University of Leicester in 2014 as a lecturer in Marketing, has developed a thorough expertise in the area of "place branding", which is an umbrella term for research in place marketing, destination image, and place-of-origin effect(s). He has been involved in advanced training programs targeting emerging countries (among others too numerous to name). In addition, Massimo also worked as Public Relations Account Executive for local administrations and organized special stakeholder engagement events, such as the recent workshop, "Let's Go to Town", delivered in collaboration with Historic England and the Municipality of Leicester. Email: m.giovanardi@leicester.ac.uk

Ross Gordon is an Associate Professor at Macquarie University in Sydney. He is also President of the Australian Association of Social Marketing (AASM). Ross is a social change activist. His work focuses on social issues and social change, through a critical, reflexive, and multi-perspective lens. His discipline expertise lies in social marketing, consumer cultures, and critical marketing teaching and research. He works across various social change topic areas including energy efficiency, environmental sustainability, alcohol and alcohol marketing, gambling, tobacco control, mental health, and workplace bullying. He is also interested in critiques of neoliberalism and related social activism. Email: ross.gordon@mq.edu.au

Chris Hackley is Professor of Marketing at Royal Holloway University of London. His research interests include advertising and the agency system, marketing, consumer policy, and interpretive research methods. Recent projects have revolved around theorizing the new advertising environment under media convergence. The fourth edition of his text, *Advertising and Promotion*, jointly authored with A.R. Hackley, was published in 2018 by Sage, and a new edition of his qualitative methods text, *Doing Research Projects in Marketing, Management and Consumer Research* is in preparation with Routledge for 2019. Email: Chris.Hackley@rhul.ac.uk

Kathy Hamilton is a Reader in the Department of Marketing, University of Strathclyde, UK. Key research projects have focused on consumer vulnerability, poverty, and the role of community in contemporary culture. Kathy is interested in interdisciplinary research and her work has been published in a variety of journals including the *Annals of Tourism Research*, *Journal of Marketing Management*, *Sociology*, *European Journal of Marketing*, *Marketing Theory*, *Journal of Macromarketing*, *Journal of Consumer Behaviour*, and *International Journal of Sociology and Social Policy*. Kathy was co-editor of *Consumer Vulnerability: Conditions, Contexts and Characteristics*, published as part of the Routledge Studies in Critical Marketing series and was co-chair of an ESRC seminar series on Vulnerable Consumers. Email: kathy.hamilton@strath.ac.uk

Matthew Higgins has spent over 19 years at the University of Leicester trying to promote an approach to the study of marketing that incorporates the imagination of social theory. He has previously co-edited *Marketing: A Critical Textbook* (2010, SAGE) and *Science Fiction and Organization* (2001, Routledge).

Aliakbar Jafari is a Reader in Marketing at the University of Strathclyde Business School. His research focuses on consumer culture, market dynamics, multiculturalism, politics and policies of consumption, and the intersections of religion and the market. He sits on the editorial board of several journals including *Journal of Marketing Management*, *Marketing Theory*, and *Iranian Journal of Management Studies*. He also sits on the editorial review board of *Consumption, Markets & Culture* and the senior editorial advisory board of *Journal of Islamic Marketing*. He has co-edited

Islam, Marketing and Consumption: Critical Perspectives on the Intersections (Routledge, 2016) and the four-volume set of *New Directions in Consumer Research* (Sage, 2015). He has received the Consumer Culture Theory Conference's 2016 Best Special Session Award, Emerald's 2015 Citation of Excellence Award for his single-authored journal article "Islamic Marketing: Insights from a Critical Perspective", and Consumption, Markets & Culture's 2014 Honourable Mention Award for his co-authored journal article "Globalization, Reflexivity and the Project of the Self: A Virtual Intercultural Learning Process". Email: aliakbar.jafari@strath.ac.uk

Mihalis Kavaratzis is Associate Professor of Marketing at the University of Leicester School of Business. His research focuses on place branding and tourism destination marketing. Mihalis is Founding Board Member of the International Place Branding Association and a Senior Fellow of the Institute of Place Management. He has published extensively in various academic journals and he is co-editor of *Inclusive Place Branding* (with M. Giovanardi and M. Lichrou, 2017), *Rethinking Place Branding* (with G. Warnaby and G.J. Ashworth, 2015), and *Towards Effective Place Brand Management* (with G.J. Ashworth, 2010). Email: mk302@leicester.ac.uk

Finola Kerrigan is a Reader in Marketing and Consumption at Birmingham Business School, University of Birmingham. Finola researches marketing and consumption in the arts with a particular focus on branding, marketing through the arts, and issues of representation. She has edited a number of books on arts marketing and is the author of *Film Marketing* (2010/2017). Finola is a Fellow of the Royal Society of the Arts, President of the International Society of Markets and Development, and Secretary of the Academy of Marketing. Email: F.Kerrigan@bham.ac.uk

William E. Kilbourne, Ph.D., received his degree from the University of Houston in 1973. He is a Professor Emeritus of Marketing at Clemson University, and his research interests are in materialism, globalization, inequality, and environmental issues in marketing. Most recently, his attention has been directed to developing, both theoretically and empirically, the role of a society's Dominant Social Paradigm in environmentally relevant consumption behavior and in materialistic values. The research agenda entails the cross-cultural comparison of both environmental and materialistic values. Email: kilbour@clemson.edu

Olga Kravets is a Senior Lecturer at Royal Holloway University of London. She holds a Ph.D. in Economics from the University of Sydney, Australia. Her research interests lie with the historical, socio-cultural, and political aspects of consumer culture and markets. Her previous research examined classed consumption, materialities of marketing, and the intersection thereof with politics and state ideologies, and has been published in the *Journal of Marketing, Journal of Macromarketing, Journal of Marketing Management, Ephemera, Journal of Material Culture, Business History Review* as well as within edited books. She has recently co-edited *The SAGE Handbook of Consumer Culture*. Email: Olga.Kravets@rhul.ac.uk

Gretchen Larsen is an Associate Professor of Marketing at Durham University. Gretchen's research is located within interpretive and critical consumer research, at the intersection of consumption, markets, and the arts. She examines the importance of the arts, particularly sound and music, in helping consumers experience and make sense of their world. Gretchen's research focuses specifically on how the position of the consumer in a socio-cultural world is constructed, performed, interpreted, questioned, and experienced through, and in relation to the arts. Email: gretchen.larsen@durham.ac.uk

Maria Lichrou is a Lecturer in Marketing at the University of Limerick. At present, she is a Visiting Researcher at the University of Brighton. Her research focuses predominantly on narratives of place and generally speaks to an emic perspective in understanding the connections between place, tourism, and consumption. Her work on place has appeared in the *Journal of Strategic Marketing, Journal of Marketing Management, Place Branding and Public Diplomacy, Tourism and Hospitality Planning & Development*, and *Journal of Place Management and Development*, and she is co-editor of *Inclusive Place Branding* (with M. Kavaratzis and M. Giovanardi, 2017). Email: Maria.Lichrou@ul.ie

Pauline Maclaran is Professor of Marketing and Consumer Research at Royal Holloway, University of London. Her research interests focus on cultural aspects of contemporary consumption, and she adopts a critical perspective to analyze the ideological assumptions that underpin many marketing activities, particularly in relation to gender issues. She is a co-editor in chief of *Marketing Theory*, a journal welcoming alternative and critical perspectives in marketing and consumer research. Email: Pauline.MacLaran@rhul.ac.uk

Chris Miles is Senior Lecturer in Marketing and Communication in the Department of Corporate and Marketing Communication, Bournemouth University, where he teaches creative and persuasive strategies for marketing communications. His research deals with the discursive construction of marketing theory and practice, particularly as it relates to communication and control. His current book, *Marketing, Rhetoric, and Control: The Magical Foundations of Marketing Theory*, is published by Routledge. Email: cjmiles@bournemouth.ac.uk

Renata Couto de Azevedo de Oliveira is a Ph.D. student at the Universidade do Grande Rio (UNIGRANRIO). She is currently investigating how the consumer society and its practices normalize objective violence, with an emphasis on dehumanization and the forgetfulness of Others. Her key research interests are the dehumanizing practices perpetrated by marketing tenets; psychoanalytic perspective of consumer practices and beliefs; and embodied consumption, especially the relationship between body modifications, fashion, body/skin, and identity. Email: renata.boop@gmail.com

Lisa O'Malley is a Critical Marketing scholar who has been interrogating relational perspectives in marketing for over 20 years. Her work has evaluated the utility of underpinning theories, myths and metaphors in Relationship Marketing and has critiqued applications of RM (and CRM) to consumer marketing contexts. Recent work has considered the impact of marketing relationships on the co-creation of value. Professor O'Malley has published in *Marketing Theory, European Journal of Marketing, Journal of Business Research, Industrial Marketing Management, Consumption, Markets & Culture, Journal of Macromarketing*, and the *Journal of Marketing Management*. Email: Lisa.OMalley@ul.ie

Bernard Paranque is Professor of Finance at KEDGE Business School. His research focuses on finance and employee ownership organization. He has been published in *Organization, Research in International Business and Finance, International Review of Financial Analysis*, and the *Revue des Organisations Responsables*. His most recent book, *Finance Reconsidered New Perspectives for a Responsible and Sustainable Finance*, was co-edited with Pr. Roland Pérez. Email: bernard.paranque@kedgebs.com

Notes on contributors

Maurice Patterson is an interpretive consumer researcher at the University of Limerick. Maurice's key research interest centers on the relationship between consumption, embodiment, and identity, and his work uncovers the connections between body-related consumption, individual identity projects, and marketplace cultures. This research acknowledges how cultural capital endowments systematically structure consumer preferences and thwart explicit social mobility goals. Maurice's other work addresses the representation of gendered bodies in advertising, the affective potential of bodies, and, more recently, embodied responses to sonic phenomena. Email: ei.lu@nosrettap.eciruam

Maria Piacentini is Professor of Consumer Research at Lancaster University Management School and Director of the Centre for Consumption Insights. Her research focuses on consumer vulnerability, and she has explored this theme in a number of contexts of public policy concern, with a focus on the strategies employed by consumers in difficult consumption contexts and situations. Her work has been published in *Sociology of Health & Illness, Journal of Business Research, Journal of Marketing Management* and *Marketing Theory*. Maria was co-editor of *Consumer Vulnerability: Conditions, Contexts and Characteristics*, published as part of the Routledge Studies in Critical Marketing series. Maria was a co-chair of the ESRC seminar series on Vulnerable Consumers, and she also co-chaired the TCR track on Consumer Vulnerability in 2013. Email: m.piacentini@lancaster.ac.uk

Lorna Stevens is an Associate Professor of Marketing in the School of Management at the University of Bath. Her primary research interests are in consumer culture, experiential consumption and media consumption. Her work is interpretive and critical, often drawing on feminist perspectives to explore gender issues and underpinning ideological assumptions in the marketplace. Email: l.m.r.stevens@bath.ac.uk

Peter Svensson is Associate Professor at the Department of Business Administration at the School of Economics and Management, Lund University, Sweden. His research interests include discourse analytical and rhetorical approaches to organizational and business life, the development of qualitative methods, and critical social theory and its relevance for marketing and management studies. He serves on the editorial board of *Marketing Theory* and as associate editor on *Qualitative Research in Organization and Management*. Email: peter.svensson@fek.lu.se

Mark Tadajewski is the editor of the *Journal of Marketing Management* and two book series for Routledge. Currently he is Visiting Professor of Marketing at the University of York, UK. He has also written and edited numerous books along with a substantial number of path-breaking articles. He is widely known for his work on critical marketing and the development of marketing theory. Email: marktadajewski@gmail.com

Özlem Sandıkcı Türkdoğan is a Professor of Marketing at the Adam Smith Business School, University of Glasgow, UK and the School of Management and Administrative Sciences, Istanbul Şehir University, Turkey. Her research addresses socio-cultural dimensions of consumption and focuses on the relationship between globalization, marketing, and culture. Her work has been published in the *Journal of Marketing, Journal of Consumer Research, Journal of Business Research, Marketing Theory, Business History Review*, and *Fashion Theory*, along with several other journals and edited collections. She is the co-editor of the *Handbook of Islamic*

Marketing (Edward Elgar, 2011) and *Islam, Marketing and Consumption: Critical Perspectives on the Intersections* (Routledge, 2016). Email: sandikci@gmail.com

Rohit Varman is Professor of Marketing at the Indian Institute of Management, Calcutta. His research interests are broadly in the fields of Critical Marketing and Consumer Culture. He uses interpretive methodologies and his current research focuses on corporate violence, marketization, modern slavery, and structures of subalternity. He has recently co-edited (with Devi Vijay) the book *Alternative Organizations in India: Undoing Boundaries* (Cambridge University Press, 2017) and is currently working on another book that examines sites of resistance to neoliberal capitalism in India. Email: rohit.varman@gmail.com

Detlev Zwick is an Associate Professor of Marketing and Faculty in the Graduate Program in Communication & Culture at York University, Toronto. His research explores how ideology functions in marketing practice. His works have been published widely in marketing, communication, media culture, and sociology journals, as well as in several edited collections. Email: dzwick@schulich.yorku.ca

1
INTRODUCING AND ADVANCING CRITICAL MARKETING STUDIES

Mark Tadajewski, Matthew Higgins, Janice Denegri-Knott, and Rohit Varman

Introduction

In this chapter we aim to accomplish a number of objectives. We will weave a history of marketing theory and practice that permits us to juxtapose the views of mainstream and Critical Marketing scholarship. In doing so, we will contribute to existing genealogical accounts of the development of critical perspectives in marketing (e.g. Tadajewski, 2010b), but without traversing exactly the same terrain. Nor will we recount the various pedagogic methods through which Critical Marketing can be incorporated into the curriculum as this has been undertaken elsewhere (Tadajewski, 2016a). Instead, this historical introduction will enable us to unpack core assumptions underwriting Critical Marketing Studies including ontological denaturalization, defatalization, epistemological reflexivity, conflict and critical performativity.

The difference between the current chapter and previous historically oriented accounts is that we explicate the above concepts using a different range of authors to those normally consulted in depth. This thereby extends existing debates in Critical Marketing Studies, hopefully adding value for the audience of this book. Since a great deal of this material will be new to many readers, we will strive to be as clear as possible and provide as many direct quotes of long out of print texts as is appropriate. Following this, we will introduce each chapter in this volume.

A history of marketing

To begin with, marketing as a practice has a long history, and can be traced back to ancient times. It has been discussed in various ways, but prior to the emergence of institutionalized definitions of the subject, basically referred to the processes involved in selling and buying. Subsequent definitions promoted by the American Marketing Association throughout the twentieth and twenty-first centuries have built upon this edifice. Initially, the definitions were more macro-focused. They talked about flows within the market, rather than specific interest groups.

Harry Tosdal, most prominently, started using the terms marketing management and related language in the 1920s. By 1927, Percival White was penning one of the most explicitly managerial texts of the time, making a case that business people should – as Adam Smith, Daniel Defoe and numerous others had already registered – start with the consumer and work backwards. It was not a matter of producing what industry wanted to produce, but about understanding and delivering what the consumer desired. This, as most students of marketing know, is the marketing concept. It is the axis around which the discipline turns and the viewing glass that we are encouraged to use when thinking about the marketplace.

Clearly, there is much value in pursuing such a strategy, but there are other approaches depending on the nature of the market, the competition being faced, and the power relations embedded therein. So, it only represents a partial account of the role of marketing in society. It is a theory – a story – that effectively helps marketing shed any connotations of manipulation.

Ask most people what image the practice of marketing conjures up in their minds and it will not be very positive. The image of the pushy salesman, forcing unwanted goods and services on to an unwitting customer, is probably going to figure prominently in their collective consciousness. Levitt (1960), of course, sought to cleave a distinction between marketing and sales that reflects, in reality, a succinct summary of the ideas presented above. Marketing, he maintained, was not simply about pushing products on to consumers. It was about meeting specific needs. Levitt's ideas, while important for the continued legitimation of the subject, are a simplification. Simplification is necessary in the classroom. It is handy for practitioners in the boardroom when they require soundbites to justify their role and accumulate political power. But it easily shades into misrepresentation.

Fred Borch (1958), a practitioner working and writing around the same time as Levitt, presents arguably a more accurate picture of the nature of marketing. This is something Chapter 12 – by Mark Tadajewski – explores in some depth. Suffice to say, Borch argued that good marketers do not simply listen to their customers and produce what they want and stop there. They listen and then they communicate. They engage in the marketing concept and the much derided sales concept (i.e. trying to stimulate demand via effective marketing communications). But, this active selling element tends to be underplayed. It is too easily associated with the idea of "hidden persuaders" (Packard, 1960) plumbing the depths of our minds to identify weaknesses that can be mobilized in the service of organizational objectives such as profit.

What we must always bear in mind when consulting any academic literature is that there is a great deal of self-legitimation and self-justification going on. This has been necessary at various points in the history of the marketing discipline, most notably during the 1960s when students were starting to look at marketing askance, perceiving it to be a conduit through which the status quo was reaffirmed. Within that context, legitimation was undertaken via the "broadening" movement. This involved the promotion of the utility of marketing for organizations and groups outside of the for-profit realm (e.g. charities) (Hackley, 2001). To say the least, this has been well received by academics who are able to point to it as a way of underlining their positive contribution to wider society.

Within most schools of business, critical accounts are given limited, if any, attention. Marketing education more often reflects the balance of focus found in Wilkie and Moore's (1999) celebration of marketing's contribution to society. This long paper devotes considerable – and somewhat justifiable attention – to the positive contributions the discipline and practice has made in this world. Tacked right on to the end of the paper and given very short shrift is a limited discussion of the criticisms it has faced. Although we believe that marketing does have much to contribute to society, as scholars and lecturers we have an ethical responsibility to present an accurate, more balanced picture of the discipline, its core assumptions, and effects across the world. This is what Critical Marketing aims to accomplish. Certainly, we must be wary of assuming that the way resources are allocated at present is necessarily the most appropriate for the population of the world as a whole.

For example, there has been a long history of criticism associated with the cost of advertising, its utility, necessity and whether there are more useful ways of spending the huge sums allocated for marketing communications. To start to foster the kind of critical reflexivity (i.e. thinking about our role in the world and how it, in turn, influences us) that is part and parcel of Critical Marketing, the following quotation should encourage us all to question whether the economy should be modified:

> The sophistication and subtlety, complex and clever symbolism, needed to convince a consumer that a tub of vegetable fat can give us something special, is a truly difficult task. Hundreds of thousands of individuals must devote their lives to helping corporations manipulate people into buying more margarine or a pair of sneakers at the expense of another corporation selling an almost identical item . . . As Held . . . has calculated, humanity could have used 1 year [of] global advertising revenue to completely eliminate hunger and malnutrition, provided reproductive health care for all women, distributed clean drinking water to all people, achieved universal literacy, doubled the budget of the United Nations, and immunized every child – *twelve times over.*
>
> Scarpaci, Sovacool & Ballantyne, 2016, p. 128; emphasis in original

You do not see commentary like that in marketing textbooks. So, to set the scene for what follows, a brief definition is in order. Now, a note of caution, a definition by definition effectively closes down debate, and that is not what we want to encourage. The chapters that follow are introductions to various topics and they are not the final word on the matter they discuss. Only those with a profound sense of egotism would assume otherwise. Critical Marketing,[1] then, "is concerned with challenging marketing concepts, ideas and ways of reflection that present themselves as ideologically neutral or that otherwise have assumed a taken-for-granted status" (Tadajewski, 2011, p. 83).

Now, despite the fact that the critique we have in mind is largely absent from much conventional marketing education, there is a large literature that engages in some element of critical reflection on marketing. What is different about the type of critique we are talking about here is that the material we, and our colleagues in this collection explore, usually draws upon some form of critical social theory. This could include the writings associated with the Frankfurt School, Pierre Bourdieu, Frantz Fanon, bell hooks or Michel Foucault among many others (Tadajewski, 2010b).

Critical reflection upon marketing is not a new practice nor has it been restricted to the publications of marketing academics (Caplovitz, 1967; Huxley, 1932/2007, 1958/2004; Klein, 2005; Lasn, 1999; Packard, 1960). We need to widen our perspective considerably if we are to make sense of the types of critiques that marketing has faced. As such, we begin with material that has taken a critical look at marketing, yet without engaging with the critical social theory characteristic of Critical Marketing Studies. The mists of time await.

Roman and medieval reflections

As Dixon (2008) has revealed, marketing has received both praise and criticism since ancient times. This continues to the present day. The role of an individual in facilitating the exchange process – that is, marketing – was heralded as a positive contribution by Plato. It was an essential part of what Adam Smith later called the division of labor, that is, where people with specific skills or attributes undertake certain types of work because they are the most efficient and effective at it. Aristotle, likewise, echoed these views.

At various junctures, notably in Roman times (from the classical era to the middle ages), but particularly in the medieval period – around the fifth to fifteenth centuries – selling practices tended to attract more mixed attention. Some writers bemoaned the practices as failing to add value; for them it appeared that the marketer was more parasitic upon society than a contributor to social welfare. In contemporary language, it was sometimes considered similar to a zero sum game. In other words, for one individual to make a profit, someone else had to take a loss. There was no mutual benefit. There was always a loser in an exchange situation.

Other thinkers – specifically Herodotus and Cicero – disdained certain facets of manual labor and particular forms of mercantile activities (particularly small-scale selling). These types of arguments were often linked to more focused criticisms about the effects that selling was having within cities and towns (i.e. merchants crowding streets with seating and their wares). Moreover, there were concerns about traders who sought to take advantage of their customer base by misrepresenting their products. They tried to do so by hiding in darker parts of the marketplace so that product adulteration, faults and outright misrepresentation were more difficult to discern. For example, Plato, along with Aristotle and various biblical sources, were all scathing about attempts to manipulate the purchaser through the use of deliberately modified weighing scales. Legislation was invoked or demanded to prevent such activities (Dixon, 2008).

Typically, however, the person occupied in selling was viewed in a largely positive light. They accepted risk in travelling to foreign locations, selecting merchandise that might or might not sell, that might perish on the return journey, and incurred considerable cost in transportation to the location that had the best remunerative possibilities. The profit that they made on these items was considered their salary (Dixon, 2008). In a refrain that sounds remarkably contemporary, Plato concluded that people try to be honest. But, we are all human, and temptation is never far away. This was especially problematic within the marketplace. It presented frequent opportunities to encourage even the most virtuous to stray from the path of "moderation"; to try to make as much money as they could. As these early scholars realized, the profit motive exerts a considerable pull for some, and it has led to much reflection on how the economic and social system could be rethought and reoriented, most notably in the late nineteenth, early twentieth centuries.

Nineteenth century: Edward Bellamy

There have been numerous writers who have offered critical commentary on marketing in some respect. Many of them have received little attention thus far, so we will pause to introduce a number that do not figure prominently in the chapters in this volume or feature elsewhere in any significant detail.[2] Generally speaking, we can differentiate the literature we explore below into two strands. There might be a utopian aspect to these writings in that they seek to envision another world; alternatively, they represent subversive commentaries on changing consumption patterns and the industrial control of production, prices and consumption. Edward Bellamy (1888/1996), for instance, famously writes about the travails of Julian West in his book *Looking Backward*, his sketch of a utopia.[3] A subscription to socialism underwrites the two books by Edward Bellamy that we will review.

Socialism entailed a belief that society should rest on egalitarian foundations. There should be no single privileged class taking advantage of other groups. This differentiated it from capitalism, where the ownership of production rested in the hands of a limited number of people who received the majority of the wealth derived from production and consumption. As Veblen (1923/2009) famously unpacked, this capitalistic group were often "absentee owners", that is, the people who owned a corporation or company frequently did little or none of the actual labor involved in the creation of value, while profiting immensely from it.

Socialism wanted to expand the ownership of industry to encompass the whole of society. It differs slightly from communism in this respect. Social change was likely to be a slower process under socialism than communism (Newman, 2005). Where these views of society align is that industry would be collectively owned and all would benefit from it (with certain provisos). Cooperation rather than competitive, capitalist individualism was to be the order of the day. As part of this social change agenda, the gender stratification of capitalism was to be abolished. Men and women would occupy equal status, with social solidarity functioning as a guiding principle.

In Bellamy's (1888/1996) *Looking Backward*, the central character, Julian West, was the beneficiary of the largesse of capitalism and the wealth accumulated by ancestors. His life was easy, carefree and on a positive trajectory. But he suffered from insomnia and sought treatment for his condition. It was a little too effective. Going to sleep in 1887, he awakes in September 2000 to find the world completely transformed. The political and business landscape was redefined. Corporations no longer controlled the production process; people did not have to work for these "soulless machines". They labored for the government, with all members of the active work force receiving the same wage, albeit with hours of work modified according to the nature of the labor (i.e. less pleasant jobs have to be performed for fewer hours per day).

In this new environment, advertising has disappeared. There are no signs blighting the cities and we are far removed from any presence of a sales orientation (i.e. high-pressure selling – something that John Wanamaker famously remarked was a feature of the retailing environment that he hated as a youth in the nineteenth century). As a replacement, the government provides cards with full and complete product information to guide consumer decision-making. Upon entering retailing emporiums, people are able to examine a sample item, with store workers only present to take the relevant order: "What a prodigious amount of lying that simple arrangement saves!" Julian opines (Bellamy, 1888/1996, p. 50). Orders are sent via pneumatic tubes to a central warehouse which distributes the product quickly and efficiently to the individual's home. We can read this as a pre-emptive response to emerging debates about the costs of marketing and sales that were beginning to take hold just after the period Bellamy was writing his best-selling classic (it sold hundreds of thousands of copies very quickly according to Morgan (1944)).

Throughout his book, Bellamy offers a critical perspective on his own economic, political and social climate, and outlines how his utopia would result in less crime, poverty, the elimination of competitive individualism, greater levels of efficiency in terms of product and service selection, and real distributive justice (i.e. with equal incomes they have access to whatever goods they desire; envy is also concomitantly undermined). His ideas were explosive, influencing public consciousness. His writing, in fact, stimulated the growth of Nationalist Clubs circa 1888 (Morgan, 1944). Basically, these were groups seeking to forward the socialist agenda being articulated in *Looking Backward* and various other sources. They grew numerically very quickly and disappeared from the scene equally so (Bellamy provided considerable funds for their support, but with the decline of his bank balance and health, the Clubs suffered from his enforced departure from social life).

A number of years later, Bellamy (1897) theoretically fleshed out his ideas in sophisticated economic terms in another fictional narrative that builds upon *Looking Backward* (i.e. it is presented as contextually based in the year 2000). This book is entitled *Equality*. In it, we receive greater discussion about the nature of the capitalist system, the market and its asymmetries, along with an explication of the wastes accompanying consumption. He describes in detail the economic and social revolution that Julian West had missed – literally by a few years – as a result of his mesmeric slumber. The revolution jettisoned an economic system based on private ownership, possessive individualism and the pursuit of wealth, replacing it with one defined by governmental management of the publicly owned means of production. It was a slow-burning revolution. It began incoherently.

West's interlocutor, Dr. Leete (a major figure in the earlier novel as well), explains that the type of system they were living in could be genealogically traced to Plato. As the working classes were exploited, they also became disgruntled. First in Europe, later in America where standards of living were higher and thereby diffused social tension for some time (until the 1940s). However, by the 1980s, the economic and political landscape was starting to be redrawn:

> It was not till the close of the eighties that the total and ridiculous failure of twenty years of desperate efforts to reform the abuses of private capitalism had prepared the American people to give serious attention to the idea of dispensing with capitalism altogether by a public organization of industry to be administered like other common affairs in the common interest.
>
> Bellamy, 1897, p. 332

Bellamy's discussion of the market prior to the revolution is telling. It resonates with much contemporary Critical Marketing scholarship – especially with Fuat Fırat's work (see Fırat, 2018; Tadajewski, 2010b), Ruby Roy and Nik Dholakia's reflections on choicelessness (Chapter 20, this volume), as well as that dealing with vulnerable consumers. Since Bellamy's book will have been read by few marketing academics, an extended quotation is in order given its connection to a key concept and the idea of consumer sovereignty:

> The market was the number of those who had money to buy with. Those who had no money were non-existent so far as the market was concerned, and in proportion as people had little money they were a small part of the market. The needs of the market were the needs of those who had money to supply their needs with. The rest, who had needs in plenty but no money, were not counted.
>
> Bellamy, 1897, p. 168

By contrast, "general welfare" is a focus for Bellamy, with "economic equality" being hailed as highly desirable. This is essential as he sees the working class being exploited under capitalism and let down by the education system (i.e. their thinking patterns are structured by the "learned and professional classes"). In fact, his empirical experience during a trip to Europe in 1868 sensitized him to the fact that the capitalist system was founded upon an "inferno of poverty" and that this "social problem" required resolution (Bellamy in Morgan, 1944, p. 45). Note that his focus is largely systemic.

While he does not exonerate all employers or manufacturers, he is astute enough to frame them as participants in a system that structured their actions. Speaking through Dr. Leete the account provided sounds a little Foucauldian (i.e. it does not have the negative connotations we would expect in a Marxist account) in terms of the process of subjectification being outlined: "The capitalists . . . were not persons of a more depraved disposition than other people, but merely, like other classes, what the economic system had made them" (Bellamy, 1897, p. 345). An interaction between two characters continues this thread:

> The root of evil lay in the tremendous difficulties, mistakes, risks, and wastes with which private capitalism necessarily involved the processes of production and distribution . . . it seems it is not necessary to consider our capitalist ancestors moral monsters in order to account for the tragical [sic] outcome of their economic methods . . . By no

means. The capitalists were no doubt good and bad, like other people, but probably stood up as well as any people could against the depraving influences of a system which in fifty years would have turned heaven itself into hell.

Bellamy, 1897, pp. 165–166

But, like other people, the capitalists were incapable of withstanding the tide of public opinion as it axiologically shifted, although there were hold outs:

A bitter minority of the capitalist party and its supporters seems indeed to have continued its outcry against the Revolution till the end, but it was of little importance. The greater and all the better part of the capitalists joined with the people in contemplating the installation of the new order which all had come to see was to redound to the benefit of all alike.

Bellamy, 1897, p. 345

In this dense volume, he continues to be critical of advertising. It is presented as increasing prices and Bellamy condemns the levels of wasteful expenditure and consumption by the wealthy – his views chime with Thorstein Veblen, another figure of some significance in the history of Critical Marketing Studies in the late nineteenth, early twentieth centuries. Bellamy, as we shall see, was a major influence on Veblen.

In *Equality*, Bellamy underlines the importance of ethics, that is, adherence to the Golden Rule (i.e. do unto others as you would have them do unto you) at the governmental and individual level; stresses the necessity of equality between the sexes; recycling is mentioned in the context of the re-use of clothing; vegetarianism is universally accepted in this socialist utopia for its health-enhancing properties and because the residents of his hoped for year 2000 have registered the self-centered nature of their humanism. Describing the feelings of shame that people felt after giving up meat eating, he writes in a manner that is redolent of themes later found in Ray Benton's (1985) call for marketing to undergo an ethical reorientation and register the rights of non-human members of our ecosystem to life:

[T]he abandonment of the custom [of carnivorism] was chiefly an effect of the great wave of humane feeling, the passion of pity and compunction for all suffering – in a word, the impulse of tender-heartedness – which was really the great moral power behind the Revolution. As might be expected, this outburst did not affect merely the relations of men with men, but likewise their relations with the whole sentient world. The sentiment of brotherhood, the feeling of solidarity, asserted itself not merely toward men and women, but likewise toward the humbler companions of our life on earth and sharers of its fortunes, the animals. The new and vivid light thrown on the rights and duties of men to one another [i.e. his version of socialism] brought also into view and recognition the rights of lower orders of being . . . The new conception of our relation to the animals appealed to the heart and captivated the imagination of mankind.

Bellamy, 1897, p. 286

Humanity was literally transformed after the revolution. The economic, political and social environment shifted on its gyros. Sociality took the place of individualism. The citizenry were better educated, more informed, and engaged in greater levels of individual decision-making, rather than following the dictates of a "leisure class".[4] We use the latter terminology deliberately.

Nineteenth and twentieth centuries: Thorstein Veblen

The informed marketing scholar will register the source as Thorstein Veblen, "one of the strongest pro-feminists of the nineteenth century" (Jorgensen & Jorgensen, 1999, p. 77), a major critic[5] of the profit motive and the deliberate "sabotage" of the industrial process to enhance prices and desirability (Veblen, 1921/2006). The wastes associated with advertising and salesmanship figured prominently in his writings (Veblen 1923/2009) and he was famous for his analysis of the "leisure class" and their "conspicuous waste". Let us unpack these terms a little. With respect to the leisure class, these were people who engaged in practices that were noticeably non-productive; they indicated that an individual could and was able to spend their time doing something other than work, and thus had the pecuniary resources that others did not possess. Veblen lists a variety of non-productive activities: knowledge of "dead languages", art, music, and especially an engagement with "the latest properties of dress, furniture, and equipage; of games, sports, and fancy-bred animals, such as dogs and race-horses" (Veblen, 1899/1994, p. 29).

"Conspicuous waste" referred to the ability of the financially well-endowed to spend money on products, services or leisurely activities to enhance the individual concerned, but which lacked utility or had negative ramifications for wider society. "Conspicuous consumption", another central element of Veblen's lexicon, relates to the overt consumption of usually expensive, sometimes "beautiful" items that served to differentiate the individual and their partner (i.e. a wife's dress, style and comportment served to enhance the self-image of her husband as well as herself).

Veblen has received far more attention within marketing and consumer research than Bellamy. His ideas were perhaps more easily incorporated into the types of empirical research favored in our subject. Veblen's scholarship on the leisure class was foundational for trickle-down theory (i.e. that people look to the class above them for guidance when making consumption decisions), and offered opportunities for further refinement in that the leisure class would change over time in terms of composition and internal differentiation, and display varying degrees of conformity and creativity.

There is a clear link between the two thinkers that has not been appreciated by experts within our subject and a long out of print biography of Bellamy makes this apparent. Again, since this material is difficult to obtain, we draw from Morgan's (1944) remarkable account in some detail. Unlike Morgan, we prefer to be a little more charitable about Veblen's originality in terms of his extension of Bellamy's ideas (for a contemporary example, see Martin, 2015). It takes preparation, attention to detail and skilful extrapolation to generate the extension that Morgan refers to, and Veblen had these in spades. Moreover, his analysis focused far more on conformity and social pressures to adhere to certain forms of "fashionableness" (Veblen, 1899/1994) than we see in Bellamy.

There are additional differences we must appreciate. Bellamy depicts a utopia; Veblen paints the tapestry of the world he confronted on the city streets on a daily basis and which – as Leo Lowenthal (1961) fleshed out using data from the period 1900 to 1941 – was going to expand its sphere of influence. With these caveats in mind, Morgan's identification of the connections between Bellamy and Veblen is genealogically instructive:

> Thorstein Veblen ranks as one of America's most original and creative thinkers in the fields of sociology and economics. As a young man he was at a loss to choose a life calling. Philology seemed most feasible . . . Then he and his wife read *Looking*

Backward together. She wrote of the experience, "I believe that this was the turning point in our lives." Veblen thereupon adopted the social sciences as the field of his life['s] work, and, in one of his first pieces of economic writing . . . he took an idea presented in *Looking Backward* and developed its significance with greater detail and emphasis. This idea – that social injustice is partly due to the fact that men strive not only for physical needs but for favorable economic standing as compared with other men – was the most widely recognized theme of Veblen's provocative and creative career. His *Theory of the Leisure Class*, and his discussions of "conspicuous waste" as a method of social competition, are little more than elaborations of Bellamy. He found the remedy for existing social evils to be Bellamy's program of the public conduct of industry, and equal division of income. With such division, he held, as did Bellamy, that economic emulation would cease, and that ambition would find more useful channels of expression.

Morgan, 1944, pp. x–xi

Edward Bellamy and Thorstein Veblen provide us with much food for thought. Bellamy can be read as encouraging us to remember that the business inflected social system we inhabit is not the only one possible. This connects us with a core concept that underwrites Critical Marketing and Critical Management Studies, namely ontological denaturalization (Fournier & Grey, 2000; Tadajewski, 2010a). This refers to the idea that we are socialized into a political-economic-social world that pre-exists us. It therefore seems to reflect the natural order of things; it is simply the way the world works. However, this is not the case. As Bellamy and Veblen both signaled, the world can be organized differently. Furthermore, it takes the considerable efforts of many groups to maintain the status quo, that is, the apparent "normality" of capitalism.

The ways in which capitalism is maintained and alternative economic systems are undermined have been discussed in various ways. Ewen (1988) takes an historical approach to highlight the growth of advertising and consumer culture. His account reflects the sentiment found in other historically oriented studies with the consumer being viewed as malleable (e.g. Domosh, 2006); their behavior channeled through marketing communications; and these, in turn, were slowly being subject to greater levels of psychological testing and analysis, so that they could be refined to appeal to the target audience (Tadajewski, 2016c). As Veblen had realized, appeals to sociality and the prestige that comes from ownership were prevalent. Connected to this point – although the historical record does vary slightly on this matter – it was thought that human practice in the marketplace was becoming more irrational. In other words, people were not the conscious, rational decision-makers that we find in Bellamy's account. They were more like the picture painted by Veblen, more irrational than rational.

Their decision-making was manipulated by the capitalist class who used their emerging communications skills to encourage people to view their desires as their personal desires, not imposed from the outside by a skilled marketer. Ewen (1988), however, displays limited sensitivity to the nuances of consumption behavior when he homogenizes buying behavior. Veblen appreciated the fact that there would be different patterns of consumption within the same class as well as between classes. Even so, Ewen (1988) offers a commensurate account to that of Edward Bernays – one of the architects of the public relations industry – by proclaiming that the role of marketing, advertising and public relations was not one of responding to the consumer, as the marketing concept claims (e.g. White, 1927): "To make customers is the new problem"

(Bernays, 1928/2005, p. 84). Making customers was enabled by the efficiencies associated with Henry Ford,[6] the growth of the factory system and installment selling.

But, the idea of "making customers" is a vague way of describing what was going on. To be sure, Ewen, Bernays, Veblen and Bellamy all indicate that some element of manipulation was occurring during the time periods they were writing about or against which they sought to contrast their accounts. No doubt there is some truth to all of these narratives. They do not provide us with the whole story, however. Tadajewski and Jones (2016) diagnose the important role played by the banking industry in cementing the circuits of capitalism. They were major factors defining the ontology we inhabit, influencing the way business was undertaken, employees were managed, the consumer was studied and targeted.

Veblen, once again, had been prescient in this regard. He appreciated how the banking industry operated behind the scenes of everyday capitalist endeavors. They funded and thereby determined which businesses would survive or not (if they had needed financial assistance in some respect). Bankers, such as Fred Shibley, were knowledgeable about marketing practice. They stressed the need to understand the customer and cater to their requirements (provided it was profitable to do so). This goes part way to emplacing capitalism as we know it – they are performing the naturalization of our ontology using their knowledge of marketing. This had been gained through direct exposure to many different businesses, across various industries.

What Tadajewski and Jones (2016) reveal is that the banking community shared a similar axiology to Frederick Taylor (1911/1998), the father of Scientific Management. Taylor was worried that socialism might replace capitalism. His system of efficiency, with its emphasis on paying the worker for the amount of labor they performed, thereby increasing their salaries if they operated at a high level (i.e. quickly and efficiently) was meant to undermine the tensions between labor and management. The former saw the latter as reaping the rewards of their work (i.e. receiving a disproportionate amount of what Marx called surplus value).

Taylor came up with an ingenious idea. Workers should forget about the current surplus – the size of the economic pie, as he put it – and think about how it could be expanded to benefit all. In this sleight of hand, Taylor hoped to defuse the appeal of socialism. Shibley, the banker, developed these ideas along a marketing trajectory. First, he underlined the importance of organizational efficiency. Second, efficiency in marketing was enabled by research, salesforce discipline and by knowing about the customer, their needs, wants and requirements. Third, he made the case that workers should purchase the goods and services provided by the firm that employed them and ideally buy shares in the organization as well. This would give them an additional reason to knuckle down in the service of the company. He provided this advice to many different organizations, wrote about it frequently in the popular and business presses and published his core arguments in a 1928 book that distilled his views about workplace surveillance, outlined what would effectively become the marketing concept, and explained how to tie the employee to the circuits of capitalism.

Published in the 1920s and 1930s, White's and Shibley's ideas would become common currency among marketing scholars and practitioners during the 1950s (Hunt, 2017; Tadajewski & Jones, 2012). The marketing managerial view of the world was thus firmly cemented. Consumerism and materialism had great appeal and thinking differently about the capitalist system given the profusion of material wealth it provided was marginalized (Tadajewski, 2010b). It is an ontology that continues to be promoted on a massive scale via business schools, consultancy organizations, self-help manuals, TED Talks and related content today. As you read this, the congeries of capitalism are striving to enroll the so-called "bottom" or "base" of the pyramid in their snare (Varman, Skålén & Belk, 2012).

Conflict

This process has not occurred unopposed. There have been many critical voices pointing out how the growth of marketing, consumerism and the "culture industries" has had negative effects on social life. Capitalism only remains ontologically stable by neutralizing criticism, often by initiatives such as stressing self-regulation, the invocation of codes of ethics (or "corporate social responsibility"), and via the extensive use of government lobbying. Organizational collusion and the violation of anti-trust statutes are another way companies have sought to avoid conflict. This formation of close relationships is rarely remarked upon in the relationship marketing literature. Yet, relationship marketing and organized collusion are points on a continuum.

Since this is a marketing book we would be remiss in failing to point out that attempts to defuse systemic conflict are made by reiterating the connection between consumption and the good life, even though empirical evidence highlights that greater levels of consumption do not lead to greater satisfaction (Scitovsky, 1976). The conflicts of the future, however, are likely to be far harder to defuse, especially those liable to take place over natural and essential, life-giving resources, such as water.

Epistemological reflexivity

With the *continued* growth of the marketing management approach in the 1950s (see Tadajewski & Jones, 2012), marketing scholarship moved partly away from the assumptions about knowledge production that informed the earliest research in our discipline at the cusp of the twentieth century. We are referring to the writings of the German Historical School. This group of scholars had discernible ontological commitments (i.e. beliefs about the nature of reality), epistemological viewpoints (i.e. a theory of knowledge), view of human nature (i.e. are we all made equal) and a theory of society (i.e. their politics).

Let us be transparent, we are summarizing a complex body of literature succinctly. This involves the elision of detail and different scholars in this tradition embodied divergent views. Richard T. Ely, for instance, had a more radical stance than Henry Charles Taylor, and both differed epistemologically from David Kinley. Reading across this group of academics, though, there are parallels (Jones & Tadajewski, 2018). What emerges is that they wanted to find some "middle-ground" between socialism and capitalism; a position most forcefully expressed by Ely, but shared by Kinley.

They considered an historical understanding of the development of the market essential. This was because they did not believe that the current structure of the market was unproblematic. Not all benefitted equally, particularly the farming community. Nor were all consumers considered essentially alike in terms of cognitive processing power. They took a realistic view of human nature and intelligence. Some people were more gifted than others and consequently would find negotiating the marketplace less onerous; others would require help and assistance (i.e. formal education about buying and selling). This view of human nature could shade into questionable territory, reflecting the racist and eugenicist discourses in circulation at the time (and which continue to appear today).

They studied each respective market in considerable historical depth (i.e. historicism), and spoke to relevant industry and consumer groups (i.e. exhibited empiricism) in an attempt to determine how the market worked and where it could be improved (i.e. via a combination of inductive and deductive reflection). In theoretical terms, they were epistemologically relativistic. They did think it might be possible to derive "laws" about the market. These would always be contingent laws, dependent on the context from which they were generated (hence "relative" to the context).

Collecting this material about the functioning of the market was of utility for pedagogic purposes. But there are more interventionist values underpinning why the German Historical School were undertaking their research. They wanted to use it to inform government policy-making, to literally help reshape the marketplace so that it moved toward a state of distributive justice. Not all were convinced that government actors were necessarily well informed or a panacea; they could be extremely self-interested or just plain ineffective in their roles. This interpretation was more often found in the writings of David Kinley (1949). Overall, intervention via governmental action was believed to be a fruitful avenue for political-economic change.

Distributive justice, in this case, means that the benefits of the exchange process should be distributed fairly and that no one group should receive undue benefits while another group suffered. What we can say is that in the terminology of Critical Marketing, the German Historical School was oriented toward a combination of ontological *naturalization* and *denaturalization*. With respect to naturalization, they wanted to retain those elements of a market system that did function efficiently and effectively and helped realize distributive justice. Similarly, where there were problems that required action, they moved to denaturalize the status quo, to make it appear dysfunctional and an unnatural order of exchange that required rectification.

While there was little use of the critical social theory that we have said is a characteristic of Critical Marketing Studies, there was some engagement with relevant perspectives. Ely, most notably in his relative youth before the "academic trials" which could have curtailed his career led him toward a more conservative orientation (see Jones & Tadajewski, 2018), did engage extensively with the literatures on anarchism and socialism. His research on this front remains deeply impressive and well informed. Even though critical social theory is largely absent, we would do well to consider this community part of the genealogy of Critical Marketing Studies. In spite of the fact that Tadajewski (2010b) suggested that the influence of this school of thought was relatively limited, this interpretation has since been revised. Now, the German Historical School's impact has been described as feeding through the genealogy of marketing thought. Their historical, institutional, empirical and critical view of the marketing system has been resurrected, often without citation (for the reason that they remain largely unread), in the macromarketing, Consumer Culture Theory and Critical Marketing literatures (Jones & Tadajewski, 2018).

What might be a point of contention is that their scholarship was framed as "positivist" in that they were looking for relative laws of the market and the underlying relationships between marketing phenomena. For Shankar (2009), if there is anything that Critical Marketing is not, it is definitely not positivist. This seems plausible at first glance, given the way positivistic thought and associated methodologies have been incorporated into the marketing literature after the negative evaluations of business education in the late 1950s by the Ford and Carnegie reports (i.e. with accompanying assumptions about the importance of objectivity, political neutrality, use of quantitative methods and mathematical symbolism). These reports bewailed business education as descriptive, unscholarly, and said that those teaching these subjects lacked appropriate certification (i.e. the Ph.D. degree).

The problem is that the understanding of positivism that Shankar (2009) is citing is a far cry from the way it was understood by our predecessors. David Kinley, as a case in point, adopted many of the tenets of the German Historical School outlined above and made use of quantitative measures (i.e. surveys and statistics). For most readers, this would appear to be a paradigmatic example of contemporary positivistic research. This was not the way Kinley positioned his work. The approaches he used enabled him to penetrate and understand the social world in a way otherwise not possible. Insights generated in this manner would then inform recommendations to government. As Jones and Tadajewski (2018, p. 88) put it, "Kinley self-associates with a politically oriented positivism". Since Critical Marketing Studies conceptualizes all knowledge production as political in nature, Kinley's "positivism" is not incommensurable with the political values of Critical Marketing Studies.[7]

More on "positivism"[8]

We would also do well to avoid assuming that the "positivism" that permeates the marketing academy is actually consistent with the way it was envisaged by those most closely associated with it, namely the Vienna Circle. Again, this was a varied group of intellectuals, each with slightly different views about philosophy and its relationship with the world. Connections can also be made to the German Historical School in that Otto Neurath studied under Gustav Schmoller for a time, being exposed to the historicist approach typified by the "leader of the younger school" (Jones & Tadajewski, 2018, p. 32). Neurath's education was also heavily inflected by sociology.

When exploring the work of Otto Neurath, a prominent figure in the Vienna Circle, Tadajewski (2010a) made the case that he was politically vocal, committed to ethics, critical thought, scholarly pluralism and reflexivity. There was little expectation that universal laws – in our case, of the marketplace – would be developed. All knowledge for Neurath was conditional on the context being studied, with claims to knowledge scrutinized via intersubjective deliberation. Such processes of deliberation would be shaped by politics (Tadajewski, 2010a, p. 212). No claims to knowledge could ever be fully accepted – they should and could not be treated as if they were tablets sent from God. Any claims to knowledge that are made, therefore, should be justified by observation (this is somewhat removed from most Critical Marketing epistemological positions), but it was not possible, he argued, for us to presume that our assumptions and observations were always correct. There is a great deal of epistemological contingency in play here. Moreover, arguably, there is evidence of a critical performative stance being deployed by Neurath (Spicer, Alvesson & Kärreman, 2009). Before we continue further, we should explain what is meant by this term.

Critical performativity

The debates on critical performativity are subject to a significant degree of contestation in the wider management literature. Their nuances need not concern us here. Marketing and management scholarship, and business education more generally, is frequently depicted as performative (Fournier & Grey, 2000). What Fournier and Grey (2000) mean by this is that it aims at increasing the efficiency of firm practice. In the case of marketing, this could signal an interest in producing students with the greatest level of knowledge about, for instance, consumer buying behavior so that they are better able to "educate" the customer. Mainstream marketing education has this as a foundational value.

To do this in the present context, students would need to understand the importance of "Big Data" – the collection of huge amounts of information about the consumer that is beyond the comprehension of an individual human being to analyze. Reflecting the volume of material, computer algorithms are used to sift this content in order to generate and deliver marketing communications through geotargeting (i.e. determining when a consumer enters a retail store and sending appropriate messages via their mobile phone which is being tracked through the global positioning system). All of these data are used to weave a web of surveillance technologies around the individual, encouraging them to act in store and at the point of purchase in a manner consistent with organizational needs.

Big Data and the various tools that accompany it, has the potential to skew existing and future power dynamics between the marketer and customer significantly. The danger, as Montgomery, Chester, Nixon, Levy and Dorfman (2017) register, is that it makes it relatively easy to discriminate against certain groups or to target vulnerable populations with material that does not serve their long-term interests (thereby violating the "societal marketing concept").

A critical performative stance does not take this kind of efficiency as the objective of marketing education or practice. Instead, it wants to challenge the way marketing managers think about their role in society, providing them with different interpretations that move them beyond a focus on the bottom line, to engage more seriously with ethics and social responsibility (e.g. Tadajewski, 2016b). It is on the basis of these kinds of axiological values that a critical performative approach might be described as fairly leftist in political orientation (cf. Grey, 2018). Importantly, it differs from the type of perspective that is often associated with Critical Theory in that practitioners and their techniques are not *a priori* assumed to be a negative force in the social world. Rather, engagement and a willingness to listen to managers is a driving force, before critique can commence.

This said, one of the dangers of critical performativity is that it tends to position the academic or some other actor as an almost heroic individual, capable of making major changes, with little "friction", to otherwise sedimented political-economic regimes, corporate value systems and managerial practices (Butler, Delaney & Spolestra, 2018). On the one hand, we cannot expect too much change. Yet, nor do we want to sound defeatist. There have been individuals who have made serious moves to modify the axiological and political values being employed in society – Otto Neurath is one such case.

It should also be noted that the arguments found in the critical literature, such as those flowing from the pen of Veblen, tended to aver that social change would be slow, piecemeal, and involve multiple actors, from multiple interest groups – groups that would presumably conflict in some way – working together to achieve some shared objective (Tadajewski, 2010a). These conjunctions of interest groups were not intended to continue *aeternum* (i.e. forever). Grey (2018) appears to assume that associations between different groups – whether big business and critical academics or some other group – have to exist in perpetuity. This is an odd perspective. Associations can be strategic, limited and break up when appropriate. At this point it is likely that the critically minded academic returns to a position of challenging the status quo and the interests they had previously worked alongside – again, this is not a position that will exist in perpetuity. As the political-economic system shifts, so will alliances (e.g. Parker & Parker, 2017).

To return to Neurath, he was politically active, serving in a socialist government (whose role, he asserted, should be one of "manufacturing happiness"), subscribed to economic planning and held the belief that society could be transformed for the better (Vossoughian, 2011). Part of this project involved developing museums and the production of a visual language to assist workers with little education to understand the macro-economic and political context which structured and shaped their lives, in order to foster "solidarity and a sense of belonging" (Vossoughian, 2011, p. 51). As Vossoughian (2011, p. 49) explains, Neurath's involvement in the founding of museums and their role as a pedagogical vehicle

> emphasized the central role that the mass media and popular culture could play in shaping public space. Museums should exhibit the aspirations and achievements of the masses . . . [and they] provided an infrastructure within which large groups of people could gather, learn and ultimately organize their goals and interests.

These museums were not vehicles for the indoctrination of capitalist values; far from it. Neurath provided information about how people could limit their interactions with the market, outlined informal bartering techniques, detailed how they could recycle products for other uses, and in doing so achieve some level of "independence" and self-determination outside of traditional channels (Vossoughian, 2011). The success of such endeavors, it must be admitted, was limited, but nevertheless they chime with the ideal of defatalization (Bourdieu, 1998; Tadajewski, 2016a). In other words, we are not fatalistic about our current circumstances. We can think and act differently within whatever political-economic context we find ourselves.

Neurath, in short, wanted to foster rationality, critical reflection and institutional transparency much in the tradition of Austro-Marxism. His visual dictionary and establishment of museums to encourage social literacy were key contributions in this regard. Information was, he firmly believed, a means to emancipation (Vossoughian, 2011). And, as indicated above, unlike the Frankfurt School, he seems to have assumed that what they referred to as the "culture industries" (i.e. certain forms of media, marketing, advertising, movies, music, etc.) usually in a negative fashion, were the most effective vehicles to enlighten the general population.

"Mass culture" was the means to forge bonds with the populace at large, it was not something to be derided (Vossoughian, 2011). Scientific information, knowledge about the economy and social life in general could be transmitted through precisely those communication methods that the Critical Theorists thought were a distraction from the reality of everyday life. To put this another way, "positivism" as originally conceived does have affinities with Critical Marketing Studies. There is no reason why they cannot cross-fertilize in future.

Marketing, as has been amply demonstrated elsewhere, has a rich history of critique (Tadajewski, 2010b). Obviously, the discipline remains deeply managerialist in orientation (Hackley, 2001). The focus is on the views of the marketing-led organization and usually stresses the heroic role of the marketing manager. At the same time as this perspective was rising to prominence, it was accompanied by a shadow, that is, the critical literature which sought to challenge core concepts, epistemological assumptions and the methodologies characteristic of managerial research (e.g. quantitative methods). In terms of the critical literature, there still remains much to be done: more theoretical work, empirical scholarship and greater effort at producing counter-concepts that challenge those currently employed in marketing pedagogy.

Marketing, then, is not necessarily a blight on society. Rather, engaging in this practice places people, with all their desires and deficiencies, in a context where immoderation is always on offer. As we have seen, these are very old arguments. Yet they resonate in the aftermath of the recent financial crisis whose rumblings appeared in 2007, but became monumental in 2008, when governments had to start buffering the financial system because they feared total economic collapse. Once again, we hear the "bad apples" argument. This is used with some regularity, and when it is uttered we should look to systemic failures being hidden behind an ideological move that tries to displace responsibility on to a few individuals. In the case of the financial crisis, it was not allegedly the capitalist system that was at fault, just a small number of institutions, and often just a limited number of "bad apples" within these firms that were responsible for poor decisions that made the lives of many millions of people highly precarious in various ways. Always treat such arguments with serious caution.

Naturally, there are many differences between the medieval period and contemporary times. Bad apples in the former could be identified and punishment delivered reasonably easily. Importantly, the effects of their actions were likely to be localized. They did not reverberate around the world, shattering the lives and livelihoods of huge numbers of people. But scholars in medieval times and contemporary Critical Marketing thinkers have argued that a devotion to profit as the sole motivator for business activities is probably going to lead to harm. The effects are now likely to be highly systemic, that is, ripple around the world, through various industries, due to the interconnected nature of the economic system.

For Critical Marketers, perhaps, their most explicit axiological assumption is that marketing is embedded within society. Practitioners have to contribute to society in a beneficial fashion, offering products and services that ensure we leave this planet in a better shape than we found it. This suggests a subscription to intergenerational justice. If corporations transgress societal legal and moral frameworks and unfortunately marketing practitioners are often central figures in such transgressions (Tadajewski, 2010c), then they can expect that society will judge them accordingly. Corporate charters can be withdrawn; individuals thrown in prison. Business practitioners are, we must remember, given sanction to perform their activities within legal frameworks and they are expected to abide by them.

Marketers often face the brunt of criticism because the discipline and its accompanying practices (i.e. advertising) are prominent. Equally, though, when corporations have faced legal action for whatever reason (i.e. various forms of anti-competitive behavior), it is the marketing executive that is usually held to account. They are frequently mid-level figures, expected to operate in a boundary-spanning role, engaging with other corporations and firms, and this – as medieval writers and Adam Smith alike remind us – places them in a position of temptation (Ashton & Pressey, 2008; Tadajewski, 2010c). They might be set sales figures or profit expectations which are high – figures that are determined by their bosses who are far distant (i.e. to ensure some semblance of legal deniability) – and so they can and do engage in acts that break the law to meet their objectives.

Before we rush to condemn such acts as a function of individual irresponsibility, we need to remember that we are dealing with people operating within a wider capitalist system. They might inhabit a corporate culture that fosters certain values, and these can and do reinforce questionable practices. The life insurance industry is notorious for structurally embedding deceptive selling practices in its training programs for new agents (Ericson & Doyle, 2006). This is buttressed by the commission system which effectively encourages the sale of policies to people who simply do not need them or for whom there are better alternatives. Obviously, we do not wish to endorse such actions, but we can understand that people might be pushed into questionable practices due to managerial pressure, combined with the need to feed their own families. This is part of the violence of the market (Fırat, 2018). Moreover, decision-making within larger companies and corporations is highly specialized and diffused. This gives rise to problems of its own. A simple request from a senior figure to lower manufacturing costs, for instance, could lead production and marketing to seek cheaper locations and labor to produce their offerings. They might never visit these locations. They sit in an office, sign a form, and meet the targets set by their managers. They are cognitively and spatially distant from the ramifications of their seemingly benign actions.

However, as Nike (among others) found out, small decisions can have horrific consequences. The "conditions of possibility" for those expensive sneakers included global inequality, long hours, unpaid overtime and, no doubt, sweat, tears and blood as well. There have been many other similar examples (Klein, 2005). We might hope that corporations would learn that globalization enables them to source goods, lower costs, market to much larger audiences than was possible previously, but it also brings considerable attention. With the internet, negative commentary spreads like wildfire. But, sadly, the individuals that steer these organizations seem reluctant to give much time to reflect upon these issues (e.g. Knight, 2016). Poor labor practices, dubious marketing messaging (e.g. involving racist stereotypes), as well as steadily increasing corporate power (e.g. Walmart's persistent environmental and labor transgressions, harm to local communities, poor pay (with the firm effectively receiving state subsidization) and operationalization of its own moral code to determine its product range), requires more than ever that we do not take what marketing textbooks say at face value. We must confront the world for what it is. Only then can we start to try to change it.

Frankly, though, even those not welcoming of the level of critique that we propose in this book, and which is embedded in Critical Marketing Studies at the axiological level, need to register that poor corporate practices can lead to what is called the "scandal effect" (Groysberg, Lin, Serafeim & Abrahams, 2016). If a specific company is embroiled in illegal, fraudulent and amoral activities, this can rebound not only on the firm, but on those working for it. This might not seem surprising. What is more unexpected is the fact that even if you are not employed by the transgressor at the time, the scandal effect can still influence your job mobility and remuneration. The taint of corporate malfeasance can lead to reductions in compensation when compared to an individual from a firm with an unblemished record, so that when a candidate moves to their next job they are paid between 3% and 7% less than someone with equivalent qualifications (Groysberg et al., 2016). Over the course of a career, the financial differential that this leads to can be eye watering.

So, Critical Marketing basically asks us to remember that the world in which we live is complicated, temptation is rife, and the pressures to perform are high as a concomitant of the needs of the capitalist system. The capitalist system, if we must be reminded, is predicated upon the generation of profit and returns to shareholders. As an approach, then, it wants to encourage us to appreciate that there might be some distance between what textbooks say about marketing and marketers and what they actually do in practice.

The contents of this collection

Exploring the terrain of Critical Marketing Studies

No volume dealing with Critical Marketing Studies would be complete without a submission from Nik Dholakia and Fuat Fırat. In their chapter, they provide us with an overview of postmodernism and its relationship to Critical Marketing. It becomes apparent fairly quickly that there are more connections between postmodernism and Critical Marketing Studies than has been appreciated. Rethinking marketing, its core concepts, and relationship to society are important elements of a postmodern critique. While Fırat has expressed his concern that the various aspects of postmodernism that he and Alladi Venkatesh (1995, p. 252) articulated were inappropriately reified, namely, hyperreality, fragmentation, reversal of production and consumption, decentered subject, juxtaposition of opposites (Bradshaw & Dholakia, 2012), itself representing a lack of criticality, there have been changes in the political and social environment which suggest we should not jettison postmodernism too quickly. Their reasoning is persuasive. Even those who typically avoid politics must have witnessed the rise of Donald Trump and his embodiment of the features that Fırat and Venkatesh listed in relation to hyperreality. Put differently, we are living in an age where the real and unreal are blurring; where fiction substitutes for fact, at least by those within Trump's circle, and presumably among some of those who voted for him.

In their analysis, Dholakia and Fırat provide an overview of the development of modernism and its connection to postmodernism. Their explication of the ganglions is superb, with numerous tables presenting core concepts and themes in an easily accessible fashion. This makes their work an ideal introduction to this topic for new students and established academics alike. Modernism and postmodernism cannot be cleanly parsed; elements of the former continue into the latter, while sometimes being negated. In a fascinating twist, they propose that some of the features widely associated with postmodernism – particularly hyperreality and the fragmentation of the social world – are not original to postmodernity.

Rather, the historical development of capitalism, the growth of consumption, with the latter sometimes even being viewed as compensation for a life of work-related drudgery, heightened our attention to the role of marketing in society. The spectacularization of the social environment, of course, has been with us for some time. John Wanamaker's retailing environments of the late nineteenth, early twentieth centuries were truly amazing to view. One of their core arguments, then, is that the rise of postmodern theoretical and conceptual discourse enabled scholars to appreciate some of the core facets of postmodernism that were already present, but not theorized, framed and labeled as such. Importantly, their chapter illuminates the politics of postmodernism in a manner that is rarely undertaken and they extend these ruminations to outline the challenges that a "radical" postmodernism poses for our future. Issues of consumer literacy, resistance, the production of counter-narratives and destabilization of the power relations accompanying media concentration and political oligarchy are flagged as central issues that we need to tackle. In addition, ongoing conceptual development intended to sensitize all of us to changes in the social environment and facilitate opportunities to think differently about the marketplace are essential, they opine. This chapter represents a call to theoretical, conceptual, empirical and political action.

Rohit Varman has been a passionate advocate of postcolonial perspectives in marketing and consumer research. His work has been important in many different ways. Being largely based in India, he has been able to draw attention to an empirical landscape that has previously been misinterpreted through Western eyes – especially during the 1960s – and in doing so takes marketing away from its largely U.S. and Eurocentric orientation. However, as he underlines in his chapter, when we look at the top journals in our discipline, they continue to focus on a very limited section of the global population. It is not an exaggeration to say that the white, middle-class, affluent, able consumer is the archetype that peppers our academic outlets. When attention is paid to non-Western contexts, they are usually presented as some kind of supplement, that is, as a means to highlight the boundary limits to existing theories or concepts, instead of being valued in their own right.

Varman's chapter can, in many respects, be read as a response to the rise of postmodernism and its focus on – mainly – Western, affluent contexts. Such theoretical orientations, while of utility in some locations, are not easily transposable (unless we ignore the empirical realities we confront) to other areas of the world. Varman is, of course, talking about the Global South. Both marketing and consumer researchers alike have been largely inattentive to nations outside of their immediate purview or which exhibit significant cultural distance. This is not to say that there is not a vibrant stream of research being published that focuses on these contexts, only that it typically appears in languages other than English and this limits its impact on scholars whose attention span is already usually strained by the profusion of material appearing with regularity in their own language.

Varman critiques postmodernism. He makes a case that other contexts exhibit far more complexity than is assumed, often fusing capitalist and non-capitalist elements. In a sophisticated analysis, Varman subjects some of the core theoretical resources drawn upon by postmodern and Consumer Culture Theorists to critical evaluation. The way Foucault has been utilized is unpacked and compared against the realities of the Indian context. This is useful in that it does mirror the argument presented by Dholakia and Firat who discourage us from moving beyond theoretical and conceptual resources too quickly (in Varman's case he takes us back to disciplinary power). This desperate need to find new theorists (ideally untranslated into English to make them that bit more special) or contexts to study is a function of various pressures.

Academics, after all, are constantly looking for the next contribution and a new theorist or conceptual architecture is often a means to publish rather than perish. Marketing has not quite caught up with organization studies in terms of its rapid consumption and disposal of theorists, but our intellectual speed-up is certainly becoming more noticeable. Varman calls upon scholars to remember that while thinkers such as Foucault move through a particular intellectual lifecycle, changing their tools accordingly, this does not mean that their earlier ideas lack utility. As he points out, while attention is increasingly focused upon Foucault's later work (i.e. biopower), his earlier scholarship retains considerable applicability in the Indian context.

Varman's analysis could not be further from our textbook narratives of the marketing concept and corporate social responsibility if he tried. What he makes abundantly clear is that some of the biggest brands on the market are engaged in practices that they would simply not be able to pursue in countries with strict legislation, the effective policing of human rights and a strong (less corrupt) political class. Throughout his chapter, he draws upon postcolonial theory, carefully defining the key concepts and terms associated with this tradition (e.g. ambivalence, mimicry, hybridity) and provides numerous examples taken from interdisciplinary sources to illustrate the value of this paradigmatic perspective.

Across all of this material is an image of the marketplace which is far removed from that normally sketched in marketing theory. His picture is much darker, riven with dubious corporate and governmental practices, and he challenges the discourse of friction-free development found in "base-of-the-pyramid" accounts. He concludes by articulating a research agenda that demands to be taken seriously.

Maclaran and Kravets explore the history of feminism and its connection to the marketplace. They remind us that the links between feminism and the market are actually far more complicated than we might expect. Not all feminists have been vociferously critical of the market. Some have used it to their advantage. This was notable in the early twentieth century, when a number of retailers courted the patronage of feminists and were willing to advance female employees by providing them with well-paying jobs as well as offering the possibility of career advancement. Their opportunities were, as is probably predictable, not as numerous as those available to men, but John Wanamaker and Harry Gordon Selfridge were quick to appreciate the value of female employees, especially as buyers. Perhaps with some degree of instrumentality, Selfridge was a vocal advocate for the suffragettes.

Taking us through numerous waves of feminist thought, Maclaran and Kravets present a structured narrative that is remarkable for its coverage of a complex literature, yet with an enviable degree of clarity. By the time we get to the late twentieth, early twenty-first centuries, feminism has been transformed in various ways. The experiences of white women are no longer treated as if they represent a standard narrative. Research has instead focused on the life-worlds of a plurality of groups. This is a valuable turn in the feminist literature. It follows from the recognition of the pioneers who promoted feminist thought within marketing (e.g. Bristor & Fischer, 1993) that they had focused too much on a limited subsection of women's experiences in society.

Maclaran and Kravets note the bifurcation of feminist discourse in the period between 1988 and 2010, with some academics making a case for the importance of the market in advancing a feminist agenda, while others saw the embrace of feminism and associated argumentation as a form of co-optation that diluted the political edge of this "big tent" of perspectives. A number of thinkers in this domain went further, underlining that the growing use of feminist tropes and imagery was regressive and commensurate with patriarchal views of what constituted appropriate forms of femininity. Post 2010, there has been a reaction to the individualized, market-based conceptualization of feminism (we can think of this as a reaction to "*Sex in the City*-type" forms of female sexual and fashion oriented "empowerment") toward a far more politically vocal, intersectional critique of social structures, ongoing misogyny, assumptions of male entitlement, and the high-profile cases of sexual harassment that appear in the media with depressing frequency. They conclude by outlining important research directions for those interested in pursuing feminist scholarship. This is a cutting-edge agenda and presents many opportunities for doctoral candidates and scholars looking to follow up promising lines of study.

Ross Gordon is rapidly becoming one of the foremost voices in Critical Social Marketing. Social marketing has historically been a counterpoint to mainstream marketing. It is our discipline's way of being able to respond to the critiques that confront it (i.e. of encouraging excessive and unhealthy consumption patterns). In terms of a definition, we can think of social marketing as dealing with behavioral change. It strives to lead people to reflect upon their consumption habits, most notably those deemed deleterious by the individual or some external stakeholder (e.g. government, doctor, family members, etc.). As a perspective, it differs from the marketing concept in the sense that as a body of literature it is often willing to prescribe, explicitly and overtly, how people should think or live differently.

Gordon begins by reminding us that social marketing, while it might have been defined more formally in the latter half of the twentieth century by such luminaries as Kotler, Levy and Zaltman through their broadening of the marketing concept (i.e. expanding marketing's purview beyond the for-profit realm to the non-profit community and associated social causes), there is evidence that related practices were being undertaken far in anticipation of these definitional moves. This historical account is useful in its own right, as is Gordon's correction of the genealogical lineage of social marketing. For most academics working in this area or teaching it, Kotler and Levy are the joint promoters of the broadening concept. This is not entirely accurate.

Levy's experience with Social Research Incorporated revealed the extent to which non-commercial entities were engaged in what was conventionally considered marketing. Yet, their practices failed to be given sufficient attention by the marketing discipline. Politically, broadening the marketing concept to include a pro-social orientation (i.e. changing people's behavior in ways likely to enhance their quality of life), shifted the discipline from its close ties with the military-industrial-commercial complex in the eyes of many students. Marketing was not, in other words, quite so tainted with a capitalist agenda and this was important during the 1960s and 1970s to prevent declines in student enrolments (Kassarjian & Goodstein, 2009).

Gordon takes a slightly different approach to many within the social marketing community in terms of where he positions his work. He does not herald Kotler and Levy as his foundational sources. His influences come from Lazer and Kelley. This is notable, as their definition of social marketing called attention to the use of marketing tools and techniques to enhance human well-being. But they went further than this by proposing that a crucial element of social marketing was the analysis of the actual effects of marketing on society. They wanted people to explore the "social consequences" of marketing practice. This keys into various strands of marketing thought including macromarketing (which deals with the influence of marketing on society) and Critical Marketing (which questions who benefits from marketplace exchanges and focuses on power relations). Gordon charts the development of critical perspectives in social marketing, unpacks the conceptualization of "Critical Social Marketing", subsequently explaining the commitments that underwrite this activist approach. He strives to encourage Critical Marketing thinkers to revisit their understanding of social marketing and Critical Social Marketing more generally.

What, in effect, he submits is that neither domain is monolithic and that within them there is much greater theoretical variety than has been supposed to date. Using this as a springboard, he takes us on a journey through an emerging literature on Critical Social Marketing. While quantitatively this body of scholarship is small, it is rich in terms of the wealth of insights it presents, is gaining sophistication in theoretical, conceptual and empirical terms, and those pursuing this system of thought deserve kudos for doing so in an academic environment that is not always favorable to their work.

One of the pioneers of critical perspectives in macromarketing provides the next contribution to this volume. Bill Kilbourne has been pushing the boundaries of macromarketing research for some time now, offering theoretically and empirically nuanced work that has advanced our understanding of the assumption bases that underwrite capitalism. In this chapter, his approach is theoretically and conceptually rich, yet eminently accessible. Kilbourne differentiates two types of macromarketing scholarship.

The first he labels "Developmental Macromarketing"; the second is "Critical Macromarketing". Developmental Macromarketing is more conservative and largely inattentive to issues such as the violence routinely found in the marketplace and which is often a condition of possibility for its ongoing operation (Fırat, 2018). But what is central to both of these schools of thought is that they do not focus on the individual firm. This is why they use the term "macro" in their titles. Their analytic level is the market, how it operates, whether it can be made more efficient and, in the more critical tradition, reoriented so that sustainability and ecological preservation and recuperation take precedence over the short-term demands of shareholders and firms.

This need to ensure that marketing practice does not adversely influence the natural environment is a concomitant of the ethics of Critical Macromarketing. As Kilbourne and others have posited, social and distributive justice is important, that is, we need to ensure that people have access to the resources they need to sustain a decent quality of life. But so is intergeneration justice. We cannot harm the planet via our consumption patterns if it will leave later generations – those still to be born – dealing with the consequences; consequences that we are already seeing in terms of climate change, the devastation caused by severe weather conditions and the problems that will accompany the melting of the polar ice-caps.

In unraveling these issues, Kilbourne adopts a distinctly philosophical approach. He is well versed in political philosophy and able to translate developments in the legal foundations of capitalism to elucidate how our current worldview – what he terms the "dominant social paradigm" – came to occupy ideological center stage. Where Critical Macromarketing and Critical Marketing Studies differ is that Critical Macromarketing shares with its developmental cousin a belief in the ultimate efficacy of markets.

Postmodernism and Critical Marketing, by contrast, discourage us from taking concepts such as the "market" or its current role in provisioning as an historical constant, something that need always exist. Instead, they call for new vocabularies, new concepts, and new ways of life. They want us to think beyond markets. Critical Macromarketing positions itself apart from the consumerist and materialistic axiology that underwrites mainstream marketing, but still remains wedded to the concept and function of the market. This is a point of contention between the perspectives mentioned above.

Tracing place marketing's roots to the post-Keynesian economic environment post 1970, Giovanardi, Kavaratzis and Lichrou outline how the broadening of marketing debate provided for an overly narrow, simplistic and prescriptive framework that rendered the place-as-an-object that was amenable to the tools and techniques of marketing. Drawing on an interdisciplinary perspective of the concept of place they outline how managerial accounts of place branding and selling fail to account for the concerns over place and economics, place and culture, place and politics, and place and image. The impact of this on local communities, the identity and wellbeing of its members and collective histories is discussed, and new methods to capture the contested domain of place from the perspectives of multiple stakeholders are outlined.

Larsen and Kerrigan argue that arts marketing has always provided a position for critical engagement with marketing theory and practice due to the vexed question over the nature of the arts and the relationship between the market and the artist. Moving the debate beyond the functional broadening of marketing perspective, the chapter opens up a far more fluid, complex and nuanced engagement at the intersection of the arts and markets, an approach that unsettles boundaries between producer and consumer and production and consumption. In doing so, it brings to the fore the inherent politics of arts marketing. The chapter provides the reader with an account that is at the forefront of challenges in contemporary marketing theory, research methods and practice.

Critical Marketing: marketing practices in focus

In his chapter, Svensson puts forward the proposal that it is indispensable that critical research of marketing work, understood as practices consisting of actions, interactions, decisions and deeds, explore it in situ. This, he submits, requires a critical attitude and commitment to observation-based field work. He provides an exemplary overview of the main theoretical sources for the study of marketing work, engaging with Marxist, Critical and Foucauldian theories as well as Critical Sociology. If research into marketing work is to have a critical edge, he believes that Critical Marketing needs to develop a methodological language of its own. His guidance on this front is valuable. There is much of interest to be mined here. One area that he indicates merits future research is the business school itself, since it functions as a production line for future marketing workers.

In her chapter, Coskuner-Balli offers a critical overview of cultural approaches in consumer lifestyle(s) research. Drawing on prominent examples from the literature, she demonstrates how cultural research can help us better understand how lifestyles operate as symbolic boundaries between different consumer segments, the dynamics steering the transformation and legitimation of emerging and stigmatized practices and the macro and institutional forces shaping them. In this regard, she provides a highly valuable complement to extant research which has reviewed the "political economy of social choice" and the "structure of available alternatives" (e.g. Tadajewski, 2010b). The thematic areas surveyed by Coskuner-Balli open up potential fields for a wealth of new directions for scholars to pursue, including studies on how consumer goods become material substantiations of cultural ideals through which desired lifestyles can be enacted. Associated with this, she calls attention to the need to historicize the emergence and evolution of lifestyles and how they are influenced by value systems such as neoliberalism, political Islam or socialism.

Focusing on advertising practice and its connections to Critical Marketing, Chris Hackley urges us to shift our attention from studying advertisements to advertis*ing*, that is, we need to better understand the nature of advertising production. After all, there is a relative paucity of empirical research that actually looks at how advertising is produced, the politics that accompany it, and this, in turn, will most likely deflate Critical Theory accounts of the power of the "culture industries" to some extent. Hackley, of course, has been at the cutting-edge of this type of research for some time, as have a number of other notable figures such as Arthur Kover and Brian Moeran.

In other words, we must not assume that the meanings that advertisers try to embed in their communications are necessarily received as intended by the ultimate consumer. Marketing communications are far more polysemic (i.e. they communicate different messages to different groups and mean different things to an individual at different points over the course of their life span) than is usually suspected (Puntoni, Schroeder & Ritson, 2010) and the process of trying to persuade the consumer to do anything is actually much harder than many traditional information-processing models assume. As an important area that desperately requires theoretical, conceptual and – especially – empirical attention, he points the reader to the related topics of digitalization and media convergence. He concludes that what is needed to deal with this new communications order is a new theoretical and methodological toolkit. Literary theory and methods hold out much promise in terms of enabling us to make better sense of emergent modes for producing and consuming advertising.

In an expansive review of multiple literatures, Tadajewski points out that Critical Theory cautions us to be on our guard about embedded assumptions regarding marketing theory and practice. Writers in marketing are not neutral commentators. They are part of a generative force within society; they are merchants of values and beliefs. Accepting this means that the role of the academic is to subject their claims to scrutiny for any ideological intent. Holding up some of the central concepts within marketing thought to question, Tadajewski explores how the idea of consumer sovereignty, the evolutionary model of marketing development, and exchange theory offer partial representations of how marketing operates in theory and practice.

There is a great need for these kinds of detailed critiques of core concepts. It is wise to anticipate that intelligent students will call into question overly effusive accounts of marketing practice. Telling them that practitioners want to give them what they need, want and desire is likely to be met with some degree of circumspection. For those lacking appropriate finances – as Bellamy (1897) and Fırat (2018) both registered – the market offers only a cold shoulder. Uncritically presenting the idealization of consumer sovereignty is also ethically questionable in the present climate given the rise of food poverty and increased usage of food banks among those on low incomes (Livingstone, 2015).

Moreover, those experiencing bereavement are easy prey for unscrupulous marketers who trade on the misery and ignorance of the consumer to maximize their incomes. We might recall that Mitford (2000) was unstinting in her critique of this industry, calling attention to manipulation, deliberate attempts to confuse the already cognitively overloaded individual, along with the fraudulent activities undertaken by some practitioners of this trade. Furthermore, the opioid crisis that is wrecking lives and hammering communities in the United States (and elsewhere), is a definitive case where people are no longer making their own choices due to addiction. Addiction to opioids such as heroin, OxyContin and Vicodin crosses class boundaries without stalling. The effects are devastating and will influence the way people live their lives. Talking about the sovereign, king or queen-like consumer seems inappropriate in these contexts. As "John" described his experience, "When you're dope sick, like bad, you're not making your own decisions any more. Your decisions are made for you" (in *Time*, 2018, p. 21). Touching upon some of these points, as well as incorporating more contemporary trends within marketing, Tadajewski outlines how issues of power, transparency and fairness are often lost if the multi-dimensional natures of our key concepts are not explored.

Vargo and Lusch's writing on Service Dominant Logic (S-DL) has been extremely influential, yet subject to relatively little critique. In easily the best close reading of this body of scholarship available at present, Chris Miles demonstrates how the authors employ strategies of persuasion and rhetoric to compete in a congested marketplace of ideas very successfully. The chapter details the evolution of S-DL and Vargo and Lusch's handicraft in ensuring that the foundational premises of their academic branding exercise are more readily subsumed within the disciplinary canon.

O'Malley has been at the forefront of critical research on relationship marketing for 20 (or so) years. She has been one of the few scholars who have rigorously questioned this perspective from multiple angles, producing excellent theoretical, conceptual (O'Malley & Tynan,

1999) and – highly unusually – empirical accounts of consumer–marketer engagement. We say "unusually" with respect to the latter as it is often assumed that people want to have relationships with companies. This, at least in part, is a bit of a marketer fantasy, rather than reflective of consumer engagement with firms (e.g. O'Malley & Prothero, 2004).

She interrogates how the marriage metaphor destabilized conventional constructions of the marketing function, directed attention toward the interaction between buyers and sellers, and framed market exchanges within the context of relationships and networks. In a fascinating account, she offers multiple insights into how metaphor functions as a tool of thought and basis for academic discourse. O'Malley concludes the chapter by pointing to the limitations of the marriage metaphor and calls for alterative conceptualizations of interpersonal relationships in markets (e.g. Tynan, 1997).

Carrington and Chatzidakis adopt an interdisciplinary perspective to unravel the core contextual threads that are emerging in critical studies on ethical consumption. They observe that sites of ethical consumption have been appropriated, marketized, and governed by neoliberal corporate interests (cf. Chatzidakis, Maclaran & Bradshaw, 2012). Such appropriation makes ethical consumption elitist, ecologically unsustainable, and casts in high relief the limitations of consumers and consumption in changing the contours of neoliberal capitalism. Moreover, the creeping responsibilization of consumers leads to even greater levels of consumption in the guise of ethical choice-making.

In seeking to broaden the analytical lens we can usefully turn on to capitalism, Ali Jafari reminds the reader that religion as an institution and set of teachings occupies a powerful position within both secular and non-secular societies. Proceeding from the stance that the world's major religions have a complex, and at times paradoxical, relationship with capitalism, the chapter examines how religious and secular critiques of the market often have more in common than usually thought. This is a wide-ranging, theologically rich survey that merits the close attention of all scholars, whether religious or not. Taking a critical stance and subscribing to the tenets of one of the world's religions is not, Jafari explains carefully, incommensurable.

Rethinking consumers and markets: critiques of markets

In a hugely impressive literature review, Denegri-Knott offers an updated map for the study of power in marketing. Utilizing her extensive knowledge of political and social theory, she delineates three approaches to the study of power: sovereign, hegemonic and discursive. Within these terrains, Denegri-Knott provides a theoretically and conceptually rigorous review of the key literatures that should form the springboard for anyone wanting to adopt the theoretical frameworks increasingly being applied to a range of marketing and consumption phenomena.

The map that she generates provides the reader with a general impression of affiliations between core power concepts and linkages within marketing and consumer research. It reveals the prominence of the sovereign and discursive models of power, and the waning of the hegemonic model. The latter does not necessarily signal a lack of utility in the present context. As Denegri-Knott concludes, there is still much work to be done across all three models in terms of adopting a more critical orientation and increased methodological rigor in their application and extension.

In their chapter on ideology and Critical Marketing Studies, Eckhardt, Varman and Dholakia, challenge the taken-for-granted status of marketing as an ideologically neutral toolkit. There is, they aver, nothing neutral about marketing. It operates as a blunt instrument, exerting tremendous violence and death upon subaltern groups who must produce the surplus value for capitalism to survive and thrive. While these acts of violence are committed in what Goffman (1959) might term the backstage of marketing practice, namely within value and supply chain networks, in the front of house, corporate brand strategies project "lovable" brands for the benefit of the well-endowed stakeholder constituencies of brand-owning corporations and their customers in the West. In advancing our understanding of marketing and ideology, Eckhardt and her colleagues force us to confront what marketing ideology hides behind the optimism of branding.

Despite evidence that the practice of inter-continental commerce was undertaken by the earliest civilizations, the theoretical development of international marketing as a field of scholarly pursuit is a relatively recent affair. Özlem Sandıkcı Türkdoğan draws parallels with the disciplinary development of marketing, managerialism and prominent geo-economic and political interests post-1900. A result of this is that the theoretical and conceptual underpinning of international marketing is burdened with a perspective that frames the discussion into a binary distinction of sameness (Western) and difference (non-Western). Drawing upon Critical Marketing Studies and Consumer Culture Theory, Sandıkcı Türkdoğan problematizes the unreflexive application of international marketing in non-Western contexts. This project to appreciate the multiplicity of local perspectives and challenge dominant universalizing narratives is, nonetheless, hampered by the geo-politics of knowledge production in our discipline and the ability of researchers from non-English speaking developing economies to engage with the relevant literatures as well as overcome hurdles to publication.

Ruby Roy Dholakia, Fuat Fırat and Nik Dholakia have been pioneers in exploring the issue of choicelessness in the marketplace. This is in stark contrast to much marketing theory which devotes a great deal of attention to the issue of choice, often uncritically valorizing it (see Kasabov & Warlow, 2012). Nevertheless, there is a growing appreciation that choice is not an unalloyed good. Similarly, not all people have equal access to the resources provided by the marketplace (Arnould, 2007). Nor should they necessarily, especially with respect to the all too prevalent trafficking of human beings to provide forced labor and sexual services to paying customers (Pennington, Ball, Hampton & Soulakova, 2009). Indeed, the provision of prostitutes to help smooth a business transaction is starting to gain academic attention, as is slavery in supply chains (e.g. Smith & Betts, 2015).

If you are wealthy, then the marketplace offers its cornucopia up for attention. Those who lack financial resources, the affordances of education or who are disabled in some way, find the marketplace much harder to negotiate. One of the limitations of consumer research to date has been its focus on those with the resources to exercise a fairly wide latitude in terms of their consumption options. This is starting to change with the attention being given to those considered "vulnerable" in some way. Poverty, certainly, makes one less secure, and open to predation by those offering loans at exorbitant interest rates (e.g. the recent Netflix documentary, *Dirty Money*). For Dholakia and colleagues, we need to pay attention to the delimited experiences of people within the market. Choicelessness, they write, is something that many people will experience at some point in their lives. Certainly, those located in poorer nations, with lower average per capita income levels, are probably exposed to choicelessness with some frequency.

In exploring the topic, the authors take us from mainstream perspectives that herald choice, positioning it as one of the core attributes that a capitalist (versus communist) market provides to all those willing to enroll in its production and consumption circuits. Closely related is the concept of consumer sovereignty – a subject explored in depth by Tadajewski in this volume. The idea that we have freedom within the marketplace and, through our spending power, are able to influence firm decision-making has been questioned by many different groups, including mainstream and critical academics alike.

For example, recent research that explores the lived experience of larger consumers (i.e. the "Fatshionista" movement) has documented that the availability of disposable income and a will-to-spend does not necessarily mean that companies will cater to your requirements (Scaraboto & Fischer, 2013). Sovereignty is, Dholakia et al. remind us, limited. Many other chapters in this collection would concur with this analysis. But, Dholakia et al. do not wish to suggest that choice is necessarily always a bad thing or that it is never present in the marketplace. Such generalizations are likely to misrepresent the experiences of various groups. Their point is that we need to attend to the benefits of choice, any associated costs and the ways in which people do negotiate the marketplace (e.g. satisficing, making compromises and so forth).

What we need to register, appreciate and research far more thoroughly than has been the case to date is the structuring of consumption. The necessity of doing so becomes apparent when we realize that our agency functions in a similar way to the computer game analogy used by Arvidsson (2005) and repeated in his chapter with Alex Giordano in this volume. Programmers define the landscape in which a computer game character can move; the same is roughly found in the marketplace. As Dholakia, Fırat and Dholakia put it:

> Consumers in contemporary market structures . . . are able to make choices from among the many alternatives, but these alternatives are predetermined for them – the palette to choose from is fixed . . . Co-creation processes, as articulated by marketing and business researchers, seemingly open up spaces for consumers to craft choice options, focus on the attribute rather than at the macro level. Rarely are consumers able to construct "real" alternatives (by and for) themselves . . . the alternatives offered are always limited to those that the producers-providers find feasible. In a market economy, those alternatives that rise to the top are profitable (or cost efficient) for the producer-provider.

For his contribution, Crockett focuses on how racial stigma in consumer culture can be understood by investigating boundary work, that is, work carried out to reinforce and challenge social distinctions that separate realms of the self. Such work, as he finds in his study of middle-class African Americans living in the USA, produces practices such as being cosmopolitan, with status-oriented consumption used to make everyday life more tolerable and as a way of managing stigma. Crockett identifies that the most prevalent stigma this community faces are attributions of low status (among others). As a way forward, he suggests that we critically historicize concepts such as stigma and racism.

Susan Dunnett, Kathy Hamilton and Maria Piacentini contribute a critical overview of consumer vulnerability and the insight generating potential of non-conventional methods. Their chapter draws attention to the value of "found secondary data" in documentaries and autobiographies as sources for research as well as storied and visual representations as optimal tools to expose and help remedy consumer vulnerability. They close by calling for a more reflective consideration of the social impact of our intellectual labor in the study of vulnerability, and outline possible areas for inquiry including how deprivation and disadvantage are represented in the media.

The aim of Maurice Patterson's chapter is to firmly position embodiment as a core concern for consumer research. To do this, he discusses differences between the natural, socially constructed and lived bodies. Concentrating his attention on Merleau-Ponty's intentional arc and corporeal schema and Bourdieu's habitus and field, he illustrates how these concepts have shaped key themes in consumer research including bodies of/in representation, the body project and the agency of bodies. He suggests that those interested in pursuing this topic should prioritize the study of what it means to "experience in" and through the body and the kinds of consumption it makes possible.

Critical Marketing: marketing practices in focus

In their chapter, Arvidsson and Giordano provide an overview of two critical perspectives on brand management. The first approach suggests that brands form an ideology and thereby obfuscate social reality. This view, of course, calls forth Marx, commodity fetishism and related ideas. Put simply, when we purchase a brand, all we see are the images and symbolism that manufacturers and retailers want to promote. It is extremely difficult to secure a realistic representation of the constitution of the product – the conditions under which it was produced, the people who were involved and the ecological impact of its distribution or disposal. Brand images are essentially the shiny surfaces that help divert us from what can be unpleasant realities.

On the other hand, the second approach emphasizes how people use brands as symbolic resources to (re)produce their identities. While certainly not a new perspective (Ladik, Carrillat & Tadajewski, 2015), this viewpoint has gained considerable purchase on the thought communities in marketing who draw upon postmodernism and various facets of Consumer Culture Theory. Arvidsson and Giordano propose that these two approaches have to be expanded to include critical analyses of the contemporary features of capitalism, such as social media, the ubiquity of brands, and self-branding. Accordingly, there is a need to understand how consumers actively create self-alienation and apparatuses of self-surveillance in the contemporary world of branding.

In a wide-ranging review, Lorna Stevens delivers a critical discussion of gender in marketing. This is an important topic. Let us be clear: sex is a biological distinction; gender is a social construction. Erving Goffman (1979) illuminated this issue superbly in his work on gender and advertising. It is produced, circulated and reaffirmed by social relations and the expectations of many stakeholders, some more powerful than others. Unsurprisingly, given the tenacity of extant power structures, the dichotomy between what constitutes masculine and feminine practices continues to reinforce traditional gender roles in marketing practice, leading to delimited opportunities for women. Historically, this has been a problem (Tadajewski & Maclaran, 2013). Throughout the twentieth century, opportunities for women in marketing practice have been restricted. Those with the tenacity – and it took a great deal of it – to break through the glass ceiling that prevented them accessing appropriate training courses usually found themselves involved with product lines that were considered traditionally feminine (Tadajewski, 2013; Zuckerman, 2013). Bigger accounts were beyond their purview in many cases. These difficulties were compounded when race was a factor (e.g. Davis, 2013, 2017).

Stevens' chapter reviews the literature on services marketing and emotional labor with a focus on the higher education sector. Emotional labor is a concept associated with the writings of Arlie Russell Hochschild (1983) and basically involves an individual (i.e. an airline attendant) suppressing their real emotions and performing those that are expected in a certain situation. Its close cousins are positive thinking, positive psychology and related discourses which place undue emphasis on the individual and their ability to adjust the self and neglect the work environment and wider social changes that deserve critical reflection (Ehrenreich, 2009).

Put otherwise, if we feel unhappy, but emotional labor is an expectation, we have to present ourselves as happy, smiling, and performing the bodily routines demanded by our bosses. It is potentially exhausting (think about smiling all day at customers) and alienating. The latter is especially likely to manifest if emotional labor is required from certain groups and not others. For Stevens, a paradigmatic case of the skewed requirement of emotional labor and its accompanying forms of "surface" (i.e. very superficial presentations of a certain form of self) and "deep acting" (i.e. where we truly try to present a picture of sincerity and shared emotional feeling) is the academic world. It is a problem in the sense that Stevens quite rightly pinpoints an unequal division of labor in the scholarly community and she outlines these debates in an exemplary fashion.

Our next chapter is by two highly knowledgeable marketing thinkers, Detlev Zwick and Alan Bradshaw. Both have been pushing the theoretical and conceptual boundaries of our discipline for some time now. In this contribution, they develop their account of biopolitical marketing. This concept represents a critical response to the growth of interest in, and utilization of, brand communities and the labor of consumers. Marketers like to believe that we are all avid fans of their brands. To be sure, some people are prominent and vocal influencers when it comes to brands such as Apple. Stephen Fry is an example that comes to mind. However, what Zwick and Bradshaw question is the extent to which discrete entities such as brand communities really exist. How many people, in reality, do you know who participate actively in brand-related activities – not just brand sponsored, but brand focused, travelling to the headquarters of the organization or engaging in closely tied corporate events. Probably relatively few.

Even so, one of the objectives of brand management is to get as close to the consumer as possible. With the profit motive driving their behavior, marketers have started to develop platforms on which people can engage with their brands, deepening their immersion into the world of the product, sharing their experiences with others, and – hopefully – offering product development advice and inspiration to corporations free of charge or in exchange for limited remuneration (e.g. free products like Lego). Tapping into user experience, into the lifeworld of the individual, and using their knowledge, insights and social connections to advance corporate objectives is what is meant by the term "biopolitical marketing". For Zwick and Bradshaw, it is part of an effort to distance marketing practice from any manipulative associations. Practitioners strive to enable user creativity, foster the imagination of their customer base and thereby extract value – financial, cultural and symbolic value. In this process, the boundary between producer and consumer is blurred.

In the writings about the "working consumer", these types of processes raise the specter of exploitation (Cova & Dalli, 2009). Cova and Dalli's (2009) position is comparable to the idea of "false consciousness" articulated by the Critical Theorists, that is, where people do not understand how they are being manipulated by outside forces such as marketing professionals. Clearly, this was and remains a strong argument to make as it tends to smack of elitism. Scholars peering from the lofty heights of the ivory tower can discern that people are being manipulated, but those actually being manipulated cannot.

Moving away from this position, Cova, Pace and Skålén (2015) now claim that brand communities are not manipulated in the strong sense assumed by the working consumer thesis. Rather, those involved register that companies are using them for their immaterial labor (i.e. their knowledge and insights) but undertake these activities willingly as they provide close bonds with the company and access to advanced knowledge about new products and services. As Zwick and Bradshaw explain, this process of value extraction has been greatly enabled by the internet, particularly Web 2.0. There are various implications that can be drawn from this technological revolution: power relations within the marketplace have shifted and innovation can just as easily come from outside an organization as from within it.

What companies have to do is find ways to capture and extract consumer-driven innovation. Despite what the first generation of Critical Theorists might have supposed, the ability of corporations to do so is somewhat limited. The people they would like to use to generate value for the firm often do not adhere closely to corporate policies, guidelines or timelines. They cannot be as easily controlled as a traditional workforce. As such, the desire of marketers to extract value in a seamless, almost Fordist-like process, is unlikely to happen apart from in limited circumstances. Whether we believe these processes are manipulative, coercive, or involve some kind of compromise is, as academics like to say, probably only discernible on a case-by-case basis. Cova and Paranque, in their chapter on exploitation and emancipation, offer the interested reader further theoretical and empirical insights into related issues.

Cova and Paranque provide us with a theoretical exegesis of the topics of exploitation and emancipation as the key building blocks of Critical Marketing. This review is deeply indebted to Marxist and Post-Marxist theory. In their chapter, we are effectively encouraged to think beyond the type of elective postmodernism that rose to prominence in the 1990s of which Cova was a proponent. What Cova embodies, for us, is the type of scholar who is willing to revisit his ideas and assumptions and challenge them. He does not rest on his laurels, but maneuvers around the world of marketing theory and practice, turning a variety of theoretical approaches on to related phenomena. The difference in interpretation that results can be striking.

The work on emancipation has focused on freedom from the marketplace. This notion of freedom, or escaping the constraints of the market, needs much further research. We have to register that "escape" is a relative notion. In other words, not everyone wants to escape the market (Arnould, 2007). There are some products – anti-retroviral drugs, for instance – that consumers in emerging economies wanted at appropriate price points. The pharmaceutical industry, however, had another agenda in mind entirely, leading to the preventable deaths of many millions of people (Gray, 2013). These wanted the market to cater to their needs; it did not.

Of course, the concentration of industry often reduces the power of consumers, so the reality is that there is a political economy of choice within which we exist, with more powerful actors dictating the offerings that are available. We, in turn, select from the limited subset ultimately presented to us (Tadajewski, 2010b). And, if large companies – indeed, whole industries – decide to withdraw a particular choice option from us, there is often relatively little that can be done, even when people mobilize in fairly substantial groups, as the case of the electric car underlined when it was first introduced in California and then recalled (e.g. Paine, 2007).

Notwithstanding the above, many companies trade on the notion that they are helping emancipate us, helping us achieve our goals. The reality is often far different. Anti-competitive practices, discrimination, environmental pollution and heavy-duty lobbying by firms help reaffirm the political-economic status quo, prevent some people from accessing services, lead to a deterioration in the natural environment and continue to cement marketplace asymmetries (e.g. Greenwald, 2006). But it is not all doom and gloom. Cova and Paranque examine some of the more recent approaches to resistance and emancipation that interpret consumers as prosumers and co-creators. This type of language is useful for marketers. It flattens the ontology of the marketplace. The dominant logic of capitalism is, they conclude, remarkably resilient.

Fougère delivers a seminal overview of the international political economy literature. When we consult most marketing scholarship, it is often the case that few links are made between the wider sphere of capitalism, production relations, consumption decision-making and their interconnected ramifications. As a way of encouraging Critical Marketing scholars to expand their intellectual horizons, he accentuates the need to combine insights from economics and international relations, using these to examine marketing practices across the globe. His example is extremely contemporary and of considerable significance – politically, economically and environmentally – namely the global palm oil market. Fougère deploys a variety of perspectives on international political economy that range from those informed by Marxist dependency theory and world-systems theory, the analysis of fictitious commodities, neo-Gramscian approaches, post-foundational discourse theory, sustainability studies, and the analysis of global commodity chains to illuminate how we can better understand (un)sustainable marketing practice when we look at it via the prism of political economy.

Our penultimate chapter is authored by one of the leading lights in communications studies, Christian Fuchs. It is actually hard to place Fuchs in a single discipline since his work is resolutely interdisciplinary, incorporating a detailed knowledge of philosophy, social theory, communications theory, marketing and consumer research. His expertise on social media and "Big Data" is unparalleled. So, we were glad when he accepted our invitation to write the chapter on the connections between social media, Big Data and Critical Marketing. Fuchs submits that some of the most visible companies in the world – companies whose services most people probably use on a daily basis, including Facebook and Google – are not in fact platforms for social engagement with peers or a search engine, but actually some of the biggest advertising agencies on the planet. They sell eyeballs, not interaction or the ability to search for pictures of cats.

As a result of our continued interaction with them, they generate huge amounts of data, more information than a human being could possibly process in any vaguely reasonable time. They are storehouses of what has been called Big Data – vast swathes of information that can only be effectively mined using advanced algorithms. This data is, as Fuchs notes correctly, the product of human agency. Yet, we are probably only dimly aware of how much information we give away to these organizations. These topics, of course, speak to the issues of manipulation and control that have appeared throughout multiple chapters in this book. Facebook has, after all, been in the media for a variety of reasons connected to the U.S. elections of late. Of equal, if not more significance to people using these platforms, is the extent to which they can be subject to subtle forms of manipulation; manipulation that targets their emotions and feelings. One of the problems with this is that using a news feed to modify the emotions someone is feeling can be both positive and negative. It can influence consumer buying behavior (depressed people tend to be pretty good consumers (Rossini, 2015)). But it does not merely influence behavior on-line, it shapes behavior off-line too. After we switch off our computers, our emotions do not necessarily change. As a consequence, the power of these social media companies, with their armory of Big Data, raises a host of ethical questions.

Fuchs provides detailed insights into these interconnected issues. He presents the ideas of a number of influential thinkers whose views can help us understand what these companies are doing; how they conceptualize the consumer; and what methods they use to extract value from them. We are thus treated to reviews of the work of Dallas Smythe, Karl Marx and Sut Jhally, and Fuchs carefully unfolds his own treatment of the concept of digital labor – an analysis that usefully supplements the work of Zwick, Bradshaw, Cova and Paranque. He concludes in Aldersonian fashion by outlining a large number of topics that warrant research. Those looking for undergraduate, postgraduate or research degree projects should consult these for inspiration.

Capitalism, for many social thinkers, is founded upon and fosters violence (Livingstone, 2015). In the final chapter, Ayrosa and Oliveira provide a theoretically advanced study which proposes that consumer culture plays an important role in the establishment of a "plateau of indifference", a level of violence that seems natural or passes unnoticed. They review different theories of violence and build propositions that summarize the processes involved in the creation of "subjective" and "objective" forms of violence. Certainly, the marketplace is rife with acts of violence. As Fırat (2018) appreciates, there are many people around the world working in unhealthy and dangerous conditions to produce the goods we desire. The same can be said of those disposing of the items we have consumed, handling harmful chemicals and materials, thereby endangering their health and the natural environment in which they live (e.g. Hill & Dhanda, 2004). Taking this even further, those facing the greatest level of financial precarity may find themselves experiencing "bioviolence". This is where people literally sell their organs in the marketplace, with advertisements in Bangladesh calling for such "donations" (Moniruzzaman, 2012). The violence that accompanies these trades is sometimes quite literally physical and often has mental repercussions. More generally it could be claimed that the overwhelming majority of us suffer – to some extent – from the violence of the market (e.g. Ehrenreich, 2002). We have to sell our labor power, otherwise we cannot obtain the resources necessary to sustain our lives. With the rollback of social safety nets courtesy of neoliberal economic policies in "developed" and "developing" countries, implied and explicit threats can be remarkably effective in rendering us the docile bodies needed by capitalism.

Notes

1 This definition is an orientation device, nothing more.
2 Other books, such as Henry George's *Progress and Poverty*, published in a similar period to Bellamy's (i.e. the 1880s) could be linked with the emergence of the critical sensibilities of other actors in our intellectual genealogy. Helen Woodward retired from her advertising career relatively early, turning to critical evaluations of the role of advertising in society. She cites Henry George's book as an important influence in focusing her attention on the inequities of the social world and how they are reaffirmed (Tadajewski, 2013). Morgan (1944) sees both *Looking Backward* and *Progress and Poverty* as seminal products of a period of social upheaval when attempts were being made to rethink the economic and social system along more equitable and progressive lines.
3 *Looking Backward* and *Equality* are far removed from other books that the reader might have consulted at some time. Freedom, the encouragement to use one's cognitive skills, independent choice-making, and personal self-development figure far more prominently in these books than is found in the "behavioral engineering" characteristic of Skinner's (1948/2005) *Walden Two*.
4 Regarding the use of consumption for the symbolic representation of status differentiation, the literature is actually far more complex than we can possibly unpack here. There were various thinkers beginning to explore similar lines of thought to Veblen, John Rae being one of the most well explicated (e.g. Alcott, 2004). This said, these issues are not a feature solely of industrial life, although this was the period when they were being most problematized (e.g. Ladik, Carrillat & Tadajewski, 2015).
5 Although we should add that Veblen was often careful when using terminology that might otherwise sound critical – invidious, for example – to stress that he was using it in a technical sense, that is, there should be no imputation of judgment, positive or negative. His sarcasm and wit, though, often shine through his work, lending it a deeply critical edge.
6 For example, the production line, extreme specialization, repetitive work, leading to efficient manufacturing processes and lower prices, thereby expanding the market.
7 The point of divergence hinges on how radical we think social change needs to be. If we expect wholesale radical change along the lines of a sudden transformation to socialism – something very unlikely to happen – then Kinley and the German Historical School appear less radical. But no scholar to our knowledge actually subscribes to this position. The most radical argument that we know of asks us to question the idea that "markets" and "marketing" as they currently stand are "a non-contested starting point" (Tadajewski, 2014). Critical Marketing Studies, by its very nature, is contesting some element of markets, marketing and the assumptions that underwrite that scholarly discipline that helps legitimate, justify and expand their currency in policy debates.
8 Neurath and related figures often used the terminology "logical empiricism" to describe their school of thought; the boundaries between this and "logical positivism" are far from easily parsed however.

References

Alcott, B. (2004). John Rae and Thorstein Veblen. *Journal of Economic Issues*, 38(3), 765–786.
Arnould, E. (2007). Should consumer citizens escape the market? *The Annals of the American Academy of Political and Social Science*, 611(1), 96–111.
Arvidsson, A. (2005). Brands: A critical perspective. *Journal of Consumer Culture*, 5(2), 235–258.
Ashton, J.K., & Pressey, A. (2008). The regulatory perception of the marketing function: An interpretation of UK competition authority investigations 1950–2005. *Journal of Public Policy & Marketing*, 27(2), 156–164.
Bellamy, E. (1888/1996). *Looking backward*. London, Dover.
Bellamy, E. (1897). *Equality*. New York, D. Appleton and Company.

Benton, R. (1985). Alternative approaches to consumer behaviour. In N. Dholakia & J. Arndt (Eds.), *Changing the course of marketing: Alternative paradigms for widening marketing theory* (pp. 197–218). Greenwich, JAI Press.

Bernays, E. (1928/2005). *Propaganda*. New York, Ig Publishing.

Borch, F.J. (1958). The marketing philosophy as a way of business life. In E.J. Kelley & W. Lazer (Eds.), *Managerial marketing: Perspectives and viewpoints. A source book* (pp. 18–24). Homewood, Richard D. Irwin.

Bourdieu, P. (1998). *Acts of resistance: Against the tyranny of the market*. New York, The New Press.

Bradshaw, A., & Dholakia, N. (2012). Outsider's insights: (Mis)understanding A. Fuat Fırat on consumption, markets and culture. *Consumption Markets & Culture, 15*(1), 117–131.

Bristor, J.M., & Fischer, E. (1993). Feminist thought: Implications for consumer research. *Journal of Consumer Research, 19*(4), 518–536.

Butler, N., Delaney, H., & Spolestra, S. (2018). Risky business: Reflections on critical performativity in practice. *Organization*. Retrieved from https://doi.org/10.1177/1350508417749737

Caplovitz, D. (1967). *The poor pay more: Consumer practices of low-income families*. New York, Free Press.

Chatzidakis, A., Maclaran, P., & Bradshaw, A. (2012). Heterotopian space and the utopics of ethical and green consumption. *Journal of Marketing Management, 28*(3–4), 494–515.

Cova, B., & Dalli, D. (2009). Working consumers: The next step in marketing theory? *Marketing Theory, 9*(3), 315–339.

Cova, B., Pace, S., & Skålén, P. (2015). Brand volunteering: Value co-creation with unpaid consumers. *Marketing Theory, 15*(4), 465–485.

Davis, J.F. (2013). Beyond 'caste-typing'? Caroline Robinson Jones, advertising pioneer and trailblazer. *Journal of Historical Research in Marketing, 5*(3), 308–333.

Davis, J.F. (2017). Selling whiteness? A critical review of the literature on marketing and racism. *Journal of Marketing Management*. Retrieved from https://doi.org/10.1080/0267257X.2017.1395902

Dixon, D.F. (2008). Prejudice v. marketing? An examination of some historical sources. In M. Tadajewski & D. Brownlie (Eds.), *Critical marketing: Issues in contemporary marketing* (pp. 33–44). Chichester, Wiley.

Domosh, M. (2006). *American commodities in an age of empire*. London, Routledge.

Ehrenreich, B. (2002). *Nickel and dimed: Undercover in low-wage USA*. London, Granta Books.

Ehrenreich, B. (2009). *Smile or die: How positive thinking fooled America & the world*. London, Granta Books.

Ericson, R.V., & Doyle, A. (2006). The institutionalization of deceptive sales in life insurance. *British Journal of Criminology, 46*(6), 993–1010.

Ewen, S. (1988). *Captains of consciousness: Advertising and the social roots of consumer culture*. New York, McGraw-Hill.

Fırat, A.F. (2018). Violence in/by the market. *Journal of Marketing Management*. Retrieved from https://doi.org/10.1080/0267257X.2018.1432190

Fırat, A.F., & Venkatesh, A. (1995). Liberatory postmodernism and the reenchantment of consumption. *Journal of Consumer Research, 22*(3), 239–267.

Fournier, V., & Grey, C. (2000). At the critical moment: Conditions and prospects for critical management studies. *Human Relations, 53*(1), 7–32.

Goffman, E. (1959). *The presentation of self in everyday life*. New York, Doubleday.

Goffman, E. (1979). *Gender Advertisements*. New York, Harper & Row.

Gray, D.M. (2013). *Fire in the blood*. Northampton, Media Education Foundation.

Greenwald, R. (2006). *Wal*Mart: The high cost of low price*. London, Tartan Video.

Grey, C. (2018). Does Brexit mean the end for critical management studies in Britain? *Organization*. Retrieved from https://doi.org/10.1177/1350508418757567

Groysberg, B., Lin, E., Serafeim, G., & Abrahams, R. (2016). The scandal effect. *Harvard Business Review*, September, 90–98.

Hackley, C. (2001). *Marketing and social construction: Exploring the rhetorics of managed consumption*. London, Routledge.

Hill, R.P., & Dhanda, K.K. (2004). Confronting the environmental consequences of the high technology revolution: Beyond the guise of recycling. *Organization & Environment, 17*(2), 254–259.

Hochschild, A.R. (1983). *The managed heart: Commercialization of human feeling*. Berkeley, University of California Press.

Hunt, S.D. (2017). Advancing marketing strategy in the marketing discipline and beyond: From promise, to neglect, to prominence, to fragment (to promise?). *Journal of Marketing Management*. Retrieved from https://doi.org/10.1080/0267257X.2017.1326973

Huxley, A. (1932/2007). *Brave new world*. London, Vintage Books.
Huxley, A. (1958/2004). *Brave new world revisited*. London, Vintage Books.
Jones, D.G.B., & Tadajewski, M. (2018). *Foundations of marketing thought: The influence of the German Historical School*. London, Routledge.
Jorgensen, E.W., & Jorgensen, H.I. (1999). *Thorstein Veblen: Victorian firebrand*. New York: M.E. Sharpe.
Kasabov, E., & Warlow, A. (2012). *The compliance business and its customers*. New York, Palgrave Macmillan.
Kassarjian, H.H., & Goodstein, R.C. (2009). The emergence of consumer research. In P. Maclaran, M. Saren, B. Stern & M. Tadajewski (Eds.), *The SAGE handbook of marketing theory* (pp. 59–73). London, Sage.
Kinley, D. (1949). *The autobiography of David Kinley*. Urbana, University of Illinois Press.
Klein, N. (2005). *No logo*. London, Harper Perennial.
Knight, P. (2016). *Shoe dog: A memoir by the creator of Nike*. London, Simon & Schuster.
Ladik, D., Carrillat, F., & Tadajewski, M. (2015). Belk's 'Possessions and the Extended Self' revisited. *Journal of Historical Research in Marketing*, 7(2), 184–207.
Lasn, K. (1999). *Culture jam: How to reverse America's suicidal consumer binge – and why we must*. New York, Eagle Books.
Levitt, T. (1960). Marketing myopia. *Harvard Business Review*, 38(4), 45–56.
Livingstone, N. (2015). The hunger games: Food poverty and politics in the UK. *Capital & Class*, 39(2), 188–195.
Lowenthal, L. (1961). *Literature, popular culture, and society*. Englewood Cliffs, Prentice-Hall.
Martin, W. (2015). *Primates of Park Avenue: A memoir*. New York, Simon & Schuster.
Mitford, J. (2000). *The American way of death revisited*. London, Virago Press.
Moniruzzaman, M. (2012). 'Living cadavers' in Bangladesh: Bioviolence in the human organ bazaar. *Medical Anthropology Quarterly*, 26(1), 69–91.
Montgomery, K., Chester, J., Nixon, L., Levy, L., & Dorfman, L. (2017). Big data and the transformation of food and beverage marketing: Undermining efforts to reduce obesity? *Critical Public Health*. Retrieved from https://doi.org/10.1080/09581596.2017.1392483
Morgan, A.E. (1944). *Edward Bellamy*. New York, Columbia University Press.
Newman, M. (2005). *Socialism: A very short introduction*. Oxford, Oxford University Press.
O'Malley, L., & Prothero, A. (2004). Beyond the frills of relationship marketing. *Journal of Business Research*, 57(11), 1286–1294.
O'Malley, L., & Tynan, C. (1999). The utility of the relationship metaphor in consumer markets: A critical evaluation. *Journal of Marketing Management*, 15(7), 587–602.
Packard, V. (1960). *The hidden persuaders*. London, Penguin.
Paine, C. (2007). *Who killed the electric car?* London, Sony.
Parker, S., & Parker, M. (2017). Antagonism, accommodation and agonism in critical management studies: Alternative organizations as allies. *Human Relations*, 70(11), 1366–1387.
Pennington, J.R., Ball, A.D., Hampton, R.D., & Soulakova, J.N. (2009). The cross-national market in human beings. *Journal of Macromarketing*, 29(2), 119–134.
Puntoni, S., Schroeder, J.E., & Ritson, M. (2010). Meaning matters. *Journal of Advertising*, 39(2), 51–64.
Rossini, E. (2015). *The illusionists: A film about the globalization of beauty*. Northampton, Media Education Foundation.
Scaraboto, D., & Fischer, E. (2013). Frustrated fatshionistas: An institutional theory perspective on consumer quests for greater choice in mainstream markets. *Journal of Consumer Research*, 39(6), 1234–1257.
Scarpaci, J.L., Sovacool, B.K., & Ballantyne, R. (2016). A critical review of the costs of advertising: A transformative consumer research perspective. *Journal of Consumer Policy*, 39(2), 119–140.
Scitovsky, T. (1976). *The joyless economy: An inquiry into human satisfaction and consumer dissatisfaction*. New York, Oxford University Press.
Shankar, A. (2009). Reframing critical marketing. *Journal of Marketing Management*, 25(7–8), 681–696.
Skinner, B.F. (1948/2005). *Walden Two*. Indianapolis, Hackett Publishing Company.
Smith, K.T., & Betts, T. (2015). Your company may unwittingly be conducting business with human traffickers: How can you prevent this? *Business Horizons*, 58(2), 225–234.
Spicer, A., Alvesson, M., & Kärreman, D. (2009). Critical performativity: The unfinished business of critical management studies. *Human Relations*, 62(4), 537–560.
Tadajewski, M. (2010a). Critical marketing studies: Logical empiricism, 'critical performativity' and marketing practice. *Marketing Theory*, 10(2), 201–222.

Tadajewski, M. (2010b). Towards a history of critical marketing studies. *Journal of Marketing Management*, *26*(9–10), 773–824.

Tadajewski, M. (2010c). Reading 'the marketing revolution' through the prism of the FBI. *Journal of Marketing Management*, *26*(1–2), 90–107.

Tadajewski, M. (2011). Critical marketing studies. In M. Tadajewski, P. Maclaran, E. Parsons & M. Parker (Eds.), *Key concepts in critical management studies* (pp. 83–87). London, Sage.

Tadajewski, M. (2013). Helen Woodward and Hazel Kyrk: Economic radicalism, consumption symbolism and female contributions to marketing theory and advertising practice. *Journal of Historical Research in Marketing*, *5*(3), 385–412.

Tadajewski, M. (2014). What is critical marketing studies? Reading macro, social and critical marketing studies. In R. Varey and M. Pirson (Eds.), *Humanistic marketing* (pp. 39–52). London, Palgrave Macmillan.

Tadajewski, M. (2016a). Critical marketing studies and critical marketing education: Key ideas, concepts and materials. *RIMAR – Revista Interdisciplinar de Marketing*, *6*(2), 3–24.

Tadajewski, M. (2016b). Relevance, responsibility, critical performativity, testimony and positive marketing: Contributing to marketing theory, thought and practice. *Journal of Marketing Management*, *32*(17–18), 1513–1536.

Tadajewski, M. (2016c). Focus groups: History, epistemology and non-individualistic consumer research. *Consumption Markets & Culture*, *19*(4), 319–345.

Tadajewski, M., & Jones, D.G.B. (2012). Scientific marketing management and the emergence of the ethical marketing concept. *Journal of Marketing Management*, *28*(1–2), 37–61.

Tadajewski, M., & Jones, D.G.B. (2016). Hyper-power, the marketing concept and consumer as 'boss'. *Marketing Theory*, *16*(4), 513–531.

Tadajewski, M., & Maclaran, P. (2013). Remembering female contributors to marketing theory, thought and practice. *Journal of Historical Research in Marketing*, *5*(3), 260–272.

Taylor, F.W. (1911/1998). *The principles of scientific management*. London, Dover.

Time (2018). The opioid diaries. March 5.

Tynan, C. (1997). A review of the marriage analogy in relationship marketing. *Journal of Marketing Management*, *13*(7), 695–703.

Varman, R., Skålén, P., & Belk, R.W. (2012). Conflicts at the bottom of the pyramid: Profitability, poverty alleviation, and neoliberal governmentality. *Journal of Public Policy & Marketing*, *31*(1), 19–35.

Veblen, T. (1899/1994). *The theory of the leisure class*. London, Dover.

Veblen, T. (1921/2006). *The engineers and the price system*. New York, Cosimo.

Veblen, T. (1923/2009). *Absentee ownership: Business enterprise in recent times: The case of America*. New Brunswick, Transaction Publishers.

Vossoughian, N. (2011). *Otto Neurath: The language of the global polis*. Rotterdam, NAi Publishers.

White, P. (1927). *Scientific marketing management: Its principles and methods*. New York, Harper & Brothers.

Wilkie, W.L., & Moore, E.S. (1999). Marketing's contributions to society. *Journal of Marketing*, *63*(Special Issue), 198–218.

Zuckerman, M.E. (2013). Martha van Rensselaer and the Delineator's homemaking department. *Journal of Historical Research in Marketing*, *5*(3), 370–384.

PART I

Exploring the terrain of Critical Marketing Studies

2
POSTMODERNISM AND CRITICAL MARKETING

Nikhilesh Dholakia and A. Fuat Fırat

Introduction

In the 20th century, radical waves of postmodernism swept through various aesthetic fields – visual arts, cinema, music, dance, architecture, literature, advertising, and more. The postmodern tendencies especially accelerated following World War II, but their roots were already planted during the iconoclastic art movements of the early years of the 20th century (Hopkins, 2004).

By the late 1980s, the marketing discipline – at least the section of the discipline that is self-reflexive and is inclined to delve into deep (and not just mid-range) theory – began to examine postmodernism in earnest. Many significant writings on postmodernism and marketing appeared in the closing decade of the 20th century (Brown, 1993; Cova, 1996; Fırat, Dholakia & Venkatesh, 1995; Fırat, Sherry & Venkatesh, 1994; Fırat & Shultz, 1997; Fırat & Venkatesh, 1993, 1995; Venkatesh, Sherry & Fırat, 1993). By the advent of the 21st century, however, postmodernism had nearly disappeared from aesthetic and literary, as well as social theory, and had also dwindled in the business and marketing academic discourses (for an exception, see Fırat & Dholakia, 2006), though not from marketing practice – where it had found a comfortable niche (Czajkowski, 2015; Roth, 2010). Indeed, in terms of social practice, the rise of Donald Trump to the U.S. presidency presented a mega-example of observable – and perverse – postmodern processes and conditions, including the disturbing emergence of "post-truth" as the Oxford English Dictionary's word-of-the-year for 2016. The Trump triumph is surely going to lead to a major reexamination of the ideas of postmodernism in social theoretical fields (Dholakia & Reyes, 2018).

This chapter explores the linkages of postmodernism to critical marketing thought. Prima facie, postmodernism and critical perspectives often appear to be incompatible domains. Often it is believed, incorrectly, that the observed continuity of some conditions – that were accentuated in modern culture and persisted in the postmodern – indicate that postmodernism is not a critique, but rather an entrenchment, of modernity or modernism – an issue we discuss below. Postmodernism, in our assessment, is an intellectual approach for recognizing the illusions and shortcomings of modernism (Angus, 1989; Baudrillard, 1981; Harvey, 1989; Jameson, 1984; Lyotard, 1984). It has served as an awakening from the (unfulfilled) dreams of modernism and – in that sense – is of major critical significance. Postmodernism urges humanity to rethink its priorities and conceptualizations. In this sense, there is much untapped and latent critical potential in postmodernism: potential that needs to be developed via further critical, indeed radical, thinking.

In the prevalent technology-infused global age, reconceptualizing of postmodernism and marketing in a critical frame can provide the building blocks of a new human epoch that is less exploitative, more egalitarian, and creatively enabling and fulfilling for the billions whose present lot is to merely accept and operate within the confines of the plastic cage (Brown, 1995) of marketized consumer culture. Such unfolding and exploratory postmodern exercises – in the form of constant critical churning and fermenting – can engender new concepts and institutionalizations that capture the spirit and experiences of new epochs that transcends modernism in ways that fulfill human potential (see, for example, Boje & Hillon, 2017).

Marketing scholars, the reflective and critical ones – as inconceivable as this might seem, given the strong capitalist commercial taint of the discipline and its adherents – might have the greatest potential to lead the effort to unleash the transformative possibilities of postmodernism. It is not a quirk that we find many scholars from distinct and varied fields – anthropology, sociology, history, philosophy, literary criticism, communication studies, and more – turning to phenomena that are the natural domain of marketing. Phenomena such as branding, advertising, positioning, public relations – and similar concepts that once appeared only in marketing papers and textbooks – have become the focus of widening circles of social theory (see, e.g., Aronczyk, 2013; Aronczyk & Powers, 2010; Arvidsson, 2006, 2007; Grainge & Johnson, 2015; Moor, 2007; Zwick & Cayla, 2011). This is because such phenomena constitute key elements of the market practices that have become central to dominant cultures of our time. Who is better placed to address these phenomena than marketing theorists? The potential to uncage the transformative power of postmodernism is present in marketing, it is the will in the discipline that is missing.

In this chapter, we revisit the nexus of postmodernism and marketing, starting with a brief overview of modernity. We then present a short historical review of postmodernism, including the cognate ideas of liquid modern, hypermodern and metamodern, always keeping in view the backdrop of marketing theory and practice. Following the brief review, the bulk of the discussion addresses issues that are relevant for the future of marketing theory and practice and, indeed, for wider social theory and practice as well:

- In what ways have the ideas of postmodernism been coopted (and usually celebrated) in marketing practices and by some authors dealing with marketing theory; and what has such cooptation/celebration done to these ideas?
- Despite such cooptation/celebration, how and why do the ideas of postmodernism retain a critical-radical-transformative edge, in terms of unmasking ideological stances that mainstream marketing favors, as well as probing the core nature of contemporary marketing phenomena?
- How can the ideas of postmodernism, and cognate and successor as well as progenitor ideas, be used for critical-radical renewal of theory and practice? In what ways can postmodernism engender new principles, fresh institutionalizations that reorganize social life, stimulating processes, novel constructs, and avant-garde phenomena that can guide marketing practices and concepts in particular, social processes in general, and humanity overall – toward a fairer, freer and more hopeful future?

Modernity: liquefaction of the bedrock

Although, circa-500 BC, quasi-modern philosophical ideas as well as some quasi-modern practices emerged in Greece, China and India (see Puett & Gross-Loh, 2016), these were squelched subsequently by the rise of powerful monarchies – in Europe as well as Asia – that reinstalled and reinforced the ancient notions of invariant traditions and fatalistic lives (Davis & Puett, 2015).

Modernity – as we know it now – has been with us for over three centuries, since the Enlightenment. For over two centuries prior to the Enlightenment, however, the European Renaissance already started witnessing modernist tendencies in art. Rather than limiting their images (i.e. objects of representation) just to gods, angels and devils, painters and sculptors – even as early as the 14th century – began to depict human figures in their art. The subject of attention and agency began shifting from the divine to the human. Rapid scientific and mathematical advances in Europe in the 16th and 17th centuries – with concomitant political changes – abetted the modernist forces. The idea gained ground that human beings could take their destiny into their own hands rather than leave it at the mercy of forces above and beyond them. In effect, humanity marched ahead, to wrest control – of its fate – from nature (Angus, 1989). The modern project of building a grand future began to take shape. A new world – the modern one – began to be envisioned, a world that would liberate the human individuals from all oppression, whether it came from nature or other humans. This modern world would allow people to reach their innate potentials.

A complete upheaval – of the norms upon which traditional societies were organized – was required to realize this project of modernity (Steuerman, 1992). To organize modern society, modernist thinkers had to devise a new set of norms, based on reason and science as key intellectual pillars. The new modern norms would enable making distinctions between reasoned and unreasonable (or emotional) modes of thinking and behavior. A set of norms based on bipolar, oppositional categories (e.g., mind–body; reason–emotion; production–consumption; public–private) informed the proper mode of agency toward the grand future (see Table 2.1).

Originating from Europe and spreading – through colonialism and trade – to the rest of the world, modern culture began displacing and replacing traditional cultures that were guided by spiritual ideologies. In place of spiritualism and religion, modern culture brought a focus on the material forces of the universe, forces of nature that influenced and often thwarted human

Table 2.1 The binaries of modernity

Feminine	**Masculine**
private	public
home	workplace
consumption	production
Woman (female)	**Man (male)**
consumer	producer
passive	active
incapable	capable
Body	**Mind**
emotional	rational
sensation	reason
submissive	assertive
powerless	powerful
Moon	**Sun**
nature	culture
Profane	**Sacred**
worthless	valuable
Property	**Owner**
product (object)	person (subject)

Source: Authors' conceptualization

efforts to take control. By scientifically discovering the principles of these forces, humanity could increase its control over them. Also, from a focus on the past – that in traditional cultures largely defined people's destiny and identity – modernity brought a focus on the future. The emerging "modern humans" – fired by imaginations of ideal, autonomous identities and futures that could be realized – became engaged in transformational projects. In these modern projects, humans turned their eyes firmly to the future.

Culture, all that is humanly created, would ameliorate and eventually take control over nature, all that is a given to humanity. Modern thinkers, as articulated by Habermas (inspired by Weber's work), imagined discursive domains of culture – science, morality, and art – each with its own set of principles: reason/objectivity, fairness/equality, and aesthetics (see Table 2.2). Each discursive domain was not to be contaminated by the principles of the other domains. Especially for science, the powerful system of knowledge that was to guide human action, such contamination would produce bias instead of true knowledge.

With the growth of modernity, culture was also separated into its practical domains – political, social, and economic (see Table 2.3). These practical domains also developed their own principles – democracy, civility, and economic value accumulation through efficient allocation of material resources. The practical domains also cultivated their key institutions through which the principle of the domain could be practiced – nation-state, nuclear family, and the market (Table 2.3).

As modernity matured, the economic domain took center stage, since it was the domain concerned with material resources. The growing centrality of the economic, in modernity, eventually spawned the "business school disciplines", including marketing, in the 20th century – the first marketing courses being offered by universities in Michigan, Illinois and California in 1902 (Applegate, 2008). These developments also gave birth, eventually, to the consumer culture and to the neoliberal ideology, which elevates the market above all other modern principles and institutions with the idea that the market, working according to its own logic, will generate all the ideal conditions that modern humans sought, including democracy.

Modernity created physical and conceptual edifices unmatched by all of preceding history. Even the combined ancient architectural glories of Egypt, Greece, Rome, Mesopotamia and China are dwarfed by the magnificence of global cities, factories, and infrastructure systems of the modern age. The same can be said of modern idea systems.

The modern edifices – especially the conceptual ones – stand increasingly, however, on seismically precarious intellectual grounds. In seismically perilous zones, there are often dangerously damaging episodes of "liquefaction". With seismic shocks, soil that is otherwise solid

Table 2.2 The discursive domains of modernity

Domain	Comments
Science	Scientist's ability to pursue reason and be objective required that s/he be free of considerations of justice and beauty.
Morality	Fairness was a matter of morals, not of reason or aesthetics (whether of beauty or ugliness).
Art	The aesthetic was purely an emotional matter, which would be vitiated if evaluations based on reason or fairness were to interfere.

Source: Authors' conceptualization

Table 2.3 The practical domains of modernity

Domain	Key institutions	Comments
Political	Nation-state	Concepts of nation and democracy took root in modernity, signaling the new set of norms and organization of life.
Social	Nuclear family	The nuclear family was the key institution to pass on to coming generations how to be civil, with support from other institutions, such as public education.
Economic	The market	Value, specifically economic or exchange value was the organizing principle of the modern economy, practiced through the market, which eventually became the central institution and the locomotive of modern life.

Source: Authors' conceptualization

temporarily behaves like a viscous liquid. Structures that stand on such vulnerable soil sink into the temporary quicksand created by seismic liquefaction, crumbling and collapsing. Modernity and its structures are facing increasing episodes of seismic jolting, liquefaction, crumbling and collapse. Therefore – for practical as well as philosophical reasons – we need to revisit postmodernism seriously, and generate fresh insights for the emerging world.

Postmodernism and beyond: an overview

Postmodernity has been characterized as a late modern period (Jameson, 1984; Featherstone, 2007) or, at times, a period following the end of modernity (Harvey, 1989; Lyotard, 1984). The former characterization emphasizes the conditions intensified by modern culture and its growing dominance globally, thus focusing on a continuity from modernity. The latter characterization emphasizes the postmodernist ideological reactions to modernist ideology, focusing on the rejection of some central tenets of modernism. It is possible to characterize postmodernity as a period of transition, therefore harboring both a continuation and a repudiation of modernity, modern culture and its idea(l)s. We think that this third characterization is the most reasonable considering the contemporary signs. While undoubtedly open to the charge of simplification, Table 2.4 nonetheless provides an overview of ideas of late stages of modernity that surround postmodernity.

Fırat and Venkatesh (1993) listed the conditions intensified by modernity as hyperreality, fragmentation, decentering of the subject, reversal of production and consumption, and paradoxical juxtaposition of opposites (each of these concepts is discussed below). These conditions – inherent in, yet denied by modernist ideology – have steadily dominated human lives especially in the second half of the 20th century and, perhaps even more dramatically, in the early decades of the 21st century (e.g., Dholakia & Reyes, 2018).

At the same time that modern scientific culture insisted on the presence of a reality independent of how human beings encountered it, the modern production machine was introducing unprecedented changes to what had existed outside of human interference. Within limits of human powers – for example, limits to how fast humans could move along the space-time continuum – even the physical, biological, and chemical realities that original *Homo sapiens* experienced were being transformed rapidly and radically. With the advent of modernity, the social, political, and economic realities faced by humans were transformed wrenchingly.

Table 2.4 Concepts of transforming modernity that surround postmodernity

Concept	Comments
Late modernity	A concept that refers to the stage in modernity when risks – that humanity did not face earlier – have arisen, related to emergence of weapons of mass destruction and ecological degradation, as well as to the collapse of global economic mechanisms and rise of totalitarian superstates.
Liquid modernity	A concept that refers to later stages of modernity, when all that was deemed stable becomes fluid and chaotic. Institutions, individuals, capital – all are in flux, changing, freely re-formable, and nomadic.
Hypermodernity	Loosely used concept that could refer to states such as virtual reality, body–machine melding. A broader view refers to an intensely and pervasively marketized world, driven increasingly by not-fully-controllable techno-sciences.
Metamodernism	Disappointed by modernity and disenchanted with postmodernity, artists and aesthetic theorists have been seeking new transcendental forms and vocabularies. Metamodernism is one such term, characterized by multiple simultaneous negations: place without a place, ordered disorder, futureless future; and reemergence-rebirth of the modern-postmodern dialectic.

Source: Authors' review and summarization

Humans imagined what life could be like, often hyped certain imaginaries – the system of symbols and institutions through which existence is imagined – and communicated them powerfully. With the aid of advancing science and technologies, in most cases, these hyped potentials turned into everyday realities. With modern tools of controlling nature and producing human-made environments, a hyperreal world was created – what was hype became the reality as wastelands and forests were turned into cities and deserts became agricultural land. Thus, hyperreality is not a postmodern creation; it is just that postmodernism, rather than renouncing or denouncing it, *recognizes* it as a human condition. With this postmodern impulse, humans are now experimenting with ending death through cloning (Kaku, 2012) and with changing the structure of DNA through adding new molecules to it, as they also added elements that did not exist in nature to the periodic table. Indeed, scientific advance and postmodern conditions are intersecting continually and dramatically to reshape not just society but humanity itself (Beniger, 2009; Castells, 2010; Ferrando, 2013).

Similarly, the other conditions that find their full expression in postmodernity were also present and nurtured in modernity. For example, modernity fragmented life moments in ways not experienced before. Work and home were separated from each other, as were moments when people perceived themselves to be in a production mode versus when they were consuming. The market, as an institution, and marketing as its institutionalized set of practices, fragmented the moments that people had with products in the market. Each product required time to be spent with it. Marketing efforts presented products as separate and distinctive, needing distinct focus and attention. Lifeworld and times-of-our-lives got sliced: there was a time to concentrate and "experience" the automobile, and a different time for television. Each moment had to be appreciated for itself, each product had to be admired for the fulfillment it could provide, as marketers presented each as an icon in itself.

With such fragmentation and attention to each product, an intense focus on consumption was promoted in modernity, especially by modern marketing practices. Yet, the key motivator for the turn to consumption in modernity – when early modern culture venerated production and regarded consumption as a necessary waste – was the loss of control the majority of the population experienced in production. The workings of the market rapidly concentrated capital and, thus, control of moments of production slipped into fewer and fewer centers of decision making, eventually controlled not so much by industrial-manufacturing capital at all as by finance (Dholakia, 2011). In modern culture, which had humans taking control of their destinies as its main theme, moments of consumption seemed the only ones that most individuals felt they had any control over. Production of meaning was, then, sought in consumption, creating the consumer culture and reversing the hierarchy of production and consumption. People more readily attributed value creation to moments of consumption rather than to moments of production, focusing on sign value (the value of a commodity or experience based on the symbolic meanings it elicits resulting from cultural discourses and negotiations among economic, social, and political interests), and sign value eventually dislodged the centrality of exchange value (Baudrillard, 1981).

This reversal was also reflected in the decentering of the subject, again developed in modernity. Value, the central principle of the market, came to be perceived as imbued in the product being consumed rather than with the producer of it. Objects of desire and the system of relations they constituted (Foucault, 1972/2010) thereby determined the structure of life moments and their meaning. The human being, the subject, gradually succumbed to the needs of the system of objects and the economy that produced them. In an economy that increased its productive capabilities, individual consumption had to be stimulated to absorb the output.

Thus, paradoxically, in a culture that had a long history of revering production, consumption took center stage (Fırat & Dholakia, 1998). Modernity, which was to create an order that gave the human individual (the subject) control over her/his own destiny to fulfill the potential s/he had, instead gave power to the objects. The subject – who was to realize oneself in what s/he produced – could only express oneself through what s/he consumed. Individual identity projects became consumer projects. Paradoxes abounded as – in these various ways – opposites were constantly juxtaposed.

As this postmodern, transitional period intensified, it also provided space for discourses that repudiated the many ideological principles of modern culture. To have an order that would make it possible to reach the goals of the modern projects – be they the individual, ethnic, national, or other identity projects; or the overall cultural project of creating a grand future for all humanity – modern thought had articulated the principles of this order in terms of bipolar evaluative oppositions (see Table 2.1). In modernity, one side of the binary represented the superior, positive, good, proper qualities that would guide modern society. The other side of the binary represented qualities that were inferior, negative, bad, improper – qualities of the old and dying order that could subvert the accomplishment of modern projects. The negative qualities, therefore, needed to be kept suppressed and not allowed to influence matters of public and social progress. Postmodernism is critical of this approach to the construction of the modern order.

According to the postmodern sensibility, suppression of any human urge, such as bodily urges in opposition to the mind or emotional urges as opposed to reason, creates uncontrollable consequences instead of knowledge and understanding. Postmodernism, therefore, suggests playful and conscious engagement with all aspects of human culture instead of their suppression. This sensibility, in turn, results in seeking multiplicity instead of dualities, recognition of difference as difference rather than inferiority or superiority, and a general tolerance and appreciation for alternatives. It is this sensibility that makes postmodernism not reject modernity (or its key principles and institutions, such as democracy and the nation-state in the political domain, and economic value and the market in the economic domain) but to insist against the singular dominance or hegemony of modernist principles.

Postmodernism seeks to locate the central principles of modernity in a non-hierarchical manner, in spaces that also contain other principles and institutions. This is what makes postmodernism different from anti-modernism, which demands the erasure of all that is modern to be replaced by one alternate order. A postmodernist sensibility demands that a multiplicity of orders be tolerated and appreciated; and that it be possible to freely navigate within and across these orders (Fırat & Dholakia, 1998). This is, indeed, a critical stance. It is a stance that requires a radical transformation of principles that guide the organization of human lives.

Postmodernist sensibility also helped firmly put on the public agenda the realization that distinctions and discriminations occur based on sources other than class. Sex, race, ethnicity, gender identity, sexual orientation, and more became subjects of prominent discourses – they all entered the social and political spaces where distinctions get made. Postmodernism helped articulate these discriminations to become more prominent in public discourses. Yet, one consequence of this prominence was that, in a fragmented market culture, each basis for discrimination could be, and was, used to obscure others. They were especially deployed to obscure class, which is the primary basis for discrimination through which market forces maintain capital accumulation. Identity politics – by accentuating differences along all the new categories of separating people – rather conveniently feeds into the obfuscation of class. In the fields of marketing and the derivative field of consumer culture theory, such obfuscation helps in creating a corpus of research that has an oft-colorful and sometimes mildly critical flavor but which, in reality, just helps in widening the discursive space for identity politics (Fırat & Dholakia, 2017).

Some of the more significant critical insights contributed by postmodernist discourses have to do with the concepts of power and agency. Both constructs are seen not as absolute determinations but temporal and contextual, in effect, contingent phenomena. While the effect of power in cultural constructions is acknowledged, power is theorized more as a distributed event rather than something possessed by some and lacked by others. It is a discursive phenomenon whereby almost all members of society share in the imaginary of the necessity for decision making to be controlled by a certain group, however large or small. Accordingly, all who share this imaginary – defined as the system of institutionalizations and symbols through which people perceive and represent their worlds – contribute to the specific distribution of power; some assuming control and others giving up control. Agency, then, at each period of power distribution, comes to be defined in terms of the logic of this distribution: those who behave in controlling modes being deemed to have agency. Consequently, the bases on which a distribution of power is culturally constructed can be, and are, different according to the context. All bases of power experienced in history – and the fact that they have been varied, such as physical, military, capital, information, etc. – attest to the truism that any number of bases and their uses are possible.

Overall, with the passage of time, postmodernism has exhibited a major tendency that it is associated with, and that postmodernism dwells on, namely, fragmentation. Postmodernism has splintered into postmodernisms. Some postmodernisms are unabashedly celebratory of some forms of contemporary capitalisms; others are solipsistic, self-absorbed, and oblivious to the prevalent socioeconomic conditions of people; yet others are so insistent on endless deconstruction that they verge on nihilism (Harvey, 1989). There do remain, however, postmodern possibilities that "could be deployed to radical ends, and thereby be seen as part of a fundamental drive towards a more liberatory politics" (Harvey, 1989, p. 353). Since we are writing critically, our interest is very much in these last forms.

Concluding comments on postmodernism and marketing

We noted earlier that in modern culture, with a philosophical emphasis on people taking control of their destinies, moments of consumption seemed to be the only ones that most people felt they had any control over. In other words, the avenues for individuality disappeared under the conditions of post-Fordist production (where production is globally dispersed into flexible units but highly controlled by central corporations through economic and financial dependencies), but seemingly remained available in the consumptive sphere. Conceptualizing the world through the intersecting prismatic of aesthetics, commerce, politics, and psychology, French aesthetic and cultural theorist Bernard Stiegler (2014) has gone a step further and argued that – from the early decades of the 20th century – individuality and individuation disappeared from the consumptive sphere as well, with emergent and fast-ascendant marketing techniques playing a key role in such disappearance. In Stiegler's view, new aesthetics, new production methods, and new marketing techniques intermingled to create new forms of consumerist "proletarianization", characterized by a "loss of knowledge" – in French – of "*savoir*" (Stiegler, 2011).

The essential radical postmodern challenge, going forward, is to recapture the *savoir* – the knowledge of how to produce and consume and have revolutionary fun in these processes – not under oligarchic corporate capitalist umbrellas, but in millions of communities and by billions of "construers-in-communion", people who together are willing and able to engage in construing the possibilities of new organizations of life they find meaningful and substantive (Fırat & Dholakia, 2016). Indeed, at the individual level, the new and radical postmodern forms of *savoir faire*, skills, and orientations required are not the typical refined bourgeois ways but rather what Fırat (2005) has labeled as "multi-sign-efficacy". The new literacy needed under postmodern conditions is to not only read and write but to have the capability to gauge the strategies and hidden intentions behind written text. Furthermore, the new literacy should equip us to process and compose multi-media (sonic, visual, olfactory, etc.) communications, and be able to critically analyze these vehicles beyond simply being affected by such sensory forces.

Another essential radical postmodern challenge, more important than the new *savoir* just discussed, is to offer massive resistance to the perverse uses of postmodernity by reactionary oligarchic forces. The November 2016 electoral triumph of Donald Trump (as well as the Brexit vote earlier in 2016) showed that processes and ideas of postmodernism are not per se revolutionary or promising of a brighter future (see, e.g., Dholakia & Reyes, 2018) for the numerically vast global underclasses. The emergent mediascape formed by the intersections of traditional broadcast media, electronic social media, and augmented/virtual reality media indeed could become the stomping ground of media manipulators. Clever manipulators could promote jingoistic, xenophobic, exclusionary, misogynistic, and reactionary views; in ways that seem populist and pro-people but in fact lead to undercutting the interests of and the oppression of the most vulnerable population segments – segments that, on a global scale, are many times larger than the well-endowed middle and upper classes of advanced nations. Indeed, Stiegler (2011, 2014) seems to have foreseen the possibilities of the political shocks of 2016; he talked of the susceptibility to capture – of entrenched "genteel, modernist" platforms – by ascendant oligarchic Mafiosi (Stiegler, 2011).

The ways out of states of symbolic misery are participatory and aesthetic – calling for novel strategies, processes, and concepts that democratize the acts of aesthetic creation. There are, at present, mere pointers about how to do this. Considerable scholarly as well as practical efforts are needed to deepen the knowledge about bringing, and inter-linking, productive as well as consumptive acts, within human and humane ambits (see, e.g., Fırat & Dholakia, 2016).

Linking theory and practice under postmodern conditions is difficult, but doable. The feminist economic geography duo of Julie Graham and Katherine Gibson, writing under the pen name Gibson-Graham (2006, 2008, 2016), do not always rely on postmodern concepts (although they have done so at times, see Gibson-Graham, 1994). The approaches to practice and theory in their book *A Postcapitalist Politics*, and subsequent Gibson-Graham writings (e.g., Gibson-Graham, 2008; Gibson-Graham, Cameron, & Healy, 2016), however, have strong postmodern flavors. The palette of postmodernist ideas – conceptual as well as practical – available from the Gibson-Graham works include the following (and more):

- Post-market: Supplementing and complementing conventional market solutions and approaches for transacting with alternative-market and non-market solutions and approaches.
- Post-wage-labor: While wage labor – and its attendant prospects of exploitation and surplus extraction – might not go away, we should explore alternative-wage and non-wage ways of laboring.
- Postcapitalist: Without wasting effort to overthrow capitalism or sinking into dejection about the entrenched inevitability of capitalism, we should explore alternative-capitalist and non-capitalist political-economic ways of forming and running enterprises.
- Commoning: Moving the idea of "commons" away from the conventional contested-property capitalist view (i.e., of ownership and maximal extraction for economic benefit in the short term) and toward a multi-species, intergenerational, resource conservation and stewardship view; thereby spawning community-commons that are not prone to tragedy but bubble with felicity.

The inspiring aspect of the work being done by Gibson-Graham and cognate intellectuals and activists is that these efforts are constantly generating a growing stream of (in our view, mostly postmodern) practical examples, as well as steadily building new theories.

For applied fields in general, and for marketing in particular – given its closeness to postmodern concepts – it is imperative to engage in concerted efforts to celebrate (not berate and castigate) difference and to reinforce the rise of a system of multiple orders that are permeable, mutually tolerant, and harmoniously coexistent (Fırat & Dholakia, 2003, 2006). Indeed, for critical marketing scholars as well as for critical marketing practitioners (e.g., Adbusters), some of the main tasks are to resist the pernicious use of postmodernism for regressive and repressive ends – and to constantly keep opening theoretical and social spaces for postmodern ideas to operate in liberatory and emancipatory-harmonious ways.

The conceptual fields of postmodernism, when ploughed and cultivated critically, can produce liberating practices to better humankind as well as progressive ideas to shape and guide a more just and hopeful future. If the manipulative forms of marketing brought about the loss of individuation and symbolic misery of our times, then via the iconoclasm and the playful creativity of postmodernism, we also see strong possibilities of (critical and radical) marketing offering the ways out of our present predicament.

References

Angus, I. (1989). Circumscribing postmodern culture. In I. Angus & S. Jhally (Eds.), *Cultural politics in contemporary America* (pp. 96–107). New York, Routledge.

Applegate, E. (2008). The Development of Advertising and Marketing Education: The First 75 Years. ERIC Online Submission, September, Available at: http://files.eric.ed.gov/fulltext/ED502731.pdf.

Arnould, E.J., & Thompson, C.J. (2005). Consumer culture theory (CCT): Twenty years of research. *Journal of Consumer Research*, 31, 868–882.

Aronczyk, M. (2013). *Branding the nation: The global business of national identity*. Oxford, UK, Oxford University Press.

Aronczyk, M., & Powers, D. (2010). *Blowing up the brand: Critical perspectives on promotional culture*. New York, P. Lang.

Arvidsson, A. (2006). *Brands: Meaning and value in media culture*. London, Routledge.

Arvidsson, A. (2007). Creative class or administrative class? On advertising and the 'underground'. *Ephemera: Theory & Politics in Organization* 7, 8–23.

Baudrillard, J. (1981). *For a critique of the Political Economy of the Sign*. St. Louis, MO, Telos.

Bauman, Z. (2000). *Liquid modernity*. Cambridge, Polity Press.

Beck, U. (1992). *Risk society: Towards a new modernity*. London, Sage.

Beniger, J. (2009). *The control revolution: Technological and economic origins of the information society*. Cambridge, MA, Harvard University Press.

Boje, D.M., & Hillon, Y.C. (2017). The fifth epoch: Socio-economic approach to sustainable capitalism. *Markets, Globalization & Development Review*, 2, Article 2.

Brown, S. (1993). Postmodern marketing? *European Journal of Marketing*, 27, 19–34.

Brown, W. (1995). *States of injury: Power and freedom in late modernity*. Princeton, NJ, Princeton University Press.

Castells, M. (2010). *The rise of the networked society*, 3 volumes, 2nd edition. Oxford, UK, Wiley-Blackwell.

Charles, S. (2009). For a humanism amid hypermodernity: From a society of knowledge to a critical knowledge of society. *Axiomathes*, 19, 389–400.

Cova, B. (1996). The postmodern explained to managers: Implications for marketing. *Business Horizons*, 39, 15–23.

Czajkowski, A. (2015). We are postmodern. http://www.igbaffiliate.com/, June 2, Retrieved March 7, 2016 from http://goo.gl/VCsAQQ.

Davis, K., & Puett, M. (2015). Periodization and 'The Medieval Globe': A conversation. *The Medieval Globe*, 2(1), 1–14.

Dholakia, N. (2011). Finanzkapital in the twenty-first century. *Critical Perspectives on International Business*, 7, 90–108.

Dholakia, N., & Reyes, I. (2018). Technology and Trump triumph: A social theoretical perspective. *Preprint* Working Paper, ResearchGate, DOI: 10.13140/RG.2.2.15270.63048

Featherstone, M. (2007). *Consumer culture and postmodernism*. London: Sage.

Ferrando, F. (2013). Posthumanism, transhumanism, antihumanism, metahumanism, and new materialisms. *Existenz*, 8, 26–32.

Fırat, A.F. (2005). Consumer meaning and identity production and consumer research: Issues of literacy, gender and identity. In K.M. Ekstrom & H. Brembeck (Eds.), *European advances in consumer research*, Volume 7 (pp. 530–532). Goteborg, Sweden, Association for Consumer Research.

Fırat, A.F., & Dholakia, N. (1998). *Consuming people: From political economy to theaters of consumption*, London, Routledge.

Fırat, A.F., & Dholakia, N. (2003). *Consuming people: From political economy to theaters of consumption* (Paperback edition). New York, Routledge.

Fırat, A.F., & Dholakia, N. (2006). Theoretical and philosophical implications of postmodern debates: Some challenges to modern marketing. *Marketing Theory*, 6, 123–162.

Fırat, A.F., & Dholakia, N. (2016). From consumer to construer: Travels in human subjectivity. *Journal of Consumer Culture*, OnlineFirst [DOI: 10.1177/1469540515623605 | First published January 15].

Fırat, A.F., & Dholakia, N. (2017). The consumer culture theory movement: Critique and renewal. In J.F. Sherry, Jr., & E. Fischer (Eds.), *Contemporary consumer culture theory* (pp. 195–214). New York: Routledge.

Fırat, A.F., & Venkatesh, A. (1993). Postmodernity: the age of marketing. *International Journal of Research in Marketing*, 10, 227–249.

Fırat, A.F., & Venkatesh, A. (1995). Liberatory postmodernism and the reenchantment of consumption. *Journal of Consumer Research*, 22, 239–267.

Fırat, A.F., & Shultz, C.J. (1997). From segmentation to fragmentation: Markets and marketing strategy in the postmodern era. *European Journal of Marketing*, 31, 183–207.

Fırat, A.F., Sherry, J.F. Jr., & Venkatesh, A. (1994). Postmodernism, marketing and the consumer. *International Journal of Research in Marketing*, 11, 311–316.

Fırat, A.F., Dholakia, N., & Venkatesh, A. (1995). Marketing in a postmodern world. *European Journal of Marketing, 29*, 40–56.

Foucault, M. (1972/2010). *The archaeology of knowledge.* New York, Vintage Books (1972 publisher: Tavistock).

Gibson-Graham, J.K. (1994). 'Stuffed if I know!' Reflections on post-modern feminist social research. *Gender, Place and Culture: A Journal of Feminist Geography, 1*, 205–224.

Gibson-Graham, J.K. (2006). *A postcapitalist politics*. Minneapolis, University of Minnesota Press.

Gibson-Graham, J.K. (2008). Diverse economies: Performative practices for 'other worlds'. *Progress in Human Geography, 32*, 613–632.

Gibson-Graham, J.K. (2016). Building community economies: Women and the politics of place. In W. Harcourt (Ed.), *The Palgrave handbook of gender and development* (pp. 287–311). London, Palgrave Macmillan.

Gibson-Graham, J.K., Cameron, J., & Healy, S. (2016). Commoning as a postcapitalist politics. In A. Amin & P. Howell (Eds.), *Releasing the commons: Rethinking the futures of the commons* (pp. 192–212). London, Routledge.

Giddens, A. (1991). *Modernity and self-identity: Self and society in the late modern age*. Stanford, CA, Stanford University Press.

Grainge, P., & Johnson, C. (2015). *Promotional screen industries*. New York, Routledge.

Harvey, D. (1989). *The condition of modernity: An inquiry into the origin of cultural change*. Cambridge, MA, Blackwell.

Hopkins, D. (2004). *Dada and surrealism: A very short introduction*. Oxford, UK, Oxford University Press.

Jameson, F. (1984). Postmodernism, or the cultural logic of late capitalism. *New Left Review, 146*, July–August, 59–72.

Kaku, M. (2012). *Physics of the future*. New York, Anchor Books.

Lyotard, J.-F. (1984). *The postmodern condition*. Minneapolis, MN, University of Minnesota Press.

Moor, L. (2007). *The rise of brands*. Oxford, UK, Berg.

Puett, M., & Gross-Loh, C. (2016). *The path: What Chinese philosophers can teach us about the good life*. New York, Simon and Schuster Paperbacks.

Roth, Y. (2010). After postmodern marketing, what would Altermodern marketing look like? http://yannigroth.com/, March 9. Retrieved March 7, 2016 from http://goo.gl/NGG2dv.

Steuerman, E. (1992). Habermas vs Lyotard: Modernity vs Postmodernity? In A. Benjamin (Ed.), *Judging Lyotard* (pp. 99–118). London, Routledge.

Stiegler, B. (2011). What happened for Duchamp between *Nude Descending a Staircase and Fountain* – between 1912 and 1917? And why should it matter to us? Translated by Arne De Boever. Retrieved March 7, 2016 from www.lanaturnerjournal.com/archives/prolsensestiegler

Stiegler, B. (2014). *Symbolic misery-volume 1: The hyperindustrial epoch*. New York, John Wiley & Sons.

Varga, I. (2005). The body – the new sacred? The body in hypermodernity. *Current Sociology, 53*, 209–235.

Venkatesh, A., Sherry Jr., J.F., & Fırat, A.F. (1993). Postmodernism and the marketing imaginary. *International Journal of Research in Marketing* 10, 215–223.

Vermeulen, T., & van den Akker, R. (2010). Notes on metamodernism. *Journal of Aesthetics & Culture*, 2.

Vermeulen, T., & van den Akker, R. (2015). Utopia, sort of: A case study in Metamodernism. *Studia Neophilologica*, 87, Supplement *1*, 55–67.

Zwick, D. & Cayla, J. (Eds.) (2011). *Inside marketing: Practices, ideologies, devices*. Oxford, UK: Oxford University Press.

3

POSTCOLONIALISM, SUBALTERNITY, AND CRITICAL MARKETING

Rohit Varman

Introduction

A cursory look at the research published in the leading journals in marketing shows that the exalted spaces within the discipline are primarily confined to discussions on American and West European markets or consumers. With less than 10% of the world's population, the attention devoted to these American-West European sites or the Global North is completely disproportionate. For example, in over 150 research papers published in the last year in the three leading journals – *Journal of Marketing, Journal of Marketing Research*, and *Journal of Consumer Research* – less than 3% of the papers covered issues outside the Global North. Such a skewed attention to the Global North in the name of scientific rigor and quality of research reflects how academic privileges within the discipline in the form of Eurocentrism unfold and how they create research priorities, agendas, and dependencies across the globe.

In this chapter, I draw upon postcolonial theory to mount a critique of Eurocentrism and to offer a different imagination of the discipline. I use the term Eurocentrism broadly to include the countries in the Global North with the United States at its center. According to Amin (2009), Eurocentrism is a distortion of the social world and creation of European hegemony that helps it to dominate the world with its ideas. This prejudice translates into a consistent valorization of the Global North and devalorization of the Global South through various disciplinary procedures. Such an emphasis is academically misleading, morally unsound, and contextually ahistorical because it ignores Fanon's (1963, p. 76) observation that

> European opulence is literally scandalous, for it has been founded on slavery, it has been nourished with the blood of slaves, and it comes directly from the soil and from the subsoil of that underdeveloped world. The well-being and the progress of Europe have been built up with the sweat and dead bodies of Negroes, Arabs, Indians, and the yellow races.

Postcolonial theory is a framework for better understanding the complex relationship between the Global North and the Global South that continues to inscribe contemporary discourses of identity, race, modernity, and development (Bhabha, 1994; Chatterjee, 1992; Fanon, 1952; Loomba, 2005; Nandy, 1983). As an area of enquiry, postcolonial theory is devoted to revisiting and interrogating the colonial past to examine relationships of reciprocal antagonism and desire between the colonizer and the colonized (Gandhi, 1998). Postcolonial theory is not a unified framework of analysis, and the broad perspective of postcolonialism is applied in a variety of ways. My intention in this chapter is to summarize some of the key ideas in postcolonial theory and to help critical marketing scholarship to interrogate the relationships of power that are taken for granted.

In attending to Eurocentrism, I do not wish to rehash the emphasis on ethnic differences as is commonly done in the cultural turn of the discipline. Instead, this chapter is an interrogation of deeper power structures that constitute articulations of universal markets and consumer subjectivity in discourse of modernity that is central to marketing as a discipline. My postcolonial analysis of power structures helps to locate vectors of hegemony, control, and resistance from a non-Western perspective. It also attends to the question of subalternity in a manner that challenges the neoliberal modernist discourses of subsistence and base-of-the-pyramid (BOP) markets in the discipline.

Eurocentrism and its limitations

Most writings in marketing start with Eurocentric theories and then apply them to the rest of the world. This problem not only plagues the mainstream marketing theorization but also critical narratives of consumption and markets. In this section, I will briefly engage with some of the developments in consumer culture theory (CCT) that are more culturally informed. I will particularly focus on the postcolonial critique of Michel Foucault because his writings have inspired several critical scholars in CCT and critical marketing.

The problem of Eurocentrism is best exemplified in the early developments of CCT in the discipline. Much of the theorization inspired by postmodernism, uncritically and prematurely celebrated the fragmentation of metanarratives and possibilities of human emancipation (Firat & Venkatesh, 1995; Thompson, 2000). Such an approach does not take into account how the imposition of capitalist modernity under the aegis of European colonialism produced uneven social outcomes in colonies. Moreover, such an analysis assumes conditions of capitalism of the Global North and ignores economic and cultural conditions in the Global South. These writings fail to acknowledge how non-capitalist and capitalist aspects coexist in postcolonial societies and how they reinforce each other (Loomba, 2013). Moreover, these writings rarely interrogate how cultural logics of the Global North and the Global South are intertwined through colonial histories. Under these conditions, an uncritical adoption of the cultural logic of postmodernity is difficult to comprehend (Varman & Vikas, 2007).

The problem of Eurocentrism persists with poststructuralist CCT. For example, the research inspired by the writings of Michel Foucault often neglects the issues of race, colonialism, violence, and dependency as concrete socio-cultural conditions in the Global North and the Global South (e.g., Thompson & Hirschman, 1995; Thompson & Tambyah, 1999). Although there is much to learn from Foucault about the question of power, several postcolonial theorists have observed that he failed to account for the European colonial project and did not take into consideration how elements of imperialism and race inscribed disciplinary and biopower in Europe (e.g., Chatterjee, 1983; Stoler, 1995). According to Foucault (1977), with disciplinary power, people are controlled and regulated by hierarchical observation, normalizing judgment, and the examination. Biopower is fostering life or managing a population in a way to make it productive and to ensure its welfare, regulation, and control (Foucault, 2008). More specifically, while agreeing with Foucault's idea of colonization of body, Arnold (1997) critiquing his reading of discipline in the penal system, points to how colonial jails in India were distinct from Bentham's model of a panopticon. A panopticon is a uniquely designed jail in which guards can observe inmates without inmates becoming aware of the gaze. Such an apparatus of disciplining creates far-reaching ability to control the behavior of prisoners and 'reform' them without any explicit use of physical violence. Instead, Arnold (1997) found that Indian jails were sites of resistance and evasion with little control exercised by prison authorities on the local networks of knowledge and power. Unlike in the prison system theorized by Foucault (1977) in which the emphasis was on 'reform', the goal of colonial jails was to primarily confine people.

Prakash (1999) adds to the above critique by observing that while biopower established its full presence in the West in the 18th CE, the non-Western world remained vulnerable to famine and biological risks. While, in the Global North, a more violent form of sovereign power was gradually superseded by biopower, Prakash (1999) offers a different reading of power in colonies that were controlled by Europeans. Colonies were witness to physical violence and deaths as tools of governance. This was not because colonies were not sites for biopolitics to take deep roots, but because that occurred under the shadow of a violent colonial apparatus. And to that extent, bio and sovereign power fed into each other to produce colonial and postcolonial subject positions. This intertwining of bio and sovereign power is so often overlooked in marketing theory and leads to a lopsided understanding of power. For example, Varman and Vijay (forthcoming) show that studies on consumer vulnerability have overlooked how sovereign power is used to violently dispossess vulnerable consumers. This study explains how dehumanization of vulnerable consumers and subsequent denial of their status as subjects contributes to violence. Varman and Vijay (forthcoming) offer insights into how vulnerable consumers are exploited, displaced, and dispossessed without creating popular revulsion.

In another insightful analysis of different modes of power from a postcolonial perspective, Chatterjee (1983) applauds Foucault for offering fresh insights on power but also points to a key limitation. Accordingly, in the Global South disciplinary regimes of power are limited and qualified by the persistence of explicit use of coercion and violence by ruling classes to exercise their domination. Spivak (1988) has suggested that Foucault treats the subaltern as a sovereign subject in control of her consciousness and assumes the intellectual to be a transparent medium through which subaltern conscious can be made present. Foucault renders colonial subjects either invisible or transparent. He does this by ignoring the 'epistemic violence' of imperialism or violence in the construction of knowledge about the colonized and the international division of labor. Such invisibility is a common feature of Western (imperialist) discourse and acts to effect the silencing of the subaltern while hindering the possibility of resistance to oppression.

Such a foundational critique of postmodern/poststructuralist writings of markets has important implications in terms of how and to what we attend in our theoretical engagements. For example, in analyzing the hegemonic brandscape of Starbucks, Thompson and Arsel (2004, p. 640) write, "Through these postmodern forms of community, consumers seek a palliative for the distressing feelings of isolation, inauthenticity, and depersonalization that can be precipitated by the conditions of postmodern consumer culture." While these conditions of resistance merit attention, the emphasis on postmodernity might hide more violent forms of control exercised by global hegemonic brands. This is illustrated in the writing of Varman and Al-Amoudi (2016) who uncover the violence that marks the domination of the Indian market by Coca-Cola and show how the global brand uses different forms of coercion to quell any resistance to it. Accordingly, Coca-Cola gets away with violence by derealizing villagers. Derealization occurs whenever particular identities are excluded from discourse (Butler, 2004). Varman and Al-Amoudi (2016) examine the practices through which the firm derealizes people. First, Coca-Cola derealizes dispossessed farmers by influencing official reports. Second, the firm derealizes workers by keeping them under a continuous threat of the sack. Third, Coca-Cola derealizes citizens by bypassing local councils. Hence, while subordinate identities are deemed inferior, derealized identities are even more fundamentally excluded because they do not fit recognizable categories through which subjects may vindicate rights, express needs or even claim existence as human beings.

In summary, the above analysis of the limitations of postmodern/poststructuralist theorization surfaces the need for scholarship that explains conditions of the Global South without Eurocentric distortions. Moreover, there is a need to understand the historical legacy of European colonialism and its impact on consumers and markets in the Global South. Postcolonial theory offers such an approach.

Postcolonial theory

Postcolonial theory, as Gandhi (1998, p. 4) describes it,

> can be seen as a theoretical resistance to the mystifying amnesia of the colonial aftermath. It is a disciplinary project devoted to the academic task of revisiting, remembering and, crucially, interrogating the colonial past. The process of returning to the colonial scene discloses a relationship of reciprocal antagonism and desire between the colonizer and the colonized.

It is in the unfolding of this troubled and troubling relationship that we start to discern the ambivalent postcolonial condition. According to Go (2016), postcolonial theory is primarily an anti-imperialist discourse that critiques empire and its persistent legacies. Moreover, it critiques conventional theories in the way they cultivate knowledge about the colonized and offer prescriptions to the Global South (Go, 2016). In many ways, postcolonial theory is antithetical to social theory in its origin. As much as sociology has colonial origins and is deeply embedded within its culture, postcolonial theory emerged amid anti-imperial protest and resistance (Go, 2016). The earlier first wave of postcolonial thought included writers such as W.E.B. Du Bois, Amilcar Cabral, Aimé Césaire, Frantz Fanon, and C.L.R. James. In the later wave, postcolonial theory has been advanced by writers such as Homi Bhabha, Dipesh Chakrabarty, Partha Chatterjee, Edward Said, and Gayatri Spivak, among others.

In suggesting a future roadmap for theory development, Calas and Smircich (1999) have drawn the attention of management scholars to postcolonial theory to attend to formerly colonized people whose voice has been absent from management disciplines. Drawing upon this call, several theorists have deployed postcolonial theory in management and marketing in the last few years. For example, Mir, Mir and Upadhyaya (2003) use postcolonial theory to argue that in contemporary organizations, control systems are derived from discourses of modernity that emerge from processes of colonialism. Prasad and Prasad (2003) unpack some key concepts of postcolonial theory, such as ambivalence, mimicry, and hybridity (discussed below) that were used by the colonized to challenge the colonizer. These ideas help to broaden the understanding of workplace resistance in organizations. In a similar vein, Priyadharshini (2003) offers a postcolonial critique of texts widely used by business and management communities through the ideas of knowing and representation. She argues that the population of the Third World is often problematically represented as wild beasts in these texts originating in the West. Accordingly, such representations create a global hierarchy in which the Third World is always the less human Other. Similarly, Jack and Lorbiecki (2003) deploy postcolonial theory to critically analyze the messages, images, and symbolism contained within cross-cultural training videos. They show that the videos encode the Western fiction of the Other and draw upon

West-centric management theories that relegate non-Western forms of knowing and subjectivity to the margin.

In marketing theory, some researchers have used postcolonial theory in recent years. For example, Patterson and Brown (2007) interpret Irish pubs as postcolonial sites of resistance, which are paradoxical, parodic, provocative, and performative spaces. While Patterson and Brown (2007) have looked at postcolonial theory as a framework that highlights resistance, some other marketing theorists have used it to draw attention to global hierarchies, racism, and subordination. Costa (1998) has followed the latter approach to demonstrate how a discourse of Orientalism inheres in the consumption and marketing of Hawaii. Similarly, Jack (2008) reports a hierarchical system of colonialist binaries in a case of the marketing of soap and in the promotion of Third World tourist destinations. Kjeldgaard and Askegaard (2006) show that deprived consumers in the periphery deploy discourses of plentitude to construct postcolonial nationhood. They show how Greenlandic youth yearn for rock music because it is popular in the First World. Such a dependence on the First World culture repeats itself in many non-Western contexts (Ger & Belk, 1996; Üstüner & Holt, 2010; Varman & Belk, 2012). Moreover, Varman (2016b) suggests that marketplace icons are markers of transnational transactions engendered by commercialization and dominance of the West. Examining the case of curry as a marketplace icon, Varman (2016b) observes that the descriptor 'curry' was a British imposition shaped by colonial and commercial interests. The colonial intervention globalized Indian food as a marketplace icon. This shows that for a product from the Global South to become a marketplace icon, colonization and commercialization are necessary pre-conditions for it to gain wider acceptability. Similarly, Askegaard and Eckhardt (2012) show that the popularity of yoga in the West has added to its acceptance in India. Therefore, to achieve popularity, signs originating from the Global South are often dependent on circuits of commercialization and Westernization.

In summary, several postcolonial scholars have highlighted the hegemony of the Global North and the role of colonialism in shaping market discourses. These scholars have further highlighted the role of modernity as a hegemonic discourse in the creation of postcolonial subjectivity. Moreover, scholars have emphasized the issues of hybridity, ambivalence, and subalternity or subordination as important markers of postcoloniality. It is to these aspects of modernity, violence, hybridity, ambivalence, and subalternity that I turn in my analysis of postcoloniality.

Modernity and colonial violence

The idea of modernity with its specific origin in European history after the Renaissance was closely tied to the human ability, individually or collectively, to determine its future. Amin (2009) observes that modernity is a product of capitalism and develops in close association with the worldwide expansion of the latter. Amin further clarifies that although Enlightenment thought offers us a concept of reason that is associated with emancipation, the idea of freedom is defined and limited by what capitalism requires and allows. Therefore, in Enlightenment, a particular vision of emancipation is made into a universal reason that gets removed from its origin and history of emergence. Moreover, such a vision of modernity is closely tied to capitalism as a mode of production. As a result, modernity is closely associated with fundamental laws that govern the expansion of capitalism and is steeped in inequality and asymmetry.

There are two key features of discourse of modernity in a postcolonial society (Guha, 1997). The first is an inward-looking critique of how modernization linked with local practices. The second critique is outward looking, challenging the universality of European experience. These are contradictory moments that make modernity deeply ambivalent – simultaneously a colonizing trope as well as a site of resistance. Prakash (1999), who observes that British colonizers in

India presented the project of science as a civilizing mission, captures the inherent ambivalence of modernity. Accordingly, science was considered as a form of rationality that had to displace all other forms of reasoning and traditional understanding. This was, however, a project fraught with several contradictions because these societies had deeply entrenched cultural practices and institutions that colonizers could never understand. Describing the project of scientific modernity in the Indian context, Prakash (1999) observes a rift in the project. On the one hand, the colonial masters desired to teach the 'natives' that Western science was universal and it should be adopted by the colonized. On the other hand, for the British, Indians were primitive and backward with no ability to appreciate and develop a scientific ethos on their own. As a result, scientific modernity was a 'civilizing mission' that could only be achieved through colonialism.

Such a narrative is similar to articulatory practices in marketing in which the Global South is a laggard that is in need of Western modernity. This approach is evident in the observations made by Westfall and Boyd Jr. (1960) about marketing systems in India. Based on their rather superficial analysis, they suggest that marketing is underdeveloped in the country and in need of modernization. In this discourse of modernization, the adoption of marketing practices prevalent in the West is a sign of modernity. In these articulations, marketing becomes a civilizing mission that the Global South should adopt. It ignores the lengthy history of markets and marketing in the country. As Sreekumar and Varman (2016) show, Indian markets had a number of institutions that point to a fairly high degree of sophistication even in medieval times. Moreover, marketing evolved in India over a long period impelled by its specific historical circumstances and institutional make-up. They point out that Indian bazaars were institutionally distinct from markets in the Global North and they were labeled as unorganized because of their different forms of organization (Ray, 2011). However, much of this history is rarely interrogated in marketing discipline, and attempts are made to fit markets and marketing in the Global South in the pre-existing grids that have been developed in the West. And practices and institutional apparatuses that cannot be explained through these Western grids become unrecognizable and unintelligible. These unrecognizable and unintelligible marketing apparatuses and practices are often labeled as primitive or traditional and in need of modernization, which can be achieved by following the West (Varman & Sreekumar, 2015).

Postcolonial authors have criticized such an approach to modernity as racist and violent. As Fanon (1952, p. 191) insightfully suggests, "in the school programs, they desperately try to make a white man out of the black man. In the end, they give up and tell him: you have undeniably a dependency complex regarding the white man." Under colonialism, the colonized are made subservient in a way to support colonialist values, and native cultural values are deemed as lacking or as uncivilized (McLeod, 2013). As a result, Fanon (1963) observes, a colonized identity is defined in negative terms by the colonizer and is denied the position of a subject. Such an identity is abbreviated, violated, inferior, and imprisoned by a way of seeing that is a form of desubjectification. Here, desubjectification means that the colonized are stripped of their heritage and ethos. For Fanon (1963) colonialism was not just an economic project but was also a psychological project of dehumanization and desubjectification. And Fanon (1963, p. 114) famously observed, "the white world, the only honorable one, barred me from all participation. A man was expected to behave like a man. I was expected to behave a like a black man."

The above fixation of the colonized as traditional and primitive is richly elucidated by Bhabha (1994) in his interpretation of stereotypes. Stereotyping is not merely setting up a false image that is used for discriminatory practices, but instead an important colonial strategy that involves acts of disavowal and fixation which create conditions for colonial fantasy, violence, and civilizing missions or anti-conquests (Pratt, 1992). McLeod (2013) reminds us that under colonialism, the colonized are made subservient through the use of stereotypes that reflect and support colonist values. A particular value system of the Global North is taught as the best, truest world-view. Said (1978) offers a rich understanding of the role of discourse of Orientalism in the determination of colonized subject positions to allow the Global North to inflict colonial atrocities. Stereotypes helped the colonizers to simplify the task of governance of the people they knew little about and to use violence against them as a form of civilizing mission to make them learn Western ways of life. Such stereotyping involves a reduction of ideas to a simple and manageable form. The function of stereotypes is to perpetuate alterity and otherness (Loomba, 2005). As Judith Butler (Berbek, 2017) reminds us, "If the self is the basis of sympathy, our sympathy will be restricted to those who are like us. The real challenge occurs when that extrapolation of the self is thwarted by alterity." Therefore, stereotypes helped to create a divide between the colonizers and the colonized, us and them, and modern and primitive. These divides, in turn, were used to inflict violence in the name of modernization and civilization.

Drawing upon Said's (1978) understanding of stereotypes in representations, Costa (1998) demonstrates how Hawaii is discursively constructed as a primitive site for consumption by Western consumers. In a similar vein, Varman and Costa (2013) illustrate the manner in which American consumers and marketers draw upon discourse of development to give meaning to country-of-origin (COO). COO theory and practice draw upon stereotypes created by discourse of development to produce a sense of modern and primitive. Challenging the use of stereotypes, Varman and Costa (2013) critique the COO framework as a creator of economic difference and hierarchy. Similarly, Bonsu (2009) has shown that the colonial stereotypes of savagery and exotica inform contemporary representations of Africa in North American advertising to reinforce a global hierarchy of races, cultures, and nations.

Systems of devalorization of cultural practices of the colonized have led to long-term traumatic outcomes as they continue to reel under the spell of slavery long after formal structures of colonialism have been removed. Nandy (1983), pointing to such an outcome, laments that colonialism colonizes minds in addition to bodies and it releases forces within colonized societies that alter their cultural priorities. Such a form of colonialism shifts the modern West from a geographical entity to a psychological category. And it leads to forms of mental slavery that are difficult to dislodge even after political freedom is achieved. Nandy further helps to understand how the center–periphery relationship between the Global North and the Global South has been configured by remnants of European colonialism and neo-colonialism. In this relationship, the Global South is located at the periphery – economically, spatially, culturally, and psychologically (Gupta, 1998). As a result, postcolonial subjects yearn for the Global North as a site of development, progress, and modernity. This results in a loss of self and a neurotic existence of trying to be like another person. Drawing upon this line of analysis, Varman and Belk (2012) interpret shopping malls in India as postcolonial sites in which young consumers deploy the West in an attempt to transform their Third World identities. Shopping malls in former colonies represent a postcolonial modernity that offers consumers the illusion of being Western and developed. Moreover, consumption of postcolonial retail arenas is characterized as a masquerade through which young consumers attempt to disguise or temporarily transcend their Third World realities. As Fanon (1952, p. 2), dissecting the psycho-politics of colonialism, contends, "all colonized people – in other words, people in whom inferiority complex has taken root, whose local cultural originality has been committed to the grave – position themselves in relation to the civilizing language: i.e., the metropolitan culture." In Fanon's theorization psycho-political means that human psychology is a combination of personal and political dimensions. Therefore, race, identity, and colonial experiences have to be closely understood to comprehend how consumers and marketers behave in postcolonial settings.

It is well understood that imposition of modernity in such a form has not produced a free and liberated space. Instead, it has helped capitalism to take deeper roots and has facilitated exploitation and expropriation of resources by the Global North. Modernization often relies on violence and use of coercion of different forms. The contact between the colonizer and colonized was fraught with violence as is the case with the more recent contact between the Global North and the Global South under the aegis of neoliberal globalization. And Césaire (1972, pp. 11, 21) rhetorically asks, "has colonialism really placed civilizations in contact? . . . I answer no . . . No human contact, but relations of domination and submission." The imposition of European modernity was often justified as a civilizing mission that was steeped in racism and economic exploitation of colonies (Loomba, 2005).

Drawing upon these arguments, Varman and Belk (2009) show how an anti-consumption movement against Coca-Cola in India is impelled by fears of neo-colonialism. India was colonized by England for more than a century before it gained independence in 1947. In contemporary India, some nationalists see Western corporations as forces of neo-colonialism and urge consumers to boycott them. Varman and Belk (2009) highlight the role of a nationalist ideology that valorizes local producers over multinationals in resistance to consumption of Coca-Cola. They explain how a nationalist ideology can become a challenge to global brands that particularly manifests itself in postcolonial encounters and is an important addition to the contradictions in present-day consumer culture.

Modernization is a project marked by violence and displacement that relies on methods that are anti-modern. This is evident in marketization and privatization as they have been imposed across the Global South in the name of structural adjustment programs in the last quarter of the twentieth century. The World Bank and International Monetary Fund impose structural adjustment programs in which they enforce privatization of public assets and reduction in state support to the under-privileged on nations that seek their financial support. Sassen (2014, p. 90) reports that "the restructuring programs were about more than debt service; they aimed at shaping a political economy and a repositioning of these countries as sites of extraction." She identifies continuity across colonialism and neoliberalism in the violent dispossession and displacement of the Global South. It is a historical continuity of the capitalist dialectic of incorporation and expulsion that characterized colonial relations. In this dialectic, colonies continue to be incorporated into the colonizers' project of capitalist expansion, and the colonized people are expelled from their lands for extraction and expropriation of their resources. Capitalism is a mode of production that often requires violence to generate profits and the socio-cultural system that capitalism generates is manipulative and violent. Banerjee (2008) labels this form of capitalism as necrocapitalism.

In necrocapitalism, businesses make profits by creating death worlds, with Varman and Vijay (2018) providing us with an illustration of necrocapitalism in their analysis of how vulnerable consumers are dispossessed of their homes to create a shopping mall for elite consumers in South India. In such a context, the poor are violently cast aside by the state and private corporations to generate profits. Therefore, as an outcome of the imposition of modernity and capitalism, postcolonial sites of consumption and exchanges are arenas of violent expulsion, dispossession, and expropriation (Varman & Al-Amoudi, 2016).

Ambivalence and hybridity

Despite extensive use of violence in the spread of colonialism, there was popular resistance to it in various societies leading to ambivalent and hybrid outcomes. For example, in the spread of colonial dominance, local elites have played an active role in both siding with the European project of modernity as compradors, while resisting it as nationalists (Prakash, 1999). Compradors are individuals who work on behalf of foreign capital and help in the transfer of wealth from the Global South to the Global North. Postcolonial theory provides the analytic scheme to understand these positions through which local and global, colonial and national, and modern and traditional are intertwined to produce hybridity. Therefore, postcolonial theory enables a different kind of understanding of practices and discourses in the Global South, one which does not seek to determine whether something is authentic or uncontaminated but which accepts cultural hybridity as a starting point (Gupta, 1998). For example, neither local nor global can be understood as pure cultural containers and can only be comprehended as social registers that emerge in a dynamic interplay with each other (Wilk, 1995).

Postcolonial hybridity is not a mere coming together of different ways of life or production of a cultural mix of ideas. Instead, it is a location created by structural violence and is impelled by different forms of inequities (Gupta, 1998). Hybridity is also a site of resistance in which the colonized do not meekly surrender to different forms of dominance. Instead, we witness combinations of local and global, modern and traditional to produce outcomes that are often different from what the dominant groups visualized. These moments of slippage and destabilization are not always conscious outcomes of tactics of resistance. An illustration of such hybridity is provided by Gupta (1998) in his ethnographic work in a village in North India which shows that postcolonial subjects subvert Western narratives of the self, of progress, and of modernity through unreflexive everyday actions that are not meant to be seen as acts of resistance.

Hybridity often manifests itself as a form of mimicry. Bhabha (1994, p. 128) suggests, "Mimicry is like camouflage, not a harmonization or repression of difference, but a form of resemblance, that differs from or defends presence by displaying it in part, metonymically." Hence, mimicry is a performance that creates a surface impression of similarity and is simultaneously a form of colonial control and resistance to it. Bhabha (1994) further argues that hybridity threatens the authority of colonial command. He points out that the colonized try to copy their 'masters' and participate in the disciplinary regimes, but realize that colonialism often speaks in a tongue that is forked. In other words, Bhabha interprets hybridity as a process of strategic reversal in which knowledge created by authority gets combined with other marginal forms of knowledge and is used by the colonized to challenge colonial power. Hybridity leads to mimicry which enables the postcolonial subject to perform their contempt of the colonizer in the process of emulating it. Under these conditions, resistance is an outcome produced by a dominant discourse itself because it forces people to mimic. For instance, Varman and Belk (2012) show how young consumers interpret shopping malls in India as signifiers of Westernization, progress, and development. They deploy these signifiers to project India onto the global stage and displace the West from its position of preeminence. These young consumers claim that the future belongs to India with its ability to beat the West in the game of economic development and progress. As Gupta (1998, p. 233) observes, "through mimicry and mockery, parody and protest, riots and rebellion, the 'not-quite-indigenous' and 'not-quite-modern' disrupts the complacent march of continuous progress implicit in discourses of growth and development."

Continuing in this train of thought, Bhabha (1994, p. 122) observes that the colonizers' interpretation is refracted by ambivalence in which natives are "almost the same, but not quite." The irony in this discourse plays itself out as a colonial mimicry, in which colonizers are keen to reform and discipline the Other, but also acknowledge that the native subjects can never be like them. As a result, the governed subject is unpredictable and indeterminate. This unpredictability contributes to the creation of a paranoid authority that leads to cycles of violence through which the colonizer tries to overcome the fear of the unknowable subject (Varman & Al-Amoudi, 2016). Therefore, hybridity helps to further comprehend how domination and resistance become intertwined in postcolonial settings. A large part of this resistance is infra-political or unorganized and generates a sense of paranoia that can lead to greater violence by those in authority.

Subalternity

To understand postcoloniality in marketing theory, a considerable emphasis has to be placed on structures of subordination or subalternity. Such an imperative, inspired by a group of scholars working in the area of Subaltern Studies (Prakash, 1994), has to go beyond neoliberal discourses of the BOP and subsistence markets to attend to the wider structures of subordination as they prevail in the Global South. The idea of subaltern can be traced to the writings of Antonio Gramsci, who used the term as a form of disguise for the proletariat to overcome the problem of prison censorship. More specifically, Subaltern Studies have their origin in India. It was a project to write history from below to focus on ordinary people instead of focusing on the rulers, as is the case with conventional history. Subaltern Studies were started with the objective of overcoming colonist elitism and bourgeois-nationalist elitism in India.

I see two forms of subalternity that need to be addressed in marketing theory. First, borrowing from Chakrabarty (1997), I see subalternity of epistemology. This form of subalternity is manifest in how marketing scholars writing accounts of markets in the Global South have to always refer to the writings in the Global North. This closely resonates with the observation made by Chakrabarty (1997, p. 264) that,

> Third World historians feel a need to refer to works in European history; historians of Europe do not feel any need to reciprocate . . . they produce their work in relative ignorance of non-Western histories, and this does not seem to affect the quality of their work. This is a gesture, however, "we" cannot return. We cannot even afford an equality or symmetry of ignorance at this level without taking the risk of appearing "old fashioned" or "outdated".

As Varman and Saha (2009) show, knowledge flows in postcoloniality are disciplined by Eurocentrism. They explain marketing knowledge in India as a form of emulation of the mainstream and managerially oriented research in the Global North. Such a Eurocentric discursive approach privileges the Global North through its mystification and denigration of the Global South through distorted representations. These articulations are situated in discourse of self-orientalism that allows the domination of the colonized to be accepted as a disciplining influence. It is, to a large extent, an outcome of dependency created because of the legacy of colonialism in the Global South.

Therefore, subalternity creates unreflexive subjectivities that shape marketing knowledge flows in postcoloniality. As a result, marketing theorization and practices in postcolonial settings witness attempts to emulate the West. For example, Varman and Saha (2009) outline how, in an elite Indian business school, researchers unreflexively adopt the SERVQUAL scale developed in the United States. Despite recent attempts to include voices from the Global South in marketing, the discipline remains overwhelmingly Eurocentric, white, and primarily confined to conversations in the Anglo-Saxon world. As Burton (2009) insightfully points out, white spaces and white people dominate consumer research, and researchers perform whiteness. Most accounts of markets and consumers tend to become variations on master narrative that could be called markets of the West (Chakrabarty, 1997). As a result of the 'first in the West and then elsewhere' structure of the discipline, different non-Western societies are expected to produce local versions of the same

Western narrative of modernity, progress, markets, and reason after a time lag (Fabian, 2002). This has consigned non-Western subject positions to an imaginary waiting room of history. It has allowed Western ideas to be used as benchmarks for others as non-Westerners are treated as less modern and in need of a period of preparation and waiting before being considered as full participants in modernity. This results in an overwhelming dominance of the West and any legitimate theorization of markets has to be an extension of pre-existing theories developed by mainly white scholars. Therefore, the Global North becomes a universal referent for any theorization that happens in the Global South. However, this is a status denied to scholars from the Global South because they remain provincial and theorists of particular cultural orders that have little claim to universality outside what has been pre-determined by the West.

The second facet of subalternity that requires attention is the limited space that has been devoted in the discipline to subaltern markets and consumption. Subaltern settings have broadly remained at the margins of marketing scholarship. The problem of silence on subalterns is further exacerbated by the limitations of their representation by privileged academics. Because of their disempowered positions, subalterns do not achieve a dialogical status and are problematically represented through privileged vantage points of academic experts. In examining subalternity in India, Spivak (1988) argues that any attempt to retrieve the voice of subalterns further distorts their speech because they cannot be represented within dominant discourses (McLeod, 2013). Accordingly, scholars must subvert the representational system that rendered subalterns mute in the first place. It is not that subalterns do not speak, but others do not know how to listen and how to have a dialogue. Therefore, the silence of subalterns is a failure of interpretation in the marketing discipline.

Such an engagement is obviously necessary because conditions of subalternity require appropriate theoretical analysis. Varman and Vikas (2007) remind us that the abject poverty and abysmal living conditions of subaltern consumers necessitate a radical rethink about the role of corporations and markets under capitalism. In a capitalist society, a vast majority of the population struggles to survive because capitalist relations of production are exploitative and fetter human agency. Varman and Vikas (2007) report that subaltern groups suffer extreme exploitation with low wages and the absence of any form of social security. These conditions leave little room for freedom in the sphere of consumption. Contra some postmodern thinkers, loss of control in production cannot be compensated for via consumption. Hence, subalternity helps us to understand issues of consumer freedom and choices under conditions of material constraints. It surfaces the linkages between the conditions of production and consumption that are all too often overlooked in marketing theory.

Attention to subalternity can also help understand markets and consumption situated in conditions of social conflicts and contradictions. As Bhadra (1997) observes, submissiveness and defiance simultaneously characterize subaltern behavior. Furthermore, the disempowered positions of subaltern groups imply that many of their discourses and practices are concealed from open scrutiny. Consequently, a deeper understanding of subalterns requires closer attention to their polysemic and hidden transcripts that contain cultural codes of resistance or infra-politics, and multiple subjectivities (Scott, 1990). Such an analysis will require a critical re-reading of the foundational assumptions of the way subalternity in the form of poverty has been examined in the discipline. Stimulated and structured by neoliberal ideology, BOP and subsistence market discourses have put emphases on markets, profits, and entrepreneurialism. A key assumption in BOP discourse is that the multinational firms have ignored the poor, and thus, the poor do not have access to the benefits of markets (Prahalad, 2005). With this assumption in play, they contend that an active engagement of big private corporations with BOP markets would transform such settings with huge latent demand. Such an approach builds on neoliberal discourse which assumes that market-based engagements create choices for the poor resulting in their economic transformation. Work on subsistence markets (e.g., Viswanathan & Sridharan, 2009; Viswanathan et al., 2011) is another dominant strand of research on the poor within marketing theory. The subsistence marketplace project is positioned as a microlevel initiative complementary to the macro-level BOP approach (Sridharan & Viswanathan, 2008; Viswanathan, Seth, Gau, & Chaturvedi, 2009). Subsistence market research also heralds markets and consumer power within the logic of neoliberal ideology (Viswanathan, Rosa, & Harris, 2005). It seeks to create active, prudential, and entrepreneurial market subjects among the poor. It is often imposed by the Global North in the name of modernity against the old logic of the welfare state in the Global South. Such subsistence marketplace initiatives are extensions of the logic of social entrepreneurship that replaces traditional socioeconomic government interventions to support subaltern groups with market-based initiatives. Therefore, the logic of subsistence is deployed as a form of mystification to mask the creation of market subjectivity in support of private accumulation (Varman, 2016a). Because of this ideological mooring, there is a marginal understanding of the systemic issues that cause poverty. Khare and Varman (2016) contend that the subaltern institutional setting is fraught with Kafkaesque elements such as indecipherable legality that does not allow subalterns to access and assess the technicalities of a state's policies, fosters abusive power relations through which local elites exploit subalterns, and creates alienation that leaves subaltern subjects disenchanted in their social and professional domains. Varman, Skålén, and Belk (2012) also criticize the role of a corporate BOP initiative for exacerbating conditions of poverty and marginalization. To understand subalternity, marketing theorists have to distance themselves from the neoliberal ideological moorings of the discipline (Eckhardt, Dholakia & Varman, 2013) and there is a need to understand how capitalism systemically creates conditions of subalternity for the majority of people on this planet.

Conclusion

This chapter outlines some of the key developments in postcolonial theory and explains their usefulness for widening the purview of critical marketing. It examines the role of modernity, hybridity, ambivalence, and violence in shaping postcoloniality. It further delves into the question of subalternity to offer it as an alternative imperative for imagining the discipline in a postcolonial society.

In the Global South, a key challenge for critical marketing is to provincialize Europe. We need to decenter the West as a universal referent for the creation and understanding of non-Western subjectivities. This does not mean we abandon systemic understanding and emphasis on global forces such as capitalism. I agree with Chibber (2013) that we need to understand the logic of universals that capitalism creates as we look into the specificities of a context. However, universal aspects of capitalism such as accumulation, extraction of surplus value, alienation, etc. have to be located in conjunction with local conditions to comprehend how they interpenetrate each other. And a universal does not equate with the Global North because it is as provincial as any other location on the globe. There is a need for theoretical development that challenges the universality of Western theories about markets and consumers, and situates them instead in their specific spatial, cultural, and institutional contexts. This requires questioning the canonical status granted to Western scholars, who have little or no awareness of the Global South. Such a shift is going to be difficult because of the entrenched interests of scholars in the Global North and the dependence of scholars in the Global South on the scholarly trends in the West. However, it is a shift that is needed to make the discipline more relevant beyond the privileged circuit of a few.

References

Amin, S. (2009). *Eurocentrism*. New York, Monthly Review Press.
Arnold, D. (1997). The colonial prison: Power, knowledge and penology in nineteenth-century India. In R. Guha (Ed.), *A subaltern studies reader 1986–1995* (pp. 148–187). Minnesota, University of Minnesota Press.
Askegaard, S., & Eckhardt, G. (2012). Glocal yoga: Reappropriation in the Indian consumptionscape. *Marketing Theory, 12*(1), 43–58.
Banerjee, S.B. (2008). Necrocapitalism. *Organization Studies, 29*(12), 1541–1563.
Berbek, S. (2017). We are worldless without one another: An interview with Judith Butler. Retrieved August 1, 2017 from: www.versobooks.com/blogs/3304-we-are-worldless-without-one-another-an-interview-with-judith-butler.
Bhabha, H. (1994). *The location of culture*. New York, Routledge.
Bhadra, G. (1997). The mentality of subalternity: Kantanama or Rajdharma. In R. Guha (Ed.), *A subaltern studies reader: 1986–1995* (pp. 63–99). New Delhi, Oxford University Press.
Bonsu, S.K. (2009). Colonial images in global times: Consumer interpretations of Africa and African advertising. *Consumption, Markets & Culture, 12*(1), 1–25.
Burton, D. (2009). "Reading" whiteness in consumer research. *Consumption, Markets & Culture, 12*(2), 171–201.
Butler, J. (2004). *Undoing gender*. London, Routledge.
Calas, M.B., & Smircich, L. (1999). Past postmodernism? Reflections and tentative directions. *Academy of Management Review, 24*(4), 649–672.
Césaire, A. (1972). *Discourse on colonialism*. Transl. by Joan Pinkham. New York, Monthly Review Press.
Chakrabarty, D. (1997). Postcoloniality and the artifice of history: Who speaks for Indian pasts? In R. Guha (Ed.), *A subaltern studies reader 1986–1995* (pp. 263–293). Minnesota, University of Minnesota Press.
Chatterjee, P. (1983). More on modes of power and the peasantry. In R. Guha (Ed.), *Subaltern studies II: Writings of South Asian histories and society* (pp. 311–349). New Delhi, Oxford University Press.
Chatterjee, P. (1992). *The nation and its fragments: Colonial and postcolonial histories*. New Delhi, Oxford University Press.
Chibber, V. (2013). *Postcolonial theory and the specter of capital*. London, Verso.
Costa, J. (1998). Paradisal discourse: A critical analysis of marketing and consuming Hawaii. *Consumption, Markets & Culture, 1*(4), 303–346.
Eckhardt, G., Dholakia, N., & Varman, R. (2013). Ideology for the 10 billion: Introduction to globalization of marketing ideology. *Journal of Macromarketing, 33*(1), 7–12.
Fabian, J. (2002). *Time and the other: How anthropology makes its object*. New York, Columbia University Press.
Fanon, F. (1952). *Black skin, white masks*. New York, Grove Press.
Fanon, F. (1963). *The wretched of the Earth*. New York, Penguin.
Firat, A.F., & Venkatesh, A. (1995). Liberatory postmodernism and the reenchantment of consumption. *Journal of Consumer Research, 22*(3), 239–267.
Foucault, M. (1977). *Discipline and punish: The birth of the prison*. New York, Penguin.
Foucault, M. (2008). *The birth of biopolitics: Lectures at Collège de France 1978–1979*. Basingstoke, UK, Palgrave.
Gandhi, L. (1998). *Postcolonial theory: A critical introduction*. New Delhi, Oxford University Press.
Ger, G., & Belk, R.W. (1996). I'd like to buy the world a Coke: Consumptionscapes of the less affluent world. *Journal of Consumer Policy, 19*(3), 271–304.
Go, J. (2016). *Postcolonial thought and social theory*. Oxford, Oxford University Press.
Guha, R. (1997). *Dominance without hegemony: History and power in colonial India*. Cambridge, Cambridge University Press.
Gupta, A. (1998). *Postcolonial development: Agriculture in the making of modern India*. Durham, Duke University Press.
Jack, G. (2008). Post-colonialism and marketing. In M. Tadajewski & D. Brownlie (Eds.), *Critical marketing: Issues in contemporary marketing* (pp. 363–383). Chichester, John Wiley.
Jack, G., & Lorbiecki, A. (2003). Asserting possibilities of resistance in the cross-cultural teaching machine: Re-viewing videos of others. In A. Prasad (Ed.), *Postcolonial theory and organizational analysis* (pp. 213–231). New York, Palgrave.

Khare, A., & Varman, R. (2016). Kafkaesque institutions at the base of the pyramid. *Journal of Marketing Management*, *32*(17–18), 1619–1646.
Kjeldgaard, D., & Askegaard, S. (2006). The glocalization of youth culture: The global youth segment as structures of common difference. *Journal of Consumer Research*, *33*(2), 231–247.
Loomba, A. (2005). *Colonialism/postcolonialism*, Second Edition. London, Routledge.
Loomba, A. (2007). *Colonialism/postcolonialism*. London, Routledge.
McLeod, J. (2013). *Beginning postcolonialism*. New Delhi, Oxford University Press.
Mir, R., Mir, A., & Upadhyaya, P. (2003). Toward a postcolonial reading of organizational control. In A. Prasad (Ed.), *Postcolonial theory and organizational analysis* (pp. 47–74). New York, Palgrave.
Nandy, A. (1983). The intimate enemy: Loss and recovery of self under colonialism. New Delhi, Oxford University Press.
Patterson, A., & Brown, S. (2007). Inventing the pubs of Ireland: The importance of being postcolonial. *Journal of Strategic Marketing*, *15*(1), 41–51.
Prahalad, C.K. (2005). *The fortune at the bottom of the pyramid*. New Delhi, Pearson Education.
Prakash, G. (1994). Subaltern studies as postcolonial criticism. *The American Historical Review*, *99*(5), 1475–1490.
Prakash, G. (1999). *Another reason: Science and the imagination of another India*. Princeton, NJ, Princeton University Press.
Prasad, A., & Prasad, P. (2003). The empire of organizations and the organization of empires: Postcolonial considerations on theorizing workplace resistance. In A. Prasad (Ed.), *Postcolonial theory and organizational analysis: A critical analysis* (pp. 95–120). New York, Palgrave.
Pratt, M.L (1992). Imperial eyes: Travel writing and transculturation. New York, Routledge.
Priyadharshini, E. (2003). Reading the rhetoric of otherness in the discourse of business and economics: Toward a postdisciplinary practice. In A. Prasad (Ed.), *Postcolonial theory and organizational analysis* (pp. 171–192). New York, Palgrave.
Ray, R.K. (2011). Bazaar: 'pulsating heart' of the Indian economy. In M.M. Kudaisya (Ed.), *The Oxford India anthology of business history* (pp. 3–48). Oxford, New Delhi.
Said, E.W. (1978). *Orientalism*. New York, Random House.
Sassen, S. (2014). *Expulsions: Brutality and complexity in the global economy*. Cambridge, MA, Harvard University Press.
Scott, J. (1990). Domination and the arts of resistance: Hidden transcripts. New Haven, Yale University Press.
Spivak, G.C. (1988). Can the subaltern speak? In C. Nelson & L. Grossberg (Eds.), *Marxism and the interpretation of culture* (pp. 271–313). Urbana, University of Illinois Press.
Sreekumar, H., & Varman, R. (2016). History of marketing in India. In D.G.B. Jones & M. Tadajewski (Eds.), *Routledge companion to marketing history* (pp. 389–405). London, Routledge.
Sridharan, S., & Viswanathan, M. (2008). Marketing in subsistence marketplaces: consumption and entrepreneurship in a South Indian context. *Journal of Consumer Marketing*, *25*(7), 455–462.
Stoler, A.L. (1995). Race and the education of desire: Foucault's history of sexuality and the colonial order of things. London, Duke University Press.
Thompson, C.J. (2000). Postmodern consumer goals made easy!!!! In S. Ratneshwar, D.G. Mick & C. Huffman (Eds.), *The why of consumption: Contemporary perspectives on consumer motives, goals, and desires* (pp. 121–139). London, Routledge.
Thompson, C.J., & Arsel, Z. (2004). The Starbucks brandscape and consumers' (anticorporate) experiences of glocalization. *Journal of Consumer Research*, *31*(3), 631–642.
Thompson, C.J., & Hirschman, E.C. (1995). Understanding the socialized body: A poststructuralist analysis of consumers' self-conceptions, body images, and self-care practices. *Journal of Consumer Research*, *22*(2), 139–153.
Thompson, C.J., & Tambyah, S.K. (1999). Trying to be cosmopolitan. *Journal of Consumer Research*, *26*(3), 214–240.
Üstüner, T., & Holt, D.B. (2010). Toward a theory of status consumption in less industrialized countries. *Journal of Consumer Research*, *37*(June), 37–56.
Varman, R. (2016a). Mystifying development: Marketing capitalist enterprise as compassionate caring. *Marketing Theory*, *16*(3), 410–414.
Varman, R. (2016b). Curry. *Consumption, Markets & Culture*, *20*(4), 350–356.
Varman, R., & Al-Amoudi, A. (2016). Accumulation through derealization: How corporate violence remains unchecked. *Human Relations*, *69*(10), 909–1935.

Varman, R., & Belk, R.W. (2009). Nationalism and ideology in an anticonsumption movement. *Journal of Consumer Research*, *36*(4), 686–700.

Varman, R., & Belk, R.W. (2012). Consuming postcolonial shopping malls. *Journal of Marketing Management*, *28*(1–2), 62–84.

Varman, R., & Costa, J. (2013). Underdeveloped other in country-of-origin theory and practices. *Consumption, Markets & Culture*, *16*(3), 240–265.

Varman, R., & Saha, B. (2009). Disciplining the discipline: Understanding postcolonial epistemic ideology in marketing. *Journal of Marketing Management*, *25*(7/8), 811–824.

Varman, R., & Sreekumar, H. (2015). Locating the past in its silence: History and marketing theory in India. *Journal of Historical Research in Marketing*, *7*(2), 272–279.

Varman, R., & Vijay, D. (2018). Dispossessing vulnerable consumers: Derealization, desubjectification and violence. *Marketing Theory*. http://journals.sagepub.com/doi/10.1177/1470593117753980

Varman, R., & Vikas, R.M. (2007). Freedom and consumption: Toward conceptualizing systemic constraints for subaltern consumers in a capitalist society. *Consumption, Markets & Culture*, *10*(2), 117–131.

Varman, R., Skålén, P., & Belk, R.W. (2012). Conflicts at the bottom of the pyramid: Profitability, poverty alleviation, and neoliberal governmentality. *Journal of Public Policy & Marketing*, *31*(1), 19–35.

Viswanathan, M., & Sridharan, S. (2009). From subsistence marketplaces to sustainable marketplaces: A bottom-up perspective on the role of business in poverty alleviation. *Ivey Business Journal*, *2*(73), 1–15.

Viswanathan, M., Rosa, J.A., & Harris, J.E. (2005). Decision making and coping of functionally illiterate consumers and some implications for marketing management. *Journal of Marketing*, *69*(1), 15–31.

Viswanathan, M., Seth, A., Gau, R., & Chaturvedi, A. (2009). Ingraining product-relevant social good into business processes in subsistence marketplaces: The sustainable market orientation. *Journal of Macromarketing*, *29*(4), 406–425.

Viswanathan, M., Sridharan, S., Ritchie, R., Venugopal, S., & Jung, K. (2011). Marketing interactions in subsistence marketplaces: A bottom-up approach to designing public policy. *Journal of Public Policy & Marketing*, *31*(2), 159–177.

Westfall, R., & Boyd Jr., H.W. (1960). Marketing in India. *Journal of Marketing*, *25*(2), 11–17.

Wilk, R. (1995). Learning to be local in Belize: Global systems of common difference. In D. Miller (Ed.), *World apart: Modernity through the lens of the local* (pp. 110–133). London, Routledge.

4
FEMINIST PERSPECTIVES IN MARKETING
Past, present, and future

Pauline Maclaran and Olga Kravets

Introduction

Feminist perspectives expose many gendered assumptions embedded in marketing and consumption phenomena, as well as the unequal power relations that underpin them. Initially critiques came from outside the marketing and consumer research disciplines, led by second-wave feminists in the 1960s and 70s. Activists such as Friedan (1963) saw marketers as being complicit in a patriarchal system (discussed below) that sought to manipulate and control women through domesticity. They targeted advertising in particular where negative female stereotypes abounded, stereotypes that served to reinforce passive, decorative models of femininity.

Despite such critiques, it was not until the 1990s that scholars within the marketing discipline began to draw on feminist perspectives. Following the "cultural turn" in the social sciences – a turn that placed emphasis on subjective meaning creation rather than seeking an objective reality – this work unpicked advertising texts to reveal their hidden biases (Stern, 1992). In particular, it exposed the underpinning masculinist assumptions of both marketing (Bristor & Fischer, 1993) and consumer research (Hirschman, 1993; Joy & Venkatesh, 1994). Since this period feminist voices have waxed and waned in marketing and consumer research scholarship, reflecting also the trajectory of feminism and the (so-called) postfeminist era.

After giving a brief overview of feminism's main principles and major types, this chapter chronicles the historical intertwining of feminism with marketing and gives an overview of the contributions feminist scholarship has made to critical marketing. In order to do this, we look at what are now often referred to as the four waves of feminism and analyze the different relationship each time period has had with marketing and the scholarship therein.[1] We also highlight key theoretical perspectives within the feminist canon that have driven this work, before detailing key areas where we believe future critique is urgently required.

What is feminism?

Many misconceptions of what constitutes a feminist still endure and, sadly, the two authors frequently hear young female students using the well-worn expression "I'm not a feminist but . . . ." This denial is usually based on ill-founded assumptions such as the belief that feminists hate men or consider women to be superior to men. We believe, therefore, it is important to set out some of the basic principles of feminism to put the record straight for new readers to the topic. Part of the problem in understanding feminism is that it is not just one unified body of thought and there are many different varieties, each with their own emphasis (see Table 4.1 for examples of various types of feminism, although this is by no means an exhaustive list). Broadly speaking, however, a key principle that underpins feminist approaches and theorizing is that men and women should be equal and that currently there is an unequal relationship, although this inequality varies greatly depending on a multitude of different global contexts. Another unifying principle is that this inequality is made possible by patriarchy, a system that ensures all major social institutions – economic, political, the family, and religion – are male-dominated. Thus, feminist theory helps us understand how the workings of patriarchy permeate all aspects of our lives, being deeply embedded in wider socio-cultural and economic structures. Feminist thought also makes a key distinction between sex and gender: sex is the biological category one is assigned at birth (man/women), whereas gender is socially constructed with gender norms (masculine/feminine characteristics) varying across different cultures and time periods.

Table 4.1 Types of feminism and their key emphases

Type of feminism	Key emphases
Liberal feminism	Seeks to bring about legal changes that encourage equality (equal pay Acts, etc.) and to educate against gender prejudice.
Marxist feminism	Sees capitalism and class relationships as its main adversary. Concerned in particular with the family system under capitalism and the concept of unpaid labor that disadvantages women.
Radical feminism	Targets patriarchy (which existed before capitalism) as the root cause of women's subordination and critiques heterosexual relationships and reproduction for allowing men to control women's behaviors.
Socialist feminism	Like Marxist feminism also focuses on women's work and its lower social status but places more emphasis on capitalism and patriarchy as intersecting systems of oppression.
Cultural feminism	Argues for feminine values to be privileged over masculine ones in society – values such as caring, cooperation, and nonviolence. Often accused of being essentialist and thereby reinforcing binary gender structures.
Ludic or celebratory feminism	A postmodern perspective that celebrates the feminine and sees empowerment as rooted in identity politics and access to marketplace offerings.
Ecofeminism	Looks at the connections between feminism and ecology, seeing the oppression of women (and other marginalized groups) as linked to the patriarchal domination of nature. Demands a new worldview that challenges the humankind's "mastery" of nature.
Black feminism	Argues that race, class, and gender are inextricably interwoven and emphasizes the importance of understanding how multiple sources of oppression are experiences, a concept referred to as "intersectionality".
Poststructuralist feminism	Focuses on the relationship between discourse and subjectivities, particularly the embedded power relations they contain. Exposes processes of "othering" and the exclusion of those who do not conform to dominant (patriarchal) social norms.

The origins of feminism: the first wave (1840–1920)

Women's oppression has a long history, with women's inferiority to men being heavily encoded in many ancient texts, particularly those conveying philosophical and religious doctrine. The Ancient Greeks were no exception and Aristotle (born in 384 BC) is accredited with saying that "the courage of a man lies in commanding, a woman's lies in obeying . . . a female is an incomplete male or 'as it were, a deformity'" (in Freeland, 1994, pp. 145–146). Given this longstanding misogyny, it is scarcely surprising that there have been dissenting female voices over the centuries although most have been silenced due to the prevalent power imbalances and women's exclusion from the public sphere. For example, one of the first documented critiques of gender ideology is Rachel Speght (born 1597), a poet and polemicist who published a women's rights pamphlet in English under her own name. French playwright, Olympe de Gouges (1748–1793) wrote another influential text, the *Declaration of the Rights of Woman and of the Citizen* (1791). And, of course, Mary Wollstonecraft's (1759–1797) *A Vindication of the Rights of Woman* is one of the most important documents in the history of women's rights.

It was not until the early suffragette movement originating in the 1850s, however, that some change to the status of women in Western society began to happen. This movement comprises the first wave of feminism. The suffragettes viewed marketing favorably and used various marketing techniques to promote their activities and gain publicity for the movement (Scott, 2005). Elizabeth Caddy famously endorsed Fairy Soap; and the notion of women's empowerment was encoded into the fashion for bloomers (named after suffragette Amelia Bloomer who started the trend). Wearing bloomers to ride bicycles, suffragettes thereby signaled their independence and right to equal citizenship with men (Finnegan, 1999). A burgeoning number of department stores provided safe havens where women could meet, unescorted by a man and thus afforded new opportunities for suffragettes to get together and plan their activities. Gordon Selfridge and John Wanamaker were known to be keen supporters of the movement (Tadajewski, 2013; Maclaran, 2012), and Selfridge's store even flew the suffragette flag from its rooftop. Such stores also provided many new career opportunities for women and were seen as "women's worlds" (Bowlby, 1985).

During this first wave, marketing as a discipline was also in its inception, just beginning to break away from economics and establish itself in its own right. The first marketing courses commenced around the early 1900s and the history of marketing thought has widely documented the contributions of various scholars such as Wroe Anderson, Paul Converse, Robert Bartels as well as many other male voices from both academia and practice. Female voices are conspicuously absent, so does this mean there were no female contributors? Our answer to this question is a resounding "no": there are many female voices that have been ignored. Just as feminist literary criticism and philosophy scholars have already argued that patriarchy has constructed the literary and philosophical canons, we argue that so too has patriarchy constructed the marketing canon. This means that within marketing scholarship women's voices have been suppressed or silenced because they were not seen as sufficiently significant, while those generally held up as role models have been men.

The goal of much feminist scholarship is to uncover and highlight works by neglected female authors. To this end a special issue of the *Journal of Historical Research in Marketing* highlights the important contributions to marketing thought and practice made by Home Economists and women who were key players in the advertising industry (Tadajewski & Maclaran, 2013). The volume shows how Home Economists such as Hazel Kyrk, Elizabeth Ellis Hoyt, and Martha van Rensselaer pioneered much early work in the understanding of consumption behaviors (Parsons, 2013; Tadajewski, 2013; Zuckerman, 2013). For example, Tadajewski (2013) highlights the conceptual and theoretical sophistication of seminal texts by Hazel Kyrk, a prolific writer on marketing and consumption phenomena. The same issue also documents the contributions of women in advertising, such as Helen Landsdowne Resor who worked for J. Walter Thompson's Women's Editorial Department in the early twentieth century (Scanlon, 2013), as well as illuminating the barriers on account of gender and race that had to be overcome (i.e. Foster Davis, 2013). In a subsequent book on the topic, Foster Davis (2017) details the many remarkable achievements of Afro-American women who worked in the advertising industry. Apart from her work, this special issue and a couple of other notable exceptions (Zuckerman & Carsky, 1990; Paulson & Schramm, 2017), there is little documentation of female contributions to marketing theory or practice and there remains much to be done to emphasize women's contributions to marketing in this early period.

Second-wave feminism (1960–1988)

This era marked a much greater suspicion of marketers and marketing activities as being complicit in the oppression of women, particularly through stereotypical conceptions of women's roles that perpetuated beauty ideals and reinforced unequal power relations. Whereas suffragettes had focused on rights to full citizenship, second-wave feminists concentrated much more on the relations encouraged by capitalist configurations of the family and the material base of women's inequality. A major influence at this time was Simone de Beauvoir's *The Second Sex* (1949) in which she famously writes "one is not born but rather one becomes woman." Here de Beauvoir analyzes the social, political, and religious structures that create woman as "other," and render her as inferior to man. Marketers' role in reinforcing these patriarchal structures became heavily critiqued by anti-marketing texts such as Betty Friedan's *Feminine Mystique* (1963) and Germaine Greer's *The Female Eunuch* (1970). Goffman's (1979) study of gender representations in advertising exposed how men were more likely to be depicted as confident and in control, whereas women were most likely to be portrayed as submissive and vulnerable. Highlighting such stereotypical media portrayals, Winship (1987), a feminist media scholar, drew attention to the "work" of femininity as women seek to achieve ideals of beauty. Such critiques alongside many other feminist exposures of negative female stereotyping brought about change in the 1980s as advertisers replaced decorative, passive portrayals of women with more diverse and agentic representations of female empowerment.

During this period, most gender research in consumer behavior ignored feminist perspectives. Often, through conflating sex and gender, it merely reinforced stereotypical gender roles, positioning men as producers/breadwinners and women as consumers/homemakers (Maclaran, Otnes & Tuncay Zayer, 2017). There was a plethora of studies on the influence of sex-role norms in family decision-making (Schneider & Barich-Schneider, 1979; Meyers-Levy, 1988; Meyers-Levy & Sternthal, 1991). Heavily influenced by psychology and the information-processing paradigm, such research generally served to reinforce gender differences rather than question them or critique the role of marketing practice in creating them. There was a small stream of research that drew on feminist perspectives, particularly the feminist critiques of advertising. However, this research was mainly to assess whether contemporary advertising portrayals were keeping up with women's changing roles rather than with the aim of offering a feminist critique (i.e. Sexton & Haberman, 1974; Belkaoui & Belkaoui, 1976; Wagner & Banos, 1973). For example, Courtney and Whipple (1983) recommended different representations of women depending on product group and market segments (i.e. traditional role models for household goods and career-oriented role models for beauty products). As practitioners began to react to the "women's movement", consumer research studies increasingly reported changing portrayals of women in advertising, noting that more were set in professional contexts (Lysonski, 1983) or included expert female voices (Ferrante, Haynes & Kingsley, 1988), but any feminist critique remained limited. Thus, the consumer research of this period does little to explain why gender differences exist (Catterall & Maclaran, 2001; Artz & Venkatesh, 1991), remaining fairly superficial and descriptive rather than attempting deeper theorizing.

Third-wave feminism (1988–2010)

Reacting to the writings of authors such as bell hooks and Judith Butler, third-wave feminists put much more emphasis on queer and non-white women, critiquing second-wave feminists for assuming that all women faced the same types of oppression. Reflecting the wider cultural turn across the social sciences, the concept of multiple feminisms acknowledged the intersection of different systems of oppression such as race, gender, class, ability, and ethnicity (now termed "intersectionality"). The principle of intersectionality means trying to avoid assuming that straight middle-class white feminists can speak for all women. The writings of black feminist theorist, bell hooks, were particularly influential at this time. In her foundational work hooks (1984) explored the intersection of race, gender, and capitalism. She also paved the way for studies of masculinity by critiquing the second wave for how it treated men and ignoring how patriarchal culture prohibits men from being in touch with their feelings and emotions. The work of poststructuralist (see Table 4.1) gender theorist Judith Butler (1990) was also breaking new ground at this time, explaining how discourse creates gender identities. One of Butler's central arguments is that gender is not something we "have" but rather something we "do," and that gender identity is constructed by performing (and repeating) specific acts within a culture (see Maclaran (2018) for more a more detailed explanation of Butler's work). Butler's ideas inspired a new field of studies, Queer Theory, that challenges the validity of heteronormative discourse (the assumption that people can be categorized as either male or female and that these are complementary).

In relation to marketing, the third wave's recognition of multiple feminisms brought a period of reconciliation with consumption as different sexualities found self-expression in the marketplace. Heralding an era of identity politics and the questioning of binary understandings of men and women, women's empowerment was frequently typified by girl-power, "raunch culture" (Levy, 2005), and porno-chic (McNair, 2002), sexual expressiveness (see, for example, *Sex and the City*; Stevens & Maclaran, 2012; Walters, 2010). Some argued that the feminists need not reject consumerism in order to "be political" (Baumgardner & Richards, 2004, p. 62); in fact, for "affirmative feminism," the market simply means more opportunities for agency and possibilities for destabilization of the old social order, which associates femininity with subordination (ibid.). Nigella Lawson, "domestic goddess," is a prime example here, as well as the globally popular TV series such as *Mad Men* and *Desperate Housewives*, which (re)present an ostensibly feminine aesthetic as a way to claim and assert woman's independence and power, thereby relegating feminism to a past no longer relevant to contemporary femininities: as a battle that has now been won. Hence, Munford and Waters (2014) dubbed this turn a "postfeminist mystique" and pointed to its deeply retrogressive nature as it reverted to women's display of femininity and female sexuality as the main means of fulfillment for young women.

It took until the 1990s for feminist critique to enter the field of consumer research as a part of the burgeoning interpretivist (i.e. cultural) turn that drew on alternative modes of theorizing. This critique often drew on poststructuralism, for example, deconstructing the masculinist ideology embedded in both marketing and consumer research rhetoric (Fischer & Bristor, 1994;

Hirschman, 1993; Joy & Venkatesh, 1994; Stern, 1992). This period also introduced innovative theoretical perspectives such as ecofeminism that threw light on the feminine bias in caring for the environment and the androcentric rationale separating humans from nature and guiding marketing activities (Dobscha, 1993). In addition, feminist methodologies suggested new ways to make research more collaborative (Peñaloza, 1996).

At this time, too, there was a growing interest in the broader intersection of gender and consumption initiated by Janeen Costa's (1991) *Gender, Marketing and Consumer Research Conference* that still exists today. Although feminist voices have always been a part of this (and remain so), it is fair to say that any feminist critique became more muted during the 2000s as the broader field of gender and identity projects (in conjunction with Consumer Culture Theorists) rose to prominence and put the emphasis on individual rather than collective agency. This is despite two books on the relationship between marketing and feminism (Catterall, Maclaran & Stevens, 2000; Scott, 2005) and other notable contributions such as: Bettany and Woodruffe-Burton's (2009) call for feminist reflexivity in marketing/consumer research; Brace-Govan's (2010) feminist deconstruction of advertising portrayals of sportswomen; and Stevens, Kearney and Maclaran's (2013) ecofeminist exploration of brand mascots. Accusing postmodern marketing of diluting feminism, Catterall, Maclaran and Stevens (2005) highlight how advertisers repackaged the feminist quest for equality of choice and opportunity as lifestyles that could be achieved through consumption. Critique of wider patriarchal structures became muted as marketing practitioners successfully co-opted messages of resistance in the "rebel sell." More recently, feminist scholars such as McRobbie (2009) and Oksala (2011) point to the role of neoliberalism with its tropes of personal freedom and choice, and how it came to define third-wave feminism, masking new forms of gender power, and undermining both the work of making institutions accountable and the struggle for wide-reaching collective emancipation.

Fourth-wave feminism (2010–present)

From a surge of social media hashtag campaigns and student feminist societies to media stars and Disney princesses speaking out against misogyny and encouraging women to support one another – we are possibly witnessing the emergence of the fourth wave of feminism (e.g., Cochrane, 2013). There has been a flood of commentary on how the discussions about gender inequality in the workplaces, on the streets, and in the media, have become topical again with a slew of celebrities now proudly reclaiming the "feminist" label (e.g., Atkenhead, 2014; Magnanti, 2014). This recent re-emergence of feminism in popular culture stands in sharp contrast to what is called a postfeminist condition of the previous decade, when gender equality was thought largely achieved (at least in the West) with women's empowerment and freedom being facilitated by individual (consumer) choices (McRobbie, 2009). Indeed, the word "feminism" itself was pejoratively abbreviated into "F-word" and banished from polite conversations.

Now the F-word is back in favor as many young women declare themselves to be feminists. Activists use social media to publicize a wide variety of issues around women's inequality (Baumgardner, 2011) and have already successfully banished *The Sun*'s notorious topless female photo page in their *No More Page 3* campaign. They appear to be blending aspects of the third wave – particularly intersectionality – with the second wave's recognition of dominant patriarchal structures. For example, UK Feminista, founded in 2010, provides training and resources for activist feminists to challenge wider structural aspects of inequality. Its website offers a template to help women start an internet campaign (www.ukfeminista.org.uk/). Many of these campaigns have already forced corporations to change their ways, i.e. the #FBrape campaign that succeeded in convincing Facebook to shut down offensive pages.

Of course, many observers are skeptical of the recent cultural trending of feminism, especially as more corporations climb on the bandwagon. Campaigns for Ethical Underwear (endorsing Who Made Your Pants company), "All for #MyGirls" (Adidas promoting female camaraderie), and Let Books Be Books (big publishers dropping the gendering of children's books) as well as the recent introduction of gender-equal certification by the likes of L'Oreal (e.g., Edge) are said to be nothing more than "rebranding feminism" (Bainbridge, 2014), a perverted market strategy in an increasingly socially aware and online-connected world (e.g., Magnanti, 2014). That might be true if the logic of cultural development is seen as separate from an economic logic, rather than intertwined (Groys, 2014). Put differently, if culture and market are not neatly bounded and distinct realms, then the idea of bracketing the market to establish the existence, essence and authenticity of the newest cultural wave is problematic, as is the dismissal of the feminist activism based on its overexposure to the market.

Marketing and consumer research has witnessed a parallel resurgence of scholarship drawing on feminist theorizing. Üstüner and Thompson (2015) take a Butlerian lens to their study of the Derby Grrrls' re-signifying practices of femininity. They reveal "ideological edgework" that extends gender boundaries by, for example, the juxtaposition of physical aggression mixed with flirtatiousness and displays of playful eroticism. In a recent special issue on theorizing gender in the *Journal of Marketing Management* (Arsel, Eraranta & Moisander, 2015), feminist theory brings new insights into: person-object relations (Valtonen & Närvänen, 2015); the gendered experience of singleness (Lai, Lim & Higgins, 2015); as well as gender violence (Joy, Belk & Bhardway, 2015). In the same issue, Hearn and Hein (2015) spell out a research agenda around missing feminisms that includes critical race theory, queer theory, intersectional and transnational feminisms, material-discursive feminism, and critical studies on men and masculinities. And at the *Gender, Marketing and Consumer Behavior Conference* (Visconti & Tissiers-Desbordes, 2016), Stevens and Houston (2016) argue that fourth-wave feminism uses the body as a site for political activism rather than individual empowerment as, for example, can be seen in the activism of breast-baring feminist groups such as Femen and the protests of Russian feminist punk rock protest group Pussy Riot. Continuing this theme, Matich and Parsons (2016) explore the #freethenipple movement's embodied resistance to patriarchal control of women's bodies, while Wechie (2016) discusses the activism potential of black feminist youtubers.

Future research directions

Having reviewed the trajectory of intersections between marketing and feminism from the past up to the present, we now go on to consider future directions for research focus. Our thoughts are necessarily speculative but, taking inspiration from the recent fourth wave's use of internet technology, we have made the relationship between feminism and technology the central focus for our discussion of key areas where we identify much potential for new feminist theorizing. In this respect, we go back to earlier feminist theorizing to build a base from which to go forward. Where better to start than with Donna Haraway, a prominent feminist scholar in Science and Technology Studies?

First published in 1985, Donna Haraway's 'A Cyborg Manifesto' (1991) became a touchstone for feminist discussion of technology and people's relations with machines and non-humans. In it, the figure of the cyborg is a direct critique of biological essentialism (the belief that human nature is innate as opposed to being formed by culture), a tendency of the, at the time, emerging ecofeminism and back-to-nature countercultural movements. Haraway (1991, p. 149) defines the cyborg as "cybernetic organism, a hybrid of machine and organism, a creature of social reality as well as a creature of fiction." It is significant that the cyborg is not merely a hybrid of human and machine but a product of politics and culture. In other words, the cyborg is a fusion; a figure of unknown origin and ambiguous ontological (the nature of being) status. Haraway uses this ambiguity of the cyborg to question the totalizing narratives such as "women's experiences" and the boundaries that these narratives often evoke. She points to three crucial boundary breakdowns – human and animal, organism and machine, and physical and non-physical – that make the cyborg a potent political form.

Her ideas sparked an explosion of debate about social and political qualities of technology and the role of socio-technical relations in constituting a modern subjectivity (Wajcman, 1991). New perspectives emerged that sought to shift from thinking in terms of human identities to thinking in terms of nodes, networks, and modes of being, most notably post-humanism (a body of theorizing that critiques traditional ideas about the human condition). Some scholars have taken Haraway's ideas to envision the possibilities of creating alternative identity patterns through digital technology in particular, and more generally the liberatory potentialities of cyberspace (Plant, 1997). In this chapter, however, we would like to set aside these intellectual developments and revisit the original thesis. In the 'Manifesto', Haraway urges us to place the analytic focus on boundaries, their confusion, and the responsibilities for their construction across the locations, folding into a historical vision of women's place (in a Western society – home, market, hospital, church, and so on). She emphasizes the need to embrace partial explanations and unresolved contradictions, looking for more horizontal connections (like lateral thinking) rather than seeking to frame everything within a linear, vertical logic. In what follows, then, we concentrate on three arenas of gender performance and gender politics – media, body, and home – which are differently (re)structured by new technology (Gill & Scharff, 2011).

Media representation and a rise of selfie culture

There is a significant body of research exploring market-mediated representation of gender. As discussed above, in the past decades, advertisers notably toned down their reliance on women as props, objects of the male gaze, to sell their wares. The dominant modes of representation shifted from sexual objectification to sexual subjectification (i.e. from passive objects for men to active sexual agents whose new status rather conveniently meshes well with masculine desires) in response to changes in the economy and society (Gill, 2003; Gill & Scharff, 2011). Depictions of women as active sexual subjects, particularly in advertising targeting female consumers, became ubiquitous. Gill (2008) found three popular figures of agentic women in advertising: young (hetero)sexually desiring woman, who sees her "sexy body" as the source of capital; the vengeful woman out to punish her (ex)partner for his transgressions; and the hot lesbian, a woman of conventional attractiveness who often appears with her beautiful double. Gill's (2008) critical analysis of these tropes points to the multiple exclusions implicated in such representations and to the fact that they operate strictly within heteronormativity.

For feminist scholars, the critique of the narrow and limiting image of women and femininity is inextricably connected to the critique of corporate media; and conversely the potentialities for progressive changes in gender representation linked to development of more democratic digital media technologies, such as the internet (e.g., Fotopoulou, 2016). In recent years, the growth of social media platforms held a promise of breaking the singular hold of advertisers and corporate media on constructing and purveying the cultural representation of gender. Some cyber enthusiasts imagined the virtual world as a space for self-authoring and potentially unlimited permutations of gender identities that would render traditional gender relations meaningless, the relics of the real world. The internet indeed opened up spaces for gender-bending and opportunities for a spectrum of gender expressions. One example is *Second Life* virtual community where, the researchers found, both female and male users commonly engaged in gender play via their avatar construction. Alternative gender performances, however, tend to be short-lived, often reifying harmful gender stereotypes, and seen as deceptive by other users (see Clinnin, 2013). Still, today, mainstream social networking sites offer a range of gender identity options; *Facebook* (UK) has over 70 definitions of gender and a popular dating app *Tinder* allows users to choose from 37 options. Gender fluidity appears a familiar notion to a new generation raised on social media and online dating sites.

For many feminist scholars, however, it is not the Facebook drop-down menu options for gender but a rise of the global phenomenon of self-portraiture – the *selfie* – that harbors significant opportunities for disrupting normative representations and pushing the cultural boundaries of gender expectations. As photographer Ina Loewenberg (1999) noted, for women in particular, who frequently have been an object in art, "self-portraiture is a way to keep control of their own representation." Easy to use and affordable mobile phone technology enabled production of self-authored images, while the growth of photo-sharing platforms allowed interactive circulation of these images. It is this interactive capacity and instantaneous nature of the selfie that sets this photographic object apart from yesteryear self-portraiture. According to Senft and Baym (2015), the selfie is "a *gesture* that can send (and is often intended to send) different messages to different individuals, communities, and audiences." In his thoughtful analysis of "the cultural fascination" with the selfie, Murray (2015) submits that, contrary to the popular belief in narcissistic impulse behind selfie practice, young women view selfies as a "radical act of political empowerment: as a means to resist the male-dominated media culture's obsession with and oppressive hold over their lives and bodies." This quote echoes the sentiment of second-wave feminist visual theory where a control obtained through the act of self-imagining is a feminist tool for resistance (Mulvey, 1975). Selfies allow women to depict their lives as they see it, in its multiplicity and from various perspectives, thus become a meaning-maker, in itself an emancipatory act (ibid.). Then, casting the selfie phenomenon in postfeminist terms, Murray (2015) argues that through sharing private moments of their lives such as routines of menstruation, young women reclaim their bodies and produce a new aesthetics of the female body.

The selfie is also a means of resisting erasure. For many marginalized people, whether it is on the basis of race, ethnicity, religion, ability, sexuality, or age, the selfie is a tactic toward visibility. Those lacking representation in corporate media use selfies as a varying tool to reaffirm their very existence. Sharing selfies *en masse* amounts to an act of colonization of the societies' visual culture in a bid for recognition. Poorly or unfairly represented groups of people can now narrate their lives in their own terms and from their point of view, thus destabilizing dominant representations. For example, Nemer and Freeman's (2015) study finds that teens in Brazilian favelas use selfies to document their suffering, speak about violence, and express their spirituality. Furthermore, the selfie is an effective outlet for a social and at times politically oppositional commentary. Connected via tagging into a massive photo-album, selfies collectively speak to challenge received socio-cultural values. #TreeOfLife or #brefie, breastfeeding selfies, and #ArmPitHair selfie trends are recent examples of selfies enacting a feminist gesture against oppressive societal standards of propriety and social control exerted over female bodies.

Moreover, there are examples when the communicative potential of selfies has been used as a direct response to government legislation or a political statement. Saudi women post selfies of themselves driving a car in a country that bans women from driving. In 2014 Turkish women launched the #resistlaugh selfie campaign, posting photos of themselves laughing in response to the Turkish deputy prime minister's comment that "women should know what is decent and what is not decent. She should not laugh loudly in front of all the world and should preserve her decency at all times" (*The Guardian*, 2014). Women from other countries joined the campaign through social media in solidarity with Turkish women fighting misogyny in their country. The campaign was covered by all the major news media, thus raising global awareness about the politics of gender in Turkey. This case illustrates that the immediacy and spontaneity of the reaction makes selfies into a medium of witnessing, that is, selfies are a record of/from those who experience an event first hand and when shared collectively provide a different perspective, possibly multiple perspectives, on an event observed together. It is this quality of the selfie on which marketers are seeking to capitalize in campaigns such as the *Dove* brand's use of selfies to celebrate the 10th anniversary of their *Campaign for Real Beauty*.

Marketers' attempts to co-opt notwithstanding, the potency of the selfie as a communication tool is hard to deny. Its capacity for self-authoring gender representation is, however, less convincing. Cyberspace, it appears, is yet to provide liberation from the dominant modes of gender representation or roles. The growing scholarship on the image-centered social media, such as *Instagram* and *Facebook*, shows that traditional gender stereotypes and corporate-engineered images of femininity/masculinity are prevalent in selfie culture. For example, Döring, Reif and Poeschl (2016) found that classic gender display categories such as feminine touch, withdrawing gaze, and laying posture (Goffman, 1979) as well as new social media-related categories (e.g., kissing pout and muscle presentation) dominate self-presentation on *Instagram*. Furthermore, the comparison of gender category adherence between selfies and magazine advertisements reveal that both male and female *Instagram* users are far more gender stereotypical than advertisers (ibid.). Similarly, cultural commentators on pervasive self-sexualization in social media observe that young people, particularly women, tend to replicate normative articulations of (hetero)sexuality and even emulate representational codes of pornography (see Levy, 2005). Furthermore, the market opportunities to convert the "Instafame" into real money fosters conformity of sexual expression (Mascheroni et al., 2015; Schwartz, 2010). That is, returning to Haraway's framework (1991), while the boundaries between the digital or virtual and the real are all but breached the boundaries between the social categories persist.

Technologized body and enterprising self

The body is another key arena where the market and technology intersect and play an important role in contemporary gender politics and making of gendered subjects (Cockburn & Omrod, 1993). In consumer capitalism, the body becomes a source of symbolic capital – both appearance and bodily presentation are crucial to achieving a social status and self-actualization (Featherstone, 1982). In *Femininity and Domination*, Sandra Bartky (1990) extends this work through the idea of self-objectification; in her words, "in the regime of institutionalized heterosexuality woman must make herself 'object and prey' for the man" (p. 73), "woman thus [takes] toward her own person the attitude of the man. She will then take erotic satisfaction in her physical self, reveling in her body as a beautiful object to be gazed at and decorated" (pp. 131–132). For some third-wave feminists, Bartky's take on beauty as oppression might seem crude; still, her notion of a "fashion-beauty complex," akin to the military-industrial complex, captures well the intricate ways in which technology and production work in tandem with marketing and retailing to regulate a female body. Susan Bordo (1993) picks up on the notion to argue that this complex operates not only through beauty standards and gender norms (both often couched in scientific discourses), but through the divergent dynamics of aestheticization and rationalization of the female body that take place in women's everyday lives. The focus on aesthetics of body (e.g., slenderness, toned muscles, smooth skin) and body maintenance (e.g., dieting, physical exercise, sleep) is central to the self that is depicted across a variety of different market contexts.

Today's cosmetic surgery market presents a paradigmatic example of how this industrial complex works and the divergent dynamics therein. Over the past two decades, a business of aesthetic remaking of body has grown into a multibillion dollar industry, with heavy investments in R&D, aggressive marketing, and a predominantly female consumer base (Stein, 2015). Feminist scholars note that this complex is fueled mainly by two ideological beliefs: (a) body is plastic – it can be (re)shaped with improving technology, and (b) body is a form of capital, which is increasingly at play in a competitive labor market (Davis, 1995; Duffy, Hancock & Tyler, 2017). The first belief is most prominent in the research on meanings and experiences of cosmetic surgery. These accounts show that personal reasons for cosmetic surgery are complex and "becoming surgical" could be liberating for an individual (Blum, 2003, p. 66; Davis, 2003). Davis (2003), for example, asserts that for some women, a surgical intervention is not merely a remedy for bodily flaws but a way to actively navigate the ideals of beauty and alter their bodies in accordance with their identity projects.

Yet, feminist analyses also show that the interpretative repertoires of cosmetic surgery are fairly limited (Fraser, 2003). They pivot on either a socio-historic degradation of the female body (flawed and out of control), or a culture of narcissism, fixed on an imperative to do something for oneself, and hedonic consumption (where the body is simply a vehicle for recognizing/realizing one's desires and projects). Though they appear opposite, both situate women as "a proper object of surgical bodily intervention" and reiterate conventional femininity (ibid., p. 120). Furthermore, empirical studies of popular makeover TV shows point to class structuring of these repertoires. Researchers find that the object of intervention and transformation is almost invariably working-class women, whose bodies are deemed not to meet feminine ideals. They are thus perceived to fail as objects of desire, and are judged to be faltering in their identity projects. While coded as universal, such successful femininity is a bourgeois one, with the middle-class women serving as operatives in disciplinary processes enacted in these widely circulated shows (Franco, 2008; Gallagher & Pecot-Hebert, 2007; Ringrose & Walkerdine, 2008).

The second belief – the body as a form of capital – is most vivid in the context of a cosmetic surgery boom in so-called emerging markets, Brazil, China, and the Middle East. The neoliberal market reforms of the past decades brought in an increased sense of agency, mobility, and self-worth for many women in these regions. Some commentators celebrate the growth of body modifications as a sign of prosperity, suggesting that breast augmentation or tummy tuck is a new luxury good. Others cite the popularity of rhinoplasty (nose jobs) and liposuction as evidence of growing freedoms for women in the Middle East (Stein, 2015). More critical observers link this boom to globalization and Western-dominated media, particularly the rise of global entertainment and celebrity culture, which asserted beauty as prerequisite for success and happiness, and the good life (Edmonds, 2010). The feminist reading of the boom, however, takes this critique further, seeking to contextualize and politicize it. For feminist scholars, it is no coincidence that as women become more active in labor markets and consumer culture, more and more of them are 'going under the knife' (McRobbie, 2009). As Ong (2006) and Gershon (2011) argue, neoliberalism is a political-economic regime that evokes a distinct mode of subjectification, where an individual must become an entrepreneur (a maker and a manager) of her own life – *an enterprising self*. Within this conception of self as a flexible set of competences continuously attuned to the market, the body is valorized as a resource to be invested in and cultivated strategically in order to advance ambitions and evidence achievements (Gershon 2011; Power, 2009). Such casting of the body is perfectly aligned with cosmetic surgery's promise of a transformation for a better self and a better life through a bodily modification (Davis, 1995).

Indeed, the research on "newly arrived into middle class" in Brazil, China, and India shows that many women undergo surgery on a path to a social mobility, be it to secure their careers or advance marriage prospects (Jha, 2016; Wen, 2013). In ethnographic work conducted in Beijing, Wen (2013, p. 236) finds that women talk of cosmetic surgery as an investment choice, often painful but necessary, for "the more physical capital a woman can hold, the more ability she may have to reshape the social, cultural and economic fields around her." Such a view is not merely an internalization of the beauty industry marketing message, but endorsed by the state, which historically, since the Cultural Revolution, has conceived of women as a labor reserve and circumscribed women's bodies accordingly. Today, within the Chinese neoliberal economy, beauty, sexuality, and femininity are legitimized as a currency and a source of capital, contributing to national economic growth (also Jha, 2016). This research supports McRobbie's (2009, p. 57) conclusion that while gender regimes of the past established what women must *not* do, the neoliberal regime works through a "constant stream of incitements and enticements" and encourages capacity, enjoyment, attainment, and social mobility.

Recognizing that the body is not only an individual asset but a site of socio-cultural and political struggles (Bordo, 1993, p. 16), some feminist researchers focus on varying ways physical features are valued in different national contexts, depending on racial histories, colonial legacy, and geopolitics (e.g., Glenn, 2008; Jha, 2016). Such focus allows scholars to go beyond the claims of Western-media domination to examine the intersectionality of beauty norms (i.e. how interconnected and co-constituting hierarchies of race, class, religion, and so on are implicated in valuing some physical features as normal or desirable, while devaluing others). As an example, the empirical research of skin-bleaching practices in India reveals that privileging fair skin pre-dates Hollywood and even British colonialism, and has origins in the Hindu caste system. Then, British Imperialism and the Bollywood cinema, along with Hollywood blockbusters and the global advertising industry cemented the symbolic status of fair skin by linking it to the notions of progress, modernity, and the good life (Jha, 2016). In taking the intersectional and transnational perspective, this body of work effectively reveals structural power relations not only of gender, but class, caste, race, nation, and global inequality, and the ways these are reproduced in both national and individual beauty preferences. This research also makes clear that while cosmetic surgery promises to erase anatomically or at least make the (markers of) difference a matter of aesthetic or stylistic choices, it actually serves to reinforce symbolic difference by (re)articulating the socio-cultural values ascribed to certain (ethnic, racial, age-related, etc.) physical features.

All in all, medical technology has developed to produce a truly technologized body. Global media and celebrity culture normalized a cyborg or Tupperware body, to rephrase Joan Rivers' self-deprecating characterization. A 30-year-old face on a 70-year-old body or a 34FF-breast with a 21-inch waist is often taken as a personal eccentricity, rather than a nonhuman body modification. The plasticity of the body is touted not only by marketers for the industry but by governments and some feminists. At times ideologically divergent, these entities tend to frame this plastic or malleable body in terms of choice, where aesthetic modifications, however painful and costly, are a tool for self-creation, overcoming (physical) constraints and social boundaries. Yet, the advancement of modern medicine and assertions of progressive politics notwithstanding, much of critical feminist research shows that a cyborg, in Haraway's sense (1991), as a figure for boundary breakdowns is as unattainable as ever. The link between the transformative potentialities of cosmetic surgery and emancipated identity reproduces the body/mind duality (Ghigi & Sassateli, 2018).

Home and quantified life

Home has long been a contentious site for feminists: a primary arena for both female oppression and female liberation. To emancipate women after the October Revolution, Soviet comrades sought to dismantle the concept of home, as a bourgeois idea, by building communal kitchens, communal nurseries, and communal living. A failed experiment, it nonetheless has exposed how women joining the workforce *en masse* does not lead to full liberation, instead it often results in what is now called a double-burden or the second shift (Hochschild & Machung, 1989). The cultural counter-revolutionaries of the 1960–70s in the West had a range of ideas about the emancipatory home; one that seems to have stood the test of time was the idea of using technology to free women of domestic labor (Cowan, 1989). Today, the talks of the revolution of home center on the idea of the smart home, which, while currently something of a buzzword, is often presented superficially as a fridge talking to a phone about milk going out of date.

Feminists have always been wary of the impact of technological innovations on the home, especially those with an ostensible motive to transform a household. In contrast to tech companies, the potentialities of smart kitchen counters, smart mattresses, and smart locks fail to enthuse many feminist commentators (see *Model View of Culture*, a feminist tech magazine). Considerable historical research has been devoted to debunking the myth that modern technology eliminated or significantly reduced housework. Ruth S. Cowan (1989) examines "the industrialisation of the home" since 1860 and questions the production to consumption model of the household transformation. She argues that domestic gadgets replaced mainly the work previously done by men or servants, and facilitated women's participation in a labor force not by freeing them of housework but by making it possible to keep up with home chores while working outside the home. Furthermore, contrary to marketing promises, modern appliances did not make life more comfortable for middle-class housewives, rather more emotionally demanding as they raised standards and expectations of cleanliness. Judy Wajcman (1991) makes a larger argument that the higher standards of cleanliness and the emergent idea of "scientific motherhood," reproduced existing ideologies of gender and, indeed, increased women's work within the home by blurring the boundaries of consumption and production spheres. The transportation and delivery services (encapsulated in the soccer mom trope) is one notable example of women absorbing some of the production sphere. Another perhaps less obvious, but for Wajcman (1991, p. 85) a more significant example is a provision of emotional support, entertainment, and ultimately shelter from "the alienated, stressful technological order of the workplace." Now with the smart domestic ecosystem, women and households are incorporated into the capitalist production system arguably in more insidious ways – the home becomes a data factory. A consideration of two innovations – tracking devices and intelligent personal assistants – serves to epitomize, in a very preliminary form, some of the problems.

The development of sensor-based technology has led to creation of mobile tracking devices, allowing them to capture a wealth of physiological information about our daily lives. Tools previously available only in a hospital's intensive care unit have been transformed into home and/or wearable gadgets, with millions of people now monitoring their own vital signs and tracking steps taken, hours slept, calories consumed, time used, and so on – a phenomenon known as the Quantified Self (Wolf, 2009). Lupton (2016) analyzes the socio-cultural and political dimensions of self-tracking across social domains. She illustrates well the simultaneous pressures of voluntarily surveillance, (apps-)imposed configuration of sexuality and reproduction, and neoliberal self-responsibility in the matters of health. Beyond the issues of data security and surveillance, Lupton highlights the implications for gender politics, namely sex apps for men that focus on endurance, in contrast to a fertility focus for women.

To be sure, the notion of statistical average in establishing norms is not new and critiques abound (e.g., Creadick, 2010). As Bordo (1993) noted, women's bodies and physiological functions have historically been surveyed and subjected to social-cultural and state regulations. However, what seems to be different now is that private companies, rather than the state, are in charge of the process. Also, as "numbers are making their way into the smallest crevices of our lives" (Wolf, 2009), the normative categories generated via the magnitude of data ("big data") are far more detailed and encompassing than before. Arguably, the disciplinary effects of individualized and continuous measuring against a near-perfect, near-universal norm performed by the tracking technologies are ever more potent. In this regard, feminist researchers traditionally posit several questions, including whose universals and who is left behind, who is measuring, what is measured, and why (Harding, 1987, 2015; Wajcman, 1991). Furthermore, the concern with repurposing of personal data for commercial uses goes beyond the issue of data security to the questions of how this data feeds the production cycle of the tech industry. That is, how new products are developed to address the needs "discovered" by, for example, the quantification of usually messy and quirky sexual and reproductive activities (Lupton, 2015). In general, feminist commentators have just begun to articulate a number of urgent societal, ethical, and political concerns regarding tracking technologies. First and foremost, they foreground disciplining effects of the technologically enhanced biopower (i.e. the management of a population), and also the potential for generating a new "algorithmic subjectivity," a way of relating to the body and the self, structured by what privileged white men from Silicon Valley deem measurable (Lupton, 2016).

Artificial Intelligence (AI) is another technological development currently with more question marks than answers. The "intelligent home assistant" entered millions of homes around the world in 2016 with the news story about Alexa, Amazon's "home operating system." Apparently, it pieced together some words and phrases into a coherent (to itself) command and placed purchase orders for dollhouses on Amazon. One order was made in response to a child's play and a few more were made in response to a TV newsreader reporting on the story. Reassurances from Amazon notwithstanding, the public discomfort over the incident registered across the social media. Some commentators noted the fact that "an intelligent butler" tends to have a female name and a female voice as a default setting, thus perpetuating age-old gender stereotypes about domestic labor, child care, and service work more generally (*Slate* 2016). Still more worryingly, others noted that Alexa listens to more than it should. Enthusiasts pointed out that Alexa incorporates a machine-learning technology, thus it *needs* to be listening, recording, and analyzing data on everyday practices and social interactions in order to serve a household. That is, before one can say "Alexa, order organic quinoa" or "Alexa, make me coffee," Alexa must recognize a personalized command and have a relevant "skill" (crudely, a function) to perform the task. Skills for Alexa are developed using the information vacuumed in homes and through interactions, and could be downloaded at a *freemium* from Amazon and other app suppliers. There are thousands of skills available, ranging from providing weather and sports updates to offering insults from Shakespeare or a monkey. As with home gadgets of the past, the majority of skills are for leisure – for men and by men (Cowan, 1989; Wajcman, 1991). However, the issue is not only that domestic technology reflects existing ideologies of gender and power relations, or the amount of time needed to master the assistant in order to see the benefits of efficiency and convenience promised. The issue is that intelligent home assistants are designed to translate all home communication into purchase commands, or in fact, are programmed to articulate our desires even before we are able to put them into words. As such, Alexa and other AIs are less in the service of a household, and more that of the governing logic of consumer capitalism. Alexa effectively transforms home into the center of economic life: it mines data to feed the production cycle, while also structuring desires to spur consumption.

As we look into the expansion of information-processing technology, we see some boundaries broken, most notably the boundary between the real and the virtual worlds. Other emerging breakdowns have proven to be more ambiguous and arguably more contentious, such as the one between the private and the public. In contrast to Haraway's vision (1991, p. 151), this breakdown is not ushered in by "a revolution of social relations in the *oikos*, the household," but rather generated mainly through the logic of surveillance, produced either by the willing selfie- and Quantified Self subjects or by the entities of yet-to-be-defined ontological nature, AI assistants. The private becomes not quite the public but open and accessible to other private entities, the corporations. Typical feminist research questions about power, social-political structures of domination, and the prevalence of "the perspective of bourgeois white men," remain extremely pertinent today when our lives are increasingly governed by proprietary algorithms and network infrastructures (Harding, 1987, 2015). The implications of many tech developments discussed in this chapter are not entirely clear but what is fairly certain is the need for more feminist consumer and marketing research into the ideology, politics, and moral values of algorithms, big data, AI, technologized bodies, and quantification of everything.

Conclusion

In this chapter we used the four waves of feminism to document the relationship between marketing and feminism, both historically and in contemporary scholarship. Then, using Haraway's concept of boundary breakdowns enabled by technology, we have suggested key areas for future feminist attention to explore the blurring boundaries of selfie culture, the technologized body, and the quantified household. In addition, and as indicated earlier in the chapter, there is also a pressing need for more historical research into the role of women in influencing marketing thought both in relation to scholarship and practice. Hence, we hope this chapter will provide an inspiration for young scholars to reinstate some of the lost female voices, as well as developing their own critical lens on the many intersections of marketing and consumption that would benefit from feminist theorizing.

Note

1 Although we find the "wave" metaphor useful for this analysis – especially in connecting early suffragette activism with that in the 1960s – we also acknowledge that it risks being reductionist in simplifying historical complexities and obscuring other feminist activism/scholarship that does not fall neatly into these periods or that might risk being mis-categorized.

References

Arsel, Z., Eraranta, K., & Moisander, J. (2015). Introduction: Theorizing gender and gendering theory in marketing and consumer research. *Journal of Marketing Management, 31*(15–16), 1553–1558.

Artz, N., & Venkatesh, A. (1991). Gender representation in advertising. In R.H. Holman & M.R. Solomon (Eds.), *Advances in consumer research Volume 18* (pp. 618–623). Provo, UT, Association for Consumer Research.

Atkenhead, D. (2014, January 24). Laura Bates interview: "Two years ago, I didn't know what feminism meant." *The Guardian*. Retrieved from www.theguardian.com/world/2014/jan/24/laura-bates-interview-everyday-sexism

Bainbridge, J. (2014, March 4). Rebranding feminism: How brands change to ride the fourth wave. *Marketing Magazine*. Retrieved from www.marketingmagazine.co.uk/article/1282898/rebranding-feminism-brands-change-ride-fourth-wave

Bartky, S.-L. (1990). *Femininity and domination: Studies in the phenomenology of oppression*. New York, Routledge.

Baumgardner, J. (2011). *Fem: Goo goo, gaga and some thoughts on balls*. New York, Perseus Book Group.

Baumgardner, J., & Richards, A. (2004). Feminism and femininity: Or how we learned to stop worrying and love the thong. In A. Harris & M. Fine (Eds.), *All About the Girl* (pp. 59–69). London, Routledge.

Belkaoui, A., & Belkaoui, J. (1976). A comparative analysis of the roles portrayed by women in print advertisements: 1958, 1970, 1972. *Journal of Marketing Research*, *12*(2), 168–172.

Bettany, S., & Woodruffe-Burton, H. (2009). Working the limits of method: The possibilities of critical reflexive practice in marketing and consumer research. *Journal of Marketing Management*, *12*(7–8), 661–679.

Blum, V. (2003). *Flesh wounds: The culture of cosmetic surgery*. Berkeley, University of California Press.

Bordo, S. (1993). *Unbearable weight*. Berkeley, CA, University of California Press.

Bowlby, R. (1985). *Just looking: Consumer culture in Dreiser, Gissing and Zola*. London, Routledge.

Brace-Govan, J. (2010). Representations of women's active embodiment and men's ritualized visibility in sport. *Marketing Theory*, *10*(4), 369–396.

Bristor, J.M., & Fischer, E. (1993). Feminist thought: Implications for consumer research. *Journal of Consumer Research*, *19*(March), 518–536.

Butler, J. (1990). *Gender trouble: Feminism and the subversion of identity*. New York, Routledge.

Catterall, M., & Maclaran, P. (2001). Gender perspectives in consumer behavior: An overview and future directions. *The Marketing Review*, *2*(4), 405–425.

Catterall, M., Maclaran, P., & Stevens, L. (Eds.) (2000). *Marketing and feminism: Current issues and research*. London, Routledge.

Catterall, M., Maclaran, P., & Stevens, L. (2005). Postmodern paralysis: The critical impasse in feminist perspectives on consumers. *Journal of Marketing Management*, *21*(5–6), 489–504.

Clinnin, K. (2013). Playing with masculinity: Gender bending in second life. *Technoculture*, *3*. Retrieved from https://tcjournal.org/vol3/clinnin

Cochrane, K. (2013). *All the rebel women: The rise of the fourth wave of feminism*. London, Guardian Shorts.

Cockburn, C., & Omrod, S. (1993). *Gender and technology in the making*. London, Sage.

Courtney, A.E., & Whipple, T.W. (1983). *Sex stereotyping in advertising*. Lexington, MA, Lexington Books.

Cowan, R.S. (1989). *More work for mother*. London, Free Association Books.

Creadick, A.G. (2010). *Perfectly average*. Amherst, MA, University of Massachusetts Press.

Davis, K. (1995). *Reshaping the female body: The dilemma of cosmetic surgery*. New York and London, Routledge.

Davis, K. (2003). Surgical passing: Or why Michael Jackson's nose makes 'us' uneasy. *Feminist Theory*, *4*(1), 73–92.

Dobscha, S. (1993). Woman and the environment: Applying ecofeminism to environmentally-related consumption. *Advances in Consumer Research*, *20*(1), 36–40.

Döring, N., Reif, A., & Poeschl, S. (2016). How gender-stereotypical are selfies? A content analysis and comparison with magazine adverts. *Computers in Human Behavior*, *55*(February), 955–962.

Duffy, K., Hancock, P., & Tyler, M. (2017). Still red hot? Postfeminism and gender subjectivity in the airline industry. *Gender, Work and Organization*, *24*(3), 260–273.

Edmonds, A. (2010). *Pretty modern: Beauty, sex, and plastic surgery in Brazil*. Durham, Duke University Press.

Featherstone, M. (1982). *Body in Consumer Culture*. London, Sage.

Ferrante, C.L., Haynes, A.M., & Kingsley, S.M. (1988). Images of women in television advertising. *Journal of Broadcasting and Electronic Media*, *32*(Spring), 231–237.

Finnegan, M. (1999). *Selling suffrage: Consumer culture and votes for women*. New York, Columbia University Press.

Fischer, E., & Bristor, J. (1994). A feminist poststructuralist analysis of the rhetoric of marketing relationships. *International Journal of Research in Marketing*, *11*(4), 317–331.

Foster Davis, J. (2013). Beyond "caste-typing"? Caroline Robinson Jones, advertising pioneer and trailblazer. *Journal of Historical Research in Marketing*, *5*(3), 308–333.

Foster Davis, J. (2017). *Pioneering African-American in the advertising business: Biographies of MAD black women*. London, Routledge.

Fotopoulou, A. (2016). *Feminist activism and digital networks*. Basingstoke, UK, Palgrave Macmillan.

Franco, J. (2008). Extreme makeover: The politics of gender, class, and cultural identity. *Television & New Media*, *9*(6), 471–486.

Fraser, S. (2003). *Cosmetic surgery, gender and culture*. Basingstoke, Palgrave Macmillan.

Freeland, C. (1994). Nourishing speculation: A feminist reading of Aristotelian science. In O. Bat-Ami Bar (Ed.), *Engendering origins: Critical feminist readings in Plato and Aristotle*. Albany, State University of New York Press.

Friedan, B. (1963). *The feminine mystique*. New York, W.W. Norton & Co.

Gallagher, A., & Pecot-Hebert, L. (2007). 'You Need a Makeover!' The social construction of female body image in 'A Makeover Story', 'What Not to Wear', and 'Extreme Makeover'. *Popular Communication*, *5*(1), 57–79.

Gershon, I. (2011). Neoliberal agency. *Current Anthropology*, *52*(4), 538–555.

Ghigi, R., & Sassatelli, R. (2018). Body projects: Fashion, aesthetic modifications and stylised selves. In O. Kravets, P. Maclaran, S. Miles & A. Venkatesh (Eds.), *The Sage handbook of consumer culture* (pp. 290–315). London, Sage.

Gill, R. (2003). From sexual objectification to sexual subjectification: The resexualisation of women's bodies in the media. *Feminist Media Studies*, *3*(1), 100–106.

Gill, R. (2008). Empowerment/sexism: Figuring female sexual agency in contemporary advertising. *Feminism & Psychology*, *18*(1), 35–60.

Gill, R., & Scharff, C. (Eds.) (2011). *New femininities: Postfeminism, neoliberalism and subjectivity*. Basingstoke, UK, Palgrave Macmillan.

Glenn, E.N. (2008). Yearning for lightness: Transnational circuits in the marketing and consumption of skin lighteners. *Gender & Society*, *22*(3), 281–302.

Goffman, E. (1979). *Gender advertising*. Cambridge, MA, Harvard University Press.

Greer, G. (1970). *The Female Eunuch*. London, Harper Perennial.

Groys, B. (2014). *On the new*. Trans. by G.M. Goshgarian, London and New York, Verso.

Haraway, D. (1991). A cyborg manifesto: Science, technology, and socialist- feminism in the late twentieth century. In *Simians, cyborgs and women: The reinvention of nature* (pp. 149–181). New York, Routledge.

Harding, S. (1987). Is there a feminist method? In S. Harding (Ed.), *Feminism and methodology* (pp. 1–14). Bloomington, Indiana University Press.

Harding, S. (2015). *Objectivity and diversity: Another logic of scientific research*. Chicago, University of Chicago Press.

Hirschman, E.C. (1993). Ideology in consumer research 1980 and 1990: A Marxist and feminist critique. *Journal of Consumer Research*, *19*(4), 537–555.

Hochschild, A., & Machung, A. (1989). *The second shift*. New York, Avon Books.

hooks, bell (1984). *Feminist theory: From margin to center*. Cambridge, MA, Southend Press.

Jha, M.R. (2016). *The global beauty industry: Colorism, racism, and the national body*. London, Routledge.

Joy, A., & Venkatesh, A. (1994). Postmodernism, feminism, and the body: The visible and the invisible in consumer research. *International Journal of Research in Marketing*, *11*(4), 333–357.

Levy, A. (2005). *Female chauvinist pigs: Women and the rise of raunch culture*. New York, Simon & Schuster.

Loewenberg, I. (1999). Reflections on self-portraiture in photography. *Feminist Studies*, *25*(2), 398–408.

Lupton, D. (2015). Quantified sex: A critical analysis of sexual and reproductive self-tracking using apps. *Culture, Health & Sexuality*, *17*(4), 440–453.

Lupton, D. (2016). *The quantified self*. London, Polity Press.

Lysonski, S. (1983). Female and male portrayals in magazine advertisements: A re-examination. *Akron Business and Economic Review*, *14*(3), 45–50.

Maclaran, P. (2012). Marketing and feminism in historic perspective. *Journal of Historical Research in Marketing*, *4*(3), 462–469.

Maclaran, P. (2018). Judith Butler: Gender performativity and heteronormative hegemony. In S. Østergaard & B. Heilbrunn (Eds.), *The Routledge companion to canonical authors in social theory on consumption* (pp. 227–234). Abingdon, Routledge.

Maclaran, P., Otnes, C., & Tuncay Zayer, L. (2017). Gender, sexuality and consumption. In M. Keller, B. Halkier, T.-A. Wilska, & M. Truninger (Eds.), *The Routledge handbook of consumption* (pp. 292–302). London, Routledge.

Magnanti, B. (2014, July 21). Your guide to fourth-wave feminist underwear. *The Baffler*. Retrieved from www.thebaffler.com/blog/your-guide-to-fourth-wave-feminist-underwear/

Mascheroni, G., Vincent, J., & Jimenez, E. (2015). 'Girls are addicted to likes so they post semi-naked selfies': Peer mediation, normativity and the construction of identity online. *Cyberpsychology: Journal of Psychosocial Research on Cyberspace*, *9*(1), article 5. http://dx.doi.org/10.5817/CP2015-1-5

Matich, M., & Parsons, E. (2016, July). #freethenipple – embodied resistance in the fourth-wave feminist movement. Paper presented at the *Gender, Marketing and Consumer Behavior Conference*, Paris.

McNair, B. (2002). *Striptease culture: Sex, media and the democratization of desire*. London, Routledge.

McRobbie, A. (2009). *The aftermath of feminism: Gender, culture, and social change*. London, Sage.

Meyers-Levy, J. (1988). The influence of sex roles on judgement. *Journal of Consumer Research*, *14*(4), 522–530.

Meyers-Levy, J., & Sternthal, B. (1991). Gender differences in the uses of message cues and judgments. *Journal of Marketing Research*, *28*(1), 84–96.
Mulvey, L. (1975). Visual pleasure and narrative cinema. *Screen*, *16*(3), 6–18.
Munford, R., & Waters, M. (2014). *Feminism and popular culture: Investigating the postfeminist mystique*. New Brunswick, NJ, Rutgers University Press.
Murray, D.C. (2015). Notes to self: The visual culture of selfies in the age of social media. *Consumption Markets & Culture*, *18*(6), 490–516.
Nemer, D., & Freeman, G. (2015). Empowering the marginalized: Rethinking selfies in the slums of Brazil. *International Journal of Communication*, *9*, 1832–1847.
Oksala, J. (2011). The neoliberal subject of feminism. *Journal of the British Society for Phenomenology*, *42*(1), 104–112.
Ong, A. (2006). *Neoliberalism as exception: Mutations in citizenship and sovereignty*. Durham, NC, Duke University Press.
Parsons, E. (2013). Pioneering consumer economist: Elizabeth Ellis Hoyt (1893–1980). *Journal of Historical Research in Marketing*, *5*(3), 334–350.
Paulson, E.L., & Schramm, M.E. (2017). Electric appliance advertising: The role of the Good Housekeeping Institute. *Journal of Historical Research in Marketing*, *9*(1), 41–65.
Peñaloza, L.M. (1996). We're here, we're queer, and we're going shopping! *Journal of Homosexuality*, *31*(1–2), 9–41.
Plant, S. (1997). *Zeros + ones: Digital women and the new technocultures*. New York, Doubleday.
Power, N. (2009). *One dimensional woman*. London, Zero Books.
Ringrose, J., & Walkerdine, V. (2008). Regulating the abject. *Feminist Media Studies*, *8*(3), 227–246.
Scanlon, J. (2013). "A dozen ideas to the minute": Advertising women, advertising to women. *Journal of Historical Research in Marketing*, *5*(3), 273–290.
Schneider, K.C., & Barich-Schneider, S. (1979). Trends in sex roles in television commercials. *Journal of Marketing*, *43*(4), 79–84.
Schwarz, O. (2010). On friendship, boobs and the logic of the catalogue: Online self-portraits as a means for the exchange of capital. *Convergence: The International Journal of Research into New Media Technologies*, *16*, 163–183.
Scott, L. (2005). *Fresh lipstick: Redressing fashion and feminism*. New York, NY, Palgrave.
Senft, T., & Baym, N. (2015). What does the selfie say? Investigating a global phenomenon. *International Journal of Communication*, *9*, 1588–1606.
Sexton, D., & Haberman, P. (1974). Women in magazine advertisements. *Journal of Advertising Research*, *14*(4), 41–46.
Slate (2016, March 30). Why do so many digital assistants have feminine names? Retrieved from www.theatlantic.com/technology/archive/2016/03/why-do-so-many-digital-assistants-have-feminine-names/475884/
Stein, J. (2015, June 18). Nip. Tuck. Or else. *TIME*. Retrieved from http://time.com/3926042/nip-tuck-or-else/
Stern, B. (1992). Feminist literary theory and advertising research: A new reading of the text and the consumer. *Journal of Current Issues and Research in Advertising*, *14*(Spring), 9–22.
Stevens, L., & Houston, S. (2016, July). Dazed magazine, fourth wave feminism, and the return of the politicised female body. Paper presented at the *Gender, Marketing and Consumer Behavior Conference*, Paris.
Stevens, L., & Maclaran, P. (2012). The carnal feminine: Consuming representations of womanhood in a contemporary media text. In C. Otnes & L. Tuncay (Eds.), *Gender in consumer behavior* (pp. 63–86). New York, Routledge.
Stevens, L., Kearny, M., & Maclaran, P. (2013). Uddering the other: Androcentrism, ecofeminism and the dark side of anthropomorphic marketing. *Journal of Marketing Management*, *29*(1–2), 158–174.
Tadajewski, M. (2013). Helen Woodward and Hazel Kyrk: Economic radicalism, consumption symbolism and female contributions to marketing theory and advertising practice. *Journal of Historical Research in Marketing*, *5*(3), 385–412.
Tadajewski, M., & Maclaran, P. (2013). Editorial: Remembering female contributors to marketing theory, thought and practice. *Journal of Historical Research in Marketing*, *5*(3), 260–272.
The Guardian (2014, July 29). Turkish deputy prime minister says women should not laugh out loud. Retrieved from www.theguardian.com/world/2014/jul/29/turkish-minister-women-laugh-loud-bulent-arinc
Üstüner, T., & Thompson, C.J. (2015). Women skating on the edge: Marketplace performances as ideological edgework. *Journal of Consumer Research*, *42*(2), 235–265.
Wajcman, J. (1991). *Feminism confronts technology*. University Park, Pennsylvania University Press.

Wagner, L., & Banos, J. (1973). A woman's place: A follow-up analysis of the roles portrayed by women in magazine advertisements. *Journal of Marketing Research*, *10*(5), 213–214.
Walters, N. (2010). *Living dolls: The return of sexism*. London, Virago Press.
Wechie, T. (2016, July). A "post" post feminism: The utopian possibilities of a fourth wave of feminism and its intersections with the continued dominance of a tyrannical consumer capitalism. Paper presented at the *Gender, Marketing and Consumer Behavior Conference*, Paris.
Wen, H. (2013). *Buying beauty: Cosmetic surgery in China*. Hong Kong, Hong Kong University Press.
Winship, J. (1987). *Inside women's magazines*. London, Pandora.
Wolf, G. (2009). Know thyself: Tracking every facet of life, from sleep to mood to pain, 24/7/365. *Wired*. Retrieved January 22, 2018 from: www.wired.com/2009/06/lbnp-knowthyself/?currentPage=all
Zuckerman, M.E. (2013). Martha Van Rensselaer and the *Delineator*'s homemaking department. *Journal of Historical Research in Marketing*, *5*(3), 370–384.
Zuckerman, M.E., & Carsky, M.L. (1990). Contribution of women to U. S. marketing thought: The consumers' perspective, 1900–1940. *Journal of the Academy of Marketing Science*, *18*(4), 313–318.

5
CRITICAL SOCIAL MARKETING
Reflections, introspections, and future directions

Ross Gordon

Introduction

This chapter examines the critical social marketing paradigm, which refers to critical analysis of marketing's impact on social outcomes, as well as critical debate about and within social marketing itself. The chapter begins by explaining and briefly charting the history of social marketing and the critical social marketing concept. The chapter goes on to provide a critical analysis of the extant critical social marketing literature, considering discourse on gender, culture, power, ideology, ethics, and pluralism. Finally, some key areas where thinking, writing, research, and debate would benefit critical social marketing moving into the future are identified.

A (very) brief history of social marketing

Although there are several existing histories of social marketing available (e.g., MacFadyen *et al.*, 1999; Truss *et al.*, 2010; Dibb, 2014), it is worth briefly charting its development to inform our understanding of critical social marketing. Social marketing is a broad field focused on the use of marketing for social good and the analysis of the social impacts of marketing (Lazer & Kelley, 1973). However, social marketing is not a unitary discipline. There are different schools of thought, paradigms, and interpretations and arguments over what social marketing should or should not be (Gordon & Gurrieri, 2014). Within the social marketing domain, critical social marketing is a small, albeit nascent stream of social marketing thought (see Gordon, 2011a; Brace-Govan, 2015).

Recorded examples of using marketing to promote social goals can be found going back to the 18th century with the campaign of William Wilberforce to abolish slavery. This drew upon market research, analysis of competitors, mass media communications, and setting up of community abolition movements taking direct action such as fundraising, lobbying, and boycotts (Hastings, 2017). Other examples can be found in the 19th century with the Lights in Darkest England (LIDE) match campaign which sought to promote safer red phosphorus matches to improve the harsh working conditions of Victorian workers in the match industry and to alleviate phossy jaw (i.e. painful mouth swelling) caused by the use of white phosphorus in manufacturing (Krisjanous, 2014). The LIDE campaign involved environmental monitoring and formative research, policy advocacy, segmentation and targeting, and use of various marketing mix tools including product development, public relations, advertising and other forms of promotion, and distribution. These are all elements that can be identified with contemporary social marketing (French & Gordon, 2015).

The 'birth' of modern social marketing is commonly traced to CBS radio research psychologist G.D. Wiebe, who posed the question, "can brotherhood be sold like soap?" (Wiebe, 1951, p. 679). Wiebe was referring to using social advertising to promote social ideas, but his ruminations helped stimulate discourse within the emerging marketing discipline about whether the marketing concept should be broadened into the social arena. Social marketing more coherently emerged as a sub-discipline of marketing in the late 1960s and early 1970s as part of the 'broadening' movement led by scholars such as Sidney Levy.

Levy (2017) drew upon his experience with Social Research Inc., where he worked with schools, museums, hospitals, and government agencies who all did their own forms of marketing. Kotler and Levy (1969) subsequently proposed that marketing was a process of exchange and that exchanges were not just of goods and money but could include services, ideas, and emotions. Essentially, the broadening movement argued for the application of marketing to social problems. Kotler and Zaltman (1971, p. 5) then provided a first definition of social marketing as: "the design, implementation and control of programs calculated to influence the acceptability of social ideas and involving considerations of product planning, pricing, communication, distribution and marketing research".

This definition focused on using marketing for social good, with no mention of the analysis of the social impacts of marketing nor any reference to critical thinking. As some have argued, this might have influenced the development of the discipline over time by placing less emphasis on critique (Gordon, 2011a). Furthermore, the broadening movement, and by extension, the introduction of social marketing, was criticized by those who preferred a narrower commercial focus for the discipline (e.g., Luck, 1969, 1974).

From the 1970s, there followed various examples of marketing programs oriented toward social concerns such as family planning interventions in Sri Lanka that moved away from clinical approaches to strategies such as the distribution of contraceptives through pharmacists and small shops (Population Services International, 1977). Oral re-hydration projects in Africa began to take a more consumer-focused approach in their development (MacFadyen et al., 1999). Such projects often used a commercially focused approach and were typically funded by neoliberal institutions such as the World Bank, and the International Monetary Fund.

Much of the work discussed in the social marketing literature aligns with Kotler and Zaltman's (1971) definition, concerned with using marketing for social good, and does not engage with critical discourse. Yet, a critical dimension to social marketing thinking was evident in the 1970s in the work of William Lazer and Eugene Kelley. Lazer and Kelley proposed that social marketing is "[c]oncerned with the application of marketing knowledge, concepts, and techniques to enhance social as well as economic ends. *It is also concerned with the analysis of the social consequences of marketing policies, decisions and activities*" (1973, p. ix; emphasis added). This definition acknowledges the use of marketing for social good in the first sentence. However, the second sentence of their definition, and the reader in which it appears, contains the proposition that social marketing should *also* be concerned with investigating the impact of marketing on society and act as a form of control and social audit of commercial marketing (Lazer & Kelley, 1973). By proposing critique of marketing, the ideas of Lazer and Kelley are often referred to as the stimulus for critical social marketing (Hastings, 2010; Gordon, 2011a). These historical debates had a major influence in shaping not only social marketing, but the marketing discipline itself. The Kotler and Zaltman (1971) oriented, positivist and functional perspective of social marketing dominated, with the potential for critical discourse being side-lined until relatively recently (Gordon & Gurrieri, 2014).

The emergence of critical social marketing

Although not necessarily badged as 'critical social marketing' there has been some active critical debate *within* the field about ideas, concepts, and approaches for some time. For example, scholars have critiqued a lack of theory development and rigor (see Rothschild, 1979; Andreasen, 2002). Others have criticized the reliance of social marketing on commercial marketing concepts such as the 4Ps, and called for original theory building within the specialty (Peattie & Peattie, 2003; Gordon, 2012). Laczniak and Michie (1979) identified that social marketing generates a number of ethical quandaries. As a practice, it needs to be held to high ethical standards. Connected to this point, the tools and tactics of social marketing should be used with consideration and reflection, and potential power imbalances registered when thinking about who decides what is socially beneficial. In response, those working in social marketing have deeply reflected upon what constitutes social good (Andreasen, 1995), the development of ethical standards (NSMC, 2010), and acknowledged that fear appeal tactics might be unethical, immoral, and ineffective (Hastings *et al.*, 2004). This earlier work has offered internal critique and reflection on social marketing, but mainly focused on operational issues and was not necessarily framed through a critical social marketing lens.

Arguably, the eventual emergence of an overt critical social marketing paradigm originally had an external focus. It was linked to prior work conducted by social marketers alongside other researchers that examined the deleterious effects of commercial marketing, namely tobacco (Hastings & Heywood, 1994; MacFadyen *et al.*, 2001), alcohol (Hughes *et al.*, 1997; Goldberg *et al.*, 1994), and food marketing (Hastings *et al.*, 2003) on health and society. These researchers took on the mantle of Lazer and Kelley by examining negative impacts of commercial marketing on consumers and society and via involvement in advocacy and policy discourse (Gordon, 2011a). For example, research on the effects of tobacco marketing on youth smoking was produced as evidence during the UK House of Commons Health Committee investigation: *The Tobacco Industry and the Risks of Smoking*.

The shift to critical discourse was also stimulated by Marvin Goldberg who critiqued the conservative, individual behavior change focus of social marketing. Goldberg argued for "a more radical approach in social marketing that emphasizes efforts to change the negative or constraining social structural influences on individual behavior, particularly those that originate as a function of marketing activities" and stated that such an initiative would be "tied to the more radical critical theory approach" (Goldberg, 1995, p. 347). In doing so, he reimagined a social marketing that drew upon critical theory and would involve critique (Murray & Ozanne, 1991), conflict (Marcuse, 1964), and change (Gouldner, 1970). Despite the arguments of Goldberg, critical work remained on the fringes during the 2000s. A few scholars called for social marketing to get more critical (Hastings & Saren, 2003). But it was not until Gordon's (2011a) article that the term 'critical social marketing' emerged.

Gordon (2011a) focused on the role of social marketing in critiquing the effects of commercial marketing on health and society. This work identified with the Frankfurt School (i.e. critical theory), with emancipation assumed to flow from the external critique of problematic commercial marketing practices, combined with advocacy and lobbying to effect social change. In his work, Gordon (2011a, p. 89) defined critical social marketing as "critical research . . . on the impact commercial marketing has upon society, to build the evidence base, inform upstream efforts such as advocacy, policy and regulation, and inform the development of downstream social marketing interventions". This definition reflected the ideas of Goldberg (1995) among others. Yet, critique *within* social marketing was largely ignored.

It has only been in recent years that a more expansive critical social marketing perspective has begun to emerge in which external critiques of commercial marketing, engagement with macromarketing and social justice perspectives, and a greater level of internal reflexive debate and critique have materialized. Issues of gender politics and stigma (Gurrieri *et al.*, 2013), power discourses (Cherrier & Gurrieri, 2014; Brace-Govan, 2015), ethnocentricity (Gordon, 2013a; Martam, 2016), and cultural diversity (Gordon *et al.*, 2016) are now being foregrounded. As are topics such as divergence between social marketing paradigms (Gordon & Gurrieri, 2014), acknowledging the socio-cultural realm (Spotswood & Tapp, 2013; Waitt *et al.*, 2016), ethical and moral questions (Spotswood *et al.*, 2012; Dann & Dann, 2016; Hastings, 2017), interpretive and participatory methods (Karippanon & Narayan, 2015), reflexivity (NSMC, 2010; Gordon & Gurrieri, 2014), and unintended consequences (Gurrieri *et al.*, 2013; Peattie *et al.*, 2016).

Given the extensive rethinking of critical social marketing this literature exemplifies, it seems appropriate to revise the definition to take us beyond a sole focus on the critique of commercial marketing. The following characterization better reflects contemporary discourse:

> Critical social marketing examines the impact of commercial marketing and business on society *and/or* critically analyzes social marketing theories, concepts, discourses, and practice, to generate critique, conflict, and change that facilitates social good.

A key point in this definition is that critical social marketing work should seek an emancipatory social justice agenda with a view to changing, not managing or reproducing, the existing world. Critical theory offers one point of departure for such critique, but there are many other veins of social theory that can be mined for inspiration, including the work of Derrida and Foucault. Moreover, there is robust debate about what exactly constitutes social good and this will always be heavily contested. Ideology and politics are salient here. It is fair to say that critical social marketers are more readily identified with progressive, or social-democratic social change agenda(s), rather than conservative and neoliberal paradigms (Gordon & Gurrieri, 2014; Gordon *et al.*, 2016). Having charted a brief history of the development of critical social marketing, this chapter now explores contemporary critical social marketing discourse.

Contemporary critical social marketing

Work in critical social marketing can largely be categorized as focusing on issues of power and ideology, reflexivity, and acknowledging socio-cultural and structural forces.

Social marketing has been criticized by scholars in sociology (Shove, 2010; Crawshaw, 2012), health promotion (Buchanan *et al.*, 1994), public health (Langford & Panter-Brick, 2013), media and communications (Moor, 2011), and critical marketing (Tadajewski & Brownlie, 2008; Bettany & Woodruffe-Burton, 2009; Hackley, 2009; Tadajewski, 2010; Tadajewski *et al.*, 2014). Although these critiques are founded on various grounds there is some commonality among them. They critique social marketing for being a neoliberal device, for a failure to acknowledge power and how it is wielded, for focusing on individual responsibility and largely ignoring socio-cultural and structural forces, and for lacking internal reflexive debate and critique (Brace-Govan, 2015; Gordon *et al.*, 2016).

Undoubtedly the emergence and apparent triumph of neoliberalism (Senker, 2015) has coincided with the emergence of social marketing (Moor, 2011). The last 30 years have witnessed the collapse of welfare state politics, the promotion of individual responsibility, increasing dominance of corporate capitalism, and the ever-greater concentration of economic, social, and political power in the hands of the global elite (Piketty, 2014).

Moor (2011) points out that the emergence of social marketing in the UK was linked to the government's focus on promoting a market ideology and individual responsibility, rather than social, public, and corporate responsibility, when it came to consumption choices and health care provision, delivery, and financing. This is perhaps unsurprising as the establishment of the National Social Marketing Centre and the embedding of social marketing principles in the NHS occurred under the neoliberal Labour Government of Tony Blair. However, some social marketers would argue that citizen participation via involving people in developing research insights and identifying strategies and tactics for public health policy and programs is at least better than top-down expert-driven approaches (French et al., 2010). A number of scholars are skeptical of this, and describe certain social marketing efforts to facilitate citizen engagement as primarily a form of "pseudo-participation" (Tadajewski et al., 2014, p. 1735).

Nevertheless, acknowledging such critiques requires social marketers to focus on participatory methods (see Spotswood, 2011; Stead et al., 2013; Karippanon & Narayan, 2015; Cooper et al., 2016), shift the language of social marketing away from the logic of the market (French & Gordon, 2015), and push back against neoliberal forces where possible. The latter could be achieved by advocating against market driven policy and program directives, and for citizen and community issues and priorities to take center stage (Bellew et al., 2017; Gordon et al., 2017; Gordon et al., 2018a).

Another interesting observation that Moor (2011) makes is that since the election of the Conservative-Liberal Coalition Government in 2010, and certainly since the Conservative majority election win in 2015, social marketing has been side-lined within government circles by behavioral economics (e.g., Thaler & Sunstein, 2008). The latter takes a very limited rational economics and social engineering perspective toward social change. It could be argued that behavioral economics is a more problematic approach to social change than social marketing despite the criticisms of the latter. It is not always possible, moral or ethical to try to simply use behavioral economics to 'nudge' people into doing certain things through choice architecture (French, 2011; Dholakia, 2016). However, the de-linking of social marketing and the neoliberal UK government might provide an opportunity to reformulate social marketing as a more moral, ethical, and reflexive discipline that registers social, cultural and structural forces, issues of power, ethics and morality, and reflexive critique. Much of this work starts with appreciating power relations.

Brace-Govan (2015), for one, critiques the failure of social marketing to engage with issues of power, and the interactions between structure and agency. This neglect is perhaps reflective of the dominance of the positivistic paradigm which ignores the shaping of individual behavior at the meso and macro levels, along with issues of power and agency (Gordon & Gurrieri, 2014). However, there are signs that scholars are working to fill these voids with substantive, meaningful, and impactful contributions. This should be expected. Social marketing is not a unitary discipline. While traditionalist social marketers influenced by Kotler and Levy have long dominated the discourse, socio-ecologist and critical social marketing schools of thought are becoming more prominent. For instance, socio-ecologists argue for a broader and deeper focus beyond the individual to consider the wider socio-cultural realm (Spotswood & Tapp, 2013), social and policy discourse (Gordon, 2013b; Waitt et al., 2016), and structural conditions that delimit individual agency (Andreasen, 2002). So, while the dominant ideology is reasonably problematized in external critiques of social marketing (e.g., Crawshaw, 2012; Tadajewski et al., 2014), these scholars sometimes ignore the kaleidoscope of perspectives in contemporary social marketing.

After all, many socio-ecological and certainly most critical social marketers do not self-affiliate with neoliberal ideology and are attempting to chart alternative pathways. Among those scholars, the commitment is not really to marketing, or neoliberal institutions and language, but to effect social change. Yet, as French and Gordon (2015) point out, emancipatory change may not come about until a major disruptive event such as a war or revolution happens. The patterns of history demonstrate this. The French Revolution temporarily removed absolute monarchy and introduced a republic, and the UK welfare state was constructed after the destructive forces of WWII. Yet, it appears to be an inherent pattern of human existence that after the collapse or replacement of one social system, what follows eventually ossifies power relations, leading to the dominance of new power elites and the emergence of (possibly new) economic, health and social inequalities that are the main drivers of social problems. Indeed, Naomi Klein speculates that global elites seek to capitalize on torpor through 'disaster capitalism'. This, put very simply, involves the engineering of societies by various interest groups (e.g., academics aligned with the Chicago School and amenable dictators) recovering from the shock of war, famine or disease (Klein, 2007). Nonetheless, until such disruptive events shift us away from the neoliberal system, critical social marketers submit that some action is better than nothing (Gordon et al., 2007).

Put differently, there is a politics to, and in, social marketing. Based upon my own observations some academics appear to be (quietly) committed commercial marketers adopting the cloak of social marketing while remaining wedded to neoliberal ideals. Others might be more intrinsically motivated. They are playing the academic game and want to build and promote their profile. Some social marketers might believe they can work on changing things, but never really reflect upon ideology and critique what they do. And other social marketers might be socially oriented and critical thinkers who are uneasy about any relationship with commercial forces and the neoliberal project.

This said, with powerful interest groups come funding and research materials. One cohort of more critically oriented social marketers might be willing to associate with these groups to co-opt their resources to forward an agenda not necessarily consistent with the ideals of neoliberalism. They do so by using pertinent research insights, encouraging citizen participation, *and* by adopting a societal orientation. In more concrete terms, they work *with* people rather than direct interventions *at them*, and use a broad range of strategies and tactics to foster social change. These more progressive politics of social marketing help frame critical social marketing work (Gordon & Gurrieri, 2014).

One area in which power relations have been subject to serious attention is with respect to the topic of gender. Gurrieri *et al.* (2013) examined how social marketing programs on breastfeeding, weight management, and physical activity in effect seek to 'manage' women's bodies in line with a neoliberal vision of acceptability that can create stigma and exclusion for those women who do not conform to the ideal. They called for an expanded macromarketing-informed critical social marketing agenda that engages with issues of social justice, and fosters reflexivity, critique and awareness of unintended consequences such as stigma and social marginalization.

Martam (2016) has picked up on issues of gender politics by discussing the challenges in delivering programs in Indonesia that seek to address gender inequality and domestic violence through improving access to services, increasing sexual and reproductive rights, and promoting gender equality. She points out that there are numerous power dynamics and cultural forces that make such work challenging but also presents a different way for social marketers to think about gender issues, especially in a country like Indonesia. However, gender perspectives and feminist discourse in social marketing remain underdeveloped and much needed, reflecting a masculine dominance of the field.

In addition, there has been greater attention to the unintended consequences of social marketing. Peattie et al. (2016) reflect on the unintended consequences that emerged from a social marketing program to address deliberate fire raising in Wales. These included a reduction in other anti-social behaviors that emerged following community engagement with local youth regarding the dangers of setting fires, and improved community relations (Peattie et al., 2016). Similarly, Gordon et al. (2018a) illuminated the negative and positive unintended consequences emerging from an energy efficiency intervention. Negative effects included participants withdrawing from the project due to the time burden involved and imposition on their home environment experienced during home retrofits. Positive effects included some participants reporting that they had carried out their own additional retrofits following their involvement in the program. These unintended consequences have led to calls for a broader evaluative net that can capture unintended consequences and inform reflective learning to avoid negative effects in the future (Peattie et al., 2016; Gordon et al., 2018a).

As has been indicated above, reflexivity is a key area for critical social marketing debate. Reflexivity is defined as "the regular exercise of the mental ability, shared by all normal people, to consider themselves in relation to their social contexts and vice versa" (Archer, 2007, p. 4). Gordon and Gurrieri (2014) propose that reflexivity should be embedded as a core social marketing principle. They used assemblage theory, an ontological framework for analyzing social complexity that emphasizes that social systems are not stable but are also subject to fluidity, exchangeability, transience, replacement, and multiple functionalities between human and non-human actors within social systems (Deleuze & Guattari, 1980) to analyze power dynamics and reflexive discourse between different stakeholder groups involved in tobacco policy. They call for social marketing actors to reflect on their biases and agendas, understand how social problems are understood, consider what role institutionalized practices play in framing social problems, and negotiate divergent objectives and perspectives to build consensus. Karippanon et al. (2017) develop this debate by examining 'collective reflexivity'. This is where actors strive to appreciate and recognize the role, actions and needs of each other to facilitate a holistic understanding of their situation (Donati, 2016). Such an approach can help address issues of power and authority in consensus formation when considering public health issues in indigenous communities.

Some social marketing literature has started to move away from a manager-consumer style focus with increasing attention devoted to community-led assets-based approaches that harness existing materials, meanings and competences within a community to foster social change (Stead et al., 2013). Participatory ideas such as co-research, co-production, co-design, co-delivery and co-interpretation and representation of programs are also being discussed (Stead et al., 2013; Hastings & Domegan, 2013; French & Gordon, 2015). Work has also considered the power relations and dynamics among various actors in relation to social issues and how stakeholder, institutional and cultural biases and objectives can influence outcomes (Gordon & Gurrieri, 2014; Karippanon et al., 2017).

This represents a sea-change in thinking about power relations in social marketing. In effect, critical scholars are making the case that social marketers are not and should not be managers. Rather, they are facilitators that should acknowledge and respect the agency of citizens and relevant stakeholders. To offer an example, the community-led assets-based social marketing approach takes a subsidiarity perspective in which communities discuss at a local level what issues they think are important before harnessing existing resources and strengths in the community to work toward change, rather than being dictated to by centralized institutions (Stead et al., 2013). This helps engage citizens in the question of who decides what constitutes the 'social good' for a community. Of course, it should be acknowledged that power relations within groups are complex and there is also an argument that not all people want to be involved in these processes.

As such, social marketers must carefully reflect upon and consider how and under what ethical and moral terms to engage with people in social change strategies. Dann and Dann (2016) suggest that social marketing can learn from Catholic Social Teaching by focusing on human dignity, solidarity, subsidiarity, and the common good rather than simply on changing behaviors. Critical scholars point out that the United Nations Universal Declaration of Human Rights can function as a starting point for social marketing (Gordon *et al.*, 2016; Szablewska & Kubacki, 2017). Accordingly, programs should try to uphold or improve basic rights of dignity, anti-discrimination, freedom of choice, speech and thought, fair judicial process, privacy, marriage, property ownership, democratic process, work, access to adequate living, health and education services (United Nations, 1948). Of course, in social marketing there are still difficult ethical trade-offs to be made. For example, tobacco control efforts might improve health but impinge on dignity or introduce stigma for smokers. Such trade-offs are not easy to resolve and social marketers must carefully reflect upon how to balance collective objectives with the rights of individual people.

The gradual shift toward critical perspectives is further reflected in changing language and terminology: from target audiences to participants, from consumers to citizens, and from campaigns to initiatives and movements (Hastings & Domegan, 2013; French & Gordon, 2015). Sacrosanct concepts such as voluntary individual behavior change, the 4Ps social marketing mix, and the exchange concept are being challenged. Ideas such as using a broad, creative and ethically and morally representative selection of strategies and tactics in programs, taking a systems approach to social change, participatory methods, and value creation are attracting increased attention (e.g. Zainuddin *et al.*, 2017).

Recently, attention has been drawn to ethnocentrism in social marketing and concomitantly to a need for greater cultural diversity and an influx of 'Voices from the South' into the literature (Lefebvre, 2011; Martam, 2016; Gordon *et al.*, 2016). Most journal articles, conference keynotes, and textbooks on social marketing are written by white, Western males (Gordon *et al.*, 2016). Consequently, issues of migration, slavery, suppression, resistance, representation, difference, race, gender, space, and place are rarely considered. Clearly, these are very relevant either as social issues in themselves or as key influences on salient social issues. As the work of Martam (2016) demonstrates by considering cultural dynamics in Indonesia such as religion, traditional gender roles, access to education, and early marriages that challenge gender assumptions in the country, there is much to be learned from alternative cultural perspectives. Therefore, social marketing must move beyond a Western model and embrace greater diversity (see also Varman, this volume).

Breaking out of an ethnocentric mold is challenging, especially when the university system and publication outlets, conferences, and other resources and platforms, are dominated by white, Anglo-Saxon Western males. Gordon *et al.* (2016) suggest some ideas for tackling this delimitation of scholarly horizons including open source publishing, supporting Asian and African social marketing networks, inviting guest speakers from around the world to conferences, and funding research and writing from different countries. Providing a platform for voices from the south is one of the key areas in which social marketing can move toward paradigmatic, theoretical, and methodological pluralism (Brace-Govan, 2015; Gordon *et al.*, 2016).

Another area in which social marketing is starting to shift toward a critical agenda is by studying social, cultural, and structural forces and their impact upon individual activities. For example, social marketers are now joining conversations about using social practice theory. This discourse factors in the socio-cultural shaping of human and non-human practices. Practice theory focuses attention on how bodily and mental activities, use of materials and things, knowledge, language, structures, place, and individual and/or group agency are used to perform everyday practices (Reckwitz, 2002; Spotswood *et al.*, 2015, 2017; Gordon *et al.*, 2018b).

Spotswood and Tapp (2013), for example, draw upon Bourdieu's (1984) concept of habitus in an ethnography among low-income families to help understand how structure and agency govern local cultures and frame physical activity practices. Others have considered how access to social capital can shape people's lives and inform social action (Glenane-Antoniadis *et al.*, 2003). And, Waitt *et al.* (2016) draw on Foucault's (1991) concept of governmentality to investigate tensions between market forces, government policy, and the energy use practices of older low-income Australians. They document problems caused by thrifty energy use practices of older people who due to increasing energy costs, rising fuel poverty, and a generational commitment to thrift, use so little energy that they can experience harms to their agency, health, and wellbeing. They aver that understanding the narratives and acknowledging subjectivities of people's home-making practices is important to help (re)shape social marketing programs (Waitt *et al.*, 2016).

Finally, the call of Goldberg (1995) to move upstream has received a response in the systems social marketing literature (Domegan *et al.*, 2016). Systems thinking recognizes that systems are a cause of social issues, and encourages a move beyond operational and problem-solving thinking to non-linear, creative, holistic, and longer-term thinking (French & Gordon, 2015). Systems perspectives help focus on how structural conditions such as regulation, fiscal policy, community mobilization, research, funding, and education influence social issues (Kennedy & Parsons, 2012; Kennedy *et al.*, 2017). Related to this, organizational theory, institutional theory, and actor-network theory have been used to unpack power relations and the dynamics between actors within social systems (e.g. Domegan *et al.*, 2016; Venturini, 2016). These dialogues capture some of the extant critical social marketing discourse. The chapter concludes by referencing future directions for critical social marketing scholarship.

Future directions

Critical social marketing has untapped potential. There are several possible reasons for this. There may be a reluctance by project partners, funding bodies, authors, reviewers, and journal editors to publish critical work in social marketing (Brace-Govan, 2015; Gordon *et al.*, 2016). These stakeholders might not wish to draw attention to perceived failures or tensions in social programs, and reviewers can often be negative about articles that report null findings or work that did not have the intended impact (see Peattie *et al.*, 2016). Those wanting to engage in critical social marketing need to be aware that this could lead to challenges from those who fund or are involved in social marketing programs. Dialogue among social marketing actors will be necessary to facilitate learning from projects whether they are successful in terms of initially set objectives or not.

Moreover, the outlets for publishing critical social marketing work are limited. Social marketing has often struggled to establish legitimacy and this has limited critical debate and stopped difficult questions from being asked. Critical marketers take the view that critical social marketing is not critical enough (e.g., Tadajewski & Brownlie, 2008) and it is noticeable that most critical work in social marketing fails to draw on critical theorists such as Marx, Horkheimer, and Habermas. As a way forward, critical social marketers could be encouraged to explore the tensions, interactions, and discourses between and across critical marketing and critical social marketing. Work in TCR and how it aligns with and diverges from transformative perspectives in social marketing could also provide fertile ground for inquiry (see Lefebvre, 2012; Stead *et al.*, 2013; Tadajewski *et al.*, 2014). Macromarketing is another sub-discipline in which critical discourse on social issues and social change is occurring that has relevance to critical social marketing work and could provide another avenue for exploration (see Gordon *et al.*, 2015; Truong, 2016).

Most critical social marketing work is published in mid-ranked journals. Even then, there are more traditionalists in positions of power (e.g., as journal editors). This makes publishing critical social marketing challenging. However, one avenue is to engage in critical inquiry on topics such as alcohol consumption through lenses such as feminist theory (Griffin et al., 2013) and literary criticism (Hackley et al., 2013). Furthermore, given the importance of being interdisciplinary in the current academic climate, critical social marketers could broaden their readership by publishing in areas such as critical public health, sociology, human geography, and cultural studies (Spotswood, 2016; Gordon et al., 2017). Topic-specific journals in energy, sustainability, public health, and addiction can also provide a vehicle for critical social marketing conversations (e.g., Waitt et al., 2016).

There is also a lack of critical mass in critical social marketing. Social marketing itself is a small field, and critical social marketing even smaller still. Some critical social marketers are still early career researchers and developing their ideas. This means we should take a positive view of the future of critical social marketing. It is a vital, energized area of inquiry and holds considerable promise for continued refinement, theoretical development, and social impact. Even so, those entering the arena need to be aware of and develop strategies to cope with the politics of knowledge production in marketing (see Tadajewski, 2008). Understanding the orientation of the journal under consideration as a publication outlet is important and new researchers should familiarize themselves with what has previously been published in their target publication before submitting their work, to maximize their chances of successfully navigating the peer review process (Bagchi et al., 2017).

It is also notable that several critical social marketers do not possess traditional business backgrounds. This is valuable. We should welcome a greater influx of scholars from political science, history, sociology, and cultural studies that are able to develop the critical work that is already ongoing. Some further areas for future critical social marketing conversation are charted in the remainder of this chapter.

First, critical social marketers can continue the critique of the traditionalist (individual responsibility) paradigm in social marketing. Critical social marketing should distance itself from the neoliberal project. Opposing neoliberalism will mean underlining the importance of social cohesion, social institutions, and social and community dynamics, rather than seeing everything through the perverse lens of individual responsibility (e.g., Ozanne & Ozanne, 2016). As French and Gordon (2015) discuss, there is a need to focus on societal objectives and societal value that rejects the refrain attributed to Margaret Thatcher that there is no such thing as society. This will mean focusing more on the social, and less on the marketing, or at least the neoliberal view of marketing. Instead, the marketing dimension of a reimagined critical social marketing would be one that speaks to mutuality, social interaction, and reciprocity (Hastings & Domegan, 2013).

Critical social marketers can also help shift away from the neoliberal language of marketing and business. People are not and should not be reduced to mere consumers. Referring to people and citizens is more appropriate given the plurality of roles we have in life. Talking about a 4Ps *social* marketing mix might be good for those looking for simplistic formulas for effecting change (or for pedagogic purposes). However, complex social marketing programs would be better served by drawing on a broad, creative, ethical and moral intervention mix. People are citizens, and belong to groups, communities, and cultures who might or might not be participants in social change efforts yet still affected by them nonetheless. The idea of offering exchanges to incentivise people to change their individual behavior is open to criticism, and work that focuses on how to facilitate individual *and* societal value can help develop things in a different direction.

There is a need for theoretical pluralism and greater engagement with the ideas available courtesy of the vast range of social thinkers whose writing remains under-explored within our discipline. Some examples may include Sloterdijk, Deleuze, Bourdieu, de Certeau, Foucault, Latour, Archer, Felman, Johnson, hooks, and Shove among many others who can offer alternative understandings to those provided by economics and psychology that dominate the social marketing landscape. Critical theoretic perspectives that encourage a focus on historical context when examining the social world, and move beyond explanatory to emancipatory objectives are also needed. Therefore, critical social marketers are encouraged to engage with the ideas of critically oriented theorists such as Marx, Horkheimer, Habermas, and Žižek (among others) to consider questions about the failure to acknowledge power and ideology in the social marketing literature, and better understand how it influences the social world.

Alternative methodologies such as ethnography and historiography are being considered and offer us the opportunity to gain new insight (Kubacki & Rundle-Thiele, 2017). Greater engagement with ethical debates and the development and embedding of ethical and moral guidelines and standards into social marketing is another stream to which critical social marketers can contribute. Finally, critical social marketers have a role to play in critiquing activity that may be passed off as social marketing yet is not participatory, inclusive, ethically and morally focused, and oriented toward social justice. A particularly vivid example of this dubious practice is the case of 'corporate social marketing' (Lee, 2016), which is supposedly socially oriented, but ultimately has economic and capitalist objectives (Hastings & Angus, 2011). These are all areas in which further work would help develop critical social marketing.

To conclude, critical social marketing is at a very early stage of development, but it is an important paradigm. Critique is not an end in itself. It holds the potential to help renegotiate and reimagine a more ethical, reflexive, participatory, and social equality focused social marketing. People should therefore be encouraged to join the burgeoning critical social marketing debate.

References

Andreasen, A.R. (1995). *Marketing social change.* San Francisco, Jossey-Bass.
Andreasen, A.R. (2002). Marketing social marketing in the social change marketplace. *Journal of Public Policy and Marketing, 21*(1), 3–13.
Archer, M.S. (2007). *Making our way through the world: Human reflexivity and social mobility.* Cambridge, Cambridge University Press.
Bagchi, R., Block, L., Hamilton, R.W., & Ozanne, J.L. (2017). A field guide for the review process: Writing and responding to peer reviews. *Journal of Consumer Research, 43*(5), 860–872.
Bellew, W., Bauman, A., Freeman, B., & Kite, J. (2017). Social countermarketing: Brave new world, brave new map. *Journal of Social Marketing, 7*(2), 205–222.
Bettany, S., & Woodruffe-Burton, H. (2009). Working the limits of method: The possibilities of critical reflexive practice in marketing and consumer research. *Journal of Marketing Management, 25*(7/8), 661–679.
Bourdieu, P. (1984). *Distinction.* London, Routledge.
Brace-Govan, J. (2015). Faces of power, ethical decision-making and moral intensity: Reflections on the need for critical social marketing. In W. Wymer (Ed.), *Innovations in social marketing and public health communication: Improving the quality of life for individuals and communities* (pp. 107–132). Cham, Springer International.
Buchanan, D.R., Reddy, S., & Hossain, Z. (1994). Social marketing: A critical appraisal. *Health Promotion International, 9*(1), 49–57.
Cherrier, H., & Gurrieri, L. (2014). Framing social marketing as a system of interaction: A neo-institutional approach to alcohol abstinence. *Journal of Marketing Management, 30*(7–8), 607–633.

Cooper, P., Gordon, R., Waitt, G., Petkovic, D., Tibbs, M., Butler, K. et al. (2016). *EE3A: Pathways and initiatives for low-income older people to manage energy: Final Report*. Canberra, Department of Industry, Innovation and Science.

Crawshaw, P. (2012). Governing at a distance: Social marketing and the (bio) politics of responsibility. *Social Science and Medicine*, 75(1), 200–207.

Dann, S., & Dann, S. (2016). Exploring Catholic social teaching in a social marketing context: History, lessons and future directions. *Journal of Macromarketing*, 36(4), 412–424.

Deleuze, G., & Guattari, F. (1980). *A thousand plateaus: Capitalism and schizophrenia*. London, Continuum.

Dholakia, U.M. (2016). Why nudging your customers can backfire. *Harvard Business Review*. Retrieved 11 April 2017 from https://hbr.org/2016/04/why-nudging-your-customers-can-backfire

Dibb, S. (2014). Up, up and away: Social marketing breaks free. *Journal of Marketing Management*, 30(1–12), 1159–1185.

Domegan, C., McHugh, P., Devaney, M., Duane, S., Hogan, M., Broome, B.J. et al. (2016). Systems-thinking social marketing: Conceptual extensions and empirical investigations. *Journal of Marketing Management*, 32(11–12), 1123–1144.

Donati, P. (2016). The 'relational subject' according to a critical realist relational sociology. *Journal of Critical Realism*, 15(4), 352–375.

Foucault, M. (1991). Governmentality. In G. Burchell, C. Gordon, & P. Miller, (Eds.), *The Foucault effect: Studies in governmentality* (pp. 87–104). Chicago, University of Chicago Press.

French, J. (2011). Why nudging is not enough. *Journal of Social Marketing*, 1(2), 154–162.

French, J., & Gordon, R. (2015). *Strategic social marketing*. London, Sage.

French, J., Blair-Stevens, C., McVey, D., & Merritt, R. (Eds.) (2010). *Social marketing and public health: Theory and practice*. Oxford, Oxford University Press.

Glenane-Antoniadis, A., Whitwell, G., Bell, S., & Menguc, B. (2003). Extending the vision of social marketing through social capital theory in the context of intricate exchange and market failure. *Marketing Theory*, 3(3), 323–343.

Goldberg, M.E. (1995). Social marketing: Are we fiddling while Rome burns? *Journal of Consumer Psychology*, 4(4), 347–370.

Goldberg, M.E., Gorn, G.J., & Lavack, A. (1994). Role of wine coolers in teenage drinking patterns. *Journal of Public Policy and Marketing*, 13(2), 218–227.

Gordon, R. (2011a). Critical social marketing: Definition, application and domain. *Journal of Social Marketing*, 1(2), 82–99.

Gordon, R. (2011b). *Critical social marketing: assessing the cumulative impact of alcohol marketing on youth drinking*. PhD thesis, Stirling, University of Stirling.

Gordon, R. (2012). Re-thinking and re-tooling the social marketing mix. *Australasian Marketing Journal*, 20(2), 122–126.

Gordon, R. (2013a). New ideas – fresh thinking: Towards a broadening of the social marketing concept? *Journal of Social Marketing*, 3(3), 200–205.

Gordon, R. (2013b). Unlocking the potential of upstream social marketing. *European Journal of Marketing*, 47(9), 1525–1547.

Gordon, R., & Gurrieri, L. (2014). Towards a reflexive turn: Social marketing assemblages. *Journal of Social Marketing*, 4(3): 261–278.

Gordon, R., Hastings, G., McDermott, L., & Siquier, P. (2007). The critical role of social marketing. In M. Saren, P. MacLaran, C. Goulding, R. Elliott, A. Shankar, & M. Catterall (Eds.), *Critical marketing: Defining the field* (pp. 159–173). Elsevier, London.

Gordon, R., Jones, S., Barrie, L., & Gilchrist, H. (2015). Use of brand community markers to engage existing lifestyle consumption communities and some ethical concerns. *Journal of Macromarketing*, 35(4), 419–434.

Gordon, R., Russell-Bennett, R., & Lefebvre, R.C. (2016). Social marketing: The state of play and brokering a way forward. *Journal of Marketing Management*, 32(11–12), 1059–1082.

Gordon, R., Waitt, G., & Cooper, P. (2017). A social marketer, a human geographer, and an engineer walk into a bar: Reflections on doing interdisciplinary projects. *Journal of Social Marketing*, 7(4), 366–386.

Gordon, R., Butler, K., Cooper, P., Waitt, G., & Magee, C. (2018a). Look before you LIEEP: Practicalities of using ecological systems theory in social marketing to improve thermal comfort. *Journal of Social Marketing*, 8(1): 99–119.

Gordon, R., Waitt, G., & Cooper, P. (2018b). Storying energy consumption: Collective video storytelling in energy efficiency social marketing. *Journal of Environmental Management*, Volume 2013: 1–10.

Gouldner, A.W. (1970). *The coming crisis of Western civilization*. New York, Basic Books.

Griffin, C., Szmigin, I., Bengry-Howell, A., Hackley, C., & Mistral, W. (2013). Inhabiting the contradictions: Hypersexual femininity and the culture of intoxication among young women in the UK. *Feminism & Psychology, 23*(2), 184–206.

Gurrieri, L., Cherrier, H., & Previte, J. (2013). Women's bodies as a site of control: Inadvertent stigma and exclusion in social marketing. *Journal of Macromarketing, 33*(2), 128–143.

Hackley, C. (2009). Parallel universes and disciplinary space: The bifurcation of managerialism and social science in marketing studies. *Journal of Marketing Management, 25*(7/8), 643–659.

Hackley, C., Bengry-Howell, A., Griffin, C., Mistral, W., Szmigin, I., & Hackley, R.A. (2013). Young adults and 'binge' drinking: A Bakhtinian analysis. *Journal of Marketing Management, 29*(7–8), 933–949.

Hastings, G.B. (2010). Critical social marketing. In J. French, C. Blair-Stevens, D. McVey, & R. Merritt (Eds.), *Social marketing and public health: Theory and practice* (pp. 263–280). Oxford, Oxford University Press.

Hastings, G. (2017). Rebels with a cause: The spiritual dimension of social marketing. *Journal of Social Marketing, 7*(2), 223–232.

Hastings, G., & Angus, K. (2011). When is social marketing not social marketing? *Journal of Social Marketing, 1*(1), 45–53.

Hastings, G., & Domegan, C. (2013). *Social marketing: From tunes to symphonies*. London, Routledge.

Hastings, G., & Heywood, A. (1994). Social marketing: A critical response. *Health Promotion International, 6*(2), 135–145.

Hastings, G., & Saren, M. (2003). The critical contribution of social marketing: Theory and application. *Marketing Theory, 3*(3), 305–322.

Hastings, G.B., Stead, M., McDermott, L., Forsyth, A., MacKintosh, A.M., Rayner, M., et al. (2003). Review of research on the effects of food promotion to children: Final report and appendices. Prepared for the Food Standards Agency. London, Food Standards Agency. Retrieved from www.sfu.ca/cmns/faculty/marontate_j/801/08-spring/ClassFolders/Iwase_Masa/SelectedTopicMaterials/foodpromotiontochildren1.pdf

Hastings, G., Stead, M., & Webb, J. (2004). Fear appeals in social marketing: Strategic and ethical reasons for concern. *Psychology and Marketing, 21*(11), 961–986.

Hughes, K., MacKintosh, A.M., Hastings, G., Wheeler, C., Watson, J., & Inglis, J. (1997). Young people, alcohol, and designer drinks: Quantitative and qualitative study. *British Medical Journal, 314*(7078), 414–418.

Karippanon, K., & Narayan, V. (2015). The use of ethnographic filmmaking in social marketing design. Paper presented at the World Social Marketing Conference, April, Sydney.

Karippanon, K., Gordon, R., Jayasinghe, L., & Gurruwuiwi, G. (2017). *Collective reflexivity in social marketing through ethnographic filmmaking: The Yolngu story of Ngarali (tobacco) in Yirrkala, Australia*. Sydney, Working Paper.

Kennedy, A.M., & Parsons, A. (2012). Macro-social marketing and social engineering: A systems approach. *Journal of Social Marketing, 2*(1), 37–51.

Kennedy, A.M., Kapitan, S., Bajaj, N., Bakonyi, A., & Sands, S. (2017). Uncovering wicked problem's system structure: Seeing the forest for the trees. *Journal of Social Marketing, 7*(1), 51–73.

Klein, N. (2007). *The shock doctrine: The rise of disaster capitalism*. Toronto, Knopf Canada.

Kotler, P., & Levy, S.J. (1969). Broadening the concept of marketing. *Journal of Marketing, 33*(1), 10–15.

Kotler, P., & Zaltman, G. (1971). Social marketing: An approach to planned social change. *Journal of Marketing, 35*(3), 3–12.

Krisjanous, J. (2014). Examining the historical roots of social marketing through the Lights in Darkest England campaign. *Journal of Macromarketing, 34*(4), 435–451.

Kubacki, K., & Rundle-Thiele, S. (Eds.) (2017). *Formative research in social marketing: Innovative methods to gain consumer insight*. Sydney, Springer.

Laczniak, G.R., & Michie, D.A. (1979). The social disorder of the broadened concept of marketing. *Journal of the Academy of Marketing Science, 7*(3), 214–232.

Langford, R., & Panter-Brick, C. (2013). A health equity critique of social marketing: When interventions have impact but insufficient reach. *Social Science and Medicine, 83*, 133–141.

Lazer, W., & Kelley, E.J. (1973). *Social marketing: Perspectives and viewpoints*. Homewood, Richard D. Irwin.

Lee, N. (2016). Corporate social marketing: Five key principles for success. *Social Marketing Quarterly, 22*(4), 340–344.

Lefebvre, R.C. (2011). An integrative model for social marketing. *Journal of Social Marketing, 1*(1), 54–72.

Lefebvre, R.C. (2012). Transformative social marketing: Co-creating the social marketing discipline and brand. *Journal of Social Marketing, 2*(2), 118–129.

Levy, S.J. (2017). Sidney J. Levy: An autobiography. *Journal of Historical Research in Marketing, 9*(2), 127–143.

Luck, D.J. (1969). Broadening the concept of marketing – too far. *Journal of Marketing, 33*(3), 53–55.

Luck, D.J. (1974). Social marketing: Confusion confounded. *Journal of Marketing, 38*(4), 70–72.

MacFadyen, L., Stead, M., & Hastings, G. (1999). *A synopsis of social marketing*. Stirling: Institute for Social Marketing. Retrieved from www.qihub.scot.nhs.uk/media/162221/social_marketing_synopsis.pdf

MacFadyen, L., Hastings, G.B., & MacKintosh, A.M. (2001). Cross sectional study of young people's awareness of and involvement with tobacco marketing. *British Medical Journal, 322*(7285), 513–517.

Marcuse, H. (1964). *One dimensional man*. Boston, Beacon.

Martam, I. (2016). Commentary: Strategic social marketing to foster gender equality in Indonesia. *Journal of Marketing Management, 32*(11–12), 1174–1182.

Moor, L. (2011). *Neoliberal experiments: Social marketing and the governance of populations*. In D. Zwick & J. Cayla (Eds.), *Inside marketing* (pp. 299–319). Oxford, Oxford University Press.

Murray, J.B., & Ozanne, J.L. (1991). The critical imagination: Emancipatory interests in consumer research. *Journal of Consumer Research, 18*(2), 129–144.

NSMC (2010). *Learning together from theory and practice: The first report on the progress of the NSMC's social marketing learning demonstration sites*. London, National Social Marketing Centre.

Ozanne, L.K., & Ozanne, J.L. (2016). How alternative consumer markets can build community resiliency. *European Journal of Marketing, 50*(3/4), 330–357.

Peattie, K., Peattie, S., & Newcombe, R. (2016). Unintended consequences in demarketing antisocial behavior: Project Bernie. *Journal of Marketing Management, 32*(17–18), 1588–1618.

Peattie, S., & Peattie, K. (2003). Ready to fly solo: Reducing social marketing's reliance of commercial marketing theory. *Marketing Theory, 3*(3), 365–385.

Piketty, T. (2014). *Capital in the twenty-first century*. Cambridge, MA, Belknap Press.

Population Services International (1977). Preetni project. Transferred to Sri-Lanka FPA. *PSI Newsletter*, (November/December), 4.

Reckwitz, A. (2002). Toward a theory of social practices: A development in culturalist theorizing. *Journal of Social Theory, 5*(2), 243–263.

Rothschild, M.L. (1979). Marketing communications in non-business situations or why it's so hard to sell brotherhood like soap. *Journal of Marketing, 43*(2), 11–20.

Senker, S. (2015). The triumph of neoliberalism and the world dominance of capitalism. *Prometheus, 33*(2), 97–111.

Shove, E. (2010). Beyond the ABC: Climate change policy and theories of social change. *Environment and Planning A, 42*(6), 1273–1285.

Spotswood, F. (2011). *An ethnographic approach to understanding the place of leisure time physical activity in 'working class' British culture: Implications for social marketing*. Unpublished PhD thesis, Bristol, University of the West of England.

Spotswood, F. (Ed). (2016). *Beyond behavior change: Key issues, interdisciplinary approaches and future directions*. Bristol, Policy Press.

Spotswood, F., & Tapp, A. (2013). Beyond persuasion: A cultural perspective of behavior. *Journal of Social Marketing, 3*(3), 275–294.

Spotswood, F., French, J., Tapp, A., & Stead, M. (2012). Some reasonable but uncomfortable questions about social marketing. *Journal of Social Marketing, 2*(3), 163–175.

Spotswood, F., Chatterton, T., Tapp, A., & Williams, D. (2015). Analysing cycling as a social practice: An empirical grounding for behavior change. *Transportation Research Part F, 29*(1), 22–33.

Spotswood, F., Chatterton, T., Morey, Y., & Spear, S. (2017). Practice-theoretical possibilities for social marketing: Two fields learning from each other. *Journal of Social Marketing, 7*(2), 156–171.

Stead, M., Arnott, L., & Dempsey, E. (2013). Healthy heroes, magic meals, and a visiting alien: Community-led assets-based social marketing. *Social Marketing Quarterly, 19*(1), 26–39.

Szablewska, N., & Kubacki, K. (2017). A human rights-based approach to the social good in social marketing. *Journal of Business Ethics*, https://doi.org/10.1007/s10551-017-3520-8

Tadajewski, M. (2008). Incommensurable paradigms, cognitive bias and the politics of marketing theory. *Marketing Theory, 8*(3), 273–297.

Tadajewski, M. (2010). Towards a history of critical marketing studies. *Journal of Marketing Management, 26*(9/10), 773–824.

Tadajewski, M., & Brownlie, D. (2008). Critical marketing: A limit attitude. In M. Tadajewski & D. Brownlie (Eds.), *Critical marketing: Issues in contemporary marketing* (pp. 1–28). London, John Wiley.

Tadajewski, M., Chelekis, J., Deberry-Spence, B., Figueiredo, B., Kravets, O., Nuttavuthisit, K., et al. (2014). The discourses of marketing and development: Towards 'critical transformative marketing research'. *Journal of Marketing Management, 30*(17–18), 1728–1771.

Thaler, R.H., & Sunstein, C.R. (2008). *Nudge: Improving decisions about health, wealth and happiness.* London, Yale University Press.

Truong, V.D. (2016). Government-led macro-social marketing programs in Vietnam: Outcomes, challenges, and implications. *Journal of Macromarketing, 37*(4), 409–425.

Truss, A., Marshall, R., & Blair-Stevens, C. (2010). A history of social marketing. In J. French, C. Blair-Stevens, D. McVey, & R. Merritt (Eds.), *Social marketing and public health: Theory and practice* (pp. 19–28). Oxford, Oxford University Press.

United Nations. (1948). *Universal declaration of human rights.* Retrieved April 30, 2016, from www.un.org/en/universal-declaration-human-rights/index.html

Venturini, R. (2016). Social marketing and big social change: Personal social marketing insights from a complex system obesity prevention intervention. *Journal of Marketing Management, 32*(11–12), 1190–1199.

Waitt, G., Roggeveen, K., Gordon, R., Butler, K., & Cooper, P. (2016). Tyrannies of thrift: Governmentality and older, low-income people's energy efficiency narratives in the Illawarra, Australia. *Energy Policy, 90,* 37–45.

Wiebe, G.D. (1951). Merchandising commodities and citizenship on television. *Public Opinion Quarterly, 15*(4), 679–691.

Zainuddin, N., Dent, K., & Tam, L. (2017). Seek or destroy? Examining value creation and destruction in behavior maintenance in social marketing. *Journal of Marketing Management, 33*(5–6), 348–374.

6
CRITICAL MACROMARKETING, SUSTAINABLE MARKETING, AND GLOBALIZATION

William E. Kilbourne

Introduction

The purpose of this chapter is to examine the relationship between critical macromarketing, sustainable marketing, and globalization. While each of these topics has been written about in detail independently, the system containing the three areas is far more than the sum of the parts, as is true of all systems. To do this, the chapter will begin with critical macromarketing as a subfield of macromarketing with a different focus. This is followed by brief explanations of both sustainability and globalization through the lens of critical macromarketing.

To accomplish this objective, a brief description of critical macromarketing will be provided simply to distinguish it from developmental macromarketing and managerial marketing. The most important aspect of the distinction with managerial marketing is that in macromarketing the focus is on the function and consequences of markets rather than marketing per se. Second, and more importantly, the concept of sustainability will be examined in some detail primarily to distinguish it from the various shades of green marketing and from the idea of ecological modernization that results in the business as usual philosophy in micromarketing. The business as usual model, however, is not so easily applied when sustainability is used as it was originally described in 1987. This also opens the door to the inclusion of globalization in the system.

Because the world of yesteryear when what happened at home stayed at home is long gone, we must examine the ramifications of markets in every area of the world because ecological consequences do not respect national borders. How markets function in one nation affects the rest of the world both directly and indirectly. Sustainability cannot be viewed as a national phenomenon, and this means that the centuries old Peace of Westphalia that considers every nation as independent of others is an anachronism in this domain.

The role of markets in sustainability for an economically integrated world must be addressed from a macromarketing perspective as it is the only approach that includes the macro institutional level of analysis. The institutions of the dominant social paradigm (DSP) in a country partially determine the structure and nature of markets in that country. Without the critical macromarketing perspective, assessments of the prospects for sustainability will be over-simplified and result in ineffective solutions that generally address symptoms rather than deep-rooted problems. The goal of the chapter is to put markets, sustainability, and globalization into the proper perspective showing that none can be considered without addressing its relationship with the others. It is hoped, that this will result in a systems perspective taking into consideration both the institutions of the DSP and a framework through which the institutions underlying sustainability and globalization develop and stabilize and then recreate themselves in the cyclical development of cultures.

Critical macromarketing

Macromarketing has been evolving since the early 1970s and its various definitions have been evolving as well. The essential aspects of macromarketing have, however, persisted during the interim. Common among the definitions are references to systems and aggregations rather than the specific marketing actions by firms. George Fisk, one of the founders and leaders of macromarketing, once quipped that if it has anything to do with making a profit, it is not macromarketing. The simplest approach to capture the essence of macromarketing is using the caption on the cover of the *Journal of Macromarketing* which states that macromarketing represents the interaction among markets, marketing, and society. Because of the complexity of this interaction, it follows that it is the study of systems of interacting parts that should be examined as a whole. Fisk (1967) argued this about marketing decades ago, and it is still considered the essence of macromarketing.

But the discipline has developed even further more recently and has spun off other sub-disciplines including areas such as marketing history and markets and development. In addition, two different but related approaches to macromarketing have evolved. These are developmental macromarketing and critical macromarketing (Mittelstaedt, Kilbourne, Shultz, & Peterson, 2015), the topic of this chapter. While "critical macromarketing" has yet to be defined precisely, the phrase was first used in Kilbourne, McDonagh, and Prothero (1997) describing the path through which hyper-consumption can be transformed to sustainable consumption. This suggested that a critical analysis of modern consumption was necessary to transform modern marketing to sustainable marketing (cf. Gordon, this volume). Their paper was the first to argue that the transition would require a critical analysis of markets and society and the underlying philosophical factors that combined throughout history to create the structure and function of modern markets in Western industrial societies.

Mittelstaedt *et al*. (2015) further elaborated on the distinction between what they referred to as the critical school of macromarketing and the developmental school of macromarketing in assessing whether sustainability was a megatrend. They argued that the difference lay in whether markets were considered positive or negative influences on societal well-being. Of the developmental school, they state:

> The Developmental School argues that marketing systems play a positive role in economic development and societal well-being. This approach focuses attention on issues such as metrics for measuring quality of life (e.g., Ahuvia and Friedman (1998); Peterson and Malhotra (1997); Lee and Sirgy (2004)). Here, we see markets and marketing as necessary provisioning systems for food, shelter, clothing, health care and education, and that they are the building blocks for socioeconomic development (Dahringer and Hilger (1985); Joy and Ross (1989); Nason, Dholakia and McLeavey (1987, p. 6)).

The critical school, while not contradicting the developmental school, takes a different view of markets and their role in development. About the critical school, they state:

The Critical School, on the other hand, postulates that markets as provisioning systems are neither stable nor sustainable, and that the gains of marketing to human welfare come at the expense of others (in other societies, or in future generations) or the environment. The Critical School rejects the tenets of the Dominant Social Paradigm, opting instead for exploration of other sets of organizing principles for societal well-being. By rejecting the assumptions inherent in the Dominant Social Paradigm, the Critical School is free to operate outside many of the cornerstone axioms of positivist tradition in the social sciences, such as the assumption of natural equilibriums in economics (Mittelstaedt, Kilbourne & Mittelstaedt, 2006) or the primacy of materialism (Ger & Belk, 1996; Kilbourne et al., 2009).

Mittelstaedt et al., 2015, p. 7

These two schools, while one is critical and the other positive, should work in tandem with each other. The positions do not reflect fundamental disagreement on the role of markets in development (see Fırat & Dholakia, this volume). The difference is that within the critical school, it is argued that the first step to insuring that market development works to enhance the well-being of its participants is that conditions required for that development actually exist on the ground. Thus, a critical assessment of political, economic, and technological institutions extant is essential in determining what kinds of markets might work best in performing their magic. American style markets, for example, are simply not going to work in more underdeveloped societies (see Varman, this volume). An example of this was the belief that once the old regime was negated in Russia in 1989 free markets would spontaneously evolve and development would be effective almost immediately. This approach proved deficient, however, as the underlying conditions for the functioning of free markets simply did not exist and might take decades to develop.

The question then turns to the nature of the institutions that are necessary for variations of free markets to exist. This is what the critical school contributes to the dialogue on markets. While a complete assessment of the underlying institutions is beyond the scope of this chapter, a summary will be included to provide a basic view of the critical school's perspective. A more complete view is provided by Kilbourne (1998).

Kilbourne (1999) proposed a model of the DSP that contained two domains each with three dimensions that constitute the DSP of any society. The domains are the cosmological (structure, function, and organization) and the socio-economic (technological, economic, and political). While all societies have conceptions of the dimensions of the DSP, they do not necessarily concur on their importance or how they relate to each other. Even closely related countries will differ to some degree in their beliefs about the importance of the dimensions. We now turn to a brief description of the dimensions in the socio-economic domain and why they affect the way markets organize and function.

Within Western industrial societies, the focus of this chapter, markets function in similar albeit not identical ways under very different paradigms (see Belshaw, 1965). Each society has a position within the dimensions of the DSP, and the critical school suggests that the position helps to determine the nature of markets in that society. We now turn to each of the dimensions and offer a brief explanation of how it affects market functions.

Political dimension

The first dimension discussed is the political. It will be clear from this description that the political has a much deeper meaning in the critical school than in traditional micro marketing thought. In traditional marketing discussions, the political generally refers to rules and regulations affecting the functioning of the market. There are, for example, rules regarding what constitutes legal pricing, distribution, advertising, etc. These are well known and might be thought of as micro institutions that all are aware of and tend to follow. The critical school takes a much broader and deeper perspective than this. It looks at institutions from a macro institutional perspective in which the rules have become embedded in the thought models of individuals and have become "self-evident" requiring no justification or critical examination (Bauman, 1998). Individuals do not know when or where the rules developed and might not even know they exist or what impact they have on individual behaviors. It is argued that these political institutions form the basis for market development and that the idea of free markets would scarcely seem possible without them. The institutions referred to here form the basis for political liberalism and were the precursor for economic liberalism developed in the next century. The three fundamental political constructs were legitimized in the Western world by Locke (1963) in the late 17th century. They are the constructs possessive individualism, private property, and limited government that are the foundation of political liberalism.

Possessive individualism refers to the existence of an independent person who is in possession of both himself and the property acquired by attaching his labor to nature (MacPherson, 1962). While this might seem intuitively obvious to the contemporary reader, it is much more complex than it appears. Ullmann (1963) argues that the emergence of the individual out of the High Middle Ages (c.1000–1300) was one of the great achievements of the human mind encumbered by the past. Before, the individual was submerged in society with no separate rights or identity beyond the group. While there were markets in the traditional sense, such as the agora where people went to buy goods, there was no market as an abstract, institutional entity as markets are now conceived. This had to emerge out of feudalism through agricultural capitalism in the 15th century (Wood, 2002). This new individual was free from the constraints of religion and government and allowed to act as a free agent, or as an atomistic individual who we will see later is a necessary condition for the existence of free markets generally.

Along with the possessive individual, Locke (1963) legitimized and extended the construct of private property. Here it is important to distinguish between private property and possessions. The two are frequently conflated and used synonymously. Hodgson (2001) argues that there have been possessions since individuals could first distinguish between "mine and thine," but this does not constitute private property. Private property materialized in the High Middle Ages with the acceptance of the Magna Carta. Paragraph 52 of the Magna Carta states: "To any man whom we have deprived or dispossessed of lands, castles, liberties, or rights, without the lawful judgment of his equals, we will at once restore these." This suggests that there are legal aspects of ownership conferred to the owner. Specifically, one's property cannot be taken without due process. This distinguishes private property referred to by Locke (1963) from what Hodgson (2001) refers to as "mere possessions." Again, this represents a political precondition for the existence of free markets because if the property acquired through free exchange were always at risk, the motivation to enter into market transactions would diminish. This leads to the third Lockean condition, referred to as limited government.

An historical perspective should also be added to the idea of private property at this point. That is the notion of exclusivity relating to property. Exclusivity of property was not granted initially and evolved through more religious discussions. Initially, while the Magna Carta created property rights, there was still a religious conundrum to be solved. That was whether granting rights to property excluded others from using it. Aquinas' response to this is in Question 66, Article 7 of the *Summa Theologica*. He reasons that if one person is under extreme need and another has more than they need, then it is not theft for the one in need to take either openly or secretly what they need to survive or what their neighbor needs to survive. So, while property was then private and protected by law, there were situations in which private property was not held in exclusivity. This condition was to arrive later in history.

From Locke's perspective, a legitimate government is necessary for the preservation of rights and duties. But its functions are limited to enforcement of contracts and protection of property. This refers to property one owns and the property one has in one's self. This condition serves to protect the first two. It also is a necessary condition for the emergence of free markets in that within the realm of neoclassical economic theory, there should be no interference from sources external to the market and no exercise of power within the market. In this sense, governments are proscribed from interfering in the market and have the responsibility for ensuring that nothing else emerges that might restrain market functioning. Here we see a condition that has since raised questions regarding the "free" in free markets, and this has been largely ignored within the macromarketing literature including the critical school. This issue will be introduced briefly following the discussion of the economic dimension of the DSP.

Economic dimension

From the perspective of the critical school, the economic dimension is the one that presents much of the "critical" commentary going back more than 200 years. But it is the transition from classical to neoclassical economics that is of concern within the DSP, particularly regarding sustainability. This is because the primary aspects at issue relate to the contemporary form of economic theory. Locke (1963) set the stage for what was to come. That was the beginning of the science of economics that was to follow in the work of Smith (1937), and it is difficult to speculate on how much time would have passed before economics arose as a discipline without Locke as a predecessor. However, it is clear that the idea of a free market would not have been possible had not Locke legitimized the atomized individual, the accumulation of private property as a virtue, and limitations on government as they are the fundamental elements that make neoclassical, free markets possible. It was, however, left to Smith to put the pieces together and derive from them the idea of an abstract institution called the market within which atomized individuals (and firms) compete for scarce resources in unconstrained markets. The motivation for the exchanges is assumed to be unbridled self-interest which, if followed strictly will benefit not only the individual, but also society at large. This is predicated on the cosmological belief that the world functions through inevitable competitive forces (Smith's propensity to truck and barter), structured as a set of atomized individuals (each is completely independent of the others), and organized hierarchically (such that individuals are at the top of the hierarchy) with all non-human entities subservient to and existing for the satisfaction of human needs. Each of these assumptions built into the "science" of economics has been questioned in the interim and been shown to receive little historical support (see, for example, Hirschman, 1977; Merchant, 1980; Polanyi, 1944).

Technological dimension

The final dimension to be discussed in the socio-economic domain is the technological. This constitutes the means through which the distributive function is carried out. But here, as earlier, we will avoid the materialist conception of technology as a set of mechanical contrivances. Instead we examine the nature of technology generally and its impact on society, sustainability, and globalization. The literature on technology as mechanical contrivances is vast indeed, but its direct and indirect effects on society are not as prevalent. Three very informative books in this area are Butterfield (1949) on science, and White (1966) and Leiss (1972) on technology. They are highly recommended reading for those interested in the history of science and technology and are foundational in its study. The focus in this chapter is, however, the relationship between technology, society, and markets as this is the focus of the critical school of macromarketing.

The critical school agrees with the developmental school in its belief that markets are, as Fisk (1974) argued, a provisioning technology through which societies secure the goods they need to survive and prosper. However, technology is promiscuous in that it can be used in many ways with different outcomes, and it is not at all clear that every outcome is as benign as all the others. That is, the same technology can provide both positive (satisfying needs) and negative unintended consequences (market failures). There are many exposé type books that point out the negative and the positive consequences in detail. But in this chapter, we will focus on the critical perspective that examines Tenner's (1997) perspective on the "tyranny of unintended consequences."

This view is very complex and will not be addressed thoroughly in this chapter, but enough will be discussed to provide the perspective of the critical school. This perspective suggests that, because of the complex role technological change plays in all societies, it should not be accepted as the panacea for all problems, physical and social. Technological optimism is common in Western societies and progress has been defined as material progress since the late 19th century (Bury, 1932). The difficulty with this perspective is that in focusing on the immediate positive result of a technology one ignores the longer term social consequences of its implementation. But, more importantly, it fails to bring into consideration the complex interaction of many large-scale technologies, and it is here that the critical school takes issue with unbridled technological optimism.

As an integral part of the DSP of Western industrial societies, technology interacts with both the political dimension and the economic dimension, and it is this complex interaction from which Winner (1986) concludes that technologies create "forms of life" that transform the social contract within society. But the terms of that new contract are unknown to the citizens of the society. The conditions of everyday existence can be, and frequently are, changed with the integration of new technologies. As a simple and well-known example, even Henry Ford could not have known how American society would be transformed by the mass production of the automobile, but the changes were inevitable. And while some changes were positive and anticipated (increased mobility), others were not as easily predicted (cultural transformation in social relations because of increased individual mobility, traffic deaths, and pollution, for example). This is what Winner refers to as a new form of life. This is, of course, a simple and obvious example, but the critical school encourages us to dig deeper into the more complex relations in economics and politics that create the paradigm of a society.

Ellul (1964) was one of the first to have viewed technology with a critical eye in that when technologies pervade societies they begin to establish regimes composed of technical rules that evade human control. This view was reiterated by Postman (1993) who distinguishes between tool-using societies, technocracies in which technologies bid for dominance in culture, and technopolies in which the bid for dominance has succeeded. The latter is the state that he ascribes to Western industrial societies. There are many versions of this view generally falling under the rubric of technical control of human societies. Others have picked up on this and expanded it even further. Probably the most articulate of these was Marcuse (1964) whose concern was rational critique of technological rationality that reduces all evaluative criteria to questions of rational efficiency. He argued that any such critique would be rendered irrational so long as material progress was the sole evaluative criterion. Thus, when material progress is challenged by any competing criterion such as justice or fairness of distribution within the prevailing mode of thought, it is dismissed as irrational within that context. Material progress is thought to create a just world as all share in economic growth. To suggest otherwise is rendered irrational and against the collective interest. Kassiola (1990) argues that this has been the case in the 20th century during which economic criteria of progress have triumphed over the political in a process he refers to as depoliticization. What makes the process of depoliticization insidious is that while economic choice has consistently been presented in neoclassical economics as value free, it is nothing more than politics in disguise. This was offered as a criticism of neoclassical economics by Myrdal (1954) who argued that the political should be removed from economic theory but had not yet been. Because of this, the political ramifications of market function must be examined critically. While all of these cannot be examined in this chapter, we will examine one case as an exemplar. That is the construct, Pareto Optimality.

Functions of the DSP

Pareto Optimality is an economic criterion of market efficiency suggesting that no interpersonal exchanges between market participants can be made without one member being made better off at the expense of another who is made worse off. Thus, person A's well-being can be enhanced without limit so long as none of what A gains reduces the well-being of person B. The subtlety in this is that economic well-being is measured in terms of absolute gains and losses. Relative well-being is not considered. This is presented as a neoclassical economic criterion of effectiveness and creates the necessary condition for increased, if not desired, maldistribution of wealth in society. This is contrary to the importance of just distribution considered by the classical economists such as Mill (1909). It also provides a basis for criticism of markets by the contemporary critical school. Within the critical school, for example, criteria such as justice and fairness are added to the traditional neoclassical criterion of efficiency.

In the context of free markets proffering Pareto Optimality as an efficient solution, the elite of society are in a position to recreate their elite position in the future. And further, non-elites have no basis for reasonable critique of the unfairness of the result, because fairness is not a criterion of success in market functioning. Elites simply respond that this is the free market outcome and it should not be questioned. Here free implies freedom of opportunity not equality of outcome. Assuming political and economic liberalism as argued earlier, the market is composed of free and independent agents each with no power or advantage over the others. But this is a fallacious assumption as Pareto Optimality insures that some will consistently have advantages over the others. The only underlying condition required to make this criterion reasonable is continuous economic growth with elites having an advantage in the competition for the increases. Unlimited economic growth insures that the economic pie is always expanding, and the elite are "entitled" to receive a larger share than the non-elite so long as the non-elite do not become worse off.

Here we have the convergence of the political, economic, and technological that results in markets functioning in a way that enhances the well-being of the elite, recreating their elite status under the guise of fairness of market functioning. The political legitimizes unlimited ownership of property, the economic proclaims that competitive markets are powerless in that no entity on either the buyer or seller sides can accumulate enough power to alter market outcomes in anyone's favor. This renders all outcomes fair when there is unlimited economic growth, and the technological insures that economic growth can be maintained to further support Pareto Optimality based on absolute rather than relative outcomes. In this process, each of the dimensions of the DSP supports and reinforces the others under the guise of market freedom. And it is this ideology of the market with which the critical school takes issue.

The fundamental criticism of this process is that it presents political decisions that require reflection as economic decisions that only require choices (see Hirschman's (1970) concepts of exit and voice on this distinction). Thurow (1980) argues that because the positive sum game implied in continuous economic growth cannot be maintained indefinitely, the political institutions that will be needed in the zero-sum society have atrophied and might not be available when the time arrives that they are needed. This presents a major challenge to the proponents of limitless growth. This is an example of the challenges proposed by the critical school. It questions the DSP of Western industrial societies which is a direct challenge to capitalism itself. The question that connects critical macromarketing's critique of the DSP is its ability to produce market outcomes that are ecologically sustainable.

Sustainability

Discussions of sustainable development per se began with a document known as the Brundtland Report (Brundtland & Khalid, 1987, p. 8) which provided the first definition of sustainable development. In that report, sustainable development was defined as "development that meets the needs of the present without compromising the ability of future generations to meet their own needs." While the idea presented captured the essence of sustainability, it met with substantial criticism mostly pertaining to its vagueness. For example, one might ask what the needs of the present are, and likewise, what will the needs of the future be? We could also ask which future we are referring to and what constitutes a compromise? Clearly the critiques were well founded. But the essence of the statement was, in fact, quite clear. Questions of future resources, however, preceded the Brundtland Report by decades, going back to Carson (1962) and Meadows, Meadows, Randers, and Behrens (1972) who addressed the resource question directly. They concluded that unlimited economic growth was simply not possible given the finite availability of resources. This conclusion has both resonated and been attacked since its publication, but only more recently has the idea of sustainability been expanded to include more than just the facts of resource availability. The real questions concerning root causes of the problem have been addressed in many fields, including macromarketing. In fact, critical macromarketing grew out of this debate in Kilbourne, McDonagh, and Prothero's (1997) critique of consumption in Western industrial societies and their DSP. Consumption practices, along with their production counterpart, are now considered an essential factor in achieving sustainability. But this evades the question of what sustainability really is.

While a precise definition of sustainability meeting everyone's satisfaction has not been established, some practices in framing it have developed. The problem here is relating the longstanding conception of greening to sustainability. Reich (1970) popularized the term "greening" referring to improving the environment to make for a more liveable future. This is the term that the marketing literature picked up and used for two decades referring to making marketing systems more environmentally benign. Kilbourne and Beckmann (1998) examined the early research in marketing and found that most research at that time was on specific behaviors by market actors, but it did not ascend to the level of asking questions about root causes of environmental problems. McDonagh and Prothero (2014) followed this up and concluded that the situation had not been transcended in the succeeding decade. While the term, sustainability, is used quite frequently now, its meaning has been somewhat conflated with greening. This presents a problem in communication because it creates the impression that the two terms can be used almost interchangeably, creating the illusion that if people or firms are greening their behavior, they are behaving sustainably. Kilbourne (1995) demonstrates how this can obfuscate meaning in an analysis of the term environmentalism, demonstrating that people confuse the term with others such as conservationism and preservationism. The same seems to be true here because many firms present sustainability reports that focus on green initiatives that have little to do with sustainability.

Resolving this issue would go a long way in determining what we are talking about. Smith (1998) presents a thorough analysis of this problem as an ideological approach to watering down the meaning of sustainability. She argues that using green marketing results in behaviors that perpetuate the status quo in that it justifies increasing consumption indefinitely because it is green. This, again, redirects the criticism away from greater consumption and toward better (greener) consumption. Continued increases in consumption might be green, but they are not necessarily sustainable. So, within the framework sometimes referred to as the "Whorfian hypothesis," the language we choose helps to create the thought models through which we choose behaviors (Whorf, 1956). It is for this reason that there needs to be a clear distinction between Green and Sustainable that does not allow for the conflation of terms the substance of which is very different. Thus, within the critical school, green marketing results in business as usual whereas sustainability connotes a fundamental shift in business models. There is, however, an increasing concern for bridging the difference in such areas as the political consumer (Dickinson & Hollander, 1991) and the greening of capitalism (Prothero & Fitchett, 2000).

In the recent past, distinguishing between green and sustainable was difficult because there was no measure that could delineate between them, so researchers were left with making arbitrary distinctions. Some, like Dobson (2000), chose to use gradations such as Green with a big "G" connoting big political changes and green with a little "g" to connote small political changes. Sustainability has been used in a similar way with the small "s" relating more to greening tactics and the large "S" relating to substantive changes in individual or organizational behavior. If the Whorfian hypothesis is valid, it indicates the need for a more definitive approach to sustainability.

But this situation is changing rapidly with the development of the ecological footprint by Wackernagle and Rees (1996) and the Global Footprint Network that provides global footprint information. This information has been described as one of the leading measures of the impact of human behaviors on nature. It offers a measure of the supply and demand on nature's resources. The ecological footprint represents the amount of productive area required to provide the renewable resources to maintain current levels of supply and demand for those resources. As the footprint measures continue to improve, sustainability takes on new, and more importantly, measurable dimensions. This also helps to address the more recent critiques of the consumer culture that argue that the original versions of the American dream are failing as they are creating many problems in their wake (Stiles, 2005; Schor, 2010). This take on sustainability is calling for a revision of the dream.

This provides us with an objective definition of sustainability that can be refined to the precision desired. Sustainability is a global construct and must be measured in that context. While critics will argue that the precision desired is not attainable or that there are variables missing from the models, these are simple red herrings thrown in the path of progress by those who eschew change in the status quo. These were the same arguments leveled against the limits to growth advocates 40 years ago, and they will certainly arise again. But we can now define sustainability by applying the I = PAT equation developed by Ehrlich and Holdren (1971). This equation (an identity rather than an equation) presents environmental impact (I) as the product of population (P), affluence (A) measured as GDP per capita, and technology (T), measured as energy use per unit of GDP. This is currently being done outside the marketing or macromarketing domain and only needs to be brought into it. Members of the critical school are currently engaged in this project drawing on the work of York, Rosa and Dietz (2003). This allows for developing models of sustainability using many variables, with some measures going back to about 1960.

These methods now allow us to predict the consequences of human and organizational behaviors as they relate to sustainable resource use. This includes the production, consumption, and disposal of market-based artifacts. Because we now have estimates of all these factors, modeling becomes a valid means for determining how much is available, how much is being used, and what the environmental consequences will be. While ecological modeling is still in its infancy, sustainability is no longer an abstract notion but a clear objective. Sustainability is defined as staying within the biocapacity of earth's systems and attending assiduously to negative feedback loops provided by nature. Global warming is a clear indicator that we are currently exceeding the capacity of the earth to assimilate wastes, implying both that current anthropogenic consequences are not sustainable and that we are not attending to nature's feedback. However, we should not be overly optimistic as the game has only just begun, and history tells us that powerful agents who do not want the rules of the game to be changed will put forth their best efforts to derail or redirect progress (Veblen, 1899).

Globalization

Like sustainability, the definition of globalization has not yet been established to everyone's satisfaction. This is because there are so many possible dimensions through which globalization can be described. There are at least five dimensions that are commonly used in the description. These are economic, financial, political, technological, and cultural. Each of these results in a different conception of globalization. Thus, we are dealing with an extremely complex process as it entails these dimensions simultaneously. However, there is one term that encapsulates the essence of globalization, and that is integration. This is what sets globalization as it exists apart from mere internationalization which can be argued to have existed as far back as ancient Greece when itinerant traders brought goods from other parts of the world to be sold in the agora of Athens. The fundamental difference is that if something happened in the source country that changed availability of the product, it did not affect the people of Asia or northern Europe. Thus, as stated earlier, in the past what happened at home stayed at home, but this is no longer the case. The integration of markets and cultures changed this. The new globalization became abundantly clear during the 1997 Asian Financial Crisis when a monetary crisis beginning in Thailand in 1997 quickly spread to much of Asia and ripples were felt in the US markets as well. This consequence of globalization is best described as the creation of a world system (Wallerstein, 2004) in which all parts are interconnected in some way.

As is characteristic of the critical school, the underlying forces propelling globalization need to be a key part of its assessment as an institution. We begin with the premise that globalization is not the next phase of the development of world systems or merely an acceleration of international marketing seeking new markets for Western products. It marks a fundamental shift in the system itself. In other words, what was a loose connection of countries trading with each other is now an integrated system of components that interact and have the potential to transform each other in the process. The global system is directly involved in the production process making most products of global origin. This makes for a very complex project that is unfolding daily and changing people's lives in the process, or as was stated earlier in the chapter, creating a new social contract creating new rules and institutions the meanings of which are uncertain and little understood. This is compounded by the lack of a superordinate control mechanism that is independent of other institutions. Beck (2000) states that globalization is culminating in a "world society without a world state and without world government" (p. 13).

This is not to suggest that the globalization process is bad and that it has not resulted in improved lives for many of the world's poorest inhabitants. The developmental school of macromarketing has shown that markets can evolve and perform well in many cases. The proponents of globalization make this case frequently, and it is the ultimate objective of the process. While some might be for globalization and as many against it, the writing is on the wall. As Greider (1997) states, "One world, ready or not." Singer (2002) concurs with this, arguing that the world of the 1648 Treaty of Westphalia through which countries had no obligations to each other, is long gone. It appears that the globalization process is unstoppable now, so we need to understand it better than we do. We will briefly examine four approaches to globalization that have been used in different disciplines, or as Pieterse (1995) suggests, in a plural space. These are economic, political, cultural, and technological.

Economic

As domestic markets become more and more saturated, firms must find other buyers for their products, not because they want to expand but because the imperatives of capitalism demand that they expand. This was discussed earlier as the economic dimension of the DSP in Western industrial societies. To survive in competitive markets, Heilbroner (1985) and Daly (1991) argue that firms must expand indefinitely in order to lower costs and maintain capital accumulation. Thus, expansion into global markets was inevitable at some point in time. This is what Beck (2000) refers to as the state of globality in which world society begins to evolve. This state is confirmed by both Giddens (1990) and Sen (2002) who argue that global exchanges of products and culture have been carried out for centuries. Again, what marks the transition between globality and globalization is the integration of markets at the global level. Market integration is also what distinguishes between capitalist and pre-capitalist organization of economic society, and this is also confirmed by Heilbroner (1980). It is in these new transnational spaces that the "container" theory of society begins to disappear. The idea that culture is contained within the geographic borders of a country has been supplanted by transnational spaces created in global economic integration carried out through multinational corporations (MNCs) the political power of which transcends national borders. This carries with it the political implications of globalization sometimes referred to as globalism (Beck, 2000).

Political

The question raised in the political approach to globalization relates to the degree that globalized, integrated markets have supplanted or at least reduced democratization. We referred earlier to Kassiola's (1990) concept of depoliticization or economic reductionism in which the economic functions of society supplant the political through market imperialism in economics. He refers here to the capacity to transform political questions about what societies ought to do into economic questions answered in the market. As a well-known example, medical care can be addressed as a political or an economic question depending on whether a country considers it to be an economic right (economic) or a human right (political). Ought citizens be entitled to health care because, as humans, they deserve it or because they can afford it (see also Dholakia *et al.*, this volume)? In the USA, medical care is an economic right while in most other developed economies it is a human right. The question is whether the technological rationality (economic efficiency) in the market mentality in such cases will supplant the substantive rationality (Habermas, 1975) of the participative political process (what we would choose for ourselves and others with economic efficiency removed). Because it is the neoliberal conception of markets that is being globalized, it is reasonable for global citizens to be concerned about how far the process will go and whether they will continue to have any voice in the choices.

As the political space is diminished through the actions of global enterprises, will market fundamentalism come in its wake? Will there remain any semblance of the Habermasian (1984) ideal speech situation, and will it be followed by a crisis of legitimation (Habermas, 1975). With market fundamentalism and laissez-faire policies that accompany globalization as it is now unfolding, these are legitimate questions regarding political process. As the MNC ascends in the global political arena, what are the prospects for the continued expansion of the principles of participatory democracy into the Third World and some developing economies?

The problem can arise because there is no superordinate global political power to control and protect nations whose level of development is not sufficient to maintain counterbalancing political power. Because of the economic power of the MNC, its capacity to usurp individual political rights can be great. In areas such as taxation, employment, environmental damage, financial flight, etc. the MNCs exert tremendous political influence within a country through their economic power. This is exacerbated by the fact that MNCs, the IMF, and the World Bank are the only true political powers that transcend national borders. These institutions maintain power and influence in multiple countries while each country has little power over them because there is no higher authority to appeal to (Dryzek, 1996; Lofdahl, 2002; Ohmae, 1995). This allows them to play countries off against each other in a kind of race to the bottom in democratic principles. This leaves countries in a situation we might call the dilemma of development. They want to have the benefits of development that globalization can bring but do not want to relinquish their cultural traditions and values. It seems that one cannot do both.

Cultural

Globalization is frequently reduced to a one-dimensional construct as mentioned earlier. One of the purposes of this section is to point out that this is a very shallow view as it ignores the interaction of all the dimensions of the DSP of Western industrial societies. Tomlinson (1999) concurs with this, arguing that globalization involves complex connectivity which he describes as an "ever-densening network of interconnections and inter-dependencies that characterize modern social life" (p. 2). Harvey (1990) and Venkatesh (1999) concur and argue that it is partially a result of time-space compression accelerated by advancing technology. That is, as technologies improve and spread, the distance between things (geography), becomes less important and communications become instantaneous. Everything seems closer together in both time and distance. Robertson (1992) argues that this complex connectivity creates new forms of social life but not to the extent suggested earlier by Greider (1997) and Singer (2002) in their conception of "one world." What is noticeable here is that there are varying perspectives on the cultural dimension of globalization, with some seeing dramatic economic and political transformations negating the container theory of society, and others seeing a reflexive process in which change is, to some extent, negotiable within the culture. Similarly, some see it as primarily an economic process driven by capitalist imperatives, and others see it as a natural progression from modernity, the period usually associated with the Enlightenment, Industrial Revolution, and the evolution of capitalism, to postmodernity in which the old notions of progress are becoming obsolete. However one sees the project of globalization, the ultimate question regards the path of globalization.

If, as is typically argued by proponents of globalization, the end is to achieve a better quality of life for global citizens, then we must consider what that means from the cultural perspective. While the complexity of this dimension is too great for us to provide a full examination, a brief description of the essential elements will be offered. All accounts of globalization, to be complete, must examine the nature of freedom within cultures. This is more complex than one might think, because, contrary to most assessments, freedom is not one dimensional even though it is most often treated that way.

We will focus here on Berlin's (1969) early conception of freedom which is usually considered to be the first to discuss the concept of positive freedom, although some suggest that it was alluded to by Fromm (1966) much earlier. They essentially distinguished between two types of freedom referred to as positive and negative freedom. The most common conception of freedom in Western industrial societies is that of negative freedom. This essentially refers to one being free from external constraints on one's choices. Negative freedom then suggests "freedom from" external (or sometimes internal) constraints. This is encapsulated in the title of Friedman and Friedman's (1980) book, *Free to Choose*. This condition is referred to as procedural neutrality (Sandel, 1996) and it pervades all conceptions of the free market.

But there is also a second dimension of freedom that is critical to quality of life in any country. Sen (1999) discusses positive freedom in terms of capabilities of people to enact the life they choose to live. The importance of this in the critical school's take on globalization is that, while it has always been assumed that an abundance of negative freedom will lead inexorably to positive freedom, Sen's work disputes this assumption in examinations of developing countries. He argues that for negative freedom to lead to capabilities, there must be institutional development sufficient to allow people to enact their desired life. As examples of this, one need only examine the negative freedoms of women and African Americans in the USA over the last century. Each received an increasing number of negative freedoms enacted in law, but neither could choose their way of life. The law moved slower than the conditions inhibiting life choices, and negative freedoms moved slower than positive freedoms.

This suggests that the market freedoms offered by globalization will not necessarily lead to the ability to enact the life citizens choose to live. This is a critical question in globalization and is addressed directly in Kilbourne (2004) and Sen (1999). This relates back to the DSP of a society and whether its prevailing institutions are amenable to the development and maintenance of markets. If not, markets (or the lack of them) can become the tools of despots used for maintaining power for the few and hopelessness for the many.

Technology

There is probably no greater force in the history of human development than technology. White (1966) examines the role of technology in medieval society and shows clearly that social change follows in the wake of technological change. From a practical perspective, internationalization would scarcely have been possible without technological advances in manufacturing, infrastructure, transportation, and communication. These were the sine qua non of the internationalization of commerce. But historically, international markets were not fully integrated as they are now. What we are now experiencing is more than multinational marketing and business generally. It is, borrowing from Bentham, technology on stilts.

From the perspective of the critical school, because technology is so advanced and proceeding exponentially, the world has long passed the time when its marketing or financial impact was felt only by those involved. It is now felt simultaneously by all, or will be soon, because the effect of globalization on business is the tip of the iceberg. It now affects politics, economics, and culture as argued above. But it is in a much more complex way that includes space-time compression that frequently occurs because of technological changes (Harvey, 1990) in transportation (speed compresses distance), economics (capital is turned over more quickly), and communications (instantaneous transfer of information) all interacting with each other. The result is what Winner (1986) and Feenberg (1991) refer to as changing forms of life in which relationships, politics, economics, and other areas of life are transmogrified, creating a new social contract the terms of which no one is ever aware of. As a result, the standard modes of behavior and the nature of social relations change slowly enough that one does not even notice them until, on reflection at some later date, one wonders where the past went. It becomes one of the functions of critical macromarketing to disclose the ideologies that are created in the wake of globalization of technologies.

This also reiterates the relationship between different dimensions of the DSP and both sustainability and globalization. One of the concerns of many cultures in the globalization process is the sanctity of their cultural history. While much has been said on the technological convergence thesis in which technologies converge in similar ways when applied in different cultures, there is concern as to whether cultures built around similar technologies will become more similar (through similar global markets) to each other as part of the new social contract (Winner, 1986; Feenberg, 1991). This is still a highly contested debate, however, and will not be discussed here.

Conclusion

The purpose of this chapter was to summarize the main ideas within the contexts of critical macromarketing, sustainability, and globalization. It was clear at the outset that this was a daunting task for a single chapter in a single book given that there are hundreds of books and thousands of journal articles on both sustainability and globalization. However, the chapter was written to provide, not every thought or reference on the topics, but some of the main ideas and "classic" references to guide the reader into the fundamental background in the areas. The chapter was written from the perspective of the critical school and how it views sustainability and globalization.

A brief description of critical macromarketing, or what is sometimes referred to as the critical school of macromarketing, was provided to distinguish it from mainstream marketing and macromarketing specifically. The main difference was described as the critical view of market functioning. Markets are the provisioning technology of societies in that they provide for the needs of a society whatever form the market may take, and there are many possibilities. The focus of this chapter is not so general, however, and concentrates on the type of free markets in Western industrial societies. Within the developmental school, markets are seen as positive influences on the development of cultures. Within critical macromarketing, while the positive results are appreciated, it is also assumed that there are negative implications of markets as well. They can result in inspired solutions to societal problems, and they can result in despotic tools in cultures that do not have the institutions conducive to market functioning built into the cultural framework. It was assumed, for example, when the USSR collapsed in 1989 or so, that freeing prices was sufficient to create modern markets. This did not materialize and has not yet. Part of the reason might be that the necessary political and economic institutions referred to earlier did not then exist. These institutions relate to the political, economic, and technological functioning extant in the culture in question. When these institutions are conducive to market functioning, great things can happen, but when they are not, they can become instruments of domination and control.

From the perspective of sustainability, the chapter first drew a distinction between what is mere environmentalism and what is true sustainability. The field has been somewhat contaminated by terminology, so the chapter sought first to clarify this. The essence of the distinction is that greening of the marketing process is a necessary condition for sustainability, but it is not sufficient because the time frames in greening are too short. Sustainability is a long-range goal of global society in which long term implies centuries, not years or decades. Sustainability necessarily implies that the global system must drastically modify its normal practices to arrive at alternate systems of consumption and production as this is, at present anyway, the only viable path forward.

With new and improving measures of sustainability, a clear definition of sustainability is available. It is no longer a series of abstract euphemisms like the original IPAT equation but a precise definition of the earth's carrying capacity measured against the ecological consequences of human behavior. Both measures are developing rapidly and are becoming readily available through the Global Footprint Network. The suggestion here is that there is now the possibility for increased empirical support for prevailing theories and theory development. While it is true that there is nothing more useful than a good theory, every theory must at some point be tested for its robustness. At the same time, we do not want to work backwards developing data-driven theory as is sometimes done. This process has begun in the critical school, and it will develop further in the coming years.

Both the DSP derived in the critical school and the approach to sustainability are directly related to the globalization process. This was shown in the globalization section of the chapter. The political, economic, and technological dimensions of the DSP figure directly in the globalization process that is, for the most part, the globalization of free markets along with the consequences. These consequences result from what Stiglitz (2002) describes, not as the globalization of free markets, but as the globalization of market failures that do not result in cultural development. For markets to function properly the underlying institutions required to support and maintain them must be in place, and for many underdeveloped countries these conditions are not met. As stated earlier, it was assumed by neoclassical economists that with the fall of the Berlin wall, the Russian economy would move quickly into a free market system. This, of course, has not happened yet. It is not difficult to see why.

Hopefully the reader will glean some insights about the critical school and its approach to markets, sustainability, and globalization. Much of the research cited is from books rather than journal articles, and many of them are quite old. This is because the chapter focused on the classic underpinnings of social critique through the centuries. Much, as can be seen, still holds today. To get a clear picture of where the critical school would like to go, it needs a clear picture of the historical development of markets, property, freedom, science, political history, and economic history. And, as is often attributed to Edmund Burke, "Those who don't know history are doomed to repeat it."

References

Ahuvia, A.C., & Friedman, D.C. (1998). Income, consumption, and subjective well-being: Toward a composite macromarketing model. *Journal of Macromarketing, 18*(2), 153–168.
Bauman, Z. (1998). *Globalization: The human consequences.* New York, NY, Columbia University Press.
Beck, U. (2000). *What is globalization?* Cambridge, UK, Polity Press.
Belshaw, C.S. (1965). *Traditional exchange and modern markets.* Englewood Cliffs, NJ, Prentice-Hall.
Berlin, I. (1969). *Four essays on liberty.* London, UK, Oxford University Press.
Brundtland, G.H., & Khalid, M. (1987). *Our common future.* London, UK, Oxford University Press.
Bury, J.B. (1932). *The idea of progress.* New York, Macmillan.
Butterfield, H. (1949). *The origins of modern science, 1300–1800.* London, UK, G. Bell.
Carson, R. (1962). *Silent spring.* Boston, MA, Houghton Mifflin.
Dahringer, L.D., & Hilger, M.T. (1985). A comparative study of public food marketing as viewed by consumers in Mexico and India. *Journal of Macromarketing, 5*(1), 69–79.

Daly, H.E. (1991). *Steady state economics*. Washington, DC, Island Press.
Dickinson, R., & Hollander, S.C. (1991). Consumer votes. *Journal of Business Research, 23*(1), 9–20.
Dobson, A. (2000). *Green political thought*. London, UK, Routledge.
Dryzek, J.S. (1996). *Democracy in capitalist times: Ideals, limits, and struggles*. Oxford, UK, Oxford University Press.
Ehrlich, P.R., & Holdren, J.P. (1971). Impact of population growth. *Science, 171*, 1212–1217.
Ellul, J. (1964). *The technological society*. New York, NY, Knopf.
Feenberg, A. (1991). *Critical theory of technology*. Oxford, UK, Oxford University Press.
Fisk, G. (1967). *Marketing systems: An introductory analysis*. New York, NY, Harper and Row.
Fisk, G. (1974). *Marketing and the ecological crisis*. New York, NY, Harper and Row.
Friedman, M., & Friedman, R. (1980). *Free to choose*. New York, NY, Houghton Mifflin Harcourt Publishing Company.
Fromm, E. (1966). *The fear of freedom*. London, UK, Routledge & Kegan Paul Ltd.
Ger, G., & Belk, R.W. (1996). Cross-cultural differences in materialism. *Journal of Economic Psychology, 17*(1), 55–77.
Giddens, A. (1990). *The consequences of modernity*. Palo Alto, CA, Stanford University Press.
Greider, W. (1997). *One world ready or not: The manic logic of global capitalism*. New York, NY, Simon and Schuster.
Habermas, J. (1975). *Legitimation crisis*. Boston, MA, Beacon Press.
Habermas, J. (1984). *The theory of communicative action*. Boston, MA, Beacon Press.
Harvey, D. (1990). *The condition of postmodernity: An enquiry into the origins of cultural change*. Cambridge, MA, Blackwell.
Heilbroner, R. (1980). *The making of economic society*. Englewood Cliffs, NJ, Prentice-Hall.
Heilbroner, R.L. (1985). *The nature and logic of capitalism*. New York, NY, Norton.
Hirschman, A.O. (1970). *Exit, voice, and loyalty*. Cambridge, MA, Harvard University Press.
Hirschman, A.O. (1977). *The passions and the interests: Political arguments for capitalism before its triumph*. Princeton, NJ, Princeton University Press.
Hodgson, G.M. (2001). *How economics forgot history*. London, UK, Routledge.
Joy, A., & Ross, C.A. (1989). Marketing and development in third world contexts: An evaluation and future directions. *Journal of Macromarketing, 9*(2), 17–31.
Kassiola, J.J. (1990). *The death of industrial civilization: The limits to economic growth and the repoliticization of advanced industrial society*. Albany, NY, SUNY Press.
Kilbourne, W.E. (1995). Green advertising: Salvation or oxymoron? *Journal of Advertising, 24*(2), 7–19.
Kilbourne, W.E. (1998). Green marketing: A theoretical perspective. *Journal of Marketing Management, 14*(6), 641–655.
Kilbourne, W.E. (1999). On the role of macromarketing in the resolution of competing ecological rationalities. Paper presented at the Macromarketing Society, Nebraska City, NE.
Kilbourne, W.E. (2004). Globalization and development: An expanded macromarketing view. *Journal of Macromarketing, 24*(2), 122–135.
Kilbourne, W.E., & Beckmann, S.C. (1998). Review and critical assessment of research on marketing and the environment. *Journal of Marketing Management, 14*(6), 507–512.
Kilbourne, W., McDonagh, P., & Prothero, A. (1997). Can macromarketing replace the dominant social paradigm? Sustainable consumption and the quality of life. *Journal of Macromarketing, 17*(1), 4–24.
Kilbourne, W.E., Dorsch, M.J., McDonagh, P., Urien, B., Prothero, A., Grünhagen, M., et al. (2009). The institutional foundations of materialism in western societies: A conceptualization and empirical test. *Journal of Macromarketing, 29*(3), 259–278.
Lee, D.-J., & Sirgy, J.M. (2004). Quality-Of-Life (QOL) marketing: Proposed antecedents and consequences. *Journal of Macromarketing, 24*(1), 44–58.
Leiss, W. (1972). *The domination of nature*. New York, NY, George Braziller.
Locke, J. (1963). *Two treatises on government*. Cambridge, UK, Cambridge University Press.
Lofdahl, C.L. (2002). *Environmental impacts of globalization and trade*. Cambridge, MA, The MIT Press.
MacPherson, C.B. (1962). *The political theory of possessive individualism*. Oxford, UK, Clarendon.
Marcuse, H. (1964). *One dimensional man*. Boston, MA, Beacon Press.
McDonagh, P., & Prothero, A. (2014). Sustainability marketing research: Past, present and future. *Journal of Marketing Management, 30*(11–12), 1186–1219.
Meadows, D.H., Meadows, D.L., Randers, J., & Behrens, W. (1972). *The limits to growth: A report for the Club of Rome's project on the predicament of mankind*. New York, NY, Universe Books.

Merchant, C. (1980). *The death of nature: Women, ecology, and the scientific revolution*. San Francisco, CA, Harper and Row.

Mill, J.S. (1909). *Principles of political economy with some of their applications to social philosophy*. London, UK, Longmans, Green and Company.

Mittelstaedt, J., Kilbourne, W., & Mittelstaedt, R. (2006). Macromarketing as agorology: Macromarketing theory and the study of the agora. *Journal of Macromarketing, 26*(2), 131–142.

Mittelstaedt, J., Kilbourne, W., Shultz, C., & Peterson, M. (2015). Sustainability as megatrend: Two schools of macromarketing thought. *Journal of Macromarketing, 34*(3), 253–264.

Myrdal, G. (1954). *The political element in the development of economic theory*. Cambridge, MA, Harvard University Press.

Nason, R.W., Dholakia, N., & McLeavey, D.W. (1987). A strategic perspective on regional redevelopment. *Journal of Macromarketing, 7*(1), 34–48.

Ohmae, K. (1995). *The end of the nation state: The rise and fall of regional economies*. London, UK, Harper Collins.

Peterson, M., & Malhotra, N.K. (1997). Comparative marketing measures of societal quality of life: Substantive dimensions in 186 countries. *Journal of Macromarketing, 17*(1), 25–38.

Pieterse, J.N. (1995). *Globalization as hybridization*. London, UK, Sage Publications.

Polanyi, K. (1944). *The great transformation: The political and economic origins of our time*. Boston, MA, Beacon Press.

Postman, N. (1993). *Technopoly: The surrender of culture to technology*. New York, NY, Vantage.

Prothero, A., & Fitchett, J.A. (2000). Greening capitalism: Opportunities for a green commodity. *Journal of Macromarketing, 20*(1), 46–55.

Reich, C.A. (1970). *The greening of America: How the youth revolution is trying to make America liveable*. New York, NY, Random House.

Robertson, R. (1992). *Globalization: Social theory and global culture*. London, UK, Sage Publications.

Sandel, M.J. (1996). *Democracy's discontent*. Cambridge, MA, Belknap Press.

Schor, J. (2010). *Plenitude: The new economics of true wealth*. New York, NY, Penguin Press.

Sen, A.K. (1999). *Development as freedom*. New York, NY, Knopf.

Sen, A. (2002). How to judge globalism. *The American Prospect, 13*(1), 1–10.

Singer, P. (2002). *One world: The ethics of globalization*. New Haven, CT, Yale University Press.

Smith, A. (1937). *An inquiry into the nature and causes of the wealth of nations*. New York, NY, Random House.

Smith, T.M. (1998). *The myth of green marketing: Tending our goats at the edge of apocalypse*. Toronto, University of Toronto Press.

Stiglitz, J.E. (2002). *Globalization and its discontents*. New York, NY, Norton.

Stiles, P. (2005). *Is the American dream killing you? How "the market" rules our lives*. New York, NY, Collins Business.

Tenner, E. (1997). *Why things bite back: Technology and the revenge of unintended consequences*. New York, NY, Vantage Books.

Thurow, L. (1980). *The zero-sum society: Distribution and the possibilities for economic change*. New York, NY, Basic Books.

Tomlinson, J. (1999). *Globalization and culture*. Chicago, IL, University of Chicago Press.

Ullmann, W. (1963). *The individual and society in the middle ages*. Baltimore, MD, The Johns Hopkins University Press.

Veblen, T. (1899). *The theory of the leisure class*. New York, NY, Macmillan.

Venkatesh, A. (1999). Postmodernism perspectives for macromarketing: An inquiry into the global information sign economy. *Journal of Macromarketing, 19*(2), 153–169.

Wackernagle, M.R., & Rees, W. (1996). *Our ecological footprint: Reducing human impact on the earth*. Philadelphia, PA, New Society Publishers.

Wallerstein, I.M. (2004). *World-systems analysis: An introduction*. Durham, NC, Duke University Press.

White, L. (1966). *Medieval technology and social change*. Berkeley, CA, University of California Press.

Whorf, B.L. (1956). *Language, thought and reality*. Cambridge, MA, The MIT Press.

Winner, L. (1986). *The whale and the reactor: A search for limits in an age of high technology*. Chicago, IL, University of Chicago Press.

Wood, E.M. (2002). *The origin of capitalism*. London, UK, Verso.

York, R., Rosa, E.A., & Dietz, T. (2003). Footprints on the Earth: The environmental consequences of modernity. *American Sociological Review, 68*(2), 279–300.

7
CRITICAL PERSPECTIVES ON PLACE MARKETING

Massimo Giovanardi, Mihalis Kavaratzis, and Maria Lichrou

Introduction

The crisis in public sector planning from the 1970s onwards (Paddison, 1993), together with the disillusionment with the effectiveness of traditional urban planning regulatory instruments (Ashworth & Voogd, 1990b) paved the way for the progressive embedding of commercially oriented tools and discourses into public management and territorial governance (Gold & Ward, 1994). In this context, place marketing can be understood as the adoption of marketing business philosophy into the realm of cities, regions, nations and spatial entities in general. At a glance, the notion of place marketing may convey that – not too differently from products and services – cities, regions and countries may constitute spatially extended 'offerings' that can be managed, developed and promoted following marketing principles. In this view, place managers can adapt their policy-making activities according to the needs of different targets. Marketing strategies and objectives can involve, for example, attracting new citizens or tourists or trying to retain the current ones; bidding for international mega-events (e.g., Olympic Games, European Capital of Culture, etc.) in order to generate global visibility and obtain external political legitimation, or internal consensus; using urban design techniques to manufacture an urban fabric that is appealing to dwellers, commuters and/or transnational and creative high-skilled workers; fine-tuning the perceived image of a developing country and positioning it in relation to other perceived competitors.

To a geographer or a social scientist in general, a city, a region and a country would constitute a profoundly different geographical unit, which would result in specific arrays of social, cultural and administrative issues that need to be considered by marketing scholars. However, in spite of the presence of apparently distinctive research domains signaled by labels such as 'city marketing' or 'regional marketing', extant scholarship has tended to generate an all-encompassing assemblage of theories generally known as place marketing (e.g., Ashworth & Voogd, 1990b; Kotler *et al.*, 1999; Rainisto, 2003; Kavaratzis & Ashworth, 2007; Parker *et al.*, 2015). Consistently, the present chapter identifies *place* as a various set of geographical units that are conceptualized by marketing scholars as spatially extended offerings. As a whole, this chapter thus aims to explore *place* as a specific focus of the marketing literature. Certainly, marketing scholars have tended to prioritize an appreciation of place as a relatively conventional *object* of marketing practices (e.g., the mainstream destination management literature). And yet, a growing awareness for the peculiarities of place as a *context* for a conceptualization of marketing can be witnessed (see Giovanardi *et al.*, 2013), which contributed to the sedimentation of a *sui generis* spatially oriented marketing theory (e.g., Papadopoulos et al., 2011; Vuignier, 2017).

This chapter begins with a historical account of place marketing's development, incorporating an overview of the place marketing 'conventional wisdom' that emphasizes its prevalent prescriptive and normative character. It proceeds to offer a reconstruction of the critical voices through an account of their main arguments. In doing so, two generations of critical voices are spelled out, by offering some critical alternative perspectives that challenge place marketing's traditional managerially oriented and prescriptive foundation. In the final part of this chapter, we propose an agenda for future research that takes stock of the most recent and promising approaches to envision more inclusive forms of place marketing. Overall, this chapter intends to (a) consolidate the critique of place marketing and establish it within the marketing theory area by articulating it with clarity and (b) to formulate a research agenda that encourages scholars to pursue place marketing research in a way that is more respectful of the needs of less powerful social actors.

The historical development of place marketing

Following Rainisto's (2003) historical reconstruction of place marketing, it is probably the publication of the 'Broadening the concept of marketing' by Kotler and Levy (1969) that paved the way for the subsequent theoretical development of the place marketing concept. Kotler and Levy's seminal article was followed by Kotler's (1972) 'A generic concept of marketing', according to which marketing is a function that can be applied to any social unit that exchanges values with other social units. Accordingly, marketing methodologies and protocols can be applied not only to traditional companies, but also to non-profit organizations (Kotler, 1979) and more general societal domains (i.e. 'social marketing'). In a similar vein, two years after the broadening thesis, social marketing emerged as an "approach to planned social change" (Kotler & Zaltman, 1971, p. 3). A marketing philosophy, once having become established within traditional commercial realms of products and services, was ready to penetrate into different, more complex types of realms, such as the 'spatial' and the 'public' (Giovanardi et al., 2013).

Ashworth and Voogd (1990b) note that place marketing is most closely related to three streams of marketing, which move beyond a focus on manufactured goods: marketing in non-profit organizations; social marketing; and image marketing. Even though they see a 'customer orientation' or the 'exchange principle' as important foci, they propose that the aforementioned streams of marketing are more applicable to places because they incorporate principles that are more aligned with public governance. Specifically, marketing for non-profit organizations focuses on broader and longer term goals than are typically set by public authorities; social marketing is interested in society's wellbeing by influencing individual attitudes in order to offer solutions to various social problems; and image marketing connects because of the fact that "images [can] be marketed, while the product to which they are related [remains] only vaguely delineated in the background" (Ashworth & Voogd, 1990b, p. 20).

This does not mean that antecedents of what we call place marketing today did not exist previously, as places have historically existed within markets and vice versa. The two most commonly identified antecedents are place promotion (e.g., Gold & Ward, 1994) and place selling (e.g., Ward, 1998). Ward (1998), for instance, examines the promotion of the seaside resort, the suburb, the industrial town and the post-industrial city since the 1800s, drawing on examples from North America, Britain and Continental Europe. However, what is 'new' about place marketing is the conscious application of marketing as a philosophy of place management

(Ashworth & Voogd, 1994). Thus, the marketing of places has been turned into an increasingly professionalized, highly organized and specialized industry (Gotham, 2002).

As Barke (1999) identifies, the initial phases of place promotion and place selling were followed by the introduction of a broader concept of place marketing, which at least initially meant finding out what potential consumers wished to 'buy'. The techniques used in this phase involved new forms of representation of places with the aim to alter and improve the place's image. Thus, place marketing went beyond advertising or promotion and incorporated hallmark events and high-profile or 'flagship' developments in the built environment. This entails a particular focus on culture, heritage, development of museums and other attractions as the means through which places attempt to cultivate an attractive positioning within the global market. Today, the place-marketing efforts of local, regional and national governments involve a variety of objectives such as country positioning in international relations, enhancement of a place's exports, protection of domestic businesses from 'foreign' (including other regions in the same country) competition, attraction or retention of development factors and generally positioning the place for advantage domestically and internationally in economic, political and social terms (Papadopoulos, 2004).

Conventional marketing perspectives to places

Since the early 1970s, Philip Kotler has been influential in the advancements of place-marketing research. The efforts of marketing scholars interested in places have been consolidated through theoretical models of place marketing and in the application of marketing models to places. Examples can be found in Kotler, Haider and Rein (1993) and Kotler *et al.* (1999). A key assumption underlying early discussions of the application of marketing to places was that places could (and should) be treated as products. For example, in discussing tourism destinations, Ashworth and Voogd note:

> Tourism destinations can undoubtedly be treated as products. They are logically the point of consumption of the complex of activities that comprises the tourism experience and are ultimately what is sold by place promotion agencies on the tourism market.
> *1990a, p. 7*

Place here is understood as both an object and a location (Ashworth & Voogd, 1990a). Hence, the 'place-product' is conceived both as a set of facilities and products provided locally (Buhalis, 2000) and at the same time as a facility and a product in its own right. This applies to all places, including cities and tourism destinations. Ashworth and Voogd (1990b), in the context of city marketing, refer to Sleipen's (1988) separation of the urban product into contributory elements (such as the specific services or even a particular isolated characteristic of the city) and the nuclear product (which is the city as a whole). Furthermore, coming from a tourism perspective Murphy *et al.* (2000), building on Kotler *et al.*'s (1996) model of marketing environments, propose a model of the place-product that is a combination of the place's environments and facilities, which compose the tourist's experience of a destination. Hence, according to Murphy *et al.* (2000) the place's macro environments, i.e. the political, social, legal, technological, economic, cultural and natural environment; the products and services made available by place's infrastructure, i.e. accommodation, transportation, travel, shopping, recreation and attraction, and food facilities; and finally the tourist's experience of these elements are the place-product.

The conception of the 'place-product' entails certain challenges, because it is characterized by complexity and intangibility. This complexity calls for a collaborative effort, which acknowledges and brings together the wishes of all stakeholders involved in the process. Moreover, places are not simply physical settings with tangible attributes; the 'reality' of place is largely mental and perceived based on subjective experiences of place. Thus, the application of the expanded marketing management perspective to places proved challenging, as it failed to address the complexity and intangibility of what was being marketed. To paraphrase Kavaratzis, the object of place marketing is not the place itself, but its image (2004, p. 62).

It is also important to note that in the meantime, marketing thought was shifting attention away from products to images, experiences and interactions (O'Malley & Patterson, 1998). The shift, fueled by postmodern perspectives in marketing and consumer research (Fırat & Venkatesh, 1995; Fırat & Dholakia, 2006; Aubert-Gamet & Cova, 1999), and service and process-based definitions of value creation (Grönroos, 2006; Vargo & Lusch, 2004; Warnaby, 2009), challenges the marketing management approach for its emphasis on goods, exchange value, and relative marketer autonomy and consumer passivity. Due to these challenges, more recent developments in the place-marketing field have engendered a shift of terminology from place marketing to place branding, largely drawing on the literatures associated with organizational identity (Kavaratzis & Hatch, 2013) and corporate branding (Papadopoulos, 2004; Kavaratzis, 2004, 2005; Kerr, 2006). Organizational identity, conceptualized "as an ongoing conversation or dance between organizational culture and organizational images" (Hatch & Schultz, 2002, p. 991), appears to reflect the diversity of products and cultures encountered in large corporations (Kerr, 2006) and entails greater intangibility, complexity and social responsibility (Simoes & Dibb 2001). Thus, Kavaratzis (2004, p. 66) suggests that both corporate brands and city brands (a) have multidisciplinary roots, (b) address multiple groups of stakeholders, (c) have a high level of intangibility and complexity, (d) need to take into account social responsibility and (e) deal with multiple identities. The shift to place branding has generated both a newly found enthusiasm (e.g., Kavaratzis, 2004) and an increased mistrust (e.g., Greenberg, 2009) of this widened perspective. For Eshuis and Klijn (2012), the use of branding and its application by policy makers and public managers can be explained by the nature of current governance processes (which are more image and perception based) and by wider societal changes such as mediatization and information overload. These have led municipalities to practice "many of the same promotional and image-generation techniques as private-sector PR firms use" (Zavattaro, 2010, p. 191) to achieve similar goals. Brands are characterized by intangibility and their understanding entails multiple dimensions, involving the perceptions of both organizations and consumers (De Chernatony & Dall'Olmo Riley, 1998). Places are therefore increasingly conceptualized as brands (Kavaratzis, 2004, 2005; Kerr, 2006; Hankinson, 2010). Taking the field of city marketing as an exemplar, Kavaratzis argues that the shift from city marketing to city branding suggests a change of perspective with respect to the whole marketing effort:

> City branding is understood as the means both for achieving competitive advantage in order to increase inward investment and tourism, and also for achieving community development, reinforcing local identity and identification of the citizens with their city and activating all social forces to avoid social exclusion and unrest.
>
> *2004, p. 70*

While these ideas have helped place marketing and place branding develop a clearer set of theoretical propositions, they have, at the same time, seriously constrained a deeper understanding of the nuances of place as an 'object' of marketing. This is something that scholars have criticized heavily and the more recent literature has attempted to address (e.g., Kavaratzis & Kalandides, 2015).

In line with Kaneva's (2011) critical review of nation branding, it can be argued that the conventional prescriptive perspective offered by business scholars frames place-marketing apparatus through a "technical-economic approach" (p. 120) that sees places as functional bundles of products and services, ignoring a wider cultural-geographical understanding. Approaching place marketing in this manner, they look at places in terms of combinations of assets to be exploited and maximized, place identity included. This instrumental approach had been developed largely in the form of descriptive studies that describe case studies of 'success stories' or provide definitional frameworks that translate and adapt mainstream marketing theory to urban and regional domains. As an ultimate aim, conventional managerial perspectives seek to "advance an applied research agenda" that is intended to inform, but not to question, the practice of brand management for nations" (Kaneva, 2011, p. 122) and other applications of marketing practices to places. Usually, clear managerial recommendations as to what it is necessary to do and not to do are offered, following a traditional paradigm of a 'linear development model' in which territories are expected to evolve from less to more advanced stages of development (Mattelart, 1994).

Remnants of the 'growth machine' metaphor can be found in the treatment of city marketing and branding (Molotch, 1976; Greenbaum et al., 1988). This metaphor neatly captures the sense of development as a discourse that sustained marketing's fascination among place managers and politicians. In this view, growth is identified as the political and economic purpose of virtually any given locality at that time in the United States (Molotch, 1976, pp. 309–310). It is around this common objective that urban elites try to reach forms of cooperation and override other issues or contrasts. Furthermore, while localities compete among one another for resources (or better, for the preconditions of growth, in terms of resources allocated by the central government), within cities different stakeholders may stake their claims for different and contrasting needs, where the capacity to aggregate and form alliances turns out to be a key ability that determines success.

Unveiling place marketing's 'conventional wisdom'

Radically different accounts on place marketing emerge from those studies on place marketing authored by critical human geographers, who endeavoured to underline the idiosyncrasy of the managerial perspective and challenge its main pillars. This section presents and discusses those critical perspectives on place marketing that developed in cognate disciplines between the end of the 1980s and the present day. On the whole, the two generations of critical voices discussed below have sought to challenge the desirability and implementation of managerialism as a public management philosophy, by highlighting its drawbacks and contradictions. In particular, several scholars in the areas of geography, sociology, public affairs, media and communication, design and cultural studies have argued that the simplistic managerial perspective frames place marketing as a pragmatic, objective and apolitical activity that has led to dubious results, gentrification and even the homogenization of place identities. Critical commentators have sought to rebalance the predominant prescriptive and dogmatic attitude underpinning business studies, and to consider the social, cultural and political context where place-marketing campaigns are actually being designed and implemented, a context that had been largely disregarded as a sort of irrelevant 'vacuum'.

The first generation of critique

A first generation of critique against place marketing emerged from a large part of the geography literature that treats it with skepticism (e.g., Harvey, 1989a; Philo & Kearns, 1993; Griffiths,

1998). Here, place marketing is approached as inherently 'bad' and disruptive and only able to serve and legitimize the already dominant self-interests of urban political and cultural elites. For instance, Philo and Kearns (1993) have provided a robust argument against many components of the armoury of the managerial approach to place marketing that we examined above. Importantly, they examine place marketing (or place selling as they term it) as an ideology dictating socially insensitive and disruptive measures. Holcomb indeed suggests that marketing can destroy a city's 'soul': "[t]he city is commodified, its form and spirit remade to conform to market demand, not residents' dreams" (1999, p. 69). A big part of the problem is that "the marketing of cities tends to be generic and repetitive" (Holcomb, 1994, p. 121). As Griffiths (1998) points out, critical discussion of place-marketing strategies has focused around three main lines of argument. First, their ideological effects because "in the process of re-imaging a city, some aspects of its identity are ignored, denied or marginalised" (Griffiths, 1998, p. 53). Second, their socially regressive consequences since "not only does place marketing divert attention away from social and economic inequalities, it can also exacerbate them . . . through the reallocation of public spending necessary to secure high-profile flagship developments" (Griffiths, 1998, p. 54). Finally, their highly speculative nature as "investments in major entrepreneurial projects are contingent, for their success, on a multitude of factors over which an individual city will usually have little if any control" (Griffiths, 1998, p. 56). Harvey (1989a) adds that spatial practices (such as urbanization and urban entrepreneurialism) acquire definite class, racial, gender and bureaucratic contents and biases.

The 1973 recession and the concurrent challenges to Western economies are recognized as the impetus for the shift in urban governance toward what Harvey (1989a) termed 'entrepreneurialism'. Entrepreneurialism is characterized by a focus on attracting investment as the main preoccupation of public authorities:

> Deindustrialisation, widespread, and seemingly "structural" unemployment, fiscal austerity at both the national and local levels, all coupled with a rising tide of neoconservatism and much stronger appeal (though often more in theory than in practice) to market rationality and privatisation, provide a backdrop to understanding why so many urban governments, often of quite different political persuasions and armed with very different legal and political powers, have all taken a broadly similar direction.
>
> *Harvey, 1989a, p. 2*

Promoting and normalizing a 'growth-first' approach to urban development, neoliberalism renders issues of redistribution and social investment as antagonistic to the overriding objectives of economic development (Peck & Tickell, 2002). Peck *et al.* (2009) trace the development of neoliberalism from its emergence as an economic doctrine in the 1970s to a means of dismantling established Keynesian arrangements in the 1980s into, most recently, a reconstituted form of market-guided regulation. The resultant socio-spatial restructuring is thus not a unified or homogenous process but rather an "an uneven, contradictory, and ongoing process of *neoliberalization*" (Peck et al., 2009, p. 51, emphasis in original). The economic crisis of 2007–2009 has intensified this process through the increasing economic, social and political influence of financial markets. This is evident in the growing role of financial intermediaries and practices in our everyday lives and the "highly uneven material, social, and political ramifications for people and places" (Pike & Pollard, 2010, p. 45).

Common mechanisms of neoliberal restructuring involve the rolling back of centralized state support of municipal activities and welfare state provision; rolling forward of new forms of governance based on public-private partnerships and the incorporation of elite business interests in local political development; privatization and outsourcing of public services; speculative investment opportunities in real estate markets; reworking of labor regulations promoting precarious jobs; and the creation of 'deregulated' spaces (see Peck et al., 2009). The built environment is transformed through gentrification, creation of privatized spaces of elite consumption and gated communities and the construction of mega-projects to attract corporate investment (Peck et al., 2009). For example, luxurious skyscrapers and other high-end buildings are transforming London's cityscape – some call it the emergence of Dubai Thames (Wainwright, 2014). These developments 'squeeze out' affordable housing (Minton, 2017) and displace poorer residents (Hill, 2014).

Private funding in the form of corporate investment and sponsorship is seen as a vital source of income for development and regeneration. In *No Logo*, Naomi Klein (recounting the sponsoring by Yves Saint Laurent of Christmas decorations in Regent Street in 1997) warned that the role of the corporate sponsor is expanding toward appropriating public space and culture (Klein, 2000). More recently, in *The Shock Doctrine* (a title attributed to Milton Friedman's view of crisis as necessary for economic reform), she argues that neoliberalism exploits crises to impose fiscal austerity and attack the provision of public services (Klein, 2007). Focusing on New Orleans in the aftermath of Hurricane Katrina, she exposes the exploitation of the shock of the natural disaster in order to attack public housing and privatize the school system. Klein explains that Friedman's idea was that

> instead of spending a portion of the billions of dollars in reconstruction money on rebuilding and improving New Orleans' existing public school system, the government should provide families with vouchers, which they could spend at private institutions, many run at a profit, that would be subsidized by the state.
>
> *2007, p. 5*

It is possible to discern through these lines of argument the following areas of concern: (a) place marketing ignores the complexity of place and culture; (b) place marketing serves the interests of elites and is socially regressive; (c) place marketing misinterprets place competition; (d) place marketing produces 'sameness'. We will now explore each in turn.

Place marketing ignores the complexity of place and culture

Economic and socio-cultural perspectives are marked by different assumptions regarding the nature of place and the role of culture (in the case of tourism destinations, this is discussed by Morgan & Pritchard, 1998; Voase, 1999; Framke, 2002; Lichrou et al., 2008, to name but a few). Greenwood (1978), for instance, points out that for economists' culture is a natural resource, part of the land factor and part of the 'come-on' factor, but for anthropology it is an integrated set of meanings through which the nature of reality is established and maintained. Following a (broadly speaking) socio-cultural perspective, places exist in flux and represent specific historical and cultural phases in society (Saarinen, 1998). They are understood as fluid, changeable, dynamic contexts of social interaction, shared cultural meanings and collective memory (Stokowski, 2002). What we come to appreciate as place is "as much a symbolic order of meaning as a form of material production" (Meethan, 2001, p. 168). In this light, the marketing of places is better understood as a dialectical process between material practices and symbolic meanings. Marketing is therefore implicated in the process through which material attributes of space take on "symbolic and aesthetic value" and these "representations or narratives of people and place assume an exchange value as the objects of consumption" (Meethan, 2001, p. 37).

Resonating with Meethan's (2001) arguments, Urry notes that "it is hard to envisage the nature of contemporary tourism without seeing how such activities are literally constructed in our imagination through advertising and the media, and through the conscious competition between different social groups" (1990, p. 13). It is therefore difficult to ignore the fact that symbolic values and meanings are contested. However, the marketing of places might reflect the interests of dominant groups (Meethan, 1996). This is because the "ability to assign meaning to a place is an act of power which has real effects on the people living in it" (Human, 1999, p. 83). Philo and Kearns (1993), discussing the marketing of post-industrial cities, suggest that the selection of certain aspects of place in the process of marketing the city tends to favor certain interests over others; the interests of dominant groups in particular. Therefore, a critical understanding of the marketing of place requires the exploration of the social relations that underpin it (Gotham, 2002).

Place marketing is elitist and socially regressive

Philo and Kearns (1993) offer an historical account of the development of the urban form by tracing the mobilization of historical and cultural resources by urban elites in their efforts to advance their economic and social interests. The authors examine the city as an ideological project and an emergent socio-spatial order, reflecting the interests, ideologies and place attachments of urban elites while excluding various 'others' (e.g., the working class, women, ethnic minorities, the elderly, children and disabled). These 'other people' are actively excluded from the 'normal' spaces of urban life or they consciously "avoid the 'normalising' pressures of bourgeois expectations" (Philo & Kearns, 1993, p. 16). Place marketing also depends on mobilizing cultural and historical aspects of place in order to create and promote appealing place images. But because of the existence of these competing interpretations and attachments to place, Philo and Kearns (1993) critique the notion that the place's cultural capital can be modified by marketers in a totally consensual way that reflects the interests of all those living in a place. Those aspects of history that are relevant to the elites are likely to be officially sanctioned, while 'other pasts' are occluded. Major redevelopment projects, such as the London Docklands, can be detrimental to particular communities and their livelihoods. Building upon this logic, Miles (2010, p. 46) asserts that "cities are reduced to an idealised version of a prosperous future that has scant regard for who might be the losers". Thus, the task of critical inquiry is to:

> constantly examine and to re-examine claims about places – claims about their cultures and their histories; claims about who lives and works in them, and why and with what implications; claims about inequalities; claims about meanings – so as to question the appropriateness of a mentality that trades only in stereotypes of places with a view to enhancing their marketability.
>
> *Philo & Kearns, 1993, p. 29*

Place marketing is therefore part of the economic, cultural and political processes involved in the constant construction of places (e.g., Goodwin, 1993). Harvey (1989a, 1989b) examines these processes in the context of the conditions of social life in advanced capitalism. Advanced capitalist societies are being transformed by "the development of transnational practices which transcend individual nation states through generating immense flows of capital, money, goods, services, people, information, technologies, policies, ideas, images and regulations" (Lash & Urry, 1994, p. 280). Harvey (1989b) discusses these transformations using the term *flexible accumulation*, which refers to the increased flexibility and mobility of production processes, enabled by the rapid deployment of new organizational forms and new technologies in production. Flexibility can be seen in labor processes, labor markets, products, and patterns of consumption and in accelerated commercial, technological and organizational innovation. In terms of marketing, flexibility is witnessed in the accelerated pace of consumption across a wide range of products and activities and the shift away from the consumption of goods to services (Harvey, 1989b). Places have thus become primarily spaces for consumption (Miles, 2010), with the consumption of services, rather than the production of goods, the defining characteristic of places (Lash & Urry, 1994). This re-imaging rests largely on image and aestheticization (Miles, 2010) as places try to become attractive to tourists and visitors for shopping, entertainment and tourism activities. Finally, more diverse modes of human sociality, including new forms of communal bonds (that are not always spatially grounded) have emerged (Amin & Thrift, 2002).

Furthermore, these practices are often contingent upon the decontextualization of culture, in order to stimulate sensations, dreams and play with the sole aim to create profit (Amin & Thrift, 2002). This depoliticizes places, which can be detrimental for those living in them, as it promotes an uncritical relationship with a place's culture and the past (Philo & Kearns, 1993). Amin and Thrift (2002) therefore call for a return to the rights to the city as a politics of the commons. In discussing urban spaces, they recognize the problems of power, but at the same time they also see potentialities:

> [U]rban spaces are not predictable machines for reproducing bounded and controllable relations. Rather they are engaged in a struggle with an often-unknown endpoint, in which corporations and other assemblages constantly try to modulate the environment in order to realise gain. But they do not necessarily succeed. So far as the growth of themed parks is concerned, corporations have to deploy a whole panoply of technologies – the interview, the focus group, the poll – which will inform them about what consumers "want". Thus, themed spaces are often used in unpredictable ways by consumers, ways which have little or nothing to do with the maximal consumption they are designed to unleash. And indeed, these spaces can sometimes be the focus of explicit resistance, all the way from taking packed lunches to actual protest.
>
> *2002, p. 129*

Resistance to neoliberalism often takes the form of protests by diverse communities against gentrification. Residents and activists in East Los Angeles, East London, Dublin, Berlin and Barcelona are opposing gentrification and touristification plans, thereby attempting to reclaim their right to the city.

Place marketing misinterprets place competition

As we discussed earlier, place-marketing advocates have found in the notion of competition and the related idea of place competitiveness an argument in favor of place-marketing implementation. Nonetheless, the meaning of place competition is far from straightforward and the rhetoric of place competitiveness can be challenged. First of all, "the novelty of the situation and much of the explanation of the relevance of place marketing approaches lies not in the existence of competition as such, but in the abruptly changing rules of the competitive struggle between places" (Ashworth & Voogd 1994, cited in Kavaratzis, 2007, p. 706). It can also be argued that the understanding of interurban competition is short-sighted and leads to an equivalently partial or short-sighted understanding and implementation of place marketing.

To flesh these issues out, we need to turn to appropriate concepts. Flexible accumulation entails the intensification of what Harvey (1989b) calls 'time-space compression'. Spatial barriers are collapsing, making it easier for capital to move freely across national borders. Places are therefore increasingly finding themselves under the pressure of increased competition for the attraction of investment and the creation of economic development. This has changed the nature of place governance from a focus on the local provision of services, facilities and benefits to local populations to a preoccupation with finding new ways in which to engender development and growth (Harvey, 1989a). This underpins the intensification of place marketing as a tool of place governance. Place marketers turn to those qualities of a place that are 'special' for competitive advantage; qualities that have the potential to increase the place's attractiveness to investors, tourists and inhabitants:

> The active production of places with special qualities becomes an important stake in spatial competition between localities, cities, regions, and nations . . . Heightened inter-place competition should lead to the production of more variegated spaces within the increasing homogeneity of international exchange.
> Harvey, 1989a, p. 29)

However, this is not really the case. In an explanation of the spatial dimensions of inter-firm competition, Cox (1995) makes a distinction between 'weak' and 'strong' competition. As Jessop (1998) summarizes, "whereas strong competition refers to potentially positive-sum attempts to improve the overall (structural) competitiveness of a locality through innovation, weak competition refers to essentially zero-sum attempts to secure the reallocation of existing resources at the expense of other localities" (Jessop, 1998, p. 79). Weak competition is socially disembedding, whereas strong competition involves the territorialization of economic activity (Cox 1995 quoted in Jessop, 1998). Weaker forms of competition are usually more concerned with modifications in formal and substantive regulatory, facilitative or supportive measures aimed at capturing mobile investment, as well as simple image-building measures with the same purpose (Jessop, 1998). Cities engaged in weak entrepreneurialism are more likely to fail in the longer term because of the ease with which such activities can be copied (Jessop, 1998, p. 79). The same argument is raised for place marketing and place branding that, therefore, they need to have a firm rooting in the place's identity and local conditions and characteristics. Yet, in their struggle for differentiation places pursue similar policy formulas (Turok, 2009) and quick yield, but highly speculative and ephemeral projects (Harvey, 1989a), manifested in the serial reproduction of cultural attractions (Richards & Wilson, 2006), themed environments (Amin & Thrift, 2002), flagship projects and catchy slogans (Colomb & Kalandides, 2010). As Harvey (1989a, p. 10) predicted, "competition may even force repetitive and serial reproduction of certain patterns of development or similar forms of urban redevelopment". He proceeds to identify that "many of the innovations and investments designed to make particular cities more attractive as cultural and consumer centres have quickly been imitated elsewhere, thus rendering any competitive advantage within a system of cities ephemeral" (Harvey, 1989a, p. 12).

Critics consequently register that even though it pursues difference, the marketing of places produces sameness and homogeneity across places, which further intensifies the conditions of flexible accumulation (Harvey, 1989a). As Amin and Thrift (2002) observe, it is firms and not cities that compete, and therefore competitiveness-based policies are not likely to deliver self-sustaining local economic development.

Place marketing produces 'sameness'

One of the main arguments against place marketing is the 'sameness' resulting from the similarity of the marketing methods used and the common marketing goals set in cities all over the world, which has negative effects evident in the landscape (e.g., Griffiths, 1998). As Holloway and Hubbard (2001) suggest, attempts to reverse images of decline go hand-in-hand with the physical creation of a new urban landscape. The construction and promotion of 'spectacular' new urban landscapes have been an almost universal response to de-industrialization and frequently center on a 'flagship' project, such as a cultural center, conference suite or heritage park. Inevitably, this redevelopment and 'repackaging' of urban districts is heavily promoted by urban governors, in effect becoming a representation of the city in its own right (Hubbard, 1996). At the heart of the matter lies the interaction between the city's identity and the image of the city that is used in and, at the same time, is formed by marketing. Although there is general agreement that one of the most important assets cities possess is their distinctive and unique local character, it is evident that marketing implementation has diminished these points of substantive differentiation (Griffiths, 1998). The tension is exacerbated if the matter of 'image vs. reality' is added in to the equation. As Hall explains,

> much academic criticism of place promotion stems from the supposed dualism of image and reality implicated by projects of place promotion. Most severely place promotion and projects of economic development of which it is an integral part, have been labelled the "carnival mask" of late capitalist urbanisation, the argument being that while such images create the impression of regeneration and vibrancy within cities, they do nothing to address the underlying problems that necessitated regeneration programmes in the first place.
>
> *1998, p. 28*

To make matters worse, it is normally the same attributes, the same icons and the same "actually quite universal vocabulary of better, bigger, more beautiful and so on" (Philo & Kearns, 1993) that are included in this promotion. As Barke and Harrop (1994, p. 99) state, "despite attempts to create a distinctive image for places, no authentic sense of place is likely to emerge from the advertising copywriters. This is all the more likely if the packaging and the type of content is uniform".

Obviously, these critical reflections and the reasoning developed within critical studies point toward a very different reality of place-marketing consequences than is typically accepted by mainstream place-marketing advocates and in 'practice circles'.

The second generation of critical voices

From the beginning of the 2000s, new conceptual energy was injected into the critical literature about place marketing (and branding) by a second generation of critical voices. This includes scholars whose main research interest lies in place marketing, and not simply in general human geography or sociology. This is coupled with an increasing focus on branding, an evolution that connects with the ongoing conceptual and observational transition from marketing to branding more broadly in the wider discipline (Broudehoux, 2001; Colomb, 2012; Jensen, 2007; Gotham, 2007; Greenberg, 2009; Lichrou *et al.*, 2008; Pasquinelli, 2010; Warnaby, Medway & Bennison, 2010; Lucarelli, 2012; Johansson, 2012; Lucarelli & Giovanardi, 2016).

The starting point of these critiques is characterized by a continuation of themes from the first generation: place branding is an instrument used by urban elites to legitimize their own strategic decision making in the wider context of the hegemonic project of neoliberal urban governance (see Colomb, 2012). As Broudehoux (2001, p. 272) avers, place branding can be described as a field where "dominant groups use spatial and visual strategies to impose their views". Thus, in continuity with the previous decade, the critical coverage is provided by cognate disciplines and most of the time is permeated by the social/civic engagement of researchers, whose intention is to challenge the neoliberal attitude underpinning local policy makers and marketing consultants.

However, the second generation of critical voices provided their own novel contributions, most notably the use of more applied and empirical perspectives, which investigate an increasingly wider array of place-branding campaigns in different countries; combined with the emergence of new methodological approaches and research themes. We explore these in more detail below.

New empirical perspectives and 'situated' critique

Critical place-branding studies from the mid-2000s start adopting more varied practical observational lenses. Among others, urban design public management, communication, heritage management studies are new intriguing foci where the turbulent and uneven nature of place-branding processes is contextualized and discussed. For instance, Julier (2005) casts an alternative perspective toward design as a tricky tool for branding and urban regeneration, unmasking the elitist 'production of aesthetic consent' that underpins many so-called 'design cities'. Gibson (2005) underlines issues of class power and 'semiotic violence' that characterize the branding campaign promoting a new, vibrant and dynamic residential district in Washington DC. In a similar vein, Young, Diep and Drabble (2006) analyze how the myth of the 'cosmopolitan city' can, in actuality, be invoked as an instrumental discourse whereby real estate companies present residential districts to rich and sophisticated middle-class dwellers as reflecting a vibrant, but highly commodified, site of multiculturalism. Connections between place, catastrophes and tourism are sometimes drawn, Gotham (2007), for example, discusses how the post-Katrina rebranding strategy in New Orleans excluded the poor and homeless, focusing instead on an audience of affluent businessmen and firms. Pasquinelli (2010) shows how strong tourist brands, such as Tuscany can be two-sided coins, since the strong traditional tourist profile can lower the credibility of the place in the eyes of investors and venture capitalists. In other words, a plethora of more specific empirical problems emerge, such as the multidimensional nature and multi-stakeholder ownership of a regional brand. Slowly, but inexorably, this critical literature is beginning to exert influence on the agenda of marketing scholars and journals.

Refining the critical toolkit: research methods approaches and themes

The symbolic turn in the way place marketing is implemented and researched in the form of place branding brought with it a renewed interest for specific methodological approaches that give due recognition to the role played by language. Koller (2008), as a case in point, adopts Cognitive Critical Discourse Analysis (CDA) to study how citizen-consumers develop certain mental representations about themselves and the world when they engage with city brands created by municipalities. Defining place brands as "socio-cognitive representation[s] that fosters communication between" councils and citizens (Koller, 2008, p. 447), the author argues that, by instilling corporate brand values, the common use of city brands tends ultimately to promote "depoliticizing the polity" (p. 447).

Another language-focused methodological approach whereby place brands have been recently investigated is based on the identification of "interpretive repertoires" (Wetherell, 1998). Through this particular type of discourse analysis, Lucarelli and Giovanardi (2016) provide empirical accounts of the political (and polemic) nature of place-branding discourses produced by different regional brand stakeholders in the Italian tourist area of Romagna. Here, language-based instruments are used to identify tensions between public and private stakeholders and explore a 'politics of memory' at work within the regional branding process (Lucarelli & Giovanardi, 2016). Branding can, in fact, be considered as a way to channel tourists' and residents' attention toward specific interpretations of the past, which exclude others in the process of shaping the future development of the area (see Gotham, 2002).

Mainstream storytelling has been a popular device in general management scholarship (e.g., Boal & Schultz, 2007), used to assess the effectiveness of management and leadership processes. However, the narrative approach might also constitute an innovative tool through which critical scholars can deconstruct the contradictions inherent in the application of place branding as a place-management philosophy. By identifying two coexisting and parallel narratives that emerged within the Danish local community of Aalborg, Jensen (2007) draws on this approach to compare competing narratives and explicate how 'semiotic regimes' highlight certain cultural resources while excluding others. The narrative approach is particularly useful in understanding how place and identity are intertwined, as stories about place become stories about identity (McCabe & Stokoe, 2004).

Stories about places are constantly produced in various forms; from the arts, to mass media and popular culture, to marketing material (Hughes, 1998; Iwashita, 2006; Santos, 2004). Urry (1995) explored the influence of Romantic poetry on perceptions of the English countryside; not only in terms of meanings, but also in terms of shaping people's perceptions about how it should be appreciated. Marketing, of course, produces and circulates stories about different places, and tourists also generate and share their own stories (Bendix, 2002). Online communities, in particular, emerge as important spaces where people share personal stories and photographs of their experiences of different places (Jensen, 2008). Narratives of place can thus aid place marketers and scholars who should be encouraged to embrace and "celebrate the complex, kaleidoscopic nature" of places based on people's diverse experiences (Warnaby & Medway, 2013, p. 356) at the same time as they appreciate how particular powerful narratives shape individual stories. This involves a reflexive process that enables a closer look at how different forms of located subjectivity emerge within broader discourses about place. Narrative brings together the personal and the social; past, present and future; and place (see Clandinin & Connelly's (2000) three-dimensional narrative inquiry space).

For example, Aitken and Campelo (2011), focusing on the case of the Chatham Islands in New Zealand, examine the networks of relationships that constitute the community which are central to a sense of shared place ownership and identity. Drawing on local narratives of Santorini, Greece, Lichrou et al. (2014) reveal how the small island involves multiple senses of place, depending on the contexts in which locals experience their place. Local place meanings shift from Santorini as 'harsh beauty', to 'service business' and to 'home' (Lichrou et al., 2014). Trapp-Fallon (2003) focuses on memories of South Wales canals; these memories illustrate that canals were integrated into people's lives and help us understand how these were once central spaces of life and activity. Santos's (2004) research shows how newspaper travel articles are often powerful narratives that frame how readers understand Portugal.

Emphasis on cultural appropriation of city brands and the use of the 'circle of culture' (Johnson, 1987) as a heuristic device underpins a stream of literature that gives prominence to the "non-oppositional audiences of place marketing" (Colombino, 2009; Giovanardi, 2011).

While problematizing the lack of empirical engagement that affects some of the accounts put forward by traditional critical commentators, Colombino points out:

> [T]hese analyses are mainly the result of the interpretations offered by the academics authoring the research, and tend to neglect how residents themselves understand these representations (Burgess, 1990). Thus, we are not really sure how people engage with place-marketing images. Do they "read" into these representations the meanings that marketers inscribe?
>
> *(2009, p. 280)*

Consequently, rigorous ethnographic research must be emphasized as a crucial element of critical place-marketing scholarship (where appropriate). It can enable us to capture the multiple ways in which different stakeholders (e.g., citizens, business communities, and tourists) emotionally connect with place brands.

Innovation from within: the way forward

We have started to register and appreciate the multiple, overlapping views on the meanings and values of brand representations in place-marketing strategy and implementation. Two main factors have encouraged more critically informed reflection on place-marketing rationales and methodologies from within the marketing discipline. First, the influence of second generation place-marketing studies developed in our sister disciplines (e.g., tourism, public management), which have widened and sharpened the criticisms formulated against place marketing and branding. Moreover, collaboration between scholars from different backgrounds was facilitated in the last decade and alliances between scholars and practitioners (Kavaraztis, 2015) have led to significantly more holistic accounts of place-branding consultation approaches (Goulart Sztejnberg & Giovanardi, 2017) and place identity formation processes (Kavaratzis & Kalandides, 2015).

Second, developments in the critical marketing literature appear to have instilled a greater confidence within place-marketing and branding researchers in their efforts to question the taken-for-granted pillars of place marketing. Building from this point, an agenda for future research is proposed below.

One of the major themes we need to tackle is the further examination of the types of discourses that embed the brand in the place. This wide theme consists of several threads of investigation. On the one hand, it points to an examination of the means and ways in which place brands actually form, the manner in which the brand emerges and takes shape for different people at the same time and for the same person at different times. What factors affect this formation and what makes for the similarities and differences noted in the conceptualization of the brand of a specific place? A related line of investigation is the experience people have in a branded place and the potential differences and difficulties this creates for them. What does it mean to live in a city brand, how is that different from living anywhere else, does the brand help people bond emotionally to the place and what difference, if any, does it make for people's everyday lives or for their prospects? This will bring place-branding studies and knowledge closer to the individual and, therefore, closer to the perceptions and realities of those neglected from our empirical attention.

On the other hand, examining the discourses that embed the brand in the place means further examining the ways in which all kinds of authorities and interested parties attempt (and sometimes manage) to impose their own values and goals on these processes. While many of the critical studies mentioned above have dealt with this topic, there is a need to consolidate their findings and critique beyond narratives of single cities or single campaigns. This inevitably leads to the need to further problematize power relations not only in the realm of destination branding (Marzano & Scott, 2009) but also, more holistically, place branding. Perhaps it is worth noting here that this goes beyond the theoretical elaborations and critical reflections that sometimes dominate parts of the literature. While these are a valuable starting point, it is necessary to undertake the gruelling task of demonstrating the negative effects in a manner and a language that practitioners and politicians will comprehend. Place marketing and branding are inextricably intertwined with politics. As the literature shows, politics takes on several forms that influence both the content and the ways in which place brands are narrated. On the one hand there is the political economy of place marketing to consider (e.g., Anttiroiko, 2014). At the same time, there are the ever-present micro and meso politics to consider, namely personal re-election tactics, party lines, the financing of campaigns and interests rooted in specific real estate, media or other investments.

Another theme of elaboration is the growing understanding of the place brand (what it is and what it can do) as well as the changing roles of the people who are supposed to develop or promote it. Giovanardi *et al.* (2013, p. 368) claim that "place branding should be understood as a relationship-builder"; as "an active interface between the place and its actors". This is an attractive idea that demands examination as it has the potential to incorporate more critical understandings of the concept of the brand and, therefore, clarify it. On a related note, recent literature encourages us to think beyond branding as 'brand management' and toward branding as 'brand facilitation' or 'negotiation'. If politicians and other brand leaders are not 'managers' but 'facilitators', what does that mean for their role and how does it work in practice? Which, of course, leads to the next important question that has to do with stakeholder relationships. What are stakeholder engagement and stakeholder empowerment in the context of place marketing and how do these become meaningful in practice?

Useful signposts have been offered by Vanolo (2017) in the suggestion to think of the 'right to the brand' (based on Lefebvre's idea of the 'right to the city'). Vanolo highlights the need to examine how inhabitants and other city users can be empowered and suggests that we consider the city brand as an urban commons, meaning as "a common immaterial object, and hence a property of people" (Vanolo, 2017, p. 136). If the desirability of civic participation and bottom-up approaches to the place-branding/marketing process are not a taboo (Aitken & Campelo, 2011), an exploration of the particular obstacles hindering civic engagement in place brands should be a priority for researchers (Insch & Stuart, 2015). Further, given the specificities of and contradictions of branding as a "cognitive dimension of policy making" (Bellini, 2004), the traditional tools and protocols of participatory planning might not necessarily be applied in a straightforward manner. Thus, more attention is needed to fine-tune participatory approaches for the sake of branding cities, regions and nations in a way that can, at least to some extent, be truly defined as inclusive (see Jernsand, 2017).

We believe that significant potential might be found in the idea of inclusive place branding. The many theoretical reflections and propositions as well as practical examples included in Kavaratzis *et al.* (2018) are testimony to the value of socially responsible, participatory approaches. More importantly, they provide evidence that the years of critical reflections and fierce argumentation against the politics, tactics and ideology of place marketing have been fertile, producing alternative solutions. These, of course, need to be tested and further criticized but, at the moment, a little light can be seen at the end of the tunnel.

References

Aitken, R., & Campelo, A. (2011). The four Rs of place branding. *Journal of Marketing Management*, 27(9–10), 913–933.
Amin, A., & Thrift, N. (2002). *Cities: Reimagining the urban*. London, Polity Press.
Anttiroiko, A.V. (2014). *The political economy of city branding*. London, Routledge.
Ashworth, G.J., & Voogd, H. (1990a). Can places be sold for tourism? In G. Ashworth & B. Goodall (Eds.), *Marketing tourism places* (pp. 1–16). London, Routledge.
Ashworth, G.J., & Voogd, H. (1990b). *Selling the city: Marketing approaches in public sector urban planning*. London, Belhaven Press.
Ashworth, G.J., & Voogd, H. (1994). Marketing and place promotion. In J.R. Gold & S.W. Ward (Eds.), *Place promotion, the use of publicity and marketing to sell towns and regions* (pp. 39–52). Chichester, John Wiley & Sons.
Aubert-Gamet, V., & Cova, B. (1999). Servicescapes: From modern non-places to postmodern common places. *Journal of Business Research*, 44(1), 37–45.
Barke, M. (1999). City marketing as a planning tool. In M. Pacione (Ed.), *Applied geography: Principles and practice* (pp. 486–496). London, Routledge.
Barke, M., & Harrop, K. (1994). Selling the industrial town: Identity, image and illusion. In J.R. Gold & S.V. Ward (Eds.), *Place promotion* (pp. 93–114). Chichester, UK, John Wiley & Sons.
Bellini, N. (2004). Territorial governance and area image. *Symphonya*, 1. Retrieved July 19, 2018 from www.unimib.it/upload/Not%20Area%20Bellini_Symphonya%202005-draft01-rev.pdf
Bendix, R. (2002). Capitalising on memories past, present, and future: Observations on the intertwining of tourism and narration. *Anthropological Theory*, 2(4), 469–487.
Boal, K.B., & Schultz, P.L. (2007). Storytelling, time, and evolution: The role of strategic leadership in complex adaptive systems. *The Leadership Quarterly*, 18(4), 411–428.
Broudehoux, A.M. (2001). Image making, city marketing and the aestheticization of social inequality in Rio de Janeiro. In N. Alsayyad (Ed.), *Consuming tradition, manufacturing heritage* (pp. 273–297). London, Routledge.
Buhalis, D. (2000). Marketing the competitive destination of the future. *Tourism Management*, 21(1), 97–116.
Clandinin, D.J., & Connelly, F.M. (2000). *Narrative inquiry: Experience and story in qualitative research*. San Francisco, Jossey-Bass Publishers.
Colomb, C. (2012). Pushing the urban frontier: Temporary uses of space, city marketing, and the creative city discourse in 2000s Berlin. *Journal of Urban Affairs*, 34(2), 131–152.
Colomb, C., & Kalandides, A. (2010). The 'be Berlin' campaign: Old wine in new bottles or innovative form of participatory place branding? In G. Ashworth & M. Kavaratzis (Eds.), *Towards effective place brand management: Branding European cities and regions* (pp. 173–190). London, Edward Elgar.
Colombino, A. (2009). Multiculturalism and time in Trieste: Place-marketing images and residents' perceptions of a multicultural city. *Social & Cultural Geography*, 10(3), 279–297.
Cox, K.R. (1995). Globalisation, competition and the politics of local economic development. *Urban Studies*, 32(2), 213–224.
De Chernatony, L., & Dall'Olmo Riley, F. (1998). Defining a 'brand': Beyond the literature with experts' interpretations. *Journal of Marketing Management*, 14(5), 417–443.
Eshuis, J., & Klijn, E.H. (2012). *Branding in governance and public management*. London, Routledge.
Fırat, A.F., & Dholakia, N. (2006). Theoretical and philosophical implications of postmodern debates: Some challenges to modern marketing. *Marketing Theory*, 6(2), 123–162.
Fırat, A.F., & Venkatesh, A. (1995). Liberatory postmodernism and the reenchantment of consumption. *Journal of Consumer Research*, 22(3), 239–267.
Framke, W. (2002). The destination as a concept: A discussion of the business-related perspective versus the socio-cultural approach in tourism theory. *Scandinavian Journal of Hospitality and Tourism*, 2(2), 92–108.
Gibson, T.A. (2005). Selling city living: Urban branding campaigns, class power and the civic good. *International Journal of Cultural Studies*, 8(3), 259–280.
Giovanardi, M. (2011). Producing and consuming the painter Raphael's birthplace. *Journal of Place Management and Development*, 4(1), 53–66.
Giovanardi, M., Lucarelli, A., & Pasquinelli, C. (2013). Towards brand ecology: An analytical semiotic framework for interpreting the emergence of place brands. *Marketing Theory*, 13(3), 365–383.

Gold, R.J., & Ward, V.S. (Eds.) (1994). *Place promotion, the use of publicity and marketing to sell towns and regions.* Chichester, Wiley & Sons.

Goodwin, M. (1993). The city as commodity: The contested spaces of urban development. In G. Kearns & C. Philo (Eds.), *Selling places: The city as cultural capital, past and present* (pp. 145–162). Oxford, Pergamon Press.

Gotham, K.F. (2002). Marketing Mardi Gras: Commodification, spectacle and the political economy of tourism in New Orleans. *Urban Studies, 39*(10), 1735–1756.

Gotham, K.F. (2007). (Re)branding the big easy tourism: Rebuilding in post-Katrina New Orleans. *Urban Affairs Review, 42*(6), 823–850.

Goulart Sztejnberg, R., & Giovanardi, M. (2017). The ambiguity of place branding consultancy: Working with stakeholders in Rio de Janeiro. *Journal of Marketing Management, 33*(5–6), 421–445.

Greenbaum, R.S., Logan, J.R., & Molotch, H.L. (1988). *Urban fortunes: The political economy of place.* Berkeley, University of California Press.

Greenberg, M. (2009). *Branding New York: How a city in crisis was sold to the world.* London, Routledge.

Greenwood, D.J. (1978). Culture by the pound: An anthropological perspective on tourism as cultural commoditization. In V.L. Smith (Ed.), *Hosts and guests: The anthropology of tourism* (pp. 37–52). Oxford, Blackwell.

Griffiths, R. (1998). Making sameness: Place marketing and the new urban entrepreneurialism. In N. Oatley (Ed.), *Cities, economic competition and urban policy.* Paul Chapman Publishing, London, UK.

Grönroos, C. (2006). Adopting a service logic for marketing. *Marketing Theory, 6*(3), 317–333.

Hall, T. (1998). Introduction to part I. In T. Hall & P. Hubbard (Eds.), *The entrepreneurial city: Geographies of politics, regime and representation* (pp. 27–30). Chichester, UK, John Wiley & Sons.

Hankinson, G. (2010). Place branding research: A cross-disciplinary agenda and the views of practitioners. *Place Branding and Public Diplomacy, 6*(4), 300–315.

Harvey, D. (1989a). From managerialism to entrepreneurialism: The transformation in urban governance in late capitalism. *Geografiska Annaler, 71*(1), 3–17.

Harvey, D. (1989b). *The condition of postmodernity.* Oxford, Blackwell.

Hatch, M.J., & Schultz, M. (2002). The dynamics of organizational identity. *Human Relations, 55*(8), 989–1018.

Hill, D. (2014). Regenerating Southwark: Urban renewal prompts social cleansing fears. Retrieved June 28, 2018 from www.theguardian.com/society/2014/oct/07/southwark-london-regeneration-urban-renewal-social-cleansing-fears

Holcomb, B. (1994). City make-overs: Marketing the post-industrial city. In J.R. Gold & S.V. Ward (Eds.), *Place promotion* (pp. 115–131). Chichester, John Wiley and Sons.

Holcomb, B. (1999). Marketing cities for tourism. In D.R. Judd & S.S. Fainstein (Eds.), *The tourist city* (pp. 54–70). New Haven and London, Yale University Press.

Holloway, L., & Hubbard, P. (2001). *People and place: The extraordinary geographies of everyday life.* London, Routledge.

Hubbard, P. (1996). Urban design and city regeneration: Social representations of entrepreneurial landscapes. *Urban Studies, 33*(8), 1441–1461.

Hughes, G. (1998). Tourism and the semiological realisation of space. In G. Ringer (Ed.), *Destinations: Cultural landscapes of tourism* (pp. 17–32). London, Routledge.

Human, B. (1999). Kodachrome icons: Photography, place and the theft of identity. *International Journal of Contemporary Hospitality Management, 11*(2/3), 80–84.

Insch, A., & Stuart, M. (2015). Understanding resident city brand disengagement. *Journal of Place Management and Development, 8*(3), 172–186.

Iwashita, C. (2006). Media representation of the UK as a destination for Japanese tourists: Popular culture and tourism. *Tourist Studies, 6*(1), 59–77.

Jensen, J.L. (2008). Virtual tourist: Knowledge communication in an online travel community. *International Journal of Web Based Communities, 4*(4), 503–522.

Jensen, O.B. (2007). Culture stories: Understanding cultural urban branding. *Planning Theory, 6*(3), 211–236.

Jernsand, E.M. (2017). *Inclusive place branding: What it is and how to progress towards it.* Unpublished Doctoral Thesis, University of Gothenburg.

Jessop, B. (1998). The narrative of enterprise and the enterprise of narrative: Place marketing and the entrepreneurial city. In T. Hall & P. Hubbard (Eds.), *The entrepreneurial city: Geographies of politics, regime and representation* (pp. 77–99). Chichester, UK, John Wiley & Sons.

Johansson, M. (2012). Place branding and the imaginary: The politics of re-imagining a garden city. *Urban Studies*, 49(16), 3611–3626.

Johnson, R. (1987). What is cultural studies, anyway? *Social Text*, 6(1), 38–80.

Julier, G. (2005). Urban designscapes and the production of aesthetic consent. *Urban Studies*, 42(5–6), 869–887.

Kaneva, N. (2011). Nation branding: Toward an agenda for critical research. *International Journal of Communication*, 5, 117–141.

Kavaratzis, M. (2004). From city marketing to city branding: Towards a theoretical framework for developing city brands. *Place Branding*, 1(1), 58–73.

Kavaratzis, M. (2005). Place branding: A review of trends and conceptual models. *The Marketing Review*, 5(4), 329–342.

Kavaratzis, M. (2007). City marketing: The past, the present and some unresolved issues. *Geography Compass*, 1(3), 695–712.

Kavaratzis, M. (2015). Place branding scholars and practitioners: 'strangers in the night'? *Journal of Place Management and Development*, 8(3), 266–270.

Kavaratzis, M., & Ashworth, G.J. (2007). Partners in coffeeshops, canals and commerce: Marketing the city of Amsterdam. *Cities*, 24(1), 16–25.

Kavaratzis, M., & Hatch, M.J. (2013). The dynamics of place brands: An identity-based approach to place branding theory. *Marketing Theory*, 13(1), 69–86.

Kavaratzis, M., & Kalandides, A. (2015). Rethinking the place brand: The interactive formation of place brands and the role of participatory place branding. *Environment and Planning A*, 47(6), 1368–1382.

Kavaratzis, M., Lichrou, M., & Giovanardi, M. (2018). *Inclusive placed branding: Critical perspectives in theory and practice*. London, Routledge.

Kerr, G. (2006). From destination brand to location brand. *Journal of Brand Management*, 13(4–5), 276–283.

Klein, N. (2000). *No logo*. London, Flamingo.

Klein, N. (2007). *The shock doctrine: The rise of disaster capitalism*. London, Macmillan.

Koller, V. (2008). 'The world in one city': Semiotic and cognitive aspects of city branding. *Journal of Language and Politics*, 7(3), 431–450.

Kotler, P. (1972). A generic concept of marketing. *Journal of Marketing*, 36(2), 46–54.

Kotler, P. (1979). Strategies for introducing marketing into nonprofit organizations. *Journal of Marketing*, 43(1), 37–44.

Kotler, P., & Levy, S.J. (1969). Broadening the concept of marketing. *Journal of Marketing*, 33(1), 1–15.

Kotler, P., & Zaltman, G. (1971). Social marketing: An approach to planned social change. *Journal of Marketing*, 35(3), 3–12.

Kotler, P., Haider, D., & Rein, I. (1993). *Marketing places: Attracting investment, industry, and tourism to cities, states, and nations*. London, Simon & Schuster.

Kotler, P., Bowen, J., & Makens, J. (1996). *Marketing for hospitality and tourism*. Upper Saddle River, NJ, Prentice-Hall.

Kotler, P., Asplund, C., Rein, I., & Heider, D. (1999). *Marketing places in Europe: Attracting investments, industries, residents and visitors to European cities, communities, regions and nations*. Harlow, Financial Times Prentice-Hall.

Lash, S., & Urry, J. (1994). *Economies of signs and space*. London, Sage.

Lichrou, M., O'Malley, L., & Patterson, M. (2008). Place product or place narrative(s)? Perspectives in the marketing of tourism destinations. *Journal of Strategic Marketing*, 16(1), 27–39.

Lichrou, M., O'Malley, L., & Patterson, M. (2014). On the marketing implications of place narratives. *Journal of Marketing Management*, 30(9–10), 832–856.

Lucarelli, A. (2012). Unraveling the complexity of 'city brand equity': A three-dimensional framework. *Journal of Place Management and Development*, 5(3), 231–252.

Lucarelli, A., & Giovanardi, M. (2016). The political nature of brand governance: A discourse analysis approach to a regional brand building process. *Journal of Public Affairs*, 16(1), 16–27.

Marzano, G., & Scott, N. (2009). Power in destination branding. *Annals of Tourism Research*, 36(2), 247–267.

Mattelart, A. (1994). *Mapping world communication: War, progress, culture*. Amherst, University of Minnesota Press.

McCabe, S., & Stokoe, E.H. (2004). Place identity in tourist accounts. *Annals of Tourism Research*, 31(3), 601–622.

Meethan, K. (1996). Consuming (in) the civilised city. *Annals of Tourism Research*, 23(2), 322–340.

Meethan, K. (2001). *Tourism in global society: Place, culture, consumption*. New York, Palgrave.
Miles, S. (2010). *Spaces for consumption*. London, Sage Publications.
Minton, A. (2017). *Big capital: Who is London for?* United Kingdom, Penguin.
Molotch, H. (1976). The city as a growth machine. *American Journal of Sociology*, *82*(2), 309–330.
Morgan, N., & Pritchard, A. (1998). *Tourism promotion and power: Creating images, creating identities*. Chichester, John Wiley & Sons.
Murphy, P., Pritchard, M.P., & Smith, B. (2000). The destination product and its impact on traveller perceptions. *Tourism Management*, *21*(1), 43–52.
O'Malley, L., & Patterson, M. (1998). Vanishing point: The mix management paradigm re-viewed. *Journal of Marketing Management*, *14*(8), 829–851.
Paddison, R. (1993). City marketing, image reconstruction and urban regeneration. *Urban Studies*, *30*(2), 339–349.
Papadopoulos, N. (2004). Place branding: Evolution, meaning and implications. *Place Branding*, *1*(1), 36–49.
Papadopoulos, N., el Banna, A., Murphy, S.A., & Rojas-Méndez, J.I. (2011). Place brands and brand-place associations: The role of 'place' in international marketing. In C.J. Subhash & D.A. Griffith (Eds.), *Handbook of research in international marketing* (pp. 88–113). Cheltenham, Edward Elgar.
Parker, C., Roper, S., & Medway, D. (2015). Back to basics in the marketing of place: The impact of litter upon place attitudes. *Journal of Marketing Management*, *31*(9–10), 1090–1112.
Pasquinelli, C. (2010). The limits of place branding for local development: The case of Tuscany and the Arnovalley brand. *Local Economy*, *25*(7), 558–572.
Peck, J., & Tickell, A. (2002). Neoliberalizing space. *Antipode*, *34*(3), 380–404.
Peck, J., Theodore, N., & Brenner, N. (2009). Neoliberal urbanism: Models, moments, mutations. *SAIS Review of International Affairs*, *29*(1), 49–66.
Philo, C., & Kearns, G. (Eds.) (1993). *Selling places: The city as cultural capital, past and present*. London, Pergamon Press.
Pike, A., & Pollard, J. (2010). Economic geographies of financialization. *Economic Geography*, *86*(1), 29–51.
Rainisto, S.K. (2003). *Success factors of place marketing: A study of place marketing practices in Northern Europe and the United States*. Helsinki University of Technology.
Richards, G., & Wilson, J. (2006). Developing creativity in tourist experiences: A solution to the serial reproduction of culture? *Tourism Management*, *27*(6), 1209–1223.
Saarinen, J. (1998). The social construction of tourist destinations: The process of transformation of the Saariselkä tourism region in Finnish Lapland. In G. Ringer (Ed.) *Destinations: Cultural landscapes of tourism* (pp. 154–173). London, Routledge.
Santos, C.A. (2004). Framing Portugal: Representational dynamics. *Annals of Tourism Research*, *31*(1), 122–138.
Simoes, C., & Dibb, S. (2001). Rethinking the brand concept: New brand orientation. *Corporate Communications: An International Journal*, *6*(4), 217–224.
Sleipen, W. (1988). *Marketing van de Historische Omgeving*. Breda, Research Institute for Tourism.
Stokowski, P.A. (2002). Language of place and discourses of power: Constructing new senses of place. *Journal of Leisure Research*, *34*(4), 368–382.
Trapp-Fallon, J.M. (2003). Searching for rich narratives of tourism and leisure experience: How oral history could provide an answer. *Tourism and Hospitality Research*, *4*(4), 297–305.
Turok, I. (2009). The distinctive city: Pitfalls in the pursuit of differential advantage. *Environment and Planning A*, *41*(1), 13–30.
Urry, J. (1990) *The tourist gaze*. London, Sage Publications.
Urry, J. (1995) *Consuming places*. London, Routledge.
Vanolo, A. (2017). *City branding: The ghostly politics of representation in globalising cities*. New York and London, Taylor & Francis.
Vargo, S.L., & Lusch, R.F. (2004). Evolving to a new dominant logic for marketing. *Journal of Marketing*, *68*(1), 1–17.
Voase, R. (1999). 'Consuming' tourist sites/sights: A note on York. *Leisure Studies*, *18*(4), 289–296.
Vuignier, R. (2017). Place branding & place marketing 1976–2016: A multidisciplinary literature review. *International Review on Public and Nonprofit Marketing*, *14*(4), 1–27.
Wainwright, O. (2014). The truth about property developers: How they are exploiting planning authorities and ruining our cities. Retrieved June 28, 2018 from www.theguardian.com/cities/2014/sep/17/truth-property-developers-builders-exploit-planning-cities

Ward, S.V. (1998). *Selling places: The marketing and promotion of towns and cities, 1850–2000*. London, Taylor & Francis.

Warnaby, G. (2009). Towards a service-dominant place marketing logic. *Marketing Theory, 9*(4), 403–423.

Warnaby, G., & Medway, D. (2013). What about the 'place' in place marketing? *Marketing Theory, 13*(3), 345–363.

Warnaby, G., Medway, D., & Bennison, D. (2010). Notions of materiality and linearity: The challenges of marketing the Hadrian's Wall place 'product'. *Environment and Planning A, 42*(6), 1365–1382.

Wetherell, M. (1998). Positioning and interpretative repertoires: Conversation analysis and post-structuralism in dialogue. *Discourse & Society, 9*(3), 387–412.

Young, C., Diep, M., & Drabble, S. (2006). Living with difference? The 'cosmopolitan city' and urban reimaging in Manchester, UK. *Urban Studies, 43*(10), 1687–1714.

Zavattaro, S.M. (2010). Municipalities as public relations and marketing firms. *Administrative Theory & Praxis, 32*(2), 191–211.

8
CRITICAL ARTS MARKETING

Gretchen Larsen and Finola Kerrigan

Introduction

Business art is the step that comes after Art. I started as a commercial artist, and I want to finish as a business artist. After I did the thing called "art" or whatever it's called, I went into business art. I wanted to be an Art Businessman or a Business Artist. Being good in business is the most fascinating kind of art. During the hippies era people put down the idea of business – they'd say "Money is bad", and "Working is bad", but making money is art and working is art and good business is the best art.

Andy Warhol, 1975, p. 92

The intersection of the arts and the market has long been filled with tensions; where the stereotype of the bohemian artist who creates 'arts for art's sake' is often juxtaposed against the 'sell-out', who succumbs to "the base materiality of utility, commerce and profit" of the market (Davies & Sigthorsson, 2013, p. 22). As highlighted in the opening quote by the (now) critically renowned and commercially successful pop-artist, Andy Warhol, the relationship between the arts and the market is far from simple, and can in fact be intimately co-constitutive. Located at this same intersection, the discipline of arts marketing is complex, nuanced and, we argue, requires an inherently critical approach. Many of the issues of interest in arts marketing are rooted in the critiques of capitalism offered by critical social theory, particularly that of the Frankfurt School (as outlined in this chapter). Thus, not only has arts marketing facilitated functional and ethical critiques (Hackley, 2009) of mainstream marketing thought, but thinking about marketing through the arts has contributed to the development of critical marketing scholarship which, as defined by Tadajewski (2010), draws upon critical theory traditions to explore marketplace power relations. While arts marketing scholarship has not always followed a critical path, this chapter argues that a critical approach to arts marketing is necessary and results in a richer and more insightful understanding of the arts/marketing relationship.

Arts marketing is a relatively young area of marketing theory and practice (O'Reilly, Rentschler, & Kirchner, 2013), originating primarily in North America in the late 1970s (Fillis, 2011). Influenced by the broadening movement in marketing initiated by Kotler and Levy (1969) which sought to transfer traditional marketing principles and practices to 'nonbusiness' organizations, much early arts marketing scholarship adheres to what O'Reilly (2011, p. 26) calls the narrow view: "a discourse about the marketing management of artistic organizations and offerings". From this perspective, arts marketing is primarily treated as another context into which general marketing principles can be transposed and adapted. A standard definition of arts marketing in this vein is provided by Hill, O'Sullivan, and O'Sullivan (2003, p. 1): "arts marketing is an integrated management process which seeks mutually satisfying exchange relationships with customers as the route to achieving organisational and artistic objectives". While this definition might read as a simple transfer of general marketing principles to an arts context, the inclusion of artistic, alongside organizational objectives as the goal, indicates that marketing the arts is different from marketing traditional products. Hirschman (1983) argued that artists are product-centred marketers who place higher value on their own internal needs and fellow artists' opinions and often ignore the needs and wants of a larger audience. Thus, 'arts marketing' offered an early functional critique (Hackley, 2009) of the marketing concept approach to marketing, which Hirschman (1983) believed was not applicable to artists. In arts marketing, there is a need to reconcile the inherent tension of giving customers what they want with the artists' need to find an outlet for creative expression. The role of marketing is therefore to match the artists' creations with an appropriate audience, and this helped shift marketing thought toward a relationship marketing approach.

In recent years, there has been a move away from reductive, overly simplistic definitions that simply insert 'arts' into existing definitions of marketing, to definitions that better capture the complex character of arts marketing. This is in part due to the recognition of the wide and complex scope of the arts that goes beyond traditional distinctions of high and low art, to encompass a broad range of artistic and cultural offerings. Thus, 'the arts' reflect systems of production, dissemination, and consumption of cultural messages through their products and services (O'Reilly et al., 2013). It can also be seen as part of what Brownlie and Hewer (2007) refer to as the attempt to "foster sceptical reflexivity" (p. 45) within marketing theorizing which requires acknowledgement of the "status panic" (p. 50) that occupies a dual role in critical arts marketing. For arts marketing theorists, such status panic can be multifaceted. First, following Brownlie and Hewer (2007), we acknowledge the positioning of marketing theory as inferior in the broader social sciences by those both within and outside of the marketing academy. Equally, marketing practice within the arts has been viewed as inferior in value in comparison to the creation, staging, or critiquing of artistic work. Therefore, theorists within arts marketing must tackle the conceptualization of their home discipline within the broader social sciences, as one that is theoretically weak, alongside a practice of arts marketing within organizations which is seen as inferior to the creative roles of director, producer or performer. In highlighting marketing theorists' status panic, Brownlie and Hewer (2007) note that it is in the study of the consumer that the critical project is most apparent as consumers seek "social spaces in which they produce their own culture" (p. 56). This brings us to the arts versus entertainment distinction which is central to drawing the (unstable, unacknowledged and ever shifting) line between arts marketing and critical arts marketing. Critical arts marketing as theorizing cannot be separated from a critical treatment of the arts. Those attempting to critically engage with arts marketing have necessitated the development of definitions of arts marketing that show awareness of the wider social and political nature of the arts. In an effort to capture the dimensions of music marketing, O'Reilly, Larsen, and Kubacki (2014, p. 19) offer a definition that is equally applicable to arts marketing as a whole, as we can see if we replace 'music' with 'arts': "[Arts] marketing is the set of historically situated, social, commercial, cultural, technological and [artistic] production, performance, intermediation and consumption practices and discourses which create [artistic] and other value in the [arts] exchange relationship." This is an inherently critical position, as it moves the field beyond a focus on managerial and organization-level processes, and enables a more nuanced understanding of the complex and varied relationships, practices and discourses that emerge at the intersection of arts and the market.

A critical arts marketing begins with the conceptualization of arts marketing as a cultural practice located at the nexus of the arts, society and the market. As a cultural practice, the arts can, and often do, encompass radical demands for social transformation, but they are also subject to co-optation by the very systems they seek to critique. Thus, the arts can simultaneously challenge and reinforce the status-quo (see Said, 1994). Nowhere is this ideological tension more apparent than at the confluence of the arts and the market, where we observe the commercialization and managerialization of the arts, alongside critical reflections of such practices in the effort to rethink and rework human-social relationships. As such, this is also a position where many critical discussions of marketing theory and practice have been located, such as the longstanding debate of whether marketing should be considered as an art or a science (e.g. Sheth, Gardner, & Garrett, 1988).

Brown and Patterson (2000) convincingly make the case that marketers must learn from artists or aesthetic methods in understanding and communicating marketing. In classifying marketing scholarship which has engaged with art into 'the art school', 'the aesthetics school' and the 'Avant-Garde school', they identify the breadth of research into, about, and through art that has gained purchase within the marketing community. Similarly, the consideration of art as a product, laid the foundation for the breaking down of the production-consumption nexus which has long underpinned marketing scholarship. Venkatesh and Meamber (2006) suggest that arts transcend the nexus due to the phenomenon of cultural production which involves the interaction and collaboration of cultural producers, intermediaries and consumers. As Attali (1977/1985, p. 9) argues, art simultaneously provides "joy for the creator, use-value for the consumer and exchange value for the seller". Thus, Bradshaw (2010, p. 10) argues, "art can be thought of as a social model in which consumption and production co-exist and are mutually constitutive". With the arrival of digital technologies, the collapsing nexus is obvious in such activities as the scanlation of manga by fans (Lee, 2012) whereby consumers find ways around the failure of the market to give them access to cultural products, not in order to overturn the market, but rather to fill the gaps in provision until the market can catch up. O'Reilly and Kerrigan (2010) call for a recognition of the different facets of the relationship between art and the market that emanate from Bradshaw's (2010) review of arts marketing: the marketing *of* art, marketing *in* art, marketing *through* art, marketing *from* art, and marketing *as* art.

In addition to providing an overview of the field in this chapter, we also tease out the role and influence of arts marketing in the conceptualization and development of critical marketing. We do this by unpacking the double helix of the 'critical in arts marketing' and the 'arts in critical marketing' throughout the chapter. What is important in any review of (critical) arts marketing, is that the foundational literature is positioned as such. Our account of the development of arts marketing will indicate the roots in political, social and cultural theory and acknowledges the debt of gratitude owed to early pioneers in marketing and consumer research concerned with art and aesthetics. Thus, the chapter proceeds with a brief historical overview of the development of arts marketing theory and practice, which highlights the key themes that have emerged with regard to this double helix. Current key areas of research that emerge from this disciplinary foundation, both building on existing themes and developing new and fruitful lines of enquiry, are then identified. An up-to-date critical review of the literature is presented, which calls attention to the following current issues: (1) the arts versus markets debate; (2) creativity at the cutting edge of marketing practice; (3) the cultural practice and theory of branding; (4) the creation and formation of alternative markets; and (5) creative methods of enquiry in marketing research. The chapter concludes with suggestions and directions for future research, which seek to build and expand upon the existing body of knowledge in arts marketing.

The development of arts marketing theory and practice

As noted above, arts marketing as a field is a recent development, however, the arts marketing intersection has long been of interest to social theorists. The broader and more critical conceptualization of arts marketing enables the field to reconnect with the work of Adorno, Horkheimer, and the Frankfurt School, whose early criticisms of market capitalism were concerned with the conditions governing engagement with the arts and the impact of market systems and ideologies on aesthetic taste. While Adorno and Horkheimer were by no means arts marketers, their work on the culture industry (Adorno & Horkheimer, 1944/1972) highlights key challenges faced within arts marketing. Their work critically engaged with the idea of popular culture produced through industrialized production processes and sold to the masses. Here the culture industry is seen as a way of distracting the masses and shaping consciousness. What their work points to is the important distinction between 'the arts' and 'entertainment'. Entertainment is rarely seen as anything other than a distraction, something to allay boredom, while the arts are usually treated as more rarefied pastimes. Adorno and Horkheimer (1944/1972) were reflecting a move from arts to entertainment but it is important to interrogate this distinction. For Horkheimer and Adorno (1944/1972), culture and the economy were intertwined and an art/market distinction was impossible. What this means is that making a distinction between arts and entertainment was also impossible. However, an examination of debates around the role of public support for the arts, illustrates that such an intertwining, while evident, does not necessitate that market logic influences all artistic decisions. If this were the case, the justification of public funding for the arts would be absent.

In this regard it is interesting to consider Shukaitis (2008) who highlights the relevance of the arts in transmitting voices of resistance and inspiring resistance. Drawing on Deleuze and Guattari's (1986) idea of 'minor literature' and the subsequent development of the concept of 'minor politics' by Thoburn (2003), Shukaitis (2008) indicates the historical use of art (music, performance and so on) in political struggles. In doing so, he recognizes that while Deleuze and Guattari's (1986) idea of deterritorialization of language can result in the use of existing cultural artefacts to transmit politically motivated messages, such deterritorialization can go in multiple directions. The acknowledgement that art forms are fluid and can be reconceptualized by those engaging with them, requires a critical approach to understanding arts marketing that recognizes the political motivation underlying an arts marketing intervention.

For the Situationists such as Debord and Vaneigem, this fluidity also connects to the art/market interface. Debord (1973/2005, p. 7) notes the increase in prominence of 'the spectacle' over unified presentations of society, where the spectacle "is not a collection of images; it is a social relation between people that is mediated by images". As the arts can be viewed both as central to processes of image production as well as sites for the consumption of the image, a critical approach to arts marketing is crucial in order to understand the significance of the arts in society more broadly. Linked to ideas of the spectacle is Walter Benjamin's work on art in the age of mechanical reproduction, where Benjamin (1968/1999, p. 215) notes (among other things) the removal of a work of art from its "domain of tradition". Here Benjamin (1968/1999) means that the context within which the work was produced might not be that within which it is consumed. This echoes Shukaitis' (2008) point on fluidity of meanings and Deleuze and Guattari's (1986) on deterritorialization. A critical approach to arts marketing requires both an acknowledgement of the historical context from which the art work derives, as well as recognition that meaning attached to art through production and consumption is fluid.

While, in theory, it is possible to make a distinction between art and entertainment, positioning practices of production or consumption along a continuum from entertainment to art would be very challenging in practice. And while Bourdieu's (1979/1984) work was based on very specific classifications of high and low art, many contemporary theorists accept a convergence has occurred, not least in terms of audiences (Hand, 2011). Holbrook (1980) highlighted that consumers have aesthetic responses to both high and low arts. However, this move away from a more elitist view of the arts may be seen as coinciding with the move to viewing audiences as consumers, which is more than a semantic labelling. Similar to the Frankfurt School's critiques, the emerging field of cultural studies also pointed to the consumerist turn in the arts. As Kotler and Levy (1969) were busy broadening the field of marketing, in the UK, Williams (1976) and his colleagues in the Birmingham School of Cultural Studies, were challenging the extension of consumerism into what were previously seen as non-commercial fields such as the arts. The traditional art versus market debate rests on assumptions about the need to satisfy consumer desires (Major, 2014) which implies that market logic leads artistic decision making. This point requires a critical reflection among arts marketing scholars, many of whose work seeks to liberate arts marketing from a straitjacket of market logic. The art world combines both public and private sector rules of engagement, where many arts are funded and validated through a range of activities by public (museums, public universities and art schools, national art prizes) and private sector organizations (private collectors, private galleries) (see Rodner & Thomson, 2013). This public/private interplay has to some degree protected the arts from fully embracing market logic and, by extension, allowing (some) arts marketing scholars to challenge the application of the logic of the market and consumer centric marketing practices to the arts on the basis of the claim that art is for the social good and thus should be publicly provided. This is reflected in O'Sullivan's (2014, p. 30) statement that "arts marketers, like the artists whose work they promote, tend to be driven by a sense of mission".

The work of Pierre Bourdieu has also been foundational for those researching arts marketing and consumption. Bourdieu's (1979/1984) concepts of social, cultural, and symbolic capital shed light on the tensions in arts marketing. Social capital from a Bourdieuean perspective can be defined as the network of those to whom you are connected, with a distinction made between types of people known on the basis of social power and position. Social capital is developed through family links as well as links made in education and career. Cultural capital relates to what you know, which for Bourdieu, was transmitted through the family and supported by education, and manifested in pastimes, interests and other types of consumption. Bourdieu was particularly interested in how cultural capital located people within a particular social class. These forms of capital lead to symbolic capital, where certain types of knowledge are valued within a certain social group. Finally, economic capital unsurprisingly relates to access to material wealth and property. For Bourdieu, social, cultural and symbolic capital are closely related to possession of and access to economic capital. Bourdieu's work, based on data from the 1960s, illustrated that cultural consumption is closely linked to social class and the possession of social and economic capital. This work has underpinned much of the subsequent study of arts consumption.

Hand (2011) among others has shown how such distinctions between social classes regarding their consumption of specific arts has broken down in contemporary society, thus we should interpret arts policy and practice through a critical social lens. The traditionally conceived 'high arts' such as opera, ballet and classical European music have been positioned as arts for the privileged classes, while popular music, cinema and forms of street art and dance are seen as being for the masses. This polarization necessitates both a critical interrogation in terms of both the cyclical nature of such assumptions and the contemporary convergence between art forms.

Fraser and Fraser (2014) look at the history of opera as an art form and the connection to the nobility and royalty which came from the persistent need to gain financial subsidy in order to mount the extravagant performances. In keeping with Bourdieu's work, they note the importance of education in exposing younger audiences to opera and facilitating the development of the required cultural capital to engage with it. This reliance on learned cultural codes in order to engage with art was a central element of Bourdieu's (1979/1984) work and challenged the dominance of Kantian views of cultural consumption.

Kant's *Critique of Judgement* (1790/2009) presented a view of arts appreciation where artists were seen to possess a natural genius, which translated itself into the creation of universally agreed works of art. Kant's work is seen as popularizing the phrase 'art for art's sake', with the focus on aesthetic appreciation of art work, in and of itself. Kant's philosophy is interrogated by O'Sullivan (2014) in terms of the role of the arts marketer in broadening arts consumption. As O'Sullivan (2014, p. 44) says: "Audience development . . . is not just about growing numbers of gallery visitors or concert goers at a particular venue or for a certain art form." For him, it is about equipping the audience to engage with the arts in a way that benefits them. Again, this brings us back to consideration of what is being marketed when we speak of arts marketing. On the one hand, we see the assertion from members of the Frankfurt School, the Situationists and the Birmingham School that the arts are capable of influencing political and social reality. On the other hand, is the Kantian consideration of the arts which assumes a 'disinterestedness', or a neutral political or ideological position for the arts, where aesthetic judgement is based on a universal set of aesthetic principles. It is this distinction between art as disinterested and inherently political that distinguishes arts marketing from what can be termed critical arts marketing.

Current areas of research

Current research emerges from this disciplinary foundation, both building on existing themes and developing new and fruitful lines of enquiry. An up-to-date critical review of the literature in each of the following, current areas is presented: (1) the arts versus the market debate; (2) creativity at the cutting edge of marketing practice; (3) the cultural practice and theory of branding; (4) the creation and formation of alternative markets; and (5) creative methods of enquiry in marketing research.

The arts versus markets debate

The arts versus the market, or arts versus commerce debate as it is also known, is rooted in the idea that artistic and commercial practices have very different, and seemingly incompatible agendas and that therefore art and products are valued in divergent ways. Hirschman (1983, p. 46) argued that because art is valued for its expressive qualities and utilitarian products are valued for functional utility or technical competence, then the "marketing concept, as a normative framework, is not applicable to [artists] because of the personal values and social norms that characterize the production process". Holbrook (2005) argued that 'art for art's sake' as opposed to 'art for mart's sake', has been a theme of great importance, and remains one of the most vexed issues, particularly in macromarketing. For example, Dholakia, Duan and Dholakia (2015) examine the evolution of the Wushipu art agglomeration in China, specifically highlighting the interplay of macro-level tensions and transitions that construct, characterize and maintain this art market. These artists copy significant works of art which are then sold (as high-quality copies) within the local art market. They are not seen as forgers, but rather skilled reproducers who make otherwise restricted art available in the mass market. Dholakia *et al.* (2015) find that the tension between mass-produced popular art and high art remains; but also, that other tensions have emerged that are more specific to the particular market, such as fostering the continued development of indigenous creativity and the protection of Chinese art motifs in the face of a growing market for Western art.

While this debate persists, we suggest that it is currently characterized by a more nuanced understanding and recognition of the interactive, rather than antagonistic, relationship between art and commerce. As suggested by Bradshaw, McDonagh and Marshall (2006, p. 81) the art versus market tension "is useful in as-much as it begins a process of unpacking and learning about the complex and dialectical relationship [the relationship between two opposing, but interacting concepts] between the two". Several interesting areas of research emerge out of such efforts. First, we see the blurring of the boundaries between art and the market. Bradshaw (2010) highlights two categories of arts marketing that underpin a critically driven understanding of the arts versus commerce debate: marketing *as* art, and art *as* marketing.

At the simplest level, 'marketing as art' facilitates an acknowledgement of the symbolic and aesthetic nature of products and brands. There is a long line of anthropological thinking which acknowledges that "the things with which people interact are not simply tools for survival" (Csikszentmihalyi & Rochberg-Halton, 1981, p. 1) but that, as Dittmar (1992) argues, they have psychological, social and cultural significance that transcends their instrumental and utilitarian functions. However, it is only relatively recently, and partly through broadening the domain of marketing to encompass the arts, that marketers began to pay attention to the experiential, aesthetic and symbolic domains of products and consumption (Belk 1988; Holbrook & Hirschman 1982; Levy, 1959). The role of aesthetics in everyday life in a consumer society is such that consumers are produced as aesthetic subjects (Venkatesh & Meamber, 2008), who judge not only art objects, but also everyday objects, such as clothing and kitchen appliances, aesthetically, i.e. as sensory experience of beauty. Thus, the line between art and the market is blurred.

Further underpinning the understanding of 'marketing as art' is the acknowledgement that the practice of marketing is culturally embedded (e.g. Holt, 2003). For example, advertising and marketing communications have become a rich, intertextual blend of cultural references, where meaning is drawn in part from, and in relation to, other cultural texts (O'Donohoe, 1997). Bradshaw (2010) argues that rather than limit our understanding of marketers to that of astute readers of culture, we should acknowledge marketing practice as inherently creative in and of itself. For example, both Brown (2001) and Waksman (2011) show how some contemporary marketing practices, such as the use of promotional techniques to manage crowds, emerged from the carnivalesque aesthetics of P.T. Barnum. Both historical and future-oriented analyses see an aesthetically driven market, defined by creative intent and the pursuit of beauty (e.g. Bradshaw, 2010; Brown, 2001; Holt, 2003; Schroeder, 2002).

The second of Bradshaw's (2010, p. 12) categories of arts marketing rests on the notion that "if marketing contains aspects of artistic endeavour, then the opposite holds that artistic practice contains elements of marketing". Many artists, such as Andy Warhol, Damien Hirst, the Rolling Stones, work, and even thrive, within the commercial infrastructures of the marketplace, although the adoption of a bohemian ideology leads many artists to discursively abandon commerciality. But this is contradictory, as even the most bohemian of artists need to survive and very many adopt marketing practices to ensure they do. Artists often develop a brand, i.e. a recognizable look, name and style (Schroeder, 2005) and artists who do this well, such as Andy Warhol, can be labelled as 'culturepreneurs' (O'Reilly, 2005). This is, however, not a new phenomenon. Fillis' (2011) examination of the artist as marketer and entrepreneur explains that as early as 1550, when Vasari published 'Lives of Artists', a clear picture began to emerge of how artists operated in the marketplace. Similarly, Brown's (2015) insightful exploration of the historically unacknowledged marketing capabilities of modernist authors Ezra Pound, T.S. Eliot, and James Joyce problematizes the tension between art and commerce that is said to characterize modernism's break with classical and traditional forms of art and the self-conscious and ironic experimentation with the new. He argues that these authors used marketing to "not so much bridge the great divide [between high art and popular culture] but tunnel beneath it" (p. 18), by for example, propounding the Imagism poetry movement effectively as a promotional campaign for Pound's own literary brand. Contemporary marketers can learn from such artists and their practices.

A critical understanding of the arts versus the market debate also facilitates a more nuanced understanding of the different kinds of value that co-exist in the marketplace and how they interact with each other. For example, Holbrook (1999) identifies eight major types of value that co-exist in any consumption (market) experience (efficiency, excellence, status, esteem, beauty, fun, ethics and spirituality), which can be streamlined into four major categories: economic, social, hedonic and altruistic. While the arts versus commerce debate historically pits aesthetic value against economic value, there has been a notable amount of work recently on understanding the value of the arts for a range of audiences (e.g. Halliday & Astafyeva, 2014; Henderson, 2013; Tyrie & Ferguson, 2013) and the creation of value in art markets (Preece, Kerrigan & O'Reilly, 2016). Rodner and Thomson (2013) present the 'art machine' as the process of dynamic and interlocking mechanisms through which symbolic and economic value are combined to generate value for contemporary art. The key point of this stream of work being, that aesthetic and economic value are not at odds with each other, but are in fact co-constitutive. What this research argues, is for a broader understanding of value when it comes to art. This more sophisticated and multifaceted perspective on value is at odds with economic notions of value which dominate policy incentives that often aim at understanding the economic value of the arts, over and above wider benefits or values. This dominance of the economic rationale in understanding the value of art then leads artists to be deemed 'successful' based on their economic performance rather than their wider cultural or social impact.

Creativity in marketing practice

Following on from the prior discussion on value in arts, we turn to examining the idea of creativity. The arts have been reconceptualized as part of the 'cultural industries' (DeFillippi, Grabher & Jones, 2007; Davies & Sigthorsson, 2013; Pratt, 2005), a sector which has been acknowledged due to the importance of arts and culture in generating value in the economy and in shaping perceptions of people and places (Lash & Lury, 2007). Creativity is clearly central to the arts sector and we can see how wider marketing practice often looks to the arts in order to gain insight and inspiration. Marketing, as well as being data led and behavioural, is reliant on the visual in understanding culture and in communicating. Here we see that the arts have been used, implicitly and explicitly in marketing mainstream products, services, places and ideologies (e.g. the use of popular music in advertising, fashion brands collaborating with visual artists and developments such as branded entertainment where the lines between art film and advertisement are being blurred). As such, the arts are fundamental to creative marketing practice. Fluency in visual arts, music and so on is required in order to develop compelling creative communications and to design functional and aesthetically pleasing products. Reflecting on the arts versus market debate discussed above, such a tension plays out in the creative elements of marketing practice, i.e. between the creatives and the suits (Kelly, Lawlor & O'Donohoe, 2008). If such battles occur in non-arts marketing, they are further complicated by the centrality of creativity in the product of the arts. While Kelly *et al.* (2008) could identify the creative within advertising, in the realm of arts marketing the creatives are those originators of the central product; the visual artist, the composer, the dramatist and so on, with little space often given to the marketers to illustrate their creativity. This has often resulted in dull, procedural and tactical marketing practices coming from these industries.

Creativity intersects with market hegemony in arts marketing practice, and it is this that interested Kerrigan (2017) when considering creative practices in film marketing. Frustrated with industrial structures that can exclude non-mainstream film or make assumptions about market preferences, film maker/marketers such as MdotStrange have engaged in creative practices that bring their fans into the creative process. As well as being asked to be extras in his films, fans are given the tools and materials to create their own film and then invited to share their finished products with him; developing a form of 'new marketing' where fans' preferences for story, character and overall aesthetics are apparent. What is interesting from a critical arts marketing perspective is that this is presented as a challenge to market hegemony where his offbeat style of animated film might not have mass appeal. However, MdotStrange draws on market logic, in order to develop his own creative practice while, at the same time, working to break down the producer/consumer divide in order to provide others with the tools of production through sharing techniques and materials. These co-creative relationships that blur the boundaries between production and consumption can be viewed as the cutting edge of marketing practice, but also indicate the inevitable circle of the hegemony of market logic. Creative marketing practices aimed at opening up the market, increasing recognition for underrepresented groups, and increasing physical, financial, and cultural accessibility require critical interrogation.

Turning to the visual arts, we can see other examples of creative arts marketers, again, those who embrace marketing practice in their artistic work. As mentioned earlier, Andy Warhol, initially excluded from the art world, developed creative practices both in his art work and, notably, in his efforts to draw attention to his work, thus amassing the necessary cultural and social capital required to gain access to the art world while benefitting to some degree from his outsider status (see Fillis, 2000; Kerrigan, Brownlie, Hewer & Daza-LeTouze, 2011; Schroeder, 2005). Fillis' (2000, 2003, 2014) body of work on the intersection of arts, marketing and entrepreneurship illustrates the multiple junctions between creativity and marketing.

Cultural practice and theory of branding

Cultural capital, as noted earlier, has been seen as a central indicator of participation in the arts. Conversely, the lack of cultural capital can result in non-participation. It is for this reason that interrogation of the role of branding in the arts is necessary, as branding is seen as a technology that aids choice and understanding, thus offering shortcuts to consumers when selecting products or services. Here we see a divergence in theory between those focused on 'managing' or 'controlling' the brand, conceived of as belonging to a more managerial school of branding (see O'Reilly & Kerrigan, 2013), and the cultural approach to branding as a more consensual practice, where brand identity is collectively agreed and evolves over time.

The relevance of applying branding theory to the arts has been recognized by scholars (see Preece & Kerrigan (2015) for an overview). Despite the number of papers on branding in the arts, through the arts and on art brands, O'Reilly and Kerrigan (2016) note that applying branding to the arts is a knotty theoretical issue. They start by querying, as does this chapter, what the arts are. That in itself is a complex question that is much debated in the wider literature. Second, O'Reilly and Kerrigan (2016), noting that branding is traditionally depicted as a way to communicate the essence of a complex phenomenon through shorthand which is primarily authored by a management team, highlight the challenge of providing a rich and thick description of a brand within the branding process. If brands are there to provide a shorthand for consumers, how can they also communicate the rich, historically located nature of cultural brands? What is evident in O'Reilly and Kerrigan's (2016) chapter, and wider work cited above, is that art brands must be historically and culturally situated, to avoid becoming merely spectacles. While mainstream managerially driven brands, often those of products such as fast-moving consumer goods, are created by a company in order to appeal to a given target market, cultural brands come with complex historical and cultural meanings attached.

One of the most significant challenges lies in the ownership of the brand and therefore the legitimacy of the branding process. In a fast-moving consumer goods context, there is a parent brand and this parent brand has the legal authority to 'brand' a product. They may decide on the pricing, the visual appearance, the brand narrative, and communicate this through a range of media. However, cultural branding approaches recognize the complexity of brands in terms of meanings located within wider cultural, social, political and historical contexts, and the more dispersed nature of brand ownership (e.g. Holt, 2003; O'Reilly, 2005; Schroeder, 2009). Moves to theories of co-creation (e.g. Cova & Pace, 2006) challenge managerial branding approaches which assume that parent brands can control brand meaning in the market, arguing instead that consumers play a significant role in co-constructing meaning. In the arts, we can see that this is not a theoretical argument, but that in fact, at a fundamental level, brand ownership is a dispersed entity. In, for example, the film industry (O'Reilly & Kerrigan 2013) and the visual arts (Preece *et al.*, 2016), legal ownership of art brands is scattered among a number of stakeholders and non-owners of brands play a significant role in co-constructing brand meaning within the marketplace. Brand meaning is relational, relying on comparison, intersection and interrelationships between different stakeholders, meaning-makers and brands. Brand meaning also shifts over time, as cultural codes (Bourdieu, 1979/1984) gain new meanings (O'Reilly & Kerrigan, 2013; Schroeder, 2009).

The concept of cultural codes, derived from the Birmingham School of Cultural Studies is central to arts branding, and brings us back to cultural capital. If we accept Bourdieu's theorization of cultural capital (echoed in the Birmingham School), then class, race and other identity markers are influential in the process of encoding (i.e. embedding meaning) and decoding (i.e. understanding the intended message) (Hall, 1980), a process that is central to developing an understanding of branding in the arts (O'Reilly & Kerrigan, 2013). This again requires arts marketing researchers to reflect on their treatment of the subject of their research, in classifying certain cultural practices as art, others as entertainment, and in making distinctions between popular and high art. Therefore, as argued by O'Reilly and Kerrigan (2016), understanding arts branding, requires an understanding of and embedding meaning in the arts themselves. O'Reilly and Kerrigan (2013, 2016) highlight the relevance of the idea of circuits of culture where social interaction with art brands, conceptualized as sets of culturally bounded meanings, results in the production, reaffirmation, and sometimes the undermining of the plurality of meanings associated with those brands. This collective understanding of branding (Rodner & Thomson, 2013) is essential in considering how brand meaning is formulated within the arts, and such analysis is relevant for brands outside the arts, as has been recognized by those who argue for a culturally grounded branding theory (e.g. Holt, 2003).

Alternative markets

The way in which the arts are created, expressed, disseminated and understood is determined by systems of production and consumption (e.g. Horkheimer & Adorno, 1972). The cultural industries are composed of organizations that produce, manage and sell cultural goods, and the arts market is a complex network that exists to bring artists, arts organizations and audiences together. Hesmondhalgh (2002) explains that while theorists such as Raymond Williams and Pierre Bourdieu show the more or less permanent presence in human history of the particular kind of creativity that underpins art and culture, i.e. "the manipulation of symbols for the purposes of entertainment, information and perhaps even enlightenment" (p. 6), how this creativity is managed has taken radically different forms. For example, in Europe, systems of patronage gave way to the principles of the market in the 19th century, which eventually took the complex form of advanced consumer capitalism. The contemporary arts market is shaped by a constantly evolving socio-cultural and economic environment. Thus, arts markets are facing many changes not only in the way that art is produced and distributed, but also in the way that it is consumed. For example, O'Reilly *et al.* (2013) outline the constant evolution of the music industry that is due to changing ownership structures and fluctuations in public funding, and which has resulted in a diversification of business models and revenue streams. Most commercial artists rely on market revenue to survive, but many other artists draw upon a mix of revenue and public funding.

Shukaitis and Figiel (2013) caution against falling back on the argument that art and artistic practices merely reflect the underlying economic structures that determine them. As Attali (1977/1985) so persuasively argues, modes of artistic production can precede and even forecast broader changes in economic interactions. What is important to note here, is that

> politics is not separate from the relations of the art world, it cannot be relegated to the content of artistic production. For arts marketing politics is found in the articulation of the relationship between art and the market, and the forms of organization and sociality that emerge and that are sustained by that very conjunction.
>
> *Shukaitis & Figiel, 2013, p. 27*

Thus, arts markets are inherently political, and it is this, combined with complexity, the economic and social precarity of living without job security, and abundant creativity, which means that the arts have often been at the forefront of the exploration and development of alternative forms of markets, and are therefore an important site of critical marketing thought and action. There is some exciting and important work which specifically explores and theorizes the creation and formation of alternative markets and marketing practices.

First, there is a long history of scholarship on alternative forms of production and consumption in the arts. An enduring construct within the fields of cultural studies and popular music studies is that of 'subculture' (Bennett & Kahn-Harris, 2004) which is a cultural group within a larger culture that emerges when a group of people interact and innovate new forms of living that are different from, or even in opposition to mainstream culture. Foundational work highlighted the role of music (alongside fashion) in subcultural style, which, Hebdige (1979) argues, functions as a form of protest against hegemonic power structures. There is a considerable amount of academic writing on popular music subcultures, for example punk, goth (Hodkinson, 2002), extreme metal (Kahn-Harris, 2007), and heavy metal (Walser, 1993). However, Weinzierl and Muggleton (2003) argue that there has been a move toward 'post-subcultural' theory, which maintains that subculture has become redundant as a conceptual framework for understanding style-based youth cultures because youth identities "had become more reflexive, fluid and fragmented due to an increasing flow of cultural commodities, images and texts through which more individualized identity projects and notions of self could be fashioned" (Bennett, 2011, p. 493). This, combined with a huge proliferation and diffusion of types of music, suggests that subcultures are no longer as demarcated by music as they once were. Yet, consumption communities continue to form around music. An interesting feature of the alternative forms of exchange emergent from subcultures is the 'do-it-yourself' (DiY) ethic which steps outside of the formal capitalist structures of production and consumption, thus blurring traditional marketplace roles of producer and consumer. Fans engage in artistic and material-semiotic production, by for example producing fanzines (Atton, 2001; Rau, 1994) or, as described earlier, engaging as new cultural intermediaries in 'scanlation' – "translating, editing and disseminating overseas cultural products, without authorization by copyright holders, in order to make the products more accessible in a given language territory" (Lee, 2012, p. 131).

Second, because arts markets have often been the first to be faced with the challenges and opportunities of technological changes, such as the rise of digital technology, they have also been a crucial site for the development of alternative forms of pricing and distribution, such as file sharing (e.g. Belk, 2014; Giesler, 2006) and crowdfunding. As a form of alternative finance, crowdfunding is "a collective effort by people who network and pool their money together, usually via the Internet, in order to invest in and support efforts initiated by other people or organizations" (Ordanini, Miceli, Pizzetti & Parasuraman, 2011, p. 444). Inspired by the open-source movement and facilitated by online communities, this collaborative approach to funding the arts relies on voluntary contributions and different forms of prosocial behaviour, which Cohendet and Simon (2014, p. 4) argue is motivated by the idea that the intrinsic value of the arts lies mostly in the creative process, which people wish to witness and be a part of: "people pay for the production and promotion of an idea rather than buying it in its final form". A consequence of these collaborative and sharing-based approaches to the production, dissemination and consumption of art, is that they open up alternative market spaces and places that serve as a form of resistance to the capitalist economic model (Albinsson & Yasanthi Perara, 2012).

Creative methods of enquiry

Several scholars have sounded the call for more creativity in arts marketing research (e.g. Brown, 2011; Larsen & O'Reilly, 2010; Patterson, 2010). There are two main reasons for this. First, the aesthetic nature of the arts sets them apart from the products and services that have historically been the focus of marketing and consumer research. As outlined by Venkatesh and Meamber (2006, p. 20), the philosophical discipline of aesthetics maintains that "aesthetic experience is distinguished from the material aspects of life and privileged because of its importance in human development and metaphysical discourse". The production of art is therefore focused on aesthetic rather than utilitarian value, and the consumption of art draws on sensory, symbolic and embodied experiences (vom Lehn, 2006) that are different from those gained from the consumption of more mundane objects (Joy & Sherry, 2003). Thus, understanding the marketing and consumption of the arts requires different approaches from traditional methods of enquiry in marketing, in order to produce relevant insights. Second, arts marketing sits at the intersection of a number of related and relevant disciplines and thus attracts interest from a range of scholars outside of marketing, including arts management (Chong, 2002), cultural sociology (Spillman, 2002), the sociology of arts and culture (Tanner, 2003), cultural economy (Du Gay & Pryke, 2002), culture and consumption studies (Lury, 2004), celebrity studies (Walker, 2003), museology, performance studies (Schechner, 1993), art economics (Frey, 2003) and theoretical literatures relating to the different arts sectors, for example film, theatre, music and fine art, as well as tourism and leisure studies. This necessitates a multi-disciplinary approach to arts marketing that incorporates psychological, sociological and anthropological perspectives and the full range of research methodologies that underlie these perspectives (Larsen & O'Reilly, 2010).

To this end, a variety of creative methods of enquiry have been adopted and become embedded in arts marketing research. For example, Patterson (2010, p. 59) strongly advocates the use of introspection (e.g. Hart, Kerrigan, & vom Lehn, 2015; Wohlfeil & Whelan, 2012), which he argues is not just a singular method, but which encompasses several ideas: "introspection as an integral component of all writing and thinking; as a meta-method much like in-depth interviews or reader response; [. . . and] as a formal method where one researcher reflects on his/her own consumption experiences". Fillis (2011) is a champion of the use of biography and other narrative methods, in order to better understand the intangible, abstract and creative aspects of arts marketing practices. For example, Larsen (2017) uses biographies in a rhetorical analysis of how the label 'groupie' is used as an othering practice that upholds the gendered norms of rock music. By examining these biographies as sites of struggle that offer both preferred and oppositional readings of the groupie identity, the particular discursive practices of othering that are at work could be identified.

Art has not remained solely the subject of enquiry, but is now also used as a method and form of representation in the broader field of marketing and consumer research. Given humanity's love of narrative, Brown (2011, p. 80) argues that marketing scholars should reconsider the traditional modes of research representation and instead "embrace the foregoing facts about fiction. Maybe we should alter our preferred mode of representation, replacing hard facts with neat stories. Maybe we should 'fictionalise' our findings to make them more acceptable to consumers". While Brown acknowledges that this might not be welcomed by the academic marketing mainstream, his argument is driven by a desire to find a way of better engaging audiences with the interesting, and often challenging, ideas that critical marketing theorists have to offer. Brown has certainly put his money where his pen is, and rewarded us with his trilogy: *The Marketing Code* (2006), *Agents and Dealers* (2008) and *The Lost Logo* (2009). Since the first film festival of the Association for Consumer Research (ACR) in 2001, videography has become institutionalized as a way of presenting research additional to the traditional manuscript (see, for example, the forthcoming Special Issue on videography in the *Journal of Marketing Management*). Petr, Belk and Decrop (2015, p. 73) define videography as "the process of producing and communicating knowledge through the collection and analysis of visual material".

Recently, we have witnessed a growing interest and exploration of non-representational, or more-than-representational methods, which are modes of theorizing that go beyond representation and meaning, to focus on the embodied, sensory, affective, precognitive experience of everyday life. These methods are inherently artistic and aesthetic. With the intention of extending the toolkit for videographers in consumer research, Hietanen (2012) outlines an innovative role for videography, in moving beyond the linguistic form inherent in representational research, to a method that foregrounds bodies in action in relation to the movement of affect. Similarly, Patterson and Larsen (2017) begin to trace the possibilities for a sonic turn in marketing and consumer research, as another non-representational approach that acknowledges sound as a site for analysis and theory development and which encourages the researcher to 'listen to consumption'. And the role of poetry in marketing research is extended by Canniford (2012) through the concept of 'poetic witness' that enables representations of consumer life worlds as heterogeneous constellations of objects, emotions, narratives, discourse and physical forces. All such efforts open up the space for an aesthetically driven, critical understanding of marketing and consumption.

Conclusion and future directions for research

The chapter concludes with suggestions and directions for future research, which seek to build and expand upon the existing body of knowledge in arts marketing. What we can see above is that the notion of 'critical arts marketing' is not something around which a clear movement is centred. There is no clear beginning or borders to the field of critical arts marketing research. However, there is a genealogy which can be linked to the broader development of critical theory, and cannot be divorced from wider debates around the role of the arts within society. The arts themselves are neither critical nor uncritical, but how we engage with them is central to any critical project. We can see the arts, as Aristotle did, as valuable in providing cathartic output, or follow Boal's more active liberatory view of the potential of theatre as a way to challenge oppression, or we can recognize the capability of the arts to distract us from the real social, cultural and political issues at play in society. All views have merit in pushing forward a critical arts marketing. Greater interrogation of the process of audience development is needed, and writing this as Donald Trump follows a Reaganomic defunding of the arts, we must continue to question the value of the arts in society, the arts/market intersection, and the convergence of arts and popular culture.

In approaching the arts, class, ethnicity and gender must be acknowledged and scholars need to find new (and old) ways to bring intersectional analysis (i.e. the effort to understand how these different social identities intersect with, and constitute one another to exclude and discriminate people) to our understanding of the arts. The increasing importance of creative methods in marketing and consumer research, necessitates a critical analysis of the deployment of methods such as videography, biography, fiction and introspection. Bringing theoretical insight from cultural studies as well as the visual arts, music, film, dance and so on can enrich methodological and theoretical enquiry into wider areas such as advertising and marketing communication, and marketing practices which increasingly rely on the moving image and the combination of visual and aural communication, such as the use of social media by companies and consumers.

This whistle stop tour of the origins and current research in what can be loosely termed critical arts marketing is partial, both in terms of historical perspective, inclusion or exclusion of authors and acknowledgement of influential foundational theorists. However, it provides a starting point for further research, debate and development.

References

Adorno, T., & Horkheimer, M. (1944/1972). The culture industry: Enlightenment as mass deception. In M. Horkheimer & T. Adorno (1944/1972), *Dialectic of Enlightenment*. Trans. John Cumming. New York, Herder and Herder.

Albinsson, P.A., & Yasanthi Perera, B. (2012). Alternative marketplaces in the 21st century: Building community through sharing events. *Journal of Consumer Behavior*, 11(4), 303–315.

Attali, J. (1977/1985). *Noise: The political economy of music*. Minnesota, University of Minnesota Press.

Atton, C. (2001). Living in the past? Value discourse in progressive rock fanzines. *Popular Music*, 20(1), 29–46.

Belk, R. (1988). Possessions and the 'extended self'. *Journal of Consumer Research*, 15(2), 139–168.

Belk, R. (2014). You are what you can access: Sharing and collaborative consumption online. *Journal of Business Research*, 67(8), 1595–1600.

Benjamin, W. (1968/1999). *Art in the age of mechanical reproduction*. Trans. Harry Zohn. New York, Schocken Books.

Bennett, A. (2011). The post-subcultural turn: Some reflections 10 years on. *Journal of Youth Studies*, 14(5), 493–506.

Bennett, A., & Kahn-Harris, K. (2004). *After subculture: Critical studies in contemporary youth culture*. Basingstoke, Palgrave Macmillan.

Bourdieu, P. (1979/1984). *Distinction: A social critique of the judgement of taste*. Trans. Richard Nice. Cambridge, MA, Harvard University Press.

Bradshaw, A. (2010). Before method: Axiomatic review of arts marketing. *International Journal of Culture, Tourism and Hospitality Research*, 4(1), 8–19.

Bradshaw, A., McDonagh, P., & Marshall, D. (2006). Response to "Art versus Commerce as a Macromarketing Theme". *Journal of Macromarketing, 26*(1), 81–83.
Brown, S. (2001). *Marketing: The retro revolution*. London, Sage.
Brown, S. (2006). *The marketing code*. London, Cyan Books and Marshall Cavendish.
Brown, S. (2008). *Agents and dealers*. London, Marshall Cavendish.
Brown, S. (2009). *The lost logo*. London, Marshall Cavendish.
Brown, S. (2011). And then we come to the brand: Academic insights from international bestsellers. *Arts Marketing: An International Journal, 1*(1), 70–86.
Brown, S. (2015). Brands on a wet, black bough: Marketing and the masterworks of modernism. *Arts and the Market, 5*(1), 5–24.
Brown, S., & Patterson, A. (2000). *Imagining marketing: Art, aesthetics and the avant-garde*. Oxford, Routledge.
Brownlie, D., & Hewer, P. (2007). Concerning marketing critterati: Beyond nuance, estrangement and elitism. In M. Saran, P. Maclaran, C. Goulding, R. Elliott, A. Shankar & M. Catterall (Eds.), *Critical marketing: Defining the field* (pp. 44–68). Oxford, Butterworth-Heinemann.
Canniford, R. (2012). Poetic witness: Marketplace research through poetic transcription and poetic translation. *Marketing Theory, 12*(4), 391–409.
Chong, D. (2002). *Arts management*. London, Routledge.
Cohendet, P., & Simon, L. (2014). Financing creativity: New issues and new approaches. *International Journal of Arts Management, 16*(3), 2–5.
Cova, B., & Pace, S. (2006). Brand community of convenience products: New forms of customer empowerment – the case "my Nutella the Community". *European Journal of Marketing, 40*(9/10), 1087–1105.
Csikszentmihalyi, M., & Rochberg-Halton, E. (1981). *The meaning of things: Domestic symbols and the self*. Cambridge, Cambridge University Press.
Davies, R., & Sigthorsson, G. (2013). *Introducing the creative industries*. London, Sage.
Debord, G. (1973/2005). *Society of the spectacle*. Trans. Ken Knabb. London, Rebel.
DeFillippi, R., Grabher, G., & Jones, C. (2007). Introduction to paradoxes of creativity: Managerial and organizational challenges in the cultural economy. *Journal of Organizational Behavior, 28*(5), 511–521.
Deleuze, G., & Guattari, F. (1986). *Kafka: Towards a minor literature*. Trans. Dana Polen. Minneapolis, MN, University of Minnesota Press.
Dholakia, R., Duan, J., & Dholakia, N. (2015). Production and marketing of art in China: Traveling the long, hard road from industrial art to high art. *Arts and the Market, 5*(1), 25–44.
Dittmar, H. (1992). *The social psychology of material possessions: To have is to be*. London, Harvester Wheatsheaf, St Martins Press.
Du Gay, P., & Pryke, M. (2002). *Cultural economy: Cultural analysis and commercial life*. London, Sage.
Fillis, I. (2000). Being creative at the marketing/entrepreneurship interface: Lessons from the art industry. *Journal of Research in Marketing and Entrepreneurship, 2*(2), 125–137.
Fillis, I. (2003). Image, reputation and identity issues in the arts and crafts organization. *Corporate Reputation Review, 6*(3), 239–251.
Fillis, I. (2011). The evolution and development of arts marketing research. *Arts Marketing: An International Journal, 1*(1), 11–25.
Fillis, I. (2014). The impact of aesthetics on the Celtic craft market. *Consumption Markets and Culture, 17*(3), 274–294.
Fraser, P., & Fraser, I. (2014). Creating the opera habit: Marketing and the experience of opera. In D. O'Reilly, R. Rentschler & T.A. Kirchner (Eds.), *The Routledge companion to arts marketing* (pp. 393–404). London, Routledge.
Frey, B. (2003). *Arts and economics: Analysis and cultural policy*, second edition. Dordrecht, Springer.
Giesler, M. (2006). Consumer gift systems. *Journal of Consumer Research, 33*(2), 283–290.
Hackley, C. (2009). *Marketing: A critical introduction*. London, Sage.
Hall, S. (1980). *Culture, media, language*. London, Taylor & Francis.
Halliday, S., & Astafyeva, A. (2014). Millennial cultural consumers: Co-creating value through brand communities. *Arts Marketing: An International Journal, 4*(1/2), 119–135.
Hand, C. (2011). Do arts audiences act like consumers? *Managing Leisure, 16*(2), 88–97.
Hart, A., Kerrigan, F., & vom Lehn, D. (2015). Experiencing film: Subjective personal introspection and popular film consumption. *International Journal of Research in Marketing, 35*(2), 375–391.
Hebdige, D. (1979). *Subculture: The meaning of style*. London, Routledge.
Henderson, S. (2013). Sustainable touring: Exploring value creation through social marketing. *Arts Marketing: An International Journal, 3*(2), 154–167.

Hesmondhalgh, D. (2002). *The cultural industries.* London, Sage.
Hietanen, J. (2012). *Videography in consumer culture theory: An account of essence(s) and production.* Helsinki, Finland, Aalto University publication series.
Hill, E., O'Sullivan, T., & O'Sullivan, C. (2003). *Creative arts marketing.* London, Butterworth-Heinemann.
Hirschman, E.C. (1983). Aesthetics, ideologies and the limits of the marketing concept. *Journal of Marketing, 47*(3), 45–55.
Hodkinson, P. (2002). *Goth: Identity, style, and subculture.* Oxford, Berg.
Holbrook, M.B. (1980). Some preliminary notes on research in consumer esthetics. *Advances in Consumer Research, 7*(1), 104–108.
Holbrook, M.B. (1999). *Consumer value: A framework for analysis and research.* London, UK, Routledge.
Holbrook, M.B. (2005). Art versus commerce as a macromarketing theme in three films from the youngman-with-a-horn genre. *Journal of Macromarketing, 25*(1), 22–31.
Holbrook, M.B., & Hirschman, E.C. (1982). The experiential aspects of consumption: Consumer fantasies, feelings, and fun. *Journal of Consumer Research, 9*(1), 132–140.
Holt, D.B. (2003). What becomes an icon most? *Harvard Business Review, 81*(3), 43–49.
Horkheimer, M., & Adorno, T. (1972). *Dialectic of enlightenment.* London, Verso.
Joy, A., & Sherry, Jr., J.F. (2003). Speaking of art as embodied imaginations: A multisensory approach to understanding aesthetic experience. *Journal of Consumer Research, 30*(2), 259–282.
Kahn-Harris, K. (2007). *Extreme metal: Music and culture on the edge.* Oxford, Berg.
Kant, I. (1790/2009). *Critique of judgement.* Oxford World's Classics. New York, Oxford University Press. Revised edition.
Kelly, A., Lawlor, K., & O'Donohoe, S. (2008). A fateful triangle? Tales of art, commerce, and science from the Irish advertising field. *Advertising & Society Review, 9*(3), 1–48.
Kerrigan, F. (2017). *Film marketing,* second edition. London, Routledge.
Kerrigan, F., Brownlie, D., Hewer, P., & Daza-LeTouze, C. (2011). 'Spinning' Warhol: Celebrity brand theoretics and the logic of the celebrity brand. *Journal of Marketing Management, 27*(13–14), 1504–1524.
Kotler, P., & Levy, S. (1969). Broadening the concept of marketing. *Journal of Marketing, 33*(1), 10–15.
Larsen, G. (2017). "It's a man's man's man's world": Music groupies and the othering of women in rock. *Organization, 24*(3), 397–417.
Larsen, G., & O'Reilly, D. (2010). Editorial: Special issue on creative methods of enquiry. *International Journal of Culture, Tourism and Hospitality Research, 4*(1), 3–7.
Lash, S., & Lury, C. (2007). *Global culture industry: The mediation of things.* London, Polity Press.
Lee, H.-K. (2012). Cultural consumers as 'new cultural intermediaries': Manga scanlators. *Arts Marketing: An International Journal, 2*(2), 131–143.
Levy, S. (1959). Symbols for sale. *Harvard Business Review, 37*(4), 117–124.
Lury, C. (2004). *Brands: The logos of the global economy.* London, Routledge.
Major, S. (2014). The art of marketing arts marketing to artists. In D. O'Reilly, R. Rentschler & T.A. Kirchner (Eds.), *The Routledge companion to arts marketing* (pp. 71–77). London, Routledge.
O'Donohoe, S. (1997). Raiding the postmodern pantry: Advertising intertextuality and the young adult audience. *European Journal of Marketing, 31*(3/4), 234–253.
O'Reilly, D.T. (2005). Cultural brands/branding cultures. *Journal of Marketing Management, 21*(5): 573–588.
O'Reilly, D.T. (2011). Mapping the arts marketing literature. *Arts Marketing: An International Journal, 1*(1), 26–38.
O'Reilly, D.T., & Kerrigan, F. (2010). *Marketing the arts.* London, Routledge.
O'Reilly, D.T., & Kerrigan, F. (2013). A view to a brand: Introducing the film brandscape. *European Journal of Marketing, 47*(5/6), 769–789.
O'Reilly, D.T., & Kerrigan, F. (2016). Art brands. In F. Dall'Olmo Riley, J. Singh & C. Blankson (Eds.), *The Routledge companion to contemporary brand management* (pp. 448–457). London, Routledge.
O'Reilly, D.T., Larsen, G., & Kubacki, K. (2013). *Music, markets and consumption.* London, Goodfellows Publishers.
O'Reilly, D.T., Larsen, G., & Kubacki, K. (2014). Marketing live music. In K. Burland & S. Pitts (Eds.), *Coughing and clapping: Investigating audience experience* (pp. 7–20). London, Ashgate/SEMPRE.
O'Reilly, D.T., Rentschler, R., & Kirchner, T. (Eds.) (2013). *The Routledge Companion to Arts Marketing.* Abingdon, Routledge.
O'Sullivan, T. (2014). Arts marketing and ethics: What you can and Kant do. In D.T. O'Reilly, R. Rentschler & T.A. Kirchner (Eds.), *The Routledge companion to arts marketing* (pp. 29–47). London, Routledge.

Ordanini, A.L., Miceli, M., Pizzetti, M., & Parasuraman, A. (2011). Crowd-funding: Transforming customers into investors through innovative service platforms. *Journal of Service Management, 22*(4), 443–470.

Patterson, A. (2010). Art, ideology and introspection. *International Journal of Culture, Tourism and Hospitality Research, 4*(1), 57–69.

Patterson, M., & Larsen, G. (2017). Towards a sonic turn in interpretive consumer research. Paper presented at the 9th Workshop on Interpretive Consumer Research, Stockholm.

Petr, C., Belk, R., & Decrop, A. (2015). Videography in marketing research: Mixing art and science. *Arts and the Market, 5*(1), 73–102.

Pratt, A.C. (2005). Cultural industries and public policy: An oxymoron? *International Journal of Cultural Policy, 11*(1), 31–44.

Preece, C., & Kerrigan, F. (2015). Multi-stakeholder brand narratives: An analysis of the construction of artistic brands. *Journal of Marketing Management, 31*(11–12), 1207–1230.

Preece, C., Kerrigan, K., & O'Reilly, D.T. (2016). Framing the work: The composition of value in the visual arts. *European Journal of Marketing, 50*(7/8), 1377–1398.

Rau, M. (1994). Towards a history of fanzine publishing: From APA to zines. *Alternative Press Review*, Spring/Summer, 10–13.

Rodner, V., & Thomson, E. (2013). The art machine: Dynamics of a value generating mechanism for contemporary art. *Arts Marketing: An International Journal, 3*(1), 58–72.

Said, E.W. (1994). *Culture and imperialism.* New York, Vintage Books.

Schechner, R. (1993). *The future of ritual: Writings on culture and performance.* London, Routledge.

Schroeder, J. (2002). *Visual consumption.* London, Routledge.

Schroeder, J.E. (2005). The artist and the brand. *European Journal of Marketing, 39*(11), 1291–305.

Schroeder, J.E. (2009). The cultural codes of branding. *Marketing Theory, 9*(1), 123–126.

Sheth, J.N., Gardner, D.M., & Garrett, D.E. (1988). *Marketing theory: Evolution and evaluation.* New York, Wiley.

Shukaitis, S. (2008). Dancing amidst the flames: Imagination and self-organization in a minor key. *Organization, 15*(5), 743–764.

Shukaitis, S., & Figiel, J. (2013). Art, politics, and markets. In D. O'Reilly, R. Rentschler & T.A. Kirchner (Eds.), *The Routledge companion to arts marketing* (pp. 20–28). Abingdon, Routledge.

Spillman, L. (2002). *Cultural sociology.* Oxford, Wiley Blackwell.

Tadajewski, M. (2010). Towards a history of critical marketing studies. *Journal of Marketing Management, 26*(9), 773–824.

Tanner, J. (2003). *The sociology of art: A reader.* London, Routledge.

Thoburn, N. (2003). *Deleuze, Marx, and politics.* London, Routledge.

Tyrie, A., & Ferguson, S. (2013). Understanding value from arts sponsorship: A social exchange theory perspective. *Arts Marketing: An International Journal, 3*(2), 131–153.

Venkatesh, A., & Meamber, L. (2006). Arts and aesthetics: Marketing and cultural production. *Marketing Theory, 6*(1), 11–39.

Venkatesh, A., & Meamber, L. (2008). The aesthetics of consumption and the consumer as an aesthetic subject. *Consumption, Markets & Culture, 11*(1), 45–70.

vom Lehn, D. (2006). Embodying experience: A video-based examination of visitors' conduct and interaction in museums. *European Journal of Marketing, 40*(11/12), 1340–1359.

Waksman, S. (2011). Selling the nightingale: P. T. Barnum, Jenny Lind, and the management of the American crowd. *Arts Marketing: An International Journal, 1*(2), 108–120.

Walker, J. (2003). *Art and celebrity.* London, Pluto Press.

Walser, R. (1993). *Running with the devil: Power, gender and madness in heavy metal music.* Middletown, Wesleyan University Press.

Warhol, A. (1975). *The philosophy of Andy Warhol: (From A to B and back again).* New York, Harcourt Brace Jovanovich.

Weinzierl, D., & Muggleton, R. (2003). *The post-subcultures reader.* London, Berg.

Williams, R. (1976). *Keywords: A vocabulary of culture and society.* London, Fontana.

Wohlfeil, M., & Whelan, S. (2012). 'Saved!' by Jena Malone: An introspective study of a consumer's fan relationship with a film actress. *Journal of Business Research, 65*(4), 511–519.

PART II

Critical Marketing

Marketing practices in focus

9
CRITICAL STUDIES OF MARKETING WORK

Peter Svensson

Introduction

In this chapter I try to do two things. First, I offer an account of classical ideas that provide material for the critical perspective that is needed in order to scrutinize the practice of marketing work. These critical classics comprise ideas from Karl Marx, the Frankfurt School's critical theory, Michel Foucault and, lastly, from what could be broadly labeled "critical sociology". Critical management studies in general, and critical marketing studies in particular, would not exist as we know the field today were it not for these four classical sources of inspiration. The second aim of the chapter is to present what I see as the main areas of current critical studies of marketing work. These are: studies of the production of the seller–buyer relation, studies of the production of marketing plans and strategies, studies of the production of market intelligence and knowledge, and studies of the production of the marketing organization.

My starting point is this: critical studies of marketing work require both a critical gaze and access to in situ observations of practical work situations. It is thereby crucial to make a distinction between the study of marketing *work* and the study of marketing *workers*. Put differently, *work* is practice, *workers* are subjects, and strictly speaking the study of work is a study of certain work practices going on in organizations. The various practices considered "marketing work" comprise actions, interactions, decisions and deeds, whereas marketing workers are the agents involved in these practices. This is a point of departure that results in the exclusion from this chapter of studies primarily based on interviews. As pointed out by Silverman (1993) and others (Button, 1987; Pomerantz, 1988; Hester & Francis, 1994; Houtkoop-Steenstra, 1996), interview accounts should be seen as social situations in their own rights rather than as more or less accurate *depictions* of practices outside the interview situation. This is not to suggest that interview studies are of less value per se. Interview-based studies contribute with knowledge of how marketing practitioners talk and reason, perhaps even of how they think, which are crucial insights if we want to understand the world in which marketing people lead their lives. My point, however, is that these studies are not – again, if we want to be strict – studies of the *work* of marketing.

The chapter is structured as follows. In the next section I discuss some definitions and limitations of the notion of *marketing work*. After this, I turn to a discussion of what I see as the main premises of these critical studies of marketing work, i.e. a suspicious mind and a willingness to get one's hands dirty. This is followed by a discussion of the four main sources of inspiration for critical studies of marketing work. Then follows a presentation of some of the themes addressed in contemporary critical research on the work of marketing. Finally, I present some outlines of future avenues and challenges for this kind of research.

Marketing work

Now, what is marketing work? Taking marketing textbooks as a point of departure, there seems to be little agreement as to what should be included in the notion of marketing work. Some writers, for instance within relationship and service marketing, hold that virtually everything that takes place in an organization is to be seen as marketing work (e.g. Grönroos, 2000; Gummesson, 2002). According to Gummesson, all people in an organization whose work have some kind of effects on the sales and image of the organization operate as at least part-time marketers (Gummesson, 2002). In a similar vein, Peter Drucker suggested that:

> Actually marketing is so basic that it is not just enough to have a strong sales department and to entrust marketing to it. Marketing is not only much broader than selling, it is not a specialised activity at all. It is the whole business seen from the point of view of its final result, that is, from the customer's point of view. Concern and responsibility for marketing must therefore permeate all areas of the enterprise.
>
> *Drucker, 1954, p. x*

In one the many marketing management textbooks produced by the Kotler *et al.* collective, the work of marketing is described in a similarly all-encompassing way: "Marketing is the activity, set of institutions and processes for creating, communicating, delivering and exchanging offerings that have value for customers, clients, partners and society at large" (Kotler *et al.*, 2016, p. 6). However, these broad definitions (if that is what they are) are of little help if we want to find a way forward toward an understanding of the practices of marketing work; of what marketing workers *do* when they are doing marketing work.

As noted by Skålén and Hackley (2011, p. 191), the question "what is marketing work?" is "far more complex, contested and differentiated than conventional marketing theory allows". In order to provide an initial answer to this question, we need to turn our attention to what marketing workers actually *do* – when they do marketing work. One good potential answer to the question is offered by Skålén and Hackley themselves (see also Brown, 2005). Marketers write texts and they talk:

> Marketing professionals write reports, advertising copy, strategy documents, marketing research briefs, presentations, sales analyses, emails and sales pitches . . . When not writing, [the] marketing manager is usually in meetings, discussing the things they have written. Marketing is seen as a discipline worked up through discourse and symbolic practices.
>
> *Skålén & Hackley, 2011, p. 191*

This is a fruitful starting point. However, in this chapter I will focus on the *outcomes* of the writing and talking done by marketing workers. More specifically, marketing work is, in this chapter, defined as the various practices through which marketing products are produced. Production involves the transformation of resources and material into artifacts, e.g. the transformation of raw material into usable goods or the transformation of knowledge into tailor-made services. Examples of marketing products are campaigns, advertisements, marketing intelligence, strategies, plans, sales, relations and, also, the marketing organization as such.

The studies I bring to the fore in this chapter are good representatives of critical research that have offered valuable insights into the production of different kinds of marketing products. Yet, I am sure there are many good pieces by good researchers that I – unknowingly – have left out in this chapter. To them I apologize.

A suspicious mind and dirty hands

The critical interpretation of empirical material is a particular kind of interpretation. Ricœur (1970) wrote about the critical interpretation in terms of the hermeneutics of suspicion. The critical gaze is indeed the gaze of a suspicious mind whose purpose is to shed light on the political functions of meaning construction in social life (Itao, 2010). Simultaneously, the suspicious interpretation is an attempt to open up for new ways of thinking and doing, for new ways of being human (Stewart, 1989). Yet, insofar as the ambition of the critical researcher is to say something about marketing work, a suspicious mind does not suffice.

As pointed out by Paul Atkinson (2006), "quick and clean" research based on standardized interviews and surveys is not the best research strategy if one is interested in what people actually *do*. According to Atkinson, successful empirical fieldwork is necessarily messy and perhaps even dirty. Social life is full of complexities, inconsistencies and messiness. What could possibly be a better path to knowledge than throwing oneself into the messiness of everyday marketing work if this is truly what we take an interest in?

Observation-based studies are indeed dirty. They provide messy data that require a great amount of interpretative work and they are labor intensive. The nitty-gritty, dirty and not so well-ordered character of in situ observations of people doing whatever they are doing when they are engaging in marketing work is a good starting point for a critical analysis of the practice of work. As Moeran (2009, p. 964) puts it: "What good fieldwork reveals – among other things – is the customary discrepancy between what people *say* they do and what they *actually do* (something not discernible in interviews per se)." A great deal of research on marketing work – critical as well as not so critical – suffer from cleanliness. The research is simply too neat and clean, and contributes to, borrowing a formulation from Cornel West (2014), deodorized accounts of marketing work.

Four classical sources of inspiration for critical marketing studies

In what follows I will discuss what I see as the four, main classical theoretical domains that are the cornerstones of the research undertaken under the rubric of critical management studies (including studies of marketing work). Critical research in management and marketing has drawn upon other theoretical perspectives in addition to these four. Still, these are the points of reference that, willingly or not, are difficult to avoid in critical writings on marketing work.

Marxist theory

Karl Marx's writings on the organization of capitalism have inspired critical marketing research in many ways, albeit not always explicitly so. One of the themes drawn upon in the critical research on marketing is Marx's discussion of commodity fetishism, a theme briefly dealt with in the first chapter of *Capital*. According to Marx, a product assumes the form of a commodity when it is evaluated in relation to other commodities rather than within the social relations in which it was produced. The commodity is a fetishized product. As a consequence, at least according to Michael Billig, "the labor involved in the production of commodities is pushed from awareness" (1999, p. 315). By means of fetishizing products, marketing workers contribute to the forgetting in society of the social and political circumstances under which production of commodities takes place, for instance in sweatshop factories sited in low-wage countries.

Marx's analysis of the circulation of capital is another idea that – explicitly or not – undergirds much of what is written within the field of critical management and marketing studies. In its most basic form, Marx's famous (indeed infamous for some commentators) formula for the continuity of the circulation of capital is formulated as follows: M–C … P … C'–M'. According to Marx, the incessant circulation of capital is necessary for the survival of capital (see also Kilbourne, this volume). The circulation is the very gravity force of capitalism, and if it comes to a halt, capitalism as we know it ceases to exist. In Marx's own words:

> The circular movement of capital takes place in three stages, which, according to the presentation in Volume I, form the following series:
>
> *First stage*: The capitalist appears as a buyer on the commodity- and the labor-market; his money is transformed into commodities, or it goes through the circulation act M–C.
>
> *Second Stage*: Productive consumption of the purchased commodities by the capitalist. He acts as a capitalist producer of commodities; his capital passes through the process of production. The result is a commodity of more value than that of the elements entering into its production.
>
> *Third Stage*: The capitalist returns to the market as a seller; his commodities are turned into money; or they pass through the circulation act C–M.
>
> Hence the formula for the circuit of money-capital is: M–C … P … C'–M', the dots indicating that the process of circulation is interrupted, and C' and M' designating C and M increased by surplus-value.
>
> Marx, 1977, p. 153

The circuit of capital is ultimately designed to produce surplus value and to deliver a return on invested capital. In the first stage (M–C), monetary capital (M) is transformed into so-called productive capital (C). Thus, the capitalist purchases commodities in the form of productive capital that consists of two sub-forms: means of production (MP) and labor (L). In the second stage (P), new commodities (C') are being produced by means of utilizing means of production and exploiting human labor in order to generate surplus value (C' > C). This is the stage that commonly occupies the minds of management and human resource thinkers. Designing the optimal organization of production is a way of carving out the maximum surplus value given the specific circumstances in the organization. Finally, in the third stage (C'–M') the commodities are transformed into monetary capital (M') again. This is when the surplus value is *realized* (M' > M) and a new round of circulation begins. The transformation of commodities into monetary value – the realization of surplus value – is one of the central tasks for marketing work. Getting the products out there, bringing them to the market, generating purchases and closing deals, this is the telos of marketing management as it is habitually taught in business schools.

However, it would probably be a mistake to conceive of marketing work as a diabolic practice deviating significantly from sound moral values in society. That would be missing the target as a critical researcher. A more fruitful approach would be to interpret this engagement in the circulation of capital as part of the game marketers play: the game of realization of surplus value. Unfortunately, it seems to be difficult to play another game as a marketer.

Critical theory

Another main influence on critical studies of marketing work is the Frankfurt School and their project of critical theory. Critical theory was (and is) an ambitious attempt to synthesize Marxist theory – and a critique thereof – with cultural theory, philosophy, social psychology, Freudian psychodynamic theory and aesthetics. Insofar as there is one overriding theme in the critical theory proposed by the Frankfurt School, it is the observation that instrumental reason has turned the Enlightenment into a new, modern form of human enslavement. When mankind broke free from the subjugation to nature and mythologies, it came with a price according to the members of the Frankfurt School. Enlightenment converted human beings into objects of calculation, management and control. Adorno and Horkheimer described this change in their magnum opus *Dialectic of Enlightenment*:

> As soon as man discards his awareness that he himself is nature, all the aims for which he keeps himself alive – social progress, the intensification of all his material and spiritual powers, even consciousness itself – are nullified, and the enthronement of the means as an end, which under late capitalism is tantamount to open insanity, is already perceptible in the prehistory of subjectivity. Man's domination over himself, which grounds his selfhood, is almost always the destruction of the subject in whose service it is undertaken.
>
> *Adorno & Horkheimer, 1944/1977, p. 54*

When the members of the Frankfurt School turned their attention to the emergent consumer society in the U.S.A in the late 1950s, their critique of the Enlightenment shifted toward the logic of consumption and, more specifically, toward what Adorno and Horkheimer referred to as the culture industry. Adorno and Horkheimer, and later Herbert Marcuse, witnessed the integration of the economic system and politics. When cultural products were increasingly being measured in terms of their exchange values on the market, the standardization of culture was one of the effects (see also Larsen & Kerrigan, this volume). According to Adorno and Horkheimer, the culture industry operated by mass deception, by means of which demands, dreams and aspirations were produced and promoted throughout society. Consequently, the culture industry was pervasive; there was no way of escaping it (see Tadajewski, this volume):

> Marked differentiations such as those of A and B films, or of stories in magazines in different price ranges, depend not so much on subject matter as on classifying, organizing, and labeling consumers. Something is provided for all so none may escape: the distinctions are emphasized and extended.
>
> *Adorno & Horkheimer, 1944, p. 123*

"This inescapable force", Adorno and Horkheimer (1944, p. 125) continue, "is processed by commercial agencies so that they give an artificial impression of being in command. There is nothing left for the consumer to classify. Producers have done it for him."

So, what we are confronted with here is a depiction of consumer society that emphasizes the repressive force of marketing work. Marketing efforts provide classifications to which we are compelled to subscribe. These classifications interpellate us and produce us as consumer subjects defined by needs that can be fulfilled (only) through consumption. The consumer subject, then, is turned into one of the objects for marketing workers to *work on*. "The masses are not primary, but secondary, they are an object of calculation; an appendage of the machinery. The customer is not king, as the culture industry would have us believe, not its subject but its object" (Adorno, 1991, p. 99).

Written in a similar vein, Herbert Marcuse's influential book *One-dimensional Man* is another key inspiration for critical researchers interested in marketing work. Marcuse argues that the advanced industrial society entailed the total integration of individuals in machinery of capitalist production. Men and women born and raised in the industrialized society have, says Marcuse, become a one-dimensional creature governed by the production forces, by mass media, advertising and technological solutions. Homogeneity has replaced heterogeneity, simplicity has replaced nuances.

Evidently, the Frankfurt School did not offer a very bright picture of late capitalist society but it is an analysis that, alas one could add, is still relevant today. This is how Adorno summarizes his and Horkheimer's analysis of late capitalism:

> The total effect of the culture industry is one of anti-enlightenment, in which, as Horkheimer and I have noted, enlightenment, that is the progressive technical domination of nature, becomes mass deception and turned into a means of fettering consciousness.
>
> *Adorno, 1991, p. 106*

This is a formulation that could work very well as a slogan for much of the critical research that has been undertaken of management and marketing work. The standard critique of marketing management is often formulated in terms of mass deception, restrictions of individual autonomy and the dominance of technocratic control of consumers.

Foucauldian theory

French philosopher and historian Michel Foucault, who was a part of what has become known as "French Theory" (Cusset, 2008), offered ways of thinking, talking and writing about the relations between language, knowledge, power and subjectivity (e.g. Foucault, 1972, 1980), that fitted perfectly well with some of the emancipatory aspirations among critical management scholars. The most influential import from Foucault's work is probably the conceptualization and analysis of power as an inevitable and concrete aspect of relations and organizations (see e.g. Alvesson, 1996, p. 5). For Foucault, power was built into the very structure of social organization, and resided in the capillaries of the social relations that make up social order as we know it. Furthermore, power is not necessarily a personal issue to Foucault. It does not belong to a certain person but should rather be understood as a characteristic of the relations between different subject positions in society. Consequently, power should not be conceived of as something someone exercises over someone else – which is often seen as the pre-Foucauldian understanding of power – but rather as a "machine in which everybody is caught, those who exercise power just as much as those over whom power is exercised" (Foucault, 1980, p. 156). For critical management and marketing studies, Foucault's ideas on power have enabled researchers to focus on the micro situations in organizations in which power is being exercised, not as extraordinary and spectacular events but rather as quite ordinary aspects of the mundane work taking place in organizations.

Foucault also drew attention to the ways in which power operates through the production of subjects, i.e. individuals that can think, speak, feel and act (e.g. making decisions) in society. Power is a double-edged structural force. It is not only repressive, in the sense of restricting our autonomy and capacity to act in certain ways, but also a productive force. Power produces us as subjects, as conscious individuals with the capacity to make decisions, evaluate situations, prioritize and plan our lives. For Foucault, knowledge – and the different truths produced by established knowing – play a central role in the production of subjects. Knowledge produced by science (and indeed by business schools), provides the concepts, categories, causalities, explanations and language needed for us to develop as thinking and acting subjects. Hence, established knowledge partakes in the everyday exercise of power and in the regulation of human beings, their thoughts, emotions and conduct. These are insights that have opened up new ways for critical research of work to understand and study human behavior in organizations.

Critical sociology

A fourth source of inspiration for critical thinking and writing about marketing work is what could loosely be referred to as critical sociology. The central argument in this rather dispersed and fragmented group of writers is that marketing operates through the manipulation of the human psyche. This kind of critique partly overlaps with, but also differs from, the predominantly structuralist critique addressed by the Frankfurt School and its analysis of culture industry and consumer society. Critical sociology is an attempt to advance a relatively detailed critique of marketing practices and the role they play in consumer society. According to this critique, marketing work is best understood as the exercise of various techniques of manipulation of symbolic systems and mental processes. The marketer is depicted as a magician with exclusive access to the mysteries of the human mind. It has, for instance, been suggested that marketers have played a central role in the creation and reproduction of taste, dreams (Ewen, 1976), identities (Packard, 1957; Lasch, 1979; Willis, 1990; Kellner, 1992; Elliot, 1999), desiring consumers (Bauman, 2001), morality (Grafton-Small & Linstead, 1989), modernity (Arvidsson, 2003), hedonism (Pollay, 1986) and sign systems (Svensson, 2007).

A seminal text stemming from this tradition of critique is Raymond Williams' essay "Advertising: The magic system" (Williams, 1980). Drawing broadly upon Marx's analysis on commodity fetishism, Williams argued that advertising had developed into a craft combining magic and scientific reasoning. The work done by advertising firms transformed material goods, in almost a magical way, into cultural signifiers connoting proper values. Advertising, according to Williams, "has passed the frontier of the selling of goods and services and has become involved with the teaching of social and personal values" (p. 334). Consumer society has developed into a post-materialist society:

> It is impossible to look at modern advertising without realizing that the material object being sold is never enough: this indeed is the crucial cultural quality of its modern forms. If we were sensibly materialists, in that part of our living in which we use things, we should find most advertising to be of an insane irrelevance. Beer would be enough for us, without the additional promise that in drinking it we show ourselves to be manly, young in heart, or neighbourly. A washing-machine would be a useful machine to wash clothes rather than an indication that we are forward-looking or an object of envy to our neighbours. But if these associations sell beer and washing machines, as some of the evidence suggests, it is clear that we have a cultural pattern in

which the objects are not enough but must be validated, if only in fantasy, by association with social and personal meanings which in a different cultural pattern might be more directly available.

Williams, 1980, p. 335

Another good representative of this critical tradition is the journalist and author Vance Packard's discussion in *The Hidden Persuaders* (1957) of the methods and effects of the advertising industry (see also Tadajewski, this volume). Packard sheds light upon a world of advertising work dominated by cynicism and misanthropy. The advertisers portrayed in Packard's book treated the minds of consumers as a playground for pseudo-psychological and hobby-semantic experiments. The consumer's *need* was the target for this work, and drawing upon motivational research, depth psychology and subliminal communication, the advertising workers tried to produce desires for specific products. Packard does not offer a very sympathetic image of those targeting consumers:

Typically they see us as bundles of daydreams, misty hidden yearnings, guilt complexes, irrational emotional blockages. We are image lovers given to impulsive and compulsive acts. We annoy them with our seemingly senseless quirks, but we please them with our growing docility in responding to their manipulation of symbols that stir us to action.

Packard, 1957, p. 12

Stuart Ewen's book *Captains of Consciousness* (1976) is another text that merits attention. Investigating the history of the advertising industry, Ewen describes the advertising worker as one of the main architects of consumer culture as we know it. As captains of consciousness, the marketing worker not only navigates the mind of the consumer but also, and more importantly, manipulates consumers' inner worlds. By doing so, Ewen suggested, advertising placed itself at the very center of the lives of the American consumers, a position from where it could mold and control images of key categories in society, such as *the family, woman* and *man*. The marketing worker in Ewen's view is someone with almost magical capacities to manufacture cultural categories and rituals.

The four theoretical domains touched upon above – Marxist theory, critical theory, Foucauldian theory and critical sociology – have had a substantial impact on the formation of critically informed research on marketing work. In the next section I will turn to the more specific themes that have been addressed by critically minded researchers of marketing work.

The products of marketing work

In what follows I will focus on research that, with a critical mind, has focused on production of marketing output. This approach is largely in line with Mumby's (2016, p. 886) call for "rapprochement between critical marketing and critical organization scholarship". Even though Mumby probably over-emphasizes the sub-disciplinary boundaries within the field of critical management studies, he does have a point. Insofar as we are interested in the ways marketing work *works*, it is necessary to explore how marketing words, ideas and deeds appear in the everyday, mundane work in and in-between organizations. I will discuss four products of marketing work: the production of the seller–buyer relation, the production of plans and strategies, the production of market intelligence and, lastly, the production of organization.

The production of the seller–buyer relation

A prerequisite for marketing work is that there exists a relation between those who sell and those who buy. A seller requires a buyer and vice versa. This is a relation that, like any other kind of relation, needs to be produced. It does not exist beyond and without the actors involved, i.e. the seller and the buyer. Market work is partly involved in the production of such relations. Leidner's (1993) ethnographic study of the attempts to manage service encounters at McDonald's restaurants and in the insurance company Combined Insurance is a good example of research focusing on this production of buyer–seller relations. As a participant observer, Leidner studied how the interactions between front personnel and customers were subjected to standardization and managerial control. Drawing largely upon critical insights from Marxist analyses and labor theory, although not without critique of these ideas, Leidner shows how routinization of work, through tightly scripted interactions and manual-based service encounters, not only affects the employees' sense of autonomy, but also challenges the cultural norm of individuality being central to the American way of life. To borrow a term from Marcuse (1964), the service encounter becomes *one-dimensional*. Moreover, Leidner suggests that the routinization of the meeting between front personnel and customers normalizes a manipulative instrumentalist approach to human interactions.

Another interesting critical contribution to what we know about the production of sales is Hochschild's (1983) *The Managed Heart*. The book is based on a large ethnography of the everyday work of flight attendants at an airline, and Hochschild sets out to investigate the attempts to manage the emotional reactions of flight attendants. This work, which Hochschild refers to as emotional labor, is an aspect of the dream nurtured by marketing management to take control of the wild social life played out in service encounters. The production of the relation between seller and buyer involves this kind of attempt to manage, not only human interaction but also the inner lives of sales and front personnel, which results in the alienation of employees from their feelings and from themselves. In other words, the management of service encounters is a case in point of the backlash of the instrumental rationality discussed by the Frankfurt School, and in Hochschild's case the backlash is manifested as alienation of marketing workers.

Another in-depth ethnography in the same tradition as Leidner and Hochschild with many critical insights is offered by Prus in *Pursuing Customers* (1989a) and *Making Sales* (1989b). The first book is an analysis of the world of sales people and the second book deals with the nitty-gritty details in the process of attracting customers and preparing for a meeting with them. An overriding critical point in both of the books is articulated in Prus's skepticism of the idea that management is a well-structured and controlled practice. Prus shows that the management of marketing and sales is a somewhat chaotic exercise, a view that challenges the most dominant marketing management thoughts and their emphasis on order and control.

Another kind of seller–buyer relationship is that between marketing professionals, such as advertising workers, and their clients. Based upon an ethnographic study of a Japanese advertising agency, Moeran has shed light upon the backstage of meetings between advertising workers and their clients (Moeran, 2005). More specifically, Moeran has studied the use of "authenticity" codes used as an interactional tactic by an advertising team trying to pitch their campaign idea to a potential client. The study offers a detailed account of the dramaturgical performance, the tricks of the trade, played out in the campaign presentation at the advertising agency.

The production of plans and strategies

Marketing plans and strategies are of central importance to marketers, not only as documented ideas about what is supposed to happen in the future, but also because they assign meaning to the work of marketing. When plans for the future are formulated, the world of marketing is simultaneously described, ambitions are stated, roles are divided, priorities are established. Plans and strategies thereby contribute to the construction of the life worlds of marketing workers. Lien's (1995, 1997) ethnographic study of the everyday work at a marketing department of a Norwegian food manufacturer explores this kind of marketing work. In these studies Lien draws attention to the various uncertainties and dilemmas characterizing marketing management decision making. Lien's study is a critical exploration of the everyday work of marketing, but it is also a critical discussion of how "modern" ideas, such as authenticity, order and purity, come into play in marketing work and managerial decision making. In this sense, Lien is a good example of a study that manages to bridge the structuralist focus of critical theory and the micro-orientation of critical sociology.

The creative production of ad campaigns has also attracted some interest from researchers from various fields (e.g. Miller, 1997; Kemper, 2001; Mazzarella, 2003). Moeran (2009), mentioned above, spent 12 months in a Japanese advertising agency as a participant observer (see also Moeran, 1993, 1996). Moeran was interested in the ways in which the different structural constraints and conventions frame the creative work of translating campaign concepts into visual images. He observed that advertising work takes place in the nexus between creative art work and administrative work guided by business principles, a situation that created both constraints and possibilities for the production team at the advertising agency. In his study, Moeran draws attention to the relation between power and creativity in the production of advertisements. Advertising work is situated in the tension between at least two professional subject positions: that of the creative generator of ideas and that of the disciplined administrator. He thereby contributes to an account of marketing work that does not exclude, but rather stresses, the institutional and political conditions defining the workplace of marketers.

The production of market intelligence and knowledge

One premise for the conventional understanding of marketing work as a strategic and rational practice is that marketing workers have access to accurate market intelligence: to knowledge about the market and the consumers. As a consequence, knowledge production appears to be one of the main practices occupying people working with marketing. I am not referring here to knowledge produced by marketing researchers at universities and business schools, but to the work undertaken by marketing practitioners in order to collect and create intelligence to back up the formulation of plans and strategies.

For critical research on marketing work, the ways in which data, information – and knowledge – are manufactured and dealt with are obvious objects of critical scrutiny. One reason for this is that knowledge is, as both critical theory and Foucault have taught us, not only (or primarily) about representing the world; it is a way of organizing our perceptions, interpretations and behavior. Put differently, knowledge production involves the production of life worlds. Arguably, marketers' actions can only be understood if we understand what the world of marketing – the marketing life world(s) if you like – looks like and how it is being shaped by marketing knowledge.

Elsewhere I have referred to these marketing life worlds as the social-phenomenology of marketing work (Svensson, 2007) or as the marketing scene (Svensson, 2004). Drawing upon ideas from critical theory and critical discourse analysis, I wanted to acknowledge the micro-political nature of these life worlds and study how they enabled as well as constrained marketing work. In a similar vein, Svensson (2006) offers a study of a marketing consultancy firm trying to sell their services to a potential client. In order to accomplish this, the consultants needed to present themselves to the clients as credible and trustworthy (see Moeran, 2005), and one way of doing this concretely was to claim professional legitimacy. Marketing knowledge was one of the rhetorical resources used by the marketing consultants in their attempts to create professional legitimacy. More specifically, my study showed that consultants, when meeting their potential clients, talked about marketing knowledge in terms of scientific qualities, objectivity and robustness. These rhetorical constructions contributed to the image of credibility and trustworthiness.

Potter and Puchta provide interesting contributions to the critical research on the production of market intelligence and knowledge (Puchta & Potter, 2002; Potter & Puchta, 2007). Their studies can be seen as microscopic explorations of the social interactions combined with Foucault's ideas about the relation between knowledge and power. As they themselves put it:

> [W]e would like to highlight a link to more sociological and historical conceptualizations of the nature of social science and its objects. One of the arguments of the philosopher and discourse analyst Michel Foucault (1972) is that objects of social science study are constituted out of its discourse practices. Much work within the Foucaultian research tradition has taken an expansive historical perspective (e.g. Danzier, 1990; Rose, 1989). In this case, we have shown how the practices of focus groups moderation can constitute freestanding opinion packages as social science objects.
>
> *Puchta & Potter, 2002, p. 361*

Furthermore, Potter and Puchta's studies involve intricate critique of much of the knowledge production undertaken in marketing departments and within market research agencies. Potter and Puchta (2007) they present a detailed analysis of the interactions in a market research focus group dealing with hair products, showing how phenomena that are often treated as psychological, not least so in marketing management textbooks, are interactional accomplishments. Market researchers habitually treat focus groups (and other methods for collecting marketing intelligence) as "a way of 'eliciting' people's opinions, attitudes and beliefs about products, policies and services" (Puchta & Potter, 2002, p. 346). In contrast, Puchta and Potter suggest that knowledge, beliefs, opinions, attitudes, motives and desires are *outcomes* of the discussions in focus groups. Psychological phenomena are jointly constructed in and through the interactions in the focus group discussions, an insight that highlights the importance of subjecting these micro instances of knowledge production to critical empirical research.

The production of the marketing organization

In order to enable the production of advertising campaigns, marketing strategies and market analyses, an organization – a marketing organization – needs to be produced. A marketing organization comprises both the formal distribution of roles and work tasks and the construction of less formal organizational building blocks, such as culture, values, subjectivities, myths and moral stories. As pointed out by Kärreman and Alvesson, organizations:

> are also sites where perceptual, cultural, and ideological material is created and reproduced. Organizational outcomes are not only restricted to trains, toys and travels, they also include ideas, customs, roles, and identities, to mention but a few elements of social reality provided in and through organizations.
>
> *Kärreman & Alvesson, 2001, p. 59*

An example of the production of the marketing organization is the logic of branding, and the ways in which it shapes organizations (e.g. Mumby, 2016). A brand can produce meaning, relevance and identities in an organization (Alvesson & Willmott, 2002). Mumby suggests that the "brand now shapes the ways in which corporations organize themselves, operating . . . from the outside in — the very structure and operation of organizations are increasingly shaped by their brand identities" (Mumby, 2016, p. 900). Interestingly enough, the brands' having effects on organizations from the outside in is, in effect, an internal product. The purpose of brand management is to create and manage brands. Hence, there seems to be a dialectical relationship in place between the output of marketing work and the organizational effects thereof.

Another interesting study along similar lines is Kärreman and Alvesson's (2001) analysis of a news bill meeting at an evening newspaper. During the meeting, the rationale and meanings of being a tabloid journalist are produced. Kärreman and Alvesson conceptualize the outcome of the news bill meeting as one of shared identities, a collective sense of being a tabloid journalist. More specifically, the news bill meeting:

> provides cues and clues on how to relate to the world from this particular point of view. It provides a simple and easily understood idea about why one of the tools of trade – the news bill – is important, and a fairly sophisticated explanatory system to defend its importance. More significantly, the structure and content of the conversation tell something important about the trade, and about those who perform it, partly through the construction of the readers, the product, and the part of the external world that is worth paying attention to, etc. These constructions call for a corresponding kind of newsmaker.
>
> *Alvesson & Kärreman, 2001, p. 86*

The construction of the reader, i.e. the consumer of news, becomes a matter of organizing and identity regulation during the news bill meeting studied by Alvesson and Kärreman.

Branding logic is only one principle according to which the marketing organization can be produced. Another one is customer orientation. Skålén et al. suggest that:

> Customerism is a form of governmental rationality, that, through prescribing certain practices and technologies, aims to establish customer needs and demands as the point of reference for management, organizational behavior, the design and development of organizational forms and the products and services that organizations offer. Within marketing discourse, customerism is signified by concepts such as customer orientation, marketing orientation, market orientation, service dominant logic, and the marketing concept.
>
> *Skålén et al., 2008, pp. 152–153*

The ambition of customer orientation is to steer the attention of the employees toward consumer needs on the market. Rather than focusing on production, strategic visions and internal resources, the minds and souls of the organizational members should be oriented toward the market out there. Drawing upon Foucault's ideas, Skålén (2010) has observed the work in a service organization and suggests that customer or market orientation is a matter of cultural change. It is an attempt to regulate and manage values and norms within the organization, for instance by means of internal educational programs. Skålén conceptualizes such a market orientation program in terms of establishing a certain kind of customer-oriented ethic (or religion) and customer-oriented subjectivities.

Chalmers (2001) has offered interesting insights into how gender stereotypes play a role in marketers' strivings for professional legitimacy within organizations. With a particular focus on gender meaning, she starts from a Foucauldian analysis of the relation between discourse, knowledge, power and meaning making, and presents three case studies of marketing departments. Chalmers shows how marketing workers, by means of employing discourses of masculinity, seek to carve out a niche for themselves vis-à-vis other managerial sub-disciplines within the corporation. Chalmers gives a detailed backstage view of the gender and management politics going on in the everyday marketing work, and she summarizes her argument as follows:

> [G]ender provides particular frameworks of meaning (simultaneously intersected by meanings of race, class, age, sexual orientation etc.) that can be used as a discursive resource to articulate claims in the competitive struggles among the various management disciplines for positions of corporate power and that these gendering processes have implications for job construction and job segregation.
>
> *Chalmers, 2001, p. 7*

Chalmers contributes to a critically informed analysis of the power play of managerial occupations, a game in which marketing workers traditionally struggle to survive. Thus, marketing work is, to a substantial extent, a legitimizing practice and Chalmers demonstrates how gender discourses become crucial in this gendering work.

Moeran (1993, 1996, 2009), who has been mentioned before in this chapter, has published a number of illuminating ethnographic studies with a critical edge of the organization of advertising work. In Moeran (2009), the organization of creativity in a Japanese advertising agency is explored in detail. Moeran shows how the organization of creativity in the everyday work at the agency is a way of producing and reproducing power relations within the organization as well as in relation to clients and consumers. Like Chalmers (2001), Moeran acknowledges the inherent tensions built into the organization of marketing work, for instance between the efforts "to dream up and prepare the campaign (an account team) and freelance professional hired to assist in the creative work required to put it into effect (a production team" (Moeran, 2009, pp. 963–964). By shedding light upon internal tensions within a marketing organization, it also becomes possible to subject the micro-politics of marketing work to critical scrutiny.

The future of critical marketing studies

One of the main challenges for all kinds of research, particularly social sciences and humanities, is to remain relevant in a society that constantly changes (Alvesson, Gabriel & Paulsen, 2017). However, research is also potentially progressive in that it can contribute with knowledge that enables new ways of understanding society and acting within it. As for *critical* social science, in particular, research can be an emancipatory force in the change of oppressive social conditions and structure. Hence, the future of critical research – e.g. of marketing work – is not only a matter of being responsive to societal changes. Perhaps more importantly, critical research needs to write itself into relevancy, not only by means of addressing issues experienced as problematic in today's society, but also by means of problematizing everything in society that seems unproblematic and unquestionable. In this final section of the chapter I will highlight three areas that are particularly important to acknowledge in critical research on marketing work.

An area for future critical studies is the increasing expansion of marketing work to organizations, situations and contexts previously untouched by the logic and language of marketing. In the wake of the studies of marketization of society conducted, for instance, within Critical

Discourse Analysis (Fairclough, 1993, 1995), there is a need for detailed and nuanced empirical studies of the ways in which marketing work has come to permeate areas within social spheres previously untouched by the language and logic of marketing. These marketization tendencies manifest themselves in, for example, the increasing importance of brand management work within the public sector. Universities, municipalities, cities and the police have adopted brand management as one of the main strategic practices to work with in order to secure legitimacy and competitive advantage (see also Giovanardi, Kavaratzis & Lichrou, this volume). If we wish to increase – and deepen – our understanding of how the logic and language of marketing influence the organization of society, this kind of critical attention is essential.

Another major challenge for future critical studies of management and marketing is to develop a methodological language of its own. Since the advent of the Frankfurt School, critical research has defined itself in opposition to what was seen as traditional positivistic research within social sciences. In contrast to traditional theory and its preoccupation with finding universal causal social laws, Horkheimer (1937/1976) suggested that critical theory should go beyond the ambition to describe the nature of society. Instead the ambition of critical theory should be to contribute to the emancipation from oppressive structures and ideological practices that constrain human autonomy. The focus on emancipation requires another methodological language that transgresses the scientific language of representation, validity, reliability and generalizability. This is not an easy task since social scientists are, as is everybody, prisoners in their language and life worlds. The methodological language is particularly important in this respect since it provides the conceptual resources by means of which research questions are formulated, research designs are set up, empirical material is created and, eventually, conclusions are drawn. Insofar as critical research is concerned with the exposure of soft, hidden and internalized power, to critical scrutiny, there is a great need for a methodological reasoning that can cope with this task.

Elsewhere (Svensson, 2014) I have suggested a more forgiving, and even encouraging, view on over-interpretations, i.e. interpretations of data that transgress "the most superficial levels of meaning – i.e. what people say and what seems to happen in an organization – in order to get down to the layers of soft and silent power of social life" (Svensson, 2014, p. 179). I have suggested that critical research needs to visualize the silent forms of power, and one way of doing this is to engage in what is sometimes seen pejoratively as *over-interpretations*. Rather than seeing over-interpretations as a sign of weakness and a methodological fallacy, there are good reasons for taking the opposite standpoint: that of striving for over-interpretations. The over-interpretation is a way of supporting the critical enterprise of disclosing the silent forms of power in organizations and within society. Silent power operates through the creation of consent and common sense in society. Things we take for granted, questions we never ask, underlying structures we never observe, norms we never reflect upon (as being norms); these are what silent power is all about. Silent power is built into the nitty-gritty details of everyday lives, and most often we do not even recognize it as power.

To access the silent power, the critical researcher needs to go beyond the superficial level of empirical support. In order to do so, interpretations that violate the empirical material might be called for. Jonathan Culler captures the critical potential of over-interpretations when he suggests that:

> Many "extreme" interpretations, like many moderate interpretations, will no doubt have little impact, because they are judged unpersuasive or redundant or irrelevant or boring, but if they are extreme, they have a better chance, it seems to me, of bringing to light connections or implications not previously noticed or reflected on than if they strive to remain "sound" or moderate.
>
> *Culler, 1992, p. 110*

Lastly, it is difficult to speculate about the future of critical marketing work without taking into account studies of the production of marketing workers in educational institutions such as business schools. Decision makers, managers, Wall Street workers, accountants, strategists and marketing workers are produced in business schools so as to become easily employable and efficient in the workplace.

Business schools are, indeed, ambivalent places. They are dangerous places in that they are the factories in which the future decision makers are manufactured. Furthermore, business schools are sites in which the architects of the capitalism of the future are manufactured, trained and refined. In business schools, prospective marketers are equipped with knowledge in the most Foucauldian sense of the term. Students are exposed to knowledge that enables them to speak, think and act as marketing workers do, not only in organizations but also in schools, hospitals and municipal offices. However, business schools are also sites of hope. Since it is the future that is at stake in the discussions taking place in classrooms and in the exam papers, business schools can make a difference. If handled with great care, management and marketing knowledge can provide the foundation for thoughts, decisions and actions that are a bit less harmful than the ones that, at least up to this point, have played a decisive role in the development of global financial and environmental crises.

References

Adorno, T.W. (1991). *The culture industry*. New York, Routledge.
Adorno, T.W., & Horkheimer, M. (1944/1997). *Dialectic of enlightenment*. London, Verso.
Alvesson, M. (1996). *Communication, power and organization*. Berlin/New York, Walter de Gruyter.
Alvesson, M., & Willmott, H. (2002). Identity regulation as organizational control: Producing the appropriate individual. *Journal of Management Studies*, 39(5), 619–644.
Alvesson, M., Gabriel, Y., & Paulsen, R. (2017). *Return to meaning: A social science with something to say*. Oxford, Oxford University Press.
Arvidsson, A. (2003). *Marketing modernity: Italian advertising from fascism to postmodernity*. London, Routledge.
Atkinson, P. (2006). Why do fieldwork? *Sociologisk Forskning*, 43(2), 128–134.
Bauman, Z. (2001). Consuming life. *Journal of Consumer Culture*, 1(1), 9–29.
Billig, M. (1999). Commodity fetishism and repression: Reflections on Marx, Freud and the psychology of consumer capitalism. *Theory and Psychology*, 9(3), 313–330.
Brown, S. (2005). *Writing marketing*. London, Sage.
Button, G. (1987). Answers as interactional products: Two sequential practices used in interviews. *Social Psychology Quarterly*, 50(2), 160–171.
Chalmers, L.V. (2001). *Marketing masculinities: Gender and management politics in marketing work*. Westport, Greenwood.
Culler, J. (1992). In defense of overinterpretation. In U. Eco (Ed.), *Interpretation and overinterpretation* (pp. 109–124). Cambridge, Cambridge University Press.
Cusset, F. (2008). *French theory: How Foucault, Derrida, Deleuze, & co transformed the intellectual life of the United States*. Minnesota, University of Minnesota Press.
Drucker, P.F. (1954). *The practice of management*. Oxford, Butterworth-Heinemann.
Elliot, R. (1999). Symbolic meaning and postmodern consumer culture. In D. Brownlie, M. Saren, R. Wensley & R. Whittington (Eds.), *Rethinking marketing: Towards critical marketing accountings* (pp. 112–125). London, Sage.
Ewen, S. (1976). *Captains of consciousness: Advertising and the social roots of advertising*. New York, McGraw-Hill.
Fairclough, N. (1993). Critical discourse analysis and the marketization of public discourse: The universities. *Discourse and Society*, 4(2), 133–168.
Fairclough, N. (1995). *Critical discourse analysis: The critical study of language*. London, Longman.
Foucault, M. (1972). *The archaeology of knowledge*. London, Tavistock.
Foucault, M. (1980). *Power/knowledge*. New York, Pantheon.
Grafton-Small, R., & Linstead, S.A. (1989). Advertisement and artefacts: Everyday understanding and the creative consumer. *International Journal of Advertising*, 8(3), 205–218.

Grönroos, C. (2000). *Service management and marketing.* Chichester, Wiley.
Gummesson, E. (2002). *Total relationship marketing.* Oxford, Butterworth-Heinemann.
Hester, S., & Francis, D. (1994). Doing data: The local organization of a sociological interview. *British Journal of Sociology, 45*(4), 675–695.
Hochschild, A.R. (1983). *The managed heart: Commercialization of human feeling.* Berkeley, University of California Press.
Horkheimer, M. (1937/1976). Traditional and critical theory. In P. Connerton (Ed.), *Critical sociology: Selected readings* (pp. 206–224). Harmondsworth, Penguin.
Houtkoop-Steenstra, H. (1996). Probing behavior of interviewers in the standardized semi-open research interview. *Quality and Quantity, 30*(2), 205–230.
Itao, A. (2010). Paul Ricoeur's hermeneutics of symbols: A critical dialectic of suspicion and faith. *Kritike, 4*(2), 1–17.
Kärreman, D., & Alvesson, M. (2001). Making newsmakers: Conversational identity at work. *Organization Studies, 22*(1), 59–89.
Kellner, D. (1992). Popular culture and the construction of postmodern identities. In S. Lasch & J. Friedman (Eds.), *Modernity and identity* (pp. 141–177). Oxford, Blackwell.
Kemper, S. (2001). *Buying and believing: Sri Lankan advertising and consumers in a transnational world.* Chicago, Chicago University Press.
Kotler, P., Brady, M., Goodman, M., & Hansen, T. (2016). *Marketing management,* 3rd European edition. Harlow, UK, Pearson.
Lasch, C. (1979). *The culture of narcissism.* New York, Norton.
Leidner, R. (1993). *Fast food, fast talk: Service work and the routinization of everyday life.* Berkeley, University of California Press.
Lien, M.E. (1995). *Food products in the making: An ethnography of marketing practice.* Oslo, Oslo University.
Lien, M.E. (1997). *Marketing and modernity.* Oxford, Berg.
Marcuse, H. (1964). *One-dimensional man: Studies in the ideology of advanced industrial society.* Boston, Beacon Press.
Marx, K. (1977). *Capital, volume I.* Moscow, Progress Publishers.
Mazzarella, W. (2003). *Shoveling smoke: Advertising and globalization in contemporary India.* Durham, Duke University Press.
Miller, D. (1997). *Capitalism: An ethnographic approach.* Oxford, Berg.
Moeran, B. (1993). A tournament of value: Strategies of presentation in Japanese advertising. *Ethnos, 58*(1–2), 73–93.
Moeran, B. (1996). *Japanese advertising agency: An anthropology of media and markets.* London, Curzon.
Moeran, B. (2005). Tricks of the trade: The performance and interpretation of authenticity. *Journal of Management Studies, 42*(5), 901–922.
Moeran, B. (2009). The organization of creativity in Japanese advertising production. *Human Relations, 62*(7), 963–985.
Mumby, D.M. (2016). Organizing beyond organization: Branding, discourse, and communicative capitalism. *Organization, 23*(6), 884–907.
Packard, V. (1957). *The hidden persuaders: Influence as interpersonal accomplishment.* New York, McKay.
Pollay, R.W. (1986). The distorted mirror: Reflections on the unintended consequences of advertising. *Journal of Marketing, 50*(2), 18–36.
Pomerantz, A. (1988). Offering a candidate answer: An information seeking strategy. *Communication Monographs, 55*(4), 360–373.
Potter J., & Puchta, C. (2007). Mind, mousse and moderation. In A. Hepburn & S. Wiggins (Eds.), *Discursive research in practice* (pp. 104–124). Cambridge, Cambridge University Press.
Prus, R.C. (1989a). *Pursuing customers: An ethnography of marketing activities.* London, Sage.
Prus, R.C. (1989b). *Making sales.* London, Sage.
Puchta, C., & Potter, J. (2002). Manufacturing individual opinions: Market research focus groups and the discursive psychology of evaluation. *British Journal of Social Psychology, 41*(3), 345–363.
Ricœur, P. (1970). *Freud and philosophy: An essay on interpretation.* New Haven, Yale University Press.
Silverman, D. (1993). *Interpreting qualitative data: Methods for talk, text and interaction.* Sage, London.
Skålén, P. (2010). *Managing service firms: The power of managerial marketing.* London, Routledge.
Skålén, P., Fougère, M., & Fellesson, M. (2008). *Marketing discourse: A critical perspective.* London, Routledge.
Skålén, P., & Hackley, C. (2011). Editorial: Marketing-as-practice. Introduction to the special issue. *Scandinavian Journal of Management, 27*(2), 189–195.

Stewart, D. (1989). The hermeneutics of suspicion. *Journal of Literature & Theology, 3*(3), 296–307.

Svensson, P. (2004). *Setting the marketing scene: Reality production in everyday marketing work*. Lund, Lund University Press.

Svensson, P. (2006). Marketing marketing: The professional project as a micro-discursive accomplishment. In R. Greenwood, R. Suddaby & M. McDougald (Eds.), *Research in the sociology of organizations Vol. 24* (pp. 349–381). Greenwich, CT, JAI Press.

Svensson, P. (2007). Producing marketing: Towards a social-phenomenology of marketing work. *Marketing Theory, 7*(3), 271–290.

Svensson, P. (2014). Thickening thick descriptions: Overinterpretations in critical organizational ethnography. In E. Jeanes & T. Huzzard (Eds.), *Critical management research: Reflections from the Field* (pp. 173–188). Los Angeles, Sage.

West, C. (2014). *Black prophetic fire*. Boston, Beacon Press.

Williams, R. (1980). Advertising: The magic system. In *Problems in materialism and culture* (pp. 170–195). London, Verso.

Willis, P. (1990). *Common culture*. Buckingham, Open University Press.

10
THE CULTURAL TURN IN LIFESTYLE RESEARCH
Overview and reflections

Gokcen Coskuner-Balli

Introduction

In contemporary societies, lifestyle concerns the very core of self-identity as well as its making and remaking. We each make choices of what to eat, how to dress, and how to spend our time. These choices reflect values and tastes that comprise collectivities in which we are similar to one another and different from others, both in the distribution of disposable incomes and the motivations that underlie such distributions (Holt, 1997; Zablocki & Kanter, 1976). The premise that consumers can be grouped into meaningful clusters based on these shared values and tastes, rather than solely on their social class and demographic background led to a rich stream of research within marketing (Wells, 1975). The early scholarly research focused on developing tools to identify distinct lifestyle segments. While practical and commonly adopted, this approach did not necessarily concern itself with power relations or the institutional and historical shaping of consumption patterns (Fırat & Dholakia, 2003; Tadajewski, 2010).

In this chapter, I offer a critical reading of lifestyle research in marketing with specific attention to the cultural approach which emerged in the late 1990s. Cultural research offers insights on how lifestyles can serve as symbolic boundaries among different social groups; on dynamics of legitimacy of new and often times stigmatized lifestyle groups and on the institutional and macro shaping of lifestyles. In the following sections, I will first provide a general overview of the history of lifestyle research in marketing. I will then determine the most prominent themes and key theoretical takeaways that have emerged in the cultural approach. I will conclude with future research directions, highlighting possible critical scholarly trajectories that can arise from the study of the linkages between globalization, political ideologies, broader institutional factors, and consumer lifestyles.

A history of lifestyle research in marketing

In the theories of Marx, Poulantzas, and Wright, the distinctions among social groups were explained in terms of social class, whereby one's position is determined by his or her place in the production of goods and services, the control of the resources of production, and his or her occupation. Modernity and the increases in economic productivity and capacity for wealth creation that have taken place since World War II, have reduced the significance of the production and acquisition of basic material needs in the lives of families and individuals (to some extent and within some locations more than others). With the rise in the standard of living, issues related to consumption, rather than production become more relevant, and lifestyles, rather than classes, begin to play an increasingly important part in shaping a range of attitudes and behaviors (Crompton, 1998). Sociologists as well as consumer researchers needed another construct, other than social class, to theorize about the differences among various social groups. Accordingly, new theories started to emphasize lifestyle, which is based on cultural and social capital (Bourdieu, 1984), education and experience (Zablocki & Kanter, 1976), and subcultural capital (Hebdige, 1979; Thornton, 1995) as the sources of difference.

By the 1960s, the field of marketing came to recognize that social class, demographics, and psychological explanations were not sufficient to account for the differences in consumer behavior. Marketing researchers started arguing for the richness of the lifestyle concept for consumer analysis. Lazer (1963, p. 130) proposed a definition of lifestyle that, akin to Bourdieu's notion of habitus, highlighted the aggregate of consumer purchases and "the manner in which they are consumed", as a reflection of consumers' lifestyles. Writing at the same time as other influential marketing scholars, such as Levy (1963) and Kelley (1963), Lazer registered the symbolism of products and laid the groundwork for lifestyle branding. The new construct, lifestyle, combined the virtues of demographics with the richness and dimensionality of motivational research (Plummer, 1974; Wells, 1975).

Notably, Plummer and Wells postulated the value of lifestyle segmentation in terms of providing a more holistic understanding of the consumer. Instead of defining the target in demographic terms (e.g. middle-aged housewives with a large family and average income) or product-usage terms (e.g. the frequent user, the price buyer, the vacation traveler), lifestyle segmentation recognized the diversity elided by those terms. In addition to being middle-aged, white-collar or blue-collar housewives, lifestyle segmentation provided definitions such as "housewife role haters", "old-fashioned homebodies", and "active affluent urbanites" (Plummer, 1974, p. 35).

Concurrent with these definitions were numerous attempts to operationalize lifestyle. This early research developed survey-based inventories, such as those focused on activities, interests, and opinions (AIO) and values and lifestyle systems (VALS), that were aimed at creating psychological profiles of consumer segments. These initial applications, however, were criticized for their lack of theoretical sophistication (Wells, 1975). Wells stated that AIO and VALS research developed separately and came together only because "lifestyle" seemed to be such an appropriate shorthand expression for what the AIO research was attempting to portray. Wells noted: "Almost accidentally, the lifestyle concept has become operationalized among a certain group of researchers as AIO research conducted for a rather limited set of purposes and employing a rather limited set of techniques" (Wells, 1975, p. 498).

In the 1980s and 1990s, consumer researchers sought to integrate lifestyle into existing personality and value theories. Research under this paradigm considered lifestyle a behavioral expression of personality traits and values (Kahle, Beatty & Homer, 1986; Kamakura & Mazzon, 1991; Kamakura & Novak, 1992; Novak & MacEvoy, 1990). The Rokeach Values Survey (RVS) and List of Values (LOV) dominated lifestyle research in this era. Upon the introduction of the RVS in 1973, scholars tested and further developed value measurement scales. Notably, Kamakura and Novak collapsed the RSV into the 9-item LOV scale. The agenda underpinning this research was to measure and classify consumers into clusters on the basis of their rank orderings among a set of nomothetic values (Thompson & Troester, 2002). This approach, somewhat predictably, came under criticism from cultural researchers, as it did not account for the cultural moorings from which value systems emerged. It is this criticism, and the subsequent cultural research program which emerged, that I examine in the next section.

The cultural approach to lifestyle research

During the late 1990s and early 2000s, the personality/values approach to lifestyle research was criticized by consumer researchers (Holt, 1997; Fırat & Shultz, 1997; Thompson & Troester, 2002). As postmodernist ideas entered the marketing discipline, researchers questioned the central tenets and principles of marketing, including lifestyles (Fırat & Venkatesh, 1995). As Fırat and Shultz (1997) posited, one key tenet of postmodernity was increased fragmentation, which made traditional bases of segmentation, such as demographics and psychographics, and even the more recent typologies such as VALS, less and less useful:

> Such strategies depended on the modern premises . . . for example, a consistent, centered and unified character or self-concept for the consumer . . . For postmodern consumer markets, using segmentation strategies that try to constrain or anchor consumers to a single, consistent, stable way of behaving is likely to lead to marketing failure.
> *Fırat and Shultz, 1997, p. 194*

Other consumer researchers also criticized the nomothetic schemes and any reliance on a single value as a basis of consumers' motivations came into question (Holt, 1997; Thompson & Troester, 2002). In subsequent years, scholars started to offer more nuanced cultural analyses by investigating how consumers' values and motivations are embedded within particular social and historical contexts (Arnould & Thompson, 2005).

To account for contextualized consumer value systems and the meaning-based linkages to the particular consumption goals and practices through which these values are enacted, Holt (1997) proposed poststructuralist lifestyle analysis. The poststructuralist approach appreciates that meanings depend on social context, are historically laden, and are negotiated within a syncretic combination of available discourses. To illustrate, he explored how the value of traditionalism had different meanings and behavioral implications for different consumers who could be clustered into the same group according to the VALS. Holt (1997, p. 332) stated:

> Traditional is not an objective, univocal term and, so, gives little descriptive guidance by itself. Traditional in what sense? Compared with whom? . . . Although personality/values lifestyle analysis captures some underlying commonalities across respondents, the extreme data reduction required to identify commonalities at the level of personality and values requires abstracting away many details of the informants' tastes that are essential for describing the cultural structuring of consumption patterns.

Building on Holt's (1997) call for a poststructuralist approach to study lifestyles, Thompson and Troester (2002) criticized the conventional theories of consumer value systems, such as that of Rokeach, due to their reductionist approach to culture. Thompson and Troester (2002, p. 552) underscored that conventional value research treated relative meanings as if they were psychological universals:

> The driving research agenda is to measure, aggregate, and classify consumers on the basis of their rank orderings (or importance weightings) among a set of nomothetic values. These classifications are divorced from any situating cultural context. As a result, they are not theoretically attuned to the cultural meanings from which value systems emerge nor the meaning-based linkages between consumer values, consumption goals, and the consumption practices through which these goals are pursued.

To account for the missing cultural and historical insight of the Rokeachian paradigm, Thompson and Troester (2002) suggested the study of microcultural frames of reference to understand consumer values and goals. They posited that the meanings and narratives that organize consumers' values are linked to broader cultural discourses, such as countermodernism. Broader cultural discourses, in other words, shape the microcultural meanings that contextualize, for example, a specific belief and practice system within the natural-health community. For instance, the value of "harmonious balance" is linked to the broader discourse of countermodernism, which views "the modernist advance of science and technology as a force that disrupts the holistic balance of nature, creates divisions between individuals, and isolates humanity from its organic connections to nature" (Thompson & Troester, 2002, p. 558). In this regard, they identified consumers who pursue a natural-health lifestyle and adopt practices of purification to attain a natural balance.

In the following years, cultural marketing researchers produced a rich literature that aimed to conceptualize consumers' values and lifestyles in a manner that is sensitive to the culturally contextualized nature of consumption practices and meanings. I identify three main research programs within this emergent tradition: (1) lifestyles as symbolic boundaries, (2) legitimation and transformation of lifestyles, and (3) institutions and lifestyles (see Table 10.1).

Lifestyles as symbolic boundaries

Cultural researchers have explored the ways in which symbolic boundaries between collectivities are expressed or recreated through consumption patterns. The corollary premise is that, although fragmented, the postmodern marketplace hosts performative settings for social stratification. This research program builds upon the classical scholarship of Veblen, Weber, and, most notably, Bourdieu. These sociological works focus on the lifestyles of different social groups to understand the dynamics of social distinction. By studying the activities of the wealthy, Veblen (1899) demonstrated how the conspicuous consumption of the leisure class made them distinct from the lower classes. Simmel (1957) discussed the importance of lifestyle to explain how the dynamic of style was driven by the trickle-down emulation of elites. Weber (1978), one of the first to use the term *style of life*, also viewed consumption as a distinctive domain in which stratified relationships are formed and sustained on the basis of style, rather than position in the labor market.

Bourdieu (1984), whose work has probably been the most influential for consumer researchers, introduced a theory of cultural capital and taste as a means to understand the social patterning of consumption. He claimed that social life can be conceived as a multidimensional status game in which people draw on at least three different types of resources (which he terms *economic, cultural,* and *social capital*) to compete for status (which he terms *symbolic capital*). Economic, cultural, and social capital act together to form classifiable conditions of existence, which he terms the *habitus*. The habitus is an abstracted, transposable schema that classifies the world and structures both action and taste. Adopting Bourdieu's cultural capital framework, cultural researchers explored how different collectivities (e.g. middle-class, suburban Americans; poor Turkish immigrant women; indie consumers) attempt to mobilize their capital to (re)create status distinctions in the marketplace. As Holt (1997, p. 336) succinctly noted:

> The symbolic differences between consumption patterns are a type of symbolic boundary: differences in meanings, embedded in consumption practices, serve as a basis for affiliating with certain types of people and likewise, as a resource for distinguishing oneself from others, reinforcing positions.

Table 10.1 Cultural research programs on lifestyle

Program	Context	Author(s)	Theoretical contribution
Lifestyle as symbolic boundary	Middle- and working-class consumers in rural Pennsylvania	Holt (1997)	A proposal for poststructuralist lifestyle analysis
	Poor migrant women in Turkey	Üstüner & Holt (2007)	Bourdieu-inspired theorization of subordinate (immigrant) consumers' engagement with dominant consumer culture
	High cultural capital and low cultural capital consumers in Turkey	Üstüner & Holt (2010)	Extension of Bourdieu's theorization of status consumption through an analysis of high and low cultural capital consumers in relation to the Western lifestyle myth
	Ecologically conscious consumers	Carfagna et al. (2014)	A study of the new high cultural consumer repertoire
	Australian post-war elites	Turner & Edmunds (2002)	Application of Bourdieu's theory of taste to explore shifts in cultural taste
	Lifestyle segments in Europe	Tapp & Warren (2010)	An analysis of how capital and competition informs lifestyle clusters in Europe
	Indie consumers	Arsel & Thompson (2011)	A Bourdieuian analysis of consumer strategies to protect their status investments as the symbolic boundaries are contested in the marketplace
Future critical marketing research directions	*Lifestyle patterns and consumer well-being?*		
Legitimation of lifestyle	Stay-at-home fathers	Coskuner-Balli & Thompson (2013)	Collective legitimation of a stigmatized lifestyle through translating domestic capital to economic, social, and symbolic capital
	Freegans	Fernandez, Brittain & Bennett (2011); Pentina & Amos (2011)	Investigations of freegan ideology and practices

Women skaters	Thompson & Üstüner (2015)	Analysis of negotiation of gender boundaries through the lens of gender performativity theory
Empowered consumers	Davies & Elliot 2006	A historical exploration of the evolution of the empowered consumer and brand consciousness from 1918 and 1965 in Britain
Future critical marketing research directions		
Evolution of lifestyles over time		
Lifestyles and institutions		
Consumers' use of credit cards	Bernthal, Crockett, & Rose (2005)	Lifestyle facilitation through credit card practice
Normalization of credit/debt	Peñaloza & Barnhart (2011)	Normalization of credit/debt in the United States
Coffeehouse culture in the Ottoman Empire	Karababa & Ger (2011)	An historical account of formation of the active consumer through an interplay among multiple institutional actors
Responsible consumer	Giesler & Veresiu (2014)	A macro-level theorization of the creation of a responsible consumer through problem-solving initiatives of the World Economic Forum
Urban consumer	Miles (2012)	A reflection on the relation between neoliberal ideology, city planning, and consumer lifestyles
Future critical marketing research directions		
State and political actors' influence on cultural value systems (e.g. neoliberalism, political Islam, socialism) and consumer lifestyles		

In his analysis of middle- and working-class consumers in rural Pennsylvania, he distinguished two main symbolic boundaries, national/local and center/periphery, that demarcated four social class-based lifestyles. The middle-class consumers in the study compared their consumption patterns to their peers in large cities and tried to maintain their networks while living in their rural community. By contrast, the working-class consumers involved in the study, had little interaction beyond their local communities. Their lifestyles revolved around playing cards, camping, socializing at lodges, hunting, folk dancing, participating in local pageants, and gardening.

In subsequent research, Üstüner and Holt (2007, 2010) investigated how symbolic boundaries are enacted within Turkish society. By studying the lives of poor migrant women who live in squatter communities, they determined how migrant women engage with Turkish consumer culture and the Western (*Batıcı*) lifestyle that has become the dominant ideology, especially in the aftermath of the 1980s, with the enactment of neoliberal trade policies. Üstüner and Holt (2007, p. 46) pointed out that "*Batıcı* offers a way of living – a constellation of tastes and sensibilities and their material expressions – that expresses a particular modernist ideal of being Turkish". Within the Turkish social class structure, however, this dominant ideology creates contradictions between middle-class urbanites and rural peasants. When Turkish villagers move into the squatter communities in the city, they encounter the celebrated *Batıcı* lifestyle, in which they have limited opportunities to participate due to a lack of economic, social, or cultural capital.

Üstüner and Holt found that the mothers' they worked with in this project, engaged with the dominant lifestyle, but reaffirmed the symbolic boundaries between themselves and modern middle-class urbanites: "Mothers use their tastes and rituals and status mechanisms to maintain a symbolic boundary separating the modern village aesthetic they have nurtured in the squatter from the middle-class aesthetics of the *Batıcı* woman" (Üstüner & Holt, 2007, p. 49). For daughters, however, this symbolic boundary between the villager identity and the *Batıcı* woman presents itself as a structural barrier that they cannot circumvent. Although they look up to the *Batıcı* lifestyle and imagine themselves as leading one, economic, social, and cultural barriers inhibit them from doing so. With this realization, the daughters lead a "shattered identity project", constantly reminded of what they cannot have.

The *Batıcı*/American lifestyle myth also informs the symbolic boundary construction between high cultural consumers (HCC) and low cultural consumers (LCC) in Turkey (Üstüner & Holt, 2010). These two different groups rely on distinct consumption strategies in their status games. The HCCs emphasize cultural sophistication, whereas LCCs focus on pecuniary displays. This boundary is further situated in the status dynamics between the West and less industrialized countries. The HCCs in Turkey work hard to transform their habitus-instilled tastes, a process that, in Bourdieu's (1984) analysis, is indicative of lower cultural capital. As a result, HCCs tend to be reflexively insecure about their ability to successfully deploy the Western lifestyle in a manner that yields cultural capital.

In another Bourdieu-inspired theorization, Arsel and Thompson (2011) document how indie consumers reinstate symbolic boundaries to protect their field-dependent social and cultural capital when their investments and, therefore, status come under threat as the commercial mainstream creates marketplace myths from their countercultural lifestyle. As the marketplace appropriated indie consumption practices, the "hipster myth" emerged as a caricature of the aesthetic tastes of this lifestyle group. To protect their field-dependent investments, indie consumers employ demythologizing practices to insulate their field from the comedic and stigmatizing encroachments of the figure of the hipster.

In other Bourdieu-inflected lifestyle research, scholars investigated the construction of middle-class lifestyles in post-war Australia (Turner & Edmunds, 2002), consumer lifestyle segments in

Europe (Tapp & Warren, 2010), and ecologically conscious consumers (Carfagna et al., 2014) to list a few. Turner and Edmunds's (2002) study of elite lifestyles in Australia documents that Australia's post-war elite developed a "distaste for taste" and instead of highbrow cultural activities such as opera and classical ballet they engaged in middle to lowbrow cultural activities. The study brings attention to the generational and culture-specific factors such as popular ethos in understanding the lifestyle(s) of distinct social groups.

Legitimation and transformation of lifestyles

The key question that drives this program of research is: If habitus and consumer choices implicitly and seemingly inevitably reproduce pre-existing social conditions, how can social changes occur, and how can we account for the emergence of new lifestyles? One family of cultural research devoted to studying consumption patterns has sought to unravel the processes by which new lifestyles emerge and are legitimated. As Giddens (1991, p. 81) noted: "The more post-traditional the settings in which an individual moves, the more lifestyle concerns the very core of self-identity, its making and remaking."

Other scholars have registered the increasing fragmentation of consumers in the United States and assert that alternative lifestyles are generated as spontaneous attempts to reach consensus on standards of value in the absence of previously class-based consumption patterns (Zablocki & Kanter, 1976). The breakdown is exacerbated as it becomes difficult to rank lifestyles and tastes unambiguously. Where such a scale exists, social values are coherent.

Within marketing, whether this postmodern fragmentation leads to consumer "liberation" from traditional cultural norms and boundaries has become a widely discussed topic. Fırat and Venkatesh (1995, p. 235) stated that the fragmentation of life, experience, society, and meta-narratives allows for the liberation and acceptance of differences as well as "putting an end to the dominance of any one 'regime of truth'". They pointed to the emergence of the fragmented subject who is free to live in fluid spaces and does not need to commit to one style of being. They consider fragmentation an emancipatory response to the totalizing logic of the market; however, the market still adheres to modern criteria and "regulates consumers' desires . . . It exerts this control through the resilient co-optation of . . . countercultural expression into the mainstream culture" (Fırat & Venkatesh, 1995, p. 254). Fırat and Venkatesh suggested that, as long as the consumer is viewed as being solely within the market, they will never be fully liberated. It is, therefore, necessary to cleave a social space beyond the reach of the market. Holt (2002), however, maintained that it is the market itself that produces the experiential and symbolic freedom that Fırat and Venkatesh fetishize. Even those identity projects that seem to be based on critical reflexivity toward the market, and involve the most creative, unorthodox practices, still reproduce the system (Holt, 2002). He concluded: "What has been termed 'consumer resistance' is actually a form of market sanctioned cultural experimentation through which the market rejuvenates itself" (Holt, 2002, p. 89).

Thompson and Haytko (1997) proposed a more balanced conceptualization to understand how consumers create and contest social identities in the marketplace. They maintained that, as consumers negotiate and forge subject positions, their actions are embedded within the sociocultural trajectories of social class, gender, and market-mediated discourses related to, for example, fashion, health, and body; nonetheless, consumers also have the ability to appropriate these cultural discourses in a process whereby they are continuously engaged in an interpretive dialogue. In two studies on how consumers interpret, adopt, and adapt fashion meanings, both sets of researchers found that fashion is intertextual, consisting of hegemonic and nonhegemonic discourses (Murray, 2002; Thompson & Haytko, 1997). These authors then suggested that consumers appropriate fashion discourses with specific cultural values and subject positions. These alignments, in many cases, served to reinscribe the hegemonic meanings of fashion and to reinstate social distinctions, gender conceptions, and archetypes, but also to negotiate culturally conventional discourses and identity positions.

Highlighting the collective aspect of agency (Sewell, 1992), in their ethnographic study of the emergent lifestyle of stay-at-home fathers, Coskuner-Balli and Thompson (2013) document the collective efforts of stay-at-home fathers to transform social structures, specifically those related to gender, via the marketplace. Although contemporary social conditions have been dramatically altered by second-wave feminism and the increased presence of women in the workforce, men who opt to abdicate their breadwinner role and stay at home face stigma. To recuperate the status loss due to their stigmatized lifestyle choice, stay-at-home fathers adopt a series of "capitalizing consumption practices" that, essentially, serve to create new types of economic, social, and cultural capital. For example, they might adopt a thrifty sensibility in their shopping practices to generate revenue streams from their domesticated cultural capital. They collectively attend playgroups and organize yearly conventions, which help them to develop an unconventional gender identity as well as build social solidarity. They also seek to elevate the status position of their collective identity in the hope that their decisions to become primary caregivers will eventually elicit respect and admiration, rather than ridicule and disparagement.

In addition to converting their domesticated capital to economic and social capital, they seek to enhance the status value of their investments in the domestic realm through masculinizing domesticity. For instance, they strategically seek public spaces, rather than the private sphere of their homes for their playful performance of domesticity. Stay-at-home fathers also seek to masculinize their domesticated cultural capital by portraying themselves as adroit users of technology and as skilful, do-it-yourself practitioners. A third strategy of stay-at-home fathers for masculinizing their domesticated cultural capital involves reframing meal provision (and, by implication, provisional shopping) as a mere necessity that is secondary to their primary caregiving responsibilities and, hence, a tertiary aspect of their collective identity.

Research concerned with lifestyle legitimacy also explored the emergence of alternative lifestyles such as "freeganism", a lifestyle that originated from the voluntary simplicity movement and aims to minimize environmental impact by consuming discarded food and sharing resources (Fernandez, Brittain & Bennett, 2011; Pentina & Amos, 2011). To legitimate the freegan lifestyle, which involves participating in illegal practices such as squatting, shoplifting and cutting locks on dumpsters, freegans formulate an ideology that denounces the capitalist economy. Instead, they create and promote an alternative sign system. This stands in contrast to the dominant values of private property, individualism, hygiene, and money-based career success, and thereby attempts to transcend not only the market economy, but also the "structuring habitus" of its symbolic meanings (Pentina & Amos, 2011, p. 1772). To sustain the freegan lifestyle, Fernandez et al. (2011) suggest that they adopt a hero identity whereby practices such as creating art from trash or trading and sharing rather than buying are construed as subverting the market.

Institutions and consumer lifestyles

Critical consumer researchers have recently examined the institutional and structural influences on consumer lifestyles[1] (see Tadajewski, 2010). Some of the questions that guide this research program include: How is the responsible consumer (i.e. green, health-conscious, financially responsible consumer) created? (Giesler & Veresiu, 2014); how is an active consumer formed through the interplay of various institutional actors? (Karababa & Ger, 2011); how does a technology such as credit cards facilitate consumer lifestyles? (Bernthal, Crockett & Rose, 2005); and how do cultural meanings, reproduced in social and market domains, help to normalize credit/debt? (Peñaloza & Barnhart, 2011); how does the neoliberal city color everyday life? (Miles, 2012); how does the market as an institution impact the motherhood experience? (The VOICE Group, 2010); and how do contemporary marketing practices shape consumer subjectivities? (Zwick & Cayla, 2011).

Bernthal *et al.* (2005) noted that participation in the consumers' republic and the good life has been made possible, especially for working- and middle-class consumers, via credit card technology. Obviously, credit cards facilitate a level of participation in contemporary consumer culture, and many people have adopted this new technology to manage their lifestyles. On the one hand, both LCCs and HCCs use credit cards to build lifestyles and participate in the consumer culture via trading economic capital for cultural capital. On the other hand, consumers with insufficient economic capital eventually find themselves in a debtor's prison (metaphorically and potentially literally). Once accumulated, a high level of debt means that the lifestyles of consumers become oriented toward maintaining control of their expenditures and debts.

In a related study, Peñaloza and Barnhart (2011) discuss the broader array of cultural meanings that underlie how credit card-oriented consumption and lifestyles became normalized in the United States. They make the case that the middle-class consuming subject position is imbricated in the nation's historical legacy of abundance. The contemporary consumer lifestyle "entails a compelling form of work, perhaps even a nascent patriotism, and . . . both are implicated in the normalization of credit/debt" (Peñaloza & Barnhart, 2011, p. 758).

In addition to investigating marketplace technologies and myths, academics have explored the multi-actor dynamics that shape the broader institutional dynamics of consumers' lifestyles. This is a return to the types of scholarship that garnered some attention in the 1970s and 1980s within the "radical" marketing tradition. One exemplar will serve to illuminate this research stream. In their account of the World Economic Forum, Giesler and Veresiu (2014) drew attention to the broader institutional dynamics that help create the category of the responsible consumer. Building on Foucault's notion of governmentality, they detail the processes of consumer responsibilization, whereby adopting a healthy, green lifestyle is rendered a consumer choice *and* responsibility.

Research directions and conclusion

In this chapter, I have grouped cultural lifestyle research into three research programs. The first concerns the ways in which symbolic boundaries between collectivities are expressed/recreated through consumption patterns. These studies illuminated consumer strategies and social structuration in relation to symbolic boundaries. One interesting insight from this research program that can be further explored is the impact of lifestyle patterns for consumer well-being. For example, McCracken (1986, p. 72) suggests that dynamism makes cultural categories somewhat elective and that "social groups can seek to change their place in the categorical scheme, while marketers can seek to establish or encourage a new cultural category (e.g. the teenager, the yuppie) in order to create a new segment". McCracken further argues that consumers in North American society have the freedom to declare which cultural categories they occupy. To do so, they rely on consumer goods, as the material embodiment of cultural blueprints. Critical Marketing researchers can explore whether these blueprints act as informative and heuristic guidelines that liberate consumers and help them to craft desired lifestyles. As Tadajewski (2010) notes, Critical Marketing Studies should also consider the negative ramifications of marketing practices. Accordingly, critical researchers can also study how these blueprints are created, by whom, and toward what end, as well as how lifestyle blueprints or marketplace myths sometimes act as barriers that lead to "shattered" identity projects (e.g. Üstüner & Holt, 2007).

The second research program concerns consumer strategies to legitimate new lifestyles. Future research could focus on how other institutional actors, such as marketers, brands, and entrepreneurs, can create and legitimize new lifestyles. Such studies might focus on how dominant meanings in various fields have evolved over time, influencing consumer values and practices. Studies on market evolution can be informative in terms of theory and methodology. For example, Giesler (2012, p. 56) shows that, in new product markets, legitimization is a brand-mediated process, whereby the market evolves through a "progressive sequence of contestations between the brand images promoted by the innovator and the doppelgänger brand images promoted by other stakeholders". More recently, Ertimur and Coskuner-Balli (2015) examined the evolution of the yoga market in the United States. Drawing from archival data, the authors present the shifts in logics of the yoga market and link these to brand practices in the marketplace. These studies can offer theoretical and methodological guidelines for historical studies on the emergence and evolution of lifestyles.

The third research program offers a theoretical understanding of institutional contexts and consumer lifestyles. Outside of "mainstream" marketing, historical research has the potential to provide macro-level analyses of the sedimentation of consumer lifestyles. For example, consider how the U.S. government proposed consumption as a civic duty that helped to boost the economy and create jobs in the aftermath of World War II (Cohen, 2003). Cohen illustrates how mass consumption has become increasingly intertwined with being a good citizen in what she calls a "Consumers' Republic". In this republic, mass production and consumption were positioned as a means for a better and more egalitarian life linked to a sense of national superiority over Communism. The promises of home mortgages, credit and tax advantages, and the new shopping centers of the "Consumers' Republic" did not necessarily lead to an egalitarian society, however. On the contrary, they reinforced ethnic, social class, and gender stratifications. Cohen's historical analysis lays out how the meanings of consumption as well as consumer lifestyles were structured against the backdrop of politics and government practices (see also Dholakia et al., this volume).

Finally, critical researchers have started to question how the field of marketing, its teaching, and application in firms, is itself socially constructed (Hackley, 2001; Tadajewski, 2010). Peter Svensson (this volume) articulates this agenda in extremely lucid terms as do Zwick and Cayla (2011). Building on this research program, Critical Marketing scholars can further examine how cultural value systems (e.g. neoliberalism, political Islam, socialism) are enacted through state or national policies alongside the actions of other political actors that influence consumer lifestyles.

Note

1 This is actually a more complex point than I can fully explicate here. For example, Tadajewski (2010) outlines the stream of research associated with the structuring of consumption patterns that was indebted to Marxist, neo-Marxist, and related variants of social theory. This appeared, most notably, from the late 1970s and was a visible presence in "radical" marketing thought throughout the 1980s. Perhaps the most recent reincarnation of this approach is found in Atik and Fırat (2013) where they return to the kind of argumentation common in Fırat's earlier work – especially his 1978 doctoral dissertation – placing considerable emphasis on the structuring of consumer lifestyles that downplays the largely voluntaristic emphasis associated with Consumer Culture Theory (CCT) and foregrounds the decision making that takes place a substantial time before the consumer ever has the chance to select and purchase a given product (see also Denegri-Knott & Tadajewski, 2017). Theoretically, this is a function of Fırat's noted distaste for the mid-range theorizing associated with CCT research.

References

Arnould, E.J., & Thompson, C.J. (2005). Consumer culture theory (CCT): Twenty years of research. *Journal of Consumer Research*, *31*(4), 868–883.

Arsel, Z., & Thompson, C.J. (2011). Demythologizing consumption practices: How consumers protect their field-dependent capital from devaluing marketplace myths. *Journal of Consumer Research*, *37*(5), 791–806.

Atik, D., & Fırat, A.F. (2013). Fashion creation and diffusion: The institution of marketing. *Journal of Marketing Management*, *29*(7–8), 836–860.

Bernthal, M.J., Crockett, D., & Rose, R. (2005). Credit cards as lifestyle facilitators. *Journal of Consumer Research*, *32*(June), 130–145.

Bourdieu, P. (1984). *Distinction: A social critique of the judgment of taste*. London, Routledge & Kegan Paul.

Carfagna, L.B., Dubois, E., Fitzmaurice, C., Ouimette, M.J., Schor, J.B., Willis, M. & Laidley, T. (2014). An emerging eco-habitus: The reconfiguration of high cultural capital practices among ethical consumers. *Journal of Consumer Culture*, *14*(2), 158–178.

Cohen, L. (2003). *A consumer's republic: The politics of mass consumption in postwar America*. New York, Alfred A. Knopf.

Coskuner-Balli, G., & Thompson, C.J. (2013). The status costs of subordinate cultural capital: At-home fathers' collective pursuit of cultural legitimacy through capitalizing consumption practices. *Journal of Consumer Research*, *40*(June), 19–41.

Crompton, R. (1998). *Class and stratification*. Cambridge, MA, Polity Press.

Davies, A., & Elliot, R. (2006). The evolution of the empowered consumer. *European Journal of Marketing*, *40*(9/10), 1106–1121.

Denegri-Knott, J., & Tadajewski, M. (2017). Sanctioning value: The legal system, hyper-power and the legitimation of MP3. *Marketing Theory*, *17*(2), 219–240.

Ertimur, B., & Coskuner-Balli, C. (2015). Navigating the institutional logics of markets: Implications for strategic brand management. *Journal of Marketing*, *79*(2), 40–61.

Fernandez, K.V., Brittain, A.J., & Bennett, S.D. (2011). "Doing the duck": Negotiating the resistant consumer identity. *European Journal of Marketing*, *45*(11/12), 1779–1788.

Fırat, A.F., & Dholakia, N. (2003). *Consuming people: From political economy to theatres of consumption*. London, Routledge.

Fırat A.F., & Shultz II, C.J. (1997). From segmentation to fragmentation: Markets and marketing strategy in the postmodern era. *European Journal of Marketing*, *31*(3/4), 183–207.

Fırat, A.F., & Venkatesh, A. (1995). Liberatory postmodernism and the reenchantment of consumption. *Journal of Consumer Research*, *22*(December), 239–267.

Giddens, A. (1991). *Modernity and self-identity: Self and society in the late modern age*. Stanford, CA, Stanford University Press.

Giesler, M. (2012). How doppelgänger brand images influence the market creation process: Longitudinal insights from the rise of Botox cosmetic. *Journal of Marketing*, *76*(November), 55–68.

Giesler, M., & Veresiu, E. (2014). Creating the responsible consumer: Moralistic governance regimes and consumer subjectivity. *Journal of Consumer Research*, *41*(October), 840–857.

Hackley, C. (2001). Commentary: Towards a post-structuralist marketing pedagogy – or from irony to despair (a two-by-two matrix approach). *European Journal of Marketing*, *35*(11/12), 1184–1198.

Hebdige, D. (1979). *Subculture: The meaning of style*. London, Methuen.

Holt, D.B. (1997). Poststructuralist lifestyle analysis: Conceptualizing the social patterning of consumption in postmodernity. *Journal of Consumer Research*, *23*(March), 326–350.

Holt, D.B. (2002). Why do brands cause trouble? A dialectical theory of consumer culture and branding. *Journal of Consumer Research*, *29*(June), 70–90.

Kahle, L., Beatty, S., & Homer, P. (1986). Alternative measurement approaches to consumer values. *Journal of Consumer Research*, *13*(December), 405–409.

Kamakura, W.A., & Mazzon, J.A. (1991). Value segmentation: A model for the measurement of values and value systems. *Journal of Consumer Research*, *18*(September), 208–218.

Kamakura, W.A., & Novak, T.P. (1992). Value-system segmentation: Exploring the meaning of LOV. *Journal of Consumer Research*, *19*(June), 119–132.

Karababa, E., & Ger, G. (2011). Early modern Ottoman coffeehouse culture and the formation of the consumer subject. *Journal of Consumer Research*, *37*(February), 737–760.

Kelley, E.J. (1963). Discussion. In S.A. Greyser (Ed.), *Toward scientific marketing* (pp. 164–171). Chicago, American Marketing Association.
Lazer, W. (1963). Life style concepts and marketing. In S.A. Greyser (Ed.), *Toward scientific marketing* (pp. 140–151). Chicago, American Marketing Association.
Levy, S.J. (1963). Symbolism and lifestyle. In S.A. Greyser (Ed.), *Toward scientific marketing* (pp. 140–150). Chicago, American Marketing Association.
McCracken, G. (1986). Culture and consumption: A theoretical account of the structure and movement of the cultural meaning of consumer goods. *Journal of Consumer Research, 13*(June), 71–84.
Miles, S. (2012). The neoliberal city and the pro-active complicity of the citizen consumer. *Journal of Consumer Culture, 12*(2), 216–230.
Murray, J.B. (2002). The politics of consumption: A re-inquiry on Thompson and Haytko's (1997) speaking of fashion. *Journal of Consumer Research, 29*(December), 427–440.
Novak, T.P., & MacEvoy, B. (1990). On comparing alternative segmentation schemes: The list of values and lifestyles (VALS). *Journal of Consumer Research, 17*(June), 32–54.
Peñaloza, L., & Barnhart, M. (2011). Living U.S. capitalism: The normalization of credit/debt. *Journal of Consumer Research, 38*(December), 743–762.
Pentina, I., & Amos, C. (2011). The freegan phenomenon: Anti-consumption or consumer resistance. *European Journal of Marketing, 45*(11/12), 1768–1778.
Plummer, J.T. (1974). The concept and application of life style segmentation. *Journal of Marketing, 38*(January), 33–37.
Sewell, W. (1992). A theory of structure: Duality, agency and transformation. *American Journal of Sociology, 98*(1), 1–30.
Simmel, G. (1957). Fashion. In D.N. Levine (Ed.), *On individuality and social forms* (pp. 294–323). Chicago, University of Chicago Press.
Tadajewski, M. (2010). Towards a history of critical marketing studies. *Journal of Marketing Management, 26*(9–10), 773–824.
Tapp, A., & Warren, S. (2010). Field capital theory and its implications for marketing. *European Journal of Marketing, 44*(1/2), 200–222.
The VOICE Group (2010). Motherhood, marketization and consumer vulnerability. *Journal of MacroMarketing, 30*(4), 384–397.
Thompson, C.J., & Haytko, D.L. (1997). Speaking of fashion: Consumers' uses of fashion discourses and the appropriation of countervailing cultural meanings. *Journal of Consumer Research, 24*(June), 15–42.
Thompson, C.J., & Troester, M. (2002). Consumer value systems in the age of postmodern fragmentation: The case of the natural health microculture. *Journal of Consumer Research, 28*(March), 550–571.
Thompson, C.J., & Üstüner, T. (2015). Women skating on the edge: Marketplace performances as ideological edgework. *Journal of Consumer Research, 42*(2), 235–265.
Thornton, S. (1995). *Club cultures: Music, media, and subcultural capital*. Middletown, CT, Wesleyan University Press.
Turner, B.S., & Edmunds, J. (2002). The distaste of taste: Bourdieu, cultural capital and Australian postwar elite. *Journal of Consumer Culture, 2*(2), 219–240.
Üstüner, T., & Holt, D.B. (2007). Dominated consumer acculturation: The social construction of poor migrant women's consumer identity projects in a Turkish squatter. *Journal of Consumer Research, 34*(June), 41–56.
Üstüner, T., & Holt, D.B. (2010). Toward a theory of status consumption in less industrialized countries. *Journal of Consumer Research, 37*(June), 37–56.
Veblen, T. (1899). *The theory of leisure class*. London, Unwin.
Weber, M. (1978). *Economy and society*. Berkeley, University of California Press.
Wells, D.W. (1975). Psychographics: A critical review. *Journal of Marketing Research, 12*(May), 196–213.
Zablocki, D.B., & Kanter, R.M. (1976). The differentiation of life-styles. *Annual Reviews of Sociology, 2*(1), 269–298.
Zwick, D., & Cayla, J. (Eds.) (2011). *Inside marketing: Practices, ideologies and devices*. Oxford, Oxford University Press.

11
ADVERTISING PRACTICE AND CRITICAL MARKETING

Chris Hackley

Introduction

Advertising has been central to the commercial success of many prominent brands (Holt, 2004; Holt & Cameron, 2010), but it has also been posited as a significant factor in the establishment and evolution of Western consumer culture (Fox, 1984; Leach, 1993; Lears, 1994; Marchand, 1985, 1998; Powell, 2013). Advertising is important, not only for organizations, but for individuals and society, and it is rightly the subject of considerable interest from researchers from many disciplines. Many studies, like those cited above, consider advertising in its cultural context, and look at the full scope of the practices of advertising production and consumption. But, many other studies do not. Rather, they purport to be about advertising, but they focus, in fact, on the industry output, the published or broadcast advertisements. That is, they are about advertisements, rather than about advertising. These studies often use advertisements as evidence from which to make broader points about social relations. However, they often neglect both the social processes that led to the creation of the advertisement, and the cultural context of audience engagement. In other words, the analysis they offer is not really about the cultural, economic, and managerial aspects of advertising, but is in fact about the particular advertisements they analyze.

This chapter will suggest that research into advertising, that is, studies that embrace the full context of advertising production and consumption, are best placed to connect advertising practice with wider issues of critical marketing. The chapter will outline key trajectories of research in both areas, and it will attempt to draw out points of connection and divergence between advertising and critical marketing. The discussion will then consider how all these issues are being re-framed as contemporary advertising re-invents itself in an era of convergence (Jenkins, 2008) characterized by consumer access to all media channels via one, internet-enabled screen (Grainge & Johnson, 2015).

Trajectories of research on advertisements

Socio-cultural perspectives

Advertising research is typically associated with managerial audience effects research (Chang, 2017) that focuses on attitudinal and behavioral responses to advertisements. The key question for managerial researchers is how does advertising 'work'? (Vakratsas & Ambler, 1999). That is, how does it persuade targeted consumers to change their buying behavior? In addition to the managerial effects research, advertising has also been researched as an inherently social communication (Leiss et al., 2005) and, seen as such, it can be a prime site for a critical marketing analysis (Saren et al., 2007; Tadajewski & Brownlie, 2008). Some critical work, for example, highlights advertising's ideological influence (Davis, 2013; Elliott & Ritson, 2007; Wernick, 1991; Wharton, 2015) in both reflecting and transmitting cultural values and power relations, and in constituting subject positions and world views. Some of this critique has pointed to the serious implications for society of the unethical dimensions of advertising (Fowles, 1996; Goldman & Papson, 1994; Pollay, 1986; Samuel, 2016) that promotes materialistic values and places consumption as a universal good in and of itself. However, both research trajectories, that is, managerial audience effects research and cultural critique, often focus on the analysis of advertisements, while taking relatively little account of the practices of advertising (McFall, 2004). The complex social dynamics that surround the production of an advertisement and its reception by audiences remain enigmatically silent in much of this research.

What happens inside agencies that produce advertising is important to cultural and critical analyses. Advertising producers can be seen as cultural intermediaries (Cronin, 2004) and, as such, they act as nodes in the production of cultural meaning as well as being key players in the co-optation of the cultural industries into late capitalism (Lash & Lury, 2007). Advertising is a managerial tool, but it does not operate in a cultural vacuum. Whether the researcher's interest is in the furtherance of managerial goals through advertising, or in the ideological influence of advertising as social communication, the practices of advertising, how it is produced, and used, are part of the explanation. The intentions and motives of the actors who created the ad, the structural social and economic forces that influenced the creative execution and media selection, and the cultural context of audience reception, are all relevant to a full understanding that locates critique within the broader field of marketing practices.

The genre of critical research that focuses on advertisements rather than advertising is perhaps exemplified in Judith Williamson's (1978) seminal work on the critical semiotics of visual advertisements. Such work proceeds on the assumption that an analysis of advertisements can reveal deep insights about social relations without the researcher needing to know anything about how or why the advertisement was created, or how it was responded to by consumers. In this genre of research an advertisement is regarded as a cultural text that stands alone but speaks of the culture from which it emerges. From Barthes (1972) to Williamson (1978) and beyond (Belk, 2017; Goffman, 1976; Stern, 1993; Stevens et al., 2003), a substantial canon of research elaborates on the cultural semiotics of advertisements to develop telling analyses of advertising's ideological influence, and also about the interpretive strategies of consumers who 'read' the advertisements (Brown et al., 1999; Scott, 1994). Broader analyses have embraced the wider structural relationships between advertising and political economy (e.g. Leiss et al., 2005; Jhally, 1987).

Information processing perspectives

The managerial tradition of research noted earlier similarly focuses on advertisements, but with very different theoretical assumptions (Chang, 2017). In most managerial research, consumers are regarded not as readers of advertisements, but as processors of advertisements. The advertisement is reduced to a 'message' constructed by marketing management and transmitted to the consumer for processing. I suggest that, in fact, advertisements do not merely transmit messages, they constitute the very act of consumption and, as such, operationalize the marketing concept.

The transmission theory of communication is based on the notion that human communication, like machine communication, can be understood as an input that is designed to trigger an output (Schramm, 1948; Lasswell, 1948; Lazarsfeld, 1941; Shannon, 1948). The transmission model underpins popular hierarchy-of-effects advertising theories, such as the Attention-Interest-Desire-Action model of persuasive communication that is ubiquitous in marketing management textbooks (Barry & Howard, 1990; Hackley, 2010). Hierarchy-of-effects theories assume that a consumer will shift from indifference to purchase through being exposed to an accumulation of rationally persuasive advertising messages. The transmission model and the hierarchy-of-effects traditions of advertising theory also assume that advertising effects are primarily cognitive and individual (e.g. Thomas & Fowler, 2016; Kumar & Gupta, 2016). They assume that an advertisement can be conceptualized as an unequivocal message that is codified by the source, transmitted via a medium, and decoded by the receiver.

Criticisms of the transmission model

There are many criticisms of the influence of the transmission model in advertising theory. For example, Buttle (1995) and Stern (1993) argue that it applies a reductionist and inaccurate account of mediated communication. Other researchers suggest that advertising persuasion constitutes many things and cannot be said to 'work' (Sethuraman et al., 2011) in just one generalized way (O'Shaughnessy & O'Shaughnessy, 2004), hence the transmission model is an oversimplification. Other critics focus on another feature of the transmission model – that is, that advertising communication must be explicit and is processed consciously. Heath and Feldwick (2008) suggest that advertising is often processed implicitly and unconsciously. Just because we might not be paying explicit attention to an advertisement does not necessarily mean that we are unaware of the brand being advertised, the jingle, and the theme, just as, for example, when a TV or radio is on in the background while we pay explicit attention to something else. This idea is developed from a linguistic perspective by Tanaka (1994) who draws attention to the persuasive rhetorical force of what advertisements imply, as opposed to what they state explicitly. In other words, what is implicit in advertising communication can be as rhetorically powerful as what is explicit. The transmission model and the hierarchy-of-effects theories that it is used to underpin cannot accommodate the idea of implicit communication.

Other researchers have argued that it is incorrect to assume, as theories based on the transmission model tend to do, that the purpose of an advertisement is to provoke the consumer into action in the short to medium term by buying the advertised product or service. Advertising can be conceived as meaning, or even as beauty (Stern, 1990) rather than as rationally persuasive information (McCracken, 1987). Ehrenberg et al. (2002) showed that exposure to a single advertisement, even many times, does not usually provoke an individual consumer to buy in the short term if they were not already predisposed to doing so. Rather, they argued that advertising typically achieves its effect by reassuring consumers that the brand remains salient. Reassurance, through publicity, rather than persuasion, is, according to Ehrenberg (2000), the route through which advertising achieves a long-term effect on sales and market share. Consequently, advertising should not be understood as being analogous to an encounter with a sales person (Kennedy, 1924) but, rather, it should be understood as a form of strategic publicity that can be useful in building or maintaining brand presence and market share across large audiences.

There are other methodological criticisms of the transmission model and its derivatives. For example, anthropologists have argued that all human communication is inherently symbolic, and that brands have a powerful symbolic role in advanced economies (Levy, 1959). The machine metaphor of communication cannot capture the symbolism of brands because it allows for no interpretive flexibility in the decoding process. For many researchers, it is a mistake to conceive of an advertisement as a univocal message at all. Rather, they suggest that it should be understood as a complex of signs (Mick & Buhl, 1992) which, in aggregate, constitute a cultural system of communication (Sherry, 1987). As cultural communication, advertisements are not mere messages to be processed and decoded, but texts to be read and interpreted (Cook, 2001; Stern, 1993) just as the reader might interpret a poem, novel (Puntoni et al., 2010; Stevens et al., 2003), or other work of art, such as a piece of music (Scott, 1990, 1994). It is also important to note, though, that the reader does not construct the meaning of an advertisement in a cultural vacuum. Reading advertising is part of a process of communication that is inherently social (DeWaal Malefyt & Moeran, 2003). Consumers' interpretations of advertisements are mediated by interaction with other possible interpretations within the social and cultural context. Consumers do not only passively view advertisements: we do things with them in our social interactions, for example, we draw on them to express our sense of identity and social positioning (Ritson & Elliott, 1999; O'Donohoe, 1994). Agencies that create advertising understand this complexity. The chapter now turns to some of the studies that have explored the agencies' practices of advertising production.

Research into advertising production

Much work on the cultural semiotics of advertisements is insightful, imaginative, and rigorous, but how legitimate is the claim of a cultural semiotician about the meaning of an advertisement if the authors or consumers of the ad were to disagree with the cultural analyst on its interpretation? Interpretations of advertisements are often based on the assumed motive of the ad in cultural critique, yet in most cases this motive is inferred without any information about how the finished ad was created. An advertisement is intended to persuade buyers to buy, right? Research in advertising agency practices demonstrates that this assumption is an oversimplification. Advertising is invariably a collaborative enterprise (Hackley & Hackley, 2015) and there might be considerable uncertainty about what the motive or intention behind the finished ad actually was. Furthermore, audiences can often hold divergent views about the ad's apparent purpose. The truth about advertisements is that their motives might be more contested, confused, opaque, misunderstood or subtle than often supposed (Hackley & Kover, 2007). They are the outcome of a negotiation, or a contest, between clients, brand strategists and marketing directors, advertising account planners, creative teams, media regulators, and other stakeholders (Feldwick, 2015; Kover et al., 1995). Advertising agencies and other marketing organizations are sites of symbolic social interaction (Skålén & Hackley, 2011; Svensson, 2007). The putative intention behind the advertisement, the motive for it, might be contested, but it is not a blank space onto which one cultural authority can inscribe a hegemonic reading. Without a full account of motive and intention the cultural critique loses something of its resonance.

I suggest that critical marketing analysis of advertising, ideally, should begin inside the organizations responsible for producing the work, and end with an understanding of how that work was received by its audiences (see also Svensson, this volume). The former has been addressed by a relatively small collection of ethnographically informed research studies that examine the social and linguistic dynamics of advertising production in different countries (e.g. Alvesson, 1998; Hackley, 2000; Kelly et al., 2005; Moeran, 1996). These studies expose the machinery behind the production of advertising. In so doing they reveal that, convincing though many cultural analyses of advertising's ideological power might be, behind the ideological force of advertisements lies not a monolithic and faceless capitalist corporatism, but a bunch of people who, by and large, love their work (McLeod et al., 2009), believe that they are doing something that is constructive, and negotiate their organizational roles as consumers as well as producers of advertising. It is often forgotten in critical analyses that the people who make advertisements are consumers too. Those who produce advertising, and those who consume it, are all actors in the same cultural landscape, and it is usually too sweeping to argue, as some researchers in advertising seem to do, that one (the advertiser) imposes a world view hegemonically upon the other (the consumer). Given the cultural and commercial significance of advertising it is surprising that there have not been more attempts to expose the dynamics of advertising practices in order to more thoroughly ground critical cultural analyses.

The authority of the author of the analysis of advertisements, then, is subject to an interpretive plebiscite. If audiences, and professionals, interpret the meaning or intention of an advertisement differently to a cultural researcher, whose authority obtains? Does the deep interpretation of visual advertisements sometimes serve as a fig leaf of empirical support for cultural opinion pieces? Elegant and compelling though cultural analyses of advertisements can be, what consumers say about advertisements has always been part of the cultural constitution of the meaning of an advertisement (Tadajewski, 2013). The consumer's involvement in co-producing advertising meaning was something of a trade secret before social media rendered it more difficult to ignore. Before social media, the more far-sighted advertising agencies employed the subtle skills of account planners, if they wanted the consumer cultural perspective brought into the creative advertising development loop (Griffiths & Follows, 2016; Hackley, 2002). Today, consumers are often enlisted as putative co-authors of the advertising text to reflect the participative character of media convergence (Jenkins, 2008; Meikle & Young, 2011), although the ways in which organizations do this might not necessarily be effective (Thompson & Malavia, 2013). Consumer insight is part of the currency of contemporary marketing. What consumers actually think and do about advertisements are by no means incidental to critical analyses. User Generated Content (UGC) on social media is a feature of advertising campaigns today as consumers discuss, critique, parody, and share advertisements online, not only as material to be co-opted into brand stories by brand planners seeking creative ideas that will resonate with consumers, but as part of a constant feedback loop of reader response (Kirby & Marsden, 2006). This gives contemporary advertising a dynamic quality, as opposed to the static characterization of advertising portrayed in many cultural analyses of the 1980s. This dynamism needs to be incorporated into theorizations of advertising (see also Larsen & Kerrigan, this volume).

This brings us to another important point. What advertisements look like is changing. Marketing communication disciplines that, since the 1960s, involved different career paths in different cultural industries, such as Public Relations, script writing, copywriting, animation, digital and art production, not to mention consumer and market research and brand planning, are now often deployed under the same roof in all-purpose marketing and media content agencies that produce multi-channel promotional campaigns (Grainge & Johnson, 2015). The practices of advertising production are changing as the media landscape for advertising changes.

This renders critical analyses of advertising practices from the production side complex and problematic. Nonetheless, the processes of advertising production remain a key site with which critical marketing researchers need to engage. One reason is that a closer understanding of advertising practice reveals tensions and contradictions in managerial marketing axioms. The negotiation, power plays (Kover et al., 1995), intuition, rhetoric, compromise, guess work, and serendipity that all play a part in the production of marketing can expose the simplistic characterization it often receives in managerial texts. Marketing and advertising practices are more complex and contradictory than mainstream text book representations allow. The discourse of the marketing management text book is a rhetorical accomplishment that does not amount to an account of practice in the field (Hackley, 2016). This complexity of advertising practices does not only present a problem for managerial research. Cultural analyses that posit advertising, or marketing, or particular forms of each, as instruments of capitalist corporatist domination and/or perpetuators of social inequity, can seem simplistic when organizational efforts to control consumers are exposed for often being far less scientific, and far less effective, than often supposed. A closer, ethnographically informed examination of the practices of advertising and marketing can act as a corrective to armchair analysis of advertisements by anchoring analysis into an empirical context.

The changing forms of advertising under convergence

For the remainder of this chapter, then, I will try to explore some of these issues in the context of the changes taking place to advertising under convergence (Meikle & Young, 2011). I will suggest that, partly as a result of the convergence of media channels, there are changes in the practices of advertising production and advertising consumption that have implications for critical marketing and advertising researchers. The rise of digital communication platforms lies at the heart of these changes (Kirby & Marsden, 2006). The resulting exponential increase in consumer choice from the proliferation of cable TV and digital radio channels, news and entertainment websites, video channels and other internet-based sources of news, information and entertainment, have caused the traditional advertiser-funded business model for media brands to collapse. Mass media advertising remains important, but traditional media brands are suffering a sharply contracted audience reach from reduced sales/viewers, and they have to create new digital revenue streams to make up the shortfall in revenue from TV and radio spots and classified, display and feature advertising in print media. Witness, for example, the way that almost every print newspaper around the world, even the great organs of public record, now have digital websites that generate revenue streams through 'native' advertising, or, sponsored editorial, and advertisements that are algorithmically targeted at individual readers. Native advertising is sponsored editorial content in digital and print newspapers, blogs, and magazines that is 'native' to the page, in the sense that it looks very like editorial content (Oakes, 2015). More generally, there is a significant shift in advertising budgets from traditional mass media to iterative and transmedia brand storytelling (Jenkins *et al.*, 2013; Katz, 2016) across varied media channels and digital platforms in forms such as product placement in video blogging channels (some of which have subscribers of many millions), sponsored Tweets, and branded content (games, videos, blogs, features, memes) that is created to entertain and engage, and to generate 'earned' media presence through likes and shares.

A renewed and more detailed focus on advertising practices within this changed landscape is important to fully engage and enable critical marketing theory development. From the consumer perspective, advertising under convergence now has a fluid quality in the sense that it is no longer necessarily about one set piece advertisement that everyone in a community talks about at work or school the next day. Advertising is now typically apprehended within a stream of news, entertainment and information as branded media content. There are still individual advertisements that can create a stir, but even these are quickly located within an intertextual system and interpreted in the light of previous ads and other stories about the brand.

For example, at the time of writing (November 2017), a *Facebook* advertisement for *Dove* soap was shared thousands of times on social media because of what some felt were its racist overtones. Within a day of the first exposure, the ad was the subject of dozens of opinion pieces in the press and online media.[1] Many different interpretations were subsequently expressed on social media, and many of these were informed by a historical comparison of soap ads of the past 100 years that, in the opinion of many social media commenters, carried racist overtones. In just a few days, these paratexts (Gray, 2010) re-framed the meaning of a brand that had been associated with equality and authenticity for a decade with its Campaign for Real Beauty campaigns. The company issued an apology, and the black model in the ad appeared on TV and wrote articles in the press defending the creative idea.[2] Whether the furore was an example of a failure of creative oversight, a misconceived strategy, or a deliberately provocative execution that was designed to push the boundaries of acceptability (and the ad was aired during a well-publicized Black History Month in the UK), one thing seems clear from the incident. A cultural analyst attempting the kind of advertising critique that was popular in academic work in the 1980s would have to acknowledge the role of the social practices of production and consumption of advertising in negotiating a meaning that is contingent, provisional, iterative, and fluid. The ad itself did not tell the whole story. As each new person read a media report or heard about the controversy from a friend, and then *Googled* the topic to see what the discussion was about, the intertextual richness of the interpretive frame was deepened as each search revealed more informed professional and layperson opinion on the putative motives and meanings of the ad. Other essential elements to understanding the issue, however, were not available. For example, there was no ethnographic account of how the ad had been commissioned, briefed, created, produced, and approved, although the model did later provide first-hand accounts of how the creative execution took shape. The waves of opinion that the ad provoked also need to be fully understood within the discourse of racism in the UK – to what extent did expressed opinion on social media follow the contours of gender, race, and class?

The Dove example illustrates the role of intertexts (Gray, 2010), in this case critical ones, in shaping and changing the meaning of advertising. Another example might serve to illustrate the positive strategic value obtaining from spread-able creative ideas (Jenkins *et al.*, 2013). The price comparison website comparethemarket.com was launched with TV advertisements featuring CGI meerkats[3] in 2009. By 2017, the meerkats are manifest as movie stars, social media stars with millions of followers, action figures, online games, soap actors, and more, their everyday lives can be followed by fans online, and they, or their various manifestations, are credited with boosting the entire industry as well as their own brand. The TV advertisement spawned dozens of paratextual iterations that have created a sense of the brand for millions who might never use the website, or even understand what it is for. The challenge for researchers of advertising under convergence is to grasp the kinetic (Gray, 2010) forms of interpretation in which consumers engage when they encounter advertising executions that play out across multiple platforms. I will conclude the chapter by suggesting that literary forms of methodology offer an opportunity of theorizing the emerging, hybrid and fluid forms of advertising in the convergent media landscape.

Concluding comments: the future of advertising research

Most of the literary tradition of advertising research within marketing and consumer research has been grounded in static analyses of mass media advertising. However, some of it has hinted at the paratextual character of advertising. For example, Ritson and Elliott (1999) conducted an ethnographic examination of adolescents' talk about advertising, showing that advertisements have a life beyond the material boundaries of the text. Similarly, O'Donohoe (1994, 1997) illuminated the intertextuality of advertisements, their capacity to generate meaning by tapping into consumers' cultural knowledge to reference other texts. Advertising under convergence is characterized by a blurring of distinctions between advertising sub-disciplines such as sponsorship, celebrity endorsement, and branded content, as campaigns can now reach across multiple channels, platforms, and materials to leverage a web of intertextuality, as illustrated by the meerkat phenomenon. Advertising researchers can develop theorizations fit for the fluidity of convergence by building on the work of television and film scholars such as Gray's (2010) work on movie paratexts and Aronczyk's (2017) on brand paratexts.

The digitization of advertising is not making traditional advertising forms and craft skills redundant. Rather, it is expanding those craft skills to embrace all the skills of the cultural industries as all-purpose advertising, media and entertainment agencies emerge (Grainge & Johnson, 2015). Advertising, especially on social media, is sometimes created by bots, algorithms or amateurs, and areas of the field, such as political advertising, are now deeply propagandistic. This makes the area all the more important for critical analysis. But, for the present, most successful advertising campaigns are still given their resonance by a piece of creative work that has emerged from an advertising development process and is given a sense of coherence by a putative strategy or motive. More ethnographic studies are needed to detail how the creative advertising development process, and its practitioners, is/are adapting to the new hybrid advertising forms.

One important feature of the contemporary advertising environment demonstrated by the Dove example above is the fluid inter-penetration of advertising with news, entertainment, trade press, and social media. The distinction between editorial and advertising, never quite as clear as some might contend, is less distinct than ever, and this invites a re-framing of issues of advertising ethics as regards how media texts are read as advertisements (Hackley *et al.*, 2008; Thorson *et al.*, 2016). Advertising researchers need methodologies that can embrace the full scope of advertising under convergence rather than confining analyses to the old artificial disciplinary silos of above-and below-the-line media. The interpretive flexibility of literary methods offers some hope for achieving these new theorizations.

Notes

1 www.independent.co.uk/life-style/dove-facebook-advert-racist-many-beauty-brands-accused-unileverblack-woman-white-nivea-tarte-a7991016.html accessed October 15, 2017.
2 www.independent.co.uk/life-style/dove-facebook-advert-racism-woman-speaks-out-black-woman-white-unilever-a7992291.html accessed October 15, 2017.
3 www.theguardian.com/media/2010/jan/16/aleksander-orlov-price-comparison-ads accessed November 5, 2017.

References

Alvesson, M. (1998). Gender relations and identity at work: A case study of masculinities and femininities in an advertising agency. *Human Relations, 51*(8), 969–1005.
Aronczyk, M. (2017). Portal or police? The limits of promotional paratexts. *Critical Studies in Media Communication, 34*(2), 111–119.
Barry, T.E., & Howard, D.J. (1990). A review and critique of the hierarchy of effects in advertising. *International Journal of Advertising, 9*(2), 121–135.
Barthes, R. (1972). *Mythologies*. New York, Noonday Press.
Belk, R.W. (2017). Qualitative research in advertising. *Journal of Advertising, 46*(1), 36–47.
Brown, S., Stevens, L., & Maclaran, P. (1999). I can't believe it's not Bakhtin! Literary theory, post modern advertising, and the gender agenda. *Journal of Advertising, 28*(1), 11–24.
Buttle, F. (1995). Marketing communication theory: What do the texts teach our students? *International Journal of Advertising, 14*(4), 297–313.
Chang, C. (2017). Methodological issues in advertising research: Current status, shifts, and trends. *Journal of Advertising, 46*(1), 2–20.
Cook, G. (2001). *The discourse of advertising*. London, Routledge.
Cronin, A.M. (2004). Regimes of mediation: Advertising practitioners as cultural intermediaries? *Consumption, Markets & Culture, 7*(4), 349–369.

Davis, A. (2013). *Promotional cultures: The rise and spread of advertising, public relations, marketing and branding.* London, Polity Press.
deWaal Malefyt, T., & Moeran, B. (Eds.) (2003). *Advertising cultures.* London, Berg.
Ehrenberg, A. (2000). Repetitive advertising and the consumer. *Journal of Advertising Research, 40*(6), 39–48.
Ehrenberg, A., Barnard, N., Kennedy, R., & Bloom, H. (2002). Brand advertising and creative publicity. *Journal of Advertising Research, 42*(4), 7–18.
Elliott, R., & Ritson, M. (2007). Poststructuralism and the dialectics of advertising: Discourse, ideology, resistance. In S. Brown & D. Turley (Eds.), *Consumer research: Postcards from the edge* (pp. 190–219). London, Routledge.
Feldwick, P. (2015). *The anatomy of humbug: How to think differently about advertising.* London, Matador.
Fowles, J. (1996). *Advertising and popular culture.* London, Sage.
Fox, S. (1984). The mirror makers: A history of American advertising and its creators. New York, William Morrow.
Goffman, E. (1976). *Gender advertisements.* New York, Harper & Row.
Goldman, R., & Papson, S. (1994). Advertising in the age of hypersignification. *Theory, Culture and Society, 11*(3), 23–53.
Grainge, P., & Johnson, C. (2015). *The promotional screen industries.* London, Routledge.
Gray, J. (2010). *Show sold separately: Promos, spoilers, and other media paratexts.* New York, NYU Press.
Griffiths, J., & Follows, T. (2016). *98% pure potato: The origins of advertising account planning as told to us by its pioneers.* London, Unbound.
Hackley, C. (2000). Silent running: Tacit, discursive and psychological aspects of management in a top UK advertising agency. *British Journal of Management, 11*(3), 239–254.
Hackley, C. (2002). The panoptic role of advertising agencies in the production of consumer culture. *Consumption, Markets & Culture, 5*(3), 211–229.
Hackley, C. (2016). Marketing texts. In G. Mautner (Ed.), *Discourse and management* (pp. 159–168). London, Palgrave Macmillan.
Hackley, C. (2010). Theorizing advertising: Managerial, scientific and cultural approaches. In P. MacLaran, M. Saren, B. Stern & M. Tadajewski (Eds.), *The Sage Handbook of Marketing Theory* (pp. 89–107). London, Sage.
Hackley, C., & Hackley, R.A. (2015). *Advertising and promotion,* third edition. London, Sage.
Hackley, C., & Kover, A. (2007). The trouble with creatives: Negotiating creative identity in advertising agencies. *International Journal of Advertising, 26*(1), 63–78.
Hackley, C., Tiwsakul, A., & Preuss, L. (2008). An ethical evaluation of product placement: A deceptive practice? *Business Ethics – A European Review, 17*(2), 109–120.
Heath, R., & Feldwick, P. (2008). 50 years using the wrong model of advertising. *International Journal of Advertising, 50*(1), 29–59.
Holt, D. (2004). *How brands become icons: The principles of cultural branding.* Boston, Harvard Business School Press.
Holt, D., & Cameron, D. (2010). *Cultural strategy: Using innovative ideologies to build breakthrough brands.* Oxford, Oxford University Press.
Jenkins, H. (2008). *Convergence culture: Where old and new media collide.* New York, New York University Press.
Jenkins, H., Ford, S., & Green, J. (2013). *Spreadable media: Creating value and meaning in a networked culture.* New York, New York University Press.
Jhally, S. (1987). *Codes of advertising: Fetishism and the political economy of meaning in the consumer society.* New York, Saint Martin's.
Katz, B. (2016, September 9). Digital ad spending will surpass TV spending for the first time in U.S. history [Online]. *Forbes Magazine.* Retrieved July 6, 2018 from www.forbes.com/sites/brandonkatz/2016/09/14/digital-ad-spending-will-surpass-tv-spending-for-the-first-time-in-u-s-history/#463425184207
Kelly, A., Lawlor, K., & O'Donohoe, S. (2005). Encoding advertisements: The creative perspective. *Journal of Marketing Management, 21*(5–6), 505–528.
Kennedy, J.E. (1924). *Reason-why advertising plus intensive advertising.* Indiana, TWI Press, Inc.
Kirby, J., & Marsden, P. (2006). *Connected marketing: The viral, buzz and word of mouth revolution.* Oxford, Elsevier.
Kover, A.J., Goldberg, S.M., & James, W.L. (1995). The games copywriters play: Conflict, quasi-control, a new proposal. *Journal of Advertising Research, 35*(4), 29–41.

Kumar, V., & Gupta, S. (2016). Conceptualising the evolution and future of advertising. *Journal of Advertising*, *45*(3), 302–317.
Lash, S., & Lury, C. (2007). *Global culture industry: The mediation of things.* London, Polity.
Lasswell, H.D. (1948) The structure and function of communication in society. In L. Bryson (Ed.), *The communication of ideas* (pp. 37–51). New York, Harper.
Lazarsfeld, P.F. (1941). Remarks on administrative and critical communications research. *Studies in Philosophy and Science*, *9*, 3–16.
Leach, W. (1993). *Land of desire: Merchants, power, and the rise of a new American culture.* New York, Pantheon Books.
Lears, J. (1994). *Fables of abundance: A cultural history of advertising in America.* New York, Basic Books.
Leiss, W., Kline, S., Jhally, S., & Botterill, J. (2005). *Social communication in advertising: Consumption in the mediated marketplace.* London, Routledge.
Levy, S. (1959). Symbols for sale. *Harvard Business Review*, *37*(July), 117–124.
Marchand, R. (1985). *Advertising the American dream: Making way for modernity, 1920–1940.* Los Angeles, University of California Press.
Marchand, R. (1998). *Creating the corporate soul: The rise of public relations and corporate imagery in American big business.* Los Angeles, University of California Press.
McCracken, G. (1987). Advertising: meaning or information. In M. Wallendorf & P. Anderson (Eds.), *Advances in consumer research, Vol. 14* (pp. 121–124). Provo, Association for Consumer Research.
McFall, L. (2004). *Advertising: A cultural economy.* London, Sage.
McLeod, C., O'Donohoe, S., & Townley, B. (2009). The elephant in the room? Class and creative careers. *Human Relations*, *62*(7), 1011–1039.
Meikle, G., & Young, S. (2011). *Media convergence: Networked digital media in everyday life.* London, Palgrave Macmillan.
Mick, D.G., & Buhl, C. (1992). A meaning-based model of advertising experiences. *Journal of Consumer Research*, *19*(3), 317–338.
Moeran, B. (1996). *A Japanese advertising agency: An anthropology of media and markets.* Oxford, Routledge.
Oakes, O. (2015, November 11). Telegraph launches first UK newspaper native ad on Apple News. *Campaign Magazine* [Online]. Campaign Live. Retrieved July 6, 2018 from www.campaignlive.co.uk/article/telegraph-launches-first-uk-newspaper-native-ad-apple-news/1371857
O'Donohoe, S. (1994). Advertising uses and gratifications. *European Journal of Marketing*, *28*(8/9), 52–75.
O'Donohoe, S. (1997). Raiding the postmodern pantry: Advertising intertextuality and the young adult audience. *European Journal of Marketing*, *31*(3/4), 234–253.
O'Shaughnessy, J., & O'Shaughnessy, N.J. (2004). *Persuasion in advertising.* London, Routledge.
Pollay, R.W. (1986). The distorted mirror: Reflections on the unintended consequences of advertising. *Journal of Marketing*, *50*(April), 18–36.
Powell, H. (Ed.) (2013). *Promotional culture in an era of convergence.* Abingdon, Taylor & Francis.
Puntoni, S., Schroeder, J., & Ritson, M. (2010). Meaning matters. *Journal of Advertising*, *39*(2), 51–64.
Ritson, M., & Elliott, R. (1999). The social uses of advertising: An ethnographic study of adolescent advertising audiences. *Journal of Consumer Research*, *26*(3), 260–277.
Samuel, L.R. (2016). Distinctly un-American: Subliminal advertising and the Cold War. *Journal of Historical Research in Marketing*, *8*(1), 99–119.
Saren, M., Maclaran, P., Goulding, C., Elliott, R., Shankar, A., & Catterall, M. (2007). *Critical marketing: Defining the field.* London, Butterworth-Heinemann.
Schramm, W. (1948). *Mass communication.* Urbana, University of Illinois Press.
Scott, L.M. (1990). Understanding jingles and needle drop: A rhetorical approach to music in advertising. *Journal of Consumer Research*, *17*(2), 223–236.
Scott, L.M. (1994). The bridge from text to mind: Adapting reader-response theory for consumer research. *Journal of Consumer Research*, *21*(3), 461–490.
Sethuraman, R., Tellis, G.J., & Briesch, R.A. (2011). How well does advertising work? Generalisations from meta-analysis of brand advertising elasticities. *Journal of Marketing Research*, *48*(3), 457–471.
Shannon, C.E. (1948). A mathematical theory of communication. *Bell System Technical Journal*, *27*(July and October), 379–423, 623–656.
Sherry, J.F. (1987). Advertising as cultural system. In J. Umiker-Sebeok (Ed.), *Marketing and semiotics* (pp. 441–462). Berlin, Mouton.
Skålén, P., & Hackley, C. (2011). Marketing-as-practice: Introduction to the special issue. *Scandinavian Journal of Management*, *27*(2), 189–196.

Stern, B.B. (1990). Beauty and joy in metaphorical advertising: The poetic dimension. In M.E. Goldberg, G. Gorn, & R.R. Pollay (Eds.), *Advances in consumer research* (Vol. 17, pp. 71–77). Provo, Association for Consumer Research.

Stern, B.B. (1993). A revised communication model for advertising: Multiple dimensions of the source, the message, and the recipient. *Journal of Advertising*, 23(2), 5–15.

Stevens, L., Maclaran, P., & Brown, S. (2003). "Red time is me time": Advertising, ambivalence, and womens' magazines. *Journal of Advertising*, 32(1), 35–45.

Svensson, S. (2007). Producing marketing: Towards a social-phenomenology of marketing work. *Marketing Theory*, 7(3), 271–290.

Tadajewski, M. (2013). Promoting the consumer society: Ernest Dichter, the Cold War and the FBI. *Journal of Historical Research in Marketing*, 5(2), 192–211.

Tadajewski, M., & Brownlie, D. (2008). *Critical marketing: Issues in contemporary marketing*. London, John Wiley & Sons.

Tanaka, K. (1994). *Advertising language: A pragmatic approach to advertisements in Britain and Japan*. London, Routledge.

Thomas, V.L., & Fowler, K. (2016). Examining the impact of brand transgressions on consumers' perceptions of celebrity endorsers. *Journal of Advertising*, 45(4), 377–390.

Thompson, D.V., & Malavia, P. (2013). Consumer generated ads: Does awareness of advertising co-creation help or hurt persuasion? *Journal of Marketing*, 77(3), 33–47.

Thorson, E., Duffy, M., Choi, H., & Kim, E. (2016). The kids are different: Perceptions of advertising ethics by millennial college students and adults. American Academy of Advertising Conference Proceedings, American Academy of Advertising, 71–73.

Vakratsas, D., & Ambler, T. (1999). How advertising works: What do we really know? *Journal of Marketing*, 26(January), 26–43.

Wernick, A. (1991). *Promotional culture: Advertising, ideology and symbolic expression*. London, Sage.

Wharton, C. (2015). *Advertising: Critical approaches*. London, Routledge.

Williamson, J. (1978). *Decoding advertisements: Ideology and meaning in advertising*. London, Marion Boyars.

12
CRITICAL REFLECTIONS ON THE MARKETING CONCEPT AND CONSUMER SOVEREIGNTY

Mark Tadajewski

Introduction

At its most basic, we can understand Critical Marketing Studies as interested in challenging the status quo, that is, it questions the way marketing activities are represented by academics and observers interested in legitimizing the role of marketing in society (Tadajewski, 2010a). When scholars legitimize – when they justify and underline only the positive contributions made by marketing scholarship and practice – they present a partial and distorted image of the discipline and the practical effects of this group on the world around them. Critical Marketing does not necessarily deny the contributions marketing can make to the quality of life some people enjoy. Rather, it asks us to consider all of the ramifications of marketing, including its praiseworthy and negative effects (see also Kilbourne, this volume).

Research adopting a Critical Marketing perspective has often been undertaken via close readings of key marketing concepts. Typically, the question being asked is whether they accurately represent what practitioners do in reality. Put differently, Critical Marketing accounts highlight the disparities and inequity inherent in the capitalist system. This representation of marketplace reality is contrasted against the 'equality' (Bagozzi, 1975) or 'win-win' (Gummesson, 1999) arguments all too frequently found in mainstream perspectives which claim that all benefit from marketplace exchange. These are false generalizations which do not stand up well when juxtaposed against the lived experiences of various groups (Falchetti, Ponchio, & Botelho, 2016).

Nor are the marketing concepts being taught in business schools neutral ways of describing the world. They represent the views of specific interest groups constituted by people who have a reason for describing the world in certain ways and not others. Marketing concepts, such as relationship marketing, present the activities of practitioners in positive terms. As such, we might want to view them as counterpoints to the accusations of manipulation that are frequently targeted at the discipline and practice (see also Svensson, this volume). Indeed, academics are often explicit in presenting their work as a response to depictions of the discipline which position it as a detrimental force in the social world (O'Donohoe, 1994).

So, marketing theory, the concepts that accompany it, and the practices associated with the subject, are all political, rather than neutral. They are fundamentally concerned with encouraging people to think about their existence in circumscribed ways. At the most basic level, the logic of marketing is driven by consumption. When we look at any textbook or mainstream journal article the refrain is almost identical. Practitioners are praised for enabling people to access a vast array of goods and services; marketing's role as a mechanism of information gathering and distribution is applauded; and its function in manufacturing demand (Webster, Malter, & Ganesan, 2005) is linked to job creation and contributions to gross domestic product (Wilkie & Moore, 1999). Those who represent marketing in this way are not nefarious characters. They are advocates for their beliefs. It is when this affirmation leads to the elision of the dark-side of marketing practice that we should be concerned. When we focus on the beneficial contributions of an academic discipline or industry practice, we often fail to pay attention to alternative ways of thinking about how the economic system could function; ways that hold out the potential to benefit more people, more equally, than present methods of providing goods and services.

Questioning the role of marketing in society is an exercise in 'ontological denaturalization' (Fournier & Grey, 2000). This grand term simply refers to the fact that we do not take the present representation of marketing or the current economic ordering of society as the only way we can think about it. When we denaturalize something, we make it seem less natural. We stop taking it for granted. We ask questions about how the economic system has taken the shape it has, how it was constructed, by whom, and for what purpose. Importantly, we focus on the issue of who benefits from existing marketing and distribution methods. This encourages us to think about the economic system in terms of power relationships. Given the present structure of the economic system, who is really in the driving-seat? Do consumers really direct producers? Do manufacturers really listen to the consumer and produce what they need and want? Or do they try to shape human behavior by creating and stimulating desire?

Of course, asking questions about power relations can sound negative. To some extent this is accurate. When we look at the marketplace, critical research often finds that the consumer is not as powerful as mainstream scholars like to claim. Even so, the fact that we are seeking to engage in ontological denaturalization means that we are effectively assuming that the power relations that shape producer and consumer behavior can be changed. Critical Marketing Studies is therefore underwritten by an optimism that all too often passes unacknowledged.

If our current reality (our ontology) is not predetermined, then alternatives are available and possible (i.e. we can make the world look unnatural and change subsequently becomes more desirable). In other words, the extant economic and marketing system is not, from the perspective of Critical Marketing, necessarily the best way of achieving our distribution and provisioning requirements. Accepting this, we must continue to treat marketing theory, its associated concepts and the practical activities of business people with a skeptical eye, asking whether they are preventing us from thinking differently or working in ways more consistent with the aim of achieving distributive justice for all.

This chapter engages with mainstream concepts in marketing – the marketing concept, consumer sovereignty and exchange. We will leverage our understanding to offer a critical evaluation of their assumptions and effects in practice. As any new student is told, marketing goes back many thousands of years. As a university subject, its history is more recent. It is a product of the early twentieth century. When approaching the development of marketing we need to be on our guard. Misrepresentation is rife. It is frequently accompanied by a very positive narrative which basically refers to the various ways in which practitioners seek to assist the consumer. Reading these accounts, one would be hard pressed to understand why marketing practice has ever been presented in negative terms (i.e. as selling snake-oil or engaging in hard-selling). In this chapter we will remove our tinted glasses and look at the marketing system with fresh, critical eyes.

The marketing concept, Drucker and Keith

In many accounts, marketing moves through a trajectory that runs as follows. Practitioners once adhered to a production orientation. They produced what they could make efficiently and cheaply. They subsequently shifted to a sales orientation. They devoted a bit more attention to the customer, rather than churning out what the firm could produce, and sometimes undertook a limited amount of market research. This sales orientation could lead to hard-selling, to people pushing products aggressively irrespective of whether it was an intelligent strategy. Eventually, business people – so the progressive narrative goes (Hollander, 1986) – registered their error and saw the light of the marketing concept (but the previous concepts continue to co-exist with the marketing concept). To pinch a line from Daniel Defoe (a writer in the eighteenth century), the marketing concept assumes that the customer is the idol of business enterprise. They are the focus around which practitioners orbit (Keith, 1960). The firm is not the powerful actor here, reaping all the benefits.

Pretty much any textbook that is consulted will present the above historical narrative as leading to a specific turning point when practitioners saw the light of customer centricity. The 1950s are the turning point that is most frequently cited. But, as gestured above, related ideas can be found in the literature from the eighteenth century. Even so, the 1950s did herald a time when there was considerable attention devoted to the idea of 'creating a customer' (Drucker, 1954, p. 39) who is sold products and services to meet organizational needs for profit (Drucker, 1954, p. 45). The reasoning for this attention is easy to understand. In the post-World War II period, people were experiencing considerable levels of affluence. They had more money, more options clamoring for their attention, and this encouraged manufacturers and retailers to focus on what their customer base wanted rather than assuming that people would buy whatever was placed on shop shelves.

Usually, the marketing concept is associated with Keith's (1960) reflections on the rise of marketing at Pillsbury (the bakery products company). This is not accurate in various ways. At that juncture, there were other companies pursuing commensurate strategies. General Electric is often cited in this regard. Keith, however, was an articulate exponent of the marketing concept, promoting this in a major journal. He stressed the reversal of power relations between marketer and consumer, explaining that customers are the more powerful partner in an exchange relationship. Their needs and desires should be preeminent; their purchasing helps ensure corporate longevity; and companies needed to appreciate this shift. Practitioners, in other words, were told to look at their businesses from the customer's point of view. Were their offerings likely to appeal to their market? Was the product a financially viable proposition for the firm? Marketers sometimes get these questions badly wrong (Hult et al., 2017).

But the marketing concept was not the end-point. 'Marketing control' was the terminal station. This was where marketing directed short- and long-term decisions that had to be taken within the firm. It basically meant that marketing was the most important specialism in the company. It controlled and directed all others (e.g. it was more powerful than production, accounting and so forth). In presenting his argument, Keith wanted to ensure that marketing had influence within the firm. Naturally, organizations are not monolithic entities. They are constituted by various groups – production, engineering, purchasing, finance, accounting and credit – each of which has different political objectives that lead to 'organizational conflicts between marketing and other departments' (Kotler, 1967, p. 139). These groups can hinder the implementation of the marketing concept (see Meyerson, 2008, pp. 19–20, 74, 94; Nader, 1972, pp. 180–181, 210–211). The same is true of staff members whether they are designated as marketers or not. Those at the coalface are paid relatively little, can be apathetic about their work and have minimal power or responsibility to resolve complaints or problems (Harris, 1998). Alongside these issues, their lack of product knowledge and poor managerial guidance can all work to undermine the implementation of the marketing concept (Harris, 1998).

To make matters more complicated, the actual position of marketing professionals within firms is contested (Webster *et al.*, 2005). It is easy to decrease the credibility of marketing inside the organization by asking its advocates to demonstrate their contribution to profit, market share and shareholder value. This made the status of marketing within the C-suite (i.e. the top rungs of the firm) precarious, even when related activities are permeating organizations (Verhoef & Leeflang, 2009). Notwithstanding these worries, recent publications have empirically determined that companies with senior marketing positions (i.e. Chief Marketing Officer) do demonstrate performance gains, sometimes quite substantial gains in terms of stock market valuations over firms without related roles (Germann, Ebbes, & Grewal, 2015).

Robert Keith did provide practitioners with a narrative to help them displace other internal actors. His arguments continue to be used. It was not appropriate – he claims – for decisions to be made without marketing having a substantial input into decision-making. If marketing was the 'voice of the customer' and satisfying the consumer was the key to success, then its organizational voice demanded priority. Destabilizing company power relations, reshaping them in a way conducive to the needs of marketing management, was the hand trying to be dealt here.

Legitimating marketing practice, further delegitimating priority claims

Keith's work has been central to the ideological legitimation of marketing. It distances the practice from lay interpretations of selling (i.e. pushing products on to reluctant buyers). We should appreciate that this account has been questioned from multiple perspectives. In historical terms, using Keith's argument to suggest that the 1950s witnessed the emergence of the marketing concept is incorrect. Eighteenth-century manufacturers such as Matthew Boulton engaged in practices akin to relationship marketing, segmented their markets and used marketing communications (Robinson, 1963). Josiah Wedgwood was adept on the marketing front. He used a large range of marketing communications, patented his products, employed sales men who traveled all over the world and provided refunds if people were dissatisfied (McKendrick, 1960).

Canadian practitioners in the 1880s focused on the customer, wanted to form long-term relationships with their clients, were attentive to profit generation and engaged in market segmentation (Jones & Richardson, 2007). Those individuals thinking about and practicing various aspects of marketing in the early twentieth century articulated related ideas. Their analytic focus was slightly more sophisticated in the sense that they undermined the way some authors represented the female customer as irrational. Lillian Gilbreth, for example, portrayed female consumers as rational and intelligent (Graham, 2013). She called for practitioners to adopt the marketing concept and undertake research to inform product development, so that their offerings were consistent with the requirements of their audience. Pauline Arnold echoed this perspective (Jones, 2013). So, these ideas were not original to Robert Keith, Peter Drucker, Wendall Smith, Philip Kotler or Evert Gummesson.

We should add that the practices Keith enumerates at Pillsbury were only a partial representation of what the company was doing. Some of their activities were not pro-customer. They engaged in collusion to try to control the prices of certain ingredients essential to the manufacture of their bread products. This is price-fixing not being customer focused (Tadajewski, 2010b). This was not restricted to Pillsbury. For some companies, it seems like the law is treated as optional. It is used when it advances corporate interests, and ignored when it fetters revenues.

Price-fixing and a host of other problematic practices, such as ignoring environmental legislation which forbids pollution, continue to the present day (e.g. Greenwald, 2005). They will be a feature of business activities while there are minimal repercussions accompanying them. We do not need to look far to find further examples of poor practices (e.g. Nader, 1972; Sinclair, 1906/2010; Veblen, 1919/2005, 1921/2006). As a case in point, the pharmaceutical industry came under sustained attack during the late 1950s, early 1960s for dubious claims of efficacy, price gouging, excessive promotional spending, use of brand names to obscure non-existent product differences, and the creation of 'customer confusion' (Pressey, 2015). They exemplified the monopoly power and corporate ethical intransigence that critics like J.K. Galbraith, activists such as Senator Estes Kefauver, and later Ralph Nader (1972), lamented and tried to eradicate.

Keith also claims generalizability for his thesis about a 'marketing revolution' taking place at Pillsbury and across the wider business community. Claims like these need to be tempered. After all, production, sales and technology orientations continue to be practiced today (Webster et al., 2005). In equal measure, the idea that marketing has distanced itself from a selling orientation is dubious. Borch (1958) maintained that business practice should combine marketing and selling orientations. There was no point, he suggested, in listening to customers and developing desirable products, if they fail to communicate this fact. His argument, however, was not subject to much discussion. It was too close to views about marketing as a manipulative activity. Still, his ideas have been resurrected in modified form with the attention given to 'market driving' and 'market shaping' (Jaworski, Kohli, & Sahay, 2000) (the latter operates more at a political level, lobbying government to enact legislation to facilitate the operation of marketing. Kotler (1986) terms this 'megamarketing').

These new concepts (market driving and shaping) are meant to sensitize practitioners to move beyond being reactive, that is, continuing to perform a purist version of the marketing concept. An extreme level of customer focus is dangerous in a turbulent, competitive marketplace. People are notoriously bad at discussing their present needs, never mind those they might have in five or ten years (Hildebrand, 1951). Responsiveness to the customer is thus downplayed in current debates; stimulus is underlined. Markets and consumers are nudged in directions deemed most attractive for the firm. From this perspective, marketers are a generative force in society (Kumar, Scheer, & Kotler, 2000).

Market driving is predicated on dramatic innovation. Companies that achieve it (and it is rare) reshape their industry and (they hope) consumer subjectivity. In many cases, it involves young firms that are new to the market who do not test their ideas using traditional research methods. They literally drive the market (i.e. like a rancher drives cattle). They communicate their vision about how the industry could be different. To bring this vision into reality, they organize their production and distribution to help them achieve their objectives, often in ways that differentiate them markedly from their competitors. This is not differentiation for the sake of it. It should enable the company to provide something of value to the customer (i.e. more convenient distribution and better access to products and services; lower prices; etc.). IKEA is an example; Swatch is another. Nike did something similar courtesy of 'word of foot' advertising (Knight, 2016) (i.e. where people would see high performance athletes using their products and want to buy them).

These debates point to an important tension in marketing theory and practice. Where does the power lie? Is it with the marketer or consumer? Marketers tend to claim that the consumer is powerful. Their actual practice does not necessarily lend support to their claims. When we look back in history, for example, the eighteenth-century economist, Adam Smith, pointed out that seeing business people meeting together was not a good omen. It meant they were colluding (like Pillsbury), seeking to maximize the benefits they derived from the market, usually to the detriment of the consumer.

Thorstein Veblen, a critically oriented economist writing in the early twentieth century, casts business in a darker light than managerially minded practitioners like Keith. He did appreciate some of the benefits that the system of industry had provided (i.e. wider access to standardized goods and services at lower prices); but he was aware of the problems that accompanied the pursuit of profit (Plotkin, 2014). He realized producers did not always have the consumers' best interests in mind. They liked to restrict output to increase prices. Veblen (1919/2005) called this sabotage. Connected to this, they had to make their goods look scarcer than they really were. Limited supply and brand differentiation helped here (Plotkin, 2014). The development of brands, evocative symbolism and tiny points of difference made it harder for the buyer to objectively weigh up the benefits the product promised to deliver. Underscoring the importance of brand image and symbolism, rather than quality and price, complicated decision-making processes. Over time, we focus on the symbolism as the most salient aspect of marketing, buying products for subjective distinction (see also Coskuner-Balli, this volume). To ensure they sold their highly priced goods, manufacturers and retailers used the tools of advertising and salesmanship to manufacture demand. Sometimes these added 50% on to the actual production costs of the product (Jones & Tadajewski, 2018).

For Veblen, we can say that marketing was not a force for the creation of satisfaction. His arguments stand in marked contrast to the idea that business people listen to the consumer, react to the information elicited, and develop goods and services that aim to satisfy. Veblen reverses these power relations. Start with the pursuit of profit and treat this as the motive force. Business will do whatever is necessary to secure the returns it wants. That is the nub of his work. From his perspective, marketing and the actors who help operationalize its varied practices, mold demand which is then satisfied. To do this they use marketing communications. Advertising shapes subjectivity; it tries to cognitively confine our patterns of thought; to make non-functional attributes resonate; and foster the perception that marketing, advertising and symbolic manipulation are our routes to happiness. This is the 'web' that surrounds us (Plotkin, 2014). This is somewhat consistent with James Rorty's (1934) critique of the advertising system.

Rorty was more emotive in his questioning of capitalism. This is reflected in his conceptualization of the consumer as a 'sucker', someone who is easily primed by the advertising, movies and cultural industries to live and think in predefined terms. The Critical Theorists make related arguments. In many respects, there is a lot of similarity between their view of the impact of marketing on society and that articulated by James Rorty. The Critical Theorists sought to examine how people in a specific historical period – the first generation of thinkers in this vein were publishing between 1930 and the late 1960s – were socialized by various influences. By socialization we mean how people are told to act in a cultural environment. Our behavior, the Critical Theorists explain, is shaped by multiple factors that we often only dimly appreciate.

Put differently, we are not the monarchs of the marketplace (Adorno, 1991). Nor do we embody the characteristics of economic (rational) 'man' (Fromm, 2002). Both concepts are 'fabrications' that help support the capitalist status quo by making it appear that the economic system reflects human nature and accommodates our real needs (Fromm, 2002, p. 74). We are not in any substantive sense an isolated, self-directed individual who determines our own route through life (Horkheimer, 2004, p. 92). We exist within interconnected economic and cultural systems that dwarf and define the individual in terms of providing the opportunity to earn income (the economic system) as well as templates for living (the cultural system) (Fromm, 2002). Nor do we make consumption choices without the input of other actors into our decision-making. Looking at the changing nature of the social environment, the Critical Theorists registered that the traditional mechanisms of orienting people to the world, such as religion and the family, were becoming less significant because of the rise of the 'culture industries' (Horkheimer, 2004). This latter term refers to all those industries who were involved with shaping the cultural environment, with fostering certain ways of life that are predicated on high levels of consumption (Adorno, 1991).

Marketing, advertising and the lifestyles of the rich and famous were often features of their analyses (e.g. Lowenthal, 1961). Each of these helps shape the cultural climate that surrounds us, thereby impacting upon our processes of psychological adjustment (i.e. they tend to foster conformity) (see also Veblen, 1899/1994). As Horkheimer puts it, 'Motion pictures, the radio, popular biographies and novels have the same refrain: This is our groove, this is the rut of the great and the would-be great – this is reality as it is and should be and will be' (Horkheimer, 2004, p. 96; see also Horkheimer, 2004, pp. 107–108). This is where the Critical Theorists – at least in some of their writings (especially the work of Fromm, somewhat in Marcuse, and less so in certain aspects of Adorno's work) – connect with Rorty. They make the case that marketing and the culture industries are powerful forces: 'The customer is not king' (Adorno, 1991, p. 99). Their writing often makes it seem that the consumer is relatively powerless compared to marketers. Fromm (2001), for instance, describes the advertising and selling of consumption items as akin to the marketing of opiates. We cannot or do not want to resist them.

Marketing practice uses advertising and other communications mediums to increase the value attributed to the enjoyments and satisfactions that accompany market-based buying and consumption. These mechanisms – marketing, distribution, and exchange – help integrate people into the economic system through their consumption of a largely 'standardized' set of offerings (Adorno, 1991) which are determined – at best – via consumer participation in market research. This drives corporate decision-making based on 'the majority principle' (Horkheimer, 2004, p. 21), whereby majority decisions shape marketplace offerings and define the parameters within which people tend to conform (Adorno and Horkheimer (1997) render this in more specific terms in the *Dialectic of Enlightenment* by gesturing to a rudimentary form of market segmentation).

Eventually people start to see their life through the prism of the accumulation of consumer goods (Marcuse, 1964). This, in turn, had implications for human self-development and the cultivation of individuality (see Fromm, 2002, p. 15). Looking to the market for inspiration about how we should live our lives and what we should deem desirable entails a certain degree of homogenization. People take what the market provides, using this to fashion their lifestyle. Such products were – when Horkheimer, Adorno, Marcuse, and others were writing – the result of the expanding factory system. They were mass produced. Because they were mass produced, they could not provide any substantive degree of individuality.

While marketing and consumption were significant factors in their writings (Fromm, 2002, 2003; Horkheimer, 2004), there was a more foundational question rousing their interest in these 'superstructural' (cultural) forces in society. They were providing a response to Marxism. Marx fully expected the working class to register and revolt from their marginal position in society. As the inequalities fostered by the capitalist system made themselves increasingly apparent, they would stimulate a revolution; a revolt that would lead to the establishment of a socialist economic system in which industry was owned by the workers and the benefits of production would return to those who provided their labor power, rather than to already wealthy owners or shareholders who did very little actual work. The problem that the Critical Theorists confronted was that the working class often did not revolt.

Within the Critical Theory tradition, marketing practice and the consumption it helps encourage are some of the major mechanisms through which people are distracted from the inequality of the social world. As standards of living have grown – even for those who are relatively poor (e.g. Horkheimer, 2004, p. 67) – it ties people to the existing status quo, to the economic system as it stands. They do see the (limited) benefits they receive, often registering the 'ephemeral' nature of the satisfactions on offer (Adorno, 1991), but still do not feel strongly motivated to change it out of fear of losing what they currently possess, can consume and might consume in the future.

The Critical Theorists were not always dismissive of marketing, consumption, distribution and exchange. Adorno, as a case in point, described the emancipatory aims of Critical Theory in less grand terms than complete social revolution (i.e. from capitalism to socialism). We experience emancipation, he submitted, when we do not feel hunger pangs, when we are free from anxiety and unhappiness, and when we do not have to conform to the dictates of social convention (Kellner, 1989). Of course, marketing and advertising can foster emancipation in these terms or weaken it. For contemporary critical thinkers, marketing practice tends to undercut the types of emancipation that Adorno hoped would be felt throughout society (Kilbourne, 1999).

Fromm (2002), like Adorno, appreciates the benefits accompanying consumption. Historically, he points out, consumption did make us happy. It made our day-to-day existence bearable. He is not, in any way, making a case that we should lead ascetic lives, avoiding the pleasures of the marketplace. His real problem revolves around the fact that much of what we consume is superfluous and that we are driven to consume not by our personal needs, but because the cultural and economic systems are perverted by capitalist imperatives for greater profit. To understand the nuances of his argument, an extended quotation is in order:

> [T]here is a legitimate need for more consumption as man develops culturally and has more refined needs for better food, objects of artistic pleasure, books etc. But our craving for consumption has lost all connection with the real needs of man. Originally, the idea of consuming more and better things was meant to give man a happier, more satisfied life. Consumption was a means to an end, that of happiness. It has now become an aim. The constant increase of needs forces us to an ever-increasing effort, it makes us dependent on these needs and on the people and institutions by whose help we attain them ... Man today is fascinated by the possibility of buying more, better, and especially, new things. He is consumption-hungry. The aim of buying and consuming has become a compulsive, irrational aim, because it is an end in itself, with little relation to the use of, or pleasure in the things bought and consumed. To buy the latest gadget, the latest model of anything that is on the market, is the dream of everybody ... Modern man, if he dared to be articulate about his concept of heaven, would describe a vision which would look like the biggest department store in the world, showing new things and gadgets, and himself having plenty of money with which to buy them.
>
> *Fromm, 2002, pp. 130–131*

Like Veblen, he believes we are surrounded by images of the good life whose real purpose is to satisfy the desires of the business community for profit. This process undermines consumer sovereignty. We stop rationally evaluating our consumption practices (Fromm presents the customer as 'passive', merely 'drinking' in the imperatives provided by industry); it becomes a compulsion to get the latest, socially desirable items. This, for both Fromm and Marcuse, is irrational.

What the Critical Theorists did want to question was whether these industries delivered on the promises they were making. Generally, their response was downbeat. They were reflecting on a business system that was undergoing a period of massive expansion. And they had seen the use and ramifications of propaganda during the Nazi regime, registering how this did shape the views of the population in their home country (Germany). With this as their context, it is not surprising that the Critical Theorists held out little hope for social change via the actions of the working class (see Horkheimer, 2004, pp. 81, 97, 99). They fully appreciated the fact that social change was being defused through the satiation provided by consumer goods.

While there was some pessimism in their writings, it did not overwrite their desire for social change or their belief that it was possible to tackle the harms and injustices created by the capitalist system. Intellectuals and other informed activists could play a role in social change by fostering 'estrangement' within their networks (Marcuse, 1964). They could point out how the marketing system encourages conformity (i.e. a herd instinct) rather than individuality (Fromm, 2002); how it provided only ephemeral satisfactions (Adorno, 1991); how it kept people working to achieve these limited satisfactions and that this was not ultimately fulfilling (see also Scitovsky, 1992).

Consistent with Marcuse, and echoing Veblen, Murray and Ozanne (1991) adopt Critical Theory as their intellectual prism and claim that capitalism, marketing and advertising are 'forcefields'. They are mechanisms for social control that surround the individual (Kellner, 1989). They help inform people about what is valuable in life, what needs are most significant, and how they can achieve the satisfactions that the marketing system is responsible for creating. In combination, the 'culture industries' help define the social world, our place within it, and focus our energies and efforts on the world of consumption. In conjunction, they warp our sense of self. We no longer build character through our actions, helping our friends, families, communities and those we otherwise indirectly touch. We buy our personality and self-image, crafting the latter courtesy of the purchase and possession of goods (e.g. Marcuse, 1964). We manifest what Fromm (2007, p. 21) calls a 'having' orientation. The production of character in line with the dictates of what the market and potential employers require is termed – somewhat confusingly in this context – the adoption of a 'marketing orientation' (e.g. Fromm, 2003, pp. 56–57).

Nonetheless, we should be wary about thinking that the Critical Theorists conceptualize the consumer as a dupe. This perspective is understandable. Fromm (2001) overplays the power of marketers and Lazarsfeld's (1941) review of Critical Theory comes close to sketching a dupe-like character. If we interpret Critical Theory to include people beyond the Frankfurt School, James Rorty's writing presents a dupe-ish individual; as does Alvesson's (1993). However, overgeneralizing is not a good idea. We are dealing with many different writers, some more nuanced than others.

Neither Adorno (1975) nor Horkheimer (2004) presented the consumer as an unsophisticated dupe, although their language can be quite deterministic (e.g. Adorno, 1991, p. 105; Horkheimer, 2004, pp. 101, 107–108; cf. Adorno, 1991, p. 131). Adorno suggested that most individuals did realize the satisfaction they derived from consumption was 'fleeting'. As he puts it:

> It may also be supposed that the consciousness of the consumers themselves is split between the prescribed fun which is supplied to them by the culture industry and a not particularly well-hidden doubt about its blessings . . . People are not only, as the saying goes, falling for the swindle; if it guarantees them even the most fleeting gratification they desire a deception which is nonetheless transparent to them. They force their eyes shut and voice approval, in a kind of self-loathing, for what is meted out to them, knowing full well the purpose for which it is manufactured. Without admitting it they sense that their lives would be completely intolerable as soon as they no longer clung to the satisfactions which are none at all.
>
> *Adorno, 1991, p. 103*

Clearly, the Critical Theorists and consumers alike registered that practitioners were not complete truth-tellers; that consumption did not always causally equate with happiness (see Fromm, 2002, pp. 7, 11). The idea that it did was an 'ideology' (Adorno, 1991). It was a justification for a worldview based on consumerist satisfactions that did not generate anything like a long-term feeling of wellbeing. Its purpose was short-term in one sense. Immediate and limited gratifications were key in ensuring that the consumer returns to the marketplace as quickly as possible, thereby continuing the cycle of production and consumption. This repeated return to the marketplace hints at the long-term agenda in play.

Marketing and the advertising system partly function as ways of offsetting any 'motivation crises' that might confront people living in a capitalist system (Habermas, 1973). The social world into which we are born largely equates success with financial income (Fromm, 2003, p. 13) and we work to finance our purchasing habits – habits that are fostered by the marketing system itself (Adorno, 1991). Provided the system can continue to generate standards of living that people find appealing, it is likely to foreclose any serious reflections on its legitimacy (Habermas, 1973).

In the last twenty years, a small number of consumer researchers have taken Critical Theory as their paradigm, using it to flesh out an alternative concept of the consumer. Ozanne and Murray (1995), for example, outline the 'reflexively defiant consumer'. They position this individual within the context of the capitalist system. This actor is surrounded by the potentially distorting influence of marketing communications. This sounds reasonable. However, their work shades into idealism quickly. Ozanne and Murray sketch an account of a motivated individual who exhibits radical sensibilities. They are critical of the status quo and treat the output of industry with cynicism. We do not doubt that some people adopt this stance, but we need to be realistic. The reflexively defiant person is a collage of many desirable attributes. It describes someone who mostly exists in a vacuum unencumbered by the constraints many of us experience in our everyday lives. Ozanne and Murray's conceptual architecture is, put bluntly, far removed from the habitual, unthinking and routine nature of much human behavior (Lafley & Martin, 2017).

Each of the thinkers referred to above – Veblen, Rorty, Fromm, Marcuse, Adorno, Murray and Ozanne – points out that power dynamics in the marketplace are complex. Business people try to influence consumers; and we do not always end up satisfied or benefitted by the experience. Handily, the work surveyed so far takes us from the eighteenth to mid-twentieth century (if we selectively ignore the Ozanne and Murray work!). We are now at the juncture when the marketing concept has been rhetorically and incorrectly positioned as emerging (i.e. the 1950s). Even after this alleged turning point, Adorno claims that practitioners inaccurately depict the consumer. They are not the sovereign individual of marketing lore. With this in mind, we need to tackle the notion of consumer sovereignty.

Consumer sovereignty

Consumer sovereignty is often united with the marketing concept (Dixon, 1992). Kotler did this in his books (Reekie, 1988). This would not surprise Galbraith (1970) who saw it as an article of religious faith in textbooks. The empirical realism of the concept is another matter. The linkage of the marketing concept and consumer sovereignty is a paradox (Brownlie & Saren, 1992; Dixon, 1992). Each concept looks realistic and reasonable. Combined, they contradict or deflate each other. Marketing professionals want to influence the consumer. They want to shape demand and meaning. They want to limit the exercise of sovereignty, yet they praise its merits to the sky when necessary (i.e. usually in front of regulators).

The idea of consumer sovereignty can be traced back to William Hutt in 1931. He pointed to earlier versions, referencing 'the customer is always right' and 'the customer is king' (Hutt, 1940). Of course, the lineage of these ideas stretches back much further. Adam Smith made the same argument when he referred to smart producers delivering what their target audiences wanted (Lynd, 1934). These ideas appear more frequently in the nineteenth and twentieth centuries, notably in the retailing practices of Marshall Field, John Wanamaker and Harry Gordon Selfridge. But what is always worth doing when thinking critically about the concepts we invoke is to look at the context in which they emerged. They are influenced by the events and belief systems of the time. The same is true of the notion of the 'customer as king'.

As king or queen, the consumer is supposed to have ultimate power in the marketplace. Via their 'dollar votes' they help determine which firms survive (Dixon, 1992). Charles Coolidge Parlin is usually cited as coining the phrase the 'customer is king'. Whether this is accurate or not, his 1914 statement did attract attention. What is not regularly appreciated is that Parlin said sovereign status did not apply to everyone. His view of the consumer focused on the white middle and upper classes (Ward, 2009). If you were not part of this privileged demographic, then you fell outside of the class of sovereign individuals.

Today this concept straddles the globe. Even ostensibly Communist states have adopted the idea of the consumer 'as a god or emperor' (Gamble, 2007). Despite the fact its merits as an accurate representation of marketplace agency are questionable, it does perform other functions. Business owners, marketing managers and brand advocates use the concept to encourage employees to treat the customer well. It is a control mechanism which structures the delivery of service experiences (Gamble, 2007). It might not always succeed (Skålén, 2009), but its intent remains unchanged.

Stated simply, sovereignty entails the valuing of individual choice. It is contestable. Too much choice does not enhance human welfare. For a start, our preferences are usually vague. When excess information and multiple options are presented, they can overload, paralyze and stunt our choice-making process, leading to suboptimal outcomes (Botti & Iyengar, 2006). Choice, then, is a double-edged sword.

The concept of sovereignty is also more complicated than normally assumed. Pure sovereignty involves the individual having dictatorial power. State, government or external forces do not exist in this fantasy world as a force of control (Hildebrand, 1951). Equally dubiously, an individual is deemed sovereign when they can make rational, thoughtful decisions (Sirgy & Su, 2000). This sounds like the mostly imaginary 'economic man'. It is a caricature we are unlikely to meet in the street. We do not often engage in deliberation about our consumption choices. We are led by our emotions, habits and the opinions of influential others (Galbraith, 1958, 1970), including corporations and their staff (Dixon, Ponomareff, Turner, & DeLisi, 2017; Pressey, 2015).

Companies, of course, typically 'anticipate' (Hutt, 1940) or 'imagine' (Galbraith, 1970) 'the average consumer's wishdream' (Scitovsky, 1962, p. 267) prior to its expression in the marketplace. These 'dreams' are shaped via marketing communications. Nor should we forget that producers are attributed with sovereignty of their own – producers' (sometimes deeply questionable) sovereignty (see Galbraith, 1970, p. 475). They have sovereignty in the sense that they do not have to respond to all requests in a free marketplace (Reekie, 1988). After all, anticipated risk is often an important factor in manufacturer decision-making. It can make their actions conservative to avoid the large-scale financial mistakes (Scitovsky, 1962) which occur with some frequency (Zinkin, 1967).

Depending on who is consulted, preferences are structured in various ways. Galbraith (1958) referenced the growing centralization of power in the economy, the greater use of marketing, consumer research and advertising and the implications of this for consumption behavior (i.e. its delimitation). He talks about the 'management of consumer tastes' (Galbraith, 1970, p. 474 n.24), with Zinkin (1967) citing the performative function of marketing in relation to demand creation. Zinkin's nuance was that the demand being promoted was usually a rethinking of existing preferences, rather than truly novel.

Lerner (1972) seems to have directed his attention at Critical Theory arguments about the external shaping of decision-making. He denounced these as implausible and asserted that socialization and imitation were the major factors bounding sovereignty. Hildebrand (1951) took a different tack. He warned that producers will try to bias decision-making. This occurs whether we are talking about a multi-stage process such as that between the customer (e.g. a doctor) and the consumer (e.g. a patient), or more directly when one person is the purchaser and user. Hutt, similarly, thought producers could exert a negative influence, encouraging 'deleterious tastes' (Hutt, 1940, p. 70). This was made less likely when advertising was regulated; when product distribution and labeling were subject to legislation and control (Dixon, 1992); when fraud and adulteration were prosecuted (Hildebrand, 1951); when people were educated and informed (Scitovsky, 1962); and when a plurality of producers were engaged in effective competition (Hutt, 1940; Lerner, 1972).

This point about competition illustrates a misunderstanding about marketing. It bears little resemblance to the reality of the marketplace today as well. As a practice, marketing is about trying to minimize or avoid competition through brands, patents, contractual arrangements, habit creation and consumer lock-in. There continues to be considerable doubt over whether there is effective competition in the marketplace, especially given the growing sizes of corporations and the power they wield (see Dholakia, Dholakia, & Fırat, this volume). Indeed, practitioners surveyed when Keith (1960) was writing were quick to rally against government intervention to ensure competition and the protection of the consumer (Barksdale & Darden, 1971).

Reflecting the tenor of the time, Hutt (1940) did privilege liberty in individual decision-making. Likewise, Zinkin (1967) calls attention to resistance being manifested against the marketing and advertising machine. People were, these authors maintained, free to make bad decisions as well as good. Not all shared these views. Lynd (1934, p. 4) conceptualized the consumer as 'becoming confused and illiterate' in the face of product proliferation and savvy marketing practices. These issues remain unresolved today. Sirgy and Su (2000), for instance, unpack the complexity that confronts the consumer in medical and high technology markets. This is compounded by their limited knowledge, comparative disinterest in extended problem-solving and largely habitual behavior.

Sovereignty, then, is 'always' limited (Hildebrand, 1951; Hutt, 1940). In some contexts, the consumer is a 'serf', they are relatively powerless in comparison to their corporate overlords (Rotfeld, 2004). They could be people living in low-income areas which already suffer from limited access to products and services. Retailers that set up in these locations tend to offer a smaller selection and charge higher prices (Crockett & Wallendorf, 2004). Alternatively, in light of industry willingness to misrepresent the safety of their products, people can find themselves buying dangerous, possibly adulterated items from 'reputable' and unknown companies alike (Boyd, 2012; Hanser, 2004). Illness and death sometimes accompany corporate actions, a topic we explore in more detail below (Custance, Walley, & Jiang, 2012).

With respect to individual sovereignty, the extent to which it reflects individual choice is problematic. First, it depends on the economic system we live in (e.g. North Korea versus the United States). Second, structural, cultural, social and personal factors influence choice (Galbraith, 1970; Hildebrand, 1951; Lepisto & Hannaford, 1980). After all, many people live in economies where consumption is presented as the royal route to happiness (Galbraith, 1970).

Some pursue this individualistically. Often this is only possible when we have access to middle-class, rather than working-class incomes. Others live in cultural environments founded upon the notion of the 'interdependent model of self' (Markus & Schwartz, 2010, p. 346). Community orientation, adherence to norms, a certain degree of inconspicuousness (Eckhardt, Belk, & Wilson, 2015), rather than self-definition and individuality, are more highly prized in these environments (Markus & Schwartz, 2010). Even if they are available, we do not necessarily make individual decisions about our consumption choices. This is true whether we live in individualistic nations (e.g. the United States) or collectivist countries (e.g. China). We are influenced by other people, sometimes following the crowd as described by the 'herd instinct' or 'trickle across' theories (Atik & Fırat, 2013).

We must acknowledge that while scholars talk about the consumer as if they are a monolithic entity, this neglects the substantive differences between people. The population of China, for instance, is marked by large income disparities. High levels of wealth are routinely contrasted against those 'clad in rags and begging for alms' (Hanser, 2004, p. 15). The shopping experiences, service levels and product safety that various groups can expect are deeply stratified by income and perceived levels of wealth. Less affluent people often visit (former) state-run department stores. They have shabby interiors, customers can expect a limited degree of politeness from staff, but nothing like the 'asymmetrical deference' found in luxury establishments built in the post-reform era (Hanser, 2007, p. 416). In these, the affluent sometimes act like misbehaving children, ignoring or treating service staff badly, shouting their requirements and calling for management to shame the worker (Hanser, 2007). The poor, on the other hand, are ignored or treated with high levels of disdain.

Third, there needs to be effective competition. Without competition, it is highly unlikely that manufacturers will willingly produce a large range of items for various market segments. This is because they seek to maximize their profit levels and restricting supply to a limited range that satisfies enough consumers to meet organizational targets will suffice. Other customers can be expected to either satisfice (i.e. buy the nearest equivalent to their requirements that is 'good' enough) or forgo consumption. If the market segments that are not being serviced become large enough or sufficiently profitable so that they attract new entrants to the market, the firm might change its approach to block new competitors from gaining a foothold.

Fourth, industry might refuse to use the most efficient and effective production techniques. Closely related is a 'vested interests' argument. Cartels are not unusual. Exploring this issue, Baker and Faulkner (1993) enumerate the ways firms try to control their markets. Some of these go beyond legal measures (e.g. political lobbying), straying into illegal territory by violating laws meant to discourage collusion (e.g. sharing future pricing strategies to limit competition). Marketing and sales managers have been implicated in formalized business-to-business price-fixing, the planned distribution of market shares and other restrictive activities (Faulkner, Cheney, Fisher, & Baker, 2003). Equally, they can be involved in 'informal' relationships (e.g. in the pharmaceutical and the insurance industries) (Lakoff, 2004). Their involvement reflects their comparatively low organizational position. This keeps them at a distance from senior management who can deny knowledge of any cartel-like activities (Baker & Faulkner, 1993). A cartel often frustrates the consumer, increases organizational profits and cements its power base. This said, they are not all-powerful. Incumbents can always be replaced by entrepreneurial firms (Zinkin, 1967).

Fifth, organizational 'ignorance' and 'fraud' likewise bound effective producer and consumer sovereignty. Sixth, the wealthy have a disproportionate influence on production; the poor are neglected in certain cases (Lerner, 1972; Karnani, 2017), feel their financial restrictions acutely, and are subject to exploitation (Bailey, 2000; Elliott & Leonard, 2004; Schulman, 2016). As a way beyond this, Hutt (1940) left room for government intervention to restructure inequalities of income, wealth and resources that were being controlled by powerful groups. Finally, sovereignty differs depending on the nature of firm–consumer interaction. Large firms can be less amenable to consumer articulations of their needs and desires; smaller companies may be more responsive (Etzioni, 1958).

It is often noted that critical researchers depict marketers as quite powerful. Mainstream scholars sometimes make remarkably consistent arguments, so we must refrain from positioning the former as making outlandish claims about marketing theory or practice. But it is clearly not only marketers who shape the cultural environment in which we live. They play a major role, but are only part of an orchestra of taste mediation (Arsel & Bean, 2013). Their activities are assisted by magazine editors, bloggers, celebrities and related figures that are called cultural intermediaries. They act as intermediaries between the culture industries (e.g. large corporations with deep marketing budgets) and the ultimate consumer (Negus, 2002). They take the free (seeded) products and information provided by the companies and translate this – sometimes complex, sometimes not – material for the people who watch their YouTube channels, read their magazines or otherwise engage with their content. In effect, these groups try to shape the way we think and act. For example, the fashion industry receives ongoing criticism for devaluing normal physiology. This affects those who look to these sources for guidance. We peer at our non-airbrushed body and wince. Creating dissatisfaction like this is undertaken as it keeps the magazines in business, giving them content and stories they can purvey. And dissatisfaction generates a response. We look for a product or service to deal with the condition being perpetuated by the magazine; a condition that can be treated with the products being heavily advertised in the pages of the same dissatisfaction-creating machine.

A recent film by Elena Rossini called *The Illusionists* (2015) unpicked this process. It referred to the stigmatization of cellulite – a normal accumulation of fatty tissue that was not considered troublesome in the past – and traced its elevation as a problem that required a marketer-delivered solution. This is 'market creation' at its most dubious. Creating a problem, making people feel unhappy, and then selling them satisfaction. For commentators like Kilbourne (1999), marketing creates unhappiness. It cleaves voids to fill with consumption. This is a process that goes on throughout our lives. Where, we might ask, is the sovereign consumer here?

What seems odd given the centrality of consumer sovereignty to marketing theory is that it has been regularly undermined. There are prominent marketers who now question its empirical reality despite their earlier support. For instance, Kotler and his co-authors sound almost Veblenian at times. Marketing is not a reactive activity in their view. Now, for them, marketing is not about pandering to the customer. It is about managing them, shaping their demand and determining whether their needs and desires should be fulfilled (Kotler, Armstrong, Harris, & Piercy, 2013). Profit generation, in this context, assumes priority. This is a problem as accruing profit and ensuring customer satisfaction do not map on to each other perfectly. The marketplace is a domain where conflict between marketers and consumers is likely to occur. Houston (1986) famously says that firms will only satisfy needs when it enables them to achieve their objectives. This bounds sovereignty, with the firm as the locus of decision-making and the font of power. This is the opposite of Keith's (1960) suggestion that power relations have shifted toward the customer.

Early authors registered the power dynamics and limitations facing the consumer (e.g. Lynd, 1936). They called the individual a compromiser, not a sovereign (Tadajewski, 2016). We have Harry Tosdal to thank for this insight. Compromise, he maintains, is a major feature of organizational and consumer decision-making, irrespective of whether the customer was routinely invoked as the 'boss' of the firm for public relations and labor management purposes (Tadajewski & Jones, 2016).

Businesses make choices about the markets they will serve in view of their technological, economic, supply chain and distributional capabilities. Reflecting the costs of information gathering, they cannot usually obtain full information about their target market and need to hedge their bets (i.e. they compromise). Limits confront the customer as well. 'Mr. Average' cannot buy everything he wants. Nor is their decision-making totally self-directed. They compromise on their desires to meet the needs of their families. Their bank statement helps force compromise. So, people make acceptable (satisficing) decisions. And let's be honest, we can all be a little lazy. But, rationally so. After all, life is too short to devote hours to weighing up minor consumption choices.

Consumer sovereignty and marketplace reality

The assumptions associated with consumer sovereignty are shaky to say the least. The idea that marketers try to enable effective decision-making should make a novice student incredulous. Sure, the marketing concept is about listening to the customer (i.e. potentially enabling sovereignty). It is questionable whether this exercise leads to products that are consistent with the requirements of the individual. To reiterate a point made above, marketers want to structure and modify demand, not merely cater to the whims of the public.

Even more questionable are arguments that mass-produced items enable the production of a unique sense of self. This thesis weaves through much of the Consumer Culture Theory (CCT) literature. As mentioned above, Critical Theorists suggest that marketing does not enable the crafting of an individual identity, rather it promotes conformity. This should not be understood as a deterministic argument. Marketing is not a monolithic force (Holbrook, 1987; Pollay, 1987). Instead, we need to appreciate the varied nature of power relations in the marketplace and examine how these are stratified. This stratification – i.e. various levels of power and influence – means that those situated at different points will have different abilities to shape the thoughts, behaviors and practices of people at other levels. This process is not uni-directional and it is context and case specific.

Focusing on the individual and their playful modification of the items they buy ignores the fact that many of these goods are mass produced. This is one of the critiques of postmodernism and CCT. As specialisms, though, they are attuned to and affirm capitalistic dynamics. Their work re-describes and promotes the status quo (see Dholakia *et al.*, this volume). And they can be subject to managerial co-optation. Sometimes this is a function of interpretive researchers wanting to commercialize their skills. Their training, knowledge and wisdom are used to study consumers in situ to produce more marketable goods and services (Fitchett, Patsiaouras, & Davies, 2015). They help define the field for channeled imagination that trades on 'the illusion of difference' (Evers, 2016).

CCT advocates miss this channeling point when they stress the agency of the ultimate consumer. They largely ignore the political-legal-economic context and the supply chains that help constitute the goods we buy (Denegri-Knott & Tadajewski, 2017). These have a major role in defining what we can buy in store or online. Atik and Fırat (2013), for example, point out that fabric producers often forecast trends years in advance of the goods arriving in store. Their choices form the base options for the designers and magazine editors who promote the products that are eventually manufactured. The customer only makes their selection out of choices that have previously been winnowed down before they appear in stock.

Even those ordinarily depicted as 'influencers', the celebrities who grace the pages of prominent magazines, are not exemplars of the postmodern or CCT consumer. To be sure, they are provided with whatever goods a company seeks to promote. In some respects, their sovereignty is limited to what they are given. In other circumstances, their choices are preformatted by stylists who have a major input into their decisions (i.e. French Montana is a good example). The fanciful conceptual architecture of the postmodern consumer or the CCT bricoleur thus needs to be scrutinized, rather than applied as a template (this has been a major problem with postmodern research). Basically, this means that concepts have shaped a version of reality without substantially being undermined by the empirical contexts (not) being confronted.

Uncritically asserting extensive levels of sovereignty is remarkably naive. We know that practitioners want to limit it by creating and affirming habitual behavior (Berinato, 2017; McGrath, 2017). We are not particularly rational, or computer-like information processors. The same goes for the postmodern identity-shifting chameleon. We get stuck in routines and ruts, constrained by our finances, interests and attention span (Wood & Neal, 2009). To state the obvious, creating habits means tying the consumer to the firm (Champion, 2017); it constrains the ability of other companies to effectively target the patron and access the profit stream they generate (McGrath, 2017). The overall effect is a reduction in competitor and consumer sovereignty.

Having now examined the marketing concept and consumer sovereignty in detail, we need to probe the connecting concept. This is the idea of 'exchange'. In this material, the textbook façade of 'win-win' discourse associated with marketing practice falls away in surprising ways.

Rethinking marketing as exchange

Exchange is the link in the chain between the marketing concept and sovereignty. It connects the two (or more) parties involved. What is glaring about some of the material on exchange is its disconnection from reality. Exchange is presented as benefitting both groups equally. For Bagozzi (1975) the 'rule of equality' frames the marketing concept. This ignores the power relations that exist in the marketplace. Even managerial writers find this argument uncompelling. Houston and Gassenheimer's (1987) *Journal of Marketing* paper is a good counterpoint. They say that the marketing concept is 'a myth' intended to legitimate the practices of marketing in society. At a minimum, it offers practitioners a narrative they can use at dinner parties when they are asked to justify what they do.

If marketers consulted some of the articles available, they would find a representation of their practice that seriously diverges from mainstream accounts. For instance, Hirschman (1991) explores the concepts, assumptions and power relations embedded in articles published in the *Journal of Marketing*. Where marketers paint pictures of equality (Bagozzi, 1975) or 'mutual gain' in exchange (Fischer & Bristor, 1994), Hirschman identifies managerial fantasies of omnipotence and marketplace power coalescing in the hands of vested interests.

She finds that marketers elevate themselves to the dominant partner in an exchange; they understand their activities as controlling the consumer, rather than responding to their 'target market'. This concept itself signifies a certain way of thinking about the customer. They are not understood as active. They are the target. They are the enemy in business warfare and practitioners use sexualized language to describe their customer interactions (Hirschman, 1991). Rather than 'win-win' statements (Fischer & Bristor, 1994), we hear about penetration, thrusting and forcing the consumer to do managerial bidding (Fischer & Bristor, 1994). Marriage is not the metaphor of choice as is usually invoked in relationship marketing discourse, but stalking (via database technology) (Tynan, 1997). All in all, the individual is dehumanized (Hirschman, 1991). They are an object to be manipulated, a means to an end – the end being profit, which is equated with success.

To be clear, Hirschman (1991) and Fischer and Bristor (1994) provide feminist analyses. This situates their work within Critical Marketing Studies as they are using a form of critical social theory to highlight the biases, blind-spots and unequal power relations that permeate marketing theory and consumer research. They are aware that their scholarship could be controversial. Saying that, there are markets where references to violence, rape and death reflect 'norms'. The market for methamphetamine is an exemplar (Brownstein et al., 2012). Beyond the extreme, there is support for their findings in mainstream research. Gentry, Kennedy, Paul and Hill (1995) examine the experiences of people undergoing traumatic events in their lives (e.g. the deaths of loved ones). Such upheavals make these individuals vulnerable to predation. Most grieving people engage in limited decision-making and reflection, with 'mental confusion . . . common' (Gentry et al., 1995, p. 132). This opens the door to manipulation, profiteering and heartache. Indeed, some funeral home operators do not come out of the study well. Greed and systematic lying to their customer base were unearthed.

For Houston and Gassenheimer (1987), marketing is about skewing the market. It is about the production of the appearance of difference in product offerings. Veblen could not have said it better. If business people were given the super-power to enact markets in the idealistic terms found in debates on economic performativity (where they conjure up a market to maximize their own benefit), they would envision a much less competitive arena, probably one in which they were the monopolist (e.g. Houston & Gassenheimer, 1987, p. 15). While Houston and Gassenheimer were writing for a mainstream audience, their appraisal of marketplace dynamics brings them into the orbit of critical thinkers. Thorstein Veblen and Fuat Fırat would applaud the honesty of their analysis.

Both Veblen and Fırat have – in their own respective ways – pointed out that marketing is about the avoidance of competition while presenting a veneer of competition (Plotkin, 2014, p. 512). This veneer is thin. As a case in point, when we walk around the supermarket it appears that the marketplace is highly competitive. There are many different product offerings from various providers. This semblance of profusion hides high levels of industrial concentration'. The documentary, *Food Inc.* (Kenner, 2009), highlights that a small number of very large producers own many different brands. Behind this pluralistic surface is an industrial complex that mass produces food as cheaply as possible. Accompanying low prices is a series of problems. Manufacturing concentration means that any sanitation problems (i.e. animal feces in the meat) and bacterial infections (e.g. *Salmonella, Campylobacter*) can overrun the slaughterhouses and factories quickly. These can affect large swathes of the population, giving them serious health conditions.

Their immense size and lobbying power means that meat companies have substantial political sway vis-à-vis regulators. Power relations in the market are not equal. Those engaged in farming have limited power. If they are supported by loans for equipment and infrastructure by the industry, they must follow the guidelines demanded by their supply-chain partner. This means agricultural production on a scale where appropriate care for the animals can fall by the wayside. Concern for livestock, farmers and the customer are secondary factors in the pursuit of profit.

Choice and sovereignty

Choice facilitates sovereignty. We need alternatives for sovereignty to be meaningful. Marketplace stratification plays a role here too. These assumptions contrast those of some interpretive, CCT and postmodern studies that uncritically assume agency and freedom of choice. As a rough rule of thumb, CCT research tends to present the consumer as slightly more structurally constrained than does postmodern writing. Within the latter tradition, the depiction of the customer is usually detached from empirical reality, with one argument being that people are no longer restricted by tradition. Closely connected is the thesis that our class position does not exert a substantive influence on how we live and work. There are numerous problems with postmodern conceptions of agency. First, (predominantly) class-derived cultural capital will shape our selection of products and services (Holt, 1998). Second, race, ethnicity and overt religious affiliations can influence how people engage with us, affecting our opportunities in the marketplace and world of work. Third, it is not clear that many people view consumption in active postmodern terms. Regularly changing identity is cognitively demanding, time-consuming and expensive. Most people probably eschew this level of commitment, preferring less involved forms of expression (Der Laan & Velthuis, 2016; Eckhardt et al., 2015).

Reading this literature, it appears that the postmodern consumer is adept at negotiating the marketplace. This is possible only with various enabling conditions. Money, finance, education and literacy skills are important. But we do not live in a world where everyone is given equal opportunity to secure high-quality education or the chance to succeed. Studies on low-literate consumers deflate the exaggerated agency postmodernists espouse (Gau & Viswanathan, 2008; Viswanathan, Rosa, & Harris, 2005). The same can be said of blind consumers who demonstrate a mixture of vulnerability, creativity and skill in achieving their goals (Dunnett, Hamilton, & Piacentini, 2016). However, these individuals also suffer from degrees of depression, feel constrained by their home environment and find shopping akin to 'torture' (Falchetti et al., 2016). These groups are not the archetypical sovereign individual – if this fiction even exists.

For example, the issue of racism and its effects on product and service access are long-standing. Racism means that people are attributed different value because of their skin color. Legislation was enacted in the United States to segregate races (i.e. so-called 'Jim Crow' laws). This prevented equal access to public services, retailing locations and private service environments. Marketing theory, in turn, reflected the racist assumptions and values circulating in the cultural environment. Mirroring this, since Parlin first uttered the phrase – the customer is king in 1914 – certain groups have been pushed to the edge of the marketplace (Ward, 2009). No matter what time period we consult, it is not difficult to find racist ideas and imagery infecting theory and practice. This is true from the turn of the twentieth century and the work of Katherine Blackford (Tadajewski, 2012), through to the discrimination faced in the ghettos of the 1960s, along with the demarketing literature of the 1970s (Kotler & Levy, 1971). When we delve into all this material, the inescapable conclusion is that race has been a divisive factor in provisioning. This has not changed. 'Redlining' continues to be a feature of the housing market (as well as other markets). This refers to the refusal of loans, mortgages, insurance and related products to people living in deprived areas (Rugh & Massey, 2010).

Racial inequality shapes access to malls, the treatment people receive when shopping (Bailey, 2000; Mallinson & Brewster, 2005) and the types of disdain they face when making inquiries (Williams, 2005, 2006). It also restricts consumer choice on the internet. As the case of Airbnb made apparent, people renting out their accommodation have few qualms about adopting racist and 'looks based' discrimination (Fisman & Luca, 2016). Equally, those using Uber services appear uninhibited about proffering racist reviews about their drivers (Fisman & Luca, 2016). It is even the case that the algorithms applied in the selection of advertisements to be displayed online have used racially common names to generate marketing communications which reinforce negative stereotypes. Fisman and Luca (2016) call this 'algorithm-generated discrimination'.

Claims to sovereignty are therefore complicated. There are many ways in which we can be discriminated against, including based on our health and wellbeing. To be the idealized candidate for sovereignty we need to be wealthy, mobile, thin and healthy. Health is not something we can take for granted. Pavia (1993) explores the lives of young people living with HIV and AIDS. Their ill-health dramatically alters their circumstances. Finding it difficult to work, their disposable income dwindles. Their social networks dissolve. Friends shun them; family members brush off their advances. In one case, the scorn was extreme, with one person's obituary being published 'before' they had passed away to halt the 'death threats' aimed at her family (Pavia, 1993, p. 426). Pavia's account spotlights the trope of 'contamination' and a dearth of empathy.

Not only do they find it difficult to buy the products and services that were once available to them – thereby indicating a limit to their sovereignty – their ability to divest was constrained by antipathy to their condition. People literally would not touch their possessions or pets. Even when they had access to money, their behavior might look odd to the healthy. When their life expectancy was limited, some spent their money freely, purchasing alcohol, drugs and expensive products they would have avoided previously (Pavia, 1993). But it is not only those who are resource poor, deemed undesirable or suffering from ill-health who have their sovereignty controlled.

Let us now examine the notion of 'lock-in' – something that probably affects most people reading this chapter to some degree. 'Consumer lock-in' refers to strong connections between a customer and company (Harrison, Beatty, Reynolds, & Noble, 2012). We become 'locked-in' to these relationships when the costs of breaking them are perceived to be too high. For critics of lock-in, for instance, it means we are purchasing suboptimal technology when better options are available or could have been successful with the right promotion and product trialing programs (Stack & Gartland, 2003).

Lock-in is a function of many things. We become locked-in due to our financial investments and commitments (e.g. mobile phone packages, fixed-price energy deals); the expertise developed in using a product (e.g. the QWERTY keyboard, an Apple or Android phone); or where social propriety 'encourages' us to patronize a service provider because we know the individual, interact with them socially or have familial connections (Harrison et al., 2012). Still, when companies use contracts to lock in their audiences, it begs the question about whether the firm truly believes it is serving its audience equitably and satisfyingly. Lock-in is, in some cases, a means to prevent dissatisfied patrons from pursuing alternative options (McGovern & Moon, 2007).

Lock-in can also be a means to generate habitual behavior. In his reflection on consumer sovereignty, Hutt proposes that we are 'slaves of habit' (Persky, 1993). This is not a total exaggeration. Being slaves of habit can, of course, be very negative depending on the products and experiences we are discussing. This is especially the case when we look at products that can cause addiction.

For early writers on sovereignty, addiction was one of the examples used to question the freedom of the individual (Hildebrand, 1951). It is true that addiction will likely wreck the life of the person involved and negatively affect those around them (Moyle & Coomber, 2015). More critically oriented observers of the changing nature of industrial society see the consumption of narcotics of all kinds as an almost inevitable concomitant of the stresses and strains of modern life. People are constantly looking 'for something that will make life in an urban-industrial environment a little more tolerable' (Huxley, 2004, p. 96). Even those people who seem to have everything: affluence, social networks and fruitful lives, find themselves slipping into alcohol and drug abuse, dependence and worse.

Martin (2015), for instance, studied a group of extremely wealthy women living in New York. There was little they could not buy or consume. Her respondents – and Martin on occasion – were not satisfied people. They might be very thin, have talented children, a wardrobe full of expensive clothing and multiple Birkin bags, but their physical management of self – plastic surgery, high-energy exercise – left them like 'zombies' (Martin, 2015, p. 147). Their stress played out in predictable ways. Alcohol and a variety of prescription pills were consumed regularly. There was no time of the day that someone was not using substances to obtain mental sanctuary (Martin, 2015). Of course, what initially appears to make life tolerable or interaction manageable, eventually isolates and devastates unless treated. Sovereignty dissipates. As Duff McKagan (2012, p. 195), the bassist for Guns N' Roses reveals, what was once fun and exciting, eventually takes over everyday life:

> I needed a tumbler of vodka and two lines of coke just to get off the mattress when I woke up. Alcohol and drugs were now bought in bulk. I wanted to have a sure supply around all the time. I was alone in my house and had no one and nothing to stop me ingesting bad stuff whenever I wished . . . I always took a bottle of vodka with me if I was going anywhere outside of my comfort zone, which is to say anywhere outside of a ten-block radius of my house.

This habit nearly killed him. There are many other examples taken from the world of celebrity culture and everyday life that highlight the progressive delimitation of life as well as the reduction in sovereignty caused by drugs, alcohol and various other habits (e.g. Adler, 2011; Clegg, 2012; Daly & Sampson, 2013; Detzer, 1988; Lee, Mars, Neal, & Sixx, 2002; Sixx, 2007). Literally being a slave takes us into the territory of dark marketing.

Dark marketing, human trafficking and the organs trade

Dark marketing has been defined as 'the application of marketing principles and practices to the domains of death, destruction and the ostensibly reprehensible' (Brown, McDonagh & Shultz, 2012, p. 196). Human traffickers are exemplar dark marketers (Smith & Betts, 2015). And the people who consume the sexual services provided by these actors have been equated, contra Adorno, to a 'king or queen' (O'Connell Davidson, 2004, p. 39). They select the objects of their fantasies without any discernible interest in the consequences of their actions.

Upwards of thirty million people are forced to labor or engage in sexual activities across the world. Disconcertingly, the purchasing of prostitutes is treated as an appropriate business practice in some quarters (Smith & Betts, 2015). The accounts provided by those who have escaped these horrific situations should leave us in no doubt that service provision in these contexts is not a 'choice': 'In an interview with a girl who had been rescued from a brothel, she described how customers were allowed to do whatever they wanted with her; no one came to help no matter how loud she screamed' (Smith & Betts, 2015, p. 225).

These morally repugnant distributors understand their markets and how to move their victims through supply chains with the minimum of police interference (Pennington, Ball, Hampton, & Soulakova, 2009). They know what perversions will sell and they are ruthless in exploiting opportunities. Trafficked individuals suffer profoundly. People are maimed, psychologically traumatized and killed. The exercise of sovereignty for some, stunts and denies the opportunities of others to live happy, healthy and fulfilling lives (Pennington et al., 2009). Other destructive customer–supplier relations are not hard to find. Capitalism, with its unequal distribution of income and resources, provides some people with the ability to enhance their physiological health. Others have little choice but to be an input into this circuit of consumption. We are talking about the market for human organs and body parts (e.g. kidneys, livers and corneas). This market is characterized by 'bioviolence' (Moniruzzaman, 2012), that is, where people are hurt by the consumption habits of others, often in ways that are deliberate and usually easily avoided.

Moniruzzaman (2012) points out that advertising is used to attract the poor to enter the market for human organs in Bangladesh. They are promised the chance of a better tomorrow. Debt can be repaid; funds for entrepreneurial activities can be obtained; or at least that is the hope that intermediaries in this market propagate. People are offered a limited amount of money for their organs; the consequences of donation are not well explained; the donor is transported across national boundaries and thereby distant from social networks and assistance. Once separated from family and friends, they are threatened; their fees are reduced; treatment is poor; post-surgical aftercare is non-existent; and scars, both physical and mental, are highly likely.

The visible scars which are a concomitant of the cheapest forms of surgical interventions are a signal to the donor's community that they have sold their organs. They will find it hard to secure and retain work; and selling organs can leave them vulnerable to illness. These factors weigh heavily. One individual described himself as 'subhuman' and deeply regretted his decision. Slipping into alcohol and drug abuse is not uncommon. Suicide looms large.

The trade in human beings and organs is one of the most destructive on the planet. This 'exchange' is not based on a 'principle of equity', 'equality', 'mutual benefit' or 'win-win' relations and satisfaction for all parties. One side will suffer depression and ill-health and will consider suicide.

New directions in marketing theory: perverts and biopolitics

As we have demonstrated, the topic of consumer sovereignty is complicated. From a slightly different perspective, it might even be problematic to continually reaffirm the notion that the consumer is king. If you tell people their every whim will be satisfied and that they cannot be wrong, this could manifest in difficult, dangerous and threatening behavior. Registering this, an emerging research frontier explores the topic of consumer misbehavior. This literature generally focuses on the service environment and consumer–employee interactions. It has even led to the coining of a new term: 'jaycustomers', that is, those customers who negatively influence the working and shopping experience for other people, whether management, employees or customers. Misbehavior can range from rudeness and exasperation (Dixon et al., 2017), returning products excessively frequently (Harris, 2010), all the way to swearing and making unwanted advances on employees (i.e. suggestive comments through to threats of rape). It might involve property destruction or making unwarranted claims about service provision in public forums (Harris & Reynolds, 2004).

In these situations, the consumer can be an abusive bully (Bishop & Hoel, 2008; Korczynski & Ott, 2004); someone who threatens, stalks and talks 'shit' to staff (Stein, 2007). The result can be long-term trauma and ill-health for service workers and added costs for management. They can even be 'predatory' in nature; people who it is more sensible to avoid rather than confront (Tyler, 2011). Kings can be re-conceptualized as perverts.

Biopolitics in the marketing literature refers to the idea that practitioners are interested in studying the activities of the consumer at the physiological, psychological and everyday practice levels. This interest manifests in multiple ways. Companies want to secure staff members with specific psychological (e.g. autism spectrum disorder) and lifestyle dispositions (e.g. 'hippies') who can be linked with other organizational members (e.g. 'geeks') to generate creative sparks, inspiration and commercially viable products, services and experiences. Nissan, the car manufacturer, is well-known for utilizing this process of 'creative abrasion' (Kumar et al., 2000).

As part of this wider biopolitical movement, greater attention has been devoted to the psychological unconscious, that is, influences that operate below the level of consciousness. Consciousness, in this context, is basically 'awareness' (Williams & Poehlman, 2017). Specifically, researchers are being encouraged to take seriously the physiological bases of our actions. This is not to displace the role of psychology or sociology, but to remind us that we are biological beings as well (Williams & Poehlman, 2017). Our biology and physiology do affect who we are and what we do, even if we do not fully appreciate it.

Kramer and Bressan (2015) deflate the concept of the unitary human being and (by extension) the individual as sovereign. They maintain that we are 'superorganisms' or 'holobionts'. We are constituted by many factors that we probably do not register at all. These include microbes, viruses, and genetic materials from our parents (to name a few). Basically, these influences can shape our psychology. Some impose considerable costs, others have the potential to benefit people with Parkinson's and Alzheimer's. Organisms can influence our mental condition, our moods, impulsivity, risk-taking and a host of other practices that have implications for marketing scholars and professionals. What this means is that the notion of sovereignty is shattered, with our self-concept shaped by an 'incessant struggle' of entities that constitute who we are, how we think and undertake our lives (Kramer & Bressan, 2015, p. 464).

On a related note, Durante, Griskevicius, Hill, Perilloux and Li (2011) unpack the significance of female hormones on choice-making[1] (cf. Patterson, this volume). Put simply, when women are ovulating they are more likely to select 'sexy' types of clothing over more functional attire. This reflects competition with other – locally accessible – female competitors for male attention. It is not merely dressing to impress men. This 'ovulatory effect' suggests the signal importance of female biology for debates around consumer sovereignty, with managerial implications of their own. Developing this line of thought, Durante and Arsena (2015), for example, explored the issue of variety-seeking (both product and mate-seeking) and found it associated with female fertility cycles. They coined the term 'fertility-regulated desire' to emphasize this influence.

Zwick and Bradshaw (2016) take a slightly different perspective. They describe how marketers tap into the lifeworld of individual consumers (i.e. 'biopolitical marketing'). They try to understand all facets of the lived experience of their customer base, studying their everyday behavior as well as their activities on social media, so that they can commercialize these interactions with and without the person always appreciating the value extraction processes being applied. Zwick and Bradshaw's (2016) argument is, quite clearly, a critical reading of these strategies; related ideas have – speedily enough – been communicated to practitioners. Holt (2016) describes how they can plumb the psyche of consumer tribes as reflected in social media forums.

What is interesting is that Zwick and Bradshaw puncture the brand community literature at its core. They appreciate that a 'brand community' might exist in some cases. In others, it is the projection of a marketer fantasy – the dream of a community of buyers fascinated with their brand, product or service. The reality is that few people really care very much about brands (cf. Fournier, 1998). They are less satisfied with the services being provided by firms and exhibit far less loyalty than management desires (Hult *et al.*, 2017). People, in other words, do not envisage themselves having relationships with most organizations in the vivid terms practitioners fetishize (O'Malley & Prothero, 2004). Some individuals might rally around a brand and this could be called a community in loose terms. It is the extensiveness of this phenomenon that is being critiqued by Zwick and Bradshaw (2016).

There are two sides to this debate. Some argue that appropriating the knowledge, interests and ideas of customers reeks of manipulation. Certainly, the power dynamics appear to mostly benefit the company (Cova & Dalli, 2009). One problem with this view is that it assumes a naive consumer. They rework the 'false consciousness' argument, repackaging it for a new generation. This assumed that people did not know their own real interests and could be manipulated. Cova, Pace and Skålén (2015) pull back from this original 'working consumer' thesis by suggesting that their respondents were not actually as manipulated by companies for their 'immaterial labor' (ideas and knowledge) as their original proposal supposed. Those engaging with brands (and brand management) were reflective about the power relationships involved, appreciated the benefits they received from organizations (i.e. access to staff, advanced knowledge about new products and services, financial remuneration from designs that entered production, free products and so forth). So, rather than these individuals having their ideas used without compensation or permission, Cova et al.'s new thesis averred that people 'compromise'. They provide their time willingly because they believe the benefits outweigh the costs.

It is now relatively easy for firms to dig down into our lives. Whenever we use credit and store cards, hand over coupons or request information, we participate in market research (Duhigg, 2013). Smith and Sparks (2004), for example, looked at the data collected by Tesco for their Clubcard program and found that the organization could differentiate client consumption practices in nuanced ways, identifying when female customers became pregnant and tailoring their communications accordingly. It is not only in the UK that such practices are used. The case of Target in the U.S. exposes related interests.

In Target's biopolitical exercises, marketing staff worked in conjunction with highly skilled computing and analysis teams. They examined how lifecycle status shapes purchasing habits. Like Tesco, they wanted to know when customers became pregnant. Pregnant women and new families are cash cows. Not only do expectant mothers and young families come into store for baby-related items, they are often so tired that they undertake all of their shopping in one location. Tiredness and price insensitivity do not merely lead to short-term financial gains for the company. Recall the lessons of relationship marketing, habits formed during these periods are likely to be translated into longer-term routines provided the experience is satisfying.

Target did not want to rely upon chance that their customer might announce to the firm that they were pregnant. They wanted to determine the likelihood of pregnancy before the individual knew. To do so, they produced 'a pregnancy-prediction algorithm' using data from their baby-shower service (Duhigg, 2013, p. 193). The company looked at the products and services an individual had bought prior to becoming pregnant and used this information to predict when other people exhibiting consistent consumption patterns were also likely to become pregnant. By cross-checking their databases, they identified 'hundreds of thousands of women . . . that Target could inundate with advertisements for diapers, lotions, cribs, wipes, and maternity clothing at times when their shopping habits were particularly flexible' (Duhigg, 2013, p. 195). This raises ethical concerns. A company 'spying into their wombs' is likely to be viewed – to put it mildly – as 'kind of creepy' (Duhigg, 2013, p. 204). So, Target adopted a cautious strategy by using communications that blurred their intent. They included products likely to appeal to new mothers and random items to obscure their motives. The placement of baby-related products in personal communications was thus meant to look accidental. It was successful.

In sum, the biopolitical management of consumers looks like the next ethically questionable frontier for marketing theory and practice.

Conclusion

In this chapter, we have examined the marketing concept and consumer sovereignty. Both concepts were critically evaluated. The linkage of the marketing concept and sovereignty was called a paradox and problematized. We then engaged with the connecting concept between these two ideas – the notion of exchange – and illuminated how this hinges on the rhetoric of mutual benefit and arguments about equality. This representation was undermined. Finally, we concluded with a discussion of a contemporary research direction for marketing that holds the potential to shatter the concept of sovereignty still further: the biopolitical management of populations and physiological management of the individual. This unification of biology with marketing has been cited as a potentially fruitful area of research by some; critical scholars and educated observers should view it with a great deal of concern.

Note

1 The reader might wish to consult the following article when reflecting on this work and that related to it. Please note, I am making no statements about the veracity of the above work in highlighting this article: https://www.counterpunch.org/2018/03/16/superunknown-scientific-integrity-within-the-academic-and-media-industrial-complexes/

References

Adler, S. (with L.J. Spagnola) (2011). *My appetite for destruction: Sex & drugs & Guns N' Roses*. London: Harper Collins Publishers.
Adorno, T. (1975). Culture industry revisited. *New German Critique*, 6(Autumn), 12–19.
Adorno, T. (1991). *The culture industry*. London, Routledge.
Adorno, T.W., & Horkheimer, M. (1997). *Dialectic of enlightenment*. London, Verso.
Alvesson, M. (1993). Critical theory and consumer marketing. *Scandinavian Journal of Management*, 10(3), 291–313.
Arsel, Z., & Bean, J. (2013). Taste regimes and market-mediated practice. *Journal of Consumer Research*, 39(5), 899–917.
Atik, D., & Fırat, A.F. (2013). Fashion creation and diffusion: The institution of marketing. *Journal of Marketing Management*, 29(7–8), 836–860.
Bagozzi, R.P. (1975). Marketing as exchange. *Journal of Marketing*, 39(4), 32–39.
Bailey, B. (2000). Communicative behavior and conflict between African-American customers and Korean immigrant retailers in Los Angeles. *Discourse & Society*, 11(1), 86–108.
Baker, W.E., & Faulkner, R.R. (1993). The social organization of conspiracy: Illegal networks in the heavy electrical equipment industry. *American Sociological Review*, 58(6), 837–860.
Barksdale, H.C., & Darden, B. (1971). Marketers' attitudes toward the marketing concept. *Journal of Marketing*, 35(4), 29–36.
Berinato, S. (2017). How habit beats novelty. *Harvard Business Review*, January–February, 60.
Bishop, V., & Hoel, H. (2008). The customer is always right? Exploring the concept of customer bullying in the British Employment Service. *Journal of Consumer Culture*, 8(3), 341–367.
Borch, F.J. (1958). The marketing management philosophy as a way of business life. In E.J. Kelly & W. Lazer (Eds.), *Managerial marketing: Perspectives and issues* (pp. 18–24). Homewood, Richard D. Irwin.
Botti, S., & Iyengar, S.S. (2006). The dark side of choice: When choice impairs social welfare. *Journal of Public Policy & Marketing*, 25(1), 24–38.
Boyd, C. (2012). The Nestlé infant formula controversy and a strange web of subsequent business scandals. *Journal of Business Ethics*, 106(3), 283–293.
Brown, S., McDonagh, P., & Shultz, C. (2012). Dark marketing: Ghost in the machine or skeleton in the cupboard. *European Business Review*, 24(3), 196–215.
Brownlie, D., & Saren, M. (1992). The four ps of the marketing concept: Prescriptive, polemical, permanent and problematical. *European Journal of Marketing*, 26(4), 34–47.
Brownstein, H.H., Mulcahy, T.M., Fernandes-Huessy, J., Taylor, B.G., & Woods, D. (2012). The organization and operation of illicit retail Methamphetamine markets. *Criminal Justice Policy Review*, 23(1), 67–89.
Champion, D. (2017). A conversation with Jørgen Vig Knudstorp, Cochairman of LEGO brand group. *Harvard Business Review*, January–February, 58.
Clegg, B. (2012). *Portrait of an addict as a young man: A memoir*. London, Vintage.
Cova, B., & Dalli, D. (2009). Working consumers: The next step in marketing theory? *Marketing Theory*, 9(3), 315–339.
Cova, B., Pace, S., & Skålén, P. (2015). Brand volunteering. *Marketing Theory*, 15(4), 465–485.
Crockett, D., & Wallendorf, M. (2004). The role of normative political ideology in consumer behavior. *Journal of Consumer Research*, 31(3), 511–528.
Custance, P., Walley, K., & Jiang, D. (2012). Crisis brand management in emerging markets: Insights from the Chinese infant milk powder scandal. *Marketing Intelligence & Planning*, 30(1), 18–32.

Daly, M., & Sampson, S. (2013). *Narcomania: How Britain got hooked on drugs.* London, Windmill Books.

Denegri-Knott, J., & Tadajewski, M. (2017). Sanctioning value: The legal system, hyper-power and the legitimation of MP3. *Marketing Theory, 17*(2), 219–240.

Der Laan, E.V., & Velthuis, O. (2016). Inconspicuous dressing: A critique of the construction-through-consumption paradigm in the sociology of dressing. *Journal of Consumer Culture, 16*(1), 22–42.

Detzer, E. (1988). *Monkey on my back: The autobiography of a modern opium eater.* London, Abacus.

Dixon, D.F. (1992). Consumer sovereignty, democracy, and the marketing concept: A macromarketing perspective. *Canadian Journal of Administrative Science, 9*(2), 116–125.

Dixon, M., Ponomareff, L., Turner, S., & DeLisi, R. (2017). Consumers want results – not sympathy. *Harvard Business Review*, January–February, 110–117.

Drucker, P.F. (1954). *The practice of management.* New York, Harper.

Duhigg, C. (2013). *The power of habit.* London, Heinemann.

Dunnett, S., Hamilton, K., & Piacentini, M. (2016). Consumer vulnerability: Introduction to the special issue. *Journal of Marketing Management, 32*(3–4), 207–210.

Durante, K.M., & Arsena, A.R. (2015). Playing the field: The effect of fertility on women's desire for variety. *Journal of Consumer Research, 41*(6), 1372–1391.

Durante, K.M., Griskevicius, V., Hill, S.E., Perilloux, C., & Li, N.P. (2011). Ovulation, female competition, and product choice: Hormonal influences on consumer behavior. *Journal of Consumer Research, 37*(6), 921–933.

Eckhardt, G.M., Belk, R.W., & Wilson, A.J. (2015). The rise of inconspicuous consumption. *Journal of Marketing Management, 31*(7–8), 807–826.

Elliott, R., & Leonard, C. (2004). Peer pressure and poverty: Exploring fashion brands and consumption symbolism among children of the 'British poor'. *Journal of Consumer Behavior, 3*(4), 347–359.

Etzioni, A. (1958). Administration and the consumer. *Administrative Science Quarterly, 3*(2), 251–264.

Evers, K. (2016). Resisting the hard sell. *Harvard Business Review*, October, 122–123.

Falchetti, C., Ponchio, M.C., & Botelho, N.L.P. (2016). Understanding the vulnerability of blind consumers: Adaptation in the marketplace, personal traits and coping strategies. *Journal of Marketing Management, 32*(3–4), 313–334.

Faulkner, R.R., Cheney, E.R., Fisher, G.A., & Baker, W.E. (2003). Crime by committee: Conspirators and company men in the illegal electrical cartel, 1954–1959. *Criminology, 41*(2), 511–554.

Fischer, E., & Bristor, J. (1994). A feminist poststructuralist analysis of the rhetoric of marketing relationships. *International Journal of Research in Marketing, 11*(4), 317–331.

Fisman, R., & Luca, M. (2016). Fixing discrimination in online marketplaces. *Harvard Business Review*, December, 88–95.

Fitchett, J.A., Patsiaouras, G., & Davies, A. (2015). Myth and ideology in consumer culture theory. *Marketing Theory, 14*(4), 495–506.

Fournier, S. (1998). Consumers and their brands: Developing relationship theory in consumer research. *Journal of Consumer Research, 24*(4), 343–373.

Fournier, V., & Grey, C. (2000). At the critical moment: Conditions and prospects for critical management studies. *Human Relations, 53*(1), 7–32.

Fromm, E. (2001). *The fear of freedom.* London, Routledge.

Fromm, E. (2002). *The sane society.* London, Routledge.

Fromm, E. (2003). *Man for himself.* London, Routledge.

Fromm, E. (2007). *To have or to be?* London, Continuum.

Galbraith, J.K. (1958). *The affluent society.* London, Houghton Mifflin.

Galbraith, J.K. (1970). Economics in the industrial state: Science and sedative economics as a system of belief. *American Economic Review, 60*(1), 469–478.

Gamble, J. (2007). The rhetoric of the consumer and customer control in China. *Work, Employment & Society, 21*(1), 7–25.

Gau, R., & Viswanathan, M. (2008). The retail shopping experience for low-literate consumers. *Journal of Research for Consumers.* Retrieved July 10, 2017 from www.jrconsumers.com/academic_articles/issue_15/Low_literate_consumers_academic_final3.pdf

Gentry, J.W., Kennedy, P.F., Paul, K., & Hill, R.P. (1995). The vulnerability of those grieving the death of a loved one: Implications for public policy. *Journal of Public Policy & Marketing, 14*(1), 128–142.

Germann, F., Ebbes, P., & Grewal, R. (2015). The chief marketing officer matters! *Journal of Marketing, 79*(3), 1–22.

Graham, L.D. (2013). Lillian Gilbreth's psychologically enriched scientific management of women consumers. *Journal of Historical Research in Marketing, 5*(3), 351–369.
Greenwald, R. (2005). *Wal-Mart: The high cost of low price*. Brave New Films.
Gummesson, E. (1999). *Total relationship marketing*, third edition. London, Routledge.
Habermas, J. (1973). *Legitimation crisis*. Boston, Beacon Press.
Hanser, A. (2004). Made in the PRC: Consumers in China. Contexts, *3*(Winter), 13–19.
Hanser, A. (2007). Is the customer always right? Class, service and the production of distinction in Chinese department stores. *Theory & Society, 36*(October), 415–435.
Harris, L. (1998). Barriers to marketing orientation: The view from the shopfloor. *Marketing Intelligence & Planning, 16*(3), 221–228.
Harris, L. (2010). Fraudulent consumer returns: Exploiting retailers' return policies. *European Journal of Marketing, 44*(6), 730–747.
Harris, L., & Reynolds, K. (2004). Jaycustomer behavior: An exploration of types and motives in the hospitality industry. *Journal of Services Marketing, 18*(5), 339–357.
Harrison, M.P., Beatty, S.E., Reynolds, K.E., & Noble, S.M. (2012). Why consumers feel locked into relationships: Using qualitative methods to uncover the lock-in factors. *Journal of Marketing Theory and Practice, 20*(4), 391–406.
Hildebrand, G.H. (1951). Consumer sovereignty in modern times. *The American Economic Review, 41*(2), 19–33.
Hirschman, E.C. (1991). A feminist critique of marketing theory: Toward agentic-communal balance. In J.A. Costa (Ed.), *Gender and consumer behavior*, Volume 1 (pp. 324–340). Salt Lake City, Association for Consumer Research.
Holbrook, M.B. (1987). Mirror, mirror, on the wall, what's unfair in the reflections on advertising? *Journal of Marketing, 51*(3), 95–103.
Hollander, S.C. (1986). The marketing concept: A déjà vu. In G. Fisk (Ed.), *Marketing management technology as a social process* (pp. 3–29). New York, Praeger.
Holt, D.B. (1998). Does cultural capital structure American consumption? *Journal of Consumer Research, 25*(1), 1–25.
Holt, D. (2016). Branding in the age of social media. *Harvard Business Review*, March, 41–50.
Horkheimer, M. (2004). *Eclipse of reason*. London, Continuum.
Houston, F.S. (1986). The marketing concept: What it is and what it is not. *Journal of Marketing, 50*(2), 81–87.
Houston, F.S., & Gassenheimer, J.B. (1987). Marketing and exchange. *Journal of Marketing, 51*(4), 3–18.
Hult, G.T.M., Morgeson, F.V., Morgan, N.A., Mithas, S., & Fornell, C. (2017). Do managers know what their customers think and why? *Journal of the Academy of Marketing Science, 45*(1), 37–54.
Hutt, W.H. (1940). The concept of consumers' sovereignty. *The Economic Journal, 50*(197), 66–77.
Huxley, A. (2004). *Brave new world revisited*. London, Vintage.
Jaworski, B., Kohli, A.J., & Sahay, A. (2000). Market-driven versus driving markets. *Journal of the Academy of Marketing Science, 28*(1), 45–54.
Jones, D.G.B. (2013). Pauline Arnold (1894–1974): Pioneer in market research. *Journal of Historical Research in Marketing, 5*(3), 291–307.
Jones, D.G.B., & Richardson, A.J. (2007). The myth of the marketing revolution. *Journal of Macromarketing, 27*(1), 15–24.
Jones, D.G.B., & Tadajewski, M. (2018). *The foundations of marketing thought: The influence of the German Historical School*. London, Routledge.
Karnani, A. (2017). The roles of the private and public sectors in poverty reduction. *Journal of Marketing Management, 33*(17–18), 1585–1592.
Keith, R.J. (1960). The marketing revolution. *Journal of Marketing, 24*(3), 35–38.
Kellner, D. (1989). *Critical theory, Marxism and modernity*. Baltimore, The Johns Hopkins University Press.
Kenner, R. (2009). *Food, Inc*. London, Dogwoof.
Kilbourne, J. (1999). *Deadly persuasion: Why women and girls must fight the addictive power of advertising*. New York, The Free Press.
Knight, P. (2016). *Shoe dog: A memoir by the creator of Nike*. London, Simon & Schuster.
Korczynski, M., & Ott, U. (2004). When production and consumption meet: Cultural contradictions and the enchanting myth of customer sovereignty. *Journal of Management Studies, 41*(4), 575–599.
Kotler, P. (1967). *Marketing management: Analysis, planning and control*. Englewood Cliffs, Prentice-Hall.

Kotler, P. (1986). Megamarketing. *Harvard Business Review*, March, 17–24.
Kotler, P., Armstrong, G., Harris, L.C., & Piercy, N. (2013). *Principles of marketing*, sixth edition. London, Prentice-Hall.
Kotler, P., & Levy, S.J. (1971). Demarketing, yes, demarketing. *Harvard Business Review*, November–December, 74–80.
Kramer, P., & Bressan, P. (2015). Humans as superorganisms: How microbes, viruses, imprinted genes, and other selfish entities shape our behavior. *Perspectives on Psychological Science*, *10*(4), 464–481.
Kumar, N., Scheer, L., & Kotler, P. (2000). From market driven to market driving. *European Management Journal*, *18*(2), 129–142.
Lafley, A.G., & Martin, R.L. (2017). Customer loyalty is overrated. *Harvard Business Review*, January–February, 47–54.
Lakoff, A. (2004). The anxieties of globalization: Antidepressant sales and economic crisis in Argentina. *Social Studies of Science*, *34*(2), 247–269.
Lazarsfeld, P. (1941). Remarks on administrative and critical communications research. *Studies in Philosophy and Social Science*, *9*, 2–16.
Lee, T., Mars, M., Neal, V., & Sixx, N. (with N. Strauss) (2002). *Mötley Crüe: The dirt*. New York, HarperCollins.
Lepisto, L.R., & Hannaford, W.J. (1980). Purchase constraint analysis: An alternative perspective for marketers. *Journal of the Academy of Marketing Science*, *8*(1), 12–25.
Lerner, A.P. (1972). The economics and politics of consumer sovereignty. *The American Economic Review*, *62*(1/2), 258–266.
Lowenthal, L. (1961). *Literature, popular culture, and society*. Englewood Cliffs, Prentice-Hall.
Lynd, R.S. (1934). The consumer becomes a 'problem'. *The Annals of the American Academy of Political and Social Science*, *173*(May), 1–6.
Lynd, R.S. (1936). Democracy's third estate: The consumer. *Political Science Quarterly*, *51*(4), 481–515.
Mallinson, C., & Brewster, Z.W. (2005). 'Blacks and bubbas': Stereotypes, ideology, and categorization processes in restaurant servers' discourse. *Discourse & Society*, *16*(6), 787–807.
Marcuse, H. (1964). *One dimensional man*. London, Routledge & Kegan Paul.
Markus, H.R., & Schwartz, B. (2010). Does choice mean freedom and well-being? *Journal of Consumer Research*, *37*(2), 344–355.
Martin, W. (2015). *Primates of Park Avenue*. New York, Simon & Schuster.
McGovern, G., & Moon, Y. (2007). Companies and the customers who hate them. *Harvard Business Review*, June, 78–84.
McGrath, R.G. (2017). Old habits die hard, but they do die. *Harvard Business Review*, January–February, 54–57.
McKagan, D. (2012). *It's so easy {and other lies}: The autobiography*. London, Orion.
McKendrick, N. (1960). Josiah Wedgwood: An eighteenth-century entrepreneur in salesmanship and marketing techniques. *The Economic History Review*, *12*(3), 408–433.
Meyerson, D.E. (2008). *Rocking the boat: How to effect change without making trouble*. Cambridge, Harvard Business Press.
Moniruzzaman, M. (2012). 'Living cadavers' in Bangladesh: Bioviolence in the human organs bazaar. *Medical Anthropology Quarterly*, *26*(1), 69–91.
Moyle, L., & Coomber, R. (2015). Earning a score: An exploration of the nature and roles of heroin and crack cocaine 'user-dealers'. *British Journal of Criminology*, *55*(3), 534–555.
Murray, J.B., & Ozanne, J.L. (1991). The critical imagination: Emancipatory interests in consumer research. *Journal of Consumer Research*, *18*(2), 129–144.
Nader, R. (1972). *Unsafe at any speed: The designed-in dangers of the American automobile*, second edition. New York, Grossman Publishers.
Negus, K. (2002). The work of cultural intermediaries and the enduring distance between production and consumption. *Cultural Studies*, *16*(4), 501–515.
O'Connell Davidson, J. (2004). 'Child sex tourism': An anomalous form of movement? *Journal of Contemporary European Studies*, *12*(1), pp. 31–46.
O'Donohoe, S. (1994). Advertising uses and gratifications. *European Journal of Marketing*, *28*(8/9), 52–75.
O'Malley, L., & Prothero, A. (2004). Beyond the frills of relationship marketing. *Journal of Business Research*, *57*(11), 1286–1294.
Ozanne, J.L., & Murray, J.B. (1995). Uniting critical theory and public policy to create the reflexively defiant consumer. *American Behavioral Scientist*, *38*(4), 516–525.

Pavia, T. (1993). Dispossession and perceptions of self in late stage HIV infection. *Advances in Consumer Research, 20*(1), 425–428.
Pennington, J.R., Ball, A.D., Hampton, R.D., & Soulakova, J.N. (2009). The cross national market in human beings. *Journal of Macromarketing, 29*(2), 119–134.
Persky, J. (1993). Retrospectives: Consumer sovereignty. *Journal of Economic Perspectives, 7*(1), 183–191.
Plotkin, S. (2014). Misdirected effort: Thorstein Veblen's critique of advertising. *Journal of Historical Research in Marketing, 6*(4), 501–522.
Pollay, R.W. (1987). On the value of reflections on the values in 'The Distorted Mirror'. *Journal of Marketing, 51*(3), 104–110.
Pressey, A. (2015). The man who managed your marketing? Estes Kefauver and the drug hearings on antitrust and monopoly. *Journal of Historical Research in Marketing, 7*(4), 429–451.
Reekie, W.D. (1988). Consumers' sovereignty revisited. *Managerial and Decision Economics, 9*(Winter), 17–25.
Robinson, E. (1963). Eighteenth-century commerce and fashion: Matthew Boulton's marketing techniques. *The Economic History Review, 16*(1), 39–60.
Rorty, J. (1934). *Our master's voice: Advertising.* New York, The John Day Company.
Rossini, E. (2015). *The illusionists.* Northampton, Media Education Foundation.
Rotfeld, H.J. (2004). The consumer as serf. *Journal of Consumer Affairs, 38*(1), 188–191.
Rugh, J.S., & Massey, D.S. (2010). Racial segregation and the American foreclosure crisis. *American Sociological Review, 75*(5), 629–651.
Schulman, D. (2016). PayPal's CEO on creating products for underserved markets. *Harvard Business Review*, December, 35–38.
Scitovsky, T. (1962). On the principle of consumers' sovereignty. *The American Economic Review, 52*(2), 262–268.
Scitovsky, T. (1992). *The joyless economy: The psychology of human satisfaction.* New York, Oxford University Press.
Sinclair, U. (1906/2010). *The jungle.* New York, Oxford University Press.
Sirgy, M.J., & Su, C. (2000). The ethics of consumer sovereignty in an age of high tech. *Journal of Business Ethics, 28*(1), 1–14.
Sixx, N. (with I. Gittins) (2007). *The heroin diaries: A year in the life of a shattered rock star.* New York, Pocket Books.
Skålén, P. (2009). Service marketing and subjectivity: The shaping of customer-oriented employees. *Journal of Marketing Management, 25*(7–8), 795–809.
Smith, A., & Sparks, L. (2004). All about Eve? *Journal of Marketing Management, 20*(3–4), 363–385.
Smith, K.T., & Betts, T. (2015). Your company may unwittingly be conducting business with human traffickers: How can you prevent this? *Business Horizons, 58*(2), 225–234.
Stack, M., & Gartland, M.P. (2003). Path creation, path dependency, and alternative theories of the firm. *Journal of Economic Issues, 37*(2), 487–494.
Stein, M. (2007). Toxicity and the unconscious experience of the body at the employee-customer interface. *Organization Studies, 28*(8), 1223–1241.
Tadajewski, M. (2010a). Towards a history of critical marketing. *Journal of Marketing Management, 26*(9–10), 773–824.
Tadajewski, M. (2010b). Reading 'the marketing revolution' through the prism of the FBI. *Journal of Marketing Management, 26*(1–2), 90–107.
Tadajewski, M. (2012). Character analysis and racism in marketing theory and practice. *Marketing Theory, 12*(4), 485–508.
Tadajewski, M. (2016). The alternative 'marketing revolution': Infra-power, the compromising consumer and goodwill. *Journal of Historical Research in Marketing, 8*(2), 308–334.
Tadajewski, M., & Jones, D.G.B. (2016). Hyper-power, the marketing concept and consumer as 'boss'. *Marketing Theory, 16*(4), 513–531.
Tyler, M. (2011). Tainted love: From dirty work to abject labor in Soho's sex shops. *Human Relations, 64*(11), 1477–1500.
Tynan, C. (1997). A review of the marriage analogy in relationship marketing. *Journal of Marketing Management, 13*(7), 695–703.
Veblen, T. (1919/2005). *The vested interests and the common man.* New York, Cosimo Classics.
Veblen, T. (1921/2006). *The engineers and the price system.* New York, Cosimo.
Veblen, T. (1988/1994). *The theory of the leisure class.* New York, Dover.

Verhoef, P.C., & Leeflang, P.S.H. (2009). Understanding the marketing department's influence within the firm. *Journal of Marketing, 73*(2), 14–37.

Viswanathan, M., Rosa, J.A., & Harris, J. (2005). Decision-making and coping by functionally illiterate consumers and some implications for marketing management. *Journal of Marketing, 69*(1), 15–31.

Ward, D.B. (2009). Capitalism, early market research, and the creation of the American consumer. *Journal of Historical Research in Marketing, 1*(2), 200–223.

Webster, F.E. Jr., Malter, A.J., & Ganesan, S. (2005). The decline and dispersion of marketing competence. *MIT Sloan Management Review, 46*(Summer), 35–43.

Wilkie, W.L., & Moore, E.S. (1999). Marketing's contribution to society. *Journal of Marketing, 63*(Special Issue), 198–218.

Williams, C.L. (2005). Racism in Toyland. *Contexts, 4*(Fall), 28–32.

Williams, C.L. (2006). Shopping as symbolic interaction: Race, class, and gender in the toy store. *Symbolic Interaction, 28*(4), 459–472.

Williams, L.E., & Poehlman, T.A. (2017). Conceptualizing consciousness in consumer research. *Journal of Consumer Research, 44*(2), 231–251.

Wood, W., & Neal, D.T. (2009). The habitual consumer. *Journal of Consumer Psychology, 19*(4), 579–592.

Zinkin, M. (1967). Galbraith and consumer sovereignty. *The Journal of Industrial Economics, 16*(1), 1–9.

Zwick, D., & Bradshaw, A. (2016). Biopolitical marketing and social media brand communities. *Theory, Culture & Society, 33*(5), 91–115.

13
SERVICE-DOMINANT LOGIC
The evolution of a universal marketing rhetoric

Chris Miles

Introduction

Vargo and Lusch's (2004a) *Journal of Marketing* paper, "Evolving to a new dominant logic of marketing", has had a profound influence upon the discourse of academic marketing. At the time of writing it has gathered over 7,900 citations indexed by Google Scholar, putting it far ahead of any other paper published in the discipline's foremost organ of dissemination.

In this chapter I examine the way that Service-Dominant (S-D) logic has evolved and explore the dynamic between the perspective's authors and its critics. In doing so I position Vargo and Lusch's (hereafter V&L) formulations of their self-described "pre-theoretic" perspective (Vargo, 2011, p. 218; Lusch & Vargo, 2011, p. 1299) as outstanding examples of rhetorical and persuasive narrative technique perfectly pitched for a discipline beset by self-doubt and accusations of irrelevance. I will argue that the quite substantial transformation that S-D logic has undergone since its introduction is a function of a complex rhetorical approach to dealing with oppositional readings. Consequently, this chapter investigates the way in which academic marketing knowledge is itself marketed through a detailed account of the journey of the ideas contained in the foundational V&L (2004a) paper. Brownlie and Saren (1995) have called for a greater appreciation of the ways in which academic marketing is losing out to other "competing voices" (p. 623) in the provision of (usually re-purposed or re-hashed) marketing knowledge. They note that the "final authority" of the marketing scholar has been eroded away and we find ourselves instead in a busy marketplace having to compete with a host of other knowledge brokers and using "the new armoury of persuasion technologies" (ibid.). The story of S-D logic can be seen as an instance of marketing scholarship's internal reaction to this erosion of authority, an attempt to generate an authoritative discourse that might bind marketing academics together in a united perspective that offers insights not just into problems in contemporary marketing but also into wider issues affecting society and so offer a competitive package in the wider market for marketing knowledge. That this is largely accomplished with the well-established 'persuasion technologies' of rhetoric is indicative of just how fundamental such discourse strategies remain to the contemporary generation of authority in the knowledge marketplace.

The chapter opens with a detailed reading of V&L's (2004a) *urtext*. Although the premises and emphases of S-D logic have constantly evolved I argue that the 2004a *Journal of Marketing* paper can be seen as a deliberately provocative piece of rhetoric through which all the later revisions should be interpreted. I then move on to a discussion of early reactions to S-D logic, particularly those contained in the commentaries printed alongside the 2004a article and the various contributions to the Lusch and Vargo (2006b) edited collection. In examining the evolution of S-D logic I have chosen to focus upon the most significant critical voices and the key texts by V&L that have marked the various revisions of the core perspective. As I will show, while there has been a tremendous scholarly activity around S-D logic, its evolution has been firmly in the hands of V&L. I close the chapter with a discussion of the ways that V&L have recently been extending S-D logic and how these transformations loop all the way back to Kiel *et al.* (1992) and point toward an even more audacious vision of the logic's future.

The foundational paper

As briefly recounted by the article's final editor (Bolton, 2006), the publication of V&L (2004a) in the pages of the *Journal of Marketing* was preceded by "an unusually lengthy review and revision process that spanned five years and the tenure of two *Journal* editors" (p. ix). Lusch and Vargo (2006b) state there were a total of five revisions during this period, indicating the level of debate their perspective sparked even before its publication. This debate was made public, to some extent, through the commentaries invited by Ruth Bolton to accompany the paper and "stimulate discussion and debate" (Bolton, 2004, p. 18). This frames the article as something worth talking about by presenting elders of the discipline publicly discussing it. This is a lesson in discourse building that was then repeated in even more dramatic form in the 2006 edited collection that I will discuss a little further below.

The foundational paper by V&L can be broken down into three principal sections. First, the authors provide a history of marketing thought that allows them to illuminate the existence of an emerging 'paradigm shift' in contemporary marketing theory. Second, the foundational premises of this paradigm are delineated. Finally, the implications of these premises are discussed, with reference to the form of future marketing research, practice, and education. I will now deal with each of these sections in some depth.

The persuasive power of historical narrative

One of the ramifications of the emergent logic that V&L (2004a) outline is a reframing of the idea of 'service' to include the manufacturing of goods and a reframing of the concept of 'transactions' in order to include it within the larger category of 'exchange'. In this sense the project of the paper is an entirely rhetorical one, re-defining the meaning of words and their contexts in order to change attitudes and practices within a discipline. In order to make this gambit as persuasive as possible, however, the reframing is presented within a particular (re-)telling of the history of marketing. Central to V&L's construction of this historical narrative is their use of the concept of the 'paradigm shift' as a frame for their history. Before the reader is presented with a historical schema of marketing thought they are first primed to think of this history as following the form of a procession of paradigms. At the same time, the authors instill this procession with a clear teleological focus – "the purpose of this article is to illuminate the evolution of marketing thought toward a new dominant logic" (p. 2).

The language of *paradigm shift* is drawn from Kuhn's (1962) *The Structure of Scientific Revolutions*, a work that had already received much attention from marketing scholars and was generally received as an explanation of how science advances – through the supplanting of one dominant paradigm with a newer one incommensurable with the terms of the older one. V&L (2004a) cast paradigm shift as evolutionary – and so inevitable and beneficial (for the health of the discipline). Through this frame, their history of marketing thought becomes an evolutionary arc, from humble beginnings as an offshoot of economics to a "continuous social and economic process in which operant resources are paramount" (p. 3).

The four eras of marketing thought that they identify are portrayed as an initial period rooted in Classical and Neoclassical economics, followed by the formative years of marketing proper (with a descriptive, transaction-oriented focus on institutions and commodities), shifting into the era of Marketing Management where value is understood to be determined in the marketplace and the focus becomes satisfying the consumer's need or desire for fulfillment. The final era is entitled "Marketing as a Social and Economic Process" and it is here that the authors describe the emergence of a 'new dominant logic' which unifies a number of perspectives (such as resource management, relationship marketing, and service marketing) that had emerged during the later Marketing Management era.

The periodization is presented both in prose (briefly) and then in tabulated and figured forms. The verbal and visual language used in the table and figure implies a sense of gradual movement from one period to another. So, in the Formative Marketing era we are told that "a focus on functions is the beginning of the recognition of operant resources" (V&L, 2004a, p. 3), and in the Marketing Management era we read that "Identification of the functional responses to the changing environment that provide competitive advantage through differentiation begins to shift toward value in use" (ibid.) which lays the ground for the final period's focus on the co-production of value. From a Kuhnian point of view this progression does not depict paradigm shifts. The types of scientific discoveries that lead to paradigm revolutions are made through "paradigm destruction" where a new way of thinking 'displaces' the older one which is no longer "logically compatible" with the new one (Kuhn, 1962, p. 97). The bringing together of "disparate literature streams" (V&L, 2004a, p. 3) into a meta-theory is not a particularly revolutionary method (in Kuhnian terms), especially when the authors point out that key aspects of the 'new paradigm' have been clearly foreshadowed in the previous two periods. Indeed, further consideration might cause us to remember that Arthur Frederick Sheldon had promulgated the idea of service as the fundamental perspective of business in his highly popular correspondence courses in the early decades of the twentieth century (Tadajewski, 2011). The prefigurings might be seen to be so great, in fact, that they effectively undercut the reality of the periodization. What is important, however, is not the historical veracity of the periodization but its persuasive effectiveness as a narrative. What V&L's (2004a) periodization delineates is a process of gradual expansion and refinement guided by refocusings and redefinitions (which have tended to be inclusive rather than exclusive). In the Kuhnian sense, then, the periods of marketing thought are not a procession of paradigms at all. The language of Kuhnian paradigms is taken advantage of but it is being used to describe something that might be more appropriately labeled as *gently evolutionary*.

There is also a supplementary periodization scheme advanced by V&L (2004a). This is the presentation of a change in marketing thought from a "goods-dominant view" to a "service-dominant view" (p. 2). This sits on top, as it were, of the fourfold historical periodization and is not given a clear historical boundary but, rather, emerges from changes across the 100 years of marketing evolution. This also marks it out as *not* a Kuhnian paradigm revolution. Furthermore, the service-dominant view effectively subsumes the goods-dominant view rather than overturning it. V&L (2004a) simply redefine goods as "distribution mechanisms for service provision" (ibid.) – we have not destroyed the idea of goods but rather brought them into an expanded vision of services.

What is the significance of V&L's (2004a) use of the *language* of Kuhnian paradigms while avoiding the Kuhnian sense? We can perhaps best understand the answer to this question by observing the reaction (or lack of it) displayed by Shelby Hunt toward V&L's use of Kuhn. Hunt had been loudly and publicly criticizing acceptance of Kuhnian concepts since 1991. His aversion to Kuhn's work is best summed up in a phrase from Hunt and Morgan (1997) where the authors describe Kuhn's work as "one of the most thoroughly discredited epistemologies of the 20th century" (p. 1997). It is striking that V&L were not aware of Hunt's longstanding distrust of Kuhn – not because all marketing academics should have read everything written by Hunt, but rather because Hunt is expressly thanked in the acknowledgements of V&L (2004a) as a reader of a draft of the paper. Additionally, Hunt was one of Bolton's invited commentators for the 2004 *Journal of Marketing* (hereafter *JoM*) publication and even there he makes no objection to the use of Kuhnian 'jargon'. Indeed, he manages to not use the word 'paradigm' at all throughout his contribution.

I would argue that the reason Hunt does not question the use of the dominant paradigm framework is twofold – first, he recognizes it as rhetorical strategy rather than a constituent of V&L's (pre-)theory and, second, he sees that the presentation of S-D logic itself does not depend upon a *displacement* of Goods-Dominant (G-D) logic but rather an enfolding, or subsuming, of the latter into the former. As we shall see, Hunt himself uses this argumentative strategy when positioning S-D logic as a subset of Resource-Advantage theory.

V&L (2004a) make reference to the revolutionary, discipline-changing drama of the Kuhnian paradigm shift while never actually adopting the proof that would be required to claim such a displacing shift. Instead, they offer a narrative of steady, evolutionary change in the discipline that finds important earlier concepts either redefined, refocused, or subsumed into later ones. So, the rhetoric says dramatic revolution but the details of the actual argument revolve around gradual, reasoned progression. Indeed, as V&L (2004a) state, the new logic functions to "refocus perspective through reorientation rather than reinvention" (p. 14).

Yet, the fact remains that the use of such phrasing as 'paradigm shift' and 'dominant paradigm' carries with it the resonance (and rhetorical association) of a scientific *revolution* overthrowing an older worldview that is no longer fit for purpose. V&L are taking advantage of their audience's familiarity with what Malone (1993, p. 69) has called the "standard reading" of Kuhn in order to produce this rhetorical association, yet prevent it from being highlighted as argumentation by erasing the trace of formal citation.

Foundational premises

The presentation of the 'foundational premises (FPs)' reflects a number of significant rhetorical strategies. First, we should note the contextual baggage that a 'premise' brings to any party. It immediately calls to mind the schema of the syllogism, with major and minor premises leading to a conclusion. Because V&L (2004a) frame their new perspective as a *logic* (the word is used 44 times in the paper) it would seem reasonable to expect that a word so rooted in the mechanics of logic would be used in its logical sense. Yet, the eight foundational premises of the "new dominant logic" (p. 1) do not seem to lead to a particular conclusion. In fact, the premises are conclusions themselves. In a neat display of confirmation bias, each premise is first stated and then, in the section that follows, provided with reasons for its acceptance. While this might run counter to the usual formal syllogistic presentation, this reversal of structure is an acceptable mode of *rhetorical* argumentation. But the mislabeling is not. If the premises are indeed premises – what is the conclusion that they lead to?

So, the premises look like premises but are not – in the same way that V&L's (2004a) use of the Kuhnian lexicon makes it look like they are arguing for a revolutionary paradigm shift even though they are not. They are rhetorically useful *allusions*.

A careful look at the foundational premises will give us an opportunity to further examine the way in which historical narrative is used to construct the emotional appeal of S-D logic. Foundational premise 1 (FP_1) states "the application of specialized skills and knowledge is the fundamental unit of exchange" (V&L, 2004a, p. 6). Here they seek to prove the legitimacy of their claim that marketing has "moved from" (p. 2) its product orientation. While reminding us that "the relationships between specialized skills and exchange have been recognized as far back as Plato's time" (ibid.) they cite Marcel Mauss to point out that way in which "clans and tribes" use gift giving to tender "total services" (p. 6). Even the early scholars of economics, they note, held that use value was at the heart of all exchange. Yet, something happened that served to derail this universal understanding. Adam Smith's *The Wealth of Nations*, while containing an appreciation of the division of labor and so fundamentally recognizing the importance of the value in use orientation, nevertheless focused on a very narrow aspect of skill, namely, labor that resulted in the production of tangible goods. Services were superfluous to Smith's vision of 'social well-being' which was defined as national wealth, which was in turn understood in terms of 'exportable things'. From this point onward, despite much historical thinking to the contrary, most economists have tended to acquiesce to the view that exchange value was to be found in tangible goods.

This narrative makes it natural for marketing to have labored under the impression that value resides in goods because, as V&L have already made clear, marketing was born from economics. Indeed, the authors demonstrate through reference to passages from Alderson, Shostack, and Levi, that insightful marketing academics had already been re-asserting the dominance of a services understanding of value since the 1950s. This salvational narrative trope crops up throughout the paper. It plays powerfully to an audience of marketing academics who are worried about the direction and relevance of their discipline. We see this approach again in the way that V&L reveal the "fragmented" (2004a, p. 1) marketing thought of the 1980s and 90s as, in fact, possessing an underlying unity.

FP_2 follows from FP_1 in that it seeks to provide an explanation of why a G-D view has been so prevalent for so long. It states that, "indirect exchange masks the fundamental unit of exchange" (p. 8). Once more, the historical narrative is designed to appeal to the marketing audience. Here, V&L tell how, over time, the customer became lost to business. Increasing microspecializations in the workforce meant that fewer people involved in a business ever interacted with a customer or even had knowledge of them. And so firms began to forget about the customer. The authors caution us that this is "not unique to manufacturing organizations" (p. 8). Of course, the reader will be aware that it is marketing that has been sounding this alarm all along.

FP_3 is effectively a re-wording of the second. "Goods", it runs, "are distribution mechanisms for service provisions" (p. 8). Here, products are recast as embodiments of knowledge and skill. As in the explications for the previous two premises, historical narrative and academic precedent are used in order to generate a sense of inevitable, gradual evolution rather than *revolution*. Of interest here is the metaphor that V&L embed in the premise. To portray products as 'distribution mechanisms' constructs a sense of the resulting marketing system as predictable, controllable, repairable. The range of descriptors that are used in the explanation of this premise all revolve around the same mechanistic/engineering metaphor ('platforms', 'appliance'). This serves to position the knowledge and skills that marketers (both academic and practitioner) offer – they can 'encapsulate' abstract knowledge into concrete platforms and appliances, serving as knowledge engineers who cross the divide between the tangible and intangible. This is a reminder that the engineering metaphors that Scully (1996) finds populating early writing on marketing remain as resonant with marketing scholars and practitioners as ever.

FP_4 takes the idea central to the previous three premises (that knowledge is at the heart of all exchange) and introduces to it the trope of competitive advantage. The full premise runs, "knowledge is the fundamental source of competitive advantage" (p. 9). V&L build the explanation for this on a mixture of references drawn from marketing and economics scholars (again underlining the evolutionary nature of their framework), but it is fair to say that the bulk of their reasoning rests upon the Hayek-inspired theorizing of Hunt's (2000) Resource-Advantage Theory. Of particular significance is their paraphrasing of Hunt's (2000, p. 146) line, "competition, as Hayek (1945) puts it, is a *knowledge-discovery* process". This leads them to argue that the marketing value chain should recognize that the "primary flow" in the chain is the "provision of the information to (or use of the information for) a consumer who desires it, with or without an accompanying appliance" (V&L, 2004a, p. 9) – and it is this provision that characterizes a *service*. A service, then, will thrive or fail on its ability to provide useful information to consumers who desire it. This further buttresses the vision of marketer as 'knowledge engineer' embedded in the third premise, but it also raises an issue regarding communication and manipulation which the authors will begin to address later, namely, how can a marketer go about their normal practice if they can only provide information to those who desire it? Does it not make the marketing organization an entirely *reactive* one?

FP_5 seeks to broaden the reach of the service-orientation, making it clear that "all economies are service economies" (p. 10). The explanation for this premise looks back to the point that V&L had already made regarding Adam Smith's narrowing of 'concern with manufacturing output' as a measurement of national wealth. V&L are concerned to build a model of intellectual evolution that focuses on models of explanation as points on a continuum rather than mutually exclusive worldviews. So, while they are happy to use Kuhnian rhetoric in order to amplify the significance of their thesis they are careful to construct an argument that works hard to demonstrate how a goods-orientation can still be *contained within* a service approach. S-D logic is a determinedly *conservative* program.

FP_6 has become perhaps the most famous: "the customer is always a co-producer" (2004a, p. 10). As V&L see it, co-production is a consequence of that "in using a product, the customer is continuing the marketing, consumption, and value-creation and delivery process" (p. 11). So, the customer contributes their own knowledge and skill alongside those of the firm. V&L quote Normann and Ramirez's (1993, p. 69) dictum that "the key to creating value is to coproduce offerings that mobilize customers". What exactly is involved in the process of "mobilization" is an issue that has beset the theoretical development of co-creation. The manner in which Normann and Ramirez (1993) go on to use a telling metaphor to depict the way in which the firm manages the customers' co-production provides us with an interesting insight. To "win" (in the struggle for competitive advantage) "a company must write the script, mobilize and train the players, and make the customer the final arbiter of success or failure" (p. 69). The firm takes on the role of the theatrical impresario – customers become part of its operant resources assortment, actors to be directed. While the customer is (of course) the final arbiter of success, the strategy of co-production brings the customer into the firm in order to *use* them – they are mobilized. They are *allowed* to be the final arbiter of success – as if this is part of the role they are scripted to have by the firm.

The literature on co-production and co-creation has certainly been mired in confusion and illogic around the issue of how customers are managed by marketers into being coproducers (Miles, 2017). Normann and Ramirez's metaphor of the firm as impresario or auteur seems to be enmeshed in the G-D logic of thinking about the customer as someone to control. While V&L choose not to reproduce that metaphor, the equally metaphorical depiction of the customer as a *resource for the firm* will inevitably raise the prospect of the customer being exploited by the firm. Yet, V&L (2004a) ignore such implications.

FP$_7$ states "the enterprise can only make value propositions" (p. 11). The authors explain that northern European service marketers such as Christian Grönroos and Evert Gummesson have persuasively argued that value is created by consumers during the act of consumption. Consequently, the firm cannot be seen as producing value – it can only be described as creating 'value propositions'. Marketing is no longer to be considered the activity of creating value and then distributing it to the customer but should instead be about creating offerings which are judged to have value by consumers. The question still remains, though – if value creation lies outside the firm, what does FP$_7$ really mean? The answer is hinted at in the very last line of V&L's (2004a) explication of the premise: "the enterprise can only make value propositions that strive to be better or more compelling than those of competitors" (p. 11). So, the firm's marketing function is the construction of more compelling, more attractive, *promises* of value to consumers. Here, the trope of co-production appears to come into sharper focus. The firm promises value and the consumer creates it; sometimes a firm's promise of value is particularly compelling and this persuades a consumer to patronize the firm and so create value in their consumption. If that created value is useful or pleasing to the consumer then the firm has a happy customer. The principal marketing job, however, is the creation of compelling, superior *promises* of value. The ramifications of this vision have not been very well examined in the resulting literature but it is perhaps the most important of all the premises, not least because it seems to characterize marketing as essentially a communications job (the presentation of propositions) but also because it places persuasion (those propositions have to be *compelling*) at the center of the marketing skillset.

FP$_8$ reads: "a service-centered view is customer-oriented and relational" (p. 11). The authors' goal here is to build to an argument that all encounters between firm and consumer, even simple one-off transactions, are necessarily relational. This allows V&L's logic to function more convincingly as a broad theory of contemporary marketing rather than as just a framework appropriate to a subset of the marketing endeavor. It should be noted, again, that V&L's argumentation here is based upon a mix of appeal to academic authority (Gummesson, Grönroos, Berry and so forth) and assertion. They then go on to argue that even simple, "discrete transactions" carry "social, if not legal, contracts (often relatively extended) and implied, if not expressed, warranties" (p. 12). This curious assertion does not come with any grounding citation or explication. It relies upon the audience nodding their heads at the seeming 'rightness' of the claim, comforted as they already are with the appeals to academic authority that sandwich it.

Ramifications

The premises are followed by a 'discussion' section that attempts to pull out some of the broader implications of the premises. So, for example, V&L argue that the university marketing curriculum should go through a process of "reorientation rather than revision", which "would subordinate goods to service provision" (p. 14). Yet, in keeping with V&L's conservatism, the new curriculum "would not necessitate the abandonment of most of the traditional core concepts, such as the marketing mix, target marketing, market segmentation, but rather it would complement these with a framework based on the eight FPs we have discussed" (ibid.).

The authors do not want anything from marketing's intellectual legacy to be consigned to the dustbin of history. Yes, some economists might have misled marketers in the past (and even that was the result of some entirely understandable exigencies of argumentation), but the overall message of the paper is that we, as marketing academics, have in fact been doing very well in rectifying the results of those misdirections.

Framing the debate: The *JoM* commentaries

The selection of short responses invited from celebrated marketing academics that accompany the 2004 paper has a powerful framing effect (Brown, 2007). In Hunt's contribution, we get a hint of the direction that Bolton provided. Hunt (2004, p. 22) writes that his "commentary does not nitpick their argument but, at the editor's suggestion, amplifies and extends it". However, some of the commentators are subtly obstructive of this remit. Evert Gummesson's (2004) contribution notes that "marketers need to do as V&L advocate: reinvent marketing theory to fit the present and the future" (p. 21). The phrasing here implies that what we should be learning from V&L is the necessity for reinventing marketing – it is *not* stating that V&L's reinvention is something we should adopt. His tangential approach and closing remarks betray little engagement with the terms of V&L's article. Deighton and Narayandas' (2004) commentary argues that the dicta of S-D logic might be applicable in *certain* particular market conditions but not necessarily *all* of them. A context-led approach rather than a theory-led approach should be preferable.

While V&L make much use of Resource-Advantage (R-A) theory, Hunt's (2004) commentary positions V&L's logic as R-A theory *lite*. The only point of uniqueness he allows them is the distinction between operant and operand (which, of course, is not unique to V&L (2004a), but originates in Constantin and Lusch (1994)). Even here, Hunt demonstrates he had already made the distinction in Hunt (2000), concluding that "resource-advantage theory both conceptualizes 'resource' and explicates the kind of resources that can be operand and operant" (Hunt, 2004, p. 22). Hunt continues in this vein demonstrating how the V&L paper partially suggests things which are fully explicated in the R-A literature.

Framing the debate: the edited collection

V&L clearly learned the lessons of the *JoM* invited commentaries. In their preface to the 2006 collection they claim that "only an open-source, collaborative effort can 'get right' a fully developed theoretical framework that can serve the long-term needs of the discipline" (Lusch & Vargo, 2006b, p. xviii). They also note how this approach is entirely consistent with the "S-D logic's advocacy of co-production and the co-creation of value" (ibid.). This is powerful rhetoric. While the evolution of the logic can sometimes *look* like it is co-created, V&L have kept a very firm hand on the tiller of its evolution.

The 2006b collection refines or articulates ideas that were either only partially developed or had been overlooked by V&L in the 2004 paper. It thus allows V&L to employ outsourced academic labor to flesh their theory out. Second, the 2006b book consolidates the S-D logic brand. Finally, the collection also allows for the airing of controlled critique of the emerging logic. This serves a number of strategic purposes. Rhetorically, it amplifies the *ethos* of the logic itself – the logic does not need to suppress dissenting voices, instead it generously seeks to include them. Furthermore, when surrounded by a supportive majority who are seen to apply the logic to their areas of specialization, criticisms are inevitably reduced in effectiveness.

The two most critical chapters in the book are those by Sidney Levy (2006) and Achrol and Kotler (2006) who are also, arguably, the three heaviest hitters in the roll call of the collection's contributors. Levy's (2006) chapter begins by demonstrating that the four ages historical structure that V&L (2004a) have used lacks subtlety and reminds readers that much of the new service perspective has been prefigured in earlier writing. V&L have never denied this point. It is argumentatively important to them to ground S-D logic in the writings of earlier marketing authors and perspectives as it helps generate a sense of legitimacy and inevitability for their pre-theory. At its core, however, Levy's criticism of S-D logic is that it is something that only scholars will appreciate. The distinction between operant and operand, for example, "probably will not help managers" (Levy, 2006, p. 62). For Levy, if a logic is to become dominant in marketing it must be found useful by both scholars and managers. Levy concedes that V&L's assertion that everything is a service might be interesting to academics who can "enjoy dialog about it" (p. 61). Managers, however, will find their older product orientation still far too useful to throw away. Finally, Levy makes reference to the "superior" (p. 62) promotional skill of V&L. So, S-D logic is not particularly new, or dominant, but has been promoted particularly well among scholars. It could become dominant by broadening this promotional effort to managers.

Achrol and Kotler's (2006) chapter is sub-headed 'a critique' and is openly skeptical of S-D logic's originality and significance. They echo Levy's point that while the language games of S-D logic might find an audience among "marketing scientists" the same cannot be said of "practicing managers", who can never be expected to "think of a six-pack of beer in terms of a six-server: a six-server vehicle of thirst-quenching, bitter-flavorful, pleasure-inducing, social-intoxicant" (p. 331). It is interesting that Achrol and Kotler, as well as Levy, attempt to argue against S-D logic's fitness by constructing a depiction of the practitioner/manager as a composite of simple-minded boob and pragmatic bean counter. In addition, Achrol and Kotler argue that the premise that "services are exchanged for services" "trivializes everything that has happened in between" (2006, p. 332), particularly the "enormous creative energy and technological progress represented by the tangible means of delivering services invented by the industrial revolution" (ibid.). The growth of S-D logic, consequently, represents a real danger to the future of marketing. Not only is V&L's framework "not based on a fundamental logic system" (p. 323), its principal distinction (between goods and services) is "merely stylistic and rhetorical" (p. 322). Yet, it threatens to transform the variegated perspectives of a thriving marketing discipline into a unified, unhealthy monoculture.

While there are a number of other critical entries in the edited collection, most contributions take S-D logic at face value and seek to either extend it or place their own work within its framework.

S-D logic is an attractive perspective to align with, it seems. It exhibits impressive momentum and lofty goals so it makes perfect sense even for well-established scholars to consider how they can position their own work within it (or alongside it) so that it has the most exposure and an increased chance of survival in the market for marketing knowledge. Other researchers can look at some of the promising but under-developed areas of the pre-theory and mine them for their scholarly value, secure in the knowledge that, for the moment, such topics are *en vogue*.

Even when invited authors end up largely side-stepping the terms of S-D logic, V&L can use the section introductions in order to argue for the compatibility of a rival formulation with their own understanding of S-D logic. For example, Gummesson (2006) seizes the opportunity to provide an account of his own emerging logic, which he dubs "many-to-many marketing". This perspective is based upon a valorization of the network as the principal trope of contemporary marketing. In their section introduction, Lusch and Vargo (2006b) take a page out of Shelby Hunt's playbook and state that they "believe that S-D logic provides the justification for network formation: mutual service exchange" and therefore they find "Gummesson's position very consistent with S-D logic" (p. 335).

Lusch and Vargo's (2006b) collection is, consequently, a fascinating exercise in ideology consolidation and defense. The directly critical voices to be found in the collection are deflated by V&L's initial three chapters which include significant arguments against the charges brought by Levy (2006) and Achrol and Kotler (2006). In particular, they set straight a series of "misstatements about the underlying thesis of S-D logic" that have dogged their project since the "receipt of our initial reviews of the first submission" (Lusch & Vargo, 2006b, p. 44) of the 2004 article. V&L attempt to correct ten of the "most consistent misconceptions and misunderstandings" (p. 45). While we might wonder at the existence of so many regular failures of understanding around something that is meant to be indicative of an already emerging paradigm in marketing scholarship, V&L make the argument that such misconceptions are "likely a reflection of the paradigmatic strength of G-D logic" (ibid.). V&L hold that "S-D logic inverts a paradigm that has served as the foundation" for economics as well as marketing and so its presentation is bound to lead to misconceptions in the minds of those still mired in the old, G-D logic. Yet, this radically undercuts the substance of the argumentation in their 2004a article, which is careful to build the impression that the emerging logic evolves from the old logic and has been present in major marketing scholarship since the early 1950s.

The great reversal

Related to the tension between evolution and revolution is the question of 'paradigm shift'. In a strategic move, V&L deal with the issue of whether S-D logic is a "fundamental shift in worldview" (2004a, p. 2) not under the rubric of "What It Is Not", but under the section entitled "What It Might Be". They re-assert the claim that G-D logic is paradigmatic. Yet, in the final paragraph the authors raise the far more central question, "does S-D logic represent a paradigm shift?" (p. 52). Their answer is "we do not think it does, at least presently" because it does not "reflect the values and interests of the dominant researchers in the science of marketing as a whole and does not reflect a worldview" (ibid.). This flatly contradicts the principal argument of the 2004a paper, namely that "marketing has moved from a goods-dominant view, in which tangible output and discrete transactions were central, to a service-dominant view, in which intangibility, exchange processes, and relationships are central" (V&L, 2004, p. 2).

This is a *significant* reversal of position yet it is hidden away from the reader in the subtlest of ways. V&L then go on to surround this reversal with defensively modal equivocations. The S-D logic "*could* have emerged as the basis of the guiding paradigm of economics and thus for marketing" if not for an historical accident (Lusch & Vargo, 2006b, p. 52). And, just to keep the paradigm metaphor in the back pocket, in the future S-D logic "*might* be a candidate for the foundation for the paradigmatic shift that has been called for by a number of marketing scholars" (ibid.).

So, once the rhetoric of paradigm shift had served its persuasive purpose and threatened to become more of a liability than a boon, V&L are careful for the rest of their output to use the wording only when describing the G-D perspective (i.e. Lusch & Vargo, 2006a, 2014; V&L, 2008b, 2011a). Instead, adopting another metaphor, the logic is "a mindset, a lens through which to look at social and exchange phenomena so they can potentially be seen more clearly" (V&L, 2008a, p. 9). This is a far cry from the rhetorical thrust of the 2004a foundational article.

The O'Shaughnessy affair

One further instance of criticism of the S-D logic needs attention. A heated exchange between V&L and John and Nicholas O'Shaughnessy occurred between 2009 and 2011. The sequence starts with an article by O'Shaughnessy and O'Shaughnessy (2009). One of the O'Shaughnessys' unique assertions is that S-D logic is solely concerned with a technologically oriented search for service-based 'techniques' or 'principles'. O'Shaughnessy and O'Shaughnessy (2009) demonstrate that the search for management or marketing principles is a misguided one. Principles, they argue, need to be balanced with "explanatory theory" otherwise they become "ritualised answers to perplexing situations" (p. 788). They also question the status of S-D logic as a theory or a paradigm, concluding that it is a "perspective" (p. 791). In this they are echoing V&L's (2008a) backpedalling because they are not aware of the ways in which the terms of S-D logic have already been defended, repositioned, and redefined. This is, indeed, one of the central points that Lusch and Vargo (2011) make in their reply to the O'Shaughnessys. Printed alongside this reply are two more pieces – a rejoinder to the response by O'Shaughnessy and O'Shaughnessy (2011) and a 'rejoinder to the rejoinder' by V&L (2011b). The substance of this back and forth revolves around whether it is defensible to base a critique of a perspective upon only a consideration of the original article that introduces that perspective. Lusch and Vargo (2011) argue that to ignore the literature around S-D logic published since 2004 "could be considered inconsistent with the generally accepted norms of good scholarship" (p. 1300). Many of the issues that O'Shaughnessy and O'Shaughnessy (2009) raise have already been addressed in the literature. However, the O'Shaughnessys argue that there is no need to consider this literature: "the authors describe their perspective as logic, not a piece of empirical work, and we treated it as such, claiming the logic was defective" (O'Shaughnessy & O'Shaughnessy, 2011, p. 1310). If the 'base' of the S-D logic is 'contestable' then there is 'no advantage' in reading the supplemental literature that builds upon it as it, too, must be flawed.

This is sensible, if one starts from the assumption that V&L (2004a) is indeed the foundational edifice upon which all the following work is *logically* built. However, the V&L (2004a) article does not present a logic. It constructs a rhetorical argument. And rhetorical arguments do indeed change their terms, tropes and enthymemes over time. Rhetoric must change with the audience and the seasons – this is the essence of rhetorical *kairos*, the improvisatory necessity to respond persuasively to the moment (Kinneavy & Eskin, 2000). One of the recurring motifs deployed by V&L is the portrayal of their intellectual journey. S-D logic is now a 'pre-theory', a collaborative, 'open-source' movement. This has enabled it to maintain an aura of intellectual vitality. It also enables them to quite confidently avoid the O'Shaughnessys' complaints (V&L, 2011b). The fact that they have refined and extended their perspective demonstrates their ability to be reflective upon weaknesses in the logic and repair them. The fact that they "have authored approximately three dozen service-dominant (S-D) logic publications, which have received almost 2,500 total citations (Google Scholar), and have made several dozen keynote, and over 100 total, S-D logic presentations on five continents" (V&L, 2011b, p. 1319) also demonstrates that the community of marketing scholars is interested in following this journey. The *argumentum ad populum* is clear in V&L's defense but it is difficult to counter.

Logic or rhetoric

Much of the substance of the O'Shaughnessy affair seems to center around the power of the single word "logic". It is the one word that V&L have consistently retained. Its rhetorical intention is clear – the word's associations with mathematical precision, argumentative purity, and foundational importance are strong and V&L appreciate this. Yet, the word can also be used quite vaguely. Williams (2012) has unraveled the 'classical' logical relationships between the S-D logic premises and concludes that there should only really be *two* fundamental premises to S-D logic. Yet, even Williams fails to explain to the reader why exactly the word *logic* is appropriate for this whole enterprise! V&L have never offered an explanation themselves. The 'logic' seems to be more of a 'rhetoric'.

Brown (2007) was quick to note the rhetorical nature of S-D logic, arguing that the perspective's success is down to its rhetorical presentation and its evocation of a "golden age that never actually existed" which has been able to serve as a "conceptual comfort blanket, something that helps marketers face the reality of mounting marginalization and ever-increasing irrelevance" (p. 296). The pseudo mathematico-logical language and structuring of the foundational article has served as part of that rhetorical 'comfort blanket', touching on the aspiration for scientific respectability within the discipline that still haunts so many marketing scholars.

A history of revisions

As mentioned above, V&L like to revise and tweak S-D logic. The first tweak was to the name itself, which changed from a 'new emerging logic' to 'Service-Dominant logic' in less than one year. The adoption of the name (lifted from the final line of V&L, 2004b), was a result of their "need to brand this new logic" (Lusch & Vargo, 2006b, p. xvii) as the dialogue and debate that it was generating so quickly was using a number of different names "with variously nuanced connotations" (ibid.). The branding is aimed at unifying the debate around a clear core concept and a clear brand owner.

Some of the changes to V&L's presentation of S-D logic have been dealt with above, however there are a series of revisions to the FPs as well as significant conceptual extensions that are public instances of the foundational text being reworked and it is to these that I now turn.

The first FP-related revision occurs in the Lusch and Vargo (2006b) edited collection, inside V&L's (2006a) 'clarification' chapter. Here they restate the eight foundational premises but note one change to the 2004a presentation – FP_6 now states that "the customer is always a co-creator of value" rather than "the customer is always a co-producer". The reason for this change is that they believe the original formulation of "co-producer" is too heavily grounded in a "goods-dominant and production-oriented logic" (p. 44). This reasoning is expanded in V&L (2006b). Here they note that "several marketing scholars" had pointed out that "co-production implies making something, a unit of output" (p. 284) and was therefore an inappropriate term to be at the heart of the S-D logic. This underlines how difficult it is to eradicate G-D associations from S-D discourse. Yet, again, the concentration on word-choice and the recognition of its power to influence discourse underlines the heavily rhetorical nature of S-D logic.

The second revision to the FPs, an additional premise, is also to be found in V&L (2006a). It is designed to highlight the way in which S-D logic "recognizes that there is an acceleration in the division of labor in society as individuals become increasingly microspecialized" (p. 52). The additional FP_9 states that: "organizations exist to integrate and transform microspecialized competencies into complex services that are demanded in the marketplace" (p. 53). In a strong echo of Kiel et al. (1992), this premise positions S-D logic as a possible "framework for a theory of the firm" (p. 53). This begins a pattern of influence-broadening attempts that finds S-D logic being presented as far more than just a simple unification of the marketing discipline.

For a 2008 special issue of the *Journal of the Academy of Marketing Science*, V&L contributed a 'state of the logic' paper (V&L, 2008a) which made several important alterations to the FPs. Here we learn that S-D logic is a "generalizable mindset from which a general theory of the market can be developed" (ibid.) – a theory that is not aimed at the manager specifically but which could instead function as a "revised theory of economics and society" (V&L, 2008a, p.3). The widening of the ambition for what at this stage is still a 'pre-theory' continues.

The most prominent revisions in V&L (2008a) are the severe re-wording of FP_9 and the addition of another premise, FP_{10}. Both of these revisions can be seen as efforts to avoid further misunderstandings and misstatements from others. FP_9 now becomes the far more elegant, "all social and economic actors are resource integrators" (p. 7), a formulation that harks back to the declamatory style of 2004a. The term 'actors' indicates the start of the focus on actor-to-actor theory that has become prominent in V&L's work in recent years (V&L, 2011a, 2016a, 2016b;

Vargo, 2011; Lusch & Vargo, 2014). FP_{10} adds the dictum that "value is always uniquely and phenomenologically determined by the beneficiary" (V&L, 2008a, p. 7) and is a direct attempt by the authors to clarify the 'experiential nature of value'. Earlier in the 2008 article, they explain that they assumed their phenomenological position was inherent in their definition of 'service'. However, they note that some have clearly not been able to infer this (particularly if they were only basing their understanding on the 2004a article). V&L cite Arnould (2006) approvingly, however, noting that those who have clearly conducted a "more extensive review of S-D logic literature" (V&L, 2008a, p. 4) do not find it difficult to tease out the experiential foundations of their logic. The additional FP_{10}, then, like so many of the other revisions, seems to be motivated by an attempt to slow the pace of misunderstanding.

Williams' (2012) article on the logical structure of the foundational premises argues that only two of them are truly 'fundamental' (i.e. cannot be derived from other FPs). These two are FP_3 ("goods are distribution mechanisms for service provision") and FP_{10} ("value is always uniquely and phenomenologically determined by the beneficiary"). As Williams (2012) concludes, "FP3 and FP10 are axioms (premises) and the other FPs are conclusions" (p. 478). Whether Williams (2012) has influenced V&L or not is difficult to tell (I cannot find a citation of his analysis in V&L's work) but what is definite is that V&L have recently begun to re-arrange the foundational premises in a way that recognizes that some of them are more fundamental than others. So, in Lusch and Vargo (2014) we find that there are now four axioms alongside the ten foundational premises. The authors explain that "there are four FPs in particular that capture the essence of S-D logic, and from these the other FPs could arguably be derived" (p. 15). These four axioms are FP_1, FP_6, FP_9, and FP_{10}. They explain that FP_2, FP_3, FP_4, and FP_5 can all be derived from FP_1, while FP_7 and FP_8 can be derived from FP_6. FP_9 and FP_{10} are 'axiomatic' but do not generate any further conclusions (or premises).

The Lusch and Vargo (2014) re-organization seems to be moving toward a simplification on the one hand (there are only four *main* FPs) while significantly increasing the complexity of the core presentation of S-D logic on the other. More recently, it has seemed that things have been re-organized once again and in V&L (2016a, 2016b, 2016c) we find *five* axioms as the result of an *eleventh* foundational premise being added that now apparently has axiomatic status! This new axiom/premise states that "value co-creation is coordinated through actor-generated institutions and institutional arrangements" (V&L, 2016c, p. 8) and reflects an increasing move toward the service ecosystem perspective evidenced in V&L (2011a) onwards.

In addition to the new premise/axiom, V&L's (2016c) paper also contains more re-wordings of the previous foundational premises. These changes are largely focused on clarifying how S-D logic sees the relationship between firm and consumer regarding the co-creation of value, particularly as it relates to the value proposition. FP_6, for example, has now been changed to "value is co-created by multiple actors, always including the beneficiary" (p. 8) to reflect a far more network-oriented perception of value co-creation, though one cannot help but feel that the consumer has been rather downgraded in this re-wording. Indeed, the change from 'consumer' to 'beneficiary', although designed to help S-D logic escape from G-D language and assumptions, does raise the question of who exactly benefits the most from any particular service provision? The term also (re)places the consumer in a decidedly passive position. FP_7 has also been significantly re-worded and now reads: "Actors cannot deliver value but can participate in the creation and offering of value propositions" (ibid.). The use of actors here means that the beneficiary (also an actor) becomes just another actor in the value co-creation. The idea that the "consumer must determine value" (V&L, 2004a, p. 11) has been gradually buried. This becomes all the more problematic given the new axiom/premise FP_{11} that highlights the need for value co-creation to be coordinated by institutions.

S-D logic has changed considerably since its expression in V&L (2004a). The current formation of the axioms/premises as found in V&L (2016c) is more complex and more ambiguous. Gone is the bulk of the revolutionary paradigm-shifting rhetoric and in its place is a fascination with the structures of systems theory, actor-to-actor communication and practice theory. V&L have been engaging in much extension of the logic over the past few years and yet most of it is dependent upon linking S-D logic to other, pre-existing frameworks rather than relying upon empirical testing of S-D logic's premises or axioms.

Although there is a large body of scholarship by others around the terms of S-D logic (particularly the ideas of co-creation of value and the value proposition), what is most noticeable about V&L's journey from 2004 is the way in which they are keen to generate the evolution of their logic from within their own operant resources. The Otago Forums of 2005, 2008, and 2011, along with appearances at the Forums for Markets and Marketing and countless other presentations (see sdlogic.net for an exhaustive list), provides them with the opportunity to create a large network of discussion around the principles of the service perspective. Yet, the various revisions and evolutions of the S-D logic have been generated either by a desire to avoid further misunderstandings or through the fruits of their own ruminations. Yet, given the increasingly Baroque nature of the structure of the axioms/premises it is hard to see how misunderstandings will subside. Perhaps one might even note here a future lesson for marketing scholars – the clearer your expression of your central argument, the fewer opportunities you will have to publish clarifications and elucidations. Perhaps being mired in the lexicon of G-D logic has its advantages? One further consequence of the complicated shifting of terms, premises, axioms, and foci that has occurred since the 2004a unveiling of S-D logic is that in order to competently comment upon the state of the logic a scholar needs to keep close tabs on the output of V&L. Inevitably, this means that only those who consider the framework to be (intellectually or professionally) valuable can engage with it. The increasing complexity and rate of change in the foundational premises thus has a defensive effect around the substance of the discourse.

Extensions and returns

V&L have engaged in three, tightly interconnected, areas of extension for S-D logic: (1) the actor-to-actor framework; (2) practice theory; (3) service ecosystems (and connections to systems theory in general). In the case of practice theory some of the most significant work connecting it to S-D logic (and 'service science') has been performed by other scholars. We should also note the almost simultaneous appearance of Grönroos and Ravald (2011) that outlines the contribution of practice theory to service research. V&L (2016c) themselves value practice theory for its elucidation of the interaction between actors and institutions and, so, the dynamics of service ecosystems.

The actor-to-actor framework has become essential to V&L's contemporary presentation of S-D logic. Lusch and Vargo's (2014) long-awaited S-D logic monograph is entirely couched in actor-to-actor terms – "It's all actor-to-actor", they write (p. 101). This goes hand-in-hand with the simultaneous (re-)turn toward a "systems orientation" that became clear in V&L (2011a, p. 182). They argue that "we must move toward a more macro, systemic view of generic actors in order to see more clearly how a single, specific actor (e.g. a firm) can participate more effectively" (ibid.). Moving away from identifying actors "in terms of discrete roles and functions" (Lusch & Vargo, 2014, p. 102) allows us to develop a logic "of human exchange systems that includes the economy and society and transcends academic disciplines" (ibid.). In other words, V&L want to develop a general theory of exchange at all levels of society. Marketing scholarship has not been greatly receptive to the general systems project historically. However, V&L's

re-focusing of the S-D logic toward a service ecosystems perspective might serve to change this and there are indications that the service ecosystems perspective on S-D logic is attracting some interest (Layton, 2008, 2011; Frow *et al.*, 2014).

It should also be noted that the increasing use of a systems theory perspective in the recent development of S-D logic looks back to an early paper by Kiel, Lusch and Schumacher (1992). This rather extraordinary article, published in *Behavioral Science* and only rarely cited in the S-D logic canon, gives a good indication of the way in which systems approaches have long been central to at least one of S-D logic's co-founder's thinking about marketing. The article also prefigures the ambitious aims that S-D logic has exhibited since its inception. Kiel *et al.* (1992, p. 60) situate "marketing into a universal and evolutionary exchange paradigm that integrates human exchange with that of other living and nonliving systems". They attempt this by using a combination of general systems theory and Kuhnian concepts of paradigm shift and evolution. There are tantalizing similarities of structure and argumentation on display between Kiel *et al.* (1992) and V&L (2004a) which hint at a greater significance for the earlier paper's ideas as a galvanizing influence on S-D logic than has been hitherto realized. However, from the perspective of the current chapter, it is worth noting that recent work by V&L which advances S-D logic as a potential theory of society looks back to Kiel *et al.*'s (1992) formulation of a theory of evolutionary exchange which sought to situate the building blocks of marketing deep within human society and, indeed, the universe. This perhaps indicates that the future direction of S-D logic is even further outwards, toward an understanding of marketing as something which resonates with the universal forces of exchange and attraction. However, there are voices which seek to rein in such ambitions. A recent paper by Hietanen *et al.* (2018) has argued that S-D logic is "ill-equipped to understand consumer culture" (p. 1) let alone be applied to wider social analysis, while Denegri-Knott and Tadajewski (2017) explain how S-D logic's assertion that value is always co-created with the consumer is simply incorrect and allows for "questions of power and politics in market organization" to be downplayed if not ignored. Both pieces sound a warning bell for those wishing to build a theory of society upon S-D logic's (shifting) foundational premises.

Conclusion

This chapter has sought to delineate the way in which a particular academic perspective has been 'marketed' by its authors to the wider academic marketing community through the utilization of powerful rhetorical strategies and (counter-)argumentation. In many ways, V&L's approach to the dissemination of S-D logic could be held up as a model for ambitious younger scholars and those seeking to promote a position in marketing academia. Key advice emerging from this chapter's investigation would be to construct a perspective/model/theory/pre-theory that is conservative at its core but is then presented in ways that rhetorically proclaim its radical or revolutionary nature.

Adopting language and structurings drawn from mathematics or the hard sciences, appealing to the authority of economics while at the same time appealing to the vanity of marketing scholars, and managing the inclusion of 'celebrity' contrarian voices in order to promote citation-generating dialogue all seem important components in the successful marketization of marketing theorization. At the center of all these techniques, however, lies the fundamental strategy of re-definition. The re-definition of products as delivery mechanisms for services, of consumers as producers, and of value as 'value in use' are powerful examples of how a shift in perspective can serve as the basis for a persuasive performance of scholarly argument. Re-definition is, of course, a conservative developmental strategy for it always leaves the basic building blocks intact, just shifting the way they are framed.

Yet, S-D logic is remarkable not for its rhetorical strategies but for its mastery of them. As Hunt and Edison (1995, p. 635) admit, "knowledge claims have always been marketed". The explication of knowledge claims across all academic disciplines is always accompanied by rhetorical strategies designed to persuade academic communities of their veracity, appropriateness, timeliness, and desirability (Billig, 1996; McCloskey, 1985; Nelson *et al.*, 1987; Peter & Olson, 1983). S-D logic is a masterful example of this truth and, as such, an analysis of its persuasive components affords us insight into the language, the hopes, the fears, and the myths that resonate deeply with the global community of marketing academics. Successful rhetorical persuasion will always tell us more about the audience than the rhetor.

The untimely death of Robert Lusch during the writing of this chapter inevitably brings into stark relief a number of questions regarding the shape of S-D logic's future evolution. This chapter has hopefully demonstrated just how dominating a force the two co-founders of S-D logic have been in the continuing development of the perspective. As a consequence, the direction this discourse will take under the navigation of just one of those co-founders is very much an unknown quantity. Given the evidence of some of Lusch's pre-S-D logic scholarship it is possible that the systems theory emphasis that has become evident in the perspective might begin to take more of a backseat. However, given the trajectory since 2004, it would be surprising if S-D logic did not undergo further development into a precursor for a 'general theory of society', although the exact form of its argumentation and the frameworks that it might choose to use in this journey remain to be seen. One suspects, however, that rhetorical sophistication will continue to play an important part in the perspective's evolution.

References

Achrol, R., & Kotler, P. (2006). The service-dominant logic for marketing: A critique. In R. Lusch & S. Vargo (Eds.), *the service-dominant logic of marketing: Dialog, debate, and directions* (pp. 320–333). Armonk, M.E. Sharpe.

Arnould, E.J. (2006). Service-dominant logic and consumer culture theory: Natural allies in an emerging paradigm. *Marketing Theory, 6*(3), 293–298.

Billig, M. (1996). *Arguing and thinking: A rhetorical approach to social psychology*. Cambridge, Cambridge University Press.

Bolton, R. (2004). Invited commentaries on 'evolving to a new dominant logic for marketing'. *Journal of Marketing, 68*(1), 18–27.

Bolton, R. (2006). Foreword. In R.F. Lusch & S.L. Vargo (Eds.), *The service-dominant logic of marketing: Dialog, debate, and directions* (pp. ix–xi). Armonk, M.E. Sharpe.

Brown, S. (2007). Are we nearly there yet? On the retro-dominant logic of marketing. *Marketing Theory, 7*(3), 291–300.

Brownlie, D., & Saren, M. (1995). On the commodification of marketing knowledge: Opening themes. *Journal of Marketing Management, 11*(7), 619–627.

Constantin, J.A., & Lusch, R.F. (1994). *Understanding resource management*. Oxford, OH, The Planning Forum.

Deighton, J., & Narayandas, D. (2004). Stories and theories. *Journal of Marketing, 68*(1), 19–20.

Denegri-Knott, J., & Tadajewski, M. (2017). Sanctioning value: The legal system, hyper-power and the legitimation of MP3. *Marketing Theory, 17*(2), 219–240.

Frow, P., McColl-Kennedy, J.R., Hilton, T., Davidson, A., Payne, A., & Brozovic, D. (2014). Value propositions: A service ecosystems perspective. *Marketing Theory, 14*(3), 327–351.

Grönroos, C., & Ravald, A. (2011). Service as business logic: Implications for value creation and marketing. *Journal of Service Management, 22*(1), 5–22.

Gummesson, E. (2004). Service provision calls for partners instead of parties. *Journal of Marketing, 68*(1), 20–21.

Gummesson, E. (2006). Many-to-many marketing as grand theory. In R. Lusch & S. Vargo (Eds.), *The service-dominant logic of marketing: Dialog, debate, and directions* (pp. 339–353). Armonk, M.E. Sharpe.

Hietanen, J., Andéhn, M., & Bradshaw, A. (2018). Against the implicit politics of service-dominant logic. *Marketing Theory, 18*(1), 101–119.

Hunt, S. (1991). *Modern marketing theory: Critical issues in the philosophy of marketing science*. Cincinnati, South-Western Publishing Co.

Hunt, S. (2000). *A general theory of competition: Resources, competences, productivity, economic growth*. Thousand Oaks, CA, Sage Publications.

Hunt, S. (2004). On the service-centered dominant logic for marketing. *Journal of Marketing, 68*(1), 21–22.

Hunt, S., & Edison, S. (1995). On the marketing of marketing knowledge. *Journal of Marketing Management, 11*(7), 635–640.

Hunt, S., & Morgan, R. (1997). Resource-advantage theory: A snake swallowing its tail or a general theory of competition? *Journal of Marketing, 61*(4), 74–82.

Kiel, D., Lusch, R., & Schumacher, B. (1992). Toward a new paradigm for marketing: The evolutionary exchange paradigm. *Behavioral Science, 37*(1), 59–76.

Kinneavy, J., & Eskin, C. (2000). Kairos in Aristotle's rhetoric. *Written Communication, 17*(3), 432–444.

Kuhn, T.S. (1962). *The structure of scientific revolutions*, second edition. Chicago, University of Chicago Press.

Layton, R.A. (2008). The search for a dominant logic: A macromarketing perspective. *Journal of Macromarketing, 28*(3), 215–227.

Layton, R.A. (2011). Towards a theory of marketing systems. *European Journal of Marketing, 45*(1/2), 259–276.

Levy, S. (2006). How new, how dominant? In R. Lusch & S. Vargo (Eds.), *The service-dominant logic of marketing: Dialog, debate, and directions* (pp. 57–64). Armonk, M.E. Sharpe.

Lusch, R.F., & Vargo, S.L. (2006a). Service-dominant logic: Reactions, reflections and refinements. *Marketing Theory, 6*(3), 281–288.

Lusch, R.F., & Vargo, S.L. (Eds.) (2006b). *The service-dominant logic of marketing: Dialog, debate, and directions*. Armonk, M.E. Sharpe.

Lusch, R.F., & Vargo, S.L. (2011). Service-dominant logic: A necessary step. *European Journal of Marketing, 45*(7/8), 1298–1309.

Lusch, R.F., & Vargo, S.L. (2014). *Service-dominant logic: Premises, perspectives, possibilities*. Cambridge, Cambridge University Press.

Malone, M.E. (1993). Kuhn reconstructed: Incommensurability without relativism. *Studies in History and Philosophy of Science, 24*(1), 69–93.

McCloskey, D. (1985). *The rhetoric of economics*. Madison, University of Wisconsin Press.

Miles, C. (2017). The rhetoric of marketing co-creation. In G. Siegert & M. Bjørn von Rimscha (Eds.), *Commercial communication in the digital age: Information or disinformation?* (pp. 209–226). Berlin, De Gruyter.

Nelson, J., Megill, A., & McCloskey, D. (Eds.) (1987). *The rhetoric of the human sciences: Language and argument in scholarship and public affairs*. Madison, University of Wisconsin Press.

Normann, R., & Ramirez, R. (1993). From value chain to value constellation: Designing interactive strategy. *Harvard Business Review, 71*(4), 65–77.

O'Shaughnessy, J., & O'Shaughnessy, N.J. (2009). The service-dominant perspective: A backward step? *European Journal of Marketing, 43*(5/6), 784–793.

O'Shaughnessy, J., & O'Shaughnessy, N.J. (2011). Service-dominant logic: A rejoinder to Lusch and Vargo's reply. *European Journal of Marketing, 45*(7/8), 1310–1318.

Peter, J.P., & Olson, J.C. (1983). Is science marketing? *Journal of Marketing, 47*(4), 111–125.

Scully, J.I. (1996). Machines made of words: The influence of engineering metaphor on marketing thought and practice, 1900 to 1929. *Journal of Macromarketing, 16*(2), 70–83.

Tadajewski, M. (2011). Correspondence sales education in the early twentieth century: The case of the Sheldon School (1902–39). *Business History, 53*(7), 1130–1151.

Vargo, S.L. (2011). Market systems, stakeholders and value propositions: Toward a service-dominant logic-based theory of the market. *European Journal of Marketing, 45*(1/2), 217–222.

Vargo, S.L., & Lusch, R.F. (2004a). Evolving to a new dominant logic for marketing. *Journal of Marketing, 68*(1), 1–17.

Vargo, S., & Lusch, R. (2004b). The four service marketing myths: Remnants of a goods-based, manufacturing model. *Journal of Service Research, 6*(4), 324–335.

Vargo, S., & Lusch, R. (2006a). Service-dominant logic: What it is, what it is not, what it might be. In R. Lusch & S. Vargo (Eds.), *The service-dominant logic of marketing: Dialog, debate, and directions* (pp. 43–56). Armonk, M.E. Sharpe.

Vargo, S.L., & Lusch, R.F. (2008a). Service-dominant logic: Continuing the evolution. *Journal of the Academy of Marketing Science, 36*(1), 1–10.

Vargo, S.L., & Lusch, R.F. (2008b). Why 'service'? *Journal of the Academy of Marketing Science, 36*(1), 25–38.

Vargo, S.L., & Lusch, R.F. (2011a). It's all B2B ... and beyond: Toward a systems perspective of the market. *Industrial Marketing Management, 40*(February), 181–187.

Vargo, S.L., & Lusch, R.F. (2011b). Stepping aside and moving on: A rejoinder to a rejoinder. *European Journal of Marketing, 45*(7/8), 1319–1321.

Vargo, S.L., & Lusch, R.F. (2016a). Service-dominant logic 2025. *International Journal of Research in Marketing, 34*(1), 46–67.

Vargo, S.L., & Lusch, R.F. (2016b). Service dominant logic: Status and directions. Presentation slides delivered at the *Forum on Markets and Marketing*, WMG, Venice, Italy, June 2, 2016. Retrieved from http://sdlogic.net/uploads/3/4/0/3/34033484/fmm_2016_pres.short.pdf

Vargo, S.L., & Lusch, R.F. (2016c). Institutions and axioms: An extension and update of service-dominant logic. *Journal of the Academy of Marketing Science, 44*(1), 5–23.

Williams, J. (2012). The logical structure of the service-dominant logic of marketing. *Marketing Theory, 12*(4), 471–483.

14
METAPHOR AND RELATIONSHIP MARKETING DISCOURSE

Lisa O'Malley

Introduction

The development and impact of Relationship Marketing (RM) has received a great deal of attention over the last thirty years (Bejou, 1997; Copulsky & Wolf, 1990; Egan, 2003; Harker & Egan, 2006; Hibbard *et al.*, 2001; Möller & Halinen, 2000; O'Malley, 2014; Sheth & Parvatiyar, 1995, 2002). RM is considered to be an appropriate lens when studying relationships between organizations, between people in organizations (buyers/sellers; service providers/clients), and between people and organizations or brands (consumer/organizational and brand/consumer relationships). Exploring the diversity of relational possibilities has generated a rich tapestry of theories, concepts and empirical examples that essentially frame marketing as 'interaction, relationships and networks' (Gummesson, 1987). The resulting entities are complex constructions consisting of multi-level social relations between individuals in interacting organizations (Alajoutsijärvi *et al.*, 2001; Håkansson, 1982).

Marketing understood as 'interaction, relationships and networks' contrasts starkly with the mix management paradigm which is pervasive in marketing. Indeed, many early discussions positioned RM as an alternative (see Arndt, 1983; Grönroos, 1994). The 'one actor, given goals' perspective axiomatic in marketing management (Arndt, 1983) was challenged by empirical work that demonstrated that buyers and sellers can both be active, that sellers do not make choices only on the basis of the price/quality function (as implied in microeconomic theory), and that individual firms cannot control the market through manipulating the marketing mix. Eschewing research approaches that focus on isolated transactions, researchers in business-to-business and services marketing (most notably the IMP Group and the Nordic School of Services in Europe) considered the context, history and potential future of exchange between market actors (Grönroos, 1982; Håkansson, 1982). As a result, marketing was reconceptualized as 'an interactive process in a social context where relationship building and management is a vital cornerstone' (Grönroos, 1994, p. 353).

RM is an important contemporary discourse in marketing. Discourse captures how knowledge is produced through language and representation, as well as how that knowledge is institutionalized, how it shapes social practices and brings technologies into play (Du Gay *et al.*, 1996). The RM discourse is informed by metaphor. Essentially, through a process of metaphoric transfer, market relationships are understood *as if* they are marriages (Hunt & Menon, 1995;

O'Malley & Tynan, 1999; Tynan, 1997). Metaphors are commonplace in academia, serving to stimulate creativity, interrogate existing thinking, and construct new theories (Zaltman et al., 1982). Although positioned as a compelling alternative to the marketing mix (see Dixon & Blois, 1983; Grönroos, 1994; Kent, 1986; O'Malley & Patterson, 1998; Van Waterschoot & Van den Bulte, 1992), RM failed to overthrow the marketing management discourse. Nevertheless, it has had a significant impact on the marketing discipline. Its rhetoric has proven compelling, and its language and concepts sufficiently malleable to be appropriated by the mainstream discourse.

Metaphor has played a fundamental role in shaping the RM discourse. Its language and concepts are informed both by the broad category of interpersonal relationships (superordinate level) and the more specific (and often intuitive) category of marriage (subordinate level) (Dwyer et al., 1987; O'Malley & Tynan, 1999; Tynan, 1997). The use of metaphor should not involve a search for a 'perfect fit' between source and target domain, because 'perfect fit' is impossible. However, in evaluating the impact of the language and concepts transferred in the process of using metaphor we understand that there should be sufficient distance between domains to support creative insight, and, at the same time, the domains should be sufficiently similar so that the resulting insights are helpful (Cornelissen & Kafouros, 2008). In this chapter, I explore how the marriage metaphor destabilized conventional constructions of the marketing function, directed attention toward the *interaction* between buyers and sellers and framed market exchanges within the context of *relationships* and *networks*. Central to this endeavor is to fully appreciate how metaphor functions as a tool of thought and as a basis for academic discourse. The chapter is structured as follows: first there is a brief overview of conceptual metaphor theory; second, the metaphoric roots of RM are explored; third the impact of the marriage metaphor is delineated; fourth, directions for further research are outlined; and finally concluding comments are offered.

On metaphor as a conceptual tool

Metaphors are commonly used in professional and academic discourse. They are employed when we have no language or concepts in our repertoire to help explain a particular phenomenon. Metaphors allow us to structure abstract, complex or unfamiliar concepts in terms of something with which we are more familiar (Semino & Masci, 1996). 'Metaphors connect realms of human experience and imagination' (Cornelissen et al., 2008, p. 8) and are one of the primary ways by which we frame and understand our worlds (Cornelissen, 2005; Morgan, 1980, 1983; Weick, 1989). Because language does not exist independent of thought, nor thought independent of language (Lakoff & Johnson, 1980), the language we have available to us structures our thinking in very particular ways (Brown, 1976).

The discipline of marketing is replete with metaphor, including 'the marketing mix (cooking), the 4Ps (alchemy), the Product Life Cycle (biology), marketing myopia (medicine), the wheel of retailing (transportation), viral marketing (epidemiology) . . . brand personality (psychology), guerrilla marketing (warfare), . . . relationship marketing (marriage), consumer information processing (computers)' (Brown, 2008, p. 211). Despite the proliferation of metaphors, analogical thinking is more commonplace in marketing than is rigorous evaluation grounded in metaphor theory (Arndt, 1985; Fillis & Rentschler, 2008; Hunt & Menon, 1995; van den Bulte, 1994). There are, of course, exceptions and interested readers are directed to the following works (Alajoutsijärvi et al., 2001; Arndt, 1985; Celuch et al., 2006; Cornelissen, 2003; Davies & Chun, 2003; Fillis & Rentschler, 2008; Fisk & Grove, 1996; Goodwin, 1996; O'Malley & Tynan, 1999; O'Malley et al., 2008; Rindfleisch, 1996; Winsor, 1995; Zaltman et al., 1982). Metaphors operate by transferring meaning from a source to a target domain. Metaphor is 'a literally false, declarative assertion of existential equivalence that compares two concepts or things, where one concept, called the primary concept, is claimed to be another, the secondary concept' (Hunt & Menon, 1995, p. 82).

Metaphors offer creative potential because they are denotatively false, while at least potentially connotatively true (Hunt & Menon, 1995). The process of metaphoric transfer foregrounds particular features and, simultaneously, hides others. For example, in comparing war (source domain) to marketing (target domain) (Kotler & Singh, 1981; Ries & Trout, 1986; Trout & Ries, 1986), we understand that engaging in marketing is not *literally* war, but that competitive activity can be considered 'as a state of warfare in which competitors battle for customer spoils' (Rindfleisch, 1996, p. 3). The use of the war metaphor offers access to new language and concepts to make sense of market behaviors. Similarly, in comparing interpersonal relationships (source domain) to marketing (target domain) we appreciate that the ensuing relationships are not *literally* interpersonal but that certain aspects of interpersonal relationships might be helpful in understanding market exchanges. However, the process of metaphoric thinking is complicated within the RM discourse because while some relationships are clearly metaphoric (e.g. firm-to-firm or consumer/brand) others actually exist between individuals (as, for example, between service providers and clients) creating a situation where these might literally be described as interpersonal. However, even here RM relies on the construction of a particular kind of interpersonal relationship, one that is governed by a formal contract and is intended to last over time – namely, a marriage (Tynan, 1997). Levitt (1983) is credited with introducing the *marriage* metaphor to marketing. Essentially, he argued that a seller should eschew one-night stands and extramarital affairs (one-off transactions) in favor of longer-term relationships that he described as a 'more convenient and necessary marriage'. Thus, when referring to relationships between buyers and sellers we appreciate that these are not *literally* marriages but that certain aspects of marriage might help generate insight and develop theory regarding market relations.

One way to interrogate a metaphor's creative potential is to consider the impact the concepts and ideas called forth by the metaphor have had on sense making in a discipline (Cornelissen & Kafouros, 2008; Hunt & Menon, 1995). Unfortunately, this is not a straightforward process because 'there is no objective reality that can referee which metaphorical conceptualization . . . is right or wrong' (Andriessen & Gubbins, 2009, p. 858). Thus, we can only consider how metaphor is used, evaluate what insights are generated, and, in this way, explore its impact (Arndt, 1985). Fundamentally, all we can ultimately say is whether one metaphor appears more, or less, apt than others (Andriessen & Gubbins, 2009). Recent work suggests that the most effective metaphors combine *within-domain similarity* and *between-domains distance* (Cornelissen, 2004, 2005; Cornelissen *et al.*, 2008; Cornelissen & Kafouros, 2008). *Within-domains similarity* means that a metaphorical source captures some important features of a target domain, and is therefore likely to result in higher levels of generative and explicatory impact. However, there also needs to be sufficient *between-domains distance* in order to create the semantic anomaly necessary to generate sufficient tension to inform new thinking (Cornelissen & Kafouros, 2008). When the distance between source and target domains is too close, the metaphor does little more than make the 'familiar' more familiar. The next section reviews the impact of metaphor on the emerging RM discourse.

Interrogating the impact of the interpersonal/marriage metaphor

A number of seminal empirical studies in the 1980s employed the lens of interpersonal relationships generally, and marriage in particular, to generate insights into market behaviors. Anderson and Narus (1984) employed Thibaut and Kelley's (1959) 'outcome matrix', a well-developed theory of dyadic social exchange, in their seminal study on distributor/manufacturer relationships. The 'outcome matrix' focuses attention on how relational partners evaluate the costs and rewards associated with a relationship and, based on their evaluation of alternatives, decide to remain, leave or manage that relationship. For Anderson and Narus (1984) there appeared to be sufficient *within-domains similarity* between source and target to offer creative potential in the mapping process. Equally, they found sufficient *between-domains distance* to describe and explain manufacturer/distributor working relationships in new and creative ways (semantic anomaly). As such, the authors conclude that while 'caution must be used when generalizing interpersonal constructs to an inter-organizational context, the adapted constructs . . . appear to have applicability to the study of distributor–manufacturer working relationships' (Anderson & Narus, 1984, p. 66). Although numerous theories of interpersonal relationships abound (Sheaves & Barnes, 1996), the majority of applications have relied on social exchange theory (O'Malley et al., 2008) and this has had quite significant implications for the emerging discourse.

Researchers tended to rely on social exchange theory because it had been successfully deployed in marketing to help explain the behavior of marketing channel protagonists (see El-Ansary & Stern, 1972) and therefore appeared familiar to them. For example, Dwyer et al. (1987) created their model of buyer-seller relationships with recourse to marriage theory (McCall, 1966), relationship development theory (Scanzoni, 1979) and contractual relations (MacNeil, 1980). Like Anderson and Narus (1984) they understood that such theories were 'not proximal to marketing' and, as a result, warned that their model was 'highly propositional' (Dwyer et al., 1987, p. 25). Delineating the phases of buyer-seller relationship development, they highlight the centrality of trust and commitment within this process. This model is broadly in line with other models of relationship development (Guillet de Monthoux, 1975; Ford, 1980; Borys & Jemison, 1989; Parvatiyar & Sheth, 2000) that depict relationships as developing over time as they become increasingly closer and more interdependent. While conceptualizations of the phases of relationship development are consistent with the development of a marriage, there is an important assumption that relationships are managed by the seller. This is because the discourse is rooted in an understanding of relationship quality as a function of 'how well the relationship is managed by the seller' (Levitt, 1983, p. 111). Thus, following Levitt (1983) and consistent with the marketing management discourse, the idea that relationships should be managed is axiomatic. While early studies focused on devising strategies to develop and maintain relationships (Dwyer et al., 1987; Ford, 1980), recent work has focused on the management of relationship ending(s) (Perrien et al., 1995; Hocutt, 1998; Halinen & Tähtinen, 2002; Haytko, 2004; Camarero et al., 2010).

Dwyer et al. (1987, p. 12) further advocated the extension of RM into mass consumer markets suggesting that even here, marketers could benefit 'from attention to conditions that foster relational bonds leading to reliable repeat business', etc. This ultimately led to efforts to build relationships in mass marketing contexts, using technology as a surrogate for interpersonal interaction. The promise of retaining customers and increasing value proved so compelling that relationships were pursued between consumers and firms (Copulsky & Wolf, 1990; Deighton & Blattberg, 1991) and between consumers and brands (Fournier, 1998; Fournier & Yao, 1997; Dall'Olmo Riley & De Chernatony, 2000; Patterson & O'Malley, 2006), often through the practice of customer relationship management (CRM). CRM is a hybrid discourse where the language and concepts (trust, commitment, mutuality) are inherently relational and the tools and technologies fundamentally managerial (Deighton & Blattberg, 1991; O'Malley & Mitussis, 2002; Mitussis et al., 2006) and grounded in classical economics. While efforts to manage customer relationships have attracted extensive critique (Barnes, 1994; Gruen, 1995; Iacobucci & Ostrom, 1996; O'Malley et al., 1997; Fournier et al., 1998; Möller & Halinen, 2000; O'Malley &

Tynan, 1999, 2000) CRM is widely employed in marketing. However, while there has been much progress in terms of the acquisition and interrogation of customer information (Boulding et al., 2005; Payne & Frow, 2005), CRM has not meaningfully enhanced the management of those relationships (O'Malley, 2014). This is because CRM rarely engages with the multidimensional exchange processes required to create relational outcomes (O'Malley & Mitussis, 2002; Mitussis et al., 2006) and fails to engage with the diverse relationships with which a firm is involved (Gummesson, 2002). Moreover, assumptions regarding who controls brands (Bonnemaizon et al., 2007, p. 57) and how information about brands is created and shared through social media (Deighton & Kornfeld, 2009; Hennig-Thurau et al., 2010; Kietzmann et al., 2011) highlight that consumer/brand relationships might not be manageable (Patterson & O'Malley, 2006; Fournier & Lee, 2009; O'Malley, 2014). Thus 'given . . . obvious differences between social relationships and consumer–brand relationships, it is important for researchers to not overextend the relationship metaphor when studying consumer behavior' (Aggarwal, 2004, p. 89).

Impact of metaphor on RM discourse

While the process of metaphoric transfer initially seemed to offer conceptual insight, the utility of the metaphor has been questioned both in terms of the range of applications and also in terms of what it foregrounds and what it hides. The *marriage* metaphor is considered to be too limited to capture the multiple and diverse relationships that a firm can have with, for example, different suppliers, distributors, and competitors (Hunt & Menon, 1995; Morgan & Hunt, 1994). Moreover, while marriage assumes consent between equal partners (Tynan, 1997), market actors do not always have a choice regarding which relationships they are involved with, and in consumer markets the comparisons with marriage might be unhelpful (Iacobucci & Ostrom, 1996; O'Malley & Tynan, 1999; O'Malley et al., 2008).

All (metaphoric) relationships between firms, between buyers and sellers, and/or between consumers and firms involve people at some level, and therefore necessitate interpersonal interaction. This has led to concerns that 'emotional bonding' will occur between relational parties and that these 'can transcend economic interests' (Bolton et al., 2003, p. 285). However, Blocker et al. (2011) demonstrate that although buyers frequently invoke relational language in discussing interactions with suppliers, most relationships remain instrumental in orientation. Moreover, the use of relational language 'can mask the fact that the interaction originates and is sustained to pursue instrumental goals' (Blocker et al., 2011, p. 900). Thus, we should be cautious of assuming that *relationship* is synonymous with friendship, or that such friendships would transcend instrumental goals. In contrast, empirical evidence suggests that while close interpersonal relationships can emerge as individuals interact over time, these tend to reduce role ambiguity and improve working conditions (Haytko, 2004). Despite this, contemporary efforts to improve transparency in organizations have mitigated against the formation of close relationships between actors in different organizations (see Blocker et al., 2011). Rather than assuming that relationships are good or bad, a more realistic appraisal is therefore necessary: relationships can easily turn into a burden for one or both of the involved parties. Relationships, thus, have both a huge benefit and a huge burden potential (Snehota & Håkansson, 1995).

Differences in understanding are an inevitable consequence of using the same metaphor in different research contexts. While variation in the meaning of terms in different textual contexts is inevitable, greater consideration should be paid to the consequences of this (Alvesson & Willmott, 1996). Significantly and primarily as a result of adopting social exchange theory, the propositional nature of models of relationship building (i.e. their metaphoric properties) have been lost over time. As a result, researchers began to treat exchange relationships as literal. This occurred because social exchange theory is a theory of interpersonal relationships that is based on the metaphor of the *market*. As a result, theorists investigated social exchanges *as if* they were market exchanges (Homans, 1950; Thibaut & Kelley, 1959). For example, using social exchange theory, marriage is understood as the context in which 'two individuals agree to exchange only with one another, at least until such time as the balance of trade becomes unfavourable in terms of broader market considerations' (McCall, 1966, p. 197).

Social exchange theory, therefore, produces a very particular view of interpersonal relationships, one that is 'entirely consistent with the notion of the *market*, and its fundamental axioms are consistent with self-interest seeking and a calculative approach to interaction and exchange' (O'Malley et al., 2008, p. 173). The prevalence of social exchange theory also explains why we tend to rely upon 'rational, practical and instrumental assumptions of marital arrangements rather than on assumptions of marriages as extremely emotional and exciting, non-rational and even messy enterprises' (Alajoutsijärvi et al., 2001, p. 100). Thus, while there initially appeared to be sufficient *between-domain difference* as to generate semantic anomaly (Anderson & Narus, 1984; Dwyer et al., 1987), with hindsight we can see that the adoption of social exchange theory significantly reduced the distance between domains. As a result 'the literatures on market exchange and social exchange are incestuous to the point that the process of cross-domain mapping is made redundant' (O'Malley et al., 2008, p. 173). Fundamentally, this use of the metaphor has indeed served to make 'the familiar more familiar' and, further, enhanced the assimilation of relational language and concepts into the marketing management discourse.

Directions for further research: exploring new metaphors

The deployment of the marriage metaphor in marketing has emphasized the long-term positive nature of market exchanges and simultaneously fails to capture the complexities that result when organizations are simultaneously involved in multiple relationships (Hunt & Menon, 1995; Wilkinson & Young, 1994). A focus on marriage as the idealized outcome could be inherently limiting, as it frames thinking in an overly positive way. Therefore, we can extend the marriage metaphor to incorporate ideas around polygamy, arranged marriages and mail order brides (Hunt & Menon, 1995; Tynan, 1997; Wilkinson & Young, 1994). Indeed, recent work has explored the 'dark side' of business relationships (Anderson & Jap, 2005; Grayson & Ambler, 1999) including that unrealistic expectations can be developed (Gruen et al., 2000); that relationships undermine the ability to remain objective (Moorman et al., 1992); and that self-interested firms might behave opportunistically (Johnsen & Lacoste, 2016). Appreciating the dark side of business relationships compels us to 'challenge the view that establishing deeper relationships with exchange partners can always lead to performance gains' (Hibbard et al., 2001, p. 32).

We can also explore where alternative conceptualizations of interpersonal relationships might prove fruitful. For example, there seems to be greater correspondence between consumer/organizational and buyer/seller relationships with patient/doctor than with husband/wife (see Iacobucci & Ostrom, 1996). This would direct us toward role theory and the possibilities afforded by the dramaturgical metaphor. When individuals interact in business exchanges they explicitly do so through the auspices of their roles – buyer, seller, service provider, client or customer. *Role* is what the focal actor does in a relationship with other actors (Anderson et al., 1998) and *role performance* is influenced by each episode of interaction. Roles are socially constructed clusters of behaviors expected of individuals in particular situations (Allen & van de Vliert, 1984; Goffman, 1983; Montgomery, 1998) with actors viewed as a collection of roles (Anderson et al., 1998) which are evoked by the situations in which they find themselves (Montgomery, 1998). Interaction occurs through role performances that can transform the actors, their products and services, and, ultimately their markets (see Ford, 2011). Role theory has been usefully applied to service encounters (Broderick, 1999; Solomon *et al.*, 1985) and inter-organizational networks (Håkansson, 2002; Heikkinen *et al.*, 2007; Knight & Harland, 2005; Möller *et al.*, 2005; Snow *et al.*, 1992; Story *et al.*, 2011; Tushman, 1977). Further application/interrogation of role theory will inevitably foreground the instrumental nature of market exchanges.

Individuals interact through their respective roles when engaging in market exchanges. Thus, these interactions are governed by the implied scripts of those roles (buyer/seller, client/service provider, customer/sales person), by the particular firms that they represent (industry, firm size and relative power, history between firms) and by their own individual personalities. The dramaturgical metaphor captures both the idea that actors perform roles and that role interaction is structured by scripts (Fisk & Grove, 1996). Further research is therefore required to capture this additional complexity and should pay particular attention to its implications for management (Ford & Håkansson, 2006; Möller, 2013; O'Malley, 2014). This should explore how role interaction is unlikely to be purely economic (as is assumed in microeconomic theory), nor entirely social (as has been a recent tendency in RM). Rather, a more balanced approach will allow us to better appreciate relational partners as socio-economic actors (Anderson *et al.*, 1998; Håkansson *et al.*, 2009) who can be simultaneously relational and instrumental.

The dance metaphor (Wilkinson & Young, 1994, pp. 74–75) is another novel alternative that captures important facets of relationships in ways that differ significantly from those informed by the marriage metaphor. For example, 'dancing involves an active cooperation, not a formal type of connection'; there are an infinite number of possibilities to capture relational processes – 'you cannot marry everyone but you can dance in many ways with many others', and, finally, 'the rules of the dance mimic the inherent logic of the processes that must be effected in a value chain'. Partners get to know each other through interaction and this familiarity can improve the quality of the dance. There is no implied assumption that relationships should progress to an inevitable 'marriage-like' state. The dance metaphor can also be extended to incorporate different types of dance, for example, there are obviously leaders and followers in a traditional waltz and this might reflect a relationship in which one partner is clearly in a leadership position, directing and informing strategy. However, bimodal connections between a firm and its customers occur within complex multinodal networks (Kozinets, 1999) and thus the assumption that one firm can create and implement a successful strategy without recourse to such networks is increasingly questioned (Ford & Håkansson, 2006). Thus, other examples of dance where there are few (if any) rules, where regular partner switching occurs and/or where there are no identifiable partners, could all usefully inform thinking (O'Malley, 2014). Importantly, the dance metaphor highlights that

> relationship management is not something that one firm does to another in a stimulus response manner, but a two-way process in which initiatives can be taken by either party with each responding to the problems and opportunities of the other.
>
> *Wilkinson & Young, 1994, p. 75*

Conclusion

RM has influenced the marketing discourse to such an extent that there has undoubtedly been a rhetorical shift from competition and conflict, to mutual cooperation and interdependence (Sheth & Parvatiyar, 1995). The language of transactions has also been eschewed in favor of the management of marketing relationships (Dwyer *et al.*, 1987; Hunt & Menon, 1995; Webster, 1992). Much of the appeal of RM for the mainstream has been that relational approaches frame marketing in a positive light (Fischer & Bristor, 1994; Fitchett & McDonagh, 2000; Smith & Higgins, 2000) creating the potential for win-win outcomes for all market actors (Morgan & Hunt, 1994). RM is often seen as 'a more progressive concept for marketing and a more progressive discourse for consumers' (Fitchett & McDonagh, 2000, p. 211). Despite this, RM has not emerged as the dominant discourse in marketing, rather, it co-exists alongside the more traditional marketing management discourse, and the newer hybrid discourse of CRM. This is because although the language and values introduced by relational perspective are inherently appealing, so too is the assumption that relationships can be effectively managed by the seller. However, 'we must question the view that a company can develop its own independent, entrepreneurial strategy at all, or that a supplier should, or even can develop its own general or customer-specific marketing mix to business customers' (Ford & Håkansson, 2006, p. 252). Recent thinking challenges the manageability of markets and/or marketing (Ford & Mouzas, 2013; Håkansson, 2006; Ford & Håkansson, 2006; O'Malley, 2014; Wilkinson & Young, 2013) and is thus deserving of greater attention within the academy.

The discussion highlighted that the distance between domains differs for each context in which the metaphor is applied. In situations that 'actually feature an interpersonal relationship, either between an employee of a buying organization and an employee of a selling organization, or between an employee of a service organization and a customer' (O'Malley *et al.*, 2008, p. 172), there is insufficient *between-domains distance* for the process of metaphoric transfer to be creative. While *between-domains distance* between firm-to-firm and marriage initially appeared to be sufficient, the use of social exchange theory reduced the *within-domain distance* to such an extent that it served to do little more than make 'the familiar more familiar'.

A number of alternative metaphors have been offered which might re-invigorate our thinking about exchange in different contexts. In contrast to extant use of the marriage metaphor, both alternatives eschew simplistic assumptions that interactions can be 'managed' by one of the partners, or that those interactions are part of an inevitable deterministic process toward greater interdependence. Thus, further attention is directed toward the inherent unmanageability of many exchange situations and to interrogate what this might mean for contemporary theory and practice in marketing.

References

Aggarwal, P. (2004). The effects of brand relationship norms on consumer attitudes and behavior. *Journal of Consumer Research*, *31*(June), 87–101.
Alajoutsijärvi, K., Eriksson, P., & Tikkanen, H. (2001). Dominant metaphors in the IMP network discourse: 'The network as a marriage' and 'the network as a business system'. *International Business Review*, *10*(1), 91–107.
Allen, V., & Van de Vliert, E. (1984). *Role transitions: Expectations and explanations*. London, Plenum Press.
Alvesson, M., & Willmott, H. (1996). *Making sense of management: A critical analysis*. London, Sage.
Anderson, E., & Jap, S.D. (2005). The dark side of close relationships. *MIT Sloan Management Review*, *46*(3), 75–82.
Anderson, H., Havila, V., Andersen, P., & Halinen, A. (1998). Position and role: Conceptualizing dynamics in business networks. *Scandinavian Journal of Management*, *14*(3), 167–186.
Anderson, J.C., & Narus, J.A. (1984). A model of the distributor's perspective of distributor–manufacturer working relationships. *Journal of Marketing*, *48*(Fall), 62–74.
Andriessen, D., & Gubbins, C. (2009). Metaphor analysis as an approach for exploring theoretical concepts: The case of social capital. *Organization Studies*, *30*(8), 845–863.

Arndt, J. (1983). The political economy paradigm: Foundation for theory building in marketing. *Journal of Marketing, 47*(4), 44–54.

Arndt, J. (1985). On making marketing science more scientific: Role of orientations, paradigms, metaphors, and puzzle solving. *Journal of Marketing, 49*(3), 11–23.

Barnes, J.G. (1994). Close to the customer: But is it really a relationship? *Journal of Marketing Management, 10*(7), 561–570.

Bejou, D. (1997). Relationship marketing: Evolution, present state, and future. *Psychology & Marketing, 14*(18), 727–736.

Blocker, C.P., Houston, M.B., & Flint, D.J. (2011). Unpacking what a 'relationship' means to commercial buyers: How the relationship metaphor creates tension and obscures experience. *Journal of Consumer Research, 38*(5), 886–908.

Bolton, R.N., Smith, A.K., & Wagner, J. (2003). Striking the right balance: Designing service to enhance business-to-business relationships. *Journal of Service Research, 5*(4), 271–291.

Bonnemaizon, A., Cova, B., & Louyot, M.C. (2007). Relationship marketing in 2015: A delphi approach. *European Management Journal, 25*(1), 50–59.

Borys, B., & Jemison, D.B. (1989). Hybrid arrangements as strategic alliances: Theoretical issues in organizational combinations. *Academy of Management Review, 14*(2), 234–249.

Boulding, W., Staelin, R., Ehret, M., & Johnston, W.J. (2005). A customer relationship management roadmap: What is known, potential pitfalls, and where to go. *Journal of Marketing, 69*(4), pp. 155–166.

Broderick, A. (1999). Role theory and the management of service encounters. *The Services Industries Journal, 19*(2), 117–131.

Brown, R.H. (1976). Social theory as metaphor: On the logic of discovery for the sciences of conduct. *Theory and Society, 3*(2), 169–197.

Brown, S. (2008). Are marketing's metaphors good for it? *The Marketing Review, 8*(3), 209–221.

Camarero, C., Antón, C., & Carrero, M. (2010). Relationship exit in different legal environments: A cross-cultural analysis. *The Service Industries Journal, 30*(9), 1457–1478.

Celuch, K.G., Bantham, J.H., & Kasouf, C.J. (2006). An extension of the marriage metaphor in buyer-seller relationships: An exploration of individual level process dynamics. *Journal of Business Research, 59*(5), 573–581.

Copulsky, J.R., & Wolf, M.J. (1990). Relationship marketing: Positioning for the future. *Journal of Business Strategy, 11*(4), 16–20.

Cornelissen, J.P. (2003). Metaphor as a method in the domain of marketing. *Psychology & Marketing, 20*(3), 209–225.

Cornelissen, J.P. (2004). What are we playing at? Theatre, organization, and the use of metaphor. *Organization Studies, 25*(5), 705–726.

Cornelissen, J.P. (2005). Beyond compare: Metaphor in organization theory. *Academy of Management Review, 30*(4), 751–764.

Cornelissen, J.P., & Kafouros, M. (2008). Metaphors and theory building in organization theory: What determines the impact of a metaphor on theory? *British Journal of Management, 19*(4), 365–379.

Cornelissen, J.P., Oswick, C., Thøger Christensen, L., & Phillips, N. (2008). Metaphor in organizational research: Context, modalities and implications for research—Introduction. *Organization Studies, 29*(1), 7–22.

Dall'Olmo Riley, F., & De Chernatony, L. (2000). The service brand as relationships builder. *British Journal of Management, 11*(2), 137–150.

Davies, G., & Chun, R. (2003). The use of metaphor in the exploration of the brand concept. *Journal of Marketing Management, 19*(1–2), 45–71.

Deighton, J.A., & Blattberg, R.C. (1991). Interactive marketing: Exploiting the age of addressability. *Sloan Management Review, 33*(1), 5–14.

Deighton, J., & Kornfeld, L. (2009). Interactivity's unanticipated consequences for marketers and marketing. *Journal of Interactive Marketing, 23*(1), 4–10.

Dixon, D.F., & Blois, K.J. (1983). *Some limitations of the 4P's as a paradigm for marketing*. Presented at the Marketing Education Group Annual Conference, Cranfield Institute of Technology, UK, July.

Du Gay, P.D., Salaman, G., & Rees, B. (1996). The conduct of management and the management of conduct: Contemporary managerial discourse and the constitution of the 'competent' manager. *Journal of Management Studies, 33*(3), 263–282.

Dwyer, F.R., Schurr, P.H., & Oh, S. (1987). Developing buyer-seller relationships. *Journal of Marketing, 51*(2), 11–27.

Egan, J. (2003). Back to the future: Divergence in relationship marketing research. *Marketing Theory*, *3*(1), 145–157.

El-Ansary, A.I., & Stern, L.W. (1972). Power measurement in the distribution channel. *Journal of Marketing*, *38*(1), 47–52.

Fillis, I., & Rentschler, R. (2008). Exploring metaphor as an alternative marketing language. *European Business Review*, *20*(6), 492–514.

Fischer, E., & Bristor, J. (1994). A feminist poststructural analysis of the rhetoric of marketing relationships. *International Journal of Research in Marketing*, *11*(4), 317–331.

Fisk, R.P., & Grove, S.J. (1996). Applications of impression management and the drama metaphor in marketing: An introduction. *European Journal of Marketing*, *30*(9), 6–12.

Fitchett, J.A., & McDonagh, P. (2000). A citizen's critique of relationship marketing in risk society. *Journal of Strategic Marketing*, *8*(2), 209–222.

Ford, D. (1980). The development of buyer-seller relationships in industrial markets. *European Journal of Marketing*, *14*(5/6), 339–353.

Ford, D. (2011). IMP and service-dominant logic: Divergence, convergence and development. *Industrial Marketing Management*, *40*(2), 231–239.

Ford, D., & Håkansson, H. (2006). IMP – Some things achieved: Much more to do. *European Journal of Marketing*, *40*(3/4), 248–258.

Ford, D., & Mouzas, S. (2013). The theory and practice of business networking. *Industrial Marketing Management*, *42*(3), 433–442.

Fournier, S. (1998). Consumers and their brands: Developing relationship theory in consumer research. *Journal of Consumer Research*, *24*(4), 343–353.

Fournier, S., & Yao, J.L. (1997). Reviving brand loyalty: A reconceptualization within the framework of consumer–brand relationships. *International Journal of Research in Marketing*, *14*(5), 451–72.

Fournier, S., & Lee, L. (2009). Getting brand communities right. *Harvard Business Review*, *87*(4), 105–111.

Fournier, S., Dobscha, S., & Mick, D.G. (1998). Preventing the premature death of relationship marketing. *Harvard Business Review*, *76*(1), 42–51.

Goffman, E. (1983). The interaction order. *American Sociological Review*, *48*(1), 1–17.

Goodwin, C. (1996). Moving the drama into the factory: The contribution of metaphors to services research. *European Journal of Marketing*, *30*(9), 13–36.

Grayson, K., & Ambler, T. (1999). The dark side of long-term relationships in marketing services. *Journal of Marketing Research*, *36*(1), 132–141.

Grönroos, C. (1982). *Strategic management and marketing in the service sector*. Helsingfors, Finland, Swedish School of Economics and Business Administration.

Grönroos, C. (1994). Quo vadis, marketing? Toward a relationship marketing paradigm. *Journal of Marketing Management*, *10*(5), 347–360.

Gruen, T.W. (1995). The outcome set of relationship marketing in consumer markets. *International Business Review*, *4*(4), 447–469.

Gruen, T.W., Summers, J.O., & Acito, F. (2000). Relationship marketing activities, commitment, and membership behaviors in professional associations. *Journal of Marketing*, *64*(3), 34–49.

Guillet de Monthoux, R.B.L. (1975). Organizational mating and industrial marketing conservatism: Some reasons why industrial marketing managers resist marketing theory. *Industrial Marketing Management*, *4*(1), 25–36.

Gummesson, E. (1987). The new marketing: Developing long-term interactive relationships. *Long Range Planning*, *20*(4), 10–20.

Gummesson, E. (2002). Relationship marketing in the new economy. *Journal of Relationship Marketing*, *1*(1), 37–57.

Håkansson, H. (Ed.) (1982). *International marketing and purchasing of industrial goods: An interaction approach*. Chichester, Wiley.

Håkansson, H. (Ed.) (2002). *Industrial technological development: A network approach*. London, Croom Helm.

Håkansson, H. (2006). Business relationships and networks: Consequences for economic policy. *Antitrust Bulletin*, *51*(1), 143–163.

Håkansson, H., & Snehota, I. (1989). No business is an island: The network concept of business strategy. *Scandinavian Journal of Management*, *5*(3), 187–200.

Håkansson, H., Ford, D., Gadde, L.-E., Snehota, I., & Waluszewski, A. (2009). *Business in networks*. Chichester, John Wiley & Sons.

Halinen, A., & Tähtinen, J. (2002). A process theory of relationship ending. *International Journal of Service Industry Management, 13*(2), 163–180.

Harker, M.J., & Egan, J. (2006). The past, present and future of relationship marketing. *Journal of Marketing Management, 22*(1–2), 215–242.

Haytko, D.L. (2004). Firm-to-firm and interpersonal relationships: Perspectives from advertising agency account managers. *Journal of the Academy of Marketing Science, 32*(3), 312–328.

Heikkinen, M.T., Mainela, T., Still, J., & Tähtinen, J. (2007). Roles for managing in mobile service development nets. *Industrial Marketing Management, 36*(7), 909–925.

Hennig-Thurau, T., Malthouse, E.C., Friege, C., Gensler, S., Lobschat, L., Rangaswamy, A., & Skiera, B. (2010). The impact of new media on customer relationships. *Journal of Service Research, 13*(3), 311–330.

Hibbard, J.D., Brunel, F.F., Dant, R.P., & Iacobucci, D. (2001). Does relationship marketing age well? *Business Strategy Review, 12*(4), 29–35.

Hocutt, M.A. (1998). Relationship dissolution model: Antecedents of relationship commitment and the likelihood of dissolving a relationship. *International Journal of Service Industry Management, 9*(2), 189–200.

Homans, G.C. (1950). *The Human Group*. New York, Harcourt Brace.

Hunt, S.D., & Menon, A. (1995). Metaphors and competitive advantage: Evaluating the use of metaphors in theories of competitive strategy. *Journal of Business Research, 33*(2), 81–90.

Iacobucci, D., & Ostrom, A. (1996). Commercial and interpersonal relationships using the structure of interpersonal relationships to understand individual-to-individual, individual-to-firm, and firm-to-firm relationships in commerce. *International Journal of Research in Marketing, 13*(1), 53–72.

Johnsen, R.E., & Lacoste, S. (2016). An exploration of the 'dark side' associations of conflict, power and dependence in customer–supplier relationships. *Industrial Marketing Management, 59*(November), 76–95.

Kent, R.A. (1986). Faith in the 4Ps: An alternative. *Journal of Marketing Management, 2*(2), 145–154.

Kietzmann, J.H., Hermkens, K., McCarthy, I.P., & Silvestre, B.S. (2011). Social media? Get serious! Understanding the functional building blocks of social media. *Business Horizons, 54*(3), 241–251.

Knight, L., & Harland, C. (2005). Managing supply networks: Organisational roles in network management. *European Management Journal, 22*(3), 281–295.

Kotler, P., & Singh, R. (1981). Marketing warfare in the 1980s. *The Journal of Business Strategy, 1*(3), 30–41.

Kozinets, R.V. (1999). The strategic implications of virtual communities of consumption. *European Management Journal, 17*(3), 252–265.

Lakoff, G., & Johnson, M. (1980). *Metaphors we live by*. Chicago, University of Chicago Press.

Levitt, T. (1983). *The marketing imagination*. New York, The Free Press.

MacNeil, I.R. (1980). *The new social contract: An inquiry into modern contractual relations*. New Haven, Yale University Press.

McCall, M. (1966). Courtship as social exchange: Some historical comparisons. In B. Farber (Ed.), *Kinship and Family Organization* (pp. 190–210). New York, John Wiley & Sons.

Mitussis, D., O'Malley, L., & Patterson, M. (2006). Mapping the re-engagement of CRM with relationship marketing. *European Journal of Marketing, 40*(5/6), 572–589.

Möller, K. (2013). Theory map of business marketing: Relationships and networks perspectives. *Industrial Marketing Management, 42*(3), 324–335.

Möller, K., & Halinen, A. (2000). Relationship marketing theory: Its roots and direction. *Journal of Marketing Management, 16*(1–3), 29–54.

Möller, K., Rajala, A., & Svahn, S. (2005). Strategic business nets: Their type and management. *Journal of Business Research, 58*(9), 1274–1284.

Montgomery, J.D. (1998). Toward a role-theoretic conception of embeddedness. *American Journal of Sociology, 104*(1), 92–125.

Moorman, C., Zaltman, G., & Deshpande, R. (1992). Relationships between providers and users of market research: The dynamics of trust within and between organizations. *Journal of Marketing Research, 29*(3), 314–328.

Morgan, G. (1980). Paradigms, metaphors, and puzzle solving in organization theory. *Administrative Science Quarterly, 25*(4), 605–622.

Morgan, G. (1983). More on metaphor: Why we cannot control tropes in administrative science. *Administrative Science Quarterly, 28*(4), 601–607.

Morgan, R.M., & Hunt, S.D. (1994). The commitment-trust theory of relationship marketing. *Journal of Marketing, 58*(3), 20–38.

O'Malley, L. (2014). Relational marketing: Development, debates and directions. *Journal of Marketing Management, 30*(11–12), 1220–1238.

O'Malley, L., & Mitussis, D. (2002). Relationships and technology: Strategic implications. *Journal of Strategic Marketing, 10*(3), 225–238.

O'Malley, L., & Patterson, M. (1998). Vanishing point: The mix management paradigm re-viewed. *Journal of Marketing Management, 14*(8), 829–851.

O'Malley, L., & Tynan, C. (1999). The utility of the relationship metaphor in consumer markets: A critical evaluation. *Journal of Marketing Management, 15*(7), 587–602.

O'Malley, L., & Tynan, C. (2000). Relationship marketing in consumer markets: Rhetoric or reality? *European Journal of Marketing, 34*(7), 797–815.

O'Malley, L., Patterson, M., & Kelly-Holmes, H. (2008). Death of a metaphor: Reviewing the marketing as relationships' frame. *Marketing Theory, 8*(2), 167–187.

O'Malley, L., Patterson, M., & Evans, M. (1997). Intimacy or intrusion? The privacy dilemma for relationship marketing in consumer markets. *Journal of Marketing Management, 13*(6), 541–559.

Parvatiyar, A., & Sheth, J.N. (2000). The domain and conceptual foundations of relationship marketing. In J.N. Sheth & A. Parvatiyar (Eds.), *Handbook of Relationship Marketing* (pp. 3–38). Thousand Oaks, Sage.

Patterson, M., & O'Malley, L. (2006). Brands, consumers and relationships: A review. *Irish Marketing Review, 18*(1/2), 10–20.

Payne, A., & Frow, P. (2005). A strategic framework for customer relationship management. *Journal of Marketing, 69*(4), 167–176.

Perrien, J., Paradis, S., & Banting, P.M. (1995). Dissolution of a relationship: The salesforce perception. *Industrial Marketing Management, 24*(4), 317–327.

Ries, A., & Trout, J. (1986). Marketing warfare. *Journal of Consumer Marketing, 3*(4), 77–82.

Rindfleisch, A. (1996). Marketing as warfare: Reassessing a dominant metaphor. *Business Horizons, 39*(5), 3–10.

Scanzoni, J. (1979). Social exchange and behavioral inter-dependence. In R.L. Burgess & T.L. Huston (Eds.), *Social exchange in developing relationships*. New York, Academic Press, Inc.

Semino, E., & Masci, M. (1996). Politics is football: Metaphor in the discourse of Silvio Berlusconi in Italy. *Discourse & Society, 7*(2), 243–269.

Sheaves, D.E., & Barnes, J.G. (1996). The fundamentals of relationships: An exploration of the concept to guide marketing implementation. *Advances in Services Marketing and Management, 5*, 215–245.

Sheth, J.N., & Parvatiyar, A. (1995). The evolution of relationship marketing. *International Business Review, 4*(4), 397–418.

Sheth, J.N., & Parvatiyar, A. (2002). Evolving relationship marketing into a discipline. *Journal of Relationship Marketing, 1*(1), 3–16.

Smith, W., & Higgins, M. (2000). Reconsidering the relationship analogy. *Journal of Marketing Management, 16*(1–3), 81–94.

Snehota, I., & Håkansson, H. (Eds.) (1995). *Developing relationships in business networks*. London, Routledge.

Snow, C., Miles, R., & Coleman, H.J. Jr. (1992). Managing 21st century network organizations. *Organisational Dynamics, 20*(3), 5–20.

Solomon, M.R., Surprenant, C., Czepiel, J.A., & Gutman, E.G. (1985). A role theory perspective on dyadic interactions: The service encounter. *Journal of Marketing, 49*(1), 99–111.

Story, V., O'Malley, L., & Hart, S. (2011). Roles, role performance, and radical innovation competences. *Industrial Marketing Management, 40*(6), 952–966.

Thibaut, J.W., & Kelley, H.H. (1959). *The social psychology of groups*. New York, John Wiley.

Trout, J., & Ries, A. (1986). *Marketing warfare*. London, McGraw-Hill.

Tushman, M.L. (1977). Special boundary roles in the innovation process. *Administrative Science Quarterly, 22*(4), 587–605.

Tynan, C. (1997). A review of the marriage analogy in relationship marketing. *Journal of Marketing Management, 13*(7), 695–703.

van den Bulte, C. (1994). Metaphor at work. In G. Lillien & B. Pras (Eds.), *Research traditions in marketing* (pp. 405–434). Netherlands, Springer.

van Waterschoot, W., & van den Bulte, C. (1992). The 4P classification of the marketing mix revisited. *Journal of Marketing, 56*(October), 83–93.

Webster Jr, F.E. (1992). The changing role of marketing in the corporation. *Journal of Marketing, 56*(4), 1–17.

Weick, K.E. (1989). Theory construction as disciplined imagination. *Academy of Management Review, 14*(4), 516–531.

Wilkinson, I.F., & Young, L. (1994). Business dancing: An alternative paradigm for relationship marketing. *Asia-Australia Marketing Journal, 2*(1), 67–80.

Wilkinson, I.F., & Young, L.C. (2013). The past and the future of business marketing theory. *Industrial Marketing Management, 42*(3), 394–404.

Winsor, R.D. (1995). Marketing under conditions of chaos: Percolation metaphors and models. *Journal of Business Research, 34*(3), 181–189.

Zaltman, G., LeMasters, K., & Heffring, M. (1982). *Theory construction in marketing: Some thoughts on thinking.* Chichester, John Wiley & Sons.

15
CRITICAL PERSPECTIVES ON ETHICAL CONSUMPTION

Michal Carrington and Andreas Chatzidakis

Introduction

A growing research agenda critically examines the notions of sustainable and ethical consumption. This body of research looks beyond the practices and contradictions of individuals attempting to consume more ethically and sustainably, to critically examine how such attempts are embedded within broader socio-economic, discursive and institutional contexts. We take an interdisciplinary perspective in this chapter, to examine key contextual threads that are emerging in critical studies across disciplines. We then synthesize this emerging body of research to lay out directions for future conceptual and empirical research.

We find five key threads developing across the emergent literature that takes a critical lens to ethical and sustainable consumption. First, it is observed that as sites of ethical and sustainable production and consumption become increasingly mainstream – such as Fair Trade, local food systems and the living wage movement – these domains often shift from spaces of responsible production and equitable exchange to vehicles for growth and competitive advantage when appropriated, marketized and governed by neoliberal corporate interests (Dolan, 2010; Humphrey, 2016; Varul, 2008), and re-framed in the market logics of sustainable growth (Chatzidakis, Larsen & Bishop, 2014).

A second thread contests the notions of 'ethical' and 'sustainable' consumption – particularly when embedded in growth-oriented business logics, suggesting that humanity cannot turbo-consume its way to global sustainability, even when this consumption is draped with the legitimating guise of 'ethical' or 'sustainable' (e.g. Chatzidakis *et al.*, 2014). For example, Soper (2008) illustrates the social and environmental destructiveness of reproducing Western ideals of the 'good life' to fuel relentless corporate growth through increased consumption – even when labeled ethical or sustainable – in both affluent and developing communities. It is also noted that in its current Westernized version, 'ethical' consumption is broadly accessible only in the domains of the affluent and middle classes (Soper, 2016; Humphrey, 2016), and the consumerist societies of the Global North (Cotte & Trudel, 2009; Kleine, 2016; Luetchford, 2016; McEwan, Hughes & Bek, 2015).

A third thread observes that the dynamic relationships between producers and consumers in ethical/sustainable consumption exchanges are complex, contextual, and often governed by incommensurate logics of citizenship and capitalism. Humphrey (2016) suggests that opportunities to consume ethically are "fleeting" and that: "Much of what passes for ethical products remain nothing of the sort, while many ethical purchases remain only vaguely oppositional, if at all" (p. 151). Inevitably, broader questions are often raised about the emergence of the consumer-citizen as the appropriate agent for socio-economic change (see Bauman, 2009) and the extent to which alternative vocabularies and imaginaries are urgently needed. Graeber (2011), for instance, traces the genealogical threads of consumption, ultimately suggesting that the very employment of words such as (ethical) 'consumer' and 'consumption' means aligning with the agenda of neoliberalism.

A fourth interrelated research thread suggests that by 'responsibilizing' the individual consumer to choose ethically under the guise of consumer sovereignty and freedom of choice, while strictly controlling choice within capitalist growth agendas and admonishing consumers when they fail to enact their ethical consumption intentions within these constraints, firms create an illusion of potential salvation from the juggernaut of excessive consumption through even more consumption (Bradshaw & Zwick, 2016; Carrington, Zwick & Neville, 2016; Denegri-Knott, Zwick & Schroeder, 2006; Littler, 2011). In contrast to this mythical salvation from the externalities of turbo-consumption capitalism, however, these illusions of ethical/sustainable consumption and the fetishization of the ethical consumption 'gap' are actually working to compound the economic, social and environmental externalities of the consumerist capitalism context that ethical/sustainable consumption sits within; such as the increasing wealth divisions between the world's affluent and the world's poor, runaway climate change and the mental health issues increasingly characterizing consumerist societies (Bradshaw & Zwick, 2016; Carrington et al., 2016; Soper, 2016). Studies within this critical genre of ethical consumption research are looking beyond the choices and contradictions of individual consumers, to focus their sights on the underlying capitalist structures that create and benefit from the distractionary illusion of individualized ethical consumption – corporations (e.g. Giesler & Veresiu, 2014; Carrington et al., 2016; Kleine, 2016). This critical research thread looks beyond the myth of the sovereign ethical consumer to the structural context – corporations and their corporate social responsibility (CSR) programs.

Finally, we observe a stream of research that critically examines the intellectual and methodological traditions that underline current academic understandings of ethical and sustainable consumption. For instance, Chatzidakis (2015) notes how much of the current research remains preoccupied with socio-cognitive models of ethical decision-making assuming that consumers are agentic and rational. Somewhat provocatively, he draws insights from psychoanalysis to argue the opposite: that most consumers are largely irrational and the reasons why they consume (un)ethically might completely escape their awareness. On the methodological front, Carrington et al. (2016) note how implicit in current empirical approaches to narrowing consumers' "attitude-behavior gap" is that ethical considerations are (and should be) mediated by the marketplace, entirely ignoring the potential of different rationalities that operate in other spheres of social life.

Synthesizing these cross-disciplinary threads arising from critiques of ethical and sustainable consumption, we propose directives for future cross-disciplinary research that dissolve dichotomous boundaries and binary categorizations – such as producer/consumer and Global North/Global South. In doing so, we aim to bring sites of consumption and production together – physically and virtually – to reduce the aesthetic distance, create shared meanings, and to facilitate shifts in the loci of choice and power. We also advocate research agendas that explore alternative systems of provision and consumption as a counterpoint to the dominant logic of sustainable growth and the fetishization of the 'ethical consumption gap'.

Mainstreaming and co-optation: diluting the ethicality of consumption and production

It is observed that as sites of ethical and sustainable production and consumption become increasingly mainstream – such as Fair Trade, local food systems and the living wage movement – these domains often shift from spaces of responsible production and equitable exchange to vehicles for growth and competitive advantage when appropriated, marketized and governed by neoliberal corporate interests (Dolan, 2010; Humphrey, 2016; Varul, 2008), and re-framed in the market logics of sustainable growth (Chatzidakis et al., 2014).

Decommodification perspectives (e.g. Lekakis, 2012) – that directly link producers and consumers in alternative systems of trade – underpin a growing field of alternative market projects and trading practices (Parsons, Maclaran & Chatzidakis, 2017). Examples such as community-supported agriculture projects (e.g. Thompson & Coskuner-Balli, 2007), direct trade with indigenous Zapatistas farmers in the Chiapas region of Mexico (Chatzidakis, Maclaran & Bradshaw, 2012), and the variety of Fair Trade initiatives illustrate decommodification perspectives in action. There is significant divergence, however, in the extent to which these seemingly alternative production and trading systems challenge and operate outside of the dominant capitalist market system. For instance, systems of 'Fair Trade' are broadly represented as an example of decommodification principles in practice, where Fair Trade items are produced, exchanged and consumed outside of the dominant market structures. When cast under a more critical lens, however, Fair Trade systems and initiatives are often assessed as limited in capacity to develop alternative economic relationships, and for the greater part operate within the dominant market structures (Humphrey, 2016). In this assessment, Fair Trade initiatives divert from decommodification principles in that the trade and economic relationship between producers and consumers is generally indirect – mediated by mainstream market actors such as supermarket chains and multinational retailers, and promoted by neoliberal growth imperatives (Parsons, Maclaran & Chatzidakis, 2017; Fridell, 2006). Further, Fair Trade labeling and products can be critically viewed as being instruments of *guilt fetishism* (Cremin, 2012) for relatively affluent Western consumers. As objects of guilt fetish, Fair Trade labeled products are harnessed by wealthy Western consumers as symbolic vessels of ethical virtue to neutralize the sense of guilt experienced from the acknowledgment of the real social and economic consequences of their consumption choices (Parsons et al., 2017).

The appropriation of alternative systems of exchange and consumption into mainstream market structures is often explained through the lens of co-optation theory (e.g. Holt, 2002). Co-optation theory suggests that in scenarios where practices of consumer resistance are embedded within the dominant market logic, these practices are vulnerable to annexation, commodification and commercialization by dominant marketplace stakeholders. In this light, production, exchange and consumption practices that are initiated to resist hegemonic market structures and to create alternative systems of provision, are ironically also creative resources that can be harnessed by powerful marketplace actors to fuel the innovation of new faux counter-cultural and alternative commodities – the fodder of hipster and the essence of commodified cool (Parsons et al., 2017). These co-optation moves are evident in *cool hunting*, where commercial interests seek out and infiltrate fringe counter-cultures and alternative consumer tribes, then emulating counter-cultural sensibilities within mainstream offerings to attract elusive and lucrative market segments. Thus, co-optation theory takes a highly critical view of decommodification projects – such as Fair Trade, suggesting that operating outside of the mainstream market and economic structures is not possible, at least not in a sustained manner (Humphrey, 2016). Rather, such practices of decommodification and resistance are very often appropriated to serve as resources that prop up the dominant market structures and are annexed and converted into mainstream market commodities.

It is suggested, however, that intimate and localized alternative provision and consumption projects can be small enough, and sufficiently divergent from the operations of mainstream markets, to remain invisible to commercial interests seeking growth opportunities (Thompson & Coskuner-Balli, 2007). These human-scale initiatives – such as local food networks – remain a derivative of the prevailing economic system, yet also further remove their participants from unintended ecological and socio-economic consequences of provision and consumption. These small-scale decommodification initiatives also allow for experimentation outside of marketplace norms, and for creating cracks in dominant capitalist systems and logics (Holloway, 2010); it is these cracks that allow a break away from the amoral sensitivities of mainstream commodification and consumption (Chatzidakis et al., 2012) and toward more genuinely progressive ethics in consumption.

The embeddedness of ethical consumerism within consumer culture

A second thread contests the notions of 'ethical' and 'sustainable' consumption – particularly when embedded in growth-oriented business logics, suggesting that humanity cannot turbo-consume its way to global sustainability even (or especially) when this consumption is draped with the legitimating guise of 'ethical' or 'sustainable' (e.g. Chatzidakis et al., 2014; Carrington et al., 2016). From this perspective, ethical consumption embedded within the prevailing marketplace works to moderate some of the concerning externalities of consumption, while falling short of posing a meaningful challenge to the Western culture of excessive consumption and the dominant growth-oriented economic logic. Indeed, the limits of embedded ethical consumption have been illustrated by the efforts of current societies falling short of meeting even the modest climate change targets developed through the 1992 Kyoto Protocol and 2015 Paris Agreement. This perspective underpins two juxtaposed critical arguments: first we examine the degrowth agenda; and, second, the contrasting argument for the negation of the dominant systems of provision through excessive consumption.

One stream of critical thought proposes a *degrowth* agenda in response to the severe social and environmental consequences of the dominant growth-orientation of modern economies. Degrowth promotes decreased levels of aggregate consumption – a shift from 'ethical' consumption at sustained levels to significantly reducing consumption. This conception of market shrinkage rather than market growth is in stark contrast to the neoliberal growth agenda that draws on increasing levels of natural resources and production to meet stimulated growth in consumer demand (Chatzidakis et al., 2014). Thus, degrowth "does not only challenge the centrality of GDP as an overarching policy objective but proposes a framework for transformation to a lower and sustainable level of production and consumption, a shrinking of the economic system to leave more space for human cooperation and ecosystems" (www.degrowth.org/definition-2). This vision of production and consumption degrowth is not entirely opposed to ethical consumption. The degrowth approach advocates the reassessment and localization of everyday consumption practices and asserts a civic-minded focus on care and sharing within communities (e.g. Latouche, 2009), which also underpin common concerns of ethical consumption movements. Indeed, the degrowth model of shrinking production and consumption within Western societies is closely aligned with the ethos and practice defined in consumer research as *voluntary simplicity*, otherwise labeled as *downshifting* (e.g. Shaw & Newholm, 2002). Similarly, philosopher Kate Soper (2008, 2016) illustrates the social and environmental destructiveness of reproducing Western ideals of the *good life* to fuel relentless corporate growth through increased levels of consumption – even when labeled ethical or sustainable – in both affluent and developing communities. Soper's (2008, 2016) vision of *alternative hedonism* describes an alternative rendering of the modern good life which eschews the materialism and excessive consumption of neoliberal consumer culture, in favor of a life rich in other sources of meaning and experience.

Similarly, and critically, to Chatzidakis *et al.* (2014), consumption is still consumption even when labeled as ethical or sustainable. Chatzidakis *et al.* (2014) argue that business and institutionally driven campaigns urging consumers to switch their consumption choices to more ethical or sustainable options are still underpinned by the neoliberal growth imperative. While these alternative consumption choices might be more sustainable in nature or reduce harm in provisioning systems, aggregate consumption is maintained, as are many of the externalities and unintended consequences intrinsically linked to consumption in any form. This study explicitly juxtaposes the radical degrowth model for shrinking production and consumption with more mainstream campaigns advocating ethical and sustainable consumption. These contrasts are illustrated in Table 15.1.

Aligned with Soper's (2008, 2016) shift in the loci of meaning-making within society from consumption to alternative forms of hedonism, Chatzidakis *et al.* (2014) characterize societal shifts toward the degrowth model as post- or de-consumerism. Central to this analysis of post-consumerism is the rejection of consumption as a meaningful act in and of itself. As Table 15.1 illustrates, the core focus of post-consumerist society is in forms of collective consumption that are built on community participation, sharing and the re-imagining of local communities.

Taking a critical lens to examine ethical consumption as it is currently practiced and understood, Carrington *et al.* (2016) offer a contrasting yet complementary view to that of the degrowth movement. They notionally contend that the route to revolutionize or negate the dominant economic system based on consumption and production growth is not through current practices of ethical consumption. Indeed, they argue that current practices of ethical consumption and production embedded within capitalist systems work to reinforce, rather than deconstruct, the destructive capitalist systems of provision. They draw on Marcuse's (1972) contention that the capitalist consumer with an aggregate consumption desire that is perpetually in excess of production capacity – where demand outstrips supply in a growth economy – has the potential to become capitalism's gravedigger. The excessive consumption demand that is central to the capitalist growth imperative, could also represent a significant threat to the capitalist system that it is embedded within. The leading role of consumption in bringing the planet to the edge of ecological catastrophe is evidence of this claim (Chomsky, 1999; Klein, 2014). Thus, it is argued, capitalist growth-focused consumption also harbors the potential to bring down the capitalist system – a threat from within. A threat that also has the potential to irrevocably bring down the global ecological system.

The power of consumption to change the system has attracted the attention of consumers, academics and capitalist institutions, who ask how can consumption practices be harnessed and diverted to bring about more equitable, ecological and ethical systems of provision and consumption – still consuming, just more ethically (Harrison, Shaw & Newholm, 2005; Jones, 2012; Micheletti & McFarland, 2011; Stolle & Micheletti, 2013). Ironically, if excessive capitalist consumption holds the potential to negate the capitalist structures of which it is a product, then this shift to ethical as an alternative consumption could save capitalism from self-destruction (Carrington *et al.*, 2016). From this perspective, an unintended consequence of ethical consumption – when practiced as alternative forms of consumption – is to inadvertently save capitalism from bringing about its own destruction by reinforcing capitalist systems of consumption. Taking this view, Carrington *et al.* (2016, p. 23) note that "ethical

Table 15.1 Logics of growth in consumption

Countervailing logic	Underpinning assumptions	Actors	Implications for consumption	Identity of the consumer
Cultivated growth	Economic rationality, Adam Smith's invisible hand, neoclassical theories of economics	Multinational, world-wide market elites. Concerned primarily with maximizing economic growth and profitability, and with social order only in relationship to market threats	Use up, use more (when possible) and throw away	'Sovereign Consumer' Self-interested, position in society is defined by conspicuous consumption
Sustainable growth	Market and society interact and impact upon one another	Governments and middle class – those concerned with maintaining social order within existing nation states	Buy ethical and green; reduce, reuse, recycle	'Ethical Consumer' Socially aware, role and identity in society defined by consumption of ethical goods
Degrowth	Society resists the domination of market logics	Consumer-citizens Activists	Do not buy anything, produce what is needed within small communities; alternative hedonism	'Post- and De-consumerist'. Role in society defined by social participation rather than consumption

Source: Chatzidakis et al., 2014, p. 753

consumption promises a solution to a systemic contradiction without challenging the system itself", thus contending that ethical consumption practiced as alternative consumption offers a new and different kind of capitalism that supports, rather than counteracts, the devastating systems of capitalist consumerism. Embedded within neoliberal economic logics, even ethical consumerism must adhere to growth-oriented consumerism.

Carrington et al. (2016, p. 32) pose the question:

> Is the brutally self-interested and singularly desiring consumer that turns an instrument of oppression and destruction – mass consumption – against itself by demanding ever more and pushing the system to the breaking point (Critchley, 2007; Marcuse, 1972) not the true resistance fighter against contemporary neoliberal capitalism and all its excesses?

While this rhetorical device might seem in opposition to the degrowth agenda of radical reduction in aggregate consumption, these positions are in close parallel in their respective views of current ethical consumption practice and marketing, calling for a more radical rejection of neoliberal growth-oriented logic and consumer capitalism. This critical thread views the promise of a more equitable and ecologically sustainable market logic promised by the business and consumer proponents of ethical consumerism as an illusion that stifles a more radical critique and restructuring of the dominant and destructive logic of growth-oriented capitalism.

Shifting lexicons of producer/consumer and consumer/citizen

A third thread observes that the dynamic relationships between producers and consumers in ethical/sustainable consumption exchanges are complex, contextual, and often governed by incommensurate logics of citizenship and capitalism. Inevitably, broader questions are often raised about the emergence of the consumer-citizen as the appropriate agent for socio-economic change (see Bauman, 2009) and the extent to which alternative vocabularies and imaginaries are urgently needed. The neoliberal agenda is revealed when investigating the role that consumerism and consumption play in daily life, in particular the spreading out of these traditional producer–customer exchanges to adjacent spheres of life – such as in hospitals and educational settings (Parsons et al., 2017). For example, increasingly university students are treated as 'consumers' and patients as 'customers' within health settings. This shifting vocabulary gives primacy to consumers rather than citizens, individuals rather than collectives, a self-focus rather than other-directed orientation, and markets rather than communities (Parsons et al., 2017). This contemporary language of neoliberalism works to shape our consciousness, inform our desires, and to recreate and underpin our worldview (Massey, 2013).

Bauman (2009) illustrates the powerful role of this shifting lexicon in his notion of 'liquid modernity' – a contemporary period starting from the late 20th century. To Bauman (2009), the period of liquid modernity is characterized by a shift in Westernized societies from being societies of producers to societies of consumers, in which being labeled and assessed on the basis of our spending power is normalized. This shift has acute implications for how we make sense of our social and material life worlds. This shift also marks a widening of the physical and cognitive divisions between those who produce and those who consume (Parsons et al., 2017). These divisions fuel neoliberal interests in keeping the conditions of production shrouded and invisible to those who consume. Thus, under conditions of liquid modernity, the term 'ethical consumer' is underscored by a separation and distancing from the environmental and social problems within production that this ethical consumer is seeking to solve. Again, the very use of terms such as ethical consumer and ethical consumption align with the contemporary neoliberal schema (Graeber, 2011).

A contrasting, yet aligned, critical perspective is presented by the neo-Marxist school of thought. This perspective gives primacy to the object of consumption itself and the obliviousness – or ambivalence – of affluent consumers in capitalist societies to the social aspects inherent to these consumption objects (Parsons et al., 2017). For Marx, this comes about due to the mystical nature of commodities in capitalist societies: "A commodity appears at first sight an extremely obvious, trivial thing. But its analysis brings out that it is a very strange thing, abounding in metaphysical subtleties and theological niceties" (1976, p. 163). In pre-capitalist societies objects were viewed as products of human labor that were evaluated on their use-value – such as the usefulness of a table to eat on and write on. Once the object is commodified and acquires monetary value to be exchanged in the marketplace, however, the social characteristics of human labor are represented as objective characteristics of the product – such as aesthetics to be represented as monetary value. From this perspective, capitalist commodities are endowed with an autonomous monetary value that is separated from the social elements of production, and are evaluated relative to comparative commodities in the market (Parsons et al., 2017; Carrier, 2010).

Operating under these conditions of distanced production and consumption, we consume in ignorance of the human consequences, rarely pondering how the objects have been produced, by whom, and under what conditions. Thus, from these perspectives, engaging in the ethics of consumption begins with investigating the mechanisms of concealment – why and how social and environmental aspects of production are made invisible in capitalist markets, as well as the consequences of the consumption and production of objects. As David Harvey (1990, p. 423) suggests: "the grapes that sit upon the supermarket shelves are mute; we cannot see the fingers of exploitation upon them or tell immediately what part of the world they are from".

To this end, academic scholars and grassroots activists alike have worked toward the conceptual re-connection of consumers and the producers of their commodities: "to get behind the veil, the fetishism of the market and the commodity, in order to tell the full story of social reproduction" (Harvey, 1990, p. 423). In addition, in the web-connected world the social and environmental impacts within global supply chains are increasingly available, due to the interest of media outlets and the development of well-informed shopping guides, websites and mobile apps. The range of labeling standards such as Fair Trade and organic certifications also work to make the ethical consumer's shopping trip a much easier task (cf. Tadajewski, this volume). It is critically noted, however, that these forms of informed ethical consumption are broadly accessible only in the domains of the affluent and middle classes (Soper, 2016; Humphrey, 2016), and the consumerist societies of the Global North (Cotte & Trudel, 2009; Kleine, 2016; Luetchford, 2016; McEwan et al., 2015). Further, these actions of individual consumer-citizens to research and inform themselves of the ethicality of production and supply chains, could also be viewed as indicative of our era of "individualised collective action", that is "the practice of responsibility-taking . . . on the part of citizens alone or together with others to deal with problems that they believe are affecting what they identify as the good life" (Micheletti, 2003, p. 26). Rosol (2012) critically views this taking on of activities that were once in the domain of the state by citizens as individuals and communities to be a form of unpaid work. He suggests that these responsibilized citizens are often portrayed as agentic and well meaning, and yet are intrinsically caught-up in 'roll-out neoliberalism' where the responsibility of maintaining public space and goods is shifted to the citizen and community. In other words, aligned with the neoliberal agenda are moves to responsibilize the consumer for the ethicalities of production. We now address this critique.

Responsibilizing the consumer

A fourth interrelated research thread suggests that by 'responsibilizing' the individual consumer to choose ethically under the guise of consumer sovereignty and freedom of choice, while strictly controlling choice within capitalist growth agendas, firms create an illusion of potential salvation from the juggernaut of excessive consumption through even more consumption (Denegri-Knott et al., 2006; Littler, 2011). By admonishing consumers when they fail to enact their ethical consumption intentions within these constraints – the ethical consumption 'gap' – powerful entities such as firms and government institutions step back from their responsibilities as key stakeholders. Critical scholars argue that these illusions of ethical/sustainable consumption embedded within growth-oriented neoliberal structures and the fetishization of the ethical consumption 'gap' are actually working to compound the economic, social and environmental externalities of the consumerist capitalism context that ethical/sustainable consumption sits within; such as the increasing wealth divisions between the world's affluent and the poor, runaway climate change, and the mental health issues increasingly characterizing consumerist societies (Bradshaw & Zwick, 2016; Carrington et al., 2016; Soper, 2016). This critical research thread looks beyond the myth of the sovereign ethical consumer to the structural context and the beneficiaries of this illusion – corporations and their CSR programs (e.g. Carrington et al., 2016; Giesler & Veresiu, 2014; Kleine, 2016).

Ethical consumerism embedded within neo-capitalist logics is about individualized solutions to collective problems (Parsons et al., 2017). For many critics, it serves to transfer responsibility from the powerful institutional stakeholders – firms and government – on to individual consumers. For instance, individual consumers are called to step up and shoulder the burden of equitable trading and environmentally sustainable production with Third World producers through the choice to purchase 'Fair Trade', shifting accountability from the stakeholders (e.g. World Trade Organization, International Monetary Fund, multinational corporations) that are responsible for unfair trading arrangements, questionable employment practices and environmental degradation in developing countries in the first place (Parsons et al., 2017). This shift in responsibility toward the individual is underpinned by the parallel shift toward neoliberal marketplace logics.

While traditional forms of capitalism assumed that people possess innate individualistic, competitive and acquisitive traits, neoliberalism assumes that these human characteristics are not necessarily inherent and thus need to be cultivated by dominant institutions such as corporations and the state (Gilbert, 2013). To this end, neoliberalism actively promotes modes of thinking and being that exude entrepreneurial spirit, marketplace freedoms, consumer choice and personal culpability for the consequences of these choices. Within this logic, little attention is paid to structural constraints limiting and manipulating individual action or systemic inequities. Rather, the emphasis is placed on consumer choice as fundamental to an individual's freedoms and well-being (Parsons et al., 2017). This agenda of consumer sovereignty is central to the marketing concept (Denegri-Knott et al., 2006; see also Tadajewski, this volume). Marketing defines consumer sovereignty as "the right to choose among a sufficient range of products so that the particular demand specifications of a particular consumer can be reasonably matched" (Fisk, 1967, p. 680). From this position, firms assess consumer demand to directly produce what consumers want (Narver & Savitt, 1971; Smith, 1987), thus placing the responsibility for produce choice, demand and responsibility directly in the hands – and shopping baskets – of consumers (Dixon, 1992).

The logic of consumer sovereignty has been the subject of significant criticism from within marketing (Tadajewski, 2010). Key criticisms include the challenges to the notion that consumers innately choose and act rationally (e.g. Sherry et al., 2001); that a power imbalance exists between individual consumers and powerful corporations that restricts consumer sovereignty; and that consumer choice is significantly manipulated and limited by the pre-determined range of options that are determined by dominant actors within firms and presented to the consumer at the point of purchase (Fırat, 1996). In sum, sovereignty creates an illusion of consumer choice and agency in the marketplace that masks the manipulative control of corporations and their marketing managers (Hackley, 2003; Smith, 1987). These criticisms place dominant notions of ethical consumption into stark relief. Discourses and representations of ethical consumption represent individual consumers as sovereign actors with the agency – and responsibility – to solve dire environmental and social problems through their consumption choices. This individualization of marketplace power and ethical accountability diverts attention from realization that destructive, negative externalities are inherent to the dominant marketplace system within which these forms of consumption reside (Carrington et al., 2016).

These challenges to dominant notions of ethical consumption are illustrated through consideration of the widely documented ethical consumption 'gap'. For consumers who hold and express ethical concerns regarding production and consumption – such as waste and environmental degradation – this gap represents a failure to follow through with this concern at the cash register (Carrington et al., 2016). The logic of consumer sovereignty suggests that exhibitions of 'the gap' illustrate negligent consumer practices. This gap also enables the belief that the capitalist system can be harnessed to reverse the environmental and social destruction of its own creation. Closing this gap could be the difference between destruction and salvation – if only the responsibilized consumer was not so flawed we would be saved from the severe ills that capitalism produced in the first place. This representation of the gap rests upon flawed assumptions of consumer sovereignty and averts attention from the role of structural forces – corporate and government – in creating the gap (Giesler & Veresiu, 2014; Micheletti & Follesdal, 2007). "In this way, guilt and responsibility are personalized – it is not the entire organization of the economy which is to blame, but our subjective attitude which needs to change" (Žižek, 2010, p. 22). Thus Carrington *et al.* (2016) argue that the notion of the ethical consumption 'gap': "serves an important ideological function to help sustain exactly the kind of neoliberal market rationalities that ethical consumerism and its proponents want to alter" (p. 24). Maintaining the myth and focus on the ethical consumption gap works to maintain the logics and structures of capitalism, rather than evoking meaningful systems change (Bradshaw & Zwick, 2016).

Methodological traditions

Finally, we observe a stream of research that critically examines the intellectual and methodological traditions that underline current academic understandings of ethical and sustainable consumption. For instance, Chatzidakis (2015) notes how much of the current research remains preoccupied with socio-cognitive models of ethical decision-making assuming that consumers are agentic and rational. Instead, he proposes that most consumers are largely irrational and the reasons why they consume (un)ethically might escape their recognition. Even if partly true, it follows that there might be limited value in asking consumers about their ethical attitudes or intentions and looking for correspondence in their actual behavior. Accordingly, more psycho-analytically inspired methods would attempt to go 'beyond the surface' by employing techniques such as indirect questioning and free or implicit associations (e.g. Clarke, 2018). Through such techniques, psychoanalysis provides a lens for more 'penetrative' interpretations of textual and (even more so) visual data (Rose, 2001). More recently, this approach has been adopted by Chatzidakis, Shaw and Allen (2018) in their study of consumers' caring logics and practices. By relying on a combination of photo elicitation and visual drawing techniques, the authors develop a more psycho-social understanding of sustainable and caring consumption, one that is sensitized to both consumers' biographical accounts and broader institutional and discursive factors.

Psychoanalytically inspired methods are not the only ones suspicious of the ability of conventional experiments and surveys to access consumers' innermost thoughts, feelings and attitudes. Within psychological and attitudinal research, a distinction is increasingly made between explicit and implicit attitudes. The latter are defined as "introspectively unidentified (or inaccurately identified) traces of past experience that mediate favorable or unfavorable feeling, thought, or action towards social objects" (Greenwald & Banaji, 1995, p. 8). Implicit attitudes therefore recognize the significance of 'unconscious' processes and rely on latent or indirect methods of accessing people's thoughts and feelings, such as priming tasks (e.g. Roefs *et al.*, 2005) and the 'implicit association test' (e.g. Greenwald, McGhee & Schwartz, 1998; for an application in ethical consumerism see Vantomme & Geuens, 2006). Similarly, neuroscientific advancements offer a range of methods for moving beyond the realm of self-awareness. Within ethical consumer research, for instance, Lee *et al.* (2014) investigate the brain wave activity patterns of green versus non-green consumers. They show that when exposed to green product information green consumers' brain activity is significantly higher, whereas there are no significant differences when it comes to price information messages.

From a more epistemological perspective, Carrington *et al.* (2016) draw attention to two flawed assumptions implicit in current empirical approaches in the expanding field of academic research focused on narrowing consumers' 'ethical consumption gap'. First, this body of research largely takes four empirical approaches to examine and attribute the sources of this 'gap': (1) social desirability bias, where ethical consumption intentions are overstated in research (e.g. Auger & Devinney, 2007); (2) internal and external influences that inhibit the realization of ethical intentions into actual behavior (e.g. Carrington, Neville & Whitwell, 2014; Shaw & Shiu, 2003); (3) multiple and competing identities that impede consumers' intentions to consume ethically (e.g. Carrington, Neville & Canniford, 2015); and (4) the ability to manage guilt and dissonance by neutralizing the gap in their behavior after the fact (e.g. Chatzidakis, Hibbert & Smith, 2007). Aligned with the neoliberal agenda of consumer sovereignty, all four of these approaches share an underlying assumption that ascribes the source and the responsibility for the 'gap' with the individual consumer.

Second, it is inevitable that these studies will reveal an ethical consumption gap as a distinction is not made between: (1) the decision-making contexts external to the market where individuals form their ethical consumption attitudes and intentions governed by moralities that are separate from the market logic; and (2) decision-making contexts within the marketplace that are governed by the dominant market logic (Carrington *et al.*, 2016). Ethical consumption researchers have largely assumed that the morality logics that determine an individual's decisions and behavior outside the market are also operating inside the market. This empirical approach ignores that the market is governed by the amoral logic of money (Habermas, 2005[1985]). Thus, a gap between individuals' ethical intentions formed in the cultural and social sphere outside the economic system, and the behaviors enacted in the amorality operating inside the economic system, should be expected (Carrington *et al.*, 2016).

Conclusion

Research into ethical consumption has come a long way since the observation of a new segment of 'environmentally aware' or 'green' consumers of the late 1960s/early 1970s (e.g. Anderson Jr & Cunningham, 1972; Webster, 1975). More recently, it has also begun to move away from a single-minded preoccupation with developing ethical decision-making models and the explanation of corresponding 'attitude-behavior' gaps (e.g. Caruana, Carrington & Chatzidakis, 2016). We find that despite their diversity, current critical and nuanced understandings of ethical consumption share in common two key characteristics: *contextualizing* ethical consumption and exposing the *ideological* threads that underpin its everyday logics and manifestations.

First, there is increasing emphasis on contextualizing 'ethical consumption' recognizing that what is understood by ethics and morals and indeed 'consumption' (e.g. Graeber, 2011) varies across different times and spaces. There is emerging consensus that the intersection of ethics with consumption pre-dates the identification of a distinct segment of socially and environmentally aware consumers of the 1960s/1970s. More commonly across disciplines, the origins of what is now understood as ethical consumption are traced within 18th- and 19th-century social movements that employed forms of consumption-mediated activism. Hilton (2007), for instance, situates the emergence of the UK ethical consumer in London's first 'consumers league'; established in 1897 to address labor concerns of that time. Members of the league were asked to boycott the goods of employers who mistreated their employees and buycott those that did not through a list of 'fair' employers within the vicinity of Bond Street, Oxford Street and Regent Street. To be sure, however, what counts as 'ethical consumption' is also dependent on historically situated discourses and genealogical explorations. For example, taking a broader understanding of 'ethical consumerism', Bradshaw, Campbell and Dunne (2013) focus on discussions around ethics and everyday consumption in ancient Greece and particularly the dialogues between Socrates and Plato. Therein, the pre-conditions (that is, acceptance of slavery) for luxurious consumption were explicitly discussed and viewed as the inevitable blind spot of wealthy Athenian lifestyles.

Current critical research is also sensitized to the spaces of ethical consumption. Various anthropological and geographical studies illustrate how moral codes underpin any system of market provision (e.g. Carrier & Luetchford, 2012) as well as the possibilities for subverting it (e.g. Gibson-Graham, 1997). Accordingly, modern day consumption in the 'Global South' (ethical or otherwise) exposes alternative articulations, narratives and symbolic practices (Gregson & Ferdous, 2015). Focusing on South Africa, for example, McEwan et al. (2015) foreground thrift as a key ethical choice that is associated not only with financial responsibility but also care, habit and aspiration. A different stream of geographically inspired studies moves beyond space as the background context to consider the role of space in 'producing' particular modes and styles of ethical consumption. Within the context of a radical left-wing neighborhood of Athens, Chatzidakis *et al.* (2012) illustrate how practices such as directly trading with Zapatistas are viewed as morally superior and therefore preferable to buying 'Fair Trade' goods in conventional retail outlets.

Second, critical understandings of ethical consumption reassert it as ideological, a material and discursive construction employed at different institutional levels by a variety of actors (e.g. corporations, NGOs) other than the 'consumer' (Caruana & Chatzidakis, 2014; Carrington *et al.*, 2016). Accordingly, the increasing responsibilization and moralization of otherwise benign everyday activities is viewed as essential in new forms of neoliberal governance. What these logics share in common is a vested interest in removing responsibility from traditional top-down national and supra-national institutions and into the consumer-citizen (e.g. Bauman, 2009). The outcome of this is societies where moral responsibility for social and environmental justice is decentralized, fragmented and atomized. Rosol (2012) suggests that, from this perspective, ethical consumption can be "understood as part of a distinct political rationality which aims at passing on state responsibilities to civil society" – an effective "roll-out" of neoliberalism (p. 240). Concurrently, a different stream of studies aims at deconstructing the ideologically sustained boundaries between consumers and producers, ethical and unethical actions. At stake is the uncovering of deeper systemic tensions and contradictions that underline late capitalism (e.g. Carrington *et al.*, 2016).

What should be the future direction(s) for critically oriented ethical consumption research? Beyond the methodological innovations mentioned above – especially when used to inform more radical understandings of ethical consumer action – we conclude that there is pertinent need for further studies that investigate real alternatives (across different scales) to dominant systems of provision and consumption. Put differently, what remains less understood and under-theorized are the pre-conditions for advancing more emancipatory and radical consumer agendas: ones that move beyond the hegemonic logics of sustainable growth, market co-optation and the fetishization of ethics in consumption.

References

Anderson Jr, W.T., & Cunningham, W.H. (1972). The socially conscious consumer. *Journal of Marketing*, 36(3), 23–31.

Auger, P., & Devinney, T.M. (2007). Do what consumers say matter? The misalignment of preferences with unconstrained ethical intentions. *Journal of Business Ethics*, 76(4), 361–383.

Bauman, Z. (2009). *Does ethics have a chance in a world of consumers?* Cambridge, Harvard University Press.

Bradshaw, A., Campbell, N., & Dunne, S. (2013). The politics of consumption. *Ephemera, 13*(2), 203–216.

Bradshaw, A., & Zwick, D. (2016). The field of business sustainability and the death drive: A radical intervention. *Journal of Business Ethics, 136*(2), 267–279.

Carrier, J.G. (2010). Protecting the environment the natural way: Ethical consumption and commodity fetishism. *Antipode, 42*(3), 672–689.

Carrier, J.G., & Luetchford, P.G. (2012). *Ethical consumption: Social value and economic practice.* London, Berghahn Books.

Carrington, M.J., Neville, B., & Canniford, R. (2015). Unmanageable multiplicity: Consumer transformation towards moral self coherence. *European Journal of Marketing, 49*(7/8), 1300–1325.

Carrington, M.J., Neville, B.A., & Whitwell, G.J. (2014). Lost in translation: Exploring the ethical consumer intention–behavior gap. *Journal of Business Research, 67*(1), 2759–2767.

Carrington, M.J., Zwick, D., & Neville, B. (2016). The ideology of the ethical consumption gap. *Marketing Theory, 16*(1), 21–38.

Caruana, R., Carrington, M.J., & Chatzidakis, A. (2016). Beyond the attitude-behavior gap: Novel perspectives in consumer ethics: Introduction to the thematic symposium. *Journal of Business Ethics, 136*(2), 215–218.

Caruana, R., & Chatzidakis, A. (2014). Consumer social responsibility (CnSR): Toward a multi-level, multi-agent conceptualization of the 'other CSR'. *Journal of Business Ethics, 121*(4), 577–592.

Chatzidakis, A. (2015). Guilt and ethical choice in consumption: A psychoanalytic perspective. *Marketing Theory, 15*(1), 79–93.

Chatzidakis, A., Hibbert, S., & Smith, A.P. (2007). Why people don't take their concerns about fair trade to the supermarket: The role of neutralisation. *Journal of Business Ethics, 74*(1), 89–100.

Chatzidakis, A., Larsen, G., & Bishop, S. (2014). Farewell to consumerism: Countervailing logics of growth in consumption. *Ephemera, 14*(4), 753–764.

Chatzidakis, A., Maclaran, P., & Bradshaw, A. (2012). Heterotopian space and the utopics of ethical and green consumption. *Journal of Marketing Management, 28*(3–4), 494–515.

Chatzidakis, A., Shaw, D., & Allen, M. (forthcoming, 2018). A psycho-social approach to consumer ethics. *Journal of Consumer Culture.* DOI: 10.1177/1469540518773815

Chomsky, N. (1999). *Profit over people: Neoliberalism and global order.* New York, Seven Stories Press.

Clarke, S. (2018). *Researching beneath the surface: Psycho-social research methods in practice.* London: Routledge.

Cotte, J., & Trudel, R. (2009). Socially conscious consumerism: A systematic review of the body of knowledge. *Network for Business Sustainability.* Retrieved January 5, 2018 from https://nbs.net/p/systematic-review-socially-conscious-consumerism-e201164a-9ce8-484f-90a2-d99e5dbf3e84

Cremin, C. (2012). The social logic of late capitalism: Guilt fetishism and the culture of crisis industry. *Cultural Sociology, 6*(1), 45–60.

Critchley, S. (2007). *Infinitely demanding: Ethics of commitment, politics of resistance.* London, Verso.

Denegri-Knott, J., Zwick, D., & Schroeder, J.E. (2006). Mapping consumer power: An integrative framework for marketing and consumer research. *European Journal of Marketing, 40*(9–10), 950–971.

Dixon, D.F. (1992). Consumer sovereignty, democracy, and the marketing concept: A macromarketing perspective. *Canadian Journal of Administrative Sciences, 9*(2), 116–125.

Dolan, C.S. (2010). Virtual moralities: The mainstreaming of Fairtrade in Kenyan tea fields. *Geoforum, 41*(1), 33–43.

Firat, A.F. (1996). The unmanageable consumer: Contemporary consumption and its fragmentations. *Journal of Consumer Policy, 19*(3), 393–399.

Fisk, G. (1967). *Marketing systems: An introductory analysis.* New York, Harper & Row.

Fridell, G. (2006). Fair trade and neoliberalism: Assessing emerging perspectives. *Latin American Perspectives, 33*(6), 8–28.

Gibson-Graham, J.K. (1997). The end of capitalism (as we knew it): A feminist critique of political economy. *Capital & Class, 21*(2), 186–188.

Giesler, M., & Veresiu, E. (2014). Creating the responsible consumer: Moralistic governance regimes and consumer subjectivity. *Journal of Consumer Research, 41*(3), 840–857.

Gilbert, J (2013). What kind of thing is 'neoliberalism'? *New Formations, 80*(1), 7–22.

Graeber, D. (2011). Consumption. *Current Anthropology, 52*(4), 489–511.

Greenwald, A.G., & Banaji, M.R. (1995). Implicit social cognition: Attitudes, self-esteem, and stereotypes. *Psychological Review, 102*(1), 4–27.

Greenwald, A.G., McGhee, D.E., & Schwartz, J.L. (1998). Measuring individual differences in implicit cognition: The implicit association test. *Journal of Personality and Social Psychology*, 74(6), 1464–1480.

Gregson, N., & Ferdous, R. (2015). Making space for ethical consumption in the South. *Geoforum*, 67(December), 244–255.

Habermas, J. (2005[1985]). *The theory of communicative action: Lifeworld and system – a critique of functionalist reason*. Boston, Beacon.

Hackley, C.E. (2003). *Doing research projects in marketing, management and consumer research*. New York, Routledge.

Harrison, R., Shaw, D., & Newholm, T. (2005). *The ethical consumer*. London, Sage.

Harvey, D. (1990). Between space and time: Reflections on the geographical imagination. *Annals of the Association of American Geographers*, 80(3), 418–434.

Harvey, D. (2010). *Social justice and the city*. Athens, University of Georgia Press.

Hilton, M. (2007). Social activism in an age of consumption: The organized consumer movement. *Social History*, 32(2), 121–143.

Holloway, J. (2010). *Crack capitalism*. London, Pluto.

Holt, D.B. (2002). Why do brands cause trouble? A dialectical theory of consumer culture and branding. *Journal of Consumer Research*, 29(1), 70–90.

Humphrey, K. (2016). Buying a better world. In D.C. Shaw, A. Chatzidakis & M. Carrington (Eds.), *Ethics and morality in consumption: Interdisciplinary perspectives* (pp. 138–152). London, Routledge.

Jones, E. (2012). *The better world shopping guide: Every dollar makes a difference*. Gabriola Island, New Society Publishers.

Klein, N. (2014). *This changes everything: Capitalism vs. the climate*. Toronto, Knopf Canada.

Kleine, D. (2016). Putting ethical consumption in its place: Geographical perspectives. In D.C. Shaw, A. Chatzidakis & M. Carrington (Eds.), *Ethics and morality in consumption: Interdisciplinary perspectives* (pp. 116–137). London, Routledge.

Latouche, S. (2009). *Farewell to growth*. Malden, Polity.

Lee, E.-J., Kwon, G., Shin, H.J., Yang, S., Lee, S., & Suh, M. (2014). The spell of green: Can frontal EEG activations identify green consumers? *Journal of Business Ethics*, 122(3), 511–521.

Lekakis, E.J. (2012). Will the fair trade revolution be marketised? Commodification, decommodification and the political intensity of consumer politics. *Culture and Organization*, 18(5), 345–358.

Littler, J. (2011). What's wrong with ethical consumption? In T. Lewis & E. Potter (Eds.), *Ethical consumption: A critical introduction* (pp. 27–39). London, Routledge.

Luetchford, P. (2016). Market, society and morality: Towards an anthropology of ethical consumption. In D.C. Shaw, A. Chatzidakis & M. Carrington (Eds.), *Ethics and morality in consumption: Interdisciplinary perspectives* (pp. 153–170). London, Routledge.

Marcuse, H. (1972). *Counterrevolution and revolt*. Boston, Beacon Press.

Marx, K. (1976). *Capital*, vol. 1, trans. Ben Fowkes. London, Penguin.

Massey, D. (2013). Vocabularies of the economy. *Soundings*, 54(54), 9–22.

McEwan, C., Hughes, A., & Bek, D. (2015). Theorising middle class consumption from the global South: A study of everyday ethics in South Africa's Western Cape. *Geoforum*, 67(December), 233–243.

Micheletti, M. (2003). Shopping with and for virtues. In M. Micheletti (Ed.), *Political virtue and shopping* (pp. 149–168). London, Springer.

Micheletti, M., & Follesdal, A. (2007). Shopping for human rights: An introduction to the special issue. *Journal of Consumer Policy*, 30(3), 167–175.

Micheletti, M., & McFarland, A.S. (2011). *Creative participation: Responsibility-taking in the political world*. Boulder, Paradigm Publishers.

Narver, J.C., & Savitt, R. (1971). *The marketing economy: An analytical approach*. New York, Holt, Rinehart and Winston.

Parsons, L., Maclaran, M., & Chatzidakis, A. (2017). *Contemporary issues in marketing and consumer behavior*. London, Routledge.

Roefs, A., Herman, C., MacLeod, C., Smulders, F., & Jansen, A. (2005). At first sight: How do restrained eaters evaluate high-fat palatable foods? *Appetite*, 44(1), 103–114.

Rose, G. (2001). *Visual methodologies: An introduction to the interpretation of visual methodologies*. London, Sage.

Rosol, M. (2012). Community volunteering as neoliberal strategy? Green space production in Berlin. *Antipode*, 44(1), 239–257.

Shaw, D., & Newholm, T. (2002). Voluntary simplicity and the ethics of consumption. *Psychology & Marketing, 19*(2), 167–185.

Shaw, D., & Shiu, E. (2003). Ethics in consumer choice: A multivariate modelling approach. *European Journal of Marketing, 37*(10), 1485–1498.

Sherry, J.F., Kozinets, R.V., Storm, D., Duhachek, A., Nuttavuthisit, K., & Deberry-Spence, B. (2001). Being in the zone: Staging retail theater at ESPN zone Chicago. *Journal of Contemporary Ethnography, 30*(4), 465–510.

Smith, N.C. (1987). Consumer boycotts and consumer sovereignty. *European Journal of Marketing, 21*(5), 7–19.

Soper, K. (2008). 'Alternative hedonism' and the citizen-consumer. In F. Trentmann & K. Soper (Eds.), *Citizenship and consumption* (pp. 50–76). London, Palgrave.

Soper, K. (2016). Towards a sustainable flourishing: Ethical consumption and the politics of prosperity. In D.C. Shaw, A. Chatzidakis & M. Carrington (Eds.), *Ethics and morality in consumption: Interdisciplinary perspectives* (pp. 11–27). London, Routledge.

Stolle, D., & Micheletti, M. (2013). *Political consumerism: Global responsibility in action*. New York, Cambridge University Press.

Tadajewski, M. (2010). Towards a history of critical marketing studies. *Journal of Marketing Management, 26*(9), 773–824.

Thompson, C.J., & Coskuner-Balli, G. (2007). Countervailing market responses to corporate co-optation and the ideological recruitment of consumption communities. *Journal of Consumer Research, 34*(2), 135–152.

Vantomme, D., & Geuens, M. (2006). Explicit and implicit determinants of fair-trade buying behavior. *Advances in Consumer Research, 33*, 699–703.

Varul, M. (2008). Consuming the campesino: Fair trade marketing between recognition and romantic commodification. *Cultural Studies, 22*(5), 654–679.

Webster, F.E. (1975). Determining the characteristics of the socially conscious consumer. *Journal of Consumer Research, 2*(3), 188–196.

Žižek, S. (2010). *Living in the end times*. New York, Verso.

16
RELIGIOUS CRITIQUES OF THE MARKET

Aliakbar Jafari

Introduction

A few years ago, I was invited to give a talk at a doctoral colloquium aimed at enhancing students' critical thinking. For discussion, the organizers had chosen Thomas Piketty's *Capital in the Twenty-First Century*, which had just taken the world by storm. In my talk, I referred to the economic philosophy of Islam to draw attention to those schools of thought that have challenged capitalism but remain largely overlooked by critical marketing scholars. After the talk, two colleagues expressed concern about my approach, which, in their view, was an attempt to 'theologize' the social science and to refute the status quo (i.e., Marxism, in their view). I tried to clarify that this was not my intention and that including religious critiques of the market in discourse on capitalism can broaden our analytical lens. However, we could not reach an agreement. For these fellow scholars, theories emerging from non-secular thinking were simply unworthy of studying.

Regardless of our subjective views, religion continues to occupy a substantial place in discourses on capitalism (Anderson, 2016; Bell, 2012; Sandel, 2012; Tawney, 1920; Wallis, 2010). As I will discuss in this chapter, along with non-secular societies (e.g. in the Middle East), which are typically associated with religious dominance and governance, secular[1] contexts (e.g. in Western Europe and North America) are also witness to the rise of various anti-capitalist voices that are either religious in orientation (e.g. Cort, 1988; Pabst, 2011) or largely influenced by religious rhetoric (e.g. Bauman, 2000; Kozinets & Handelman, 2004).

Understanding the religious critiques of the market requires acknowledging the fact that there are multiple relationships between religion and the market. On the one hand, religion has allegedly paved the way for the rise of capitalism (the Weberian view) and is therefore accountable for its negative consequences (e.g. ecological calamities) (Feuerbach, 1957; Nash, 1991; White Jr., 1967). Religion itself has been significantly marketized (McAlexander, Dufault, Martin, & Schouten, 2014; Usunier & Stolz, 2014); religious enterprises broadly utilize the tools and rules of neoliberalism to grow and compete with one another and with non-religious institutions (Gauthier & Martikainen, 2013; Jafari & Sandıkcı, 2016). This means that religion is not, as commonly perceived, the antithesis of capitalism. Conversely, religious critiques of the market raise issues that are also reflected in the established secular traditions (e.g. Marxism). The existence of certain similarities (e.g. debate on social solidarity, poverty and social justice, and unleashed materialism) between the two camps indicates that they are not in total discord.

It is because of such complex and, at times, paradoxical interactions between religion and the market that this chapter argues for the inclusion of religious critiques of the market in debate on capitalism. At its core, this chapter argues: (1) religious and secular critiques of the market have more in common than usually thought. Analyzing each stream can help understand the other one and eventually draw a broader picture of the critiques of capitalism. (2) Religious critics of the market are not uniform in their approach toward capitalism. For example, while revolutionaries (the religious left) (e.g. Tawney, 1920) fervently argue for religious socialism as a viable alternative, reformists (e.g. Bell, 2012) call only for reconfiguring capitalism.

Given the diversity of religious orientations and their historical developments in relation to economy, policy, culture and society, this chapter does not intend to present a comprehensive review of the extant literature on religious critiques of the market. What the chapter covers, however, is a set of main issues that are expressed by religious critics of the market. These discussions can hopefully show that religious critiques of the market are not exclusively concerned with the sacred (i.e., the world hereafter); they also tap on issues that relate to the profane (i.e., life in the here and now). At the core of these agendas are poverty and social injustice, ill-being, state intervention, ecological degradation and unsustainable growth, and loss of human dignity and solidarity, all of which recur in secular critiques of capitalism too.

The chapter is organized in three sections. First, a summary of the key perspectives on the relationship between religion and the market is presented. This overview explains that religion and the market are not necessarily in opposition. It also sets the ground for understanding the reason why religious critiques of the market adopt different approaches (e.g. revolutionary or reformist) toward capitalism. The second part focuses on the most recurrent themes in the literature that generally echo the critiques of the market from the lens of major world religions such as Christianity, Judaism, Buddhism and Islam. This spectrum should not be seen as a deliberate exclusion of other faiths; rather, it should be related to the limitations of writing a book chapter and the trade-off between depth and breadth of discussion. I hope that other colleagues will embark on analyzing other faiths not covered in this chapter. The third and final section will propose areas for future research.

Religion and the market

In a typology, Haddorff (2000) presents three theoretical perspectives on the relationship between religion and the market: opposition, absorption, and the ambiguous tradition. Religion represents the sacred and the market represents the profane. From the 'opposition' viewpoint, religion and the market are in conflict (Weber, 1958/1904–1905; Marx & Engels, 1967/1848). This means that "the triumph of a market society would lead to the destruction of the fabric of civil society, including the secularisation of religion, and a dystopian collapse of communal solidarity traditional values" (Haddorff, 2000, p. 487). Capitalism frames people through an economic lens that encourages more consumption. The rationale is that consumption would accelerate the wheels of commodity production (Marx & Engels, 1967/1848). Through the establishment of this rationality, people's traditional values (including religious) and social relationships are overshadowed by market-generated values and short-term economic relationships with the market (Bauman, 2000; Bocock, 1993).

For Weber (1993), while the rationalization of human relations represents a historical progress in terms of economic and political organization, it also leads to the disenchantment of the world by stripping human existence of its mystical but inwardly genuine elasticity (i.e., the influence of the sacred on the private lives of the individuals). Weber argues that capitalism, which owes its triumph to the work of religion, inevitably marginalizes religion because the modern administration system gradually replaces the role of religion in organizing societies' day-to-day activities. In contrast to Weber's pessimism, for Marx the decline of religious values is a positive development because the desacralization of human relations prompts the questioning of the capitalist production relations and, therefore, would lead to a quest for the replacement of religious cohesion by secular forms of social solidarity. Marx's skeptical view of religion (as "opium of the people") drives his quest for revolutions that would replace the oppressed people's passive grieving over their miseries and instead energize them to revolt against the ruling class. For both Weber and Marx, with the progress of capitalism, religion fades away from the public sphere because they are not compatible with each other.

As regards the second perspective, Emile Durkheim's (1984/1893, 1915/1912) 'absorption theory' "attempts to reframe the triumph of market society and *homo economicus* in light of the symbolic boundaries of the 'sacred' and the 'profane'" (Haddorff, 2000, p. 490). Instead of opposition between religion and the market, there is a symbiotic relationship between the two. Durkheim's religion is not transcendental. For him, religion is a socially constructed phenomenon, which uses a 'symbolic-expressive system' to assign values and meanings to people's life goals in society. The values it promotes, therefore, do not necessarily stand above the culture of society; rather, they are (re)defined by the society itself. From this perspective, a healthy society will depend on maintaining balance between the sacred and the profane. As such, the market becomes "a historically conditioned way of construing the world, a way of organizing and reorganizing our core religious beliefs and practices in a secular society" (Haddorff, 2000, p. 491). The market itself becomes a religion because it produces a series of life goals, meanings, symbols and values that usurp the values and meaning systems that were traditionally assigned by religion. Via the market system, the profane produces the sacred (Muñiz & Schau, 2005). For example, as Belk, Wallendorf and Sherry (1989) show, by blessing objects through rituals, people can sacralize profane objects and create transcendental meanings in their lives.

Finally, with reference to Polanyi's (2001) thesis of 'double movement', Haddorff (2000) explains that 'the ambiguous tradition' has both similarities and differences with the opposition and absorption perspectives. While the development of capitalism affects society, it does not result in the alienation of religion. Polanyi also believes in the symbiotic relationship between the market and religion; yet, for him religion is a transcendental reality (i.e., a spiritual realm connected to God). With the development of capitalism and the subsequent changes that occur in human relations, society too develops decommodification strategies as a self-defense mechanism either through redistribution (e.g. almsgiving) or reciprocity (e.g. gift giving) against the commodification of human relations. While redistribution occurs within the realm of welfare politics, reciprocity occurs in the realm of culture. For example, sacralization of certain objects (e.g. souvenirs) or activities (e.g. rituals and ceremonies) can safeguard human relations against the commercialization of society imposed by capitalism. This means that people give sacred meanings to the profane.

As this analysis suggests, along with the market that pursues its own objectives (e.g. maximization of profit), as an agentic entity, society maintains its social order. As such, society deploys a variety of resources such as welfare politics, religion and culture to establish order. Polanyi argues that "since the problems of society are inherently social rather than political or economic, it is through a rediscovery of society (or community) that persons begin to engage, resist, and even transform market society" (quoted in Haddorff, 2000, p. 494). This is the reason why capitalism cannot outweigh religion. Religion persists because it supplies human society with the values that endure and respond to people's communal and individual needs in their everyday life.

Given the self-defense mechanism of society, the market abides by the rules of society because "the market is infused with moral values, principles, and virtues, which draws from the 'public' role of religious and ethical discourse" (Haddorff, 2000, p. 498). This means that neither the market is completely profane, nor is religion entirely sacred. Several scholars (Wuthnow, 1994a, 1994b, 1996; Marty, 1995; Schmidt, 1995) also endorse this statement by demonstrating that the material consumption rituals in Americans' daily lives do not estrange them from their religious beliefs. Indeed, people realize moral and social values such as 'freedom', 'success', and 'well-being' through their consumption of the material, the profane.

> The philosophy of hedonistic materialism does not drive the practice of consumption. Rather, consumption is linked with the basic life values of health, security, being loved, beauty, knowledge, relaxation, and social solidarity. Through consumption persons embody these non-market 'values' or 'goods', which ironically assists persons in attaining the 'non-material' good life.
>
> Haddorff, 2000, p. 497

To these three perspectives (opposition, absorption, and the ambiguous tradition), Jafari and Süerdem (2012) add the 'authorized selection' view. The authors critique the Weberian rigid analysis of the relationship between religion and the market and explain that Islam refutes asceticism. They show that, historically, economic activities have been part of the Muslim tradition and Islamic teachings regard economic prosperity an important and valued aspect of human life. Supporting Polanyi's analysis, the authors argue that, as interpretive agents, people selectively choose and adapt the cultural codes of religion to justify their own life conditions and preferences. As such, the same religion may be practiced differently around the world. People authorize themselves to adopt lifestyles that might seem even contradictory to the principles of a given religion. To elaborate on their thesis, the authors refer to several controversial examples, such as the unveiling of Muslim women, consumption of alcohol, and immersion in luxury consumption. "Such practices are common among those Muslims who pursue their own ways of religiosity. They may no longer feel the need for the traditional religious institutions to exclusively describe and prescribe religious practices for them" (Jafari & Süerdem, 2012, p. 72).

The presence of multiple and, at times, conflicting forms of religiosity in society is because religion plays a variety of roles in people's life. People do not have a uniform relationship with religion. With reference to Soroush (2000), the authors contend, "Some people commit themselves to religion because they fear God, others do so because they love God, and there are also those who carry the label of religiosity because it gives them a sense of identity" (Jafari & Süerdem, 2012, p. 71). In their everyday life situations, people define their customized relationship with God and, therefore, sacralize the profane and desacralize the sacred in order to actualize their own ideal self. In this self-actualization quest, the market plays an important role as it avails people with the means to organize their lives in ways that do not stand opposite to the enduring values (e.g. salvation and well-being) of religion. The authors emphasize that the market acts as a platform on which people can seek salvation by strengthening the foundations of a healthy life. They can practice ethics, brotherhood, almsgiving, wealth creation and poverty alleviation, entrepreneurship, innovation and improving life standards, and so forth. Achieving such ends only becomes possible when balance is created between the sacred and the profane.

Religious critiques of the market

I now proceed to examine the religious critiques of the market. Three points need to be emphasized. First, as mentioned in the introduction, religious critiques of the market converge on several points with one another and also with the non-religious critical accounts of capitalism.

These similarities provide a fertile ground for gaining a more holistic view of the critiques of the market. In order to achieve this goal, I will present a thematic discussion of such similarities that overlap in several areas. Yet, this thematic categorization is not meant to homogenize these perspectives; rather, it serves only as a means to maintain the focus of the chapter. In developing the discussion, I will make several references to Christianity, Judaism, Buddhism, and Islam. These references can help associate the existing views with certain faiths without delving into their specificities. This is because within each faith, there are several sects and within each sect there are multiple voices that are not necessarily similar in their approach toward the market (e.g. Christian left, Christian right, and Christian libertarian).

Second, religious critiques of the market, themselves, are subject to criticism. For example, as Jafari and Sandıkcı (2015, 2016) argue, religious critics of the market often fail to acknowledge that religion itself has become substantially marketized. Therefore, cosmetic surgeries of the market, in the name of religious reformism, are less likely to result in structural changes in the market system. To elaborate, the authors critique the emergence of academic and managerial practices that use religious terminology and symbolism to promote Islamic marketing and branding. Since such practices do not work outside the neoliberal economy, they cannot contribute to the creation of 'perfect' markets built upon religious utopias. The same view is shared by Süerdem (2013, 2016) who criticizes the commoditization of religion by those who endorse Islamic marketing as an alternative for the mainstream marketing anchored in the principles of capitalism. In the following pages, some critique of the religious critiques of the market will be discussed, but a detailed critical review of such critiques remains beyond the objective of this chapter (for detailed analysis see Jafari, 2012; Jafari & Sandıkcı, 2015, 2016; Süerdem, 2013, 2016).

Third, it is important to recognize the institutional role of religion in shaping critiques of the market. As Geertz (1968) explains, religion is an abstract symbol system for people to make sense of their everyday activities. This conceptualization of religion makes it subject to multiple interpretations. Yet, religion should also be viewed as an institution in itself. That is, it is comprised of a set of actors (e.g. religious leaders, organizations, and their networks of media and politics) that give particular meanings to the abstract and promote specific ways of thinking and interpreting the symbols (see Soroush, 2000; Jafari & Süerdem, 2012). Acknowledging the institutional role of religion in society and the institutional dynamics (e.g. political and socio-economic) that (re)shape religious discourses can help us understand the reason why religious critiques of the market might highlight certain issues at the expense of others. For example, as Kruse (2015) reports, one of the main reasons for the triumph of modern capitalism in the United States is that during the 1930s, corporations such as Hilton Hotels and General Motors financed the Congregational Church in return for their support of capitalism per se. Figures such as Rev. James W. Fifield used the slogans of "The blessings of capitalism come from God" and "Freedom under God" to convince the public that socialism was bad and Christian libertarianism was good. Therefore, the religious critiques of the market are underpinned by different political orientations. Next, I will discuss some of the main themes that recur in the literature on the religious critiques of the market.

Loss of social solidarity

Religious critics of the market regard the loss of social solidarity as one of the main vices of capitalism. They believe that by initiating the project of the 'self', capitalism disrupts social ties, nurtures extreme individualism, and harms the social fabric of society. Capitalism uses the slogan of freedom of choice to alienate members of society from one another; it encourages an unlimited pursuit of self-interest through property ownership, utilization of natural resources, accumulation of wealth and consumerism (Anderson, 2016; Bell, 2012; Changkhwanyuen, 2004; Kalantari, 2008; Kaplan, 2010/1934). While these concerns are shared among different faith groups, certain aspects of them gain more importance in different scholars' thinking. For example, Changkhwanyuen (2004, p. 248) argues:

> Buddhism can accept individualism only on the concept of personal inequality based on personal uniqueness, opportunity differences caused by personal intellects, social or family background, and environment. But Buddhism cannot accept personal exploitation of public resources or free competition leading to certain personal advantages and disadvantages. Persons who get better chances by differences are obliged to share them back to general society. Beneficiaries must be responsible for damages to society and nature because it is shared duty for all to preserve public resources.

For the followers of Abrahamic faiths, capitalism's primacy of the individual over the community threatens the foundations of societal integrity and family values. A key aspect of this belief is that human beings are created in the image of God. From a Christian perspective, Bell (2012) argues that through its project of consumerism, capitalism 'deforms humanity'. Neoliberalism disciplines society in such ways that human beings get agonistically involved in competition over quenching their desire for more possessions. This competition results in viewing other human beings not as creatures of God that should live in a harmonious society but as rivals in a purely economic system. Similarly, from an Islamic lens, Motahari (2000) criticizes capitalism for its commoditization of every aspect of life to an extent that human beings become products for sale in the market. Capitalism turns human beings into the slaves of its own consumerism; the more individuals bow to this ideology, the more they turn their back on the values of their society. In order for capitalism to maximize its financial gains, the values that keep members of a community together need to be eradicated so that individuals become liberated from their established traditions and follow those offered by the market. From a Jewish perspective, too, capitalism becomes problematic when individuals forget that God has bestowed wealth to human beings in order to strengthen the foundations of their social solidarity (Levi, 1993).

Poverty and social injustice

There is a general consensus among scholars that social injustice is an outcome of capitalism because of its emphasis on the motto of 'what is mine is mine and what is yours is yours' (Anderson, 2016; Asutay, 2007; Bell, 2012; Changkhwanyuen, 2004; Levi, 1993; Sarao, n/d; Yusuf, 1971). In a capitalist system, whose objective is economic growth, the accumulation of wealth in the hands of elite groups and certain corporations creates monopolies that use the available resources (e.g. natural or common) in order to maximize their profit. In other words, capitalist enterprises use whatever means are available to reduce their cost (e.g. cutting wages and attempting to access cheaper raw materials) and increase their profit. "Capitalism is the most centralized economic system of all by attracting capital to the center and distributing out in the least degree in order to cut cost, produce more, dump market, and profit the most" (Changkhwanyuen, 2004, p. 254). While capitalist enterprises enjoy the conditions of free market economy, the economically vulnerable strata of society feel the pressure of poverty on them. As distribution of wealth is unbalanced to the advantage of the rich, in a vicious circle, then the exploited poor become poorer and the exploiting rich become richer. Through its privatization project, capitalism leaves no room for communal ownership; neither does it recognize distribution without a financial exchange value (Anderson, 2016; Asutay, 2007; Yusuf, 1971).

To address the problem of social inequality and poverty, different faith groups agree that there should be a balanced distribution of wealth in society; yet, the solutions they offer to implement this are slightly different. For example, some scholars of Islamic economics (e.g. Afzal-ur-Rahman, 1975; Siddiqi, 1972; Yusuf, 1971) suggest a series of means such as prohibitions (e.g. of extravagance), restrictions (e.g. on income), obligations (e.g. charitable donations), and responsibilities (e.g. behaving altruistically). Such measures in Kuran's (1989) critical analysis are problematic because they lack consistency and fail to address the principles of issues of fairness and equality in Islam:

> By and large, I go on to argue, these injunctions rest on a faulty model of human civilization, and they leave far more room for interpretation than the Islamic economists acknowledge. In many contexts, moreover, the injunctions bring the principles of justice into conflict, both with one another and with other Islamic principles.
>
> p. 171

The above-mentioned measures for Kuran are only cosmetic surgeries because they do not address the structural problems (e.g. politics of economic distribution) in society. A majority of Islamic economics scholars fail to acknowledge that the state cannot and should not impose certain lifestyles on people, believing that this will bring justice to society. Similarly, Jafari (2012) argues that many such scholars overlook issues of corruption and cronyism that increasingly contribute to the failure of economic systems and the growth of injustice in Muslim contexts.

From a Buddhist viewpoint, Changkhwanyuen (2004) and Sarao (n/d) argue that measures such as simplicity, downsizing, and localization of economies are sustainable ways of preventing the gap between the poor and the rich from widening. For less-developed economies, in particular, turning away from international investment and globalization can save them from falling into debt. Economic growth, in the name of globalization, only paves the way for big organizations to access the cheap natural resources of other countries and turn them into their own consumers. It is at this point that people become enslaved by capitalism and start to witness the gap widening between the rich and poor. From Christian (Anderson, 2016; Bell, 2012; Sandel, 2012; Wallis, 2010) and Jewish (Levi, 1993) standpoints, since the problem of capitalism is its separation of economy from morality, there is an urgent need to return to the principles of religion. In their view, almsgiving can significantly contribute to the redistribution of wealth in society. Yet, figures such as Bell and Wallis specifically argue that, even if under capitalism all members of society become rich, capitalism is still problematic because it makes people greedy for more economic gains. Therefore, there is a need for the state to intervene in the economic system and establish balance in society. This will be discussed further in the next section.

State intervention

Religious views about alternative political systems are diverse. For example, in the 20th-century United States, the Christian right movement has shifted orientation from full support for laissez-faire to support for conservative economic policies (e.g. tax cuts and child benefits). The religious left argues that capitalism is a totalizing regime that aims to govern all aspects of socio-economic life (e.g. Shariati, 1988; Tawney, 1920; Thomas, 1932; West, 1991). This system oppresses the masses in order to exploit them for its profit maximization. Under capitalism, the power of the state is minimized and restricted to the regulatory bodies that only partly control the market.

As a result, the economic system actually works to the advantage of the rich as the poor become subject to minimum benefits received from the state, depending on the social welfare of the country. This is the reason why the religious left calls for state intervention in economy and the establishment of religious socialism. What differentiates it from secular socialism, however, is the governance of the system by the spiritual principles of religion. In other words, the state abides by the religious belief that all human beings are equal in the eyes of God and the state should be responsible for a just distribution of wealth.

In contrast to the revolutionary standpoint of the religious left, reformists (e.g. Bell, 2012; Levi, 1993) call for reconfiguring capitalism. Bell takes a reformist position because he believes that capitalism is an inevitable reality that cannot be destroyed. Therefore, for practical reasons, what we can do is to find ways to re-embed it in moral values. Bell, of course, puts the 'Kingdom of God' above all the ruling systems to suggest that if the actors in the capitalism system work with faith in God and mercy toward his creatures, then society can experience salvation. For Levi, the market and religious values need to go hand in hand in order for society to run. For both Bell and Levi, the state should devise some mechanisms to support the needy without taking property rights from individuals.

From a Buddhist perspective, Changkhwanyuen (2004) suggests that the state should take part in administrating production and consumption in order to ensure that the order of the economic system is based on a balanced consumption-production. That is, real consumption should determine enough production not vice versa. Otherwise, if production creates consumption, the system will lean toward capitalism that encourages consumerism based on artificial needs. The state is also responsible for tighter controls of the production, distribution and marketing of processes:

> For example, bank and financial institution[s] should be managed not to take advantage of their clients, to curb financial power with no production base, recapitalize for cooperative activities, control currency flow, and establish knowledge and development of production for community. So it can be self-reliant, and knowledgeable enough to grow in its own strength. This control should extend to product quality control, consumer protection, production volume, environment safety, waste volume, and so on. This control is possible through legal mechanism such as labor law, consumer protection law, law protecting small and medium size enterprise, product standard law, law on service business, etc.
>
> *Changkhwanyuen, 2004, p. 257*

Overall, religious perspectives' discontent with the state's minimal intervention in the market arises from criticizing the totalizing greed of a capitalist regime that irresponsibly takes advantage of the resources (e.g. natural) that belong to the whole society. The capitalist system also manipulates state regulations in the interest of profit maximization for the ruling class. While revolutionaries propose socialism as an alternative, reformists suggest that the free market economy needs to be reconciled with morality, and states should take the necessary steps to ensure that market rules are fair.

Ill-being

Capitalism brings a wide variety of ills for society. Again, the common belief among religious critics is that capitalism contaminates human life by its emphasis on materialism (Anderson, 2016; Bell, 2012; Changkhwanyuen, 2004; Kalantari, 2008; Kaplan, 2010/1934; Levi, 1993;

Motahari, 2000; Sandel, 2012; Sarao, n/d; Wallis, 2010). Neoliberalism makes a consumerist life plausible and even necessary in the market. In a market society, people engage in never-ending status competitions with one another in order to increase their material possessions. As competitive individualism expands, people gradually lose the meaning of life and happiness is described and prescribed in terms of the accumulation of valued assets and consumerism.

Materialism imposes several problems on human beings. As individuals agonistically race with each other, they go into debt in order to buy the things that are not really needed but are wanted because in their absence there would be a feeling of losing the competition to their rivals. Such an economic burden is exacerbated when people struggle with psychological ill-being. The anxiety and depression that arise from the desire of continuing the race can remove happiness from people's lives. Although individuals find temporary happiness in having their material possessions, under a neoliberal economic system, their relationships with people around them will also depend on their ability to maintain material equivalence. The end result is that human beings lose peace inside them and harmony with the external environment.

All faith groups reject the idea that happiness solely lies in materialism, but they also agree that the lack of sufficient financial means can result in poverty and ill-being. The key point in maintaining happiness is to create balance between the spiritual and the material. For example, in Buddhism, "an ideal society would follow the motto of happiness and welfare of maximum number of people" (Sarao, n/d, p. 7). Such an ideal situation can be embraced only when members of society consume mindfully and refrain from greed. The same notion finds support in other faith groups.

With reference to the concept of 'sin', Bell (2012) and Anderson (2016) argue that human beings are born with certain characteristics that make them susceptible to failure. Greed is one of them. It is claimed that people are faced with the unquenchable desire to possess, and capitalism targets this aspect of human nature, provoking them to ask for more. From this perspective, therefore, capitalism is the 'economy of desire' that directs happiness through materialism (Bell, 2012). Motahari (2000) and Kalantari (2008) also emphasize that the most tragic part of materialism is self-alienation. That is, by becoming materialistic, they lose their connection with their true self, created in the image of God.

Ecological degradation and unsustainable growth

Religious critics of the market, commonly hold capitalism accountable for the rapid ecological degradation and waste of natural resources (e.g. Nasr, 1997; Sarao, n/d; Wallis, 2010). With its emphasis on rapid economic growth, capitalism utilizes natural resources much faster than they can be replaced. Economic growth also brings with it different types of demands such as water and air pollution and waste (both industrial and domestic). Economic growth is not against the principles of religion as far as it maintains a harmonious relationship with nature: "Buddhism does not mind wealth and prosperity as long as they are acquired and used in accord with the ethical norms. The real problem lies in the human tendency to have which the Buddha called craving (taṇhā)" (Sarao, n/d, pp. 5–6). From a Buddhist perspective, "apart from taking into account the profitability of a given activity, its effect upon people and environment, including the resource base, is equally important" (Sarao, n/d, p. 6).

Some secular critics of capitalism (e.g. Feuerbach, 1957; Nash, 1991; White Jr., 1967) associate such problems with the Judeo-Christian notion of anthropocentrism, arguing that it was religion that put humanity above nature and facilitated the exploitation of natural resources. El-Jurdi, Batat, and Jafari (2017, p. 13) summarize the response of faith groups as follows:

Bouma-Prediger (2009) in particular rejects the accusations made against Christianity for their shaky rationale [i.e. its importance as a precondition for capitalism]. Such accusations, he argues, fail to acknowledge the 2000 year gap between the advent of Christianity and today's ecological crisis. Natural degradation, in Bouma-Prediger's view, is a direct result of mankind's divorce from nature in search of economic gain. This is a similar theme in Nasr's (1997) thesis. Nasr forcefully argues that in its applications, modern science has lost touch with the divine. Ecological crisis in modern society is due to human beings' spiritual vacuum and detachment from nature and the sacred and their overreliance on materialism, scientism, and positivism. In other words, by abandoning the sacred and secularization of science man declared "war against nature". Nasr deems the reconciliation of science with the spiritual traditions of religions pivotal to combating ecological crises.

Scholars from across Judaism (Freudenstein, 1970; Tirosh-Samuelson, 2001), Christianity (Grønvold, 2013; Sandelands & Hoffman, 2008; Wirzba, 2003) and Islam (Afrasiabi 2003; Dien 1997; Foltz, Denny, & Baharuddin, 2003; Ozdemir, 2003) all argue that anthropocentrism is misunderstood by the critics of religion. Indeed, God created mankind in his own image and made them his stewards on earth. With such stewardship came the responsibility of protecting nature and the environment. As such, it is not religion but its absence that made mankind exploit the environment. Religious critiques of the market endorse the claim that ecological crisis is rooted in human beings' pursuit of happiness through materialism and consumerism (Assadourian, 2010; Hurst, Dittmar, Bond, & Kasser, 2013; Sandel, 2012), over-reliance on science as the magic wand of well-being (Nasr, 1997), and people's market-oriented narcissism and the collapse of morality (Wallis, 2010).

Loss of human dignity

According to faith groups, capitalism renders human beings as goods for sale in the market. Capitalism applies its monetary value system to human dignity. This is done via the relativization of morality (Wallis, 2010). In the name of economic productivity and growth, capitalism exploits human beings both as subjects and objects of consumption. For example, Motahari (2000) argues that by viewing human beings only as the market-made consumers of a neoliberal system, capitalism dehumanizes human beings by playing with their unquenchable desires (e.g. greed, arrogance and sexuality). It detaches individuals from their position as citizen-members of human society and makes them slaves of its own realm of consumerism. Via its marketization mechanism, it also puts human beings up for sale. This is more common in the media and advertising industry which commoditize human beings as images for sale, particularly when women are packaged as sexual commodities (e.g. images of desire). This kind of aesthetic commodification restricts human beings to a physical entity (e.g. the body image) sold within the market. For example, in pornography, human beings literally become the object of consumption as a means to satisfy human lust. For capitalism, this kind of economy is accepted because it generates its producers, consumers, price mechanism, and, of course, significant revenue streams.

Bell (2012), Wallis (2010) and Sandel (2012) also aver that capitalism relativizes morality. In their view, the neoliberal market economy creates its own vices and virtues through, for example, the production of media celebrities for the masses to follow. It also defines human dignity in relation to their material achievements in the economic system, that is, it distinguishes between the haves and have-nots. In contrast to this, religion recognizes human dignity in and of itself.

Under capitalism, human dignity is at risk when it comes to power relations between those who have economic power and those who do not (Wallis, 2010). In a situation where everything is for sale, those who cannot afford to meet their basic needs become vulnerable to losing their human dignity (Sandel, 2012). Bell (2012) contends that the biggest problem with capitalism is that it separates human beings from God. Instead of bowing to the Creator, human beings idolize the market and materialism.

Conclusion and areas for future research

This chapter began with a suggestion that including religious perspectives in critical marketing can help us gain a more holistic understanding of the critiques of the market. An overview of the relationship between religion and the market was presented to demonstrate that these two are not necessarily in opposition. As the religious critiques of the market were discussed, it became apparent that despite some similarities, religious discourses do not equally oppose the market. While some critics totally reject the free market economy, others seek to reform it (see Orwig, 2002).

The discussions under 'Religious critiques of the market' reflected some of the main themes that recur in religious discourses. These themes are also shared in secular critiques of the market. For example, the alienation of human beings and the problem of social injustice are best exemplified in Marx's works. Neoliberalism is widely criticized by many scholars including Trentmann (2004, 2006) and Gill (1995). These similarities can be seen as opportunities for a better understanding of the extant discourses shaped around the critique of capitalism. These discussions indicate that religious perspectives on the critique of the market cannot and should not be overlooked because they reflect some of the general concerns (e.g. social justice, well-being, and ecology) about how society works under capitalism. Regardless of our subjective views about, and potential skepticism toward, religion, it continues to shape the worldviews of a large number of people around the world. Therefore, scholars in general, and critical marketing thinkers in particular, need to acknowledge the importance of understanding the viewpoints of those whose critique of the market is fueled by religious discourses. Such scholars' approach to knowledge generation should not be driven by their (dis)belief in religion; rather, they should endeavor to understand how research on critiques of the market can be enriched by incorporating a diversity of critiques (i.e. secular and religious).

There are several areas for future research. It would be of particular interest to explore the changes (e.g. political and socio-economic) religious critiques of the market undergo over time. The example of the Christian libertarianism in this chapter can be specifically insightful. Closely related to this is to understand whether or not such critiques mobilize the masses against capitalism. What kind of techniques do they employ? How do they interact with non-religious critiques of the market? Are they as isolated as they are in the academic literature? If yes, why? If no, why are they less represented in the field? If religious critics of the market are powerful in religious societies, are these societies free from poverty and social injustice? Have they managed to establish an ideal economy? What are the expected outcomes of generating knowledge on the critiques of the market? How can the knowledge generated in this area be enacted to benefit society at large?

Note

1 Non-religious governance.

References

Afrasiabi, K.L. (2003). Toward an Islamic ecotheology. In R.C. Foltz, F.M. Denny & A. Baharuddin (Eds.), *Islam and ecology: A bestowed trust* (pp. 282–296). Cambridge, MA, Harvard University Press.

Afzal-ur-Rahman (1975). *Economic doctrines of Islam*. Lahore, Islamic Publications.

Anderson, K. (2016). *Christians and economics: A biblical point of view*. Cambridge, OH, Christian Publishing House.

Assadourian, E. (2010). Transforming cultures: From consumerism to sustainability. *Journal of Macromarketing*, *30*(2), 186–191.

Asutay, M. (2007). Political economy approach to Islamic economics: Systemic understanding for an alternative economic system. *Kyoto Bulletin of Islamic Area Studies*, *1*(2), 3–18.

Bauman, Z. (2000). *Liquid modernity*. Cambridge, Polity.

Belk, R.W., Wallendorf, M., & Sherry, J.F. (1989). The sacred and the profane in consumer behavior: Theodicy on the odyssey. *Journal of Consumer Research*, *16*(1), 1–38.

Bell, D.M. (2012). *The economy of desire: Christianity and capitalism in a postmodern world*. Grand Rapids, MI, Baker Academic.

Bocock, R. (1993). *Consumption*. London, Routledge.

Bouma-Prediger, S. (2009). Is Christianity to blame? The ecological complaint against Christianity. Creation Care Conference, Southeastern Baptist Theological Seminary, October, 30–31.

Changkhwanyuen, P. (2004). Buddhist analysis of capitalism. *The Chulalongkorn Journal of Buddhist Studies*, *3*(2), 247–259.

Cort, J.C. (1988). *Christian socialism: An informal history*. Maryknoll, NY, Orbis Books.

Dien, M.I. (1997). Islam and the environment: Theory and practice. *Journal of Beliefs and Values*, *18*(1), 47–57.

Durkheim, E. (1984/1893). *The division of labor in society*. New York, Basic Books.

Durkheim, E. (1915/1912). *The elementary forms of religious life*. New York, Free Press.

El-Jurdi, H., Batat, W., & Jafari, A. (2017). Harnessing the power of religion: Broadening sustainability research and practice in the advancement of ecology. *Journal of Macromarketing*, *37*(1), 7–24.

Feuerbach, L. (1957). *The essence of Christianity*. New York, NY, Harper and Row.

Foltz, R.C., Denny, F.M., & Baharuddin, A. (2003). *Islam and ecology: A bestowed trust*. Cambridge, MA, Harvard University Press.

Freudenstein, E. (1970). Ecology and the Jewish tradition. *Judaism* (fall issue), 1–11.

Gauthier, F., & Martikainen, T. (Eds.) (2013). *Religion in consumer society: Brands, consumers and markets*. Surrey, Ashgate Publishing Limited.

Geertz, C. (1968). *Islam observed: Religious development in Morocco and Indonesia*. Chicago, IL, University of Chicago Press.

Gill, S. (1995). Globalisation, market civilisation, and disciplinary neoliberalism. *Millennium – Journal of International Studies*, *24*(3), 399–423.

Grønvold, J. (2013). Theology and sustainability in oil-producing Norway. *Nature & Culture*, *8*(3), 265–281.

Haddorff, D.W. (2000). Religion and the market: Opposition, absorption, or ambiguity? *Review of Social Economy*, *58*(4), 483–504.

Hurst, M., Dittmar, H., Bond, R., & Kasser, T. (2013). The relationship between materialistic values and environmental attitudes and behaviors: A meta-analysis. *Journal of Environmental Psychology*, *36*(December), 257–269.

Jafari, A. (2012). Islamic marketing: Insights from a critical perspective. *Journal of Islamic Marketing*, *3*(1), 22–34.

Jafari, A., & Sandıkcı, Ö. (2015). 'Islamic' consumers, markets, and marketing: A critique of El-Bassiouny's (2014) 'The one-billion-plus marginalization'. *Journal of Business Research*, *68*(12), 2676–2682.

Jafari, A., & Sandıkcı, Ö. (2016). The ontological pitfalls of Islamic exceptionalism: A re-inquiry on El-Bassiouny's (2014, 2015) conceptualization of 'Islamic Marketing'. *Journal of Business Research*, *69*(3), 1175–1181.

Jafari, A., & Süerdem, A. (2012). An analysis of material consumption culture in the Muslim world. *Marketing Theory*, *12*(1), 59–77.

Kalantari, A. (2008). *Eslam va Olgooye Masraf*. Qom, Boostan.

Kaplan, M.M. (2010/1934). *Judaism as a civilization: Toward a reconstruction of American-Jewish life*. Philadelphia, PA, Jewish Publication Society.

Kozinets, R.V. & Handelman, J.M. (2004). Adversaries of consumption: Consumer movements, activism, and ideology. *Journal of Consumer Research*, *31*(3), 691–704.

Kruse, K.M. (2015). *One nation under god: How corporate America invented Christian America*. New York, Basic Books.

Kuran, T. (1989). On the notion of economic justice in contemporary Islamic thought. *International Journal of Middle East Studies*, *21*(2), 171–191.

Levi, Y. (1993). Is the Torah capitalistic or socialistic? *B'Or HaTorah*, *8*, 113–119.

Marty, M. (1995). Materialism and spirituality in American religion. In R. Wuthnow (Ed.), *Rethinking materialism: Perspectives on the spiritual dimension of economic behavior* (pp. 237–253). Grand Rapids, MI, Eerdmans Publishing Company.

Marx, K., & Engels, F. (1967/1848). *The communist manifesto*. London, Penguin.

McAlexander, J.H., Dufault, B.L., Martin, D.M., & Schouten, J.W. (2014). The marketization of religion: Field, capital, and consumer identity. *Journal of Consumer Research*, *41*(3), 858–875.

Motahari, M. (2000). *Mas'aleye hejab*. Tehran, Sadra.

Muñiz, A.M., & Schau, H.J. (2005). Religiosity in the abandoned Apple Newton brand community. *Journal of Consumer Research*, *31*(4), 737–747.

Nash, J. (1991). *Loving nature: Ecological integrity and Christian responsibility*. Nashville, TN, Abingdon Press.

Nasr, S.H. (1997). *Man and nature: The spiritual crisis in modern man*. Chicago, IL, Kazi Publications.

Orwig, S.F. (2002). Business ethics and the protestant spirit: How Norman Vincent Peale shaped the religious values of American business leaders. *Journal of Business Ethics*, *38*(1), 81–89.

Ozdemir, I. (2003). Toward an understanding of environmental ethics from a Qur'anic perspective. In R.C. Foltz, F.M. Denny & A. Baharuddin (Eds.), *Islam and ecology* (pp. 3–38). Cambridge, MA, Harvard University Press.

Pabst, A. (2011). *The crisis of global capitalism: Pope Benedict XVI's social encyclical and the future of political economy*. Cambridge, James Clarke & Co.

Polanyi, K. (2001 [1944]). *The great transformation: The political and economic origins of our time*. Boston, MA: Beacon Press.

Sandel, M.J. (2012). *What money can't buy: The moral limits of markets*. London, Penguin Books.

Sandelands, L.E., & Andrew, J.H. (2008). Sustainability, faith, and the market. *Worldviews: Global Religions, Culture & Ecology*, *12*(2), 129–145.

Sarao, K.T.S. (n/d). Road blocks in sustainable development and social change: A Buddhist critique of modern capitalism and globalization. Retrieved June 6, 2017 from www.icdv.net/2014paper/ws1_01_en_Road_Blocks_in_Sustainable_Development_and_Social_Change_427447712.pdf.

Schmidt, L.E. (1995). *Consumer rites: The buying and selling of American holidays*. Princeton, NJ, Princeton University Press.

Shariati, A. (1988). Religion vs religion. Albuquerque, NM, ABJAD.

Siddiqi, M.N. (1972). *The economic enterprise in Islam*. Lahore, Islamic Publications.

Soroush, A. (2000). Reason, freedom, and democracy in Islam, ed. M. Sadri and A. Sadri. Oxford, Oxford University Press.

Süerdem, A. (2013). Yes my name is Ahmet, but please don't target me: Islamic marketing: Marketing Islam™? *Marketing Theory*, *13*(4), 285–295.

Süerdem, A. (2016). What is in a name that we call 'Islam'? A critical inquiry into the semiotic construction of super-brand Ummah. In A. Jafari and Ö. Sandıkcı (Eds.), *Islam, marketing and consumption: Critical perspectives on the intersections* (pp. 15–45). London, Routledge.

Tawney, R.H. (1920). *The acquisitive society*. New York, Harcourt, Brace and Co.

Thomas, N. (1932). *The socialist cure for a sick society*. New York, John Day Company.

Tirosh-Samuelson, H. (2001). Nature in the sources of Judaism. *Daedalus*, *130*(4), 99–124.

Trentmann, F. (2004). Beyond consumerism: New historical perspectives on consumption. *Journal of Contemporary History*, *39*(3), 373–401.

Trentmann, F. (2006). Knowing consumers – histories, identities, practices: An introduction. In F. Trentmann (Ed.), *The making of the consumer: Knowledge, power and identity in the modern world* (pp. 1–27). Oxford, Berg Publishers.

Usunier, J.C., & Stolz, J. (Eds.) (2014) *Religions as brands: New perspectives on the marketization of religion and spirituality*. London, Ashgate Publishing Ltd.

Wallis, J. (2010). *Rediscovering values: On Wall Street, Main Street, and your street: A moral compass for the new economy*. New York, Howard Books.

Weber, M. (1958/1904–1905). *The Protestant ethic and the spirit of capitalism*. New York, Scribner.

Weber, M. (1993). *The sociology of religion: Max Weber*. Boston, MA, Beacon Press.
West, C. (1991). *The ethical dimensions of Marxist thought*. New York, Monthly Review Press.
White Jr., L. (1967). The historical roots of our ecologic crisis. *Science*, *155*(March), 1203–1207.
Wirzba, N. (2003). *The paradise of God: Renewing religion in an ecological age*. New York, Oxford University Press.
Wuthnow, R. (1994a). Religion and economic life. In N.J. Smelser & R. Swedberg (Eds.), *Handbook of Economic Sociology* (pp. 620–646). Princeton, NJ, Princeton University Press.
Wuthnow, R. (1994b). *God and mammon in America*. New York, The Free Press.
Wuthnow, R. (1996). *Poor Richard's principle: Recovering the American dream through the moral dimension of work, business, and money*. Princeton, NJ, Princeton University Press.
Yusuf, S.M. (1971). *Economic justice in Islam*. Lahore, Sh. Muhammad Ashraf.

PART III

Rethinking consumers and markets
Critiques of markets

17
RE-MAPPING POWER FOR CRITICAL MARKETING AND CONSUMER RESEARCH

Janice Denegri-Knott

Introduction

Power has a prominent role in the organization and legitimacy of marketing theory and practice (Denegri-Knott, Zwick & Schroeder, 2006; Smith, 1987). Most notably, power underpins notions of consumer sovereignty which frame and legitimize the marketing function (see also Tadajewski, this volume). It has also gained analytical purchase as a conceptual vehicle through which critically inclined marketing and consumer researchers, can expose inequalities produced and maintained by marketing and markets more generally. That prominence has not always been adequately matched with an effort to come to terms with the various intellectual bases that inform its study. Mostly, power continues to be reduced to heuristic simplifications and ambiguous epithets. This makes any attempts to draw comparisons difficult. Even more challenging is undertaking the kind of theoretical development required to elevate the study of power in marketing into a programmatic area of research. In a remedial effort, this chapter re-visits an integrative framework of consumer power proposed by Denegri-Knott, Zwick and Schroeder (2006) for the purpose of redefining boundaries in the study of power for marketing and consumer research, surveying the state of research to date and suggesting new directions for research. The chapter offers an entrée for those new to the study of power and for the more familiarized reader, it provides a hopefully useful point of reference and departure.

Drawing from political and social theory, the original map focused on sovereign, cultural and discursive models of power and was used to establish familial relationships between power concepts and consumer and marketing research. It based its delimitation of sovereign-type approaches to power on a Dahlian conception of power as a zero sum, quantitative capacity, where market agents with the most individual or collective resources and skills were deemed powerful. The map also located cultural power at the level of strategic operations carried out by resource-rich businesses that have the most say in how market and consumer reality are to be ordered. Making a break with these negative conceptualizations of power as both destructive and repressive, discursive power was introduced, defining power as productive, relational and exercised across all members of a field.

Like its predecessor, the new proposed cartography described in this chapter also reflects the term's complex theoretical roots, not in the spirit of forcing convergences, but rather to help critical marketing and consumer researchers engage with the study of power more rigorously.

Cognizant that power is variously defined according to its theoretical roots (Dowding, 2012; Clegg, 1989; Haugaard, 2002), the formulation of an exact definition of power is omitted in favor of carrying out a comparative analysis of theories of power and discussing their implications for critical marketing and consumer research. The result of this exercise is a conceptual map that provides a contextualized and applied understanding of power. The framework is updated in two significant ways.

To begin with, the power territories mapped out in the original cartography have been repopulated to reflect research carried out since the first map was published. Second, in order to achieve greater distinction between cultural and discursive models of power and be consistent with theories of power in use in our field, cultural power is now replaced by hegemonic power. This provides a clearer demarcation between the theoretical traditions that inform these two models and enables a more precise articulation and differentiation of agendas, including a clearer identification of steering concepts and preferred methodological approaches.

Reading the map

There are still only a handful of comprehensive studies of power in consumer and marketing research (e.g. Denegri-Knott *et al.*, 2006; Desmond, 2003; Hopkinson & Blois, 2014). More generally, the term appears tangentially linked to other related concepts such as consumer resistance, empowerment, sovereignty or agency. In revisiting the map, Haugaard's (2002) conceptual map to power is once again borrowed. The starting point is the partitioning of two broad territories depending on their theoretical origins either in social or political theory. In the social theory tradition, definitions of power are dependent on broader explanations of how society works. Historically, social theories of power have dealt with structural inequalities embedded in society, and sought to expose the ways in which these are reproduced and how they may be subverted. Political theory, in turn, has pursued the development of a more precise and scientifically grounded way of measuring power. From these two branches, and in order to provide a more useful guide to critical marketing and consumer researchers, three further distinct models have been identified.

1 Sovereign power model (political theory)
2 Hegemonic power model (social theory)
3 Discursive power model (social theory)

This revised map, as its precursor did, provides a necessarily selective overview of some key literature. The map is not a comprehensive survey of all work that alludes to the study of power in marketing and consumer research, nor does it provide a synthesis of all power theories. Instead, it offers an impression of what the field looks like and draws on some illustrative examples to indicate how concepts have been used. Thus, the relationships that are presented for each stream are selective and by no means complete. The filial bonds are of first degree, for example, between de Certeau and a wide range of consumer researchers who have found his concepts of strategy and tactics of important analytical and theoretical value when approaching consumer power and resistance. A bold arrow links such first order affiliations. Dotted lines are used to show weaker relationships. This is the case for many marketing studies located in the sovereign power model, where power, while not defined, appears to adhere to a quantitative definition of power typical of the political tradition (see Figure 17.1).

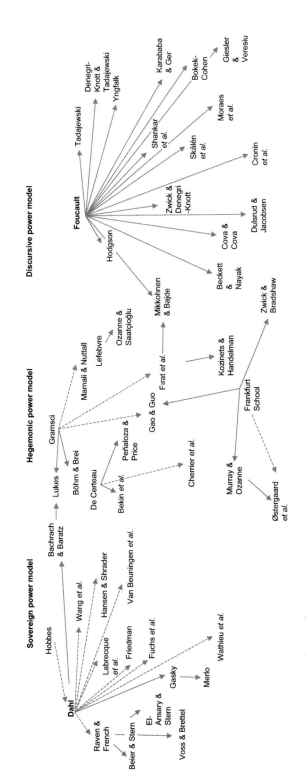

Figure 17.1 Conceptual map of power

Sovereign power model

Sovereign power is the first and most enduring model of power in the field of marketing. Power in the sovereign tradition is simply expressed as a force exerted *over* others. In this sense, social or political power is no different to the mechanical power of a machine. More wattage will yield a stronger tool for example, as much as a more resource-rich individual will be able to outflank a less powerful one. In political theory, this thinking can be traced back to Thomas Hobbes's (1651/1968) account of sovereign power. Hobbes provided the first modern theory of power as an aggregate of individuals' power into a power greater than any of them held individually. His power theoretic introduced a first model of power as a quantity capacity deployed to attain a personal advantage as well as distinguishing those powers that are innate to people, like their physical strength or talents, and those that are instrumentally obtained, such as riches and reputation. Importantly, Hobbes also conferred legitimacy to the sovereign as the rightful owner of power. For Hobbes, the collective power of people was consensually transferred to a sovereign by a Covenant to preserve peace and avoid war.

Some of these ideas endure in more contemporary theories of power within political theory and, in the marketing field, persist in the liberal concept of consumer sovereignty. By consumer sovereignty, as Slater (1997) explains, two key things are meant. First, that consumer needs are private and endogenous. They are immune to external manipulation and thereby consumer choices in the marketplace are genuine manifestations of free agency. Second, consumer sovereignty can only be fully realized in a competitive market society where producers, vying for consumers' 'dollar votes' (Dixon, 1992), can best respond to their preferences (see also Tadajewski, this volume and Dholakia *et al.*, this volume). This is a truly collective achievement made possible through the coordinated action emerging from the anarchic coalescence of individual desires and needs. Just like Hobbes's sovereign, sovereign consumers, as a block, are more powerful than individual producers because they amass more individual powers. However, this is also a power that is legitimated by way of agreement. Such agreement is granted by liberalism, which elevates free choice as the highest expression of personal freedom (Friedman & Friedman, 1990; Slater, 1997).

It follows that when looking for power in market relations, power is assumed to rightfully reside in the aggregate, with free choices made by autonomous and self-interested consumers directing the market's invisible hand. This assumption is of course wedded to liberal and neoliberal views of markets as optimal (and morally superior) allocation mechanisms of goods, services and societal wellbeing (Friedman & Friedman, 1990). The doctrine of consumer sovereignty is the product of a market constructed in these political and moral terms and in awarding power to the consumer without questioning his authority, legitimizes the market as highly democratic and participative. Yet, it also provides a convenient ideological smokescreen to cover all sorts of corporate ill doings (Hansen & Schrader, 1997; Smith, 1987). Despite being much maligned (see Tadajewski, this volume), consumer sovereignty makes possible a study of power for marketing research that can bypass any serious consideration or theoretical discussion of power. Symptomatic of this is our methodological response – the belief that consumers are *de facto* rightful owners of power and that whatever allows for improved choice making, means increased power. This has meant that all too often consumer sovereignty has been too quickly used as a heuristic to assign power to consumers.

With very few exceptions, most studies operate with an implicit and taken-for-granted definition of power as an ability to enforce change in the marketplace through sovereign consumer agency. Generally, we find cases studies of consumer boycotting activity (Friedman, 1991, 1996; Smith, 1987), collective purchasing to reduce market asymmetries (Wang, Zhao &

Li, 2011), enhanced decision-making (Broniarczyk & Griffin, 2014), increased control in the choice environment (Fuchs, Prandelli & Schreier, 2010; Wathieu *et al.*, 2002) and collective protest on social media (Yuksel, Milne & Milner, 2016). Frequently, power appears only as a footnote in these works, or simply equated to consumer empowerment. A good illustration of this treatment can be found in the following definition: 'Consumer empowerment results from products, services and practices that expand consumers' freedom of and control over the choice and action to shape their consumption experiences' (Yuksel *et al.*, 2016, p. 111). In other words, empowerment is the measure to which consumer sovereignty can be carried out. Methodologically this has meant that empowerment is measured in terms of concepts such as self-efficacy, involvement, and autonomy in choice making (see Fuchs *et al.*, 2010; Harrison & Waite, 2015). Indeed, power is not the subject of study, but rather seen only in conjunction with other empirical market-related phenomena such as boycotts, decision-making and reduction of market asymmetries.

While often unacknowledged, the model of power alluded to in these studies, is a zero sum, quantity capacity most often associated with the work of political pluralist, Robert Dahl (1957). In this model, power is defined as a quantifiable and accumulative essence that is distributed asymmetrically in any given system (Dahl, 1957; Clegg, 1989; Hindess, 1996) where A has the ability to make B do something that he/she would otherwise not do (Dahl, 1957). In theory, the measurement of power is empirically possible and can be done analytically. Within this framework, power is very specific and can be brought into sharp focus in key decision-making moments or episodes where outcomes can be determined. The implication of this is that we must rigorously test for causality in very specific contexts where powerful and less powerful actors are identified and decision-making outcomes ascertained. For example, in his famous study of community power in New Haven, Connecticut, Dahl identified who initiated and vetoed key decision-making processes in public education, urban development and public nominations for office. This allowed him to conclude that there wasn't one ruling elite in New Haven, but rather a plurality of elites.

In consumer and marketing research, this model of power continues to be popular, although progress toward more empirically focused and rigorous studies as envisioned by Dahl, has been uneven. There have been some positive developments since the publication of the first map in 2006, with many studies now disclosing definitions of power informing their work. Labrecque, vor dem Esche, Mathwick, Novak and Hofacker (2013, p. 257), for instance, provide a clear definition of power – as an asymmetric ability to control resources and people – that is then used to offer a framework to link 'consumer digital participation with evolving sources of power'. Merlo's (Merlo, Whitwell & Lukas, 2004; Merlo, 2011) studies of marketing's influence within organizations is also based on a definition of power as the 'capacity of one actor to make another do something that the other would not otherwise do' (2011, p. 1153). A similar concept is used by Voss and Brettel (2013) and others in a specialized manner to consider how the marketing department's power might be affected by the availability of alternatives within the firm to provide a customer connection, that is, whether the firm has a marketing orientation or the political acumen of those leading the marketing department. In this marketing management literature in particular, we find a more robust measurement of power. Here, the Dahlian framework has been used to inform an influential bases of power approach devoted to the measurement of five sources or bases of power – coercive, reward, referent, legitimate and expert – within organizational contexts (see Hopkinson & Blois, 2014). This approach was introduced in 1969 with the publication of a study by Beier and Stern, who transposed work originally used to explain power between individuals to an organizational context. Those ideas were subsequently tested by El-Ansary and Stern (1972) in a paper measuring power in distribution channels. In other studies, the focus is on strategies of power acquisition and maintenance, like those we first proposed in the 2006 paper, based on quantity capacity principles of power and subsequently tested by Kerr, Mortimera, Dickinson and Waller (2012) in their study of Australian bloggers. There are a handful of variations of the above work, with many studies latching upon related concepts of empowerment to measure distribution of power in consumer–producer dyads (Pires, Stanton & Rita, 2006) or as resulting in greater feelings of control and the acquisition of choice-making skills (Harrison & Waite, 2015; Harrison, Waite & Hunter, 2006; Labrecque et al., 2013; Wathieu et al., 2002). What is consistent across these investigations is the overall aim of cataloguing sources of power and strategies through which power can be either measured or increased.

New research directions

Given that a key goal of this model is the precise measurement of power, there are opportunities for further conceptual and methodological refinement. To begin with, the principle of causality which requires a cause-effect assessment, needs to be more clearly expressed in our research designs. This means that more work needs to assess how power is distributed across a range of stakeholders beyond that which is assumed legitimately belongs to consumers as sovereign agents. That is, we must approach the study of power, freed from the underlying assumption that power is possessed by consumers *only*. This will see the horizon of our empirical contexts substantially expanded to consider power distribution among a range of actors, including, but not limited to, businesses, government agencies, environmentalists, local governments, charities, consumer defense leagues and volunteer groups.

This means that going forward we should supplement emphasis placed on consumer–company dyadic relationships (even when studying collective actions such as boycotts and class action-suits) with studies that include a broader range of agents. Consider the case of decisions made about the privatization of health or education, governmental legislation banning diesel cars, or disputes over copyright resulting in products being withdrawn from the market. In all of these different scenarios power is distributed in various locations. Likewise, we find campaigns aiming to change a company's position will often involve a range of different actors. In the 2001–03 Stop Esso campaign, a coalition against Exxon, included a number of stakeholders such as Greenpeace, Friends of the Earth, high-profile celebrities, journalists and consumers who wanted to change the company's policy on climate change. Even the service dominant logic (S-D Logic) paradigm where value in co-creation is generally described as resulting from the harmonious collaboration between multiple actors operating in a marketing system or service ecosystem (Vargo & Lusch, 2004) has evolved into a consideration of disruption produced by conflict between different actors. For example, Corvellec and Hultman's (2014) study of the politics of value in a Swedish Waste Management service system is a good illustration of how competing actors operating in a market context (households, companies producing waste, municipalities) are said to draw from different institutionalized regimes of value to express and communicate value. In this work, the act of valuation itself is construed as political because it creates conflict among actors (given their different ways of appraising what is valuable and good). This kind of dynamic can be re-appraised by a closer examination of power distribution in specific value co-creation systems.

In better understanding power distribution, we return to Dahl's (1961) studies of New Haven politics, for guidance. Our empirical focus should be on the consequences of decision-making. This is best done by observing decision-making events as it is 'in cases involving key political decisions in which the preferences of the hypothetical ruling elite run counter to those of any other likely group that might be suggested' (Dahl, 1958, p. 466). For instance, in the

UK, opposition to the opening of a new McDonald's restaurant could aggregate small business owners, anti-McDonald's activist groups, council members, consumers, the parish council and neighborhood associations around a council's decision to grant permission for operating.

Such work can be organized according to Dahl's descriptive (magnitude, distribution, scope and domain) and exploratory characteristics (resources, skill, motivations and cost). First, *magnitude* must be established. We must answer, who has more power? Going back to our example of McDonald's opening a new outlet; do McDonald's, the councilors, the parish council, or the local neighborhood association have more power in determining the outcome of the application? Second, we must determine how power is *distributed* among stakeholders. What are each group's defining characteristics? Is it a Conservative council? Is it a low-income neighborhood? We also need to qualify power further by studying its *scope*, meaning what specific behaviors or aspects are affected. For example, a company might exert power when fixing high prices for pharmaceuticals, but cannot determine their classification as over-the-counter medication. An individual consumer can boycott McDonald's, but they cannot impede the opening of its new outlet if permission by the council is granted. Market actors will have a specific *domain* over which they can exercise power. Do they exercise power over consumers, marketing professionals, local communities, city planners, local businesses or a selection of these?

Upon this initial determination of the system where power operates, a more granular analysis of power can be performed by looking at Dahl's explanatory characteristics made up of *resources, skills, motivations* and *costs*. The characteristics of *motivations* and *costs* in particular can help enrich existing focus on *resources* and *skills*. By looking into motivations, we can better account for intentionality to act upon power. This means that the motivations of powerful and less powerful market actors need to be determined or measured. What is the neighborhood association's motivation to oppose the opening of a McDonald's? Why is this issue of importance to the parish council and small businesses opposing the application? The question of who has more resources is one of importance too, as it is expected that those with more resources are more likely to be more powerful. A group opposing the expansion of McDonald's might find it difficult to win over the hearts of undecided stakeholder groups, the neighborhood, parish council or councilors if they cannot afford to fund their campaign, or if they do not have the political skills. In order to provide a clearer picture of power, future research could map out the different resources and skills available across different stakeholder groups. Last, opportunity costs can be factored in order to assess a powerful agent's likelihood to act over a weaker one, or likewise, the opportunities less powerful actors have to resist. How far is McDonald's likely to go, or invest in this new restaurant, taking into account the general animosity the plan is generating among their desired potential market?

Hegemonic power model

The hegemonic model of power is informed by critiques of the market as a culturally authoritarian force systematically corroding communal embeddedness and encouraging excessive individualism (Murray & Ozanne, 1991; Ozanne & Murray, 1995; Peñaloza & Price, 1993). In this model, consumer sovereignty is not a means to exercise individual or collective power in the marketplace, but rather a chimerical and ideologically potent myth that free choice is a self-determined act of autonomy and power (Carrington, Zwick & Neville, 2016). In this model power is a *power to* that creates optimal opportunities for A, who has the power to make X happen (Pansardi, 2012). This means that power is not observable or quantifiable as in the sovereign power model, but rather is a latent capability to implant 'enabling or disabling strategies vis-à-vis protagonists' (Clegg, 2002, p. 89).

In critical marketing and consumer research, our understanding of hegemonic power is largely framed by concepts derived from Antonio Gramsci and Frankfurt School theorists including Adorno, Horkheimer, Althusser, Marcuse and Fromm (see Izberk-Bilgin (2010) for a comprehensive overview) and more recently de Certeau and Lefebvre. Gramsci (1971) provides us with a definition of hegemony as the permeation of an entire system of values and morality through societal structures such as schools, churches, family and trade unions, which allow for the domination of one class over another. When fully internalized, hegemony is accepted as a 'common sense' directing people toward desired behaviors, even when these run counter to what is good for them. In this model, power operates through a culture industry, including the media and advertising, tasked with inculcating a sense of individualism via consumption choices (Adorno & Horkheimer, 1997), elevating 'having' rather than 'being' as a meaningful mode of existing (Fromm, 1976/2007) and creating false needs, so that unequal participation in capitalist relations of production can be maintained (Marcuse, 1964/1991). Simply put, power inhibits the identification and realization of real needs and instead implants desires and thoughts which serve the long-term interests of a ruling class (see also Tadajewski, this volume).

Power is given more material force in the writings of Lefebvre (1991) and de Certeau (1984). In Henri Lefebvre's (1991) *The Production of Space*, space is defined as a unitary body which brings in together place, abstraction and social action. In this modality, the mental components, the ideological nature of markets as they are thought of and planned by entrepreneurs, the built environments through which exchange can take place as well as the social action within that domain, would be distinguishable, but not separable dimensions of market space. In order to account for the complex production of space he drew up a conceptual triad. His spatial project subsequently unfolds in the intertwining of the physical space (nature), mental space (abstraction) and social space (human action). For Lefebvre, the first dimensions, the abstract space and that of the built environment, are products of power. These spaces were the spaces of commodities and capital. These dimensions cohere with de Certeau's (1984) concept of power as strategy. Strategy, he wrote, was an expression of will and power of subjects such as an enterprise or proprietor who postulate a place as his own, and from which relations with exterior others (consumers, competitors, clients) can be managed. Places are designed and controlled by a ruling class for the purpose of steering individuals to believe that acquisitiveness and consumption are the paths to a good life, in this way hindering their ability to make critical and progressive choices (Murray & Ozanne, 1991; Ozanne & Murray, 1995).

These ideas have shaped criticisms against markets as a cultural authority in the marketing academe with Ozanne and Murray (1995) having been most vocal in charging the market with restricting communicative openness and semiotic diversity. Here, hegemonic power is seen as operating in the articulation of research problems such as the ethical consumption attitude–behavior gap popular in the business scholarship (Carrington et al., 2016), the commodification of historic sites (Gao & Guo, 2017) and in the perpetuation of discourses that benefit owners of capital (Böhm & Brei, 2008).

Generally, these critiques have stopped short of disclosing the kind of power theory that is driving analysis, opting instead to use Marx's concept of class struggle to explain how owners of capital are able to retain their position of power and influence. In that relationship, it is the ruling class who is presented as powerful and actively pursuing the protection of that position through a series of strategies designed to maintain the status quo. That is, class struggle incorporates aspects of domination, meaning strategies used by a ruling class such as coaxing, persuasion, violence or prohibition, to maintain and enhance its privileged position as well as to prevent resistance. Such descriptors bring to mind a power–resistance couplet, where power is something that is 'owned' by a ruling class and utilized to maintain an existing social order and resistance is what an oppressed, subaltern class does in order to resist existing social arrangements.

In Gramscian theory resistance is possible through the creation of a counter-hegemony to challenge the false world of established appearances embedded in the dominant belief systems. This task is delegated to organic intellectuals (Gramsci, 1971), who must 'incite critical reflection in subaltern groups, and develop an alternative hegemony' (Boggs, 1976, p. 42). Resistance also requires critical reflection. Ozanne and Murray (1995) see this in a reflexively defiant consumer, capable of challenging existing structures to assert her or his independence from the marketplace in defining and meeting needs. Such aspiration is present in the consumer resistance movements described by Kozinets and Handelman (2004) or Canadian-based Adbusters (Østergaard, Hermansen, & Fitchett, 2015), which aim to denaturalize consumer culture and create more humane socio-economic systems. Resistance can also be parodic in nature. As Mikkonen and Bajde (2013) show, parodies can be powerful vehicles to help people imagine other ways of being that run contrary to dominant consumer culture expectations.

For Lefebvre (1991), resistance should culminate not only with ideological changes to existing superstructures, but produce new spaces to realize its full potential. These ideas are taken by Saatçioğlu and Ozanne (2013) to envision the production of counter-spaces of hope that can be more democratic and counter marketplace exclusion. More specifically, they invite policy makers to adopt a more humane approach that incorporates input from marginalized groups when designing fair housing policies, for example. In a more extreme vision of resistance found in the writings of Fırat and Venkatesh (1995), emancipation requires stepping outside the market altogether so that alternative life-worlds can be built. As Izberk-Bilgin (2010 p. 311) explains, resistance understood in these terms 'is achievable only if the consumer, rather than mastering the code, breaks away from it'.

In de Certeau (1984) resistance is much more prosaic in scope. Where power is strategic, resistance is tactical. As de Certeau explains, resistance is present in mundane consumption practices, through which consumers *make do* with 'products imposed by a dominant economic order' (1984, p. xix). So, while consumers might have limited opportunities to change a market and the capitalist system that sustains it, they can subvert intended product uses by incorporating them in their own idiosyncratic ways. These tactics of resistance are, indeed, not radical and do not need to amount to a frontal challenge to power. Thus, although tactics remain inscribed in the territory of power, these allow consumers to transverse it, imposing their own interests and desires. Resistance, as Peñaloza and Price (1993) describe, can be found in mundane everyday acts such as using a refrigerator as a communal bulletin board. These small acts of subterfuge alter meanings and objects, transforming them into singular possessions or experiences. In critical marketing and consumer research this has also shaped a liberatory agenda (e.g. Ozanne & Murray, 1995; Fırat & Venkatesh, 1995), where resistance is emancipatory in its rejection of the market's cultural authority. In particular, Dholakia and colleagues' postmodern agenda for consumer and marketing research rendered consumers as agentic manipulators of meaning, and not powerless victims of marketing (Fırat & Dholakia, 1998; Fırat & Venkatesh, 1995). Resistance, here, does not have a strategic intent, but rather hijacks power through playful, irreverent behaviors. However, they can be more purposeful too. For example, inspired by de Certeau (1984), Bekin, Carrigan and Szmigin (2005) detail the micro-level simplifier strategies in New Consumption Communities – such as buying second-hand goods, recycling products, avoiding processed or non-organic food, growing their own fruit and vegetables and sharing one car – that allow members to restructure their production systems so as to redefine their position in the marketplace.

We see such ideas present in descriptions of consumers purposefully distancing themselves away from the market to experience other forms of exchange and more authentic ways of being, such as those offered by the Burning Man festival (Kozinets, 2002) or in simplifier strategies (Bekin et al., 2005), non-consumption for sustainability (Cherrier, Black & Lee, 2011), downshifting (Cherrier & Murray, 2002), culture jamming and anti-branding (Østergaard et al., 2015), deviant behaviors (Amine & Gicquel, 2011), purification and transformation of hegemonic practices by resisting organizations (Mamali & Nuttall, 2016) or through consumer cynicism (Mikkonen & Bajde, 2013; Odou & Pechpeyrou, 2011).

New research directions

As Tadajewski (2010) concludes in his assessment of the state of critical theories as a series of perspectives for use in marketing, the hegemonic model of power continues to be underutilized. While, no doubt, this model has resulted in rich empirical accounts of consumer resistance in particular and arresting critiques of marketplace inequalities, power defined in these terms, has a somewhat opaque explanatory value (Hindess, 1996). This is because, in privileging class and ideology as taken-for-granted motives for power, power becomes empirically opaque. The reduction of hegemonic power to the study of resistance has meant a reduction of our field of study to adversarial or reactive consumer actions. The problem in focusing on resistance is that these studies say very little about the hegemonic powers that provoke it. Put differently, we are left with moralizing condemnations devoid of analysis. That is, we enter the field looking for evidence of pre-established assumptions as to where power is located and we find it.

There are, however, some encouraging developments in our field that we can take as useful footings for further work. To begin with, in order to get a more precise articulation of the functioning of hegemonic power, studies could refine their conceptual tools by way of theoretical integration. Such work has been carried out effectively by Carrington et al. (2016) in their joint use of Althusser and Žižek, which they use to challenge the status of ethical consumption as a means to resist or negate global capitalism, to reveal it, instead, as producing a hysterical consumer subject that sustains global capitalism in their ethically led consumption choices. Likewise, in their study of Red tourism to the birthplace of the Chinese Communist revolution in the Jianggang Mountains, Gao and Guo (2017) draw from both Althusser and Williams to provide a measured account of the complex constitution of hegemonic power, not as a homogenous ideological form, but rather a hybrid of emergent and dominant ideologies. They illustrate how competing ideologies such as Confucianism, capitalism and communism exert influence in the shaping of consumption practices. As they explain, 'some local consumer practices may be oppositional to capitalism and globalization but, by mobilizing various forms of nationalism . . . they also take on the ideological baggage of nationalism, which may facilitate, rather than resist, the rule of the state' (Gao & Guo, 2017, p. 252). In furthering our understanding of resistance, longitudinal studies that shed light on how hegemonic power is contested could be pursued. Such work could, as Mamali and Nuttal (2016) have done in their study of a community cinema, focus on how hegemonic practices are appropriated and purified in order to be congruent with the anti-consumption space they enter. This allows us to better understand how practices of resistance themselves are transformed through the integration of hegemonic practices.

If the focus is to be power, future work could change its secondary role, to one that is more methodologically meaningful. A way of doing this work is to engage with Stephen Lukes's radical vision for the study of power. Lukes's (1974, p. 22) radical and three-dimensional view of power folds in the empiricism of the Dahlian approach with a critical predisposition to expose structural inequalities through which power is deployed without 'being recognized by those who are subject to its effects'. In Lukes's three-dimensional view of power, Dahl's empirical-causal model of power makes up the first dimension. The second dimension incorporates Bachrach and Baratz's (1962) corrective to expose the institutional biases that limit agents' participation in the political process through agenda setting. Lukes (1974, p. 25) adds a third (radical) dimension to deal with the cultural structuration of power relations, where power is exercised in 'influencing, shaping . . . determining wants'. This means bringing to the fore latent conflicts and distinguishing between the real interests of those who do not exercise power and those who do. Power here is not simply exercised covertly by a powerful individual, but rather resides in 'socially structured and culturally patterned behavior' (Lukes, 1974, p. 22). This position is commensurate with explanations articulated by Gramsci and the Frankfurt School, as it argues that the working classes (powerless) internalize values that are contrary to their long-term wellbeing. Empirical cases could include contentious areas involving a range of different stakeholders, such as the future of diesel cars or privatization of public services. Based on this first-dimension assessment, analysis would progress to expose overt conflicts, items for example that a stakeholder group considers important, and which are not timetabled for discussion. A third-dimension analysis would move onto the more challenging differentiation between real and false needs from those who are deemed powerless and affected by decision-making outcomes.

Discursive power model

In the last decade, Michel Foucault's concepts, histories and methodologies have provided the most productive framework for critical marketing and consumer research (Denegri-Knott et al., 2006; Shankar, Cherrier & Canniford, 2006; Denegri-Knott, 2004; Tadajewski, 2006). Together, this work has focused our attention on power as channeling our way of thinking about consumers, producers, markets and marketing. This critical attitude has also sensitized researchers in the field about the operation of power relations in enabling and denying forms of thinking and being as well as the spaces of resistance they open (e.g. Denegri-Knott & Tadajewski, 2017; Giesler & Veresiu, 2014; Skålén, Fellesson & Fougère, 2006; Tadajewski, 2006, 2011). These papers have done so by subscribing to a productive and relational understanding of power. Power is not, as the sovereign or hegemonic model of power would have us believe, a destructive force that can be held and lost by a sovereign or ruling elite. It cannot be measured or located in one site. Causal relationships between those who have power and those who do not cannot be empirically determined, or inferred simply from coercive actions. Rather, what makes power effective is its productive and creative quality (Foucault, 1994). Its study requires a general suspicion toward what is believed to be a universal truth to expose the power relations that legitimated ways of understanding and acting upon the world and ourselves.

For Foucault (1976/1998, 1994), power is creative in that it directs practices, desires, norms and morals through the production of discourse. These, he defined as a collection of identifiable utterances bound by rules of construction and evaluation, which make it possible to say and do within a particular field of action (Foucault, 1982). That is, behavior is not guided by an internal moral compass, but rather an external code that has been internalized. Such effects are achieved by the ongoing administration of discipline across a range of institutions and by the subject himself, with the aim of producing a certain type of person (Foucault, 1976/1998, 1977/1991). Discourses themselves are products of power, inasmuch as only certain knowledges gain legitimacy as truthful, and the way in which they attain this status is politically motivated and enacted (Foucault, 1977/1991, 1979, 1980a). Marketing discourses, as epistemologically linked to those which arouse greatest suspicion from Foucault – medicine, economics, and the social sciences (Tadajewski, 2011) – have a considerable effect on shaping how we come to understand and act upon ourselves, and thus demand our attention.

This model's popularity coincides with the growing prominence of S-D Logic studies and other systemic perspectives, such as Actor Network Theory, in the marketing field that flatten distinctions between producers and consumers and position them rather as co-creators of value in market processes. Such narrative runs counter to binary oppositions pitting marketers against consumers, and is more amenable to an inclusive and productive vision of power. The model encourages a view of power as creating the very conceptual categories through which distinctions between consumers, producers and market practices can be made. This model of power also rejects any definition of power as a fixed quantity held by a powerful sovereign. Instead, power is conceived as relational and distributed across the social body in a network-like way. It can only be exercised by means of securing alignments between the actions of network actors (Foucault, 1976/1998). This means that the actions of a dominant actor are constrained by the need to sustain that alignment in the future, but at the same time are resisted by agents challenging that alignment. Power is thus co-constituted by those who support and resist it (Foucault, 1976/1998).

One way of studying power has been to bring to the fore the historic conditions that enabled certain knowledges to emerge and gain currency, as well as the various disciplinary mechanisms through which these truths operate across populations to produce desired subjects and practices. Rather than passively accepting claims to truths such as the universality of consumer sovereignty, or service excellence, for example, studies within this model have drawn attention to the power-infused processes through which certain knowledges gained their discursive legitimacy (Cova & Cova, 2009; Denegri-Knott & Tadajewski, 2017; Tadajewski, 2006; Skålén et al., 2006; Skålén 2009; Tadajewski & Jones, 2016).

This kind of sensitivity has generated work that reimagines developments in theory and practice as being discontinuous, rather than evolutionary (Denegri-Knott & Tadajewski, 2010; Tadajewski & Jones, 2016). For example, Denegri-Knott and Tadajewski (2010) have shown in their critical history of MP3 technology, that new products are discontinuous and respond to certain orders of knowledge and do not naturally follow an organized or logical development. This, and other work in this model, sees marketing as a form of government that mobilizes reflexive capabilities in both consumer and market employees by encouraging agency in line with consumption opportunities. To illuminate this, there are now various theoretical and empirical accounts of how consumers (Beckett, 2012; Beckett & Nayak, 2008; Bokek-Cohen, 2016; Moraes, Shaw & Carrigan, 2011; Shankar et al., 2006; Zwick & Denegri-Knott, 2009) and market workers (Tadajewski & Jones, 2016; Skålén et al., 2006; Skålén 2009) are governed and self-managed through marketing discourse.

We have also increased our commitment to deal with discursive power more generally, to focus on how normality operates through market-sanctioned discourses in the family, the media, branding and other institutions. In contemporary consumer cultures, people are subject to neoliberal ideals which are perpetuated across societal institutions, including advertising and marketing, which govern people as consuming, self-enterprising subjects (Rose, 1999). By 'govern', Foucault (1991), referred to those calculated efforts to control and regulate people's conduct through technologies of domination and technologies of the self. From this vantage point, consumer sovereignty is a condition to power, where individuals are invited to act in self-enterprising ways to maximize the quality of their own lives through choices they make in the marketplace (Rose, 1999; Shankar et al., 2006). This requires a continual exercise over ourselves, a form of self-elaboration that is increasingly reliant on promotional discourses that provide us with morally viable ways of being. Ideal standards of what we can be are present in a steady supply of possible lifestyles, glamorized through advertising and other promotional discourses. Thus, to know ourselves, becomes a practice mediated by a range of market resources;

the kinds of lives we want to lead will therefore require purchasing products and brands that help actualize desired ideals. In this modality, power operates through a discourse of consumer sovereignty, where one is given a degree of autonomy so that human potentiality and self-actualization can be reached through self-determined acts of choice (Rose, 1999). Consumer subjects defined in these terms are subject to a range of marketing technologies such as branding, advertising, sales, database and behavioral marketing techniques, and self-governing via free exercise of choice in the marketplace. Together, these power technologies have colonized everyday life in ways that encourage people to see themselves as consumers when dealing, not only with their purchasing decisions in the marketplace, but also their medical care, politics and education (Shankar et al., 2006).

In critical marketing and consumer research these ideas have steered studies into the emergence of consumer subjects and practices (Karababa & Ger, 2011), self-governing in choice making (Cronin, McCarthy & Delaney, 2015; Moraes et al., 2011), governing through marketing technologies such as club cards (Beckett & Nayak, 2008), databases (Zwick & Denegri-Knott, 2018) and in-store surveillance (Dulsrud & Jacobsen, 2009). Consumers are, as Beckett and Nayak (2008) as well as Zwick and Denegri-Knott (2018) have shown, subjected to disciplinary marketing technologies such as databases and CRM which govern by way of increased objectivization of the consumer by ever more precise behavioral profiling, but also in subjectivizing the consumer with identity forms they are encouraged to appropriate and internalize. More recently a number of studies have provided a more nuanced understanding of how whole populations of consumers are governed by drawing on Foucault's concept of bio-power (see Zwick & Bradshaw, 2016; Yngfalk, 2016). The concept covers the various ways in which populations are acted upon, including visualization, discipline and manipulation and the direct regulation of health and life expectancy. An effective application of the concept in marketing is provided by Zwick and Bradshaw (2016). They use the term to develop their own definition of biopolitical marketing, which they describe as strategies seeking to capture and manage consumers in intensive networks of production, consumption, surveillance and entertainment. They show how biopolitical marketing functions within the context of online communities, by 'inserting the object for sale directly into the social fabric and, thus, renders the production of consumer subjectivity as contributive to the continuous dynamic reproduction of value competitive' (Zwick & Bradshaw, 2016, p. 96).

New research directions

Foucault is best approached as providing a tool box or scaffolding for undertaking studies of power. In that spirit, new directions for research could include: (1) studies that problematize or challenge taken-for-granted assumptions, (2) comprehensive studies into the different technologies of power and (3) legitimation of value-creating processes.

Archaeology and genealogy are two means to problematize existing assumptions in marketing knowledge. To do this requires that at an archaeological level we pay attention to the 'conditions under which certain relations between subject and objects are formed or modified, to the extent that these relations are constitutive of a possible knowledge' (Foucault, 1994, p. 314). We must draw more careful attention, as has Tadajewski (2006), to the historic conditions enabling the emergence of discourse, to include an account of political, economic and social factors, accepted means of generating knowledge, and available institutional frameworks for the provision of marketing education, which enabled the emergence of marketing as a field of knowledge. In sharpening our study of discursive power, we must demonstrate a commitment to undertake genealogical work. Without revealing the histories of embattlements which led to the production of what counts as truth, our work will lack critical edge. This means that we must be suspicious of any universal and essentialist claims about marketing concepts, objects, practices and subjects. Instead we should view them as political products, bound to their own historical milieu and legitimated within domains of normality within power relations. This can be done by unearthing the conditions that made the production of knowledge and their accompanying artifacts possible and by considering the whole range of mechanisms that are brought to bear upon individuals in order to produce docile consumers and disciplined marketing workers.

This means that in radicalizing our senses toward deeply held assumptions about what marketing is and does, we must examine those knowledges that had been actively filtered out and historically buried for being located 'beneath the required level of cognition and scientificity' (Foucault, 1980a, p. 82). Subjugated, naive knowledges are underused, but vital, resources for understanding discursive power, as they have the ability to disrupt the dynamic flow between power and knowledge, and expose the 'ruptural effects of conflict and struggle that the order imposed by functionalist and systematising thought is designed to mask' (Foucault, 1980a, p. 82). What Foucault means is that we must unravel why a certain discourse and not others attains analytic purchase by drawing attention to the denials of validity, and challenges of appropriateness they face within an established order of marketing discourse.

Such subjugated knowledges in marketing could include failed theoretical developments, in the shape of work that has been excluded from entering the marketing canon. These could be, for example, new steering concepts or more process-based accounts of how marketing is to be performed that were dismissed as unscientific or not relevant (see Denegri-Knott & Tadajewski (2017) for an example). They could also be the popular knowledge of marketing held by consumers themselves or people who have not received a formal education in marketing. The aim is to unsettle the sedimented taken-for-granted truths that have currency in present scholarship, as a means to draw a baseline for further critique, reflection and, ultimately, re-development. These types of studies continue to be limited. This task is more pressing when we consider how new marketing knowledge, such as value co-creation, celebrates participatory consumer engagement and seeks to redefine marketplace relations in terms of sharing and equality (see Zwick & Bradshaw, 2016). There is, therefore, plenty of scope to question how a range of marketing concepts and practices, such as co-creation, relationship making and branding, emerge and take hold on our imagination and become taken-for-granted aspects of what counts as marketing and the legitimation function they serve.

More specifically, the emergence of co-creation of value as participatory can be challenged in ways that extend work already undertaken by Zwick and Bradshaw (2016) and Denegri-Knott and Tadajewski (2017). S-D Logic's new emphasis on operant, or knowledge-based resources in co-creation, should be matched with studies that deal with the power relations through which legitimacy is constructed and maintained. In the case of the S-D Logic paradigm, practices, it is claimed, add value by making certain actions reproducible and repeatable. For example, Schau, Muñiz and Arnould (2009) illustrate the various practice-based processes undertaken by brand community members that might constitute collective value co-creation. This means that the more a practice is sedimented in a meso context, such as a brand community, the more a greater number of consumers can derive value from that brand. How legitimate value-creating consumer practices attain their legitimacy is ill defined. Practices described by Schau *et al.* (2009) such as championing a brand or showing Mini owners how to best look after their car, as well as those practices through which communities themselves are maintained (greeting, motivating participation), are assumed as legitimate. Thus, work so far has been politically conservative. Explicit attention could be placed on the discursive arrangements enabling the justifications needed to distinguish between practices that can create or destroy value, and those that are deemed unacceptable altogether. Without understanding the kind of conditions that underwrite legitimate co-creating practices we cannot understand their political relevance. Doing this requires questioning the taken-for-granted legitimacy warranted to them and focusing instead on the power relations leading to their emergence and legitimation.

Discursive studies of power could also be extended to include work appraising the currency of marketing's own explanatory power in relation to other fields of knowledge. In their study of the legitimization of digital music consumption, Denegri-Knott and Tadajewski (2017) show how in determining the legitimacy of file sharing and as source of value, competing communal discourses were denied any currency, allowing for an articulation of legality to be established by an interpolation of digital libertarianism and market conservatism. The power of market conservatism was exposed by showing the ease with which it was accepted as the reasonable and truthful justification for why file sharing should be treated as a deviant practice.

There is also an acute need for studies dealing with the intersection of competing discourses acting upon consumption practices. Often, consumer sovereignty is mobilized as totalizing, denying the operation of other discourses, thus reducing the complexity of the knowledge systems in operation. A good example of work that is beginning to address this is Yngfalk's (2016) study of how the intersection of marketing and state discourses shapes food consumption choices through food labeling. That work shows there is an enmeshing of state and marketing discourses in driving consumption choices that is not only meant to be individualized as per a neoliberal marketing discourse, but also to bio-politicize consumption at a macro, population level. That bio-politicization is achieved by the authority of the label that dictates when produce must be sold and consumed by. As Yngfalk (2016, p. 283) explains: 'date labelling actualizes an anatomo-politics that manipulates and utilizes individual bodies in food consumption and it provides companies with the means by which to govern, in detail, the pace of food consumption and production in the market.'

Likewise, new research directions can catalogue the multitude of technologies that are deployed (and to what effect) as well as the forms of self-governing required from people subjecting themselves as consumers or market employees. Such a shift will also allow us to consider the range of technologies of domination and of the self which are deployed and how they work together in dispensing power. Here Foucault's concept of the *dispositive* – 'a heterogeneous ensemble consisting of discourses, institutions, architectural forms, regulatory decisions, laws, administrative measures, scientific statements, philosophical, moral and philanthropic propositions which are mobilized to produce and maintain power' (Foucault, 1980b, pp. 194–195), can provide a useful framework for further work. Such scholarship could locate the different legal, disciplinary and security *dispositives* modulating power in a given field of market action (see Raffnsøe, Gudmand-Høyer & Thaning, 2016). So, research could ask what rules and regulation shape market practices, what are the systems of legal mechanisms that can be enforced to produce desired practices? What disciplinary *dispositives* – education, timetabling of activity, examination, surveillance, training, pedagogy are in place? And what are the *dispositives* of security, such as self-regulation, bio-power, technologies of self and pastoral power, in operation?

Conclusion

This chapter provides a revised edition of a cartography of power models for marketing and consumer research first published in 2006. The key reason for doing this was to offer some definitional clarity and identify various entry points from which to navigate the complex political and social theory on power and to show how these ideas had shaped, or could shape still, our research priorities.

In returning to the field, the need to redefine power territories, in light of developments since its publication, was made apparent. The first realization was that the cultural power heading initially utilized was not sufficiently distinct from the discursive model of power, and that definitions of power were not sufficiently clear or anchored in political and social theory. This was evident in the boundary-spanning theories of de Certeau and Foucault which could be, to lesser or greater degree, connected to work assigned to cultural and discursive models of power included in the 2006 map. A second observation is that the first framework was too narrowly focused on the question of consumer empowerment, and this told an incomplete picture of power. A re-reading of classic texts of power across the three domains, suggested that even situations where power could be reduced to a quantity capacity definition demanded a consideration of greater number of actors beyond consumers and businesses. This broadening coheres with present concerns in the marketing discipline, in particular those emerging from the S-D Logic tradition, and Actor Network Theory and Practice Theory interventions. A common complaint in those works has been our disciplinary emphasis on producer or consumer agency which is seen as eclipsing the role of other actors; a point not missed by Vargo and Lusch (2015), who have argued recently that the more important extension of S-D Logic has been a zooming out from its original narrow focus on dyadic interactions between firms and consumers to produce a more realistic, dynamic and holistic perspective of how value is created across a range of agents. Another realization was that by enlarging the domain of power beyond the consumer, the marketing management literature initially overlooked in the first map, showed how since the 1970s a rigorous measurement of marketing power within organizations had been flourishing.

A last observation was that progress across models had been patchy. Changes in the landscape have not been uniform. Areas of interest over time had shifted toward the discursive model. The hegemonic model, hampered by the apparent waning of the postmodern project, has lost some of its vitality and momentum, with little theoretical or empirical development. The specter of sovereign power still looms large. It is, by and large, the idea of power that dominates and is invoked to demonstrate who has power in the marketplace.

The chapter also outlines directions for future research. These should be taken as suggestions for future work. Over time the hope is that, based on a sturdier edifice for the study of power, we collectively will be willing and able to adopt a more courageous, less prescriptive attitude toward how we go about framing our projects and justifying their importance. An unintended consequence of embracing models in overly prescriptive ways is the limiting of our imagination by importing programmatic research agendas from social and political theory into the domain of marketing. Our own critical ambition becomes secondary or subject to a ready-made perspective with stock questions, methods and modes of interpretation. As this re-mapping exercise has also revealed, that ambition, is beginning to be realized. That map, however, is yet to be drawn.

References

Adorno, T.W., & Horkheimer, M. (1997). *Dialectic of enlightenment*. London, Verso.
Amine, A., & Gicquel, Y. (2011). Rethinking resistance and anti-consumption behaviors in the light of the concept of deviance. *European Journal of Marketing*, 45(11–12), 1809–1819.
Bachrach, P., & Baratz, M.S. (1962). Two faces of power. *American Political Science Review*, 56(4), 947–952.
Beckett, A. (2012). Governing the consumer: Technologies of consumption. *Consumption Markets & Culture*, 15(1), 1–18.
Beckett, A., & Nayak, A. (2008). The reflexive consumer. *Marketing Theory*, 8(3), 299–317.
Bekin, C., Carrigan, M., & Szmigin, I. (2005). Defying marketing sovereignty: Voluntary simplicity at new consumption communities. *Qualitative Market Research: An International Journal*, 8(4), 413–429.

Boggs, C. (1976). *Gramsci's Marxism*. London, Pluto Press.

Böhm, S., & Brei, V. (2008). Marketing the hegemony of development: Of pulp fictions and green deserts. *Marketing Theory, 8*(4), 339–366.

Bokek-Cohen, Y. (2016). How are marketing strategies of genetic material used as a mechanism for biopolitical governmentality? *Consumption, Markets & Culture, 19*(6), 534–554.

Broniarczyk, S., & Griffin, J. (2014). Research review: Decision difficulty in the age of consumer empowerment. *Journal of Consumer Psychology, 24*(4), 608–625.

Carrington, M.J., Zwick, D., & Neville, B. (2016). The ideology of the ethical consumption gap. *Marketing Theory, 16*(1), 21–38.

Cherrier, H., & Murray, J. (2002). Drifting away from excessive consumption: A new social movement based on identity construction. *Advances in Consumer Research, 29*(1), 245–247.

Cherrier, H., Black, I.R., & Lee, M. (2011). Intentional non-consumption for sustainability: Consumer resistance and/or anti-consumption? *European Journal of Marketing, 45*(11/12), 1757–1767.

Clegg, S.R. (1989). *Frameworks of power*. London, Sage.

Clegg, S.R. (2002). *Frameworks of power*. London, Sage Publications.

Corvellec, H., & Hultman, J. (2014). Managing the politics of value propositions. *Marketing Theory, 14*(4), 355–375.

Cova, B., & Cova, B. (2009). Faces of the new consumer: A genesis of consumer governmentality. *Recherche et Applications en Marketing* (English Edition), *24*(3), 81–99.

Cronin, M., McCarthy, M., & Delaney, M. (2015). Deconstructing consumer discipline: How self-management is experienced in the marketplace. *European Journal of Marketing, 11*(12), 1902–1922.

Dahl, R. (1957). The concept of power. *Systems Research and Behavioral Scientist, 2*(3), 201–215.

Dahl, R. (1958). A critique of the ruling elite model. *The American Political Science Review, 52*(2), 463–469.

Dahl, R.A. (1961). *Who governs? Democracy and power in an American city*. New Haven, CT, Yale University Press.

de Certeau, M. (1984). *The Practice of everyday life*. Berkeley, CA, University of California Press.

Denegri-Knott, J. (2004). Sinking the online music pirates: Foucault, power and deviance on the web. *Journal of Computer Mediated Communication, 9*(4). Retrieved from http://onlinelibrary.wiley.com/doi/10.1111/j.1083-6101.2004.tb00293.x/full

Denegri-Knott, J., & Tadajewski, M. (2010). The emergence of MP3 technology. *Journal of Historical Research in Marketing, 2*(4), 397–425.

Denegri-Knott, J., & Tadajewski, M. (2017). Sanctioning value: The legal system, 'hyper-power' and the legitimation of MP3. *Marketing Theory, 17*(2), 219–240.

Denegri-Knott, J., Zwick, D., & Schroeder, J. (2006). Mapping consumer power: An integrative framework for marketing and consumer research. *European Journal of Marketing, 40*(9/10), 950–971.

Desmond, J. (2003). *Consuming behavior*. London, Palgrave.

Dixon, D.F. (1992). Consumer sovereignty, democracy, and the marketing concept: A macromarketing perspective. *Canadian Journal of Administrative Science, 9*(2), 116–125.

Dowding, K. (2012). Why should we care about the definition of power? *Journal of Political Power, 5*(1), 119–135.

Dulsrud, A., & Jacobsen, E. (2009). In-store marketing as a mode of discipline. *Journal of Consumer Policy, 32*(3), 203–218.

El-Ansary, A., & Stern, L.W. (1972). Power measurement in the distribution channel. *Journal of Marketing Research, 9*(February), 47–52.

Fırat, A.F., & Dholakia, N. (1998). *Consuming people: From political economy to theatres of consumption*. London, Routledge.

Fırat, A.F., & Venkatesh, A. (1995). Liberatory postmodernism and the reenchantment of consumption. *Journal of Consumer Research, 22*(4), 239–267.

Foucault, M. (1976/1998). *The history of sexuality, Volume 1*. London, Penguin Books.

Foucault, M. (1977/1991). *Discipline and punish: The birth of the prison*. London, Penguin-Allen Lane.

Foucault, M. (1979). Truth and power: An interview with Michel Foucault. *Critique of Anthropology, 4*(January), 131–137.

Foucault, M. (1980a). Two lectures. In C. Gordon (Ed.), *Power/knowledge* (pp. 78–108). New York, Pantheon Books.

Foucault, M. (1980b). The confession of the flesh. In C. Gordon (Ed.), *Power/knowledge* (pp. 229–260). New York, Pantheon Books.

Foucault, M. (1982). The subject and power. In H.L. Dreyfus & P. Rabinow (Eds.), *Michel Foucault: Beyond structuralism and hermeneutics* (pp. 208–226). Hemel Hempstead, Harvester Press.

Foucault, M. (1991). Governmentality. In G. Burchell et al. (Eds.), *The Foucault effects: Studies in governmentality* (pp. 87–104). Hemel Hempstead, Harvester Wheatsheaf.
Foucault, M. (1994). Maurice Florence. In G. Gutting (Ed.), *The Cambridge companion to Foucault* (pp. 314–319). Cambridge, Cambridge University Press.
Friedman, M. (1991). Consumer boycotts: A conceptual framework and research agenda. *Journal of Social Issues, 47*(1), 149–168.
Friedman, M. (1996). A positive approach to organized consumer action: The buycott as an alternative to the boycott. *Journal Consumer Policy, 19*(4), 439–451.
Friedman, M., & Friedman, R. (1990). *Free to choose: A personal statement*. San Diego, CA, Harcourt Brace Jovanovich.
Fromm, E. (1976/2007). *To have or to be?* London, Continuum.
Fuchs, C., Prandelli., E., & Schreier, M. (2010). The psychological effects of empowerment strategies on consumers' product demand. *Journal of Marketing, 74*(1), 65–79.
Gao, Z., & Guo, X. (2017). Consuming revolution. *Journal of Macromarketing, 37*(3), 240–254.
Giesler, M., & Veresiu, E. (2014). Creating the responsible consumer: Moralistic governance regimes and consumer subjectivity. *Journal of Consumer Research, 41*(3), 840–857.
Gramsci, A. (1971). *Selections from the prison notebooks.* Q. Hoare and G. Nowell-Smith (Eds.). New York, International Publishers.
Hansen, U., & Schrader, U. (1997). A modern model of consumption for a sustainable society. *Journal of Consumer Policy, 20*(4), 443–468.
Harrison, T., & Waite, K. (2015). Impact of co-production on consumer perception of empowerment. *Service Industries Journal, 35*(10), 502–520.
Harrison, T., Waite, K., & Hunter, G.L. (2006). The internet, information and empowerment. *European Journal of Marketing, 40*(9/10), 972–993.
Haugaard, M. (2002). *Power: A reader.* Manchester, Manchester University Press.
Hindess, B. (1996). *Discourses of power: From Hobbes to Foucault.* Oxford, Blackwell.
Hobbes, T. (1651/1968). *Leviathan.* Baltimore, MD, Penguin Books.
Hopkinson, G., & Blois, K. (2014). Power-base research in marketing channels: A narrative review. *International Journal of Management Reviews, 16*(2), 131–141.
Izberk-Bilgin, E. (2010). An interdisciplinary review of resistance to consumption, some marketing interpretations, and future research suggestions. *Consumption, Markets & Culture, 13*(3), 299–323.
Karababa, E., & Ger, G. (2011). Early modern ottoman coffeehouse culture and the formation of the consumer subject. *Journal of Consumer Research, 37*(5), 737–760.
Kerr, G., Mortimera, K., Dickinson, S., & Waller, D. (2012). Buy, boycott or blog: Exploring online consumer power to share, discuss and distribute controversial advertising messages. *European Journal of Marketing, 46*(3/4), 387–340.
Kozinets, R.V. (2002). Can consumers escape the market? Emancipatory illuminations from Burning Man. *Journal of Consumer Research, 29*(2), 20–38.
Kozinets, R.V., & Handelman, J.M. (2004). Adversaries of consumption: Consumer movements, activism, and ideology. *Journal of Consumer Research, 31*(3), 691–704.
Labrecque, L.I., vor dem Esche, J., Mathwick, C., Novak, T.P., & Hofacker, C.F. (2013). Consumer power: Evolution in the digital age. *Journal of Interactive Marketing, 27*(4), 257–269.
Lefebvre, H. (1991). *The production of space.* Oxford, Basil Blackwell.
Lukes, S. (1974). *Power: A radical view.* London, Macmillan Press.
Mamali, E., & Nuttall, P. (2016). Mobilizing hegemonic practices in trajectories of conspicuous resistance. *European Journal of Marketing, 50*(9–10), 1629–1651.
Marcuse, H. (1964/1991). *One dimensional man.* London, Abacus.
Merlo, O. (2011). The influence of marketing from a power perspective. *European Journal of Marketing, 45*(7/8), 1152–1171.
Merlo, O., Whitwell, G., & Lukas, B. (2004). Power and marketing. *Journal of Strategic Marketing, 12*(4), 207–218.
Mikkonen, I., & Bajde, D. (2013). Happy festivus! Parody as playful consumer resistance. *Consumption, Markets & Culture, 16*(4), 311–337.
Moraes, C., Shaw, D., & Carrigan, M. (2011). Purchase power: An examination of consumption as voting. *Journal of Marketing Management, 27*(9–10), 1059–107.
Murray, J., & Ozanne, J. (1991). The critical imagination: Emancipatory interests in consumer research. *Journal of Consumer Research, 18*(2), 129–144.

Odou, P., & Pechpeyrou, P. (2011). Consumer cynicism: From resistance to anti-consumption in a disenchanted world. *European Journal of Marketing*, 11(12), 1799–1808.

Østergaard, P., Hermansen, J., & Fitchett, J. (2015). Structures of brand and anti-brand meaning: A semiotic square analysis of reflexive consumption. *Journal of Brand Management*, 22(1), 60–77.

Ozanne, J., & Murray, J. (1995). Uniting critical theory and public policy to create the reflexively defiant consumer. *American Behavioral Scientist*, 38(4), 516–525.

Pansardi, P. (2012). Power to and power over: Two distinct concepts of power? *Journal of Political Power*, 5(1), 73–89.

Peñaloza, L., & Price, P. (1993). Consumer resistance: A conceptual overview. *Advances in Consumer Research*, 20(1), 123–128.

Pires, G.D., Stanton, J., & Rita, P. (2006). The internet, consumer empowerment and marketing strategies. *European Journal of Marketing*, 40(9/10), 936–949.

Raffnsøe, S., Gudmand-Høyer, M., & Thaning, M.S. (2016). Foucault's dispositive: The perspicacity of dispositive analytics in organizational research. *Organization*, 23(2), 272–298.

Rose, N. (1999). *Governing the soul: The shaping of the private self*, second edition. London, Free Association Books.

Saatçioğlu, B., & Ozanne, J. (2013). A critical spatial approach to marketplace exclusion and inclusion. *Journal of Public Policy & Marketing*, 32(Special Issue), 32–37.

Schau, H., Muñiz, A., & Arnould, E. (2009). How brand community practices create value. *Journal of Marketing*, 73(September), 30–51.

Shankar, A., Cherrier, H., & Canniford, R. (2006). Consumer empowerment: A Foucauldian interpretation. *European Journal of Marketing*, 40(9/10), 1013–1030.

Skålén, P. (2009). Service marketing and subjectivity: The shaping of customer-oriented employees. *Journal of Marketing Management*, 25(7–8), 795–809.

Skålén, P., Fellesson, M., & Fougère, M. (2006). The governmentality of marketing discourse. *Scandinavian Journal of Management*, 22(4), 275–291.

Slater, D. (1997). *Consumer culture and modernity*. Cambridge, Polity.

Smith, N.G. (1987). Consumer boycotts and consumer sovereignty. *European Journal of Marketing*, 22(5), 7–19.

Tadajewski, M. (2006). Remembering motivation research: Toward an alternative genealogy of interpretive consumer research. *Marketing Theory*, 6(4), 429–466.

Tadajewski, M. (2010). Towards a history of critical marketing studies. *Journal of Marketing Management*, 26(9/10), 773–824.

Tadajewski, M. (2011). Producing historical critical marketing studies: Theory, method and politics. *Journal of Historical Research in Marketing*, 3(4), 549–575.

Tadajewski, M., & Jones, D. (2016). Hyper-power, the marketing concept and consumer as 'boss'. *Marketing Theory*, 16(4), 513–531.

Vargo, S.L., & Lusch, R.F. (2004). Evolving to a new dominant logic for marketing. *Journal of Marketing*, 68(1), 1–17.

Vargo, S.L., & Lusch, R.F. (2015). Institutions and axioms: An extension and update of service-dominant logic. *Journal of the Academy of Marketing Science*, 44(1), 5–23.

Voss, C., & Brettel, M. (2013). Conditions of departmental power: A strategic contingency exploration of marketing's customer-connecting role. *Journal of Strategic Marketing*, 21(2), 160–178.

Wang, J.J., Zhao, X., & Li, J.J. (2011). Team purchase: A case of consumer empowerment in China. *Journal of Consumer Affairs*, 45(3), 528–538.

Wathieu, L., Brenner, L., Carmon, Z., Chattopadhyay, A., Wertenbroch, K., Drolet, A., et al. (2002). Consumer control and empowerment: A primer. *Marketing Letters*, 13(3), 297–305.

Yngfalk, C. (2016). Bio-politicizing consumption: Neo-liberal consumerism and disembodiment in the food marketplace. *Consumption Markets & Culture*, 19(3), 275–295.

Yuksel, M., Milne, G., & Milner, E. (2016). Social media as complementary consumption: The relationship between consumer empowerment and social interactions in experiential and informative contexts. *Journal of Consumer Marketing*, 33(2), 111–123.

Zwick, D., & Bradshaw, A. (2016). Biopolitical marketing and social media brand communities. *Theory, Culture & Society*, 33(5), 91–115.

Zwick, D., & Denegri-Knott, J. (2009). Manufacturing customers. *Journal of Consumer Culture*, 9(2), 221–247.

Zwick, D., & Denegri-Knott, J. (2018). Biopolitical marketing and technologies of enclosure. In Kravets et al. (Eds.), *The Sage handbook of consumer culture* (pp. 333–348). London, Sage.

18
IDEOLOGY AND CRITICAL MARKETING STUDIES

Giana M. Eckhardt, Rohit Varman, and Nikhilesh Dholakia

Introduction

Within mainstream marketing, the domains of ideology and marketing are seldom seen in a holistic frame. For mainstream scholars, ideology and marketing are from the distinct domains of politics and economy, respectively, and are rarely analyzed and discussed with reference to each other. In contrast, this chapter argues that ideology and marketing have a complex palette of relationships. In exploring the ideology–marketing nexus, we focus on three places on this palette. First, we take a brief look at the mainstream marketing view that holds – along with mainstream business disciplines in general – an instrumental view of marketing: that the discipline simply provides a toolkit, which is ideologically neutral, and employable in the service of any ideological position that is of interest at a particular point in time (Kotler & Keller, 2016).

Next, we provide a detailed look at the range of nuanced views that acknowledge the innately ideological character of marketing concepts and practices, including a far-reaching position that characterizes marketing as the prevailing ideology of the *Zeitgeist*, i.e., exploring 'marketing as ideology' rather than 'marketing and ideology'. In pursuing this objective, we not only examine some of the important writings in marketing (e.g. Eckhardt, Dholakia & Varman, 2013; Dholakia, 2016; O'Reilly, 2006), but also draw upon some of the seminal works on ideology in critical theory (Althusser, 1971; Eagleton, 1991; Gramsci, 1971; Adorno & Horkheimer, 1989; Marx, 1968; Žižek, 1989). In particular, we examine the political economy underpinning the contemporary neoliberal marketplace, exemplified in areas of marketing involved in the production of culture, such as advertising agencies (Eckhardt & Bradshaw, 2014), and 'new markets' such as the sharing economy (Eckhardt & Bardhi, 2016).

Third, we engage in an exploration of the functioning of contemporary capitalism on a global scale, and delve into how businesses deploy extra-ideological violence against subalterns. Indeed, in subaltern imagination, naked use of force reduces marketing ideology to a mere tool for accumulation of capital; in essence a turned-on-its-head radical return to the instrumental view of marketing. In many oppressive subaltern settings, marketing is not just an illusion or dreamlike state of brand bonhomie; rather, it is one of the blunt instruments to advance corporate profits. This section draws attention to the extra-ideological violence that is commonly present in the Global South. We conclude with suggestions as to how researchers interested in the nexus between marketing and ideology can further this nascent research agenda.

Ideology

Ideology is a set of ideas that can be false and deceptive, which emerges from the material structure of society. We do not attribute ideology to any one particular group or a class of actors but understand ideology as the systemic necessity in any socioeconomic order. Although a functionalist reading is misleading, ideology can be unifying, rationalizing, legitimizing, universalizing, and naturalizing in a social setting. Despite its significance in any social order, ideology does not inform every social practice and is not present everywhere. We concur with Eagleton (1991, p. 8) that, "the force of the term ideology lies in its capacity to discriminate between those power struggles which are somehow central to a whole form of social life, and those which are not." As Giddens (1984) observes, reification of social relations and the discursive naturalization of the historically contingent circumstances are some of the main dimensions of ideology.

Geuss (1981) describes three distinct interpretations of ideology in social theory. According to the first interpretation, ideology is descriptive and creates a shared sense of purpose for a social group. In this form, ideologies are universal and present in every social setting. Second, ideology in its programmatic sense is about creating delusions that allow dominant interests to prevail. Such a usage is pejorative and reflects a critical reading of ideology. Third, ideology is used positively to indicate how alternative sets of ideas can be used to mobilize people and to raise their consciousness. An example of such an effort is Lenin's 'What is to be done' that delves into how a revolutionary consciousness of the proletariat can be created. In this chapter, we confine our reading of ideology primarily to the second form in which it is used to create distorted representations of capitalism and to disguise the destruction caused by corporations.

The second reading of ideology as a form of delusion goes back to Karl Marx (1968) and subsequent developments in critical theory. Although Marx uses ideology in multiple ways, the most overwhelming usage of ideology is as constitutive naivety, as it becomes a form of misrecognition of power structures and social domination. Therefore, ideology creates a gap between a social reality and its representations. A dominant ideology expresses the material interests of a ruling social class, and which are useful in promoting its control. Two key Marxist scholars who inform our understanding of ideology are Antonio Gramsci and Louis Althusser. In the early 20th century, Gramsci (1971) advanced Marx's idea of ideology with his emphasis on the role of civil society in creating consent of the under-classes in producing structures of their exploitation. However, Gramsci does not use ideology in a pejorative manner. According to Gramsci (1971, p. 707), "one must therefore distinguish between historically organic ideologies, those, that is, which are necessary to a given structure, and ideologies that are arbitrary, rationalistic, or 'willed'." Instead of ideology, Gramsci (1971) uses the idea of hegemony, which means a ruling elite wins consent to its rule from those it subjugates. Drawing upon the work of Gramsci, Althusser (1971) questions the rationalistic theory of ideology that interprets it only as a collection of distorting representations of reality and false propositions. Accordingly, ideology is chiefly about lived relations and materiality of existence. Althusser (1971) differentiates between theoretical ideology and practical ideology of social life and emphasizes the significance of material expression of ideology. An ideology makes its belief system appear natural and self-evident in the everyday lives of its subjects. Moreover, ideology interpolates or hails individuals to single them out as uniquely valuable subjects. Therefore, for Althusser, ideology is not just about a distortion or a false reflection, but a form of creation of subjectivity.

Scholars from the Frankfurt School in attending to critical analyses of ideology have further contributed to our understanding. According to these critical theorists, reality cannot reproduce itself without ideological mystification (Adorno, 1960; Adorno & Horkheimer, 1989). In this interpretation, the mask of ideology is not hiding a reality, but distortion is the very essence of the capitalist social world. In an important development in critical theory, Adorno (1960) reads ideology as a form of identity thinking that homogenizes the world and tries to repress differences. Furthermore, Adorno and Horkheimer (1989) argue that reason has become violent and manipulative, which is best reflected in the ideological control exercised by the culture industry. Taking this further, Marcuse (1964) suggests that capitalist ideology is a totalitarian system that has managed all social conflicts out of existence to create a one-dimensional subject.

A problem with the early Frankfurt School, particularly in the writings of Adorno, Horkheimer, and Marcuse, is that they take ideology at face value and assume that a capitalist society languishes in the grip of an all-pervasive reification (Eagleton, 1991). In this view, a dominant ideology is apparently devoid of contradictions. They overlook several important writings on ideology from a critical perspective that challenge such a view. For example, Gramsci (1971) notes that an ideology is rarely pure and unitary because it exists in relation to other ideologies. A dominant ideology has continually to negotiate with the ideologies of its subordinates. Similarly, Williams (1977), in highlighting the three forms of residual, dominant, and emergent consciousness, emphasizes past, present and future ideologies, respectively, in terms of their domination at a given point in time in any society. Based on Williams' emphases on resistance and counter-hegemony, it is essential to situate any society in an inter-ideological space within which ideologies and counter-ideologies are constantly struggling for control. As Eagleton (1991, p. 45) observes,

> a successful ruling ideology . . . must engage significantly with genuine wants, needs, and desires; but this is also its Achilles heel, forcing it to recognize an "other" to itself and inscribing this otherness as a potentially disruptive force within its own form.

Therefore, Eagleton (1991) maintains that an ideology is never a monolithic entity and is often fraught with contradictions and social dissent of various forms. Within the domain of critical theory, Habermas (1981) offers a corrective to such a reified understanding by interpreting ideology as a form of communication systematically distorted by power. Habermas suggests that to move to an order that overcomes ideological distortions there is a need for a rationality that is based on collective self-reflection. However, consistent with the critical tradition, Habermas (1981) interprets ideology as a distortion that leads to thought control of under-classes.

Some scholars question such a reading of ideology as a system of thought control and its role in creating false consciousness. For example, Sloterdijk (1987) believes that under-classes do not have a false consciousness because they have the ability to create distance and see through dominant ideologies. Calling this keynicism, Sloterdijk becomes an advocate of the end of ideology thesis. According to Sloterdijk (1987, p. 110), "the power of the underdog comes into its own individuality as that cheekiness that constitutes the core of power in keynicism. With it those who are disadvantaged can anticipate their own sovereignty." Such a conclusion can be misleading as ideology continues to influence our social imagination and practices. Rising consumerism and popular support for markets across the world are examples of how dominant neoliberal ideology continues to shape the behaviors of under-classes. Therefore, we agree with Žižek (1989) that ideology influences social practices by safeguarding dominant interests in different life situations. According to Žižek (1989, p. 29), "the cynical subject is aware of the distance between the ideological mask and the social reality but he nonetheless insists upon the mask." In other words, one is aware of a particular interest hidden behind an ideological universality, still one does not renounce it. "It is therefore a kind of perverted 'negation of negation' of the official ideology" (Žižek, 1989, p. 30). In this manner, ideology is not a matter consciousness, false or otherwise, but its distortions are inscribed in our everyday life situations of reading, writing, teaching, or publishing.

Drawing upon these developments, several marketing scholars have highlighted the importance of ideology in markets (Crockett & Wallendorf, 2004; Eckhardt & Bradshaw, 2014; Hirschman, 1993; Kozinets & Handelman, 2004; Thompson & Haytko, 1997; Thompson & Tambyah, 1999; Varman & Belk, 2009; Zwick & Cayla, 2011). Crockett and Wallendorf (2004) describe the role of normative political ideology in consumer behavior and suggest that African American political ideology plays an important role in determining black consumption practices. Although the emphases on Black Nationalism and ideology in consumption are significant, in treating ideology as a "world view" it takes a "benign stance" toward the concept (Crockett & Wallendorf, 2004, p. 512). Similarly, Marion's (2006) interpretation also situates ideology in the rather sterile domain of ideas, stripping it of its deeper systemic roots and ramifications. We are more in agreement with O'Reilly (2006, p. 266), who contends that "a deeper engagement with the imagination and with quotidian practices is necessary for an understanding and critique of ideology." This leads to a more nuanced, critical, and deeper understanding of ideology like that of Kozinets and Handelman (2004), who are concerned with the processes through which anti-consumption activists represent their goals, themselves, and their adversaries.

For example, Varman and Belk (2009) examine the role of a nationalist ideology in an anti-consumption movement and show that its deployment is linked to the experiences of colonialism, modernity, and globalization in India. And Varman and Saha (2009) point to the role of postcolonial epistemic ideology in shaping marketing thought in India as it becomes an appendage of the West. In a similar critical tradition, Hirschman (1993) draws upon the Gramscian conceptualization of hegemony to uncover the ideologies of capitalism and patriarchy inherent in much consumer research theorization. In concurrence with Heath and Potter's critique (2004), O'Guinn and Muniz (2005) demonstrate the co-optation of brand communities with alternate beliefs and ideologies into the larger process of consumption. Similarly, Thompson and Haytko (1997) and Thompson and Tambyah (1999) further our understanding by offering a post-structuralist critique and in highlighting the role of ideology in the consumer identity-building process. In some other works Thompson demonstrates the influence of ideology in consumer risk perceptions and in the development of resistance to co-optation of alternate beliefs (Thompson, 2005; Thompson & Coskuner-Balli, 2007). Finally, Zwick and Cayla (2011) look behind the curtain of marketing practice to reveal how marketing works as an ideology; looking particularly at how marketing has shaped how we think about modernity, and how marketing appropriates the creativity of consumers for profit. Similarly, Eckhardt and Bradshaw (2014), using Adorno and Horkheimer's (1989) cultural industry thesis, conclude that the ideological consequence of the non-problematic use of music in advertising is an enactment of the industrialization of culture.

In this chapter, we specifically seek to understand the role of ideology in the context of mainstream marketing thought that has largely ignored critical writings. We find that distorted representations of corporate interests and capitalist relations are evident in mainstream marketing theory. These distortions take two forms in the discipline. First, early scholarship sanitizes the discipline internally by marginalizing discussions on the harmful impact of capitalist enterprises. In this process, the discipline uncritically adopts the dominant ideology of capitalism and claims to be a-ideological. Second, governments, non-governmental organizations, and corporations deploy marketing tools to shape institutions, state policies, and private behaviors. In this form, marketing becomes ideology as it serves the function of an ideological veil to disguise dominant interests outside the discipline. It is to these readings of ideology in mainstream marketing theory that we turn next in our analysis.

Marketing as bereft of ideology

The notion of scrubbing ideology from the conceptual repertoire and managerial toolkits of marketing was not a part of the early development of marketing concepts, but the early marketing theorists were quite sensitive in terms of portraying marketing concepts in salutary rather than objectionable ideological frames; and paved the way for later ideology-masking representations of marketing. For example, Wroe Alderson, writing in the third issue of the inaugural volume of *Journal of Marketing*, offered a strong justification of marketing in essentially ideological terms, claiming that marketing methods and practices offered benefits of quick adaptation to changing conditions, strong operating efficiencies, and general economic welfare (Alderson, 1937, p. 190):

> Semi-permanent pairings grow up between each segment of the market and certain specialized suppliers . . . [Unfortunately, such] (s)emi-permanent pairings have been called quasi-monopoly or monopolistic competition, terms which are misnomers since entrenchment of specialized suppliers in separate segments of the market is a great obstacle to the growth of true monopoly . . . The specialized supplier in the segmented market does not behave like a monopolist [but rather] . . . seeks profits of adaptation, which are profits of efficiency but broader in scope, involving not only the idea of doing a job well but also that of picking the right job to do . . . The firm which seeks profits of adaptation is obliged to serve general economic welfare more directly and less wastefully than under orthodox [economic] analysis . . . Market research, cost analysis and consumer advertising receive proper recognition under such a view as important tools of business adaptation . . . Price adjustments are also a basic aspects of business adaptation.

Although the article from which the quote above is drawn is only two pages long, it is evident how much ideological punch Alderson packs in this short article. He is: (a) setting up the evil strawman of "true monopoly" and arguing that marketing is a bulwark against it; (b) rejecting the use of then-prevalent (and negatively valenced) economic terms 'quasi-monopoly' and 'monopolistic competition' as descriptors of marketing practices and institutions; (c) introducing salutary terms such as 'adaptation', 'efficiency', and 'welfare' as descriptors and consequences of marketing actions; (d) enshrining the strategic pre-eminence and superiority of marketing actions as focused on the 'right job' rather than the wrong job; and (e) justifying and advocating the greater use of marketing tools such as market research, cost analysis, product differentiation, consumer advertising, and price adjustments.

A few years later, Wroe Alderson and Reavis Cox, the pioneering scholars who wrote the first major theoretical treatise on marketing (Alderson & Cox, 1948), were well aware that many marketing practices fitted closely with the type of economy that was called 'monopolistic competition', and that this term had ideologically negative connotations. They argued instead for giving prominence to product differentiation practices and the concept of 'heterogeneous competition'; ideas that reflected the increasing sophistication of marketing practices, and were ideologically more palatable than concepts that invoked the idea of monopoly:

> Certainly the last word has not been said on product differentiation as a factor in . . . heterogeneous competition – a term, incidentally, which well might replace "monopolistic competition" as being more descriptive [of prevailing marketing practice] and

not so weighted with objectionable connotations . . . it may be said that differentiation is a basic function which is carried out primarily through channels of distribution and which is intimately related to the problem of efficiency in marketing.

Alderson & Cox, 1948, p. 48

In this important pioneering paper, Alderson and Cox provide many useful linkages to a wide range of behavioral and social science theorists. The ideological stance, however, is clear: to scrub the odious idea of monopolistic positions and actions from marketing theory, and to inject edifying and reinforcing notions of 'efficiency', 'balance', and 'welfare' into the discipline's theoretical foundation.

It is interesting to explore why early marketing theorists, while not dwelling on ideology, were at least trying to associate salubrious ideological ideas with marketing; while the post-World War II theorists felt no such compulsions. The latter period – when, eventually, neoliberalism achieved high ascendancy and indeed even stranglehold – is discussed in the next section. The 1930s and 1940s, the formative years of marketing theory, fell in the historically anomalous phase of America that Cowie (2016, p.9) has called "the great exception":

[T]he political era between the 1930s and 1970s marks what might be called a "great exception" – a sustained deviation, an extended detour – from some of the main contours of American political practice, economic structure, and cultural outlook. During this period, the central government used its considerable resources . . . on behalf of non-elite Americans.

Cowie is especially emphatic about the exceptionalism of the 1930s and 1940s. A juggernaut-like

combination of power and political vulnerability . . . burst upon the national stage in the 1930s and 1940s. The New Deal alliances seemed to come together in an all-powerful force capable of implementing progressive liberal policies with limited regard for conservative opposition.

Cowie, 2016, p. 10

Perspicacious marketing theorists such as Alderson and Cox must have been well aware of this juggernaut-like (but, in retrospect, highly fragile and exceptional) progressive force; and they ensured that – by bleaching out monopolistic competition notions – marketing would not fall prey to excessive regulation (see especially Alderson, 1937, p. 189). From the end of World War II to the 1970s (and beyond) – what can be called the Kotler era of marketing (Kotler, 2005) – the threat of radical progressive reforms and regulation was gone, aided in great part by the intense Cold War against communist USSR. In the United States, especially, only general notions of public and consumer welfare remained; which found some receptivity in the ideas of social marketing (Kotler & Zaltman, 1971).

Indeed, the powerful appeal by Kotler and Levy (1969) to broaden the concept of marketing was, in a sense, the closing argument to shut out anyone who still thought of marketing in an ideological commercial-capitalist way. Although the practices of marketing had started seeping into non-commercial domains by the late 1950s (Cohen, 2004; Schwarzkopf, 2011; see also Gordon, this volume), the conceptual frames of marketing were still welded to commercial settings. Kotler and his associates set a blowtorch to melt away these welds: they argued forcefully that not only were marketing methods spreading beyond commercial domains, but such a conceptual centrifuge – to diffuse marketing tools and concepts widely – should be revved up and accelerated. Indeed, if marketing methods could be employed equally well to sell goods and to do good then, *ipso facto*, marketing had become a-ideological. Marketing approaches could inject rational planning and responsive, caring service to non-commercial, oft-bureaucratic fields, and like good screwdrivers and wrenches – had become neutral tools. In a very short period, the 'broadening movement' had become a practical success worldwide and conceptually deeply ingrained in marketing books and articles (Fox & Kotler, 1980). The obvious – and intended – side effect of this was to strip any residual ideological trappings away from marketing, and to make the field a universally appealing source of tools and techniques to serve humanity (Kotler, 1972).

Marketing as innately ideological

There is a paradox – perhaps somewhat understandable from the viewpoint of locations and politics of disciplines within the university – in the discussion of marketing and ideology. While most disciplines outside of the business school are quite clearly – and plainly and simply – aware of the ideological character of marketing, and some of these scholars openly discuss this issue (e.g. Aronczyk & Powers, 2010), there is either a studied silence or an active denial of this issue within the marketing discipline (Hunt, 2002). Located in business schools that are often dependent on capitalist corporate patronage and largesse, marketing departments cling to the a-ideological view of marketing that emerged from the 1950s and was reinforced strongly from the 1970s. In marketing departments and their published outputs, discussions of marketing and ideology are essentially absent (for an exception, see Brownlie & Saren, 1995; cf. Tadajewski, 2010).

Despite its efforts – more accurately, the pretense – to be non-ideological, marketing, and especially its practices, turned intensely ideological from about the same juncture when the 'broadening' movement was launched in marketing. The tidal wave of Reagan–Thatcher neoliberal 'reforms' (Hacker & Pierson, 2010; Harvey, 2005; Mirowski & Plehwe, 2009) engulfed and incorporated the relatively modest moves by marketing practitioners and academics to spread marketing ideas to non-commercial fields (see also Gordon, this volume). Marketization and consumerization – not because of the proselytizing and evangelizing efforts of marketing academics but because of globe-spanning changes in political economy and culture (Hardt & Negri, 2001) – turned into key pillars of the ascendant neoliberalism, with punitive consequences for those resisting such ascendance.

The drivers of neoliberalism are economic and financial, with the growing financialization of all institutions at the core. While Finanzkapital is in the driver's seat and the global puppet master (Dholakia, 2011, 2012), most public-facing institutions in the West feel the need to put a softer, humane-appearing veneer on the hard, harsh, efficiency-seeking, ambiguity-intolerant juggernaut of neoliberal strategies and actions. In other words, neoliberalism – powerful and pervasive as it is – requires actions that legitimize it (Harvey, 2005). Marketing concepts offer some of the ready, handy forms of legitimizing neoliberalism and mask its harsh edges. Marketing concepts and ideas such as customer focus, consumer orientation, market orientation, customer relationship, and customer intimacy serve very well in handmaiden roles with respect to Finanzkapital-driven neoliberalism. Such ideas from marketing provide the silken, soft swaths to swaddle the unflinchingly harsh financial-economic core of neoliberalism. As we have noted elsewhere:

> Bedecked in the floral metaphors that marketing and branding provide, the advancing neoliberal behemoths look less like threatening army tanks and more like delighting Rose Bowl parade floats. Marketing theories and practices often provide a soothing layer of fantasy to hard-edged neoliberal agendas.
>
> *Eckhardt, Dholakia & Varman, 2013, p. 8*

Indeed, as Žižek (1989, p. 45) observes, "ideology is not a dreamlike illusion that we build to escape insupportable reality; in its basic dimension it is a fantasy-construction which serves as a support for our reality itself."

In all this, the consumer role – which is in essence a crassly transactional mode of human interaction – is lifted up to become noble, autonomous, infused with ideas of freedom and awesome power over the corporate sector (e.g. Vargo & Lusch, 2004). To ennoble and hold aloft the consumer role, a well-established older role, that of the democratic citizen – one with a history going back to the Enlightenment, and with an unshakeable, built-in legitimacy – had to be invoked. Leading members of advertising and market research fields worked hard to build a false equivalence between the consumer role and the citizen-voter role:

> Advertising agencies in particular were at the forefront of attempts to revive and popularize the concept of the consumer as sovereign voter in a market structure that resembled the political process. These attempts to culturally and socially legitimize advertising communication received political-philosophical credibility from a new generation of economists spearheaded by the Hayek-pupil William Harold Hutt. Both advertising and market research practitioners and academics for different reasons reinforced the myth that capitalism and "free markets" were merely the economic equivalent of democracies.
>
> *Schwarzkopf, 2011, p. 15*

A mythical 'consumer-citizen' role was crafted, a role that – prima facie – appears nobler and loftier than the crassly transactional consumer role (Jubas, 2007).

Individual consumers usually cannot counter the intense demands of the ascendant consumer culture, and even collective attempts at anti-consumption and resistive strategies remain feebly at the margins of the market (Devinney, Auger, & Eckhardt, 2010). From a critical perspective, within the marketing discipline, the insights into, as well as the solutions to, such issues need to be sought at systemic, macro levels (Zwick & Cayla, 2011).

Are marketing theorists beginning to tackle such challenges? In the large mainstream, the answer is that they are not. There is, however, definite hope, springing from the fact that at the critical and – in our view – the leading edge of marketing theory, there are very insightful scholars addressing these challenges. For example, Levy and Luedicke (2012) examine the historical trajectory of a marketing ideology, tracing it from mercantilism to a production ideology, to a consumer ideology, and finally to a branding ideology. Expanding on the current branding ideology so prevalent in today's marketplace, Bandinelli & Arvidsson (2012) argue that self-branding for the purposes of getting ahead in the workplace is an effect of the neoliberal regime of governmentality. Fitchett, Patsiaouris, and Davies (2014) go even further in terms of their use of ideology as an analytic tool to argue that the domain of consumer culture theory (CCT) is an inherently neoliberal one, as it reifies the 'consumer as hero', which reinforces the neoliberal logic of bringing all human action into the domain of the market (Harvey, 2005). Although Askegaard (2014) argues that CCT is trying to understand how and what the consequences are of a neoliberal world in which everyone is a consumer at all times, rather than trying to reinforce that agenda. Finally, Eckhardt and Bardhi (2016) interrogate the political economy of the sharing economy using Polanyi's (1944/2001) distinction between economic and social exchange. In doing so, they demonstrate that the sharing economy does not encompass social exchange, or sharing at all, but rather is based on economic exchange. The consequence of this is that the sharing economy is not an anti-consumerist revolution that will lead to the end of market capitalism via social collectives and sharing, as argued by Rifkin (2014) for example, but rather serves to prop up today's neoliberal marketplace. What these papers have in common is that they are openly addressing the innately ideological character of marketing, and exploring the consequences of that, for individuals as well as for society.

Recognizing and confronting the innately ideological character of marketing is an imperative, but this does not cover the whole ground of marketing and ideology. In particular, such efforts remain – in epistemic, ontological and teleological terms – oriented to the essentially Western center of Empire (Hardt & Negri, 2001), with only minor attention paid to the numerically vast but politico-economically marginal periphery of the Empire. The next section brings in perspectives on marketing and ideology in subaltern settings.

Marketing as a blunt instrument of ideology

In this section, we turn to critical lines of analyses that have begun examining extreme forms of capitalist organization. These focus on totalitarian forms of capitalism that have taken root as extensions of liberal capitalism (Sassen, 2014). It helps to attend to how marketing as ideology in liberal settings is often based on the use of extra-ideological forms of coercion against subalterns. According to Žižek (1989, p. 30):

> Totalitarian ideology no longer has a pretention. It is no longer meant, even by its authors to be taken seriously—its status is just that of a means of manipulation, purely external and instrumental; its rule is secured not by its truth value but by simple extra-ideological violence and promise of gain.

Therefore, there is no ideological masking of the real nature of exploitation in such a context and the consent of those who are exploited is not required, as Gramsci (1971) had explained. We draw attention to the idea of necrocapitalism in which death and violence are commonly associated with how businesses operate for the benefit of the upper classes (Banerjee, 2008, 2011; Varman & Al-Amoudi, 2016). In such settings, subaltern lives become unworthy or ungrievable with the normalization of violence against them. As Evans and Giroux (2015, p. 7) have argued, "when violence becomes normalized and decentered, the disposability of entire populations becomes integral to the functioning, the profiteering, and the entrenchment of the prevailing rationalities of the dominant culture." Varman and Al-Amoudi (2016) draw upon this line of analysis and examine how Coca-Cola uses violence in a village in India for the purpose of accumulation. Accordingly, subaltern groups are derealized and made into ungrievable lives through practices that keep violence unchecked. In such a context of necrocapitalism, markets and marketing may function without any attempt to mystify to subalterns the real nature of accumulation. Socioeconomic participation of subalterns in such a setting may be achieved through the use of violence without illusory masking of social realities. On the other hand, for the massively well-endowed and influential so-called 'stakeholder' constituencies of major brand-owning corporations, constituencies located in safe, advanced nation settings – including investors and brand consumers – the need for projecting an ideologically pleasant brand-corporate 'face' becomes, paradoxically, quite important. In other words, in conditions of or resembling necrocapitalism, there emerge Janus-faced corporate brand strategies – nakedly violent in the practically invisible remote markets but well-groomed and amiable in the moneyed and politically important constituencies of the brand's home markets.

Marketing and ideology: discussion

In this chapter, we have introduced what ideology is, and how it has been used in marketing to date. We then traced how the ideological nature of marketing has been portrayed in the marketing literature in three different ways: (1) in mainstream marketing, particularly in the early days of the field, marketing's inherently ideological nature was scrubbed from literature. Marketing was portrayed as being ideologically neutral, as a tool which can be used by anyone for any purpose. Later it was acknowledged within the marketing literature, although still not the mainstream literature, that (2) marketing is inherently ideological, and we outlined the ways in which this has been recognized and explored. Finally, (3) we pointed out that this acknowledgment tends to stem from a Western perspective, and in the subaltern we can see the results of necrocapitalism, an ideology whereby the subaltern experiences death and violence in order for brands to present a whitewashed front to the Western world. An example of this would be the working conditions and deaths that take place in the Foxconn factories in China to produce Apple iPhones. We would suggest that the Apple brand image of enabling consumers to 'Think Differently' cannot be understood without the full picture of what occurs in the subaltern to make this happen. While scholars are beginning to write about this (e.g. Bannerjee, 2011; Varman and Al-Amoudi, 2016), this acknowledgment of the Janus-faced nature of how marketing ideology plays out in the subaltern has yet to be explored in the mainstream marketing literature.

In pointing out these ways in which the ideological nature of marketing has and has not been acknowledged within the literature, we hope to inspire marketing researchers to explore ideology and marketing, in the West and the subaltern, in more depth in the future. For example, Eckhardt and Bardhi (2016) point out that the ideology behind the sharing economy is one of extreme neoliberalism, in that it promotes the idea that everyone must monetize all aspects of their lives, and be micro-entrepreneurs in order to succeed. Scholars such as Bauman (2000, 2007) and Ritzer (2015) have pointed out that this mentality reinforces alienation, and ultimately exploits consumers, who end up doing jobs that previously have been done by companies. Henwood (2015, p.1) notes that

> [t]he sharing economy is a nice way for rapacious capitalists to monetize the desperation of people in the post crisis economy while sounding generous, and to evoke a fantasy of community in an atomized population. The sharing economy looks like a classically neoliberal response to neoliberalism: individualized and market driven, it sees us all as micro-entrepreneurs fending for ourselves in a hostile world.

We see this type of engagement with the ideological background and consequences of current market trends such as the sharing economy as an example of how marketing scholars can make further inroads into understanding the nature of the relationship between marketing and ideology. There is evidence that the intersection of marketing and ideology is becoming more topical within the discipline of marketing, with the inaugural Marketing, Capitalism and Critique conference happening at Royal Holloway University of London in 2017.

Conclusion

Summing up, we see ideology in liberal capitalism and necrocapitalism in the subaltern as two sides of the same coin. In this way, ideology can be a mask for violence; witness, for example, marketing practices that project 'lovable' brands in consumer marketspaces while committing acts of violence in the background value chains. In advancing understanding of marketing and ideology, this chapter examined theoretical positions that offer a range of views and cast in high relief settings in which the role of ideology is deliberately denied, regarded as deeply infused, is limited or callously ignored, or Janus-faced.

We want to debunk the disingenuous position that applied disciplines 'should not bite the hand that feeds them' and, therefore, marketing practice and theory should steer clear of discussions of ideology. To the contrary, it is not only an intellectual necessity but also a moral duty of marketing academics, and also marketing practitioners, to examine and question the ideological aspects of marketing. Would it be acceptable, for example, for a mechanical engineer to overlook the shady manufacturing practices of an automaker or for a civil engineer to turn a blind eye to the adulteration of cement by a bridge-building authority? It is high time for marketing academics and practitioners to reclaim and stand their moral ground, and to confront ideology head on.

References

Adorno, T. (1960). *Negative dialectics*. London, Verso.
Adorno, T., & Horkheimer, M. (1989). *Dialectic of enlightenment*. New York, Continuum.
Alderson, W. (1937). A marketing view of competition. *Journal of Marketing*, *1*(3), 189–190.
Alderson, W., & Cox, R. (1948). Towards a theory of marketing. *Journal of Marketing*, *13*(2), 137–152.
Althusser, L. (1971). *Lenin and philosophy*. New York, Monthly Review Press.
Aronczyk, M., & Powers, D. (Eds.) (2010). *Blowing up the brand: Critical perspectives on promotional culture*. New York, Peter Lang.
Askegaard, S. (2014). Consumer culture theory: Neoliberalism's 'useful idiots'? *Marketing Theory*, *14*(4), 507–511.
Bandinelli, C., & Arvidsson, A. (2012). Brand yourself a changemaker! *Journal of Macromarketing*, *33*(1), 67–71.
Banerjee, B.S. (2008). Necrocapitalism. *Organization Studies*, *29*(12), 1541–1563.
Banerjee, B.S. (2011). Voices of the governed: Towards a theory of the translocal. *Organization*, *18*(3), 323–344.
Bauman, Z. (2000). *Liquid modernity*. Cambridge, Polity.
Bauman, Z. (2007). *Liquid times: Living in an age of uncertainty*. Cambridge, Polity.
Brownlie, D., & Saren, M. (1995). On the commodification of marketing knowledge: Opening themes. *Journal of Marketing Management*, *11*(7), 619–627.
Cohen, L. (2004). A consumers' republic: The politics of mass consumption in postwar America. *Journal of Consumer Research*, *31*(1), 236–239.
Cowie, J. (2016). *The great exception: The new deal & the limits of American politics*. Princeton, Princeton University Press.
Crockett, D., & Wallendorf, M. (2004). The role of political ideology in consumer behavior. *Journal of Consumer Research*, *31*(December), 511–528.
Devinney, T., Auger, P., & Eckhardt, G.M. (2010). *The myth of the ethical consumer*. Cambridge, Cambridge University Press.
Dholakia, N. (2011). Finanzkapital in the twenty first century. *Critical Perspectives on International Business*, *7*(1), 90–108.
Dholakia, N. (2012). *Finanzkapital* and consumers: How financialization shaped twentieth century marketing. *Journal of Historical Research in Marketing*, *4*(3), 453–461.
Dholakia, N. (2016). Marketing as mystification. *Marketing Theory*, *16*(3), 401–426.
Eagleton, T. (1991). *Ideology: An introduction*. London, Verso.
Eckhardt, G.M., & Bardhi, F. (2016). The relationship between access practices and economic systems. *Journal of the Association of Consumer Research*, *1*(2), 210–225.
Eckhardt, G.M., & Bradshaw, A. (2014). The erasure of antagonisms between popular music and advertising. *Marketing Theory*, *14*(2), 167–183.

Eckhardt, G.M., Dholakia, N., & Varman, R. (2013). Ideology for the 10 billion: Introduction to globalization of marketing ideology. *Journal of Macromarketing, 33*(1), 7–12.

Evans, B., & Giroux, H. (2015). *Disposable futures: The seduction of violence in the age of spectacle*. San Francisco, City Lights Books.

Fitchett, J., Patsiaouris, G., & Davies, A. (2014). Myth and ideology in consumer culture theory. *Marketing Theory, 14*(4), 495–506.

Fox, K.F.A., & Kotler, P. (1980). The marketing of social causes: The first 10 years. *Journal of Marketing, 44*(Fall), 24–33.

Geuss, R. (1981). *The idea of a critical theory*. Cambridge, Cambridge University Press.

Giddens, A. (1984). *The constitution of society: Outline of the theory of structuration*. Cambridge, Polity Press.

Gramsci, A. (1971). *Selections from the prison notebooks of Antonio Gramsci*. Translated by Quintin Hoare & Geoffrey Nowell Smith. New York, International Publishers.

Habermas, J. (1981). *The theory of communicative action (volume two): Life world and system — A critique of functionalist reason*. Boston, Beacon Press.

Hacker, J.S., & Pierson, P. (2010). Winner-take-all politics: Public policy, political organization, and the precipitous rise of top incomes in the United States. *Politics & Society, 38*(2), 152–204.

Hardt, M., & Negri, A. (2001). *Empire*. Cambridge, Harvard University Press.

Harvey, D. (2005). *A brief history of neoliberalism*. Oxford, Oxford University Press.

Heath, J., & Potter, A. (2004). *The rebel sell: How the counterculture became consumer culture*. New York, Harper Business.

Henwood, D. (2015). What the sharing economy takes. *The Nation*. February 16.

Hirschman, E.C. (1993). Ideology in consumer research 1980, and 1990: A Marxist and feminist critique. *Journal of Consumer Research, 19*(March), 537–556.

Hunt, S. (2002). *Foundations of marketing theory: Toward a general theory of marketing*. London, Routledge.

Jubas, K. (2007). Conceptual confusion in democratic societies: Understandings and limitations of consumer citizenship. *Journal of Consumer Culture, 7*(2), 231–254.

Kotler, P. (1972). A generic concept of marketing. *Journal of Marketing, 36*(April), 46–54.

Kotler, P. (2005). The role played by the broadening of marketing movement in the history of marketing thought. *Journal of Marketing & Public Policy, 24*(1), 114–116.

Kotler, P., & Keller, K. (2016). *Marketing management*, 15th edition. New York, Prentice Hall.

Kotler, P., & Levy, S.J. (1969). Broadening the concept of marketing. *Journal of Marketing, 33*(January), 10–15.

Kotler, P., & Zaltman, G. (1971). Social marketing: An approach to planned social change. *Journal of Marketing, 35*(July), 3–12.

Kozinets, R., & Handelman, J. (2004). Adversaries of consumption: Consumer movement, activism, and ideology. *Journal of Consumer Research, 31*(December), 691–704.

Levy, S.J., & Luedicke, M. (2012). From marketing ideology to branding ideology. *Journal of Macromarketing, 33*(1), 58–66.

Marcuse, H. (1964). *One dimensional man*. Boston, Beacon Press.

Marion, G. (2006). Marketing, ideology and criticism: Legitimacy and legitimization. *Marketing Theory, 6*(2), 245–262.

Marx, K. (1968). *The German Ideology*. Retrieved July 8, 2018 from www.marxists.org/archive/marx/works/download/Marx_The_German_Ideology.pdf

Mirowski, P., & Plehwe, D. (2009). *The road from Mont Pelerin*. Cambridge, Harvard University Press.

O'Guinn, T.C., &. Muniz, A.M. Jr. (2005). Communal consumption and the brand. In S. Ratneshwar & D.G. Mick (Eds.), *Inside consumption: Consumer motives, goals, and desires* (pp. 252–272). Abingdon, Routledge.

O'Reilly, D. (2006). Branding ideology. *Marketing Theory, 6*(2), 263–271.

Polanyi, K. (1944/2001). *The great transformation*. New York, Ferrar & Rinehart.

Rifkin, J. (2014). *The zero marginal cost society*. New York, Palgrave Macmillan.

Ritzer, G. (2015). The new world of prosumption: Evolution, return of the same, or revolution? *Sociological Forum, 30*(1), 1–17.

Sassen, S. (2014). *Expulsions: Brutality and complexity in the global economy*. Cambridge, Harvard University Press.

Schwarzkopf, S. (2011). The subsiding sizzle of advertising history: Methodological and theoretical challenges in the post advertising age. *Journal of Historical Research in Marketing, 3*(4), 528–548.

Sloterdijk, P. (1987). *Critique of cynical reason.* Trans. Michael Eldred. Minneapolis, University of Minnesota Press.

Tadajewski, M. (2010). Towards a history of critical marketing studies. *Journal of Marketing Management, 26*(9–10), 773–824.

Thompson, C. (2005). Consumer risk perceptions in a community of reflexive doubt. *Journal of Consumer Research, 32*(September), 235–248.

Thompson, C.J., & Coskuner-Balli, G. (2007). Countervailing market responses to corporate co-optation and the ideological recruitment of consumption communities. *Journal of Consumer Research, 34*(August), 135–152.

Thompson, C.J., & Haytko, D.L. (1997). Speaking of fashion: Consumers' uses of fashion discourses and the appropriation of countervailing cultural meanings. *Journal of Consumer Research, 24*(1), 15–42.

Thompson, C.J., & Tambyah, S.K. (1999). Trying to be cosmopolitan. *Journal of Consumer Research 26*(3), 214–241.

Vargo, S.L., & Lusch, R.F. (2004). Evolving to a new dominant logic for marketing. *Journal of Marketing, 68*(1), 1–17.

Varman, R., & Al-Amoudi, I. (2016). Accumulation through derealization: How corporate violence remains unchecked. *Human Relations, 69*(10), 1909–1935.

Varman, R., & Belk, R. (2009). Nationalism and ideology in an anti-consumption movement. *Journal of Consumer Research, 36*(4), 686–700.

Varman, R., & Saha, B. (2009). Disciplining the discipline: Understanding postcolonial epistemic ideology in marketing. *Journal of Marketing Management, 25*(7/8), 811–824.

Williams, R. (1977). *Marxism and literature.* Oxford, Oxford University Press.

Žižek, S. (1989). *The sublime object of ideology.* London, Verso.

Zwick, D., & Cayla, J. (2011). *Inside marketing: Practices, ideologies, devices.* Oxford, Oxford University Press.

19
NON-WESTERN CULTURES AND CRITICAL MARKETING

Özlem Sandıkcı Türkdoğan

Introduction

In this chapter, I explore the study of consumption and marketing in non-Western cultures. Specifically, I trace the trajectory of research on marketplaces that fall outside the Western world and discuss the potentialities and possibilities of critical research approaches in studying these contexts. In pursuing these goals, the terms West and non-West present many challenges. My intention here is not to submit to a dichotomic view of the world and reproduce an illusionary separation between the West and the non-West. Rather, I use the terms to refer to characteristics commonly attributed to the West and the non-West in the social sciences and primarily as analytical signposts.

As I discuss in detail, the emergence of international marketing as an independent field of inquiry is a relatively recent phenomenon. While worldwide commercial interactions have a long history, systematic inquiry of marketing in 'foreign' contexts dates back only to the mid-twentieth century. In what follows, I first offer a brief overview of the development of the field with a focus on its historical roots and theoretical and methodological orientations. The analysis shows that the growth of international marketing research has been tightly connected to the history of marketing thought and closely linked with the interests of Western, and especially American, businesses. Over the years, international marketing researchers adopted an overtly managerial focus and became preoccupied with delineating the similarities and differences between the Western and non-Western contexts.

In the next section, I discuss the scope of critical approaches in marketing and outline the principle tenets of Critical Marketing Studies and Consumer Culture Theory as alternative ways of seeking and producing knowledge in the marketing discipline. I highlight the relationship between these two perspectives and their implications for the study of non-Western marketplaces. I then focus on research that has emerged in the last two decades and challenged the cultural difference/similarity prism dominating international marketing studies. I outline the growth of the situated, critical and socio-historically driven approach to studying consumption and marketing in the non-West and review the key research interests and findings of this body of work. I conclude the chapter by arguing that despite the growing interpretive research on the topic, the potential of developing a truly critical perspective to non-Western marketplaces remains unfulfilled.

Development of the field of international marketing

Global trade and commerce date back millennia (Frank & Gills, 1992; Hopkins, 2002; Pieterse, 2012). Archeological studies show that agriculture and migration connected people in disparate locations since the Bronze Age. By 3000 BC, olive oil, wine and grains were regularly traded among the peoples of the Mediterranean Basin (Haldane, 1993). The foundations of the Silk Road were established around 100 BC and, by 1000 AD, commodities of various sorts were circulating between the emergent empires in what we now refer to as Asia, the Middle East and Europe. However, while worldwide commercial interactions have a long history, development of international marketing as a field of scholarly inquiry is a relatively recent phenomenon and is tightly connected to the evolution of marketing thought (e.g. Cavusgil, Deligonul & Yaprak, 2005; Cunningham & Jones, 1997).

The history of marketing as an academic discipline goes back a little more than a century. Studies document that the earliest lectures on the subject were offered in the U.S. around the 1890s and marketing education gained momentum after the 1900s (Bartels, 1962; Berghoff, Scranton & Spiekermann, 2012; Jones & Shaw, 2002). In the 1902–1903 academic year, the Universities of Illinois, Michigan, and California offered marketing-related courses (Bartels, 1962; Jones, 2004). Among other early teaching centers were Harvard University, the University of Wisconsin, the Ohio State University and New York University (Maynard, 1941). Early marketing educators were influenced by the philosophy of the German Historical School of Economics which emphasized pragmatism, positivism and statistical methodologies and adopted a macro orientation to the study of the marketplace (Jones & Monieson, 1990). As Witkowski (2005) notes, issues of marketing and society were central to the work of the pioneering scholars. They were concerned not only with profit and managerial efficiency but also with the ways in which more efficient marketing activity could increase societal welfare in general.

As marketing teaching and research progressed, views on the nature of the subject diversified. By the 1920s, there were four major perspectives on marketing – commodity, institutional, regional, and functional schools (Dixon, 1999; Jones & Monieson, 1990; Sheth & Gross, 1988). The commodity school was concerned with classifying products (e.g. convenience, shopping and specialty goods) and linking them to particular forms of consumer behavior. The functional school focused on understanding different marketing functions, such as transportation, advertising and sales, performed by different market actors. The institutional school sought to justify the economic and societal utility of marketing and marketing intermediaries. Finally, the regional school "viewed marketing as [an] economic activity designed to bridge geographic or spatial gaps between buyers and sellers" (Sheth & Gross, 1988, p.13).

The interest in analyzing trade flows among different regions and commercial activities across boundaries was evident in the early marketing education and writing. For example, George M. Fisk and Simon Litman, pioneering educators of marketing in the USA, "were specifically interested in international marketing and wrote about marketing in the context of international commerce" (Cunningham & Jones 1997, p. 88). Fisk published *International Commercial Policies* in 1907 and discussed issues such as commodities, merchandise and distribution in relation to the international political environment. Litman began writing on international commerce in the early 1900s and published his book *Essentials of International Trade* in 1923. Moreover, American and Canadian schools, such as the University of California, the University of Illinois, the Harvard Business School and Queen's University, began to offer courses on 'foreign trade', 'international trade' and 'foreign marketing' from the 1900s (Cunningham & Jones, 1996).

It is no coincidence that the disciplinary origins of marketing were rooted in North America. During the 1920s, the U.S. economy boomed. While the European economies were struggling to recover from the debts of World War I, the so-called Roaring Twenties brought a dazzling and expanding variety of goods, locally produced or imported, to the attention of the American public (Leach, 1993). American companies also took advantage of the advancements in mass production techniques, namely the increasing supply and lower product costs, and intensified their internationalization initiatives and export operations. As domestic and foreign commercial activities increased, so did the demand for college-trained marketing experts and academic insights into different aspects of marketing.

However, the Great Depression of the 1930s and World War II interrupted economic growth and the expansion of international trade. The crash of the U.S. stock market in October 1929 and the ensuing Great Depression led to sharp drops in manufacturing output and general employment in the United States. In order to promote sales of locally produced goods, the U.S. Congress raised tariffs on imports, up to 50% in some categories (Hall & Ferguson, 1998). The sharp decline in export revenue along with the withdrawal of American foreign capital investments eventually pushed European and other countries into the depression. A major outcome of the protectionist policies was a collapse of world trade – a decline of over 40% was reported (Kindleberger, 1986). The economic difficulties caused by the Great Depression intensified social unrest and nationalist movements, eventually leading to World War II.

Following the war, the shift in production capacity from military goods to consumer products stimulated economic growth in the United States. The surplus in supply, pent up demand in many countries, and technological advances that enabled development of new and better products, motivated American companies to revitalize their international operations and expand globally (Marglin, 1990). However, in the post-war era, marketing assumed a role greater than merely provisioning and selling goods; it has become an instrument for the advancement of American interests abroad. As Tadajewski (2006) notes, the period between 1945 and 1975 had a major impact in shaping marketing research and education. The general atmosphere of the Cold War demanded "academic research to be geared towards the promotion of American interests, aimed at keeping America economically strong in the face of the ideological appeal of Communism" (Tadajewski, 2006, p. 172). Business schools were instrumental for training business leaders who would effectively manage the increasingly complex American marketplace, spread American ways of marketing and consumption to other parts of the world, and help bolster the image of capitalism against communism. In order to fulfill such goals, the academic quality of business schools needed to be improved.

The Ford and Carnegie foundation reports published in the 1950s criticized the business schools for failing to equip their students with proper intellectual and scholarly abilities and for generating research that was largely descriptive and 'unscientific' (Pierson, 1959). In the following years, the funding provided by these principal philanthropic foundations were channeled to develop scientific bases for marketing, with an emphasis on prediction and control (Gemelli, 1998). This funding had significant impact on the development of the field (Tadajewski, 2006). It helped form a generation of marketing scholars that viewed logical empiricism as the appropriate methodological approach and managerial focus as the relevant scope of theorization.

Research and teaching on international marketing reflected the prevailing sentiments of the time and also became predominantly concerned with providing insights that would help managers expand the commercial interests of American companies abroad. To improve the quality of education and strengthen collaboration among researchers and practitioners, a number of professional bodies were set up. For example, the USA International Marketing Institute, a nonprofit foundation located at the Harvard Graduate School of Business Administration, was established in 1958. The Institute aimed at providing research and training on issues pertaining to international marketing practices. Edward Collins Bursk, Professor of Marketing at the Harvard Business

School and the editor of *Harvard Business Review* from 1946 to 1972, served as its educational director. Prof. Bursk, who was also a member of the Council of Economic Advisers during the Kennedy administration, was a keen advocate of international cooperation. In the following years, the Institute, often in collaboration with various state agencies, produced manuals, case studies and publications on topics such as export marketing, international distribution and market development and provided training to managers located both within and outside the USA. For example, a 1963 publication titled *Export Marketing for Smaller Firms*, prepared for the Small Business Administration, an agency of the U.S. federal government, offered guidelines on assessing the attractiveness of foreign markets, establishing or expanding export operations, and determining effective strategies to achieve profits. Around the same time period, in 1959, the Association for Education in International Business, which then became the Academy of International Business, was founded in the USA. The idea was inspired by a task force that had been set up by the American Marketing Association to "study the international aspects of the association work" (Fayerweather, 1974, p. 70). The central function of the association was to facilitate the interchange of ideas among educators and create a platform for the training of managers.

By the 1960s, research on various aspects of international marketing (i.e. export behavior, market entry modes, and internalization strategies of companies) began to appear in marketing and management journals (Aulakh & Kotabe, 1993; Cavusgil & Li, 1992; Cavusgil et al., 2005). As Cavusgil et al. (2005) observe, scholars perceived international marketing as an extension of domestic marketing and sought to "project existing marketing knowledge from their home to a host country" (p. 3). Researchers compared foreign markets' infrastructures, marketing institutions, consumer behavior and competitive dynamics with those in the United States and offered strategy recommendations to companies on how to enter into and expand within foreign markets. As the field evolved, research attention extended to issues such as consumer ethnocentrism and nationalism, globalization of marketing strategy, management of brand equity across markets and marketing in economies in transition (Cavusgil et al., 2005). Several journals introduced in the 1980s (e.g. *International Marketing Review, International Journal of Research in Marketing, Journal of Global Marketing*) and 1990s (e.g. *Journal of International Marketing, International Business Review, Advances in International Marketing*) provided new outlets for the dissemination of research on international marketing.

Overall, since its roots in the early twentieth century, international marketing developed as a field concerned with the production of knowledge that will help managers effectively navigate the uncertainties and unknowns of foreign marketplaces. Research reflected the interests of Western, mostly American, businesses and focused on their operations and strategies in unfamiliar contexts. Foreignness is conceptualized mainly through a similarity-difference prism. That is, the focus has been on understanding how foreign markets compared to the home market in terms of their marketing infrastructure, consumer behavior, competitive environment, cultural dynamics, economic variables, and political and legal institutions. The comparative approach rested on two assumptions. First, it is assumed that theories and conceptual categories developed in the West could be unproblematically applied to the non-West and used to explain phenomena observed there. Second, it is expected that economic progress would diminish the sociocultural differences between the West and the non-West and create uniformly modern marketplaces worldwide.

Levitt's (1983) seminal paper "The globalization of markets" had been pivotal in advocating the idea that while cultural differences exist, they could be ignored because globalization would homogenize tastes and preferences. Levitt saw technology as the most important driving force of globalization and argued that it would drive commonality in consumption and marketing. From his perspective, "different cultural preferences, national tastes and standards, and business institutions" were "vestiges of the past" destined to disappear (1983, p. 96). Thus, he argued for a completely standardized approach to marketing and business strategy as the way forward. Such an approach would allow global corporations to operate "as if the entire world . . . were a single entity" and unburden them from the mistake of wasting resources to cater for superficial differences (pp. 92–93).

In contrast to Levitt's strong position on global homogenization, in another seminal study of the period, *Culture's Consequences: International Differences in Work-Related Values*, Geert Hofstede (1980) endorsed the importance of cultural differences and argued that culture has consequences that cannot be overlooked by business practitioners. Based on a worldwide survey of employee values at IBM, Hofstede developed a model of cultural differences. The original model identified four dimensions along which cultural values could be analyzed: individualism-collectivism, uncertainty avoidance, power distance, and masculinity-femininity. Later two more dimensions, long-term orientation and indulgence versus self-restraint were added. Hofstede (1980) defined culture as the "collective programming of the mind which distinguishes the members of one human group from another" (p. 13). His conceptualization privileged a cognitive, immutable and geographically bounded – national – view of culture (Nakata, 2009). The focus has been on identifying shared thoughts and values characterizing countries and then comparing them with each other along the value dimensions. Hofstede's model has been criticized for reducing culture to a simple set of dimensions, failing to account for the malleability of culture over time, and ignoring within-country cultural heterogeneity (e.g. Askegaard, Kjeldgaard & Arnould, 2009; Erez & Early, 1993; Schwartz, 1994; Sivakumar & Nakata, 2001). Nevertheless, it has become the dominant culture paradigm in international marketing research, inspiring thousands of empirical studies (Kirkman, Lowe & Gibson, 2006).

International marketing scholars employed Hofstede's framework to understand the influence of culture on consumption and marketing across different countries and regions. The nature and extent of cultural differences and similarities across markets have been used to determine the optimal level of standardization or adaptation of marketing strategies and practices (e.g. Jain, 1989; Papavassiliou & Stathakopoulos, 1997). Overall, utilizing a set of value dimensions to study cultural influences has provided a pragmatic approach for conducting cross-cultural research. Quantitative measures of cultural differences and similarities have helped scholars explain and predict a wide range of phenomena such as advertising appeals, innovation, service performance, brand imagery, and product diffusion in the context of global marketing (e.g. Ganesh, Kumar & Subramaniam, 1997; Lynn, Zinkhan & Harris, 1993). However, the preoccupation with differences and similarities has reflected and reinforced the field's orientation toward a binary understanding of the world – home-host, domestic-foreign, Eastern-Western. Such conceptualization, although in line with the managerial perspective underlying much of the marketing literature, has privileged Western models and theories of marketing and consumption as indisputable universal truths that would apply unproblematically in non-Western contexts. As I discuss in detail in the next sections, various streams of research within marketing have called for critical, reflexive, situated perspectives that are attentive to the complexity and multiplicity of cultural practices, power dynamics, contextual histories in studying consumption and markets. The growth of alternative approaches has also had an impact on how non-Western cultures are understood and studied by marketing scholars.

Critical approaches to culture, markets and marketing

Despite the continuing dominance of the managerial perspective in marketing theory and research, there have been critical approaches since the beginnings of the discipline. In the early years of the development of marketing thought, scholars were interested in issues beyond business concerns (Tadajewski & Brownlie, 2008; Witkowski, 2005, 2010). At the University of Wisconsin, for example, academics such as Henry Charles Taylor and Edward David Jones had "an explicit concern with ethics, sometimes manifested in social activism" (Jones, 1994, p. 70). The economic fall of the 1930s intensified criticism of marketing and big businesses. Journalists and activists such as James Rorty and Robert Lynd questioned the assumptions that supported the legitimacy of business and marketing practices (Tadajewski, 2010). During the boom years following World War II, critical analyses of marketing and business systems were far fewer. Outside the marketing field, the works of the Frankfurt School writers and social critics such as Vance Packard and David Caplovitz offered disparaging analyses of marketing practices and the consuming subject (Monieson, 1988; Tadajewski, 2010).

Within the marketing discipline, the interest in critical perspectives was revitalized in the late 1970s (e.g. Fırat, 1978). Seminal publications appeared in the 1980s (e.g. Dholakia & Arndt, 1985; Fırat, Dholakia & Bagozzi, 1987) and 1990s (Brownlie, Saren, Wensley & Whittington, 1999), and the literature has flourished since the 2000s (e.g. Hackley, 2009; Saren et al., 2007; Tadajewski, 2009, 2011; Tadajewski & Brownlie, 2008). As Tadajewski (2011) observes, Critical Marketing scholarship is "concerned with challenging marketing concepts, ideas and ways of reflection that present themselves as ideologically neutral or that otherwise have assumed a taken-for-granted status" (p. 83). Critical Marketing Studies has advocated theoretical and methodological pluralism and is committed to ontological denaturalization, epistemological reflexivity and a non-performative stance (e.g. Brownlie, 2006; Fırat et al., 1987; O'Shaughnessy & O'Shaughnessy, 2002).

Ontological denaturalization calls for acknowledging that the current social order which is structured around the notion of consumer society is not a natural state of affairs but an outcome of particular historical processes (Tadajewski & Brownlie, 2008; Atik & Fırat, 2013). Thus, Critical Marketing Studies draws attention to the power relations that structure and maintain the claims made in support of the market system and questions "whether or not it is possible to envision an alternative structure of market relations" (Tadajewski & Brownlie, 2008, p. 10). Critical Marketing Studies also rejects the notion that reality exists external to the researcher and, instead, recognizes the role of the researcher in the production of knowledge. Finally, the non-performative position suggests that research should not be solely interested in generating knowledge that helps managers maximize sales of products, but should be geared toward problematizing and questioning capitalist values and the individualistic conception of consumer behavior.

The non-performative stance is also acknowledged in Consumer Culture Theory (CCT), an interpretive research approach to the study of consumption that emerged in the 1990s (Arnould & Thompson, 2005). The term CCT was coined by Arnould and Thompson in their 2005 *Journal of Consumer Research* article and used to refer to studies that address the sociocultural, experiential, symbolic and ideological aspects of consumption. As Arnould and Thompson (2005, pp. 868–869) explain:

> [R]ather than viewing culture as a fairly homogenous system of collectively shared meanings, ways of life, and unifying values shared by a member of society (e.g. Americans share this kind of culture; Japanese share that kind of culture), CCT explores the heterogeneous distribution of meanings and the multiplicity of overlapping cultural groupings that exist within the broader sociohistoric frame of globalization and market capitalism.

By valorizing a 'distributed view of cultural meaning' (Hannerz, 1992), CCT has drawn attention to the importance of the lived experiences of consumers and the fragmented, plural and fluid nature of consumption. While the CCT tradition represents a plurality of theoretical traditions, CCT-oriented studies have shared a common interest in studying consumption as "a historically shaped mode of sociocultural practice that emerges within the structures and ideological imperatives of dynamic marketplaces" (Arnould & Thompson, 2005, p. 875). CCT research has distanced itself from the overtly managerial approach that characterized mainstream marketing research; nevertheless, it has also recognized that socio-historically situated, interpretive accounts of consumption and markets can generate highly managerially relevant insights.

Overall, Critical Marketing Studies and CCT approaches have problematized the dominance of logical empiricism and managerial focus, and instead advocated methodological and theoretical pluralism to the study of consumption, markets and marketing (see also Tadajewski *et al.*, this volume). The developments within the social sciences, especially in relation to the theorizations of culture, knowledge and globalization, have further inspired some marketing scholars to adopt interpretive, situated and critical perspectives while studying non-Western marketplaces. In particular, theories of globalization challenged the relevancy of linear development and modernization models and highlighted the multidirectional and multilayered flows and the complex interactions between the local and the global (e.g. Appadurai, 1990; Robertson, 1995; Pieterse, 1995). Similarly, postmodern theorization emphasized multiplicities, fragmentations and contingencies, and challenged the hold of "totalizing visions" and "the general paradigmatic style of organizing research" (Marcus & Fischer, 1986, p. 8; also Jameson, 1987; Lyotard, 1984). Thus, critically oriented scholars have started to question the prevailing dichotomic conceptualization of the Western and non-Western marketplaces and the unreflexive use of Western models and theories of marketing in non-Western contexts.

Re-thinking consumption and marketing in non-Western cultures

Among the pioneering work to address the significance of context and demonstrate the limitations of applying theories and models developed in the West to other cultures were Arnould's (1989) analysis of the processes of innovation diffusion among the Hausa in the Republic of Niger and Ger, and Belk's studies on globalization of consumer culture (Ger & Belk, 1996; Ger, 1997). Arnould used the case of preference formation to critique the ethnocentric assumptions on which models of preference formation are based as well as to reconfigure the 'standard' models of innovation diffusion. His analysis revealed that a traditional pre-market model, the Western market-based model and an Islamic-nationalist model inform behavior of the Hausa toward new products. Arnould's study has provided evidence that consumer behavior in non-Western contexts cannot simply be assumed to replicate Western models and that systematic study of particular macro-economic, social structural, political and cultural variables are needed to generate contextualized insights. Similarly, Ger and Belk (1996) and Ger (1997) objected to the tendency to conceptualize non-Western consumer culture as a mere imitation of the Western consumer culture and called for research that is attentive to the multiplicity and complexity of the articulations of consumption in the non-West. Ger and Belk (1996) made a strong case against the view of a homogenized, one-world consumer culture that is either passively adopted or staunchly resisted and instead discussed other possible alternatives such as recontextualization and creolization, through which local and global intermingle and inform consumption practices.

Around the same time period, Venkatesh (1995) offered a systematic approach, named 'ethnoconsumerism', to facilitate socio-culturally and historically embedded cross-cultural research.

Venkatesh described ethnoconsumerism as "a conceptual framework to study consumer behavior using the theoretical categories originating within a given culture" (1995, p. 27). In other words, ethnoconsumerism emphasizes that researchers need to study behavior on the basis of the cultural realities of individuals, rather than imposing pre-existing categories to explain that behavior. This approach recommends beginning with the basic categories of a given culture and subsequently studying the actions, practices, words, thoughts, language, institutions and interconnections between these categories. However, ethnoconsumerism goes beyond a 'field view' level analysis that recounts the native's point of view to a 'text view' level analysis that delves into "the development of knowledge constructed from the culture's point of view" (Venkatesh, 1995, p. 29; also Meamber & Venkatesh, 2000). That is, in addition to describing current practices and impressions, ethnoconsumerism involves the identification of the historical and sociocultural themes of a culture.

In the years following, a socio-culturally driven and critically oriented stream of research on the dynamics of consumption and marketing in non-Western contexts has emerged (e.g. Izberk-Bilgin, 2012; Jafari & Goulding, 2008, 2013; Jafari & Maclaran, 2014; Joy, 2001; Karababa & Ger, 2011; Karatas & Sandıkcı, 2013; Kravets & Sandıkcı, 2013, 2014; Sandıkcı & Ger, 2002, 2010; Üstüner & Holt, 2007, 2010; Varman & Vikas, 2007; Varman & Belk, 2008; Yazıcıoğlu & Fırat, 2007; Zhao & Belk, 2008a, 2008b). Studies conducted in diverse settings such as Turkey, India, Iran, China and Russia appeared in prominent journals (see also Varman, this volume). Workshops, conference sessions, edited collections and journal special issues dedicated to the study of non-Western consumer cultures and marketplaces enabled the exchange of ideas among researchers and inspired new research avenues. A complete overview of the entire catalog of this work is naturally beyond the scope of this chapter. However, a critical assessment of the literature indicates that researchers have been particularly interested in understanding the nature and dynamics of the interactions between the global and the local and their implications for the consumption cultures and consumer subjectivities in the non-West.

A prominent concern characterizing much of this research has been identifying and analyzing local interpretations and experiences of modernity in non-Western consumer cultures. Building on the preliminary work that drew attention to the limitations of the emulative model in accounting for the consumption practices observed in the non-Western contexts (e.g. Fırat, 1997; Ger & Belk, 1996), these studies have taken issue with the concept of modernization. Rejecting the view of a single path of modernization and the assumption of the eventual homogenization of Third World consumption cultures (e.g. Belk, 1988; Joy & Wallendorf, 1995), scholars have instead adopted the perspective of 'multiple modernities'. The concept of multiple modernities rests on a view of culture as a dynamic constellation of diverse practices and transnational flows of meanings, styles and conventions and suggests that differentiated forms of modernities emerge through the interaction of local and global cultures (e.g. Appadurai, 1990; Friedman, 1994; Hampden-Turner & Trompenaars, 1993; Hannerz, 1992, 1996; Miller, 1998; Pieterse, 1995; Robertson, 1995; Wilk, 1995). In the marketing field, scholars have explored how the meanings of consumption objects and practices are appropriated and reconfigured in non-Western contexts and used as resources to negotiate and resolve identity tensions.

For example, in a series of studies Sandıkcı and Ger (2001, 2002, 2005, 2010) have explored different articulations of local/global, East/West, and modern/traditional that characterized consumption in Turkey. The authors observe that different consumption styles operate as microcosms in which a diverse set of claims to a modern identity are acted out. As globalization, marketization and neoliberal restructuring open up new spaces for political, economic and cultural expressions, even practices that were once stigmatized, such as veiling, can become attractive and viable routes for constructing and performing a modern identity. Similarly, Jafari and Goulding (2008, 2013) explored how Iranian middle-class consumers use consumption discourses to tackle a series of ideological tensions. As they show, individuals living in a theocratic state use commodified cultural symbols not only to construct and reaffirm a sense of self, but also to covertly resist the dominant order. Global cultural flows thus stimulate an ongoing intercultural learning process through which people reconstitute their lives and change their everyday consumption practices and lifestyle choices (Jafari & Goulding, 2013).

Studies have also focused on understanding the ways consumers in non-Western contexts interact with global brands and use them as resources when negotiating the modern and the traditional. For example, in their research on the evaluation of McDonald's in China, Eckhardt and Houston (2002) found that the brand had triggered contradictory meanings. When families eat together at a McDonald's it becomes an instrument to sustain traditional values, but when young people go on unchaperoned dates there, it is used as a place to challenge traditional practices. Another study by Venkatraman and Nelson (2008) also reported similar results for Starbucks. People experience Starbucks both as a home-like secure, warm and comfortable place and a threatening, frustrating and exotic place. They suggest that the paradox over Starbucks reflects the "tension between the excitement of constructing new identities as modern, Western-looking professionals and the traditional pull of maintaining their role as dutiful, Chinese family members" (Venkatraman & Nelson, 2008, p. 1022). Relatedly, Dong and Tian (2009) and Eckhardt and Mahi (2012) discuss how consumers in China and India, respectively, transform the meanings of global brands and use them to assert particular forms of national and traditional identities. While these accounts have tended to conceptualize cultural globalization as the export of Western products to other countries and focus on non-Western consumers' responses to the arrival of global brands, Cayla and Eckhardt's (2008) analysis of the creation of regional Asian brands has called for a 'decentering' of globalization studies. That is, research on global consumer cultures needs to acknowledge the multiplicity of influential cultural centers and the diversity of cultural flows originating from many, non-Western places.

However, while global cultural flows enable multiplicity, fluidity and hybridity, scholars have also reported that political, economic and sociocultural structures continue to operate and constrain consumption choices. Institutional dynamics and power relationships shape individuals' interactions with products, ideas and images and influence their identities and reflexive abilities (Askegaard et al., 2009; Jafari & Goulding, 2013). As such, glocalization of consumption and local appropriations themselves become a 'global structure of common differences' (Wilk, 1995). That is, while the global cultural system promotes difference, the dimensions across which cultures vary become more limited – "cultures become different in very uniform ways" (Wilk, 1995, p. 118). In the domain of consumption, although plural and different interpretations are possible at the individual level, homogenization occurs at the structural level (Kjeldgaard & Askegaard, 2006).

In line with this view, several studies look into the dynamics and potential of local resistance to global consumer culture. For example, Izberk-Bilgin (2012) found that low-income Turkish consumers draw from the religious ideology of Islamism to construct global brands as infidels and wage a consumer jihad against them. Varman and Belk (2009) examined the role of the nationalist ideology of swadeshi in an anti-consumption movement opposing Coca-Cola in India. They noted that a nationalist ideology is an unarticulated challenge to global brands that particularly manifests itself in postcolonial encounters. On the other hand, Zhao and Belk's research on the discourses of advertising in China (2008a, 2008b) revealed that the advertising industry itself had appropriated the dominant political ideology and played a key role in promoting consumption in post-Communist China.

Research also indicates that the constraining effects of globalization and marketization in non-Western contexts have been particularly visible among the less advantaged consumer groups. As Varman and Vikas (2007) aver, the types of consumerist freedom reported in many prior studies have been an elitist privilege, available only to those who have the resources to exercise their freedom of choice. For subaltern consumers who live in abysmal material conditions production continues to define their state of unfreedom. The authors demonstrated that lack of empowerment in the domain of production translates into a lack of freedom in the sphere of consumption. Furthermore, Üstüner and Holt's (2007) study of poor migrant women living in a Turkish squatter neighborhood and Varman and Belk's (2008) study of working-class consumers in India have suggested that while television, popular culture and the material environment promoted a lifestyle centered around products, participation in a consumption culture might be difficult and even impossible for subordinate groups, resulting in 'shattered identity projects' and 'dialectics of turmoil and tranquility'.

As more research delved into non-Western cultures, it became apparent that understanding the sociocultural context of consumption is crucial because it frames possibilities for thought, beliefs and actions, and makes the emergence of certain meanings more likely than others. Situated analyses of consumption and consumers have rendered the applicability of existing theories outside the West more and more questionable. For example, Üstüner and Holt (2007) proposed a 'dominated consumer acculturation model' to account for consumer acculturation in non-Western contexts; Üstüner and Holt (2007), Kravets and Sandıkcı (2014) and Vikas, Varman, and Belk (2015) criticized top-down class emulation and status consumption models for their inadequacies in explaining consumption dynamics in the developing world and proposed alternative frameworks; and Joy (2001) offered a critique of existing theories of gift-giving and showed that in Hong Kong gift-giving involves exchanges between individuals, but not family members, as family falls outside the realm of reciprocity.

Moreover, historical studies of consumption in non-Western contexts challenged the implicit yet fundamental assumption that consumer culture originated in the West and then spread throughout the world (Zhao & Belk, 2008b; Karababa, 2012; Karababa & Ger, 2011; Kravets & Sandıkcı, 2013). This assumption has rested on a belief that conditions necessary for the emergence of consumer culture (i.e. the absence of a bourgeois class, a public sphere, Protestant ethic, capitalist economy, and a rational subjecthood) had been missing in non-Western societies (e.g. Slater, 1997; Weber, 2002). Assuming that the modern culture of consumption in the non-West only began in the post-World War II era, much marketing research has focused on contemporary expressions of consumption in the developing world. In contrast, Zhao and Belk's (2008b) work on China revealed the striking similarities between the commercial forces shaping Shanghai in the 1930s and the commercialism found in China today. Moreover, work on the Ottoman Empire (Karababa & Ger, 2011; Karababa, 2012) has traced the formation of a consumer subject back to the sixteenth century and showed that the presence of hybrid global-local forms of consumption objects in Ottoman society goes back to the early modern period. Finally, when looking at the marketing practices of a Soviet state trust in the 1930s, Kravets and Sandıkcı (2013) found that while the marketing techniques utilized by the trust were comparable to those of Western companies, its logic had been entirely different. In the Soviet context, marketing was used to frame consumption as a productive, progressive social activity, rather than a hedonistic, bourgeois, individualistic one and helped promote the state's ideological policies.

Overall, in the past two decades, research that goes beyond the prevailing theoretical and methodological boundaries of the international marketing literature has developed. These studies have called into question an essentialist view of culture and sought to understand consumption and marketing dynamics in non-Western contexts by exploring the lived experiences of consumers, as well as the local and global structural forces shaping their marketplaces. However, as I elaborate next, much of this research has adopted an interpretive rather than critical perspective and failed to provide an analytical engagement with the Western imaginations of power, market, or subjectivity as universal meta-narratives. In other words, research continues to be fixated on Western conceptualizations of the market and marketing and preoccupied with understanding the construction of identity through consumption.

The potential of critical marketing beyond the West

The growth of interpretive research on non-Western contexts has sensitized scholars to the complex and multilayered cultural interactions between the local and global, the dynamics of socio-historical and ideological forces shaping consumption practices, and the multiplicity of ways objects are used in constructing, communicating and negotiating identities in the non-West. However, despite the fact that studies have gone beyond a managerially driven interest in understanding the non-West, they have not adequately engaged with issues about knowledge production. In other words, while the world that consumers live in is recognized as glocal, inter-connected and fluid, the production and circulation of knowledge has continued to be organized alongside an asymmetrical distribution of academic power (see also Varman, this volume). Non-Western contexts have been explored mainly from a Western perspective and different forms of knowledge circulating in different parts of the world have remained largely unknown to Western academic audiences (Jafari *et al.*, 2012; Varman & Saha, 2009).

In their discussion of the geopolitics of knowledge in the field of sociology, Miskolci, Cortes, Scalon and Salata (2016, p. 2) argue that

> besides the concentration of research in the Global North, there is a tacit division of intellectual work: European and US scholars produce "legitimate" theory and research methods while sociologists from the "rest of the world" dedicate their efforts to gathering data, analyzing case studies, or on applied research.

A similar observation applies to the field of marketing. Despite the increase in scholarly attention on non-Western cultures, which has resulted in articles appearing in prominent academic outlets (see also Varman, this volume), the research agenda continues to be established by the priorities of the Global North/West (i.e. the American Marketing Association, Marketing Science Institute and related journals etc.). The focus of inquiry and the underlying theoretical frameworks adopted converge with the prevailing (Western) theoretical models of marketing and consumption. The once prominent, and still existing, concern in applying and testing theories developed in the West in non-Western contexts reflects and endorses the West's position as the historical center of scientific knowledge. Even when researchers explore the consumption cultures of the non-West using socio-historically and locally developed conceptual categories and constructs, they still continue to operate along the lines set by the extant academic (hegemonic) structure. That is, while these studies provide context-specific understanding of meanings and practices, the not context-specific rationality continues to be based on the criteria of Western knowledge (Holmwood, 2009).

While the 'non-West' is far from being a homogeneous set of countries, as this review indicates, representations of non-Western cultures in marketing theory remain confined to a very limited number of contexts. Research tends to concentrate on only a few places (i.e. Turkey, China, India, Brazil) and scholars from a limited number of countries appear to be present in the international scientific arena. There are several reasons for this (Jafari *et al.*, 2012; Alcadipani, Khan, Gantman & Nkomo, 2012). Besides financial limitations and difficulties in accessing academic resources, the dominance of the English language in the circulation of knowledge shapes both the content of the discussion and the extent of participation. The language barrier works in two ways. It limits the ability of non-Western academics to publish in the 'top journals' and it restricts Western academics' access to knowledge produced and disseminated in local languages. As such, a two-way interaction and communication between Western and non-Western academics becomes almost impossible. Furthermore, being able to speak and write in English to acceptable academic standards requires years of study abroad, an opportunity that is typically available only to a privileged few. It is no surprise that the 'few' are often from the so-called emerging markets (EMs). What characterizes these countries is their adherence to neoliberal capitalism, increasing economic affluence and growing middle-class consumer segments. As key trading partners of the U.S. and Europe, they attract increasing managerial attention. Research that provides insights into the EMs, whether mainstream or interpretive, appears to enjoy a more welcoming presence in the Western academic outlets than research on other non-Western contexts.

In recent years, alternative frameworks concerned with fostering dialog between different ways of knowledge production have emerged (e.g. Comaroff & Comaroff, 2015; Connell, 2007; de Sousa Santos, 2007). Referred to as the theories of south or epistemologies of the south, this perspective calls for decolonizing knowledge by "uncovering its sociocultural and ideological origins and, simultaneously, conceive alternative spaces for thinking and acting outside mainstream systems of thought" (Glaveanu & Sierra, 2015, p. 345). A key premise of this approach is that the diversity of being, thinking and feeling needs to be recognized and alternative ways of knowledge production and valorization should be acknowledged. Beyond sociology and anthropology, such calls have been made in management studies, encouraging researchers to embrace diverse epistemological possibilities (e.g. Seremani & Clegg, 2016; Westwood & Jack, 2007). Advancing intellectual dialogue between the West and non-West can also play a productive role in the marketing field and contribute to the decolonization of knowledge generation. To this end, postcolonial theory can provide a useful toolkit. And yet, postcolonial theory has enjoyed only a marginal position in the marketing literature (e.g. Brace-Govan & de Burgh-Woodman, 2008; Jack, 2008; Patterson & Brown, 2007; Varman & Belk, 2012), with the result that postcolonial studies of non-Western marketplaces have remained largely absent from academic discourse (for exceptions, Varman & Saha 2009; Varman & Sreekumar, 2015).

The full realization of the potentialities of a critical engagement with different epistemologies is yet to be witnessed. However, Wallerstein's (1991) distinction between *re-thinking* and *un-thinking* social sciences can provide some insights into how 'southern' perspectives can contribute to Critical Marketing Studies. Re-thinking implies reconsidering taken-for-granted categories and phenomena in light of new evidence. Un-thinking, however, entails exposing the embedded assumptions upon which these very categories, as a set of 'givens', rest. Wallerstein suggests that we need to deconstruct and rework many of the presumptions that still remain the foundation of dominant perspectives in social sciences. The implications of Wallerstein's distinction for research on consumption and marketing are evident. Re-thinking non-Western consumer cultures indicates a reconceptualization of consumption by taking into account the experiences of non-Western consumers and the dynamics of local market structures and thus seeing non-Western consumption cultures as a derivative of (Western) consumption. However, un-thinking non-Western consumer cultures means moving beyond consumption as the telos of modernity and seeing marketplaces as articulations and materializations of multiple ways of imagining society, economy and politics.

As is now apparent, globalization is not only promoting consumerist lifestyles but affecting the way knowledge is created and circulates. The existence of 'multiple modernities' suggests that there might be not only multiple routes to modern consumer cultures, but multiple routes to theorizing consumption. However, as Varman and Saha point out, "the Eurocentrism of critical marketing theory has meant that marketing knowledgescapes in the Third World countries have been overlooked" (2009, p. 811). Thus, the challenge remains for marketing scholars as they engage with non-Western cultures to figure out ways to un-think consumption and marketing.

Conclusion

In this chapter I have focused on research devoted to non-Western marketplaces. While the historical roots of international marketing go back to the early twentieth century, systematic inquiry about marketing in foreign markets gained momentum in the late 1950s. From the very beginning, international marketing thought and practice have been connected to Western, and mostly American, commercial interests. Scholars have adopted a managerial perspective and sought to generate knowledge that would guide companies in their international operations.

Since the 1990s, research on non-Western markets expanded beyond a limited managerial focus to understanding the socio-historically shaped dynamics of marketing and consumption in these contexts. This body of work has significantly expanded our knowledge of non-Western marketplaces and highlighted the drawbacks of essentialist and ahistorical conceptualizations of culture which characterize much of the mainstream research on the topic. Indeed, the need to go beyond a Hofstedian notion of culture has also been voiced in the mainstream international marketing literature (e.g. Craig & Douglas, 2006; Douglas & Craig, 2011; Nakata, 2009). For example, Craig and Douglas (2006) have called for research designs that take into consideration processes of deterritorialization and define the appropriate unit on a cultural basis. Likewise, Nakata (2009) has maintained that interdependencies created through globalization have rendered a nationally based notion of culture increasingly limiting. More recently, Chelekis and Figueiredo (2015) drew attention to "critical regionalities" and called for greater sensitivity to regional consumer culture as a potential analytical lens to study non-Western contexts. However, despite theoretical and methodological advancements, research on non-Western contexts has not fully benefited from a truly critically oriented approach. Going beyond the hegemonic Western imaginations of market, marketing and consumption remains a key challenge.

References

Alcadipani, R., Khan, F.R., Gantman, E., & Nkomo, S. (2012). Southern voices in management and organization knowledge. *Organization*, *19*(2), 131–143.
Appadurai, A. (1990). Disjuncture and difference in the global cultural economy. *Theory, Culture and Society*, 7(2–3), 295–310.
Arnould, E.J. (1989). Toward a broadened theory of preference formation and the diffusion of innovations: Cases from Zinder Province, Niger Republic. *Journal of Consumer Research*, *16*(2), 239–267.
Arnould, E.J., & Thompson, C.J. (2005). Consumer Culture Theory: Twenty years of research. *Journal of Consumer Research*, *31*(4), 868–883.
Askegaard, S., Kjeldgaard, D., & Arnould, E.J. (2009). Reflexive culture's consequences. In C. Nakata (Ed.), *Beyond Hofstede* (pp. 101–122). London, Palgrave Macmillan.
Atik, D., & Fırat, A.F. (2013). Fashion creation and diffusion: The institution of marketing. *Journal of Marketing Management*, *29*(7–8), 836–860.
Aulakh, P.S., & Kotabe, M. (1993). An assessment of theoretical and methodological development in international marketing. *Journal of International Marketing*, *1*(2), 5–28.

Bartels, R. (1962). *The development of marketing thought.* Homewood, Richard D. Irwin.

Belk, R.W. (1988). Third world consumer culture. In E. Kumcu & A.F. Fırat (Eds.), *Marketing and development: Towards broader dimensions* (pp. 103–127). Greenwich, JAI Press.

Berghoff, H., Scranton, P., & Spiekermann, U. (2012). The origins of marketing and market research: Information, institutions, and markets. In H. Berghoff, P. Scranton & U. Spiekermann (Eds.), *The rise of marketing and market research* (pp. 1–26). New York, Palgrave Macmillan.

Brace-Govan, J., & de Burgh-Woodman, H. (2008). Sneakers and street culture: A postcolonial analysis of marginalized cultural consumption. *Consumption Markets & Culture, 11*(2), 93–112.

Brownlie, D. (2006). Emancipation, epiphany and resistance: On the underimagined and overdetermined in critical marketing. *Journal of Marketing Management, 22*(5–6), 505–528.

Brownlie, D., Saren, M., Wensley, R., & Whittington, R. (Eds.) (1999). *Rethinking marketing: Toward critical marketing accountings.* London, Sage.

Cavusgil, S.T., & Li, T. (1992). *International marketing: An annotated bibliography.* Chicago, American Marketing Association.

Cavusgil, S.T., Deligonul, S., & Yaprak, A. (2005). International marketing as a field of study: A critical assessment of earlier development and a look forward. *Journal of International Marketing, 13*(4), 1–27.

Cayla, J., & Eckhardt, G.M. (2008). Asian brands and the shaping of a transnational imagined community. *Journal of Consumer Research, 35*(August), 216–230.

Chelekis, J.A., & Figueiredo, B. (2015). Regions and archipelagos of consumer culture: A reflexive approach to analytical scales and boundaries. *Marketing Theory, 15*(3), 321–345.

Comaroff, J., & Comaroff, J.L. (2015). *Theory from the South: Or, how Euro-America is evolving toward Africa.* London, Routledge.

Connell, R. (2007). *Southern theory.* London, Polity Press.

Craig, S.C., & Douglas, S.P. (2006). Beyond national culture: Implications of cultural dynamics for consumer research. *International Marketing Review, 23*(3), 322–342.

Cunningham, P., & Jones, D.G.B. (1997). Early development of collegiate education in international marketing. *Journal of International Marketing, 5*(2), 87–102.

de Sousa Santos, B. (Ed.) (2007). *Another knowledge is possible: Beyond northern epistemologies.* London, Verso.

Dholakia, N., & Arndt, J. (Eds.) (1985). *Changing the course of marketing.* Greenwich, JAI Press.

Dixon, D.F. (1999). Some late nineteenth-century antecedents of marketing theory. *Journal of Macromarketing, 19*(2), 115–125.

Dong, L., & Tian, K. (2009). The use of Western brands in asserting Chinese national identity. *Journal of Consumer Research, 36*(3), 504–523.

Douglas, S.P., & Craig, S.C. (2011). The role of context in assessing international marketing opportunities. *International Marketing Review, 28*(2), 150–162.

Eckhardt, G.M., & Houston, M.J. (2002). Cultural paradoxes reflected in brand meaning: McDonald's in Shanghai, China. *Journal of International Marketing, 10*(2), 68–82.

Eckhardt, G.M., & Mahi, H. (2012). Globalization, consumer tensions, and the shaping of consumer culture in India. *Journal of Macromarketing, 32*(3), 280–294.

Erez, M., & Early, C. (1993). *Culture, self-identity, and work.* Oxford, Oxford University Press.

Fayerweather, J. (1974). The birth of the AEIB. *Journal of International Business Studies, 5*(2), 69–80.

Fırat, A.F. (1978). *The social construction of consumption patterns.* Unpublished Ph.D. Dissertation. Northwestern University.

Fırat, A.F. (1997). Globalization of fragmentation: A framework for understanding contemporary global markets. *Journal of International Marketing, 5*(2), 77–86.

Fırat, A.F., Dholakia, N., & Bagozzi, R.P. (1987). Introduction: Breaking the mold. In A.F. Fırat, N. Dholakia & R.P. Bagozzi (Eds.), *Philosophical and radical thought in marketing* (pp. xii–xxi). Lexington, Lexington Books.

Fisk, G.M. (1907). *International commercial policies.* New York, Macmillan Co.

Frank, A., & Gills, B. (1992). The five thousand year world system: An interdisciplinary introduction. *Humboldt Journal of Social Relations, 18*(1), 1–79.

Friedman, J. (1994). *Cultural identity and global process.* New York, Sage.

Ganesh, J., Kumar, V., & Subramaniam, V. (1997). Learning effect in multinational diffusion of consumer durables: An exploratory investigation. *Journal of the Academy of Marketing Science, 25*(3), 214–228.

Gemelli, G. (1998). From imitation to competitive cooperation: The Ford Foundation and management education in western and eastern Europe (1950s–1970s). In G. Gemelli (Ed.), *The Ford Foundation and Europe (1950s–1970s): Cross-fertilization of learning in social science and management* (pp. 167–306). Oxford, Peter Lang.

Ger, G. (1997). Human development and humane consumption: Well-being beyond the 'good life'. *Journal of Public Policy & Marketing, 16*(1), 110–125.

Ger, G., & Belk, R.W. (1996). I'd like to buy the world a Coke: Consumptionscapes of a less affluent world. *Journal of Consumer Policy, 19*(3), 271–304.

Glaveanu, V.P., & Sierra, Z. (2015). Creativity and epistemologies of the South. *Culture & Psychology, 21*(3) 340–358.

Hackley, C. (2009). *Marketing: A critical introduction.* London, Sage.

Haldane, C. (1993). Direct evidence for organic cargoes in the Late Bronze Age. *World Archaeology, 24*(3), 348–360.

Hall, T.E., & Ferguson, J.D. (1998). *The great depression: An international disaster of perverse economic policies.* Ann Arbor, The University of Michigan Press.

Hampden-Turner, C., & Trompenaars, F. (1993). *The seven cultures of capitalism.* New York, Doubleday.

Hannerz, U. (1992). *Cultural complexity: Studies in the social organization of meaning.* New York, Columbia University Press.

Hannerz, U. (1996). *Transnational connections.* London, Routledge.

Hofstede, G. (1980). *Culture's consequences: International differences in work-related values.* London, Sage.

Holmwood, J. (2009). The challenge of global social inquiry. *Sociological Research Online, 14*(4). Retrieved April 21, 2016 from www.socresonline.org.uk/14/4/13.html

Hopkins, A.G. (2002). The history of globalization – and the globalization of history? In A.G. Hopkins (Ed.), *Globalization in world history* (pp. 11–46). London, Pimlico.

Izberk-Bilgin, E. (2012). Infidel brands: Unveiling alternative meanings of global brands at the nexus of globalization, consumer culture, and Islamism. *Journal of Consumer Research, 39*(4), 663–687.

Jack, G. (2008). Postcolonialism and marketing. In M. Tadajewski & D. Brownlie (Eds.), *Critical marketing: Issues in contemporary marketing* (pp. 363–383). Chichester, Wiley.

Jafari, A., & Goulding, C. (2008). 'We are not terrorists!' UK based Iranians, consumption, and the 'torn self'. *Consumption Markets & Culture, 11*(2), 73–93.

Jafari, A., & Goulding, C. (2013). Globalisation, reflexivity and the project of the self: A virtual intercultural learning process. *Consumption Markets & Culture, 16*(1), 65–90.

Jafari, A., & Maclaran, P. (2014). Escaping into the world of make-up routines in Iran. *The Sociological Review, 62*(2), 359–382.

Jafari, A., Fırat, F., Süerdem, A., Askegaard, S., & Dalli, D. (2012). Non-western contexts: The invisible half. *Marketing Theory, 12*(1) 3–12.

Jain, S.C. (1989). Standardization of international marketing strategy: Some research hypotheses. *Journal of Marketing, 53*(1), 70–79.

Jameson, F. (1987). The politics of theory: Ideological positions in the postmodern debate. In P. Rabinow & W. Sullivan (Eds.), *Interpretive social science: A second look* (pp. 351–364). Berkeley, University of California Press.

Jones, D.G.B. (1994). Biography and the history of marketing thought: Henry Charles Taylor and Edward David Jones. In R.A. Fullerton (Ed.), *Research in marketing, supplement 6: Explorations in marketing thought* (pp. 67–85). Greenwich, JAI Press.

Jones, D.G.B. (2004). Simon Litman (1873–1965): Pioneer marketing scholar. *Marketing Theory, 4*(4), 343–361.

Jones, D.G.B., & Monieson, D.D. (1990). Early development of the philosophy of marketing thought. *Journal of Marketing, 54*(January), 102–112.

Jones, D.G.B., & Shaw, E.H. (2002). A history of marketing thought. In B.A. Weitz & R. Wensley (Eds.), *Handbook of marketing* (pp. 39–65). London, Sage.

Joy, A. (2001). Gift giving in Hong Kong and the continuum of social ties. *Journal of Consumer Research, 28*(September), 239–256.

Joy, A., & Wallendorf, M. (1995). Development of consumer culture in the third world: Theories of globalism and localism. In R.W. Belk, N. Dholakia & A. Venkatesh (Eds.), *Consumption and marketing: Macro dimensions* (pp. 104–142). Cincinnati, Southwestern.

Karababa, E. (2012). Approaching non-western consumer cultures from a historical perspective: The case of early modern Ottoman consumer culture. *Marketing Theory, 12*(1), 13–25.

Karababa, E., & Ger, G. (2011). Early modern Ottoman coffeehouse culture and the formation of the consumer subject. *Journal of Consumer Research, 37*(5), 737–760.

Karatas, M., & Sandıkcı, O. (2013). Religious communities and the marketplace: Learning and performing consumption in an Islamic network. *Marketing Theory, 13*(4), 465–484.

Kindleberger, C.P. (1986). *The world in depression, 1929–1939.* Berkeley, University of California Press.

Kirkman, B.L., Lowe, K.B., & Gibson, C.B. (2006). A quarter century of culture's consequences: A review of empirical research incorporating Hofstede's cultural values framework. *Journal of International Business Studies, 37*(3), 285–320.

Kjeldgaard, D., & Askegaard, S. (2006). The glocalization of youth culture: The global youth segment as structures of common difference. *Journal of Consumer Research, 33*(2), 231–247.

Kravets, O., & Sandıkcı, O. (2013). Marketing for socialism: Soviet cosmetics in the 1930s. *Business History Review, 87*(3), 461–487.

Kravets, O., & Sandıkcı, O. (2014). Competently ordinary: New middle class consumers in the emerging markets. *Journal of Marketing, 78*(4), 125–140.

Leach, W.R. (1993). *Land of desire: Merchants, power, and the rise of a new American culture.* New York, Pantheon.

Levitt, T. (1983). The globalization of markets. *Harvard Business Review* (May–June), 92–102.

Litman, S. (1923). *Essentials of international trade.* New York, John Wiley & Sons.

Lynn, M., Zinkhan, G.M., & Harris, J. (1993). Consumer tipping: A cross-country study. *Journal of Consumer Research, 20*(3), 478–488.

Lyotard, J.-F. (1984). *The postmodern condition: A report on knowledge.* Minneapolis, University of Minnesota Press.

Maynard, H.H. (1941). Marketing courses prior to 1910. *Journal of Marketing, 5*(April), 382–384.

Marcus, G.E., & Fischer, M.M.J. (1986). A crisis of representation in the human sciences. In G.E. Marcus & M.M.J. Fischer (Eds.), *Anthropology as cultural critique: An experimental moment in the human sciences* (pp. 7–16). Chicago, University of Chicago Press.

Marglin, S.A. (1990). *The golden age of capitalism: Reinterpreting the postwar experience.* Oxford, Oxford University Press.

Meamber, L.A., & Venkatesh, A. (2000). Ethno-consumerist methodology for cultural and cross-cultural consumer research. In S.C. Beckmann & R.H. Elliott (Eds.), *Interpretive consumer research: Paradigms, methodologies and applications* (pp. 87–108). Copenhagen, Copenhagen Business School Press.

Miller, D. (1998). Coca-Cola: A black sweet drink from Trinidad. In D. Miller (Ed.), *Material culture: Why some things matter* (pp. 169–187). Chicago, University of Chicago Press.

Miskolci, R., Cortes, S.V., Scalon, C., & Salata, A.R. (2016). Sociologies in dialogue. *Sociologies in Dialogue, 2*(1), 1–15.

Monieson, D.D. (1988). Intellectualization in macromarketing: A world disenchanted. *Journal of Macromarketing, 8*(2), 4–10.

Nakata, C. (Ed.) (2009). *Beyond Hofstede: Culture frameworks for global marketing and management.* London, Palgrave Macmillan.

O'Shaughnessy, J., & O'Shaughnessy, N. (2002). Postmodernism and marketing: Separating the wheat from the chaff. *Journal of Macromarketing, 22*(1), 109–135.

Papavassiliou, N., & Stathakopoulos, V. (1997). Standardization versus adaptation of international advertising strategies: Towards a framework. *European Journal of Marketing, 31*(7), 504–527.

Patterson, A., & Brown, S. (2007). Inventing the pubs of Ireland: The importance of being postcolonial. *Journal of Strategic Marketing, 15*(1), 41–51.

Pierson, G.W. (1959). *The education of American businessmen.* New York, McGraw-Hill.

Pieterse, J.N. (1995). Globalization as hybridization. In M. Featherstone, S. Lash & R. Robertson (Eds.), *Global modernities* (pp. 45–68). London, Sage.

Pieterse, J.N. (2012). Periodizing globalization: Histories of globalization. *New Global Studies, 6*(2), 1–25.

Robertson, R. (1995). Glocalization: Time-space and homogeneity-heterogeneity. In M. Featherstone, S. Lash & R. Robertson (Eds.), *Global modernities* (pp. 25–44). London, Sage.

Sandıkcı, O., & Ger, G. (2001). Fundamental fashions: The cultural politics of the turban and the Levi's. *Advances in Consumer Research, 28*(1), 146–150.

Sandıkcı, O., & Ger, G. (2002). In-between modernities and postmodernities: Investigating Turkish consumptionscape. *Advances in Consumer Research, 29*(1), 465–470.

Sandıkcı, O., & Ger, G. (2005). Aesthetics, ethics and politics of the Turkish headscarf. In S. Kuechler & D. Miller (Eds.), *Clothing as material culture* (pp. 61–82). London, Berg.

Sandıkcı, O., & Ger, G. (2010). Veiling in style: How does a stigmatized practice become fashionable? *Journal of Consumer Research*, 37(1), 15–36.

Saren, M., Maclaran, P., Goulding, C., Elliott, R., Shankar, A., & Catterall, M. (Eds.) (2007). *Critical marketing: Defining the field*. Amsterdam, Elsevier.

Schwartz, S.H. (1994). *Beyond individualism/collectivism: New cultural dimensions of values*. London, Sage.

Seremani, T.W., & Clegg, S. (2016). Postcolonialism, organization, and management theory: The role of 'epistemological third spaces'. *Journal of Management Inquiry*, 25(2), 171–183.

Sheth, J.N., & Gross, B.L. (1988). Parallel development of marketing and consumer behavior: A historical perspective. In T. Nevett & R.A. Fullerton (Eds.), *Historical perspectives in marketing* (pp. 9–33). Lexington, D.C. Heath and Company.

Sivakumar, K., & Nakata, C. (2001). The stampede toward Hofstede's framework: Avoiding the sample design pit in cross-cultural research. *Journal of International Business Studies*, 32(3), 555–574.

Slater, D. (1997). *Consumer culture and modernity*. Cambridge, Polity Press.

Tadajewski, M. (2006). The ordering of marketing theory: The influence of McCarthyism and the Cold War. *Marketing Theory*, 6(2), 163–199.

Tadajewski, M. (2009). Editing the history of marketing thought. *Journal of Historical Research in Marketing*, 1(2), 319–329.

Tadajewski, M. (2010). Towards a history of critical marketing studies. *Journal of Marketing Management*, 26(9–10), 773–824.

Tadajewski, M. (2011). Producing historical critical marketing studies: Theory, method and politics. *Journal of Historical Research in Marketing*, 3(4), 549–575.

Tadajewski, M., & Brownlie, D. (2008). Critical marketing: A limit attitude. In M. Tadajewski & D. Brownlie (Eds.), *Critical marketing: Issues in contemporary marketing* (pp. 1–29). Chichester, Wiley.

Üstüner, T., & Holt, D.B. (2007). Dominated consumer acculturation: The social construction of poor migrant women's consumer identity projects in a Turkish squatter. *Journal of Consumer Research*, 34(1), 41–56.

Üstüner, T., & Holt, D.B. (2010). Toward a theory of status consumption in less industrialized countries. *Journal of Consumer Research*, 37(1), 37–56.

Varman, R., & Belk, R.W. (2008). Weaving a web: Subaltern consumers, rising consumer culture, and television. *Marketing Theory*, 8(3), 227–252.

Varman, R., & Belk, R.W. (2012). Consuming postcolonial shopping malls. *Journal of Marketing Management*, 28(1–2), 62–84.

Varman, R., & Russell, B. (2009). Nationalism and ideology in an anticonsumption movement. *Journal of Consumer Research*, 36(4), 686–700.

Varman, R., & Saha, B. (2009). Disciplining the discipline: Understanding postcolonial epistemic ideology in marketing. *Journal of Marketing Management*, 25(7/8), 811–824.

Varman, R., & Sreekumar, H. (2015). Locating the past in its silence: History and marketing theory in India. *Journal of Historical Research in Marketing*, 7(2), 272–279.

Varman, R., & Vikas, R.M. (2007). Freedom and consumption: Toward conceptualizing systemic constraints for subaltern consumers in a capitalist society. *Consumption Markets & Culture*, 10(2), 117–131.

Venkatesh, A. (1995). Ethnoconsumerism: A new paradigm to study cultural and cross-cultural consumer behavior. In J.A. Costa & G.J. Bamossy (Eds.), *Marketing in a multicultural world* (pp. 26–67). Thousand Oaks, Sage.

Venkatraman, M., & Nelson, T. (2008). From servicescape to consumptionscape: A photo-elicitation study of Starbucks in the New China. *Journal of International Business Studies*, 39(6), 1010–1026.

Vikas, R.M., Varman, R., & Belk, R.W. (2015). Status, caste, and market in a changing Indian village. *Journal of Consumer Research*, 42(3), 472–498.

Wallerstein, I. (1991). *Unthinking social science: The limits of nineteenth-century paradigms*. Philadelphia, Temple University Press.

Weber, M. (2002). *The Protestant ethic and the spirit of capitalism and other writings*. Penguin, London.

Westwood, R.I., & Jack, G. (2007). Manifesto for a post-colonial international business and management studies: A provocation. *Critical Perspectives on International Business*, 3(3), 246–265.

Wilk, R. (1995). Learning to be local in Belize: Global systems of common difference. In D. Miller (Ed.), *Worlds apart: Modernity through the prism of the local* (pp. 110–133). London, Routledge.

Witkowski, T.H. (2005). Sources of immoderation and proportion in marketing thought. *Marketing Theory*, 5(June), 221–231.

Witkowski, T.H. (2010). The marketing discipline comes of age, 1934–1936. *Journal of Historical Research in Marketing*, 2(4), 370–396.

Yazıcıoğlu, E.T., & Fırat, A.F. (2007). Glocal rock festivals as mirrors to the future of culture(s). In R.W. Belk & J.F. Sherry (Eds.), *Consumer culture theory, research in consumer behavior, Vol. 11* (pp. 85–102). Oxford, Elsevier.

Zhao, X., & Belk, R.W. (2008a). Politicizing consumer culture: Advertising's appropriation of political ideology in China's social transition. *Journal of Consumer Research*, 35(2), 231–244.

Zhao, X., & Belk, R.W. (2008b). Advertising consumer culture in 1930s Shanghai: Globalization and localization in Yuefenpai. *Journal of Advertising*, 37(2), 45–56.

20
CHOICE AND CHOICELESSNESS IN CONSUMER PRACTICE

Ruby Roy Dholakia, A. Fuat Fırat, and Nikhilesh Dholakia

Introduction

Embedded deeply, semi-unconsciously, and ideologically in commonplace practices – be they in marketplaces or political arenas – is the idea of the goodness and salubriousness of choice. Notions of the probity of plentiful choice are also abundant in theories in social sciences and in applied fields such as marketing. The availability and abundance of choice are regarded as unequivocally good, and are readily conflated with the celebrated ideas of freedom and democracy (Amadae, 2003; Riker, 1982), and (for many) with the idea of unfettered capitalism (Friedman & Friedman, 1990). The opposite idea – of choicelessness – is associated with totalitarianism and tyranny, and is shunned and rejected (Amadae, 2003). Indeed, the value and worth of individuals, groups and nations are measured by the amount of choice they have. While for the vast majority, the degree of choice is the metric for assessing their socioeconomic and politico-cultural status and success, choicelessness is often a stark reality for the underprivileged and marginal groups within the same society (Nathan, 1998; Holme, 2002).

There are, of course, concerns about choice overload (Chernev, Böckenholt & Goodman, 2015; Iyengar & Kamenica, 2010; Scheibehenne, Greifeneder & Todd, 2010) and with the difficulty as well as goodness of choice decisions (Ariely, 2008; Cho, Khan & Dhar, 2013; Parker & Schrift, 2011) but – in ideological terms – these concerns are raised to shore up the pinnacle position of choice. In most empirical work, the focus is to assess whether people make choices that are well-considered, satisfying, confident, regret-free, and stable (Ariely, 2008; Gourville & Soman, 2005; Sela & Berger, 2012). Overall, in the vast and interdisciplinary literature on choice, the issue of choicelessness receives short shrift. Yet, when we look at fundamental issues that affect everyday life, in many parts of the world – including in some economically advanced nations (especially in the United States, the largest among the affluent and advanced nations) – choiceless conditions, as well as conditions of confusing difficult-to-compare privatized options, arise in vital life contexts such as these:

- Guarantees of basic universal health care;
- Access to reasonably priced, convenient public transport;
- Assurance of clean air and water;
- Adequacy of food and shelter;
- Pathways to relevant literacy and education.

In far too many instances, such contexts shape up in ways such that the rich and the privileged have plentiful and good choice options, while the poor and underprivileged are trapped in choiceless states. Indeed, and ironically – given the tremendous techno-scientific progress we have witnessed in the past few centuries – in a rising number of cases even the privileged segments, subject to the same great contradictions of neoliberal capitalism as the rest of the people are, are sometimes stuck in choiceless states. As an example, one venture capital entrepreneur in USA, a socio-politically liberal individual known to the authors – although he owns multiple luxury homes and cars – is waiting desperately to reach age 65. This is because, despite his affluence, the healthcare insurance options for him are rather expensive or under-featured. At age 65 he will cross over into the demographic category where he will become eligible for the governmental (and relatively generous, by U.S. standards) Medicare health insurance program. In his case, there is evident preference for the reduced-choice state of Medicare – which critics dubbed as a socialist program at the time of its creation (reported in Shaffer, 2016) – than for the 'free choice' insurance options, all of which this individual finds expensive and suboptimal.

In this chapter, we explore and explode the nexus of choice and choicelessness, specifically in the contemporary consumptionscapes and marketscapes, but with implications for society at large. We examine the concept of choice at a level that recognizes its complex systemic character, rather than at a level where each set of choices is isolated. When viewed in an isolated manner, in many micro contexts, one can imagine an almost endless set of choices in each aspect of life. For example, if we think of buying personal, private vehicles for transportation, an endless number of choices regarding each feature of an automobile and, therefore, an endless number of combinations of features as well as a vast number of brands attached to combinations can be imagined. A typical U.S. supermarket, on average, carries over 40,000 items (Bishop, 2014); a New Age Walmart over 100,000 items; and it is impossible to count the product list at Amazon.com or iTunes. This abundance leads to questions about how a rational consumer – with limited cognitive and other resources – can navigate such choice contexts and arrive at a destination that maximizes his/her welfare. Yet, imagining that there can be endless choice in every aspect of life is simply illusory. Indeed, the ontology of the market – as it functions in reality and not as it is mythically and ideally (ideologically) imagined – "is riven by compromise" (Tadajewski, 2016, p. 308). Tradeoffs will always exist – requiring communal or social choices among resources allocated to different aspects of life – tradeoffs that indeed limit individual choice in all aspects of life. We simply cannot isolate each set of choice(s) from all others unless we wish to oversimplify our understanding of human existence. Of course, from certain ideological standpoints, compartmentalizing and isolating of choice sets makes perfect sense: disaffection with choicelessness in vital life spaces can often be deflected by pointing to a surfeit of choice in another (often non-central and trivial) life spaces. Also, often welfare-enhancing choiceless states – such as guaranteed universal healthcare or retirement pensions – are denounced on ideological grounds as being socialistically constraining and inferior to a situation of multiple, privatized options that are frequently confusing and suboptimal.

In the sections to follow, beginning with a brief review of the 'choice as pinnacle' positions, we turn to multiple positions about choice and choicelessness that shed light on the nature of contemporary markets, consumption, and society in various parts of the globe. In structuring the discussion, we ascend analytic levels, from micro brand or variant level choices to macro choices at the level of major patterns of consumption that shape, even define, sociocultural and politico-cultural systems. At all levels, there are evident – in extant research –attempts to problematize the concepts of choice, and to deal with aspects of choicelessness. These attempts, however, lose momentum quickly when exploring the issues surrounding – sometimes causing, oft-times compounding and exacerbating – choicelessness. Choice is the supreme Regina, and choicelessness the backroom handmaiden; and we make the critical case to redress this imbalance. The critical part of our argument focuses on the political, economic, social, and cultural factors that abet certain very basic forms of choicelessness – factors that are either deliberately ignored for ideological reasons or benignly neglected for epistemic-ontological reasons. Our critique also touches on the post-Thatcher–Reagan politics of replacing safe, guaranteed, welfare-preserving choiceless states with confusing, infra-optimal, privatized choice options.

Choice as the moral pinnacle

While we do not endorse or agree with most of the material reviewed in this brief section, it is nonetheless essential to deal with it. The bulwark of social science argumentation, political posturing, and moralizing in the neoliberal contemporary world is shaped by the zenithal positioning of (free) choice in public discourse; and especially in marketplace discourses.

Milton Friedman was of course the greatest modern crusader for freedom of (consumer) choice, with an unshakeable belief in the self-correcting nature of markets. In his iconic *Capitalism and Freedom*, he wrote (Friedman, 1962/2002, p. 14):

> [T]he central feature of the market organization of economic activity is that it prevents one person from interfering with another in respect of most of his activities. The consumer is protected from coercion by the seller because of the presence of other sellers with whom he can deal. The seller is protected from coercion by the consumer because of the presence of other consumers with whom he can deal.

Transcending his scholarly brilliance, Friedman was able to deploy jargon-free language that reached the general consumer, voter, businessperson, and politician – and to 'seal the deal', ideologically, for unfettered libertarianism, for all those inclined that way. In the simple statement above, in one fell swoop, Friedman dismisses the 'voice' and 'loyalty' options of the exit-voice-loyalty trio suggested by Hirschman in his seminal book *Exit, Voice, and Loyalty* (1970). Instead, Friedman emphasizes the idea of an always-available cost-and-friction-free 'exit' option and ignores situations where 'exit' options are simply not available, as in the case of oligopolistic and monopolistic markets. His assumption of an atomistic market structure with countless competing players does not accommodate any notion of the manipulability of the choice made available to the consumer. In effect, there is no role for marketers and marketing, except to "give people what they want" (Friedman, 1962/2002, p. 15). And, of course, the issue of 'options not appearing at all' – (unseen) options, if they were there, that would be intensely desirable and sought after – does not appear in such discourses because the efficient market is somehow able to 'divine' anything that is desirable and make it available. The idea that certain choice options might not (be allowed to) appear simply does not find any space or support in capitalist discourses.

Furthermore, Friedman's emphasis on exit only – as if it were the always possible, practical, and meaningful option – robs any party involved in a relationship from the option of engaging in discourse and dialogue. Such a world – where the only option is discontinuation of one relationship in favor of another – is neither democratically desirable nor possible given the evidence of history.

With masterful equating and conflating of 'freedom', 'liberty', and 'choice' Friedman and others of similar ideological persuasion (e.g., Gellhorn, 1969; Simon, 1992) skyrocketed the moral position of 'choice' to the very top of many academic, popular, and policy discourses; along with the idea that free and abundant choice is only possible under totally unfettered capitalism. Following the Austrian School of neoclassical economics and Hayek's thoughts on individual choice (Hayek, 1948), they recommended a world of individual choice, unconcerned about its implication for others, as the height of freedom, also played out in Ayn Rand's best-known novel, *Atlas Shrugged* (Rand, 1957).

Consumer sovereignty

Closely allied with the idea of freedom of choice, and of abundance of choice, is the concept of consumer sovereignty. The idea of consumer sovereignty has also been elevated to celestial heights. In neoclassical microeconomics, a neat circular logical loop is set up in such a way that efficient markets produce preferred consumer choices, and catering to revealed consumer preferences makes markets efficient, thereby enshrining the idea of consumer sovereignty – not just as a desired condition but as the only (natural) condition for well-working market capitalism (Trigg, 2002). Underlying this condition are the assumptions of consumer rationality, ability, motivation, and freedom of choice (Broniarczyk & Griffin, 2016; Kohn, 1986; Penz, 1986; Sirgy, Lee & Yu, 2011). Technological developments such as the Internet are seen to empower consumers as they are able to search and compare alternatives, customize, complain, and advocate – all in order to maintain their power over the market transaction (Franke, Schreier & Kaiser, 2010; Simonson & Rosen, 2014). Some authors even propose that the individual agency felt by consumers (Balsamo, 2000) – by using the Internet and overcoming information asymmetries – allows consumers to 'band together' (Rezabakhsh et al., 2006); and this has led to the greatest transition of power to consumers at the expense of corporations (Murphy, 2000).

Some key economic and organizational scholars – those who employ analytical models that are broader than merely economic, and who add social and political dimensions to their work – have questioned the mythology of consumer sovereignty. Reviewing some of the most significant critical studies of consumption in the 20th century, Juliet Schor is baffled by the glaring contradiction – of the same space of public and intellectual discourse being cohabited by two opposite phenomena – the rising power of corporations and the persistent myth of a sovereign, powerful, in-control consumer. Schor (2007, p. 28) writes:

> For my part, the view that corporations have grown more rather than less powerful is the more compelling one. And in that light, it is striking that this growing power has been accompanied by the dominance of an ideology that posits the reverse – that the consumer is king and the corporation is at his or her mercy.

In the pharmaceutical industry, for instance, increased producer concentration has reduced the power of the consumer and undermined consumer sovereignty (Cockburn & Henderson, 2001). Newer industries such as Internet-based search engines, auction and social media platforms, have seen increased concentration – often because of the winner-take-all strategies prevalent in such industries (Noe & Parker, 2005). While concentration might be efficient because network effects are maximized (Haucap & Heimeshoff, 2013), Noam (2003) argues that the 'newer the medium, the more concentrated it is' – with implications for society and economy in terms of market power, innovation and consumer prices. Some of the negative implications are already evident in broad sectors of the U.S. economy where the 'high profits across a whole economy can be a sign of sickness' rather than a positive sign of entrepreneurial innovativeness (*The Economist*, 2016).

Working at a more micro level, Korczynski and associates (Korczynski, 2005; Korczynski & Ott, 2004, 2006) have explored the ways in which the myths of consumer sovereignty come into play at the point-of-sale interactions in retailing, restaurants, hotels, and similar settings. The explorations by Korczynski and others find a number of things happening, sometimes sequentially and at other times simultaneously. According to the work by Korczynski and associates, promotion of the idea of consumer sovereignty by the service industry is a way to enchant consumers into thinking that they are all-powerful and are the deserving recipients of the kinds of service that, in the past, only feudal overlords received. Of course, promotion of such an idea does not mean that it always takes hold. Bonsu and Darmody (2008) argue, for example, that consumers feel 'entrapped' rather than 'empowered' in these relationships; and Zwick and Dholakia (2004) critically evaluate the use of information by marketers to control and construct consumer identity.

The mythology of clinging to the enchanting idea of sovereignty is of course soon self-evident, to the non-sovereign customer as well as to the harried frontline worker (Singh, 2000). In some cases, the consumer–producer interactions turn empathetic as they both realize that they are just pawns in this enchantment game.

The merits of choice

We do want to point out here that – while the moral pinnacle positioning of choice, employed liberally in neoliberal discourses, is an ideological hyperbole – there is social and psychological merit in providing good choices (Lefcourt, 1973).

In psychology, reactance theory suggests that limiting someone's choices (as in over-strict parenting) often leads to oppositional, conflictual, and negative behaviors; rather than to the desired positive behaviors (Brehm & Brehm, 2013; Miron & Brehm, 2006). Fears of reducing perceived choice have limited retailers' ability to reduce product assortment (choice), particularly in grocery retailing. The consequences of limiting choice in the marketplace vary, however.

Limiting consumer choice appears to have two varied consequences. First, it can increase the value and desirability of the 'scarce' object (Aggarwal, Sung & Jong, 2011; Lynn, 1991) particularly when choice limitation is perceived to be driven by market forces (Verhallen & Robben, 1994). Then it tends to have a positive effect on consumer preferences, intentions, and purchase behaviors (Boatwright & Nunes, 2001; Broniarczyk, Hoyer & McAlister, 1998; Crawford et al., 2002). In fashion and apparel retailing as well as in popular consumer electronic products, supplier-induced scarcity – by limiting supplies or frequent reshuffling of merchandise – appears to be common practice in influencing perceptions of choice.

Second, as predicted by reactance theory, it might trigger defensive behaviors – to hold-at-bay or counter threats to perceived freedom of choice (Brehm & Sensenig, 1966). It can even lead to deviant behaviors such as in-store hoarding (e.g., hiding a desirable garment in an obscure place, to prevent others from getting it) or competitive buying due to perceived threats to freedom of buying decisions (Gupta, 2013). On occasions, it can backfire when consumers move away from the scarce good (Min, 2003; Stiller, 2011). Our understanding of choice and choicelessness, at micro as well as at macro levels, therefore has to be nuanced and multidimensional.

Choice and choicelessness: micro levels

The overwhelming weight of research on choice, of course, is on its micro aspects. When study of consumer choices focuses on branded products, the emphasis is on how consumers make choices. Studies deal with the evaluative criteria they use, the consequences of the choice in terms of satisfaction, repeat purchases, and loyalty (which is measured as the propensity to repurchase, rather than in ways that reflect traditional sociocultural meanings of 'loyalty', see for example Erickson &

Pierce, 2005). The implicit assumption is that when an individual has choice/agency, then that individual is intrinsically motivated to engage in the activity: "The sense of control, the illusion that one can exercise personal choice, has a definite and positive role in sustaining life" (Lefcourt, 1973, p. 424). When choices are multiple, consumer utility is likely to increase because of the positive effect on 'freedom of choice' (Kahn, Moore & Glazer, 1987), shopping enjoyment (Babin, Darden & Griffin, 1994), and overall consumer satisfaction (Botti & Iyengar, 2006).

Are there limits to the beneficial effects of increased choice? Can there be too much choice? Siegel and Etzkom (2013) counted 45 Medicare D Plans (privatized supplements to the governmental Medicare health insurance program in the U.S.) and Updegrave (2011) reported an average number of 20 options for 401K funds (privatized retirement savings plans). Some recent work has explored how overchoice dilutes the quality of consumer choice – especially in choice settings that have deep financial or health implications (Botti & Iyengar, 2006). Research on 'overchoice' situations, using experimental as well as field research, has shown that an overly large choice set "increases the appeal of simple, easy-to-understand, options" that might indeed be inferior and suboptimal for the consumer (Iyengar & Kamenica, 2010, p. 538). In more frequent – and less life-critical – choice settings, increased choice seems to affect quality of decisions based on individual consumer characteristics (Broniarczyk & Griffin, 2016; Chernev, 2003; Cho et al., 2013) as well as the assortment and choice framing characteristics (Boatwright & Nunes, 2001; Chernev, 2003; Mogilner, Shiv & Iyengar, 2013).

Beliefs that we would be better off if choices were limited, with 'good enough' options (Schwartz, 2004), do not seem to receive consistent empirical support in ordinary brand choice settings. Meta analyses of choice overload did not find conclusive evidence that choice overload exists or that it has particular effects on consumer behavior (Chernev et al., 2015; Scheibehenne et al., 2010). Certain conditions of increased choice are beneficial while other conditions are detrimental to various measures/outcomes of choice overload such as consumer satisfaction/confidence, regret, choice deferral, and switching likelihood. Sometimes consumers even attempt to 'complicate' rather than 'simplify' choices (Schrift, Netzer & Kivetz, 2011); and it is 'perceived' difficulty that determines how consumers actually allocate cognitive effort. Sometimes they even voluntarily seek more options, which can further increase decision difficulty (Sela & Berger, 2012).

All these micro-empirical results emerge from a less-than-critical examination of how choice is framed or made available. In most branded choice settings, there are systemic incentives for retailers and manufacturers to increase the variety of assortment (Gourville & Soman, 2005) even though evidence exists that reducing assortment does not necessarily lead to lower consumer satisfaction or sales (Boatwright & Nunes, 2001; Broniarczyk et al., 1998; Chernev, 2003). In fact, retailers and manufacturers increase the variety of assortment to increase perceived choice and shift emphasis from 'real' to 'meaningless' choices. Instead of considering fresh fruits and vegetables, consumers might be happy to spend more time choosing among a variety of sugared cereals or fruit-flavored yogurt. Sela and Berger (2012), for instance, demonstrate how consumers avoid important choices because they perceive them to be difficult; yet they voluntarily spend much more effort processing information on 'easier' choices, requesting additional information and increasing the difficulty of 'trivial choices'.

Choices can affect the very trajectory and quality of people's lives in settings where there are potentially momentous financial or health implications. There may be two approaches to affect the quality of choices. In one setting, a traditional approach is used to increase choice. For instance, efforts to improve school performance are guided by offering increased choices – education savings accounts, school vouchers, tax credits, scholarships and tax deductions. Rose (1998, p. 482) argues that tax credits and other such financial incentives only serve to help "those that need help the least". Even in the use of school vouchers, the assumption of increased choice overlooks the lack of evidence on school performance and ignores the reality of students and their families who are supposed to benefit from such choices (Nathan, 1998; Rouse, 1998). Even in Chile, where school voucher programs have been available since 1981, vouchers have not been able to improve performance metrics; indeed, the outcome has been for the 'best' public school students to leave and join the private sector schools (Hsieh & Urquiola, 2006). Similar results have been reported for measures to improve healthy food availability in 'food deserts' (inner-cities that lack fresh, healthy grocery options) where retailer and consumer characteristics in these areas restrict the likelihood of success (Hanbury, Rahkovsky & Schnell, 2015; Ebel et al., 2015).

In other settings, there are some admonitions to choice-offering entities – such as health and social welfare agencies, insurance firms and investment houses – to keep the choice sets to a manageable size so as not to tax overly the "cognitive and emotional resources" of the consumers (Botti & Iyengar, 2006, p. 35). While well intentioned, the implied benign paternalism of such a position does not get at the critical heart of the macro-level issue that we address later: why, in the first place, for deep welfare-affecting aspects of life, do the choice-offering entities create overly large choice sets with many suboptimal and confusing (mentally taxing) options?

There is clearly a need for strong critical perspectives to bear upon micro-level choice making, something that most marketing and consumer researchers shy away from. Indeed, the more life-shaping and welfare-determining a choice setting is, the greater the need for a strongly critical view of the entire choice-shaping and choice-making system and process. We turn to this research challenge in the next section as well as in the reflections section at the end.

Choice and choicelessness: meso and macro levels

At the meso and macro levels – levels that define life itself, rather than mere lifestyle – the research on choice, unfortunately, really thins out; with the research field drying out completely in some cases. Through denial, deliberate exclusion, or simple benign neglect, choice and choicelessness phenomena at more macro levels disappear behind ideological smokescreens (Dholakia, Dholakia & Fırat, 1983; Dholakia & Dholakia, 1985; Fırat & Dholakia, 1982). Commenting on the large and multidisciplinary contemporary field of consumption studies (including studies in marketing), Juliet Schor (2007, p. 17) notes that:

> [T]he field has ended up with a certain depoliticization and difficulty examining consumption critically. Interpretive accounts, while important, have their own limitations, including the tendency to accept consumers' own accounts of themselves without a critical or more complex and macroscopic lens.

Schor (2007) goes on to observe that while some of the best 20th-century critical analyses of consumer choice – the works of Veblen, the Frankfurt School, John Kenneth Galbraith – had some epistemic deficiencies, on the whole such works did grasp the key political and cultural dimensions of choice (or lack of it). She says that:

> [A] return to the critical traditions of the early twentieth century . . . is a necessary first step to recovering a tradition of engaged, critical scholarship at the macro level. From here [onward] the task is to construct a truly twenty-first-century approach, a new critical paradigm that [explores] the ways in which consumption has grown and radically transformed notions of individuality, community, and social relations.
>
> *2007, pp. 28–29*

In this section, we peer behind the smokescreens that obfuscate the meso-macro views of choice processes, and make a start toward presenting a more comprehensive, multi-level view of choice and choicelessness than found in extant work. In choice contexts at the macro level, a number of things happen:

- Choices become social and political rather than economic and psychological;
- Choice options are framed by political (Riker, 1982), ideological and media-driven processes;
- Choice is not an individual but a group act – the group being remote from the vast majority of individuals affected by the choice;
- Choice making is often done by entities that might be dictatorial, unelected, or elected-but-unaccountable;
- Choices are often manipulated by special interests and influenced by money flows that could be possibly corrupt;
- Choices sometimes shape markets rather than being shaped in or by markets.

In all settings, and especially in macro settings, it is important to acknowledge the nature of choice available to choice-makers. Consumers in contemporary market cultures, for example, are able to make choices from among many alternatives, but these alternatives are predetermined for them – the palette to choose from is fixed (see, e.g., Atik & Fırat, 2013). Co-creation processes, as articulated by marketing and business researchers, seemingly opening up spaces for consumers to craft choice options, focus at the attribute rather than at the macro level. Rarely are consumers able to construct 'real' alternatives (by and for) themselves (for an argument to transcend this state, see Fırat & Dholakia, 2016). No matter how much market research business entities and even public organizations perform, to find all the different alternatives consumers might wish to consume, in the end, the alternatives offered are always limited to those that the producers-providers find feasible. In a market economy, those alternatives rise to the top that are profitable (or cost efficient) for the producer-provider. In affluent settings, the consumer segments at the margins of the mass-mainstream are shut out or poorly served (e.g., the predicament of obese fashion-seekers in America, discussed in Scaraboto and Fischer (2013)). For most people on the planet, this logic gets turned on its head. With the exception of about three-dozen affluent countries, the profitable segments in about 200 other countries are the upper-crust high-income segments. This leaves large segments of the world population with unavailable or limited (Prahalad, 2005) or unaffordable (Karnani, 2007) choices.

At the societal level, it would be insincere not to acknowledge the fact that many people seeking alternatives outside the 'acceptable' norms and morals of dominant cultural ideologies are pressured to abandon their preferences, thus being left choiceless in an abundance of 'acceptable' choices. In contemporary society, for example, we see ample examples of this condition in regards to sexual preference and family composition choices, as well as often in what people can ingest or wear. There is often a heavy price to pay (in some societies, punitive incarceration or even death) for acts of choice that deviate from socio-politically acceptable – indeed, often dictatorially prescribed – ones.

As suggested earlier, given the triumph of neoliberal ideology, the market has increasingly come to be seen as the source of true choice and, thereby, the locomotive of freedom. This, of course, is greatly illusory as is the suggestion that freedom can be attributed to any single source. Limiting freedom to a single source is, by definition, a limitation, but this is hardly noticed by those blinded by the market ideology and its logic; a logic in which all human advancement is dependent on continual expansion of the market. This is a logic that has reversed the relationship between the end for modern thought – liberating humanity from all oppression to enable pursuit of lives organized according to independent and free wills – and the means – putting all cultural (that is, including political, social, and economic) institutions in the service of market forces. With neoliberalism, human beings are now in the service of the expansion of the market, the preeminent modern institution of the economic domain (Fırat & Dholakia, 2003).

This hegemonic logic of contemporary life limits and structures choice in at least two ways. First, since the expansion of the market is the end, attempts at creating non-market choices are suppressed, as all human relations that were non-market relations are increasingly converted into market transactions, and redistributive and reciprocal systems of allocating resources (Polanyi, 1944) are diminished, if not entirely dismissed. Consequently, choice among these different resource allocation and distribution systems – market exchange, redistribution, reciprocity – is blunted despite numerous attempts at creating alternative forms of distribution (e.g., Ozanne & Ozanne, 2016). Throughout history people have tried to escape being trapped in any one of these systems or to employ them under different situations and conditions (e.g., Marcoux, 2009), but this is no longer possible with the hegemonic presence of the market. Examples of this "New Great Transformation" – to the singular choice of market exchange – abound (e.g., Ozgun, Dholakia & Atik, 2017). As people are pulled into the market economy, options to obtain education, healthcare, clothing, and food provisions, among many others – that were earlier afforded through kinship, communal support, and tribal relations – can now only be afforded through the market. These transformed conditions require resources exchangeable in the market; and the kinship, communal, and tribal relations are degraded and destroyed, leaving no choice but to look to the market in areas central to the lifeworld. Second, since the expansion of the market is dependent on exchanges of resources that have market value, the choices in the market are structured to respond to the needs of those who have more of such resources, namely the rich. Thus, this structure of choices privileges the rich and disadvantages the poor. The needs of the poor are not represented in the choices available in the market, while the desires of the privileged rich find ample choices. In the market for good schools, the rich in the U.S. appear to have ample choice in deciding where to live, thus having the freedom to determine the schools their children attend (Nathan, 1998); and the quality of schools appears to reflect the socioeconomic status of the families they serve (Jankowski, 1995; Metz, 1990). Poor families, most often racial minorities as well, are stymied by their lack of choice and suffer from the status ideology that privileges the white and the rich (Holme, 2002). To say that there is ample choice for the people, under such circumstances, is uninformed at best, but mostly insincere and morally reprehensible.

The market logic and its companion neoliberal ideology promised choice, freedom, and control over one's life for modern humans. Instead, a relentless pursuit of this singular logic has created a new form of slavery for all humanity: enslavement to the neoliberal market economy – a system that cuts no slack for the socially, culturally, economically, and politically underprivileged. Almost everyone is now in fear that the economy will collapse; and believes that when and if the economic collapse comes, all will go to pieces. The fact that we have created such a monster that is now in so much control of our lives makes this belief at least partially true; if the economy fails, many lives will be hurt. The alternatives to catastrophic economic collapse are either slavish adherence to the dictates and discipline of the neoliberal market economy, with the attendant cycles of bubble build-up and burst (Dholakia & Turcan, 2013); or else slippage into severe socioeconomic marginalization. Of course, we believe it is imperative to create fundamental choices beyond these stark ones.

Choice and choicelessness: reflections and way forward

In contemporary settings, there is often an ironic juxtaposition of a surfeit of micro choices coupled with extreme limitations on macro choices, often bordering on stark choicelessness.

Even more paradoxically, as a consequence of the neoliberal regimes ushered in following the Reagan–Thatcher political ascendancy, particularly in the United States (but with echoes worldwide), there is often a surfeit of choice options in the maddeningly complex neoliberal public–private choice systems (see Megginson & Netter, 2001). In the U.S., this is the case for health insurance plans, for retirement savings methods, for college savings, and more – areas of life that have make-or-break effects on people's health, finances, employability, and even survivability (Starr, 1990). In a sense, a bewilderingly complex palette of suboptimal choice options has often supplanted the choicelessness – in many cases a risk-free, safe, socially optimized form of choicelessness – of the past. In the neoliberal political framing of things, rather than examining the potential dark side of such suboptimal choice palettes (Botti & Iyengar, 2006), since the very act of offering choices is deemed desirable, such palettes are celebrated. Even more darkly, from their globally central cultural positions, the United States and U.K. urge their vast network of global allies and followers to abandon their preexisting low-cost or cost-free choices of extensive public transport, guaranteed pensions, public health systems, and public education in favor of privatized systems with complex, suboptimal, confusing, and costly choice options.

In the commercial spaces also, the cross-level choice dynamics work in ways that disadvantage the poor, and often even the non-poor. Choice for those who can afford it has increased manifold at the brand and sub-brand levels, including minutely fine-grained differentiations within these categories. Even as such granular choices explode, choice at levels of product category and mode of consumption has progressively declined. In the very affluent economy of the United States, for example, it is hard to find any longer neighborhood stores that provide relief to residents of the neighborhood by providing consumption items on interest-free loans (a practice still commonplace in less affluent nations). This causes those living in poorer neighborhoods to pay more for their needs, a condition recognized by Caplovitz (1963) as early as the 1960s. In the U.S., except for a few large cities, public modes of transportation – very prevalent even into the first quarter of the 20th century – no longer exist. The market offers choice only in categories that assure profit, capital accumulation, and the enlargement of the market (Fırat & Dholakia, 1982).

To put the various political and (supposedly) apolitical perspectives in a comparative frame, we present two summary tables. Both of the tables deal with how 'choice abundance' and 'choiceless states' are viewed from such perspectives. Table 20.1 presents the ontological view, the way the very nature of choice/choicelessness is viewed. Not surprisingly, in the conservative neoliberal view, choice is as natural as air and water, and choicelessness is an asphyxiating state created by 'socialist' policies.

Table 20.2 presents the ideological stances that arise (or do not arise, or are irrelevant, in claimed-apolitical discourses) as a result of the respective ontologies. Once again, the conservative neoliberal position is staunchly in favor of choice abundance; even when psychologically oriented studies might find problems in overchoice settings, and socio-political studies often find severe damage to people's welfare.

In the conventional research in marketing, consumer behavior, and economic psychology – in settings that we are labeling as the 'mid-ground, claimed-apolitical empirical positions' – choice abundance is associated with greater perceived freedom of choice, shopping enjoyment and overall consumer satisfaction. Also, under abundance, empowered consumers – searching, comparing, and customizing alternatives – are likely to arrive at optimal choice solutions.

Table 20.1 Ontological positions on choice

Ontology regarding:	Conservative politically neoliberal position	Progressive politically liberatory position	Mid-ground, claimed-apolitical empirical positions
Choice abundance	Free and natural state	Driven by specific public and private policies	Choice is a psychological process influenced by social pressures. Choice abundance depends on competitive market structure
Choiceless states	Unfree and unnatural state; often because of contrived socialist policies	Result of public policies	Choiceless states arise when the market structure does not respond well; or when policy decisions limit choice

Source: Authors' conceptualization

Table 20.2 Ideological stances on choice

Ideological stance about:	Conservative politically neoliberal position	Progressive politically liberatory position	Mid-ground, claimed-apolitical empirical positions
Choice abundance	Always welfare-enhancing	Good in moderation; and then confusing, taxing, welfare-diminishing	Except under conditions of excessive overchoice or a proliferation of trivial differences across options, choice abundance is welfare-enhancing
Choiceless states	Always welfare-diminishing	Could be welfare-enhancing – via rock solid guarantees – in life-critical spheres such as health, education, transportation	Choiceless states are psychologically problematic; and should be considered only when there are considerations of overall social good

Source: Authors' conceptualization

By contrast – in these conventional research settings in marketing, consumer behavior, and economic psychology – choiceless states arise due to market-induced scarcity. Sometimes, these reflect deliberate strategic moves by brands, aiding the perception of increased value and desirability of the scarce good (see Brown, 2013). Also, under choiceless states, behaviors of compliant customers – who become compliant mostly because they are facing situations where non-compliance has a high cost – has the appearance of consumers making 'considered and informed choices', which results in reinforcing a smug sense of the 'customer is always right' sensibility, on the part of 'free market' enthusiasts.

From each of these tables, the research and practical implications that flow are quite straightforward: there are imperatives to boost research efforts as well as practical solution efforts in the progressive and politically liberatory category. What prevails at present – massive research efforts in the mid-ground, claimed-apolitical, academic choice investigation settings and the rising tendencies, in the public arena, to formulate choice policies informed by the conservative, neoliberal political positions in ruling circles – will not resolve the dilemmas of choice and choicelessness that we have profiled in this chapter.

Conclusion

Writing in 1985, Dholakia and Dholakia (pp. 182–183) made these six concluding observations about choice and choicelessness:

1. With increasing capitalist development, the degree of macro choice declines.
2. Increased micro choice is usually accompanied by decreased macro choice.
3. In any society, the overall structure of choice (macro/micro, actual/perceived) is determined by that society's organization of productive activity and by its ideology.
4. The more democratic the organization of productive activity in a society, the greater the degree of satisfaction with the overall structure of choice.
5. In advanced industrial societies, ideology has an increasing influence on the overall structure of choice.
6. Decentralization of productive activities help decrease the ideological influence on the structure of choice.

Almost four decades have passed since that writing, and these six observations about choice and choicelessness, by and large, continue to ring true. A substantial change that has happened, with oft-negative consequences for people's health and financial well-being, is what Jacob Hacker (2006) has termed the 'great risk shift': removal of guarantees and safety nets about healthcare and pensions. In effect, the comfortable choicelessness of guaranteed healthcare and guaranteed pensions has been replaced by risky choices of privatized options; or, worse, for many at the bottom of the pyramid, by the abject choicelessness of 'no options available' (as, for example, in the United States, millions being left without any health insurance).

The core ideological and philosophical issue of choice is the unavailability of options that are desirable and life-fulfilling, i.e., the core issue is that of choicelessness. Solnit (2014, p. 6) lays the blame for this on multiple things: the 'tyranny of the quantifiable', failure of language and discourse, and the (in our view, ideologically 'very deliberate') failure of key decision makers to understand and make available life-affirming choice options.

What can be measured almost always takes precedence over what cannot: private profit over public good; speed and efficiency over enjoyment and quality; the utilitarian over the mysteries and meanings that are of greater use to our survival and to more than our survival, to lives that have some purpose and value that survive beyond us to make a civilization worth having.

There are no compelling social, cultural, economic or political reasons why we cannot develop the language and the consensus-building methods to deal with – typically macro-level – choice options that contribute to an enduringly peaceful and sustainable world.

One dimension of human freedom might indeed involve choice, when choice is articulated in ways that examine and express its complex nature and consequences for humans. If freedom is to have control over one's life – being able to participate in matters when one desires or not participating (Fromm, 1969), having both freedom to and freedom from (Fırat & Dholakia, 1998) – then the falsity of relating 'freedom' solely to magnitudes of choice becomes transparently evident. Can we say, for example, that consumers of the richest economies today are freer than Mahatma Gandhi, who lived – of his own volition, with ascetic simplicity – in a sparse ashram in India with very little choice of consumables?

References

Aggarwal, P., Sung, Y.J., & Jong, H.H. (2011). Scarcity messages: A consumer competition perspective. *Journal of Advertising*, 40(3), 19–30.

Amadae, S.M. (2003). *Rationalizing capitalist democracy: The Cold War origins of rational choice liberalism.* Chicago, IL, University of Chicago Press.

Ariely, D. (2008). *Predictably irrational.* New York, HarperCollins.

Atik, D., & Fırat, A.F. (2013). Fashion creation and diffusion: The institution of marketing. *Journal of Marketing Management*, 29(7–8), 836–860.

Babin, B.J., Darden, W.R., & Griffin, M. (1994). Work and/or fun: Measuring hedonic and utilitarian shopping value. *Journal of Consumer Research*, 20(4), 644–656.

Balsamo, A. (2000). The virtual body in cyberspace. In D. Bell & B.M. Kennedy (Eds.), *The cybercultures reader* (pp. 489–503). London, Routledge.

Bishop, W. (2014). Data from 'the future of food retailing' at Food Marketing Institute (FMI) site. Retrieved September 19, 2015 from https://goo.gl/hf0HiX

Boatwright, P., & Nunes, J.C. (2001). Reducing assortment: An attribute-based approach. *Journal of Marketing*, 65(3), 50–63.

Bonsu, S.K., & Darmody, A. (2008). Co-creating Second Life: Market-consumer cooperation in contemporary economy. *Journal of Macromarketing*, 28(4), 355–371.

Botti, S., & Iyengar, S.S. (2006). The dark side of choice: When choice impairs social welfare. *Journal of Public Policy & Marketing*, 25(1), 24–38.

Brehm, J., & Sensenig, J. (1966). Social influence as a function of attempted and implied usurpation of choice. *Journal of Personality and Social Psychology*, 4(6), 703–707.

Brehm, S.S., & Brehm, J.W. (2013). *Psychological reactance: A theory of freedom and control.* Cambridge, MA, Academic Press.

Broniarczyk, S.M., & Griffin, J. (2016). Decision difficulty in the age of consumer empowerment. *Journal of Consumer Psychology*, 24(4), 608–625.

Broniarczyk, S.M., Hoyer, W.D., & McAlister, L. (1998). Consumers' perceptions of the assortment offered in a grocery category: The impact of item reduction. *Journal of Marketing Research*, 35(2), 166–176.

Brown, S. (2013). Torment your customers (they'll love it). *Harvard Business Review*, October, 83–88.

Caplovitz, D. (1963). *The poor pay more.* New York, The Free Press.

Chernev, A. (2003). When more is less and less is more: The role of ideal point availability and assortment in consumer choice. *Journal of Consumer Research*, 30(2), 170–183.

Chernev, A., Böckenholt, U., & Goodman, J. (2015). Choice overload: A conceptual review and meta-analysis. *Journal of Consumer Psychology*, 25(2), 333–358.

Cho, E.K., Khan, U., & Dhar, R. (2013). Comparing apples to apples or apples to oranges: The role of mental representation in choice difficulty. *Journal of Marketing Research*, 50(4), 505–516.

Cockburn, I.M., & Henderson, R.M. (2001). Scale and scope in drug development: Unpacking the advantages of size in pharmaceutical research. *Journal of Health Economics*, 20(6), 1033–1057.

Crawford, M.J., McConnell, A.R., Lewis, A.C., & Sherman, S.J. (2002). Reactance, compliance and anticipated regret. *Journal of Experimental Social Psychology*, 38(1), 56–63.

Dholakia, N., & Dholakia, R.R. (1985). Choice and choicelessness in the paradigm of marketing. In N. Dholakia & J. Arndt (Eds.), *Changing the course of marketing: Alternative paradigms for widening marketing theory* (pp. 173–185). Greenwich, CT, JAI Press.

Dholakia, N., & Turcan, R.V. (2013). Bubbles: Towards a typology. *Foresight*, 15(2), 79–88.

Dholakia, R.R., Dholakia, N., & Fırat, A.F. (1983). From social psychology to political economy: A model of energy use behavior. *Journal of Economic Psychology*, 3(3–4), 231–247.

Ebel, B., Moran, A., Dixon, L.B., Kiszko, K., Cantor, J., Courtney Abrams, C., & Mijanovich, T. (2015). Assessment of a government-subsidized supermarket in a high-need area on household food availability and children's dietary intakes. *Public Health Nutrition*, 18(15), 2881–2890.

Erickson, K., & Pierce, J.L. (2005). Farewell to the organization man: The feminization of loyalty in high-end and low-end service jobs. *Ethnography*, 6(3), 283–313.

Fırat, A.F., & Dholakia, N. (1982). Consumption choices at the macro level. *Journal of Macromarketing*, 2(2), 6–15.

Fırat, A.F., & Dholakia, N. (1998). *Consuming people: From political economy to theaters of consumption.* London, Routledge.

Fırat, A.F., & Dholakia, N. (2003). *Consuming people: From political economy to theaters of consumption*. London, Routledge.
Fırat, A.F., & Dholakia, N. (2016). From consumer to construer: Travels in human subjectivity. *Journal of Consumer Culture*, 17(3), 504–522.
Franke, N., Schreier, M., & Kaiser, U. (2010). The 'I designed it myself' effect in mass customization. *Management Science*, 56(1), 125–140.
Friedman, M. (1962/2002). *Capitalism and freedom*. Chicago, IL, University of Chicago Press.
Friedman, M., & Friedman, R. (1990). *Free to choose: A personal statement*. Boston, MA, Houghton Mifflin Harcourt.
Fromm, E. (1969). *Escape from freedom*. New York, Henry Holt and Co.
Gellhorn, W. (1969). *Individual freedom and governmental constraints*. Westport, CT, Praeger.
Gourville, J.T., & Soman, D. (2005). Overchoice and assortment type: When and why variety backfires. *Marketing Science*, 24(3), 382–395.
Gupta, S. (2013). The psychological effects of perceived scarcity on consumers' buying behavior. *Unpublished Doctoral Dissertation*. Retrieved September 21, 2015 from http://digitalcommons.unl.edu/businessdiss/41.
Hacker, J.S. (2006). *The great risk shift*. New York, Oxford University Press.
Hanbury, J., Rahkovsky, I., & Schnell, M. (2015). Is the focus on food deserts fruitless? Retail access and food purchases across socio-economic spectrum. *NBER Report*. Retrieved September 21, 2015 from www.nber.org/papers/w21126
Haucap, J., & Heimeshoff, U. (2013). Google, Facebook, Amazon, eBay: Is the Internet driving competition or monopolization? DICE Discussion Papers 83, Düsseldorf, Germany, University of Düsseldorf, Düsseldorf Institute for Competition Economics (DICE).
Hayek, F. (1948). *Individualism and economic order*. Chicago, IL, University of Chicago Press.
Hirschman, A.O. (1970). *Exit, voice and loyalty: Responses to decline in firms, organizations, and states*. Cambridge, MA, Harvard University Press.
Holme, J.J. (2002). Buying homes, buying schools: School choice and social construction of school quality. *Harvard Education Review*, 72(2), 177–205.
Hsieh, C.-T., & Urquiola, M. (2006). The effects of generalized school choice on achievement and stratification: Evidence from Chile's voucher program. *Journal of Public Economics*, 90(8–9), 1477–1503.
Iyengar, S.S., & Kamenica, E. (2010). Choice proliferation, simplicity seeking, and asset allocation. *Journal of Public Economics*, 94(7–8), 530–539.
Jankowski, M.S. (1995). The rising significance of status in U.S. race relations. In M.P. Smith & J.R. Feagin (Eds.), *The bubbling cauldron: Race, ethnicity and the urban crisis* (pp. 77–98). Minneapolis, MN, University of Minnesota Press.
Kahn, B., Moore, W.L., & Glazer, R. (1987). Experiments in constrained choice. *Journal of Consumer Research*, 14(1), 96–113.
Karnani, A. (2007). The mirage of marketing to the bottom of the pyramid: How private sector can help alleviate poverty. *California Management Review*, 49(4), 90–111.
Kohn, A. (1986). *No contest: The case against competition*. Boston, MA, Houghton Mifflin Co.
Korczynski, M. (2005). The point of selling: Capitalism, consumption and contradictions. *Organization*, 12(1), 69–88.
Korczynski, M., & Ott, U. (2004). When production and consumption meet: Cultural contradictions and the enchanting myth of customer sovereignty. *Journal of Management Studies*, 41(4), 575–599.
Korczynski, M., & Ott, U. (2006). The menu in society: Mediating structures of power and enchanting myths of individual sovereignty. *Sociology*, 40(5), 911–928.
Lefcourt, H.M. (1973). The function of the illusions of control and freedom. *American Psychologist*, 28(5), 417–425.
Lynn, M. (1991). Scarcity effects on value: A quantitative review of the commodity theory literature. *Psychology and Marketing*, 8(1), 43–57.
Marcoux, J.-S. (2009). Escaping the gift economy. *Journal of Consumer Research*, 36(4), 671–685.
Megginson, W.L., & Netter, J.M. (2001). From state to market: A survey of empirical studies on privatization. *Journal of Economic Literature*, 39(2), 321–389.
Metz, M.H. (1990). Magnet schools and the reform of public schooling. In W.L. Boyd & H.J. Walberg (Eds.), *Choice in education: Potentials and problems* (pp. 123–147). Berkeley, CA, McCutchan.
Min, K.S. (2003). Consumer response to product unavailability. Unpublished Doctoral Dissertation, Ohio State University.

Miron, A.M., & Brehm, J.W. (2006). Reactance theory – 40 years later. *Zeitschrift für Sozialpsychologie, 37*, 9–18.

Mogilner, C., Shiv, B., & Iyengar, S.S. (2013). Eternal quest for the best: Sequential (vs. simultaneous) option presentation undermines choice commitment. *Journal of Consumer Research, 39*(6), 1300–1312.

Murphy, T. (2000). *Web rules: How the internet is changing the way consumers make choices*. Chicago, IL, Dearborn.

Nathan, J. (1998). Heat and light in the charter school movement. *Phi Delta Kappan, 79*, 499–505.

Noam, E. (2003). The internet: Still wide open and competitive? *OII Internet Issue Brief No. 1*, August. Retrieved October 1, 2015 from www.oii.ox.ac.uk/archive/downloads/publications/OIIIB1_0803.pdf

Noe, T., & Parker, G. (2005). Winner take all: Competition, strategy, and the structure of returns in the internet economy. *Journal of Economics & Management Strategy, 14*(1), 141–164.

Ozanne, L.K., & Ozanne, J. (2016). How alternative consumer markets can build community resiliency. *European Journal of Marketing, 50*(3–4), 330–357.

Ozgun, A., Dholakia, N., & Atik, D. (2017). Marketisation and Foucault. *Global Business Review, 18*(3), S191–S202.

Parker, J.R., & Schrift, R.Y. (2011). Rejectable choice sets: How seemingly irrelevant no-choice options affect consumer decision processes. *Journal of Marketing Research, 48*(5), 840–854.

Penz, G.P. (1986). *Consumer sovereignty and human interests*. Cambridge, Cambridge University Press.

Polanyi, K. (1944). *The great transformation*. Boston, MA, Beacon.

Prahalad, C.K. (2005). *The fortune at the bottom of the pyramid: Eradicating poverty through profits*. Upper Saddle River, NJ, Wharton School Publishing.

Rand, A. (1957). *Atlas shrugged*. New York, Random House.

Rezabakhsh, B., Bornemann, D., Hansen, U., & Schrader, U. (2006). Consumer power: A comparison of the old economy and the internet economy. *Journal of Consumer Policy, 29*(1), 3–36.

Riker, W.H. (1982). *Liberalism against populism: A confrontation between the theory of democracy and the theory of social choice*. San Francisco, CA, Freeman.

Rose, L.C. (1998). The tax credit: Another wolf in sheep's clothing. *Phi Delta Kappan, 79*, 482.

Rouse, C.E. (1998). Private school vouchers and student achievement: An evaluation of the Milwaukee parental choice program. *The Quarterly Journal of Economics, 113*(2), 553–602.

Scaraboto, D., & Fischer, E. (2013). Frustrated fatshionistas: An institutional theory perspective on consumer quests for greater choice in mainstream markets. *Journal of Consumer Research, 39*(6), 1234–1257.

Scheibehenne, B., Greifeneder, R., & Todd, P.M. (2010). Can there ever be too many options? A meta-analytic review of choice overload. *Journal of Consumer Research, 37*(3), 409–425.

Schor, J.B. (2007). In defense of consumer critique: Revisiting the consumption debates of the twentieth century. *The Annals of the American Academy of Political and Social Science, 611*(1), 16–30.

Schrift, R.Y., Netzer, O., & Kivetz, R. (2011). Complicating choice. *Journal of Marketing Research, 48*(2), 308–326.

Schwartz, B. (2004). *The paradox of choice*. New York, Ecco.

Sela, A., & Berger, J. (2012). Decision quicksand: How trivial choices suck us in. *Journal of Consumer Research, 39*(2), 360–370.

Shaffer, R. (2016). Socialism in the United States: Hidden in plain slight. *Social Education, 80*(1), 31–35. Retrieved October 1, 2015 from https://lawcha.org/wp-content/uploads/Shaffer-SE-Socialism-2016.pdf

Siegel, A., & Etzkom, I. (2013). When simplicity is the solution. *Wall Street Journal*, March 30, C1.

Simon, Y.R. (1992). *Freedom of choice*. Edited by P. Wolff, New York, Oxford University Press.

Simonson, I., & Rosen, E. (2014). *Absolute value: What really influences customers in the age of (nearly) perfect information*. New York, HarperCollins.

Singh, J. (2000). Performance, productivity and quality of frontline employees in service organizations. *Journal of Marketing, 64*(April), 15–34.

Sirgy, M.J., Lee, D.-J., & Yu, G.B. (2011). Consumer sovereignty in healthcare: Fact or fiction? *Journal of Business Ethics, 101*(3), 459–474.

Solnit, R. (2014). *Men explain things to me*. San Francisco, CA, Haymarket Books.

Starr, P. (1990). The new life of the liberal state: Privatization and the restructuring of state-society relations. In J. Waterbury & E. Suleiman (Eds.), *Public enterprise and privatization* (pp. 22–54). Boulder, CO, Westview Press.

Stiller, M. (2011). *Is less more? The influence of scarcity strategies on variety seeking*. Unpublished Doctoral Dissertation, Maastricht University.

Tadajewski, M. (2016). The alternative 'marketing revolution': Infra-power, the compromising consumer and goodwill creation. *Journal of Historical Research in Marketing*, 8(2), 308–334.

The *Economist* (2016). Too much of a good thing. March 26. Retrieved July 7, 2016 from www.economist.com/news/briefing/21695385-profits-are-too-high-america-needs-giant-dose-competition-too-much-good-thing

Trigg, A. (2002). Consumer sovereignty. In S. Himmelweit, R. Simonetti & A. Trigg (Eds.), *Microeconomics: Neoclassical and institutionalist perspectives on economic behavior* (Chapter 3). London, Cengage.

Updegrave, W. (2011). Overwhelmed by too many 401(k) options? *CNN Money*, October 25. Retrieved October 1, 2015 from https://goo.gl/evQaa9

Verhallen, T.M., & Robben, H.S.J. (1994). Scarcity and preference: An experiment on unavailability and product evaluation. *Journal of Economic Psychology*, 15(2), 315–331.

Zwick, D., & Dholakia, N. (2004). Whose identity is it anyway? *Journal of Macromarketing*, 24(1), 31–43.

21
MANAGING RACIAL STIGMA IN CONSUMER CULTURE

David Crockett

Introduction

Racial inequality in the United States persists despite areas of meaningful and sustained progress largely because new forms emerge to replace those that have withered or been defeated (Bloome, 2014). Racial inequality in the marketplace often takes the form of stigmatized encounters (Henderson, Hakstian & Williams, 2016). Stigma is traditionally thought of as a discredited or disgraced identity and is experienced as an 'assault on worth' (Lamont et al., 2016). Any encounter in the marketplace can invoke stigmatized treatment (possibly accompanied by discriminatory treatment) whose effects on well-being the stigmatized must then try to minimize. Thus, it is important to understand how people manage stigma in the marketplace, a crucial site for the maintenance of racial inequality and anti-racist resistance.

Researchers have generated much insight into resistance, especially through collective political action such as formal protests and boycotts (e.g., Wolcott, 2012; Glickman, 2009; Cohen, 2004). However, such actions are not always accessible or they might simply be an ill fit for quotidian encounters where stigma might be operating. For instance, Lamont et al. (2016) cite a stigmatized service encounter involving a Black business professional in Brazil. Upon checking into an upscale hotel, the male desk clerk, relying on prevalent gender and racial stigma about Black women, assumed that she was a sex worker there to see a client. Although he was embarrassed by his faux pas, she was humiliated. Such encounters can be narrow in scope and brief in duration, not always rising to the level of illegal discrimination. They call for immediate reliance on interpersonal rather than collective action if stigma's impact on well-being is to be limited. They do not easily lend themselves to protest or boycott. As such, they are usefully described as 'micro-political.'

In this chapter I explore racially stigmatized interactions to better understand the role of marketplace consumption in managing them at the micro-political level, as described. To that end, I investigate the relationship between social boundaries and consumption behaviors. I first provide historical context for the struggle against stigma specific to the Black middle class in the USA. I then provide a brief overview of the dominant approaches in the field for understanding the relationship between the marketplace and racial inequality. One approach conceptualizes the marketplace as a site where racial inequality is produced. The other conceptualizes status-oriented consumption among Blacks as a longstanding (if problematic) challenge to racial inequality. Although many researchers would readily acknowledge that the marketplace both produces and challenges racial inequality, prior research (with notable exceptions) has largely not synthesized the two approaches.

In this chapter I conduct such a synthesis using interviews from a sample of middle-class Blacks in the USA about their efforts to manage racial stigma through status-oriented consumption. I highlight the creation of very basic subjective boundaries around these efforts (e.g., what 'works' vs. what doesn't). Boundary theoretic approaches contribute to a general understanding of how people utilize symbolic resources (e.g., conceptual distinctions, interpretive strategies, cultural traditions, etc.). Such approaches draw attention to subjective and intersubjective distinctions embedded in everyday action, typically through evidence from the field in the form of narrative and observation. In this chapter I place a sharp focus on people's subjective assessments of their own efforts to manage (if not dissolve) institutionalized social inequality, of which racism is a particularly troublesome type. In this way the study also contributes to sociological literature on anti-racist resistance. Much prior research either ignores anti-racist action altogether, or focuses entirely on macro-political (collective) action. As 20th-century US historian Robin D.G. Kelley (1996) notes, doing so undertheorizes anti-racist action, which is often embedded in the everyday consumption practices.

Background: the Black middle class and consumer culture

A Black middle class emerged in the USA first as a petit bourgeoisie during Reconstruction (1865–1877). The nation's brief experiment with social justice inaugurated unprecedented opportunity for Black economic and social advancement (DuBois, 1935/1999; Ownby, 1999). Much of that newfound opportunity accrued to the same free Blacks and mulatto slaves that had been the highest status group during antebellum. Nevertheless, a small cadre of former field slaves joined this new Black petit bourgeoisie through the skilled trades, as land owners, ministers, entrepreneurship, and elected office and sought to advance its status (Anderson, 2000; Frazier, 1957/1997).

Reconstruction's expansion of roads and railroads also benefitted the South broadly, facilitating widespread access to consumer goods. This literally brought meaningful choice to consumers in backwoods towns and villages outside the port cities for the first time (Richter, 2005; Wilson, 2005). In the USA, this new Black petit bourgeoisie and consumer culture were born at the same historical moment. Moreover, they grew up together, overtly aware of each other's existence.

From petit bourgeoisie to middle class

Historian Lizbeth Cohen (2004) cogently argues that consumer culture held in tension egalitarian and anti-egalitarian discourses about race, gender, and other social identity categories throughout its early development in the USA. Although billed as a 'new democracy of goods,' it built on top of existing practices as much as it gave rise to new ones. Historians commonly mark the period from the end of Reconstruction in 1877 until the Civil Rights Movement's emergence in the mid-20th century, as the nadir of race relations in the USA (e.g., Foner, 1988/2011; Logan, 1954). In addition to rampant violence, Blacks were effectively barred from opportunities to amass wealth. Thus, they had little material basis for building the intergenerational social mobility that had been part of the promise of consumer culture.

By the time of the *Brown* v. *Board of Education* decision nearly a century after the end of the Civil War, a more egalitarian cultural logic facilitated numerous social justice reforms (Cohen,

2004; Ikenberry, 2011). In this new social milieu, a new Black middle class emerged to replace the old petit bourgeoisie (Landry, 1987). This was a proper social class rather than a privileged status group, with class consciousness and material interests distinct from (though related to) the Black working class. Compared to the old petit bourgeoisie, the Black middle class is larger, better off financially, and more disbursed geographically (see Patillo, 2000).

Black consumers, racial inequality, and anti-racist action

Exercising the rights and privileges of consumption has always been a tangible expression of equality and thus a major feature of anti-racist action in the USA, but their exercise has been hard won (Wolcott, 2012; Ownby, 1999). Researchers highlight the two distinct ontological orientations toward consumption and racial inequality. In one, consumer culture is a site where racial inequality is created and maintained. In the other, consumption is a practice through which Blacks resist or manage inequality.

Consumption is a site for racial inequality

In this respect, consumer culture is no different from other social domains. Researchers highlight marketplace discrimination (and stigmatized encounters) and corporate appropriation as the two primary means by which consumption maintains and reinforces racial inequality. Marketplace discrimination and stigmatized treatment remain significant features of the contemporary marketplace and have harmful economic, social, and personal consequences (e.g., Henderson, Hakstian & Williams, 2016; Bone, Christensen & Williams, 2014; Ouellet, 2007). Likewise, the notion that cultural appropriation, as enacted by global corporations such as Nike, creates a 'false connection' between Black youth culture and the presumptively White mass market is conventional wisdom. Such studies typically adopt a version of the Frankfurt School view that mass market consumption is itself alienating, as popularized by Adorno and Horkheimer (2002/1972). To wit, Kotlowitz's (1991) pioneering ethnographic account of two boys from Chicago's inner city posits that firms such as Nike appropriate Black inner-city youth cultural styles, infuses them into its brand, which it then promotes to the mass market. Goldman and Papson's (1999) advertising-focused account of this process, *Nike Culture*, is built on Kotlowitz's premise, and Patillo's (2013/1999) ethnographic account of Groveland's Black youth strikes a similar tone. She describes them as conspicuous consumers who use material goods to challenge White supremacy but who are nevertheless vulnerable to being duped by mass market messages about what to buy and be. Notably, this view of consumption has been criticized for its determinism, for downplaying subjectivity, or ignoring it outright (Arnould, 2007; Tate, 2003, p. 11).

Black consumption challenges racial inequality

Scholars suggest that Blacks have utilized consumption to compensate for low-status stigma, and more recently as a basis for social identity. It has long been conventional wisdom that Blacks emphasize conspicuous consumption to shield the self from stigma, and this spending is often characterized as understandable but dysfunctional (e.g., Charles, Hurst & Roussanov, 2009; Hannerz, 1969; Lewis, 1968; Liebow, 1967). In a useful departure, some have challenged the consumption-as-compensatory conventional wisdom. They argue that mass market consumption can at times be considered reasonable and effective anti-racist action (Branchik & Davis, 2009; Chin, 2001; Ownby, 1999; Weems, 1998). To cite two key examples, Chin's (2001) ethnographic study of poor Black girls in Newhallville details the complex ways they bend ideology, hegemony, and power to make them fit within the contours of their lives, even if only for brief moments (pp. 178–179). She argues that failure to assess their consumption in relation to the powerful social forces arrayed against them leads to a conclusion that it is only compensatory and maladaptive. But, any consideration of the inequality-exacerbating power of the market forces arrayed against these children necessitates a conclusion that their consumption is more than sensible and normative under the circumstances. She describes it as hopeful. In another example, Lamont and Molnar (2001) show that members of the Black middle class in the USA use the marketplace to engage in social identity construction. Further, they note that this has no inherently anti-racist character. They critique the consumption-as-compensatory view for overstating consumption's anti-racist qualities. Instead they focus on the ways Blacks use consumption practices and identification processes to make nuanced in-group/out-group distinctions, without predefining them as anti-racist. Though insightful, their study is unfortunately limited by its purposive sample of Black corporate marketing specialists.

Consumption as boundary work

Building on Lamont and Molnar (2001), this chapter utilizes theory on boundary-making to illuminate certain aspects of anti-racist resistance in consumption. Exploring boundaries helps us understand the role of symbolic resources (e.g., conceptual distinctions, interpretive strategies, cultural traditions, etc.) in producing institutionalized social difference. Boundaries reveal the nature of social interactions and their use of symbolic resources. The approach originates with Durkheim (1915) and is usefully extended by Weber's (1922/1978) analysis of ethnic and status groups (see Lamont & Molnar, 2002).

What are boundaries and boundary work?

The substantial sociological literature on boundaries suggests that they come in two basic types: blurry (symbolic) and bright (social) (see Fox & Guglielmo, 2012). *Blurry boundaries* are intersubjective conceptual distinctions made to categorize objects, people, practices, time, and space. Individuals and groups operating within blurry boundaries experience feelings of similarity and belonging, but they compete to draw the boundaries in ways that legitimize their classification schemes. *Bright boundaries* are objectified forms of social difference. They are manifested in inequality and revealed in identifiable and stable patterns of association, exclusion or segregation.

Boundary work consists of the interactions that lead to the creation, maintenance, and modification of boundaries, of which two types are important to this analysis. *Boundary placement* involves the act of drawing mental, emotional, and social distinctions that separate realms of the self. *Boundary transcendence/transition* involves navigating back and forth across the realms (Nippert-Eng, 1996). Stigma management in the domain of consumption necessarily involves both types of boundary work, which may reinforce or challenge boundaries. In the findings, I detail instances from a sample of middle-class Blacks in the USA of boundary work intended to manage stigma in order to make everyday life more tolerable. Before detailing the findings, I describe the empirical context, data collection, and analysis.

Methodology

The data corpus for this research consists primarily of semi-structured interviews that I conducted alone with 20 adult members of the Black middle class in the USA between 2008 and 2013.

This includes 12 family households and a focus group consisting of four professional men who meet monthly as an informal lunch group. I buttressed interviews with numerous observations and unrecorded conversations with other members of the Black middle class for purposes of triangulation over the multi-year data collection period. Because the empirical context is a significant aspect of this research, I elaborate on it further.

The informants all reside in the southeastern USA in small- to medium-sized communities in North and South Carolina and Northern Florida. Blacks, who have flowed steadily southward since 1990 (Frey, 2004), now comprise 20% of the region's population (Rastogi, Johnson, Hoeffel & Drewery, 2011). Notably, the small- to medium-sized communities in this sample are likely to have the lowest Black–White residential segregation in the country (Lichter, Parisi & Taquino, 2015; Scommenga, 2010). Thus, these ethno-racial groups are more likely to interact in their daily routines in the setting than in other regions of the country. Recent research in political science (Acharya, Blackwell & Sen, 2016) shows that anti-Black stigma is deeply infused into those routines.

Sample

I considered only individuals who self-identify as Black/African-American and who are also readily categorized as middle class for inclusion into the sample. Racial classification in the USA is a quintessentially bright boundary, lacking in substantial nuance (Saperstein & Penner, 2012). For the most part, anyone with discernible (sub-Saharan) African ancestry is classified as Black/African American. Nevertheless, I exclude Black immigrants to the USA from Africa, Latin America, and the Caribbean, as well as persons who self-identify as multiracial from the sample in order to (partially) relegate to the background the complexities of immigration, nationality, language, and alternative systems of ethno-racial self-identity.

The other criterion for inclusion in the sample is middle-class status. Since my interest is in consumption, I emphasize lifestyle rather than income as the basis for classification. Therefore, I rely on occupation and education rather than income cut-offs to make class distinctions. These more reliably indicate the high cultural capital lifestyle indicative of middle-class status across a broad range of incomes. I defined 'middle class' for purposes of this study using the following criteria: (1) an undergraduate or advanced degree, or (2) white-collar/managerial work, or entrepreneurship. These are expansive criteria that better reflect the various mixtures of socio-economic privilege and cultural capital capable of sustaining what most in the USA would consider a middle-class lifestyle.

Data collection and analysis

From 2008 through to 2013 I recruited informants via direct referrals using the friend-of-a-friend approach. I initially asked contacts in my personal and professional networks to refer me to members of the Black middle class who might be amenable to interviews, with the proviso that they not refer any of our mutual friends or acquaintances. After locating the first five informants this way, I asked them to refer family, friends, and colleagues (with the same proviso), adding to the sample this way to capture variance on relevant dimensions of idiographic detail (e.g., stage of family life cycle, sexual orientation, age, and engagement with Black civic organizations).

I conducted personal interviews primarily in informants' homes and offices. I also conducted a focus group at a local restaurant with four professional Black men who regularly meet as a lunch group. This allowed me to capture gender dynamics that were less evident in interviews. Following Thompson and Tambyah (1999), I began with a grand tour probe for general consumption. I asked about family life, finding a home, favorite objects, vacations, etc. I continued to probe to elicit consumption narratives and meaning about lifestyle. When informants would invariably broach the topic of ethno-racial identity or everyday racism I encouraged them to elaborate as much as possible in the context of consumption. I recorded each interview and the focus group, which ranged from 1–3 hours. Similar to Lacy (2007), I buttressed informants' talk with observations of social interaction at events where the Black middle class is prone to gather, such as those sponsored by Black social and civic organizations.

I conducted analysis in part-to-whole fashion, using Atlas.ti software for coding and analysis. From informants' stories, I searched for emergent meanings and relevant underlying structures that help explain general patterns of discourse but that are also flexible enough to account for idiographic sources of variation. My goal was to interpret informants' consumption stories in the context of their everyday lives. To help refine my interpretations I used informal conversations and formal presentations to members of my professional network.

Additionally, I attempted to account for my role in social interactions as a fellow member of the Black middle class. This certainly facilitated entrée and helped elicit narratives about racial inequality. However, being an interloper and complete stranger allowed me to ask about features of daily life they might commonly take for granted. Unfortunately, this status engendered enough apprehension in some that they refused my requests for a formal interview, preferring to speak only conversationally. Thus, they are not included in the sample total.

Findings

American sociologist W.E.B. DuBois famously quipped that the problem of the 20th century would be the problem of the color line (DuBois, 1903). As the century, unfolded race-as-biology was exposed as scientific fiction but White supremacy revealed as Durkheimian social fact. Even after the demise of the slave system, racialized debt peonage, and legal apartheid in the South, blackness remains heavily stigmatized and racial inequality stagnant (Kendi, 2016; Bloome, 2014). Against this backdrop I draw attention to the consumption-focused boundary work employed by the Black middle class to manage racial inequality.

Racialized stigma most directly reinforces blurry boundaries, and as such is managed directly by these informants. I characterize their boundary work as boundary placement and boundary transcendence, which are of course ideal types that overlap in the empirical world. In the former, actors seek to draw 'visible' lines that they can expand or contract. In the latter, actors seek to navigate back and forth across boundaries by changing affiliation or altering a boundary's meaning. Boundary work is typically useful in understanding identity construction, but I use it similar to Lamont and Fleming (2005) in their study of anti-racist repertoires.

Boundary placement

This form of boundary work marks off strategies of action and tactics for inclusion in a given anti-racist repertoire that reinforce or maintain existing boundaries. To illustrate, in this excerpt from the focus group I prompt the participants with a reference to Bill Cosby's now infamous 'poundcake' speech at the NAACP's annual convention in 2004. The speech echoed a longstanding class-inflected criticism of Black popular culture's presumed preoccupation with entertainment and disdain for cultural capital-building opportunities.

Moderator: [. . .] Is that what you see going on in Black America?

Male 4: I do. I do. In fact, I watched that video of people in Ohio. The new Jordans that came out—a big fight broke out and they tore the place down. Had to call the police. These shoes were $300, $200? [. . .] You're going to put them on your feet.

Male 3: Some people are not. They just want to put them in the closet. Not just that. Look how many kids have iPhones and cell phone plans that get Internet? If you took that money and spent it on any type of an educational product—

Male 4: My daughter, we had this conversation as well. She's got two sons. She buys the handheld Gameboys and what-do-you-call-it. I don't even know the name of a lot of them. I don't buy them. My grandson wanted to—the school was having an afterschool science program for a week. He wanted to go, but she didn't have the money for that. We said, "Well, [sign] him up for it and we'll pay for it." That I'll pay for. But the bottom line is, it was a double issue. I think she used the money issue [as an excuse for] not wanting to do it. When we said we'll pay for it, now she's coming up with a different excuse . . . It's not just the kids.

This critique of Black popular culture has its origins in the nation's Puritan religious and cultural heritage (Lears, 1981). Though it is also levied at US popular culture generally, Black popular culture is thought especially frivolous and openly disdainful of cultural capital-enhancing opportunities (especially related to education). This has long been a standard trope in White supremacist discourse and in Black intra-racial class politics (Mullins, 1999).

The men in the focus group, particularly Male 4, reinforce a boundary thought to have blurred over time that conforms to this trope. Their tactic of story-telling and testifying combats racial stigma (i.e., Blacks as excessively frivolous) by assigning explicit moral superiority to utilitarian consumption (e.g., education products) over morally questionable hedonic consumption. In doing so, the men construct a moral consumption hierarchy that anyone can (and should) adopt to reject the stigma. Male 4 even implicates his adult daughter's suspect morals for failing to subscribe to the hierarchy, despite his tutelage and financial support. He casts her failure as individual because he cultivated a habitus that should dispose her to properly appreciate education's cultural capital-enhancing capacity. Consequently, he resolves to finance only consumption that conforms to the right moral values in the future.

Another way of managing the stigma of excessive frivolity is trying to be cosmopolitan (Thompson & Tambyah, 1999). Omnivore tastes are a hallmark of cosmopolitanism. They are thought to signal high cultural capital because they are eclectic but distinct from frivolity because they are pulled from a deep reservoir of knowledge and experience. In one instance from the data, Shante put her omnivore tastes on display in her interview, jumping from one topic to the next; the sorry state of local cuisine, her love of Japanese décor, her most cherished possession—a 9mm Berretta—and what it means to be a responsible gun owner. When I asked how she cultivated such tastes, she cited her college experience living on the designated international floor of a residence hall where a coterie of students from around the world routinely shared foods from their respective cultures of origin:

Eventually from the food perspective I just went through phrases. Like I went through the phase where I was eating nothing but Indian food, and that was just it. Then I had the West Indies phase, and then Korean. Then I started mixing things. I'd have Korean for breakfast, and that was just completely weird from where I grew up. It's funny, because I can remember coming home once for Thanksgiving and my mom—we'd get there a couple of days before. She had the spread ready, because Thanksgiving's not just a single day. It's like—a week of eating. I was completely unimpressed. It was like, "Macaroni and cheese? Whatever." It had no taste whatsoever. It tasted good, but relative to kimchi it's just different. As far as the food is concerned, my palette was broadened. I really loved it, because I'll try anything.

She expresses pride in her ability to code switch, to navigate diverse social groups without losing her sense of self. As a child, she was the only Black and female basketball player in her youth league. She chose to attend an elite private school over a Historically Black school (HBCU) that she very much admired. She thought that matriculating at the elite school would demonstrate her ability to navigate the 'real' (i.e., predominantly White) world. She offered the anecdote about cultivating omnivore tastes, which caused her to initially disavow (but later reclaim) her family's low-brow cuisine. Thus, her consumption practices, originating with a head-long dive into global foodways, helped reinforce (at least temporarily) a class-inflected boundary between the cosmopolitan and the low-brow but also helped her avoid racial stigma.

Boundary transcendence/transition

Boundary transcendence/transition includes strategies of action and tactics in the anti-racist repertoire that 'blur' existing boundaries by emphasizing fluidity or by changing meanings. In this excerpt from an interview, Adam spoke extensively about finding his neighborhood and home. Through his preferences in this consumption category he seeks to transcend intra-racial social class distinctions by glossing over them:

Adam: [. . .] My sister and I talked about this this morning. She and I feel like we're quite different from our other siblings, because they're so busy trying to run away from their roots, and she and I seem like we're trying to connect to ours . . .

Interviewer: So tell me a little bit about this conversation you were having with your sister about your other siblings . . .

Adam: [. . .] We started having the conversation about where we live, because my sister lives in a house probably a little larger than this one. She lives in the deep country. I mean, I'm in a subdivision in the country [but] she's got lots of land, and they have to have a tractor to mow their grass kind of country. But, all of my other siblings just seem to— . . . My sister and I talk about the way we live and where we live, how it does remind us so much of the neighborhood and the country that I grew up in, and the same style houses. And no negative reflection on my siblings, but my siblings have become—they like living in your more upscale neighborhoods. And I don't know if they really go back and spend time in the community like my sister and I do. You know, I think for them, it's kind of like, "I've been there. I want to move forward." And with my sister and I it's like, "Came from there. Still have a fondness for it, and will always keep that connection or ties with it."

Adam says his family bought the very first home in a subdivision marketed toward first-time Black homeowners—a first in that part of the state—in the late 1960s. He joked that at the closing his older brothers seated their mother on the 'For Sale' sign and carried it like a chariot around the yard as she waved imperiously, "because we were finally homeowners."

Sociologists generally agree that as upward social mobility increases so does the likelihood that persons will, where possible, identify as White (or as not Black) (Saperstein & Penner, 2012). This ethno-racial fluidity is generally less available to persons characterized as Black in the USA, which reinforces the stigma of blackness as inherently low-status. In fact, some upwardly mobile Blacks are especially desirous to increase their social distance from low-status Blacks to be closer to their White middle-class counterparts (see Frazier, 1957/1997). I should note that middle-class people generally seek distance from lower status people, but among African Americans strong countermanding norms exist against such distancing. Political scientist Michael Dawson (2002) calls this a sense of 'linked fate.' Adam and his sister adhere to these norms while their siblings do not to the same degree.

Adam uses consumption to combat low-status stigma by blurring neighborhood-level race and class boundaries. He enacts linked fate in his neighborhood choice, but engages in boundary work that allows him to gloss over crucial points of social difference. His descriptions of his childhood home contrast with his current home, which I visited. They do not seem especially similar. Although both are semi-rural, he exaggerates the extent to which that equalizes them. He describes his childhood neighborhood as consisting entirely of full-nest Black working-class families while his current neighborhood is predominantly White and mixed income, with few full-nest families. For Adam, this boundary transition work allows him to avoid low-status stigma while maintaining his sense of linked fate (and avoiding being overly desirous of social contact with Whites, an accusation he and his sister aim at their other siblings).

Sterling and Jamie engage in boundary work that blurs boundaries to manage a different stigma. This couple moved to the South from careers in Midwestern cities that featured either few Blacks, or a very small Black middle class. They shared their prodigious efforts at boundary transcendence to combat the stigma that 'Blacks don't fit in' at predominantly White settings. In the instance from the data, they share the origin story of a holiday tradition where they take a family Christmas photo at the homes of neighbors. During the interview at their home they showed me a photo album with annual Christmas letters and photos. Some were studio photos while others were clearly shot in homes, but different homes:

Jamie: We borrowed friends' houses. That started because we always went to Florida [to visit family], and I thought, "Why decorate my house since we aren't going to be here?" We'd go for two weeks or something.

Sterling: [Didn't this start with] our neighbors across the street? What was her name? [. . .] I think that's the first time. All the ones before this, we had them done in a studio. Then something happened. We were dressed and we couldn't get an appointment or something like that. So we went up to our neighbor's house. Then we started going to neighbors' houses.

Jamie: Oh, yeah. People get so excited. They'd say, "Where are you going to take your picture this year?"

Moderator: That's good.

Jamie: They get really excited to do that. I had one family, we'll show you—they wanted to get their tree [into the photo]. I'm like, "No, focus on our face."

Moderator: Their tree. That's good.

Sterling: This [photo] is in front of our—is that in front of—

Jamie: the coach's—

Sterling: Yeah. He was an assistant coach at [State U]. He's the assistant coach at Notre Dame now.

Moderator: That's great. That's great.

Jamie: That was taken at Dr. McDonald's. He's our local doctor . . . *That's* the tree; the Martin's. They're doctors too.

Moderator: Like, "We have to get our tree in. Could you [move] a little to the left?"

Jamie: Yeah, that's right. Oh, that's at the McDonald's house again. We've been there three times.

Blacks are by far the least desired neighbors in the USA, a fact that does not vary with social class position (Charles, 2005). Middle-class Blacks living in predominantly White neighborhoods report occasional harassment, but most often stigmatized exclusion where they are made to feel unwelcome (Lacy, 2007; Patillo, 2000). Sterling and Jamie combat this stigma by crossing this exclusionary boundary. They make this odd annual request of neighbors, asking them for a level of engagement in their family life that is uncommon. Interestingly, they do not report that this practice has cultivated deep, lasting friendships. Nevertheless, as a stigma-management tactic it helped make daily life more tolerable.

Conclusion: boundary work as surgery

The most prevalent stigma aimed at Blacks, and shaping many of their social encounters, strongly associates blackness with low status and various forms of dysfunction. Many engage in various forms of boundary work intended to combat such stigma. Sociologist E. Franklin Frazier (1957/1997) famously dismissed the boundary work of the mid-20th-century Black petit bourgeoisie as mere pretension. Deftly capturing the contradictions of their status-inflected challenges to White supremacy, he strongly castigated them for internalizing the behavioral norms of Victorian elites. Performing these norms did little to alter the basic contours of racial stigma, but did much to further stigmatize the Black working class and poor. Roughly 60 years on, many in the Black middle class engage in status-inflected boundary work. At times they prevail on existing status differences just like the old petit bourgeoisie, but it would be mistaken to reduce their boundary work to only this.

Nippert-Eng (1996) in her study of how people use mundane objects to establish categories of the self (such as 'home' and 'work') that impose order on everyday life, compares boundary work to the act of sculpting. Actors use boundary work to impose order on the raw symbolic materials of everyday life, cutting away what is not needed until a work of art remains. Though cogent, that metaphor does not precisely capture the purposes or spirit of boundary work that is directed at managing stigma's assaults on worth. The stigmatized typically seek to remove rather than sculpt the symbolic substance of stigma where possible. Thus, their boundary work often emphasizes cutting away and mending.

Boundary placement is largely focused on imposing boundaries that isolate stigma's symbolic harm and cut it away. Boundary transcendence/transition is comparatively focused on making connections across boundaries by mending together what is healthy. The challenges for the would-be surgeon are in the symbolic substance of boundaries and skill in their placement. Social boundaries, though in some instances mobilized to challenge racial stigma, are comprised of symbolic materials that often prevail on other forms of social difference. Moreover, they can cut away what is healthy when used by the unskilled, as when Shante disavowed her mother's mac and cheese while trying to be cosmopolitan.

I close with a note to readers interested in pursuing future research on this topic. The insights in this chapter extend beyond this specific empirical context. Yet this sample of middle-class African Americans in the Deep South emerges in a very specific socio-historic context that I have attempted to account for through a research design that is explicitly non-comparative. This of course should not be construed as any sort of admonition against comparative designs. The benefits of comparative research that explores other stigmatized communities in the marketplace, particularly those stigmatized on the basis of ethno-racial, gender, and social class identity, in other empirical contexts are beyond question. In fact, interested readers would do well to refer to the previously cited Lamont *et al.* (2016) multi-national comparative study of stigma. However, I would caution readers that there remains much we can learn from deeply historicizing key constructs (such as stigma, racism, sexism, heteronormativity/homophobia, etc.) so that we can recognize the deeply contextual distinction between a 'wink' and a 'nod' and its implications. Such insight is easily lost in comparative analysis, given its often enormous data collection and analysis requirements, and more likely to emerge in a single empirical context with a sharply delimited sample.

References

Acharya, A., Blackwell, M., & Sen, M. (2016). The political legacy of American slavery. *Journal of Politics*, 78(July), 621–641.
Adorno, T.W., & Horkheimer, M. (2002/1972). *Dialectic of enlightenment*. Trans. E. Jephcott. Stanford, CA, Stanford University Press.
Anderson, E. (2000). The emerging Philadelphia African American class structure. *The Annals of the American Academy of Political and Social Science*, 568(March), 54–77.
Arnould, E. (2007). Should consumer citizens escape the market? *The Annals of the American Academy of Political and Social Science*, 611(May), 96–111.
Bloome, D. (2014). Racial inequality trends and the intergenerational persistence of income and family structure. *American Sociological Review*, 70(December), 1196–1225.
Bone, S.A., Christensen, G.L., & Williams, J.D. (2014). Rejected, shackled, and alone: The impact of systemic restricted choice on minority consumers' construction of self. *Journal of Consumer Research*, 41(August), 451–474.
Branchik, B.J., & Davis, J.F. (2009). Marketplace activism: A history of the African American elite market segment. *Journal of Macromarketing*, 29(March), 37–57.
Charles, K.K., Hurst, E., & Roussanov, N. (2009). Conspicuous consumption and race. *The Quarterly Journal of Economics*, 124(2), 425–467.
Charles, C.Z. (2005). Can we live together? Racial preferences and neighborhood outcomes. In X.N. DeSouza Briggs (Ed.), *The geography of opportunity: Race and housing choice in metropolitan America* (pp. 45–80). Washington, DC, Brookings Institution Press.
Chin, E.M. (2001). *Purchasing power: Black kids and American consumer culture*. Minneapolis, University of Minnesota Press.
Cohen, L. (2004). *A consumers' republic: The politics of consumption in post-war America*. New York, Vintage Books.
Dawson, M.C. (2002). *Black visions: The roots of contemporary African-American political ideologies*. New York, Oxford University Press.
DuBois, W.E.B. (1903). *The souls of black folk: Essays and sketches*. Chicago, IL, A.C. McClurg & Company.
DuBois, W.E.B. (1935/1999). *Black reconstruction in America 1860–1880*. New York, Simon & Schuster.
Durkheim, E. (1915). *Elementary forms of religious life: A study in religious sociology*. New York, Macmillan.
Foner, E. (1988/2011). *Reconstruction: America's unfinished revolution, 1863–1877*. New York, Harper & Row.
Fox, C., & Guglielmo, T. (2012). Defining America's racial boundaries: Blacks, Mexicans, and European immigrants, 1890–1945. *American Journal of Sociology*, 118(2), 327–379.

Frazier, E.F. (1957/1997). *Black bourgeoisie*. New York, Free Press.
Frey, W.H. (2004). The new great migration: Black Americans' return to the South, 1965–2000. *The Brookings Institution: Center on Urban and Metropolitan Policy*. Retrieved 25 July, 2018 from www.brookings.edu/research/the-new-great-migration-black-americans-return-to-the-south-1965-2000/
Glickman, L.B. (2009). *Buying power: A history of consumer activism in the United States*. Chicago, IL, University of Chicago Press.
Goldman, R., & Papson, S. (1999). *Nike culture: The sign of the swoosh*. London, Sage Publications.
Hannerz, U. (1969). *Soulside: Inquiries into ghetto culture and community*. Chicago, IL, University of Chicago Press.
Henderson, G.R., Hakstian, A.M., & Williams, J.D. (2016). *Consumer equality: Race and the American marketplace*. Santa Barbara, CA, Praeger.
Ikenberry, G.J. (2011). *Liberal leviathan: The origins, crisis, and transformation of the American world order*. Princeton, NJ, Princeton University Press.
Kelley, R.D.G. (1996). *Race rebels: Culture, politics, and the Black working class*. New York, Simon & Schuster.
Kendi, I.X. (2016). *Stamped from the beginning: The definitive history of racist ideas in America*. New York, Nation Books.
Kotlowitz, A. (1991). *There are no children here*. New York, Anchor Books.
Lacy, K. (2007). *Blue chip Black: Race, class, and status in the new Black middle class*. Berkeley, University of California Press.
Lamont, M., & Fleming, C.M. (2005). Competence and religion in the cultural repertoire of the African American elite. *Du Bois Review*, *2*(1), 29–43.
Lamont, M., & Molnar, V. (2001). How Blacks use consumption to shape their collective identity: Evidence from marketing specialists. *Journal of Consumer Culture*, *1*(March), 31–45.
Lamont, M., & Molnar, V. (2002). The study of boundaries in the social sciences. *Annual Review of Sociology*, *28*(1), 167–195.
Lamont, M., Moraes Silva, G., Welburn, J.S., Guetzkow, J., Mizrachi, N., Herzog, H., & Reis, E. (2016). *Getting respect: Responding to stigma and discrimination in the United States, Brazil, and Israel*. Princeton, NJ, Princeton University Press.
Landry, B. (1987). *The new Black middle class*. Berkeley, University of California Press.
Lears, T.J.J. (1981). *No place of grace: Antimodernism and the transformation of American culture, 1880–1920*. Chicago, IL, University of Chicago Press.
Lewis, O. (1968). *La vida: A Puerto Rican family in the culture of poverty*. New York, Random House.
Lichter, D.T., Parisi, D., & Taquino, M.C. (2015). Toward a new macro-segregation? Decomposing segregation within and between metropolitan cities and suburbs. *American Sociological Review*, *80*(August), 843–873.
Liebow, E. (1967). *Tally's corner: A study of negro streetcorner men*. Boston, MA, Little, Brown and Company.
Logan, R. (1954). *The negro in American life and thought: The nadir, 1877–1901*. New York, Dial Press.
Mullins, P. (1999). *Race and affluence: An archaeology of African Americans and consumer culture*. New York, Kluwer Academic/Plenum Publishers.
Nippert-Eng, C. (1996). Calendars and keys: The classification of 'home' and 'work'. *Sociological Forum*, *11*(September), 563–582.
Ouellet, J.F. (2007). Consumer racism and its effects on domestic cross-ethnic product purchase: An empirical test in the United States, Canada, and France. *Journal of Marketing*, *71*(January), 113–128.
Ownby, T. (1999). *American dreams in Mississippi: Consumers, poverty, & culture, 1830–1998*. Chapel-Hill, NC, University of North Carolina Press.
Patillo, M. (1999/2013). *Black picket fences: Privilege and peril among the Black middle class*, second edition. Chicago, IL, University of Chicago Press.
Patillo, M. (2000). The limits of out-migration for the Black middle class. *Journal of Urban Affairs*, *22*(Fall), 225–241.
Rastogi, S., Johnson, T.D., Hoeffel, E.M., & Drewery, M.P. (2011). *The Black population: 2010*. Retrieved 25 July, 2018 from www.census.gov/prod/cen2010/briefs/c2010br-06.pdf
Richter, A.G. (2005). *Home on the rails: Women, the railroad, and the rise of public domesticity*. Chapel Hill, University of North Carolina Press.
Saperstein, A., & Penner, A.M. (2012). Racial fluidity and inequality in the United States. *American Journal of Sociology*, *118*(November), 676–727.
Scommenga, P. (2010). Least segregated U.S. metros located in the fast-growing South and West. *Population Reference Bureau Report*. Retrieved 25 July, 2018 from www.prb.org/us-residential-segregation/

Tate, G. (2003). *Everything but the burden: What White people are taking from Black culture*. New York, Broadway Books.
Thompson, C.J., & Tambyah, S.K. (1999). Trying to be cosmopolitan. *Journal of Consumer Research*, *26*(December), 214–241.
Weber, M. (1922/1978). *Economy and society*. Berkeley, University of California Press.
Weems, R. (1998). *Desegregating the dollar: African American consumerism in the twentieth century*. New York, New York University Press.
Wilson, M.R. (2005). *Encyclopaedia of Chicago (mail order entry)*. *Chicago Historical Society*. Retrieved 25 July, 2018 from www.encyclopedia.chicagohistory.org/pages/779.html
Wolcott, V.W. (2012). *Race, riots and roller coasters: The struggle over segregated recreation in America*. Philadelphia, University of Pennsylvania Press.

22
CONSUMER VULNERABILITY
Critical insights from stories, action research and visual culture

Susan Dunnett, Kathy Hamilton, and Maria Piacentini

Introduction

Critical marketing scholars have been encouraged to consider the experiences of consumers who encounter marketplace exclusion, consumers 'whose views are rarely heard by those in positions of power' (Tadajewski, 2010, p. 214). Our focus in this chapter is on consumers experiencing vulnerability. Baker, Gentry and Rittenburg (2005, p. 134) offer the following definition of consumer vulnerability:

> Consumer vulnerability is a state of powerlessness that arises from an imbalance in marketplace interactions or from the consumption of marketing messages and products. It occurs when control is not in an individual's hands, creating a dependence on external factors (e.g. marketers) to create fairness in the marketplace. The actual vulnerability arises from the *interaction* of individual states, individual characteristics, and external conditions within a context where consumption goals may be hindered and the experience affects personal and social perceptions of self.

Central to Baker *et al.*'s (2005) definition is the lack of control and power experienced by some consumers, but also that the experience of vulnerability is often heightened due to circumstances beyond the individual's control (e.g. how other people respond to her/him). This point emphasizes the socially constructed and interactive nature of consumer vulnerability. Since the 1990s the importance of consumer vulnerability has been recognized with research exploring its conditions and contexts (Smith & Cooper-Martin, 1997; Gentry, Kennedy, Paul & Hill, 1994; Hill & Stamey, 1990; Ozanne, Hill & Wright, 1998; Morgan, Schuler & Stoltman, 1995; Botti *et al.*, 2008; Ozanne & Ozanne, 2011; Cartwright, 2015). This work has been published in a range of outlets, including special issues of *Journal of Macromarketing* (Hill, 2005) and *Journal of Marketing Management* (Dunnett, Hamilton & Piacentini, 2016) and an edited collection (Hamilton, Dunnett & Piacentini, 2016). Much of this research stream questions and problematizes experiences of vulnerability within the marketplace.

Critical marketers have put forward contrasting opinions about the link between a critical marking perspective and marketing practice. For Bradshaw and Fırat (2007, p. 40), critical marketing should be about the empowerment of consumers so 'that they be masters of their institutions rather than simply be served by them.' In this sense, critical marketing is less about relevance to marketing managers and more about 'question[ing] the very foundation[s] of marketing's existence' (p. 31). In contrast, Tadajewski (2010) argues that critical marketers should be concerned with engaging with practice and working with both for-profit and non-profit organizations. We argue that such engagement is crucial within the context of consumer vulnerability. As Stearn (2016, p. 66) suggests, 'changes in the behavior of the companies providing essential goods and services and their regulators is as important as developing the "empowered" behavior of consumers in vulnerable situations.'

Consumer vulnerability is a broad and multi-faceted concept, which has led to a variety of research approaches. Specifically Baker, LaBarge & Baker (2016) identify three commonly used analytical perspectives: (1) isolating particular populations of people, for example, studies have focused on socioeconomic status (Hill, 2001) and literacy (Adkins & Ozanne, 2005); (2) isolating particular environmental conditions, for example, studies have focused on ghettoized neighborhoods (Crockett & Wallendorf, 2004) and natural disasters (Sayre, 1994); and (3) isolating meanings and processes of vulnerability, an approach that highlights the dynamic nature of consumer vulnerability. For example, Baker and Mason (2012) suggest that vulnerability can be a catalyst for change. Where researchers find common ground is their acknowledgment that researching consumer vulnerability requires careful methodological consideration with techniques that are appropriate for sensitive topics in challenging contexts (e.g. Hill, 1995; Turley, 2015). However, this need not create a barrier to methodological innovation, with many recent studies adopting creative approaches to consumer vulnerability analysis. We suggest that these methods have much potential, in particular for unpacking and exposing consumer vulnerability, and, in turn, laying the groundwork for transformative resolutions. In this chapter, we review consumer vulnerability studies that have drawn on non-conventional methods and, in doing so, have enriched our critical understanding of the concept.

In order to do so we open with a discussion of the role and position of context in the field of consumer vulnerability. We touch briefly on the relationship between contexts, theory and representation in order to critically examine the ways context has been viewed in consumer research more widely, particularly harnessing recent debates in the field of Consumer Culture Theory (CCT). We then move on to discuss methodologies that offer unique types of access to, and engagement with, vulnerable consumers as informants and participants. First, we consider stories (such as autobiographies) as sources of data and mechanisms of representation, we then consider the merits of action research and participant involvement and finally we outline the benefits of a visual, filmic sensibility in studies of consumer vulnerability.

The role of context

Studies of consumer vulnerability often differ from those in the wider field of consumer research in their treatment of context. For consumer vulnerability researchers, the context is the subject or focus of the study and can be the driver for transformation or impact as well as theoretical contribution. This perspective provides a contrast to wider consumer research, which emphasizes that studies are not simply of their context but rather make use of contexts for purposes of theory development. In their 2006 paper, Arnould, Price and Moisio discuss what they term the dangers of contexts, chief among these that context may overshadow the theoretical insights on offer; '[c]ontexts are dangerous not only for the way they threaten to swallow researchers, but for the way contexts can overabsorb our readers' (p. 1090). For the most part, consumer vulnerability studies do not aim to make 'use of' research contexts but rather work with and in contexts to affect positive change. Indeed, it is central to work conducted in the field of consumer vulnerability that it is contextualized, and that it offers an insight into a population, phenomenon or a feature of the marketplace. Therefore, context remains deliberately in the foreground and research questions are often framed in terms of consumer welfare and lives in context, e.g. disability studies (Kaufman-Scarborough, 1999), studies of poverty (Hamilton, 2012) and homelessness (Hill & Stamey, 1990). How far to move from this context in terms of theorization, or an etic view, can be both an intellectual challenge and a moral one for the researcher. Sure enough, the balance between context and theory, emic (participant voice) and etic (theoretical insight) must be struck, and the required balance will differ across journals and other outlets. Yet a common goal of this type of work is that it 'gives voice' to the unseen challenges of under-represented populations. Representation is therefore the aim rather than abstraction. Such a goal can often seem incommensurate with an academic culture that builds legitimacy on the sociological tradition of 'grand theorization on a more aggregate level' (Askegaard & Linnet, 2011, p. 397).

Of course, theorizing legitimizes stories for academic audiences, but as we have found in our work with practitioners, it excludes other audiences. This is more than an issue of using the right mode of communication for the right audience. We should recognize that theorization is always a retelling of the stories and experiences of others; to theorize a story is to shape it and wield power over it. Merton, writing in the 1970s, suggests that the conceptual frameworks of sociology

> serve to exclude from the attention of the social scientist the intense feelings of pain and suffering that are the experience of some people caught up in the social patterns under examination. By screening out these profoundly human experiences, they become sociological euphemisms.
>
> *1972, p. 38*

Little wonder then that we see much work in the field – including our own – which brings an agentic, neoliberal perspective (Fitchett, Patsiaouras & Davies, 2014) to the study of vulnerable consumers, focusing on how consumers cope despite their vulnerable states. CCT, in particular, has been charged with viewing the majority of consumers as 'navigating [their] way through the plethora of opportunities provided by the marketplace' (Askegaard & Linnet, 2011, p. 383). In contrast, our data often speaks of difficult lives and un-solvable problems – the lives of vulnerable consumers are, in general, contexts of constraints rather than possibilities (Moisander, Valtonen & Hirsto, 2009; Kazeminia, Del Chiappa & Jafari, 2015; Beudaert, Gorge & Herbert, 2017).

There are further conflicts and contradictions when we consider the role of context to research aims. In the CCT tradition, Arnould et al. (2006, p. 108) suggest that distance aids the construction of theoretical insights: 'distance is needed to uncover theoretical contributions and get on with the crafting of science.' Yet Hill (2016, p. 368) cautions us that to comprehend intractable problems such as poverty 'we can not understand their circumstances' without getting close to those circumstances and building a deep understanding of contexts, over time.

A move away from the view that instances of consumer vulnerability represent a case exemplar of an unusual phenomenon would go some way to ensuring that consumer research is an inclusive discipline in terms of the lives it represents. So, rather unfashionably, we propose a return to contexts. Not simply the 'how to make contexts work for you' model (Arnould et al., 2006) but one that can provide a wider representation of consumers. Further research spanning the social boundaries between researcher and context is needed, e.g. social class, income, education (Hamilton, 2012; Hill, Rapp & Capella, 2015; Piacentini, Hibbert & Hogg, 2014;

Saatcioglu & Ozanne, 2013). Such studies offer an opportunity to counter the 'heavy bias of the American middle-class in our understanding of consumer culture' (Askegaard & Linnet, 2011). Arguably it is easier to collect data in and theorize our own worlds and perhaps this meets the needs of our business schools more readily. Certainly, our individual biographies shape research relations, and knowledge construction is embedded in these biographies (Griffith, 1998). Yet Hill (2016) points to routes to effect change – his central message is that the 'beliefs and behaviors of impoverished citizens can be markedly different from affluent citizens because of the contexts and restrictions they face' (p. 368). Studies in vulnerability have much to offer CCT and critical marketing and vice versa, not least a move beyond the agentic, middle-class, American individual to explore a variety of contexts and the macro-social frameworks that shape them. The goal of the influential Askegaard and Linnet (2011) paper – to develop a contextually oriented CCT research – can be served by contextualized consumer vulnerability studies. Below we outline three methodological approaches that work to both unearth the micro lived experience and the wider macro politics at play in the lives of vulnerable consumers.

Consumer vulnerability and stories

Here we look at the ways stories have been used as both data and to represent findings. Stories can offer a form of proximity to the lived experience that might not be achievable through other means. As Hill (2016) reminds us: 'we need to get proximal' in order to have any chance of understanding complex conditions – such as entrenched poverty – and to move beyond understanding to work toward societal change.

Stories differ from data collected through traditional marketing research techniques in that they are completely told from the viewpoint of the teller. They are therefore free from some of the biases created by the research setting, types of questioning and the fragmentation of data analysis. Stories privilege the emic viewpoint and provide rich experiential knowledge (Brown, 2005). They are particularly valuable in their communication of emotion, both as data and as a mode of representing findings. In short, stories allow us to see a phenomenon through the eyes of the writer, and in the telling the condition becomes personified – poverty is no longer an intractable social problem but is the context for a life (Sajovic & Kenningham, 2014).

Stories as data

In considering stories as data this chapter will draw on two examples: first the work of Stephanie O'Donohoe and Darach Turley, and second the recent commentary by Tim Stone and Stephen Gould (2016). Using stories found in the public domain – such as autobiography – offers a way of sensitively accessing difficult human experiences and deep emotions. This has been done particularly well by Stephanie O'Donohoe and Darach Turley in their work on bereavement and grief. Turley and O'Donohoe (2012) explore the connectedness of possessions – 'things' – and bereavement using autobiography or pathographies as a data source. They describe pathography as a 'personal and often poignant account of illness, dying or bereavement' (2012, p. 1336). They note that these stories offer detailed accounts of consumer experience – consumption, objects and market interactions are woven into the narrative, just as they are woven into life. Arguably, autobiography or pathography offers the researcher a more frank and arresting glimpse into the pain of loss than other methods, such as interview, might garner. Pathographies capture the mundane detail of life alongside deep introspection. They are crafted stories that make the unfamiliar familiar and the private public. As Brown (2005) reminds us, autobiography allows us to reach elements of an experience or phenomenon that other research techniques might not.

O'Donohoe (2016) extends this technique to explore the experience of childhood grief through an analysis of a memoir written by Ben Brooks-Dutton following his wife's death. O'Donohoe (2016) considers the role of consumption and consumer culture in Brooks-Dutton's toddler son's life after the death of his mother. This method allows for insights to 'emerge organically as part of a story being told for other purposes, highlighting the seamless and salient nature of consumption in vulnerable people's lives' (p. 100). Again, O'Donohoe is concerned with our relationship to possessions and the role that these possessions play in grieving and loss. Indeed, O'Donohoe shows that trivial and mundane objects can be central to the grieving process for both adults and very young children. It seems hard to imagine uncovering such insights through the traditional research encounter, not least because it is challenging to discuss seemingly inconsequential everyday consumption in the shadow of loss. Yet O'Donohoe and Turley's work with autobiographies as data shows us the rewards of sensitively and compassionately applying the consumer lens to profound human experiences. In particular, this work on toddler grief and the role of possessions has been shared with the support agency Grief Encounter.

Also working with stories, Stone and Gould (2016) draw on an account of Sandra Bem published in the *New York Times* detailing her decision to commit suicide following a diagnosis of Alzheimer's disease. They consider her decision to 'navigate the market for suitable goods and services in order to bring about a self-determined end to her life' (p. 386). Their work is notable for its combination of sensitivity to the individuals and sources featured and the use of a powerful theoretical lens – they use terror management theory to theorize the rationale of ending one's life and the practicalities of doing so. It reminds us that telling stories need not be (and often, *should* not be) an entirely emic undertaking, and yet theory need not obliterate the ideographic lived experience. Their framing of Sandra's experience as a form of consumption allows the reader to see both the ordinariness (shopping for the wherewithal) and the extraordinariness (the power and presence of mind with which she approaches the decision and the task) of the practices of ending one's own life. Flying in the face of the assertion that 'informants' plights can overwhelm scientific goals' (Arnould *et al.*, 2006, p. 109), they allow Sandra's story to offer a critique of depictions of elderly consumers that overlook the less agentic, frail 'fourth age' and end of life.

This source of secondary data, which contained both Sandra's voice and that of her husband, allowed investigation of a phenomenon that would otherwise be near impossible to access. Using existing texts gives us admission to accounts of raw emotion and embodied life that offer deep understanding of hidden experience. The beauty of this approach is its sensitivity, particularly in contexts where the presence of a researcher could be intrusive or unethical. Indeed, using secondary sources as data removes much of the potential harm of the research encounter and can redress the power imbalance between the researcher and the researched (Jafari, Dunnett, Hamilton & Downey, 2013). Achieving access to sensitive contexts and informants can be a barrier to studies of consumer vulnerability, the above shows there are ways of accessing profound, unseen experience through autobiography and media interview.

Stories as representation

In order to explore the use of stories as representation we turn now to the poet-researcher to consider what the poetic form offers the field of consumer vulnerability. For some time now, poetry has been legitimized in the field of consumer research as an alternative mode of representation (Canniford, 2012; Downey, 2016; Sherry & Schouten, 2002; Wijland, 2011). As Downey (2016) points out, the 'poet-researcher' sits well in the often-emotive field of consumer vulnerability. Poetry provides a uniquely visceral and immediate form through which to recount the emotion in the research encounter and forms an excellent tool to aid reflexivity and data analysis (Canniford, 2012). Hilary Downey, in particular, (2016, p. 358) demonstrates the potential of poetry to offer a release for 'hidden narratives' that otherwise, might remain absent in more conventional academic outputs. Downey's (2016) recent poem stems from a two-year research relationship with a homebound consumer and effectively brings various themes to the fore, including physical bodily constraints, emotional reactions, sense of marginalization, relationships with others (including carers) and spatial surroundings (hospital, bedroom).

As a tool of representation, poetry explicitly acknowledges that it is a *reaction to* the lives of others not a retelling. The pain and suffering seen and felt are written into the account. Researchers who use stories to represent contexts weave themselves into the story. The storyteller is off-stage but their presence is strongly felt. The poem offers an attempt to weld these world views together giving insight into the experience of vulnerability and the researcher's, sometimes visceral, reaction to the context. The role of the researcher in shaping stories – in creating feeling – is perhaps more explicit here than might be in prose. As Downey observes, poetry offers a 'heady mix of sensory imagery, emotionally laden observations' (2016, p. 361). The reader is drawn in, asked to decode the imagery, and in this decoding, is made to feel some of what has been felt by both participant and researcher. The poem *Vulnerability in Parts* attempts to capture the experience of quadriplegic man, Jay:

> Floating seamlessly atop the skin-like,
> Dreamlike stretched reality, frighteningly stilled
> On a still body; the something I can be
> Made all the more chilling by ceding
> Control at the brink;
>
> 2016, p. 362

Thus, the power of Downey's poetry is its evocation of the emotional connection between researcher and researched. It does this through style, expression, imagery, cadence – poetry serves to 'unfix' the language conventions of traditional representations seen in academic research (Canniford, 2012, p. 393).

Indeed, Canniford (2012) makes the case for the use of poetry in data analysis, to represent the ethnographic encounter through both poetic field notes and data interpretation. Its value here is to capture feelings, atmosphere, preliminary interpretations and fleeting thoughts such that they can be revisited. In this way, poetry is not simply an end point but process as well. In the hands of Downey, Canniford and others, poetry offers a chance to break out of the traditions of academic representations, to take us closer to the feel, the sights, the spaces, and the experience of consumer vulnerability.

Narrative, as Visconti (2016) points out, is absorbing, convincing and memorable; whether veiled in poetry or recounted in prose the story gives voice to the vulnerable. Exploring the phenomenon of vulnerability from a conversational perspective Visconti (2016) reminds us that stories can be powerful mechanisms of change. He contends that, 'individual and social conversations on, among others, ethnic and gender diversity, illness, and poverty are powerful transformative means to subvert established positions of domination' (2016, p. 372). He notes that 'etic social representations tend to flatten vulnerable consumers to a whole, relatively homogeneous group of like-minded and like-acting individuals' (2016, p. 377). Emic social representations, instead, are bolder in documenting pluralism and difference within vulnerable consumer groups. Visconti too is concerned with notions of proximity and empathy: 'it is easier to reject a faceless group than people with names and stories' (2016, p. 377). Poetic and narrative representation offer a very good fit with the goals of most transformative research or studies of consumer vulnerability – stories inform, uncover hidden contexts and people, give voice, capture and share emotion and create empathy. Stories, then, are powerful tools of persuasion and can be used as catalysts for change.

The use of stories presents several methodological challenges for the researcher. As in all qualitative research, questions of viewpoint must be considered critically – whose viewpoint is being rendered and why, whose interests are served by the story? Narrative analysis technique (Clandinin & Connelly, 2000) can reveal how tellers position and characterize themselves in their stories, e.g. hero, victim, questing traveler, revealing what type of story is being told. Unlike observation techniques, such as ethnography, which can reveal unconscious, disordered behavior and counter intuitive insights, stories as data present honed and crafted artifacts that the researcher must unpick. Narratives are often immediate and persuasive, the temptation to take them at face value should be avoided and a critical perspective adopted, particularly in their analysis. As the above scholars show, a robust analytical lens or theoretical framework need not obliterate the narrative voice but can instead draw out insight from lengthy, subjective texts such as autobiography or media interview.

Studies of vulnerability that use autobiography or poetry, should consider the cultural context in which they were written, including the personal history of the writer and main 'characters'. The aspects of the context, such as geographical location, historical or political setting, legal and ethical issues and relevant consumer cultures should inform the treatment of the data and ideally should be considered in subsequent publications. It is worth remembering that in telling stories 'people are seen as composing lives that shape and are shaped by social and cultural narratives' (Clandinin & Connelly, 2000, p. 43). At first glance, it might seem difficult to find space for alternative forms of representation – such as poetry or narrative – in our publications, yet journals such as *Journal of Marketing Management, Marketing Theory* and *Journal of Consumer Behavior* have featured poetic work alongside discussions of the poet-researcher, and special issues continue to offer opportunities for stories to be told.

Consumer vulnerability and action research

Recent attention in the Transformative Consumer Research (TCR) field has turned toward embracing the methodological approaches captured by the term action research. Action research refers to a family of qualitative research methodologies, which are characterized by being iterative, participative and reflective. Developed post WWII, the driver for this approach was a general concern with how social change could be facilitated, and Lewin's early work (1951) was instrumental in guiding how the field evolved. Action research approaches are responsive to the research situation, and tend to be emergent and flexible (Dick, 2000). Members of the family of action research approaches include such methodologies as participatory action research, action learning, action science and soft systems approaches. Action research, in various forms, has been widely used in applied social science contexts (Nyman, Berg, Downe & Bondas, 2016; Kidd, Kenny & McKinstry, 2014), particularly in the organizational and educational sectors (Edwards-Groves & Kemmis, 2016; Dey, Bhattacharya & Ho, 2015), and has been the methodological approach adopted in a number of recent studies with vulnerable groups of the population (e.g. Clough, 2015; Hill, Cunningham & the Gramercy Gentlemen, 2016; Ozanne & Anderson, 2010).

An action research project will usually have six key stages, involving analysis, evidence/fact gathering, conceptualization, planning, implementation of action, and evaluation (Baskerville &

Wood-Harper, 1996). Although action research is typically considered a qualitative methodology, it does not rule out the use of quantitative methods for evaluatory purposes; however, the requirement to be adaptive and responsive in support of successive iterations means that qualitative methods are more commonly used. It is common to use fuzzy and heuristic methods early in the conduct of action research to allow for quick refinement of approaches and methods.

A key attraction of action research for consumer research lies with the emergent nature of the approach. This lends itself effectively to contexts where organizational and individual change is a key aim, and this includes any attempts to modify consumer behavior. A large-scale example of this was a European study of energy behavior change (Feenstra, Backhaus & Heiskanen, 2009). In this work, Feenstra and colleagues undertook an in-depth analysis of 27 European energy demand management programs, and from this developed a toolkit for practitioners to use to improve the outcomes of energy change programs. The key point here is that the toolkit to enhance the practical implementation of energy behavioral change initiatives – aimed at saving energy of the more efficient use of energy – was developed based on an emergent design from analysis of existing programs and literature.

A further advantage for consumer and marketing research is that action research is relevant to the lives of the participants and empowers them. This engenders greater engagement in participants. The work by Clough (2015) exemplifies this point, where he adopted a participatory action research approach to explore the range and types of services and facilities available to older people, and how these might support them to lead fuller lives. In Clough's study, the older people at the center of the project were involved as researchers, interviewers and commentators on the emergent findings – the research participants are not merely passive but actively involved in the research process. This has both advantages and disadvantages. While the involvement of communities of interest in all stages of the research has clear benefits in terms of representation of those voices, there are downsides linked to their status as first and foremost representatives of that community, rather than as researchers investigating a specific research problem. As Clough notes, a participant with short-term training might well be less effective and efficient as a researcher, and any assumption that there are labor and time savings in this approach could be misplaced.

This empowerment and greater engagement is further enhanced by the ways in which action research breaks down hierarchies and opens up dialogue between participants and researchers (Hill, Cunningham & the Gramercy Gentlemen, 2016). In the context of a maximum-security prison, Hill *et al.* (2016) adopted a participatory action research approach to give voice to their participants (incarcerated men), and to open up conversations about their lives in order to develop insights about the acquisition and ownership restrictions they face. In their paper, the voices of the men are clearly incorporated as research data as informants (which is expected in qualitative research) but also as inmate co-researchers, where they are in the unique position of providing insights as investigators of their own community, as well as representing the community. The following data excerpt is typical from this work:

> Base pay a month for an inmate is usually between $19.00 and $55.40. If the inmate has cable, $16.50 is automatically deducted from his account, as is any owed medical costs (they may not be aware of). The average income for an inmate with no outside support is a subsistence of extreme poverty—so medical costs affect them greatly. The income we earn has not increased in decades, though costs all around us have. Poor care for profit or the little income prisoners have causes resentment. (Inmate co-researcher no. 10).

Hill et al., *2016, p. 306*

For this work, research participants were included to the point of being co-authors on the written work relating to this study, as the Gramercy Gentlemen (Hill *et al.*, 2016).

As a result of these effects, another attraction emerges: action research has ethical advantages in that it centers on the needs of participants and is democratic, accountable and, if properly conducted, life-enhancing. Action research often centers on community engagement and empowerment, with a view to encouraging participants to actively develop interventions that will help their lives. According to Ozanne and Anderson (2010), community-based action research emphasizes the role of multiple participants from a community, often focusing on improving people's well-being, especially where they are disadvantaged or vulnerable in some way. The interventionist approach so central to action research clearly fits with the TCR agenda, where improving people's lives is a driving concern (Mick, 2008). However, this approach does not always neatly fit the broader context of academic research, and the key message with the action research approach is to keep in mind that 'good' action research has both practical and academic outcomes. The balance between these varies according to context and project aims – sometimes the practical outcomes outweigh the academic outcomes, and vice versa. The role of theory can be contentious here – rigorous academic theory might be impractical or impossible to implement. Practitioner participants might not have rigorous theoretical knowledge but might use implicit theories that are highly effective (Ozanne & Saatcioglu, 2008). As applied research, action research can seem frustrating in that it does not seek to offer general solutions outside the study context, which can be antithetical to some researchers, especially those of a positivistic or experimental disposition (Wansink, 2012).

Another key consideration around action research use relates to its resource implications. Project funding and timescales often do not allow for extensive iteration, and it is not uncommon to find action research projects that never actually manage to engage fully with later cycles of development. Gaining the trust of participants takes time and researchers need to be prepared to take a less central and controlling role, even to the extent of a complete reversal of leadership at some stages in a project (Hill *et al.*, 2016). However, in the context of working with vulnerable populations, the action research approach brings important benefits, which outweigh possible downsides.

There are a number of methodological challenges associated with action research approaches. The first links to the role of the 'participant as researcher'; how does becoming an active research participant (involved in all stages of the research) impact the participant as a study informant? Action research is, by definition, participative, and through participation study participants occupy a role as both researcher and the implementer of the program or action being investigated. Participants are also co-constructors of the data, who can facilitate access to and understanding of the socio-cultural context of the research (Alvesson & Sköldberg, 2000; Burawoy, 1998). These dual roles can provide a heightened sense of ownership of the action program, but also raise questions about the legitimacy of the researcher among the various stakeholders and those being researched. From a methodological point of view, it is important that researcher reflection and critical subjectivity (Ladkin, 2007) are factored into the program of action research.

Second, the applied nature of much action research raises the issue of emic–etic balance in terms of the research outcomes. This stems from the very advantage of the action research approach (some form of intervention within a specific context), which also serves as a limitation – the findings and contribution are often very context bound, and therefore it is difficult to get the balance of theory and empirical data unpacked to the extent that wider relevance and contributions can be noted. While this is an important aspect of the action research approach, this question is one that concerns many qualitative and post-positivist researchers more generally (Payne & Williams, 2005), and certainly not exclusive to action research approaches.

Finally, action research operating at a community level represents challenges in gaining access to all stakeholders in a community, issues of power imbalances in a community, and ensuring all voices are heard. The idea of comprehensive coverage of the community of interest is going to be influenced by local politics and power relations, which might facilitate but could also hinder access to key community members.

Consumer vulnerability and visual culture

Visual culture surrounds us on a daily basis and recent years have seen marketing and consumer researchers embrace the visual turn as they employ visual forms of analysis and dissemination. In this section, we consider what a visual approach can bring to our critical understanding of consumer vulnerability. We begin with a discussion of consumer vulnerability research that has used existing visual resources as the basis of analysis and then consider examples of researchers who have collected and produced visuals themselves. Chase and Walker (2016) consider global experiences of poverty and shame across seven countries – Britain, Norway, India, Uganda, China, South Korea and Pakistan. They draw on a range of data-collection techniques including analysis of representations of poverty in film and literature in the different cultural contexts. Although recognizing shifting attitudes toward consumerism over time, a common theme across countries was the need for impression management to 'keep up appearances' and how those experiencing poverty felt at risk of judgment from others. Interestingly, their interviews revealed synergies with these fictional accounts, demonstrating how films, short stories and poetry can be important resources for obtaining insight about experiences of vulnerability with reference to a particular cultural and historical context.

The mass media is a dominant agent in transmitting knowledge and shaping our cultural frameworks (Jansson, 2002) yet the media can commoditize the vulnerable 'other' (Coleman, 2016, p. 46). Coleman (2016) considers the documentary, as 'a media commodity working within market-based logic' (p. 48). Her focus is on *The Uncondemned*, a documentary part financed by a crowdfunding campaign, which includes accounts of women who testified at the International Criminal Tribunal for Rwanda to help secure the first successful prosecutions of rape and sexual violence as crimes of war. The documentary publicly discloses the women's identities, which were concealed during the trials, and 'is named to present the story of transition from vulnerability toward empowerment through voice' (p. 50). Drawing on Adichie's (2009) warning about 'the danger of the single story', Coleman suggests that the women's narratives in the tribunal records are only one telling of their experiences and highlights the potential of *The Uncondemned* to complement this perspective and stimulate broader conversations about sexual violence. Given the constructed nature of documentaries, and the power dynamics at play, Coleman reminds us of the need to maintain a critical and reflective stance toward the consumption of representations.

The need for a critical reading of representations is in keeping with Social Representations Theory (SRT) which has recently been proposed as a useful approach to identify and challenge dominant representations that stigmatize by reframing one-dimensional perceptions of vulnerability (Hamilton et al., 2014). Referring to the context of poverty, Hamilton et al. (2014, p. 1849) suggest that representations have transformative potential 'to provoke change in those representations that lead to social exclusion, thereby affecting how people in poverty both are viewed and view themselves.' By replacing poverty with other states of vulnerability, we could make the same argument. Vulnerability is a multi-faceted concept (Baker et al., 2016) and one-dimensional views of its various states – poverty, illness, aging, grief, etc. – risk oversimplifying consumer experiences. Dominant discourses are often disempowering because they exclude the voices of those with first-hand experience of vulnerability whereas more transformative discourses prioritize the voice of lived experience (Hamilton et al., 2014).

Visual approaches that adopt a participatory approach are one means of giving more emphasis to the voices of consumers experiencing vulnerability. One recent example is Chatzidakis and Maclaran's (2016) film, *Skoros: Anti-Consumption in Crisis*, which features an anti-consumption collective and was produced and filmed almost entirely by members of the collective. Their involvement ensures that the emic perspective of the collective is portrayed in terms of their experiences of the 'crisis' which has forced many consumers into poverty. This film is reminiscent of Bradshaw & Firat's (2007, p. 40) suggestion that a critical marketing orientation can 'inspire transformations that would empower people to shed their identities as consumers to perform a takeover of organizations and marketing to control and run them for their purposes.'

Since the Association for Consumer Research (ACR) Film Festival began in 2001, videography has gained popularity as a useful approach to disseminating research findings. Here, we consider several films that are based on contexts relevant to the study of consumer vulnerability. We begin with Caldwell and Henry's (2009), *A Right to Life: Reducing Maternal Death and Morbidity in Pakistan*, as a powerful example. Pakistan has high maternal death and morbidity statistics and the film highlights the vulnerability of women within a cultural context where family units are characterized by patriarchy and women have limited education and poor literacy skills. Shockingly there is an acceptance of women's death, particularly women living in poverty, and the film brings much-needed attention to an issue that for many remains under the radar. Featuring activists who highlight the need for the empowerment of women, the film puts forward a powerful critique of government support of the existing health care system.

Another film that also highlights the need for change is Caldwell, Kleppe and Watson's (2010) *Talk the Walk, Walk the Talk*. Filmed in Botswana, this example centers on a pageant for men who are willing to go public with their HIV/Aids status and engage in public advocacy for positive living by encouraging others to get tested and promoting safe sex. The decision to enter the pageant is particularly significant because the cultural norm, particularly for men, is not to expose their HIV status for fear of discrimination or stigmatization (cf. Tadajewski, this volume). Similar to the previous example, this film raises awareness of an issue that often remains outside of public discourse and puts forward a powerful message about the need for behavior and lifestyle changes (see also Gordon, this volume).

In reflecting on the two films discussed above, we suggest that there are various benefits of employing videography as a means of disseminating research findings of studies linked to consumer vulnerability. First, films are a useful means of learning about experiences of vulnerability in different cultural contexts and allowing viewers to see cultural traditions and rituals that might be unfamiliar to them. For example, in both films we learn about traditional health care methods that sharply contrast with Western medicine. Here we recall Moscovici (1984, p. 24) who suggests that 'the purpose of all representations is to make the unfamiliar, or unfamiliarity itself, familiar.' Films not only allow us to witness the lived experience of consumer vulnerability but to situate this within the 'context of context' (Askegaard & Linnet, 2011). Becoming sensitive to the structuring influences that constrain consumers or enhance their vulnerability is an essential stage in developing a critical understanding of their lives.

Second, such films have the potential for intense emotional impact. Although we could read about the same themes in more traditional academic outlets, experiences of vulnerability take on greater immediacy when we see them visually. The need for change is undeniable when we see with our own eyes the poor infrastructural conditions, low-quality medical facilities which have a shortage of drugs and other supplies and the tears of family members who have lost loved ones to complications during childbirth or people talking about the diagnosis and treatment of HIV (Caldwell et al., 2010).

Third, critical marketing often involves a focus on societal issues (Schroeder, 2007) and this is certainly evident in the films discussed above. Both feature ambassadors of change who are committed to improving the health and well-being of consumers experiencing vulnerability, and both have the potential to feed into social marketing campaigns. The film format is particularly appropriate because of its potential to reach a large audience, including those stakeholders who have the resources to instigate and promote behavior changes that will reduce consumer vulnerability (see also Gordon, this volume).

Fourth, reaching a broad audience is also advantageous in the sense that these films raise the profile of experiences of vulnerability of which there is little awareness. They therefore serve an important role in giving voice to aspects of vulnerability that otherwise might remain hidden. Another relevant example in this regard is Veer's (2014) "'I'm Struggling". Men's Stories of Mental Illness', which reveals the fear and shame experienced by men whose notions of masculinity have been compromised because of their mental health illnesses. It is only by making such issues visible that transformation can occur and we can take steps toward overcoming myths that stigmatize.

Hietanen, Rokka and Schouten (2014) have highlighted the potential of expressive videography. This moves beyond films as a representational tool to 'a powerful transformative tool in the production and shaping of social relations' (p. 2020). This shift is important from a critical marketing perspective as it opens up the opportunity for critiquing cultural representations. Arguably, some of the films mentioned above are already exhibiting transformative potential and we encourage future work to do the same.

In terms of methodological challenges, videography can be associated with the 'unconscious emotional manipulation' (Belk & Kozinets, 2005, pp. 133–134) of the audience, which is heightened by the visceral and sensory aspects of representation. This is particularly relevant within the context of consumer vulnerability given the potential for emotionally intense stories of illness, poverty, stigmatization and marginalization. Another key concern for researchers drawing on visual approaches is to ensure that visual interpretations and productions do not harm participants. When working with images associated with vulnerability, the potential for stigmatization is clear. For example, Fink and Lomax (2014) suggest that images of child poverty can become 'othered' because of the narrow, one-dimensional view they often depict. Images have a permanence and often resurface years after their original production when they are employed for different purposes. This points to another challenge related to the fluidity of interpretations. Again, Fink and Lomax's (2014) work on images of child poverty offers some useful advice. They suggest that semiotic readings of photographs must be combined with 'the structure of feeling in which photographs are produced.' In other words, analysis of images should not be divorced from broader cultural narratives and dominant discourses of the time as images 'become repositories for our own anxieties and those of society more broadly.'

Directions for future research

Future research can usefully borrow from critical marketers to develop a stronger critical voice for TCR and studies of consumer vulnerability (see Hein et al., 2016). For example, a program of research could be developed around poverty, consumerism and neoliberalism to explore economic disadvantage at the level of individual experience, with consideration of macro-social structuring forces.

In terms of telling stories, there is space for further researcher reflexivity in both our process and our publications (Bettany & Woodruffe-Burton, 2009). For example, if we acknowledge the gulfs and similarities between our experiences and those of our informants/participants we are better equipped to represent them.

In order to bridge some of the divide between academic merit and social impact we encourage journals, editors and reviewers to allow space in journal articles for authors to outline the value and impact of their research to the population (or phenomenon) under investigation. This is common practice in applying for research grants but is less commonly seen in published work. Allowing discussion of impact, even in highly theorized accounts, will encourage more researchers to consider the value of their work to the individuals who provide the data on which it is based.

A key aspect to the action research discussed here is the interventionist nature of this approach. This speaks directly to policy developments and interventions, and there are many possibilities for developing research projects in collaboration with practitioner engagement. The ongoing nature of the input of the participants in the community work, and also the ability to build in to the research design some longitudinal component, would be very appealing in contexts where there are deep and wide-reaching effects of a social problem. Examples might include programs aimed at improving access to healthy food in areas of economic deprivation; initiatives aimed at reducing alcohol consumption among vulnerable groups, for example underage drinkers; and financial services initiatives aimed at specific vulnerable groups, such as those living on low incomes. Such social problems would benefit from a comprehensive research approach, involving representation of community stakeholders in the evidence gathering about the design of change initiatives. Ultimately, such whole community action approaches are likely to lead to more impactful and meaningful results, with the power to effect change.

In terms of visual research, the study of representations of consumer vulnerability is in its infancy and there is much scope to further develop this line of inquiry. In particular, it would be useful to explore how various states of consumer vulnerability are represented in the media. We suggest that future marketing research could take inspiration from our colleagues in sociology and social sciences who have investigated the meanings of deprivation and disadvantage portrayed in media reporting (Fink & Lomax, 2014; Mooney, 2011). For example, Mooney (2011) discusses the sensationalist nature of 'poverty porn':

> Together with the expressions of middle class fear and distrust of poor people, there is also a fascination with poverty and the supposedly deviant lifestyles of those affected – where viewers are encouraged to find the worst and weakest moments of people's lives funny and entertaining. This is offered up for consumption on a wider, cross-class basis – yet it is clear that it reflects middle class antipathies and angst.
>
> *Mooney, 2011, p. 7*

Adopting a critical marketing perspective could add a welcome dimension to this debate – how are the consumption decisions of those experiencing vulnerability depicted? What do we learn about service interactions for consumers in poverty/other vulnerable states? How do these representations compare with existing theoretical perspectives? How do consumers understand and respond to these images? How do consumers experiencing vulnerability respond to these discourses?

Conclusion

The above has offered brief discussion of three less commonly seen methodologies that offer much value to the study of consumer vulnerability in terms of prioritizing the voices of consumers experiencing vulnerability. This chapter has particularly highlighted the significance of 'found' or secondary data, for example the use of documentary and autobiography, of visual and storied representations, and of working with participants to create change through action research. These approaches offer not just scope for insight but an opportunity to critically analyze and represent the wider ideologies and discourses that structure experiences of vulnerability in the marketplace.

Whether or not studies of vulnerability are by their nature *critical* is a matter for debate. Yet it is certainly true that studies of poverty, race, gender, class, illness and natural disaster critique norms, highlight ignorance and implicate wider market structures (Baker, 2009; Hamilton, 2012; Hill *et al*., 2015; Visconti, 2016). Yet a critical reading of extant representations of vulnerability might highlight that agentic assumptions are at work in much of our representations (Fitchett *et al*., 2014). The problem-solving orientation of many academics leads to papers that focus on how the vulnerable cope and are resilient, and in this we might be guilty of averting our gaze from the powerlessness of some consumers and the structuring forces that perpetuate disempowerment. Indeed, there is opportunity for studies of consumer vulnerability to more effectively contextualize the micro level experiences of vulnerability and consumer coping to consider meso and macro forces that structure the lives of consumers. We are not proposing a move away from the lived experience (Askegaard & Linnet, 2011), but recognizing the importance of the 'systemic and structuring influences of market and social systems' (p. 381). If, as Askegaard and Linnet (2011) suggest, research movements can be seen as a reaction to dominant paradigms, then studies of consumer vulnerability and TCR could do more to provide an alternative to the reflexive and agentic consumer.

References

Adichie, C. (2009). The Danger of the Single Story. *TED talk*. Retrieved July 20, 2018 from www.ted.com/talks/chimamanda_adichie_the_danger_of_a_single_story

Adkins, N.R., & Ozanne, J.L. (2005). The low literate consumer. *Journal of Consumer Research, 32*(1), 93–105.

Alvesson, M., & Sköldberg, K. (2000). *Reflexive methodology*. London, Sage.

Arnould, E.J., Price, L., & Moisio, R. (2006). Making contexts matter: Selecting research contexts for theoretical insights. In R.W. Belk (Ed.), *Handbook of qualitative research methods in marketing* (pp. 106–125). London, Edward Elgar.

Askegaard, S., & Linnet, J.T. (2011). Towards an epistemology of consumer culture theory: Phenomenology and the context of context. *Marketing Theory, 11*(4), 381–404.

Baker, S.M. (2009). Vulnerability and resilience in natural disasters: A marketing and public policy perspective. *Journal of Public Policy and Marketing, 28*(Spring), 114–123.

Baker, S.M., & Mason, M. (2012). Towards a process theory of consumer vulnerability and resilience: Illuminating its transformative potential. In D.G. Mick, S. Pettigrew, C. Pechmann & J.L. Ozanne (Eds.), *Transformative consumer research for personal and collective well-being* (pp. 543–563). Abingdon, Taylor & Francis.

Baker, S.M., Gentry, J.W., & Rittenburg, T.L. (2005). Building understanding of the domain of consumer vulnerability. *Journal of Macromarketing, 25*(2), 128–139.

Baker, S.M., LaBarge, M., & Baker, C.N. (2016). On consumer vulnerability: Foundations, phenomena, and future investigations. In K. Hamilton, S. Dunnett & M. Piacentini (Eds.), *Consumer vulnerability: Conditions, contexts and characteristics* (pp. 13–30). London, Routledge.

Baskerville, R.L., & Wood-Harper, A.T. (1996). A critical perspective on action research as a method for information systems research. *Journal of Information Technology, 11*(3), 235–246.

Belk, R.W., & Kozinets, R.V. (2005). Videography in marketing and consumer research. *Qualitative Market Research: An International Journal, 8*(2), 128–141.

Bettany, S., & Woodruffe-Burton, H. (2009). Working the limits of method: The possibilities of critical reflexive practice in marketing and consumer research. *Journal of Marketing Management, 25*(7–8), 661–679.

Beudaert, A., Gorge, H., & Herbert, M. (2017). An exploration of servicescape exclusion and coping strategies of consumers with 'hidden' auditory disorders. *Journal of Services Marketing, 31*(4/5), 326–338.

Botti, S., Broniarczyk, S., Häubl, G., Hill, R., Huang, Y., Kahn, B., et al. (2008). Choice under restrictions. *Marketing Letters, 19*(3–4), 183–199.

Bradshaw, A., & Fırat, A.F. (2007). Rethinking critical marketing. In M. Saren, P. Maclaran, C. Goulding, R. Elliott, A. Shankar & M. Catterall (Eds.), *Critical marketing: Defining the field* (pp. 30–43). Oxford, Elsevier.

Brown, S. (2005). I can read you like a book! Novel thoughts on consumer behavior. *Qualitative Market Research: An International Journal, 8*(2), 219–237.

Burawoy, M. (1998). The extended case method. *Sociological Theory, 16*(1), 5–33.

Caldwell, M., & Henry, H. (2009). A right to life: Reducing maternal death and morbidity in Pakistan. In S.R. Vaidyanathan & D. Chakravarti (Eds.), *Asia-Pacific advances in consumer research, Volume 8* (pp. 121–121). Duluth, MN, Association for Consumer Research.

Caldwell, M., Kleppe, I., & Watson, S. (2010). *Talk the walk, walk the talk*. Film presented at the *Association for Consumer Research ACR Annual North American Conference*, Jacksonville, United States.

Canniford, R. (2012). Poetic witness: Marketplace research through poetic transcription and poetic contexts for translation. *Marketing Theory, 12*(4), 391–409.

Cartwright, P. (2015). Understanding and protecting vulnerable financial consumers. *Journal of Consumer Policy, 38*(2), 119–138.

Chase, E., & Walker, R. (2016). Poverty, shame and the vulnerable consumer. In K. Hamilton, S. Dunnett & M. Piacentini (Eds.), *Consumer vulnerability: Conditions, contexts and characteristics* (pp. 198–208). London, Routledge.

Chatzidakis, A., & Maclaran, P. (2016). *Skoros: Anti-consumption in crisis*. Retrieved March 1, 2017 from www.youtube.com/watch?v=z8fAmi0mHgA

Clandinin, D.J., & Connelly, F.M. (2000). *Narrative inquiry*. San Francisco, Jossey-Bass.

Clough, R. (2015). Older people: Citizens in a consumer society. In K. Hamilton, S. Dunnett & M. Piacentini (Eds.), *Consumer vulnerability: Conditions, contexts and characteristics* (pp. 130–141). London, Routledge.

Coleman, C. (2016). Justice in injustice, power in vulnerability: The dialogic potential of the uncondemned. In K. Hamilton, S. Dunnett & M. Piacentini (Eds.), *Consumer vulnerability: Conditions, contexts and characteristics* (pp. 43–54). London, Routledge.

Crockett, D., & Wallendorf, M. (2004). The role of normative political ideology in consumer behavior. *Journal of Consumer Research, 31*(3), 511–528.

Dey, P.K., Bhattacharya, A., & Ho, W. (2015). Strategic supplier performance evaluation: A case-based action research of a UK manufacturing organization. *International Journal of Production Economics, 166*(August), 192–214.

Dick, B. (2000). *A beginner's guide to action research*. Retrieved March 4, 2017 from www.aral.com.au/resources/guide.html

Downey, H. (2016). Poetic inquiry, consumer vulnerability: Realities or quadriplegia. *Journal of Marketing Management, 32*(3–4), 357–364.

Dunnett, S., Hamilton, K., & Piacentini, M. (2016). Consumer vulnerability: Introduction to the special issue. *Journal of Marketing Management, 32*(3–4), 207–210.

Edwards-Groves, C., & Kemmis, S. (2016). Pedagogy, education and praxis: Understanding new forms of intersubjectivity through action research and practice theory. *Educational Action Research, 24*(1), 77–96.

Feenstra, C.F.J., Backhaus, J., & Heiskanen, E. (2009). How to change consumers' energy related behavior? Improving demand side management programs via and action research approach. *First European Conference on Energy Efficiency and Behavior*.

Fink, J., & Lomax, H. (2014). Challenging images? Dominant, residual and emergent meanings in on-line media representations of child poverty. *Journal for the Study of British Cultures, 1*(21), 79–95.

Fitchett, J.A., Patsiaouras, G., & Davies, A. (2014). Myth and ideology in consumer culture theory. *Marketing Theory, 14*(4), 495–506.

Gentry, J.W., Kennedy, P.F., Paul, K., & Hill, R.P. (1994). The vulnerability of those grieving the death of a loved one: Implications for public policy. *Journal of Public Policy & Marketing, 14*(Fall), 128–142.

Griffith, A.J. (1998). Insider/outsider: Epistemological privilege and mothering work. *Human Studies, 21*(4), 361–376.

Hamilton, K. (2012). Low-income families and coping through brands: Inclusion or stigma? *Sociology, 46*(1), 76–92.

Hamilton, K., Dunnett, S., & Piacentini, S. (2016). *Consumer vulnerability: Conditions, contexts and characteristics*. London, Routledge.

Hamilton, K., Piacentini, M.G., Banister, E., Barrios, A., Blocker, C.P., Coleman, C.A., et al. (2014). Poverty in consumer culture: Towards a transformative social representation. *Journal of Marketing Management, 30*(17–18), 1833–1857.

Hein, W., Steinfield, L., Ourahmoune, N., Coleman, C.A., Tuncay Zayer, L., & Littlefield, J. (2016). Gender justice and the market: A transformative consumer research perspective. *Journal of Public Policy & Marketing, 35*(2), 223–236.

Hietanen, J., Rokka, J., & Schouten, J.W. (2014). Commentary on Schembri and Boyle (2013): From representation towards expression in videographic consumer research. *Journal of Business Research, 67*(9), 2019–2022.

Hill, R.P. (1995). Researching sensitive topics in marketing: The special case of vulnerable populations. *Journal of Public Policy and Marketing, 14*(1), 143–148.

Hill, R.P. (2001). *Surviving in a material world: The lived experience of poverty*. Notre Dame, IN, University of Notre Dame Press.

Hill, R.P. (2005). Special issue on vulnerable consumers. *Journal of Macromarketing, 25*(2), 215–218.

Hill, R.P. (2016). Poverty as we never knew it: THE source of vulnerability for most of humankind. *Journal of Marketing Management, 32*(3–4), 365–370.

Hill, R.P., & Stamey, M. (1990). The homeless in America: An examination of possessions and consumption behaviors. *Journal of Consumer Research, 17*(December), 303–321.

Hill, R.P., Cunningham, D., & the Gramercy Gentlemen (2016). Dehumanization and restriction inside a maximum security prison: Novel insights about consumer acquisition and ownership. *Journal of the Association for Consumer Research, 1*(2), 295–313.

Hill, R.P., Rapp, J.M., & Capella, M.L. (2015). Consumption restriction in a total control institution: Participatory action research in a maximum security prison. *Journal of Public Policy & Marketing, 34*(2), 156–172.

Jafari, A., Dunnett, S., Hamilton, K., & Downey, H. (2013). Exploring researcher vulnerability: Contexts, complications and conceptualisation. *Journal of Marketing Management, 29*(9–10), 1182–1200.

Jansson, A. (2002). The mediatization of consumption: Towards an analytical framework of image culture. *Journal of Consumer Culture, 2*(1), 5–31.

Kaufman-Scarborough, C. (1999). Reasonable access for mobility-disabled persons is more than widening the door. *Journal of Retailing, 75*(4), 479–508.

Kazeminia, A., Del Chiappa, G., & Jafari, J. (2015). Seniors' travel constraints and their coping strategies. *Journal of Travel Research, 54*(1), 80–93.

Kidd, S., Kenny, A., & McKinstry, C. (2014). From experience to action in recovery-oriented mental health practice: A first person inquiry. *Action Research, 12*(4), 357–373.

Ladkin, D. (2007). Action research. In C. Seale, G. Gobo, J. Gubrium & D. Silverman (Eds.), *Qualitative research practice* (pp. 478–490). London, Sage.

Lewin, K. (1951). *Field theory in social sciences*. New York, Harper & Row.

Mick, D.G. (2008). Introduction: The moment and place for a special issue. *Journal of Consumer Research, 35*(3), 377–379.

Moisander, J., Valtonen, A., & Hirsto, H. (2009). Personal interviews in cultural consumer research: Post-structuralist challenges. *Consumption Markets & Culture, 12*(4), 329–348.

Mooney, G. (2011). *@Stigmatising poverty? The 'broken society' and reflections on anti-welfarism in the UK today*. Oxford, Oxfam.

Morgan, F.W., Schuler, D.K., & Stoltman, J.J. (1995). A framework for examining the legal status of vulnerable consumers. *Journal of Public Policy and Marketing, 14*(2), 267–277.

Moscovici, S. (1984). The myth of the lonely paradigm: A rejoinder. *Social Research, 51*(4), 939–967.

Nyman, V., Berg, M., Downe, S., & Bondas, T. (2016). Insider action research as an approach and a method: Exploring institutional encounters from within a birthing context. *Action Research, 14*(2), 217–233.

O'Donohoe, S. (2016). Consuming childhood grief. In K. Hamilton, S. Dunnett & M. Piacentini (Eds.), *Consumer vulnerability: Conditions, contexts and characteristics* (pp. 89–102). London, Routledge.

Ozanne, J.L., & Anderson, L. (2010). Community action research. *Journal of Public Policy & Marketing, 29*(1), 123–137.

Ozanne, J.L., & Saatcioglu, B. (2008). Participatory action research. *Journal of Consumer Research, 35*(3), 423–439.

Ozanne, J.L., Hill, R.P., & Wright, N.D. (1998). Juvenile delinquents' use of consumption as cultural resistance: Implications for juvenile reform programs and public policy. *Journal of Public Policy & Marketing, 17*(2), 185–196.

Ozanne, L.K., & Ozanne, J.L. (2011). A child's right to play: The social construction of civic virtues in toy libraries. *Journal of Public Policy & Marketing, 30*(2), 264–278.

Payne, G., & Williams, M. (2005). Generalization in qualitative research. *Sociology, 39*(2), 295–314.

Piacentini, M., Hibbert, S.A., & Hogg, M. (2014). Consumer resource integration amongst vulnerable consumers: Care leavers in transition to independent living. *Journal of Marketing Management, 30*(1–2), 201–219.

Saatcioglu, B., & Ozanne, J.L. (2013). A critical spatial approach to marketplace exclusion and inclusion. *Journal of Public Policy in Marketing, 32*(Special Issue), 32–37.

Sajovic, E., & Kenningham, D. (2014). *The roles we play: Recognising the contribution of people in poverty*. London, ATD Fourth World.

Sayre, S. (1994). Possessions and identity in crisis: Meaning and change for victims of the Oakland Firestorm. In C.T. Allen & D. Roedder John (Eds.), *Advances in consumer research, Volume 21* (pp. 109–114). Provo, UT, Association for Consumer Research.

Schroeder, J.E. (2007). Critical marketing: Insights for informed research and teaching. In M. Saren, P. Maclaran, C. Goulding, R. Elliott, A. Shankar & M. Catterall (Eds.), *Critical marketing: Defining the field* (pp. 18–29). Oxford, Elsevier.

Sherry, J.F., & Schouten, J.W. (2002). A role for poetry in consumer research. *Journal of Consumer Research, 29*(2), 218–234.

Smith, N.C., & Cooper-Martin, E. (1997). Ethics and target marketing: The role of product harm and consumer vulnerability. *Journal of Marketing, 61*(July), 1–20.

Stearn, J. (2016). Consumer vulnerability is market failure. In K. Hamilton, S. Dunnett & M. Piacentini (Eds.), *Consumer vulnerability: Conditions, contexts and characteristics* (pp. 66–76). London, Routledge.

Stone, T., & Gould, S.J. (2016). Vulnerable consumers in the 'fourth age': Theoretical reflections upon the case of Sandra Bem. *Journal of Marketing Management, 32*(3/4), 386–392.

Tadajewski, M. (2010). Critical marketing studies: Logical empiricism, 'critical performativity' and marketing practice. *Marketing Theory, 10*(2), 210–222.

Turley, D. (2015). Asking for trouble: Some reflections on researching bereaved consumers. In K. Hamilton, S. Dunnett & M. Piacentini (Eds.), *Consumer vulnerability: Conditions, contexts and characteristics* (pp. 55–65). London, Routledge.

Turley, D., & O'Donohoe, S. (2012). The sadness of lives and the comfort of things: Goods as evocative objects in bereavement. *Journal of Marketing Management, 28*(11/12), 1331–1353.

Veer, E. (2014). 'I'm struggling': Men's stories of mental illness. In J. Cotte & S. Wood (Eds.), *Advances in consumer research, Volume 42* (pp. 758–758). Duluth, MN, Association for Consumer Research.

Visconti, L. (2016). A conversational approach to consumer vulnerability: Performativity, representations, and storytelling. *Journal of Marketing Management, 32*(3–4), 371–385.

Wansink, B. (2012). Activism research: Designing transformative lab and field studies. In D.G. Mick, S. Pettigrew, C.C. Pechmann & J.L. Ozanne (Eds.), *Transformative consumer research for personal and collective well-being* (pp. 67–88). London, Routledge.

Wijland, R. (2011). Anchors, mermaids, shower-curtain seaweeds and fish-shaped fish: The texture of poetic agency. *Marketing Theory, 11*(2), 127–141.

23
THE EMBODIED CONSUMER

Maurice Patterson

Introduction

> While much of the people's time is devoted to economic pursuits, a large part of the fruits of these labours and a considerable portion of the day are spent in ritual activity. The focus of this activity is the human body, the appearance and health of which loom as a dominant concern in the ethos of the people.
>
> Miner, 1956, p. 503

Miner's coded description of the American populace in the 1950s reminds us of the central position occupied by our bodies in our everyday lives. As consumers, we have become obsessed with our bodies; grooming them, clothing them, beautifying them, and even modifying them in various ways. For their part, marketers offer countless products and services designed to aid us in these endeavors, they utilize the representation of bodies, both male and female, as rhetorical tools in advertising (Patterson & Elliott, 2002; Schroeder & Zwick, 2004), and, relatedly, they encourage us to attend to, manage, and care for our bodies through the prudent use of commodities. It is something of a surprise then that marketing and consumer research have been relatively slow to tackle the body as a core issue even though such a deficit was identified by Joy and Venkatesh (1994, p. 338) over 20 years ago:

> While academic consumer researchers were ignoring the body completely, the marketing industry was making billions of dollars by selling products closely tied to it and, ultimately, by selling the body itself as the central concept of contemporary life.

The lack of attention paid to bodies in marketing and consumer research owes much to the limited scrutiny of consumption activities beyond purchase, the dominance of the machine and container metaphors within consumer research, and the mind/body dualism on which these metaphors depend (Patterson & Elliott, 2002). The positioning of consumers as information processors within mainstream marketing and consumer research sees them treated as though they were machines, collecting information, processing that information and then acting upon it. Such machines "act but do not emote; they make decisions but do not feel the consequences.

When the machine metaphor is used to characterise human beings, we risk losing sight of the other significant aspects of being human" (Hirschman, 1993, p. 544). This machine metaphor is further supported by the use of the container metaphor in which the body is treated as nothing more than a container for the mind and the mind is where symbolic representations of the external world are brought into consciousness (Thompson et al., 1989).

Of particular significance to our treatment of the topic within consumer research then are the distinctions drawn between the mind and the body. A major outcome of Cartesian thought has been the conjunction of humanity and the rational mind (Burkitt, 1999) and thus the information processing school of thought continues to dominate consumer research. For example, such an approach continues to evidence itself in accounts of thinking style in consumer decision making (see Monga & John, 2007; Novak & Hoffman, 2009; Gershoff & Koehler, 2011). In contrast, the body is deemed to be corrupt and flawed, and protecting and sustaining it requires the intervention of rationality acting through science and technology (Hirschman, 1990). For instance, there has been a wealth of research that addresses the use of cosmetic surgery to fix the body's flaws (see Schouten, 1991; Askegaard et al., 2002; Mowen et al., 2009). Thus, Hirschman (1993) and Thompson et al. (1989) both highlight the problematic nature of relegating the body to the shadows. Of course, bodies have not been completely absent from the story of consumption, but, following Shilling (2012) might be considered more of an *absent presence*, for "reason is not the whole story ... in order to establish rationality, there must be a contrast with the irrational" (Longhurst, 1995, p. 99).

It might be reasonable to expect that ever since work on experiential consumption emerged (Holbrook & Hirschman, 1982; Hirschman & Holbrook, 1982), embodiment might have garnered greater attention within consumer research. After all, Hirschman and Holbrook (1982, p. 92) define hedonic consumption as "those facets of consumer behavior that relate to the multisensory, fantasy and emotive aspects of one's experience with products", thereby acknowledging the central role played by the body in terms of sensory modalities and the physiological dimensions of emotion. Nonetheless, in the wake of this work the body continued to be relegated to the periphery of consumer research discourse. For example, one early acknowledgment of the body in consumer research comes from Dennis Rook's (1987) account of the buying impulse. While Rook lavishes most attention on the psychological aspects of impulse purchasing, he is careful to note that many impulses are 'biochemically stimulated'. Indeed, some of his informants describe 'tingling sensations', 'warm feelings', 'hot flashes', 'surges of energy' and 'goosebumps' (Rook, 1987, p. 194). In the end, though, Rook cautions against the possible negative consequences of behavior that combines both somatic responses and irrationality, and in later work (Rook & Fisher, 1995) suggests "trait tendencies and normative influences mediate impulsive actions, so that rationality prevails" (Joy & Sherry, 2003, p. 261).

In this chapter, then, I work to establish embodiment as a core concern of consumer research and, thus, to draw an outline of what we might call the embodied consumer. To this end I address the question of what it means to talk about *the body*, doing so by fleshing out our ideas around the natural body, the socially constructed body, and the lived body. Next, I get to grips with two key theorists who have shaped scholarly understanding of embodiment and who are becoming ever more influential on the topic in consumer research. Specifically, I delineate the work of Maurice Merleau-Ponty in respect of his concepts of the *intentional arc* and the *corporeal schema*, and the output of Pierre Bourdieu as it relates to *habitus, field* and *capital*. Finally, I direct my attention to the treatment of *the body* within consumer research around three key themes: bodies of/in representation, the body project, and the agency of bodies.

The body

What does it mean to talk of *the body*? Ontologically we can approach the body from naturalistic, social constructionist, and lived perspectives. The *natural body* is a biological body that provides the foundation for social relations, hierarchies and inequalities (Burkitt, 1999; Shilling, 2012; Williams & Bendelow, 1998). For example, women's biological experiences of menstruation highlight the obdurate physicality of the body (Frank, 1991). But such experiences are also used to erode the position of women in society through suggestions of how their volatile and unstable bodies constantly threaten to overwhelm their 'fragile' minds. Indeed, until recent years, arguments about how Pre-Menstrual Tension drove women 'out of their minds' were used to prevent them becoming pilots in Australia and bank managers in the U.S. (Shilling, 2012). In a similar vein, work within consumer research that draws on evolutionary psychology uses experiments to contend that female fertility impacts on choices for products related to physical appearance (Durante et al., 2011), promotes variety seeking behavior (Durante & Arsena, 2015), and powers the drive for positional goods to help improve social standing (Durante et al., 2014) (see also Tadajewski, this volume).

The *socially constructed body*, in contrast, "holds that instead of being the foundation of society, the character and meanings attributed to the body, and the boundaries which exist between the bodies of different groups of people, are social products" (Shilling, 2012, p. 75). Thus, Conrad and Barker (2010) draw a distinction between diseases, as biological conditions, and illnesses, as the meanings attributed to those conditions, meanings that are shaped by cultural and social systems. In this way, menstruation, an everyday experience for women, becomes medicalized and is deemed to require intervention in the form of hormone therapy or even surgery (Howson, 2013). Within the consumer research domain, the slipperiness associated with the social construction of the body has been addressed in the consideration of media representations of the pregnant body (O'Malley, 2006), expert systems and the promotion of medically managed childbirth (Thompson, 2005), and the encroachment by the institutions of consumer culture on the spaces of pregnancy and beyond such that they demand particular types of postpartum bodies (O'Malley & Patterson, 2013).

Accounts of the body as socially constructed are driven largely by poststructuralist interests populated by what Grosz (1994, p. xiii) labels "theorists of corporeal inscription". These interests position the body "as a text of cultural meaning [that] offers important insights into the cultural underpinnings of consumers' desires" (Thompson & Hirschman, 1995, p. 140). As a reaction against modernism and Cartesianism, poststructuralism brings the body back into focus. According to Williams and Bendelow (1998, p. 135), poststructuralism "abandon[s] any notion of a core-abiding subjectivity and instead seek[s] to celebrate the corporeal intimacies and affective dimensions of social life". However, such interests tend to be cerebral, esoteric and ultimately disembodied (Davis, 1997). Burkitt (1999, p. 2) stridently argues:

> Discursive constructionism . . . has difficulties in dealing with human embodiment and also, therefore, with the multi-dimensional way in which we experience reality . . . we are not just located in the world symbolically; nor do we experience reality purely through the text . . . embodied persons are not simply constructs, but are productive bodies . . . communicative bodies . . . powerful bodies [and] thinking bodies.

In other words, a socially constructed approach effectively neglects the material dimensions of the body and its experience in the world, neglects its corporeality and its agency (Ussher, 1997).

Materiality matters in that the physical corporeality of the body makes certain kinds of experience and activity possible while preventing others. Thus, although discursive theories have helped to foreground interest in the body, their ability to adequately deal with the active role played by our bodies remains limited.

This leads us to notions of the *lived body* that bring to the fore the tensions between 'having' and 'being' a body (Lyon & Barbalet, 1994). For McNay (1999, p. 98):

> The body is the threshold through which the subject's lived experience of the world is incorporated and realised and, as such, is neither pure object nor pure subject. It is not pure object since it is the place of one's engagement with the world. Nor is it pure subject in that there is always a material residue that resists incorporation into dominant symbolic schema.

Paterson and Hughes (1999) show how the very limitations of the discursive approach to the body underline the strengths of the more phenomenological standpoint encapsulated in the lived body. They draw on Turner (1994, p. 46) who contends that the lived body "consists essentially in processes of self-productive activity, at once subjective and objective, meaningful and material, personal and social, an agent that produces discourses as well as receiving them". Consumer researchers are beginning to attend to the lived body across a wide range of contexts including the experience of ethnicity (Dion et al., 2011), the body work engaged in by salsa dancers (Hewer & Hamilton, 2010), and the exploration of an affective subjectivity that emerges in the immediate enjoyment of the world around us (Joy et al., 2010).

Taking these issues into consideration, we might begin to develop our understanding of the body as the meeting place of the physical, the symbolic and the sociological (Slutskaya & De Cock, 2008), and in bringing all these bodies together we might also move discussion away from bodies per se and toward *embodiment*, the manner by which we engage with and perceive the world (Abercrombie et al., 2000), "bridging phenomenological dimensions of the body and its situatedness ... existing at the confluence of sentience and sensation, regulation and active agency" (Tulle, 2007, p. 331). Our consideration of embodiment, rather than merely *the body*, points us toward the work of two key theorists in the field; Maurice Merleau-Ponty who exposes the nature of embodiment by focusing in on processes of perception, and Pierre Bourdieu who establishes embodiment within the idea of practice (Csordas, 1990). Merleau-Ponty's approach to the body was both groundbreaking and philosophically important (Bullington, 2013), while Chris Shilling (2004, p. 473) has referred to the work of Bourdieu as "a powerful vision of corporeal sociology."

Merleau-Ponty

> The life of consciousness - cognitive life, the life of desire or perceptual life - is subtended by an 'intentional arc' which projects round about us our past, our future, our human setting, our physical, ideological and moral situation.
>
> *Merleau-Ponty, 1962, p. 136*

Merleau-Ponty takes the Cartesian perspective on the body to task, believing the body to be the means by which we perceive the world and give it meaning (Paterson & Hughes, 1999; Styhre, 2004). He attempts to transcend the dichotomy between mind and body by introducing the concept of the body-subject (Purser, 2011) which operates as the foundation for human subjectivity (Crossley, 1995); the ground level of all knowledge (Paterson & Hughes, 1999). In so doing, Merleau-Ponty focuses attention on purposive human activity (Crossley, 2007) set in relation to a world of objects and relationships (Dion et al., 2011; de Waal Malefyt & McCabe, 2016). Consciousness, then, amounts to the body projecting itself into that world (Csordas, 1990): "Merleau-Ponty views the 'mental' aspects of the human agent as emergent properties arising out of the total structure of the organism and/in its environment" (Crossley, 2001a, p. 320).

For Merleau-Ponty the body-subject is not a static construction. Rather, embodiment captures the essence of an active engagement with the world in the present and the potential for action into the future (Purser, 2011). In addressing these issues further, Merleau-Ponty introduces the notions of the *intentional arc* and the *corporeal schema*. The intentional arc describes the relationship between the body-subject and the various objects and situations in the world around it (Chan, 2005; Dreyfus & Dreyfus, 1999). As skills are developed to cope with these objects and situations they are stored in the body as dispositions in the corporeal schema; that is, in structures of behavior (Crossley, 2001a) or bodily know-how and practical sense (Ball, 2005; Crossley, 2001b). These dispositions, in turn, represent a proneness to respond to even more refined objects and situations in the future (Dreyfus & Dreyfus, 1999). Thus, the intentional arc embodies the interrelatedness between perception, skilful action, and the intentions of individuals (Chan, 2005; Dant & Wheaton, 2007). Further, there are three levels of embodiment that determine the degree to which objects and situations present themselves to us: innate structures, general acquired skills and specific cultural skills (Dreyfus, 1996). Innate structures incorporate the size, shape and capacities of the body and these have a part to play in determining the possibilities for action (Chan, 2005). For example, the very physicality of our bodies influences the possibilities we see in terms of taking things from particular shelves in the supermarket; the highest shelves are simply not an option for some of us. General acquired skills are honed through exposure to various objects and situations. As such, the ability to drive a car will evolve over repeated interactions with the automobile itself, driving lessons, an instructor, and experience on the road. Finally, specific cultural skills, such as playing Irish traditional music on the fiddle, may be nuanced based on the particular cultural setting and require the body-subject to act appropriately to each specific cultural setting (Joy & Sherry, 2003). While the fiddle is identical to the violin it is played differently in a vast range of regional styles each of which calls upon the body-subject to make use of skills in a culturally appropriate manner. In respect of motivation, there might be no explicit goal or intention on the part of the body-subject (Joy & Sherry, 2003) other than to maintain the optimum equilibrium in the body–environment relation (Yakhlef, 2010): "Part of that experience is a sense that when one's situation deviates from some optimal body-environment relationship, one's motion takes one closer to that optimum and thereby relieves the 'tension' of the deviation" (Dreyfus, 1996, n.p.).

The notion of the corporeal schema encapsulates the extent to which our skilful activities come to be a part of us (Crossley, 2001a). In actively engaging with the world about us we develop a pre-reflective grasp both on our bodies and on our environment relative to our bodies such that we come to 'know without knowing'. In respect of our bodies, for example, we might engage with singing to such an extent that it becomes second nature and we no longer have to think about singing in the traditional sense, we just develop a feel for it. Similarly, in learning to play a musical instrument such as the guitar, the necessary skills may be incorporated into the corporeal schema such that their deployment becomes pre-reflective "where the thinking is in the feel developed for the instrument, rather than in any abstract thought about it" (Burkitt, 1999, p. 76) and in this manner the object and its use become an extension of the body (Crossley, 2001b). Crossley (2007, p. 89) further suggests that newly developed skills might be transferable to other similar domains though such transferability has limits: "We learn certain principles of use and these are transferable but acquisition of new principles may involve significant relearning."

Bourdieu

> The habitus fulfils a function which another philosophy consigns to a transcendental conscience: it is a socialised body. A structured body, a body which has incorporated the immanent structures of a world or of a particular sector of that world – a field – and which structures the perception of that world as well as action in that world.
>
> Bourdieu, 1998, p. 81

Bourdieu shares Merleau-Ponty's interest in the embodiment of experience and extends it to incorporate the reproduction of social fields (de Waal Malefyt & McCabe, 2016; Shilling, 2001). Bourdieu mobilizes the concepts of *habitus, field* and *capital* to outline a theory of embodied practice that seeks to negotiate the troublesome dynamic between structure and agency (Crossley, 2001b; Tulle, 2007): "for Bourdieu the socially informed body is the 'principle generating and unifying all practices,' and consciousness is a form of strategic calculation fused with a system of objective potentialities" (Csordas, 1990, p. 8). Bourdieu's habitus is a form of embodied skill or knowledge acquired through habituation (Gerrans, 2005), and that often unconsciously dictates an individual's action. For their part, fields are "the key arenas in which actors compete for placement in the social hierarchy through acquisition of the statuses distinctive to the field" (Holt, 1998, p. 4). Fields are heterogeneous and, as such, each is governed by its own rules and value system (Entwistle, 2009). The habitus, then, is deployed within a field in an effort to act successfully according to the rules of the field. Success lends the individual some cultural capital – "the sedimented knowledge and competence to make judgements of taste acquired through expenditure of time and money on such unproductive matters" (Jagger, 2000, p. 51) – which can then be mobilized in the competition for cultural authority within the field.

The habitus incorporates bodily hexis, which refers to the way we hold, move and use our bodies (Dion *et al.*, 2011; Sweetman, 2009): "the socially inscribed manner in which individuals carry themselves" (Williams, 1995, p. 586). Thus, even the ways in which we mobilize our bodies in everyday life is a product of our social upbringing:

> Cumulative exposure to certain social conditions instils in individuals an ensemble of durable and transposable dispositions that internalise the necessities of the extant social environment, inscribing inside the organism the patterned inertia and constraints of external reality.
>
> Bourdieu & Wacquant, 1992, p. 13

But because the habitus is transposable, it does also allow for some agency on the part of the individual. While it encourages us to act in particular ways determined by the field, it also leaves space for some improvisation and strategic maneuvering (Crossley, 2001b). For example, Wacquant (1995, p. 67) describes how the pugilist's body is simultaneously the product of his upbringing and training to date, the raw material to be worked upon further, and his means of production:

> Properly managed, this body is capable of producing more value than was "sunk" in it. But for that it is necessary for the fighter to know its intrinsic limits, to expand its sensorimotor powers, and to resocialise its physiology in accordance with the specific requirement and temporality of the game. In addition, the fighter's body is a system of

signs, a symbolic quilt that he must learn to decipher in order to better enhance and protect it, but also to attack it. For what is unique about boxing is that the boxer's body is both the weapon of assault and the target to be destroyed.

Habitus, then, represents an individual's feel for the game within a particular field. It is supported by the *illusio* or belief in the game (Crossley, 2001a) such that there is a felt connection between the habitus and underlying ideologies of certain fields. This connection grants the individual greater capacity to belong to, to act within, and to admire the activities and objects of particular fields over others. Against this backdrop, consumption can be viewed as embodied agency with a field (Styhre, 2004): "the habitus organizes how one classifies the universe of consumption objects to which one is exposed, constructing desire toward consecrated objects and disgust toward objects that are not valued in the field" (Holt, 1998, p. 4).

Individuals deploy a range of capitals within the fields to which they are bound (Holliday & Cairnie, 2007, p. 63). These capitals include, for example, cultural capital, economic capital, symbolic capital, social capital and embodied capital. With regard to embodied capital, bodies may be ascribed exchange-value within a social field. Thus, bodily attributes, such as sporting ability or aesthetic qualities, are ascribed certain value and function as capital (Crossley, 2001c), which might be subsequently converted to economic, cultural and social capital. Moreover, this value grows as those bodies move closer to a social field's normalized ideals (Featherstone, 1991). Thus, we are persuaded to devote our energies to improving our bodies and maximizing our exchange-value.

Embodiment in consumer research

In addressing the body, consumer researchers have relied rather heavily on theories of corporeal inscription. In particular, scholars have devoted much attention to the representation of bodies in advertising and the media, the interpretive repertoires utilized by consumers in making sense of such representations, and the likely effect of these representations on the bodies of consumers. In this sense, scholars in consumer research have been relatively poor at incorporating the ideas around embodiment espoused by Merleau-Ponty and Bourdieu, though such work is beginning to appear with increasing frequency. Beyond the representational focus, some researchers have considered the close alignment between the body and identity and thus have honed in on the notion of the body project. More recently, a small corpus of research work has begun to address the lived agentic body and embodiment as part of the move toward practice-based perspectives (Valtonen, 2013) and sensory ethnography (Valtonen et al., 2010). It is in these two areas in particular that we are most likely to see the influence of Merleau-Ponty and Bourdieu.

Bodies of/in representation

The institutions of consumer culture are deeply implicated in our embodiment in that marketers have always profited from the sale of products and services associated with our bodies (Joy & Venkatesh, 1994), and indeed the successful management of our bodies requires the intervention of a range of marketplace commodities from dental implants (Tepper et al., 2003) to hair removal creams (Frank, 2014), and fake tans (Kemp & Eagle, 2009) to vitamin supplements (Nichter & Thompson, 2006). In the process, representations are said to objectify bodies (Jhally, 2009) such that they are seen as subject to the gaze (Patterson & Elliott, 2002; Patterson et al.,

2009; Schroeder & Zwick, 2004), as symbols for consumption objects and thus exchangeable with those objects (Schroeder & Zwick, 2004), as fragmented collections of component parts (Schroeder & Borgerson, 1998), and as things to be used (Patterson et al., 2009). Moreover, marketing communications are primarily responsible for the constitution of body ideals (Dittmar, 2007; Ostberg, 2010): they disavow the complexity of lived embodied experience (Gurrieri et al., 2013); they promote the latest version of the body beautiful (Patterson et al., 2009; Woodruffe-Burton & Ireland, 2012); they encourage consumers to be "actively concerned about the management, maintenance and appearance of their bodies" (Shilling, 2012, p. 7); and they teach consumers how to work toward the idealized bodies they covet (Finkelstein, 1997).

In accessing the reaction of audiences to advertising's depictions of bodies, early work (e.g. Peterson & Kerin, 1977; Simpson et al., 1996) employs a series of experiments to determine the effects on attitudes. Much research contends that idealized representations of bodies in advertising and the media might cause consumers to engage in social comparison (Phillips, 2005; Richins, 1991), experience negative body images, feelings of insecurity, diminished self-confidence (Grogan et al., 1996) with possible long-term health implications (Martin & Gentry, 1997). Many such studies continue to assume, despite the weight of critical evidence, that advertising is a linear communication process in which audiences understand and acknowledge messages uniformly and uncritically. In truth, as Bulmer and Buchanan-Oliver (2004, p. 2) contend: "different audiences bring different cultural competencies to their readings [of advertising] and not everyone employs the same codes in interpreting communication". Indeed, Thompson and Hirschman (1995, p. 151) move beyond the rather one-dimensional conceptualization of body image to consider the socialized body, where:

> a complex cultural ideology of the body underlies consumers' satisfaction with their appearance, their sense of an ideal or more desirable body, and the consumption activities that these self-perceptions motivate. This cultural ideology is concretely manifested through mass media, advertising, everyday beliefs, scientific pronouncements, interpersonal relationships, and the course of social encounters. These social influences all exert a shaping influence on the ways individuals interpret the symbolic meanings of the body and the multitude of attributions about self and others that follow from these interpretations.

Moreover, Currie (1997) challenges the understanding of advertising as a gender script, whereby "bad images produce bad attitudes and behaviors" (Walters, 1995, p. 3, cited in Currie, 1997, p. 456). As such, gendered bodies are an everyday accomplishment mediated by advertising discourses but not necessarily determined by them.

Thus, a more fruitful avenue has been the inclusion of reader response analyses of body-related advertising. For example, Phillips (2005) indicates how responses to body-related representations can vary not only across a range of consumers, but also individual consumers can exhibit a range of different responses depending on the context. She demonstrates how advertising and the media use depictions of what bodies might become, focus on physical appearance, make use of fit bodies, and actively promote fun and self-understanding through the body in an effort to appeal to the disciplined body, the mirroring body, the dominating body, and the communicative body (Frank, 1991). Rokka et al. (2008, p. 87) further describe a complex relationship with advertising, highlighting tensions between local readings and global cultural flows. Here, globalized depictions of idealized bodies provide symbolic resources for consumers, but these are negotiated at the local level such that nuanced regional interpretations are produced. Similarly, research on the representation of male bodies specifically underlines the critical nature of interpretation (Holt & Thompson, 2004), and catalogues changes in traditional notions of the male gaze such that it is inverted (Patterson & Elliott, 2002), expanded (Schroeder & Zwick, 2004), and destabilized (Barry & Phillips, 2016). This work is taken up by Elliott and Elliott (2005, p. 16) whose reader response study of young British men finds:

> In an attempt to maintain a masculine persona, the respondents in this study rejected or disassociated themselves with images that did not fit masculine traits. By accepting an image that was feminine, they could risk breaking culturally established gender codes and allow suspicions of homosexuality . . . The other negative theme that emerged was "gender stereotyping", where male respondents labelled consumption and body consciousness as female traits or female problems . . . Several of the respondents evinced a disassociation with muscular body ideals, but they also displayed an association with normal bodies and were very aware of marketing ploys. They seemed to pride themselves on this fad and were quick to voice their independence and ability to resist advertisers' tricks.

In considering the motivations for the body work engaged in by men in response to idealized depictions in the media, both Patterson and Elliott (2002) and Schroeder and Zwick (2004) underline the importance of embodied capital. In sum, men who work upon their bodies are often doing so in an effort to create a "body-for-others" (Bourdieu, 1984, p. 207). In essence, then, we are left with the realization that our relationship with representations of the body is complex. While the body is a major symbol in contemporary consumer culture, deployed in a multitude of stereotypical, restricted, ironic and humorous ways (Stevens & Ostberg, 2011), consumers' interpretations of these representations are not one-dimensional. Rather, our readings of bodies represented in advertising and the media are negotiated in a whole host of interesting ways.

The body project

In the drive to fuel consumer demand, the market fosters and venerates individualization and individuality (Jafari & Goulding, 2008), qualities made manifest through freedom of choice, the 'core value and emblem' (Gabriel & Lang, 2006) of contemporary consumer culture. Through choice, consumers endeavor to 'become' (Giddens, 1991). In this regard, consumers have long been understood as identity-seekers (Arnould & Thompson, 2005). Our understanding of identity within consumer research promotes the idea that people are actively concerned about the creation, enhancement, transformation and maintenance of a sense of identity (Bardhi et al., 2012). For its part, consumption is considered to perform a vital service by anchoring and supporting identity (Bardhi et al., 2012), facilitating on-going negotiations across time (Syrjälä, 2016) that bolster past lives and pre-empt future opportunities for self-making (Epp & Price, 2008). Further, the cultural imperative to work upon identity has become inescapable, demanding symbolic work of consumers at unprecedented levels such that they process "an ever-expanding supply of fashions, cultural texts, tourist experiences, cuisines, mass cultural icons, and the like" (Holt, 2002, p. 87).

In the establishment and maintenance of our identity narratives, our bodies act as tableaux upon which we inscribe many symbols and to which we attach many meanings. Thus, a core dimension of identity in consumer culture is the idea that our bodies can be treated as projects. Indeed, engagement with the body in such projects is increasingly considered to be obligatory, "a technological-moral imperative to not just shape and discipline the body . . . but to sculpt (re-sculpt) the body into more desirable cultural forms" (Thompson & Hirschman, 1998,

p. 405). Holbrook *et al.* (1998, pp. 4–5) detail four perspectives on the relationship between the appearance of the body and consumption that suggest that not all body projects operate in pursuit of what might be traditionally considered desirable cultural forms. These perspectives include: configuration, "a situation in which some character wishes to fit in with the conventions and norms of the surrounding society – and succeeds in doing so"; transfiguration, where deviant characters strive to "live and consume in ways that will lead toward acceptance according to the conventional canons of society"; refiguration, which "occurs when a character who begins as normal in personal appearance chooses to depart from the prevailing conventions in ways that change his or her orientation towards society by introducing elements of deviance"; and disfiguration, where "a physically or psychologically deviant character may elect or be forced to remain deviant in the eyes of society and may therefore persist in a state of disfiguration". In these ways, then, bodies are not to be accepted as given; rather, they are malleable, capable of being transformed and reconstructed through industry and 'body work' (Featherstone, 1991). Further, this re-creation or transformation is achieved through the judicious use of commodities and consumption and, indeed, failure to meet with normalized ideals of the body is indicative of the inadequacy of the self and its consumption (Slater, 1997).

Brogård Kristensen *et al.* (2011) identify how contemporary consumer culture, replete as it is with all manner of scientific and non-scientific programming and advice on diet, leaves the consumer stranded in an ever more complex foodscape. Such complexity is then reflected in the relationships between our body projects and food. For example, in their exposition of *Weight Watchers*, Beruchashvili *et al.* (2015) demonstrate how diet-related weight loss may be viewed as a sacrosanct moral duty while stubborn weight gain is seen as punishment for a life of food-related sins. Moreover, Cronin *et al.* (2014) illuminate the 'cultural antimony' between food behaviors that offer a means of achieving the *right* body shape and socialized food indulgence.

In respect of sport, exercise and fitness, Thompson and Üstüner (2015) deploy Bourdieusian analysis to make sense of the transformations in embodiment and gendered habitus undertaken by women engaging with roller derby. These transformations necessitate the acquisition of new skill sets, and training the body such that it becomes stronger, more agile, and more resilient and thus more suited to playing the sport. Powers and Greenwell (2017) describe how promotional culture characterizes fitness as a route to both individual health management and a better-looking body. Further, they evidence how branded fitness programs such as *CrossFit* and *Bikram Yoga* help us to modify our bodies and to exteriorize our health and morality.

Meanwhile, in the world of fashion, Entwistle and Wissinger (2006, p. 785) identify the aesthetic labor of models who commodify the body through a variety of techniques that include "dieting, working-out, tanning, looking after one's skin, shaving, waxing, plucking bodily hair, paying regular trips to the hairdresser, the beauty salon, the gym", and that are designed not just to look good, but also cultivate a coherent identity in the absence of a corporate aesthetic. The body ideals of the fashion industry are not for everyone though. Scaraboto and Fischer (2013, p. 1236) utilize the work of Bourdieu to suggest "how some consumers within organizational fields may develop differentiated symbolic capital that can increase their potential to influence market changes". These institutional insiders, in this case *fatshionistas*, attempt to push through institutional change with regard to how we view the body. While Fatshionistas strive to do this by appealing to institutional logics, publicizing desirable institutional innovations, and aligning themselves with powerful institutional actors, they might also themselves be trapped by the fact that they have internalized the myths, discourses and values of the industry (Scaraboto & Fischer, 2013). In the end, the outcomes of such negotiations between individual goals and the opportunities afforded by the marketplace might include hegemonic, counter-hegemonic and hybrid body-related identities.

Cosmetic surgery, Schouten (1991) contends, is a product of dissatisfaction with the self and the drive toward impression management especially during periods of role transition. Dissatisfaction comes from a variety of social pressures around beauty culture and the cult of youth, while impression management is at least partially attributable to the need to express the inner self through outward appearance (Askegaard et al., 2002; Slater, 1997). Both Schouten (1991) and Sayre (1999) underline the importance of the practice as a means of exercising control over the body and, by extension, over one's destiny. Following Bourdieu, this points to a direct relationship between the body as a site for adornment and the body as seat of investment (Crossley, 2001c). As Davis (1995) argues, the body is often seen as a business venture, and so provides the means of improving life chances. The consumption of cosmetic surgery can be viewed, therefore, as an embodied practice whereby individuals not only re-shape their bodies, but also re-shape their identities.

Tattooing has also captured the imagination of consumer researchers. Sanders (1985) describes the tattoo as an 'expressive symbol', symbolizing the self to others, in a self-conscious and often highly visible act of inscribing the body (Velliquette et al., 1998). For Bengtsson et al. (2005) tattoos are believed to capture the essence of the self and, as a result, those who modify their bodies with them are driven to favor custom designs that demonstrate authenticity. Patterson and Schroeder (2010) focus attention on the experience of women who become heavily tattooed, and thus hold in tension the transgressive nature of this form of consumption and the everyday experiences of these women. The paper illuminates and complicates the relationship between heavily tattooed women and mainstream beauty culture suggesting how these women are able to re-appropriate their bodies, so often the target of objectification, and use them as the basis of agency. They position tattooed female bodies as simultaneously transgressive, docile and abject. They are transgressive in that they seek to establish alternative notions of what is aesthetically pleasing and what is beautiful. However, breaking free of the smothering inscriptions of patriarchy is difficult and many tattooed women feel the need to balance their tattoos by creating looks that otherwise adhere to normalized ideals of feminine beauty (Larsen et al., 2014). Tattooed female bodies might also be characterized as monstrous and abject. They are at once abhorrent and fascinating, attracting the gaze and challenging it. They are liminal, existing on the border but not respecting it, questioning the distinction between beauty and repulsiveness. Throughout this analysis Patterson and Schroeder are keen to connect to Bourdieu's notion of capital. After all, given the contemporary emphasis on youth and beauty, skin has come to be a major component of embodied capital and operates as a projection surface for the moral character and taste that lie within. Further, skin is also modified in myriad ways in an effort to maximize the capital it holds within particular social fields.

While each of these contexts is interesting in and of itself, Patterson and Schroeder (2010) argue that our understanding of body projects, as it is currently framed, reproduces the Cartesian mind/body dualism that envisages the body as merely an instrument of the mind: "To see the body as the introjection or internalisation of an external image is to give a highly mind-dependent account of the body" (Bray & Colebrook, 1998, p. 55).

The agency of bodies

The body remains our most immediate means of interacting with the world (Lewis, 2000). Joy and Sherry (2003) reiterate that while the body has been the object of some investigation in consumer research, much of this work has approached the body wholly as an outcome of social processes. They argue that a more comprehensive treatment of the body should incorporate analyses of embodied agency and, in such a move, they mine a rich seam of work within the social sciences that is constructed on the foundations of Merleau-Ponty's work. For Hepworth (2004, p. 125) "embodied agency requires physical competencies of the body through which the self is socially expressed". Indeed, the body is fundamental to understanding the means by which the subject is agential (McNay, 2000). Borrowing from Merleau-Ponty's conception of the corporeal schema, Crossley (2007, p. 89) indicates how Muay Thai boxers "can learn to find parts of their body and mobilise them in new ways". Further, in a manner set out in Bourdieu's treatment of capital, while those who modify their bodies are often considered dupes, we might consider that they are, in fact, able to operate within body culture in such a way as to maximize their potential by translating their embodied capital into other forms of capital (Reischer & Koo, 2004).

Perhaps the most comprehensive work in this field has been carried out by Nick Crossley (2004, 2005, 2007) for whom:

> The body is an object in practices of modification. It is reflectively thematised and worked upon. But it is equally a subject or agent in such practices. Embodied agents work upon themselves, upon their own embodiment, in body modification projects. The "I" that is aware of "my body" (qua embodied "me") is my (active and changing) body. Moreover, I modify and maintain myself, qua body, by way of bodily activities or reflexive body techniques.
>
> *2004, p. 37*

These body techniques are reflexive in that the agent utilizes the environment around her for the express purpose of working upon her body. These are techniques of the body and for the body, making use of both bodily effort and embodied competence (Crossley, 2005).

It is against this backdrop that Valtonen et al. (2010, p. 378) extend our appreciation of the embodied nature of consumption in their work on troll-fishing tournaments:

> It is, after all, the body that enters into a specific sensory, semiotic and social environment and is the medium through which practices are performed. Consider, for instance, cold hands touching slimy fish, aching buttocks after sitting in a boat in a windy weather, the touch of a warm wind on the skin, or splashes of cold water on the face. Furthermore, the sport in question is based on motion and activity: the vessel is in constant motion through the water and the crew is active in carrying out specific practices – they are handling the fishing gear, manoeuvring the boat, keeping a close watch on the changing environment, constantly controlling and adjusting their body movements in rough water, and receiving and sending kinaesthetic messages to other bodies.

In a similar fashion, Woermann and Rokka (2015, p. 1493) draw upon Merleau-Ponty by outlining how a practice enfolds consumers in a phenomenal field and allude to sensory engagement with and embodied orchestration in the consumption of freeskiing and paintball: "a 'tuned' experience of the body and the world". Further, Rantala and Valtonen (2014) expose the phenomenal field of 'bodies-in-inaction' as they address the sleeping practices of tourists on nature holidays. Meanwhile, Murphy and Patterson (2011) underline how high-speed motorcycling involves an assemblage (Dant, 2004) between body and machine such that the practice of motorcycling becomes embodied, with behavior underpinned by corporeal competencies as much as by cognitive ones. This embodiment of practice is demonstrated further by Ford and Brown (2006, p. 124) whose extended investigation of surfers attests to the fact that sustained practical engagement with the rules, knowledges and physical practices of the surfing field . . . come to inscribe certain qualities into and onto their bodies that begin to define them as surfers and also begin to orientate them towards engaging with the social world in particular ways that will further define them as surfers to themselves and others.

All of this work confirms that our bodies play a central and active role in our consumption experiences. Involvement in consumption experiences inevitably necessitates the prior development of embodied competencies, the deployment of those capabilities and the choreography of the body in the experience, and the engagement of the body's senses.

Directions for further research

While research on embodiment is beginning to find its way into consumer research with greater regularity, there is much that remains to be done. Although the representation of the body in advertising and the media appears to have been the most popular research stream within consumer research, it is possible to suggest that there still remains huge potential given the wide variety of body types and the endless potential for contextual and critical interpretations. For example, the vast majority of existing work continues to focus in on representations of idealized body types and pays less attention to the portrayal of bodies that might deviate from the ideal. Further, we need to be more critical in our treatment of advertising and the media in this regard. Advertising, for example, is not a simple, linear communication process and thus it is incumbent upon researchers to engage with the actual interpretations of real consumers.

In considering body projects there has been a similar concentration on the movements consumers make toward more culturally sanctioned body types. Nonetheless, the idea of aesthetic labor holds much potential and it could be employed to great effect in domains beyond the fashion model industry (Entwistle & Wissinger, 2006; Lonergan et al., 2012). However, given the contribution of Holbrook et al. (1998) in terms of configuration, transfiguration, refiguration and disfiguration, there is also ample space for research that addresses consumers who resist incorporation into the mainstream of body culture or who determinedly and wilfully deviate from it.

In light of the work that has been done in respect of the lived body, Budgeon (2003) urges us to view the body not as an object but as an event. Representations of bodies, and the practices that bodies engage in, come to be embodied by real people. While our treatment of the body has focused very much thus far on the issue of what bodies mean, we might do well in the future to shift our attention more to what bodies experience and what bodies do in consumption. In other words, what does it mean to experience in and through the body? How do bodies implicate themselves in consumption activities? What kinds of consumption do particular bodies make possible and do other bodies prevent?

References

Abercrombie, N., Hill, S., & Turner, B. (2000). *The Penguin dictionary of sociology*, fourth edition. Harmondsworth, Penguin.

Arnould, E., & Thompson, C. (2005). Consumer culture theory (CCT): Twenty years of research. *Journal of Consumer Research*, *31*(4), 868–882.

Askegaard, S., Cardel Gertsen, M., & Langer, R. (2002) The body consumed: Reflexivity and cosmetic surgery. *Psychology & Marketing*, *19*(10), 793–812.

Ball, K. (2005). Organisation, surveillance and the body: Towards a politics of resistance. *Organisation*, *12*(1), 89–108.

Bardhi, F., Eckhardt, G., & Arnould, E. (2012). Liquid relationship to possessions. *Journal of Consumer Research*, *39*(3), 510–529.

Barry, B., & Phillips, B. (2016). Destabilising the gaze towards male fashion models: Expanding men's gender and sexuality identities. *Critical Studies in Men's Fashion*, *3*(1), 17–35.

Bengtsson, A., Ostberg, J., & Kjeldgaard, D. (2005). Prisoners in Paradise: Subcultural resistance to the marketisation of tattooing. *Consumption, Markets & Culture*, *8*(3), 261–274.

Beruchashvili, M., Moisio, R., & Gentry, J. (2015). Cultivating hope. *Journal of Consumer Culture*, *15*(3), 307–328.

Bourdieu, P. (1984). *Distinction: A social critique of the judgement of taste.* London, Routledge.

Bourdieu, P. (1998). *Practical reason: On the theory of action.* Stanford, CA, Stanford University Press.

Bourdieu, P., & Wacquant, L. (1992). *An invitation to reflexive sociology.* Cambridge, Polity Press.

Bray, A., & Colebrook, C. (1998). The haunted flesh: Corporeal feminism and the politics of (dis)embodiment. *Signs: Journal of Women in Culture and Society*, *24*(1), 35–67.

Brogård Kristensen, D., Boye, H., & Askegaard, S. (2011). Leaving the Milky Way! The formation of a consumer counter mythology. *Journal of Consumer Culture*, *11*(2), 195–214.

Budgeon, S. (2003). Identity as an embodied event. *Body & Society*, *9*(1), 35–55.

Bullington, J. (2013). *The expression of the psychosomatic body from a phenomenological perspective.* Dordrecht, Springer.

Bulmer, S., & Buchanan-Oliver, M. (2004). Meaningless or meaningful? Interpretation and intentionality in post-modern communication. *Journal of Marketing Communications*, *10*(1), 1–15.

Burkitt, I. (1999). *Bodies of thought: Embodiment, identity and modernity.* London, Sage.

Chan, G. (2005). Understanding end-of-life caring practices in the emergency department: Developing Merleau-Ponty's notions of intentional arc and maximum grip through praxis and phronesis. *Nursing Philosophy*, *6*(1), 19–32.

Conrad, P., & Barker, K. (2010). The social construction of illness: Key insights and policy implications. *Journal of Health and Social Behavior*, *51*(1), S67–S79.

Cronin, J., McCarthy, M., Newcombe, M., & McCarthy, S. (2014). Paradox, performance and food: Managing difference in the construction of femininity. *Consumption, Markets & Culture*, *17*(4), 367–391.

Crossley, N. (1995). Merleau-Ponty, the elusive body and carnal sociology. *Body & Society*, *1*(1), 43–63.

Crossley, N. (2001a). Embodiment and social structure: A response to Howson and Inglis. *The Sociological Review*, *49*(3), 318–326.

Crossley, N. (2001b). The phenomenological habitus and its construction. *Theory and Society*, *30*(1), 81–120.

Crossley, N. (2001c). *The social body: Habit, identity and desire.* London, Sage.

Crossley, N. (2004). The circuit trainer's habitus: Reflexive body techniques and the sociality of the workout. *Body & Society*, *10*(1), 37–69.

Crossley, N. (2005). Mapping reflexive body techniques: On body modification and maintenance. *Body & Society*, *11*(1), 1–35.

Crossley, N. (2007). Researching embodiment by way of body techniques. *The Sociological Review*, *55*(s1), 80–94.

Csordas, T. (1990). Embodiment as a paradigm for anthropology. *Ethos*, *18*(1), 5–47.

Currie, D. (1997). Decoding femininity: Advertisements and their teenage readers. *Gender & Society*, *1*(4), 453–476.

Dant, T. (2004). The driver-car. *Theory, Culture and Society*, *21*(4/5), 61–79.

Dant, T., & Wheaton, B. (2007). Windsurfing: An extreme form of material and embodied interaction? *Anthropology Today*, *23*(6), 8–12.

Davis, K. (1995). *Reshaping the female body: The dilemma of cosmetic surgery.* London, Routledge.

Davis, K. (1997). Embody-ing theory: Beyond modernist and postmodernist readings of the body. In K. Davis (Ed.), *Embodied practices: Feminist perspectives on the body* (pp. 1–26). London, Sage.

de Waal Malefyt, T., & McCabe, M. (2016). Women's bodies, menstruation and marketing 'protection': Interpreting a paradox of gendered discourses in consumer practices and advertising campaigns. *Consumption, Markets & Culture*, *19*(5), 555–575.

Dion, D., Sitz, L., & Rémy, E. (2011). Embodied ethnicity: The ethnic affiliation grounded in the body. *Consumption, Markets & Culture*, *14*(3), 311–331.

Dittmar, H. (2007). The costs of consumer culture and the 'cage within': The impact of the material 'good life' and 'body perfect' ideals on individuals' identity and well-being. *Psychological Inquiry*, *18*(1), 23–31.

Dreyfus, H. (1996). The current relevance of Merleau-Ponty's phenomenology of embodiment. *The Electronic Journal of Analytic Philosophy*, *4*(Spring). Retrieved July 14, 2017 from http://ejap.louisiana.edu/EJAP/1996.spring/dreyfus.1996.spring.html

Dreyfus, H., & Dreyfus, S. (1999). The challenge of Merleau-Ponty's phenomenology of embodiment for cognitive science. In G. Weiss & H. Fern Haber (Eds.), *Perspectives on embodiment: The intersections of nature and culture* (pp. 103–120). New York, Routledge.

Durante, K., & Arsena, A. (2015). Playing the field: The effect of fertility on women's desire for variety. *Journal of Consumer Research*, *41*(6), 1372–1391.

Durante, K., Griskevicius, V., Hill, S., Perilloux, C., & Li, N. (2011). Ovulation, female competition, and product choice: Hormonal influences on consumer behavior. *Journal of Consumer Research*, *37*(6), 921–934.

Durante, K., Griskevicius, V., Cantú, S., & Simpson, J. (2014). Money, status, and the ovulatory cycle. *Journal of Marketing Research*, *41*(1), 27–39.

Elliott, R., & Elliott, C. (2005). Idealised images of the male body in advertising: A reader-response exploration. *Journal of Marketing Communications*, *11*(1), 3–19.

Entwistle, J. (2009). *The aesthetic economy of fashion: Markets and value in clothing and modelling*. New York, Berg.

Entwistle, J., & Wissinger, E. (2006). Keeping up appearances: Aesthetic labour in the fashion modelling industries of London and New York. *The Sociological Review*, *54*(4), 774–794.

Epp, A., & Price, L. (2008). Family identity: A framework of identity interplay in consumption practices. *Journal of Consumer Research*, *35*(1), 50–70.

Featherstone, M. (1991). The body in consumer culture. In M. Featherstone, M. Hepworth & T. Bryan (Eds.), *The body: Social process and cultural theory* (pp. 170–196). London, Sage.

Finkelstein, J. (1997). Chic outrage and body politics. In K. Davis (Ed.), *Embodied practices: Feminist perspectives on the body* (pp. 150–167). London, Sage.

Ford, N., & Brown, D. (2006). *Surfing and social theory: Experience, embodiment and narrative of the dream glide*. London, Routledge.

Frank, A. (1991). For a sociology of the body: An analytical review. In M. Featherstone, M. Hepworth & B.S. Turner (Eds.), *The body: Social process and cultural theory* (pp. 36–102). London, Sage.

Frank, E. (2014). Groomers and consumers: The meaning of male body depilation to a modern masculinity body project. *Men and Masculinities*, *17*(3), 278–298.

Gabriel, Y., & Lang, T. (2006). *The unmanageable consumer: Contemporary consumption and its fragmentation*. London, Sage.

Gerrans, P. (2005). Tacit knowledge, rule following and Pierre Bourdieu's philosophy of social science. *Anthropological Theory*, *5*(1), 53–74.

Gershoff, A., & Koehler, J. (2011). Safety first? The role of emotion in safety product betrayal aversion. *Journal of Consumer Research*, *38*(1), 140–150.

Giddens, A. (1991). *Modernity and self-identity: Self and society in the late modern age*. Cambridge, Polity Press.

Grogan, S., Williams, Z., & Conner, M. (1996). The effects of viewing same-gender photographic models on body-esteem. *Psychology of Women Quarterly*, *20*(4), 569–575.

Grosz, E. (1994). *Volatile bodies: Toward a corporeal feminism*. Bloomington, IN, Indiana University Press.

Gurrieri, L., Previte, J., & Brace-Govan, J. (2013). Women's bodies as sites of control: Inadvertent stigma and exclusion in social marketing. *Journal of Macromarketing*, *33*(2), 128–143.

Hepworth, M. (2004). Embodied agency: Decline and the masks of ageing. In E. Tulle (Ed.), *Old age and agency* (pp. 125–135). Hauppuage, NY, Nova Science.

Hewer, P., & Hamilton, K. (2010). On emotions and salsa: Some thoughts on dancing to rethink consumers. *Journal of Consumer Behavior*, *9*(2), 113–125.

Hirschman, E. (1990). Secular immortality and the American ideology of affluence. *Journal of Consumer Research*, *17*(1), 31–42.

Hirschman, E. (1993). Ideology in consumer research, 1980 and 1990: A Marxist and feminist critique. *Journal of Consumer Research*, *19*(4), 537–555.

Hirschman, E., & Holbrook, M. (1982). Hedonic consumption: Emerging concepts, methods and propositions. *Journal of Marketing*, *46*(3), 92–101.

Holbrook, M., & Hirschman, E. (1982). The experiential aspects of consumption: Consumer fantasies, feelings, and fun, *Journal of Consumer Research*, *9*(2), 132–140.

Holbrook, M., Block, L., & Fitzsimons, G. (1998). Personal appearance and consumption in popular culture: A framework for descriptive and prescriptive analysis. *Consumption, Markets & Culture*, 2(1), 1–56.

Holliday, R., & Cairnie, A. (2007). Manmade plastic: Investigating men's consumption of aesthetic surgery. *Journal of Consumer Culture*, 7(1), 57–78.

Holt, D.B. (1998). Does cultural capital structure American consumption? *Journal of Consumer Research*, 25(1), 1–25.

Holt, D.B. (2002). Why do brands cause trouble? A dialectical theory of consumer culture and branding. *Journal of Consumer Research*, 29(1), 70–90.

Holt, D.B., & Thompson, C.J. (2004). Man-of-action heroes: The pursuit of heroic masculinity in everyday consumption. *Journal of Consumer Research*, 31(2), 425–440.

Howson, A. (2013). *The body in society: An introduction.* Cambridge, UK, Polity Press.

Jafari, A., & Goulding, C. (2008). We are not terrorists! UK-based Iranians' consumption practices and the torn self. *Consumption, Markets & Culture*, 11(2), 73–91.

Jagger, E. (2000). Consumer bodies. In P. Hancock, B. Hughes, E. Jagger, K. Paterson, R. Russell, E. Tulle-Winton & M. Tyler (Eds.), *The body, culture and society: An introduction* (pp. 45–63). Buckingham, Open University Press.

Jhally, S. (2009). Advertising, gender and sex: What's wrong with a little objectification? In R. Hammer & D. Kellner (Eds.), *Media/cultural studies* (pp. 313–323). New York, Peter Lang.

Joy, A., & Sherry, J. (2003). Speaking of art as embodied imagination: A multisensory approach to understanding aesthetic experience. *Journal of Consumer Research*, 30(2), 259–282.

Joy, A., & Venkatesh, A. (1994). Postmodernism, feminism, and the body: The visible and the invisible in consumer research. *International Journal of Research in Marketing*, 11(4), 333–357.

Joy, A., Sherry, J., Troilo, G., & Deschenes, D. (2010). Re-thinking the relationship between self and other: Levinas and narratives of beautifying the body. *Journal of Consumer Culture*, 10(3), 333–361.

Kemp, G., & Eagle, E. (2009). The bronze debate: Looking gold versus getting old. *Journal of Research for Consumers*. Retrieved October 17, 2017 from http://eprints.uwe.ac.uk/8387

Larsen, G., Patterson, M., & Markham, L. (2014). A deviant art: Tattoo-related stigma in an era of commodification. *Psychology & Marketing*, 31(8), 670–681.

Lewis, N. (2000). The climbing body, nature and the experience of modernity. *Body & Society*, 6(3–4), 58–80.

Lonergan, P., Patterson, P., & Lichrou, M. (2012). Consuming and producing bodies: Exploring the embodied practices of male models. Paper presented at the *Academy of Marketing Annual Conference*, Southampton, 6–8 July.

Longhurst, R. (1995). The body and geography. *Gender, Place and Culture*, 2(1), 97–106.

Lyon, M., & Barbalet, J. (1994). Society's body: Emotion and the somatisation of social theory. In T. Csordas (Ed.), *Embodiment and experience: The existential ground of culture and self* (pp. 48–66). Cambridge, Cambridge University Press.

Martin, M., & Gentry, J. (1997). Stuck in the model trap: The effects of beautiful models in ads on female pre-adolescents and adolescents. *Journal of Advertising*, 26(2), 19–33.

McNay, L. (1999). Gender, habitus and the field: Pierre Bourdieu and the limits of reflexivity. *Theory, Culture & Society*, 16(1), 95–117.

McNay, L. (2000). *Gender and agency: Refiguring the subject in feminist and social theory.* Cambridge, Polity Press.

Merleau-Ponty, M. (1962). *The phenomenology of perception* (Trans. Colin Smith). London, Routledge and Kegan Paul.

Miner, H. (1956). Body ritual among the Nacirema. *American Anthropologist*, 58(3), 503–507.

Monga, A., & John, D. (2007). Cultural differences in brand extension evaluation: The influence of analytic versus holistic thinking. *Journal of Consumer Research*, 33(4), 529–536.

Mowen, J., Longoria, A., & Sallee, A. (2009). Burning and cutting: Identifying the traits of individuals with an enduring propensity to tan and to undergo cosmetic surgery. *Journal of Consumer Behavior*, 8(5) 238–251.

Murphy, S., & Patterson, M. (2011). Motorcycling edgework: A practice theory perspective. *Journal of Marketing Management*, 27(13–14), 1322–1340.

Nichter, M., & Thompson, J.J. (2006). For my wellness, not just my illness: North Americans' use of dietary supplements. *Culture, Medicine and Psychiatry*, 30(2), 175–222.

Novak, T., & Hoffman, H. (2009). The fit of thinking style and situation: New measures of situation-specific experiential and rational cognition. *Journal of Consumer Research*, 36(1), 56–72.

O'Malley, L. (2006). Does my bump look big in this? *Advertising & Society Review*, 7(3), 1–13.

O'Malley, L., & Patterson, P. (2013). Bouncing back: Reclaiming the body from pregnancy. In S. O'Donohoe, M. Hogg, P. MacLaran, L. Martens & L. Stevens (Eds.), *Motherhoods, markets and consumption* (pp. 131–144). London, Routledge.

Ostberg, J. (2010). Thou shalt sport a banana in thy pocket: Gendered body size ideals in advertising and popular culture. *Marketing Theory*, 10(1), 45–73.

Paterson, K., & Hughes, B. (1999). Disability studies and phenomenology: The carnal politics of everyday life. *Disability & Society*, 14(5), 597–610.

Patterson, M., & Elliot, R. (2002). Negotiating masculinities: Advertising and the inversion of the male gaze. *Consumption, Markets & Culture*, 5(3), 231–249.

Patterson, M., & Schroeder, J. (2010). Borderlines: Skin, tattoos and consumer culture theory. *Marketing Theory*, 10(3), 253–267.

Patterson, M., O'Malley, L., & Story, V. (2009). Women in advertising: Representations, repercussions, responses. *Irish Marketing Review*, 20(1), 9–22.

Peterson, R., & Kerin, R. (1977). The female role in advertisements: Some experimental evidence. *Journal of Marketing*, 41(October), 59–63.

Phillips, B. (2005). Working out: Consumers and the culture of exercise. *The Journal of Popular Culture*, 38(3), 525–551.

Powers, D., & Greenwell, D.M. (2017). Branded fitness: Exercise and promotional culture. *Journal of Consumer Culture*, 17(3), 523–541.

Purser, A. (2011). The dancing body-subject: Merleau-Ponty's mirror stage in the dance studio. *Subjectivity*, 4(2), 183–203.

Rantala, O., & Valtonen, A. (2014). A rhythmanalysis of touristic sleep in nature. *Annals of Tourism Research*, 47(July), 18–30.

Reischer, E., & Koo, K. (2004). The body beautiful: Symbolism and agency in the social world. *Annual Review of Anthropology*, 33(1), 297–317.

Richins, M. (1991). Social comparison and the idealized images of advertising. *Journal of Consumer Research*, 18(1), 71–83.

Rokka, J., Desavelle, H.K., & Mikkonen, I. (2008). Negotiating beauty: Local readings of global cultural flows. In C. Acevedo, J.M. Hernandez & T. Lowrey (Eds.), *Latin American advances in consumer research*, Volume 2 (pp. 84–89). Duluth, MN, Association for Consumer Research.

Rook, D. (1987). The buying impulse. *Journal of Consumer Research*, 14(2), 189–199.

Rook, D., & Fisher, R. (1995). Normative influences on impulsive buying behavior. *Journal of Consumer Research*, 22(3), 305–313.

Sanders, C. (1985). Tattoo consumption: Risk and regret in the purchase of a socially marginal service. In E. Hirschman & M. Holbrook (Eds.), *Advances in consumer research* (pp. 17–22). Provo, UT, Association for Consumer Research.

Sayre, S. (1999). Using introspective self-narrative to analyse consumption: Experiencing plastic surgery. *Consumption, Markets & Culture*, 3(2), 99–127.

Scaraboto, D., & Fischer, D. (2013). Frustrated fatshionistas: An institutional theory perspective on consumer quests for greater choice in mainstream markets. *Journal of Consumer Research*, 39(6), 1234–1257.

Schouten, J. (1991). Selves in transition: Symbolic consumption in personal rites of passage and identity reconstruction. *Journal of Consumer Research*, 17(4), 412–425.

Schroeder, J.E., & Borgerson, J. (1998). Marketing images of gender: A visual analysis. *Consumption, Markets & Culture*, 2(2), 161–201.

Schroeder, J., & Zwick, D. (2004). Mirrors of masculinity: Representation and identity in advertising images. *Consumption, Markets & Culture*, 7(1), 21–52.

Shilling, C. (2001). Embodiment, experience and theory: In defence of the sociological tradition. *The Sociological Review*, 49(3), 327–344.

Shilling, C. (2004). Physical capital and situated action: A new direction for corporeal sociology. *British Journal of Sociology of Education*, 25(4), 473–487.

Shilling, C. (2012). *The body and social theory*. London, Sage.

Simpson, P., Horton, S., & Brown, G. (1996). Male nudity in advertisements: A modified replication and extension of gender and product effects. *Journal of the Academy of Marketing Science*, 24(3), 257–262.

Slater, D. (1997). *Consumer culture and modernity*. Cambridge, Polity Press.

Slutskaya, N., & De Cock, C. (2008). The body dances: Carnival dance and organisation. *Organisation*, 15(6), 851–868.

Stevens, L., & Ostberg, J. (2011). Gendered bodies: Representations of femininity and masculinity in advertising practices. In L. Peñaloza, N. Toulouse & L. Visconti (Eds.), *Marketing management: A cultural perspective* (pp. 392–407). London, Routledge.

Styhre, A. (2004). The re-embodied organisation: Four perspectives on the body in organisations. *Human Resource Development International*, 7(1), 101–116.

Sweetman, P. (2009). Revealing habitus, illuminating practice: Bourdieu, photography and visual methods. *The Sociological Review*, 57(3), 491–511.

Syrjälä, H. (2016). Turning point of transformation: Consumer communities, identity projects and becoming a serious dog hobbyist. *Journal of Business Research*, 69(1), 177–190.

Tepper, G., Haas, R., Mailath, G., Teller, C., Bernhart, T., Monov, G., & Watzek, G. (2003). Representative marketing-oriented study on implants in the Austrian Population. II. Implant acceptance, patient-perceived cost and patient satisfaction. *Clinical Oral Implants Research*, 14(5), 634–642.

Thompson, C.J. (2005). Consumer risk perceptions in a community of reflexive doubt. *Journal of Consumer Research*, 32(2), 235–248.

Thompson, C.J., & Hirschman, E. (1995). Understanding the socialised body: A poststructuralist analysis of consumers' self-conceptions, body images, and self-care practices. *Journal of Consumer Research*, 22(September), 139–153.

Thompson, C.J., & Hirschman, E. (1998). An existential analysis of the embodied self in postmodern consumer culture. *Consumption, Markets & Culture*, 2(4), 401–448.

Thompson, C.J., & Üstüner, T. (2015). Women skating on the edge: Marketplace performances as ideological edgework. *Journal of Consumer Research*, 42(2), 235–265.

Thompson, C., Locander, W., & Pollio, H. (1989). Putting consumer experience back into consumer research: The philosophy and method of existential-phenomenology. *Journal of Consumer Research*, 16(2), 133–146.

Tulle, E. (2007). Running to run: Embodiment, structure and agency amongst veteran elite runners. *Sociology*, 41(2), 329–346.

Turner, T. (1994). Bodies and anti-bodies: Flesh and fetish in contemporary social theory. In T. Csordad (Ed.), *Embodiment and experience: The existential ground of culture and self* (pp. 27–47). Cambridge, Cambridge University Press.

Ussher, J. (1997). Introduction: Towards a material-discursive analysis of madness, sexuality and reproduction. In J. Ussher (Ed.), *Body talk: The material and discursive regulation of sexuality, madness and reproduction* (pp. 1–9). London, Routledge.

Valtonen, A. (2013). Height matters: Practicing consumer agency, gender, and body politics. *Consumption, Markets & Culture*, 16(2), 196–221.

Valtonen, A., Markuksela, V., & Moisander, J. (2010). Doing sensory ethnography in consumer research. *International Journal of Consumer Studies*, 34(4), 375–380.

Velliquette, A., Murray, J., & Creyer, E. (1998). The tattoo renaissance: An ethnographic account of symbolic consumer behavior. In J. Alba & W. Hutchinson (Eds.), *Advances in consumer research*, Volume 25 (pp. 461–467). Provo, UT, Association for Consumer Research.

Wacquant, L. (1995). Pugs at work: Bodily capital and bodily labour among professional boxers. *Body & Society*, 1(1), 65–93.

Williams, S. (1995). Theorising class, health and lifestyles: Can Bourdieu help us? *Sociology of Health & Illness*, 17(5), 577–604.

Williams, S., & Bendelow, G. (1998). *The lived body: Sociological themes, embodied issues*. London, Routledge.

Woermann, N., & Rokka, J. (2015). Timeflow: How consumption practices shape consumers' temporal experiences. *Journal of Consumer Research*, 41(6), 1486–1508.

Woodruffe-Burton, H., & Ireland, K. (2012). Lived consumer bodies: Narcissism, bodily discourse, and women's pursuit of the body beautiful. In C. Otnes & L. Tuncay Zayer (Eds.), *Gender, culture, and consumer behavior* (pp. 195–221). New York, Routledge.

Yakhlef, A. (2010). The corporeality of practice-based learning. *Organization Studies*, 31(4), 409–430.

PART IV

Critical marketing

Marketing practices in focus

24
CRITICAL PERSPECTIVES ON BRAND MANAGEMENT

Adam Arvidsson and Alex Giordano

Introduction

Brand management is no longer just the business of brand managers. The diffusion of social media, such as Facebook, Twitter and Instagram, together with the growing importance of an everyday culture of publicity has made brand management a feature of everyday life for a large and growing number of people. People use social media such as Instagram and Facebook to build personal brands in order to gain popularity and fame. Some hope to make money this way, by promoting their own micro businesses or by attracting commercial sponsorship and transforming their social media pages into venues for bottom-up corporate branding. Self-branding is particularly necessary for the growing mass of people whose careers and livelihoods no longer depend on the organizational structures of industrial modernity. Examples are the expanding range of freelance workers in the knowledge and creative industries, or the many 'platform laborers' who make a living (or part of it) by driving for Uber or renting out at Airbnb. For this new 'precariat' personal brands have become the key asset to guarantee the kinds of reputation and trust on which success depends. This is true not only for the Northern heartland of modernity, but increasingly across the 'Global South', as smartphones and internet connectivity, together with global consumer culture are spreading across the world. Across Asia and Africa young people in particular invest resources in managing social media in order to build personal brands either for themselves or for the small business by which they hope to gain a livelihood, (Lincoln & Robards, 2015). This is particularly relevant for the expanding 'hipster economy', composed of food trucks and artisan coffee houses, in which traditional forms of street vending are combined with sophisticated brand management techniques. In short, brand management has become mainstream, perhaps even a default way of relating to one's self and to others. This shift challenges our established ways of thinking about brands and brand management.

Traditionally, critical theories of brands and brand management divide into two genres. The first genre suggest that brands and consumer culture essentially form a kind of ideology, a system of signs, stories and symbols that serve to obfuscate social reality and provide people with a false, or at least distorted way of relating to their own conditions of existence. The second genre instead emphasizes how people use brands and consumer culture as symbolic resources to build and affirm their own identities vis-à-vis the institutionalized expectations of society and, indeed, of mass culture as a whole. In what follows, we will present and discuss these two consolidated approaches.

In the last section, we will suggest what new directions in critical thinking about brands might look like, in a situation like that of today, where branding has become an almost ubiquitous practice.

Early critical thought: brands and consumer culture as ideology

What is an 'ideology'? The common sense meaning of this term is something like 'a way of thinking', as in 'conservative ideology' or 'communist ideology'. In the critical (read Marx-inspired) social sciences the term has come to achieve a somewhat more elaborate meaning: An ideology is a 'truth that hides the truth', as Umberto Eco wrote in the 1970s (Eco, 1975). To say that drunk driving kills people is ideological in the sense that it is true, but it hides the truth that what really kills people is not so much alcohol as the overall reliance on private cars rather than, for example, public transport. In this sense, ideology is the necessarily distorted relation that we have to our own conditions of existence, a socially constructed filter that allows us to only see a part of the picture (cf. Althusser, 1971).

The perspective on brands and brand management as a form of ideology was pioneered already in the interwar years by exponents of the Frankfurt School, a group of German Marx-inspired intellectuals that formed in the 1930s. Even if they did not explicitly mention brands, the members of the Frankfurt School saw advertising as the business of creating artificial and false distinctions between essentially similar consumer goods. This, in turn, served to create false demands and desires, further the apparatus of consumerism and generally orchestrate an overall ideology of commodity fetishism, whereby the historical condition of industrial capitalism was naturalized and the masses pacified.

The idea of commodity fetishism originally came from Karl Marx. In the first chapter of his life's work, *Capital*, Marx argued that in what he called *bourgeois society*, the use values, or useful things that we make use of every day – such as food, cars, toothpaste or what have you – appear to us as commodities. As commodities they appear as objects of anonymous origins (we do not know who makes our toothpaste) that seem to simply be facts of nature. That the wealth of society appears principally as a great mass of commodities has consequences on our mentality, Marx suggested. We tend to understand the world as made up of objects that, like commodities, appear detached from their social origins with no particular story or identity. Furthermore, the only evident meaning that commodities have is their price (this was written in the 1850s, before branding, the business of giving artificial identities to commodities, took off in earnest). Furthermore, it is in the nature of commodities that they can be compared to each other and that their value can be determined in relation to other commodities ('Five beds equal a house', wrote Marx, citing Aristotle – beds were expensive and houses were cheap in Athens at the time, 'five iPhones equal one Prada bag', we can write today, cf. Marx (1973[1867], p. 52)). This inherent quantitative comparability leads to what the Hungarian Marxist philosopher György Lukács called reification.

Lukács (1923) argued that as use values were exclusively available as commodities, this tended to produce a 'reified consciousness'. By this he meant that as the relation between objects now appeared as a set of relations between objective values that could be evaluated and compared to each other in rational ways, so would the relations between subjects and objects as well as between subjects and other subjects take on a nature of objectivity and calculability. As a consequence of being surrounded by commodities, people would start to relate to each other, and, increasingly to themselves, as to things that could be evaluated in terms of their quantitative attributes, be this price, performance, reputation or what have you. This fundamental insight is perhaps ever more relevant today as the quantified self movement spreads the practice of evaluating one's body, psyche and even relations in terms of quantifiable indicators (Moore & Robinson, 2015).

Lukács' insights became a stepping stone for the Frankfurt School's critiques of consumer modernity on the part of Max Horkheimer and Theodor Adorno (1944) as well as, later, Herbert Marcuse (1964). They would extend his analysis by describing how the culture industries, including the emerging advertising industry, promoted the spread of an industrially produced culture made of objectified meanings and narratives, which was imposed on and sometimes replaced the subjective culture of tradition and popular culture. People would compare themselves to movie-stars or other pop cultural celebrities who, in turn, were ordered in hierarchies reflecting their quantitative attributes (number of films made, or what they were paid at the time of the Frankfurt School theorists, or the number of followers on social media today). Lukács also inspired Jurgen Habermas' (1961) analysis of the 'colonization of the life world', which described a similar phenomenon, as industrially produced cultural forms, like brands (along with the bureaucratic rationality of the welfare state), tended to invade and transform the intimate meanings of interpersonal relations. To these theorists from the Frankfurt School, commercial popular culture, including brands, was part of a whole-scale substitution of a traditional culture rooted in centuries of practice, for an industrially produced culture that had no roots but referred only to itself. (Later on, Jean Baudrillard, a somewhat extravagant French thinker would term this the culture of 'Simulacra', and argue that it had already replaced 'reality' to the extent that the very ideas of the true meaning or value of anything had already become absurd. This was in the 1970s, see below).

Another foundational thinker who, without speaking of brands, articulated the basis for contemporary critical understandings of the cultural consequences of branding was Walter Benjamin. In his essay on 'The work of art in the age of mechanical reproduction' (1936), Benjamin suggested that the 'mechanical' production of meaning, chiefly by means of film and photography, led to a cultural shift whereby art objects were dissociated from their traditional 'aura'. With this term he referred to the metaphysical significance that was given to art works by their place in traditional rituals. (For example, a crucifix in a church has an aura that conveys elaborate layers of metaphysical significance on it by virtue of its place within the ritual fabric of the Catholic liturgy.) Like Lukács, Benjamin suggested that this loss of aura tended to create a culture dominated by objective rationality, with little place for subjective meanings. He also added that the loss of traditional aura in 'the age of mechanical reproduction' entailed the possibility of the artificial production of new auratic qualities. To Benjamin, fascism was an example of how such mechanical production of aura was put to work in order to generate new myths that allowed for forms of affective identification that went far beyond the rational. By means of the swastika and the elaborate rituals created around it, National Socialism was able to mobilize the masses in ways that were more profound and engaging than could have been achieved by rational argument alone.

The post-war years and the rise of semiotics

In the post-Second World War years consumer culture reached maturity in the US and most of Western Europe. Social and cultural theorists began to look at brands and consumer goods as symbols that conveyed deep and complex meanings, as a sort of material ideology that was instrumental in maintaining consensus for what, at the time, was known as 'late capitalism' (Mandel, 1975). This semiotic perspective (from the Greek σημεῖον, sign), developed in different contexts at about the same time. In the UK Raymond Williams (1958) and Richard Hoggart (1957) started what came to be known as the 'Cultural Studies' tradition wherein popular culture, including commercial cultural practices such as consumption and mass entertainment, became the object of critical analyses. In the North American context, Marshall McLuhan (1964) popularized 'medium theory', where popular cultural phenomena such as brands and advertising received the kind of serious scholarly attention previously reserved for the classics of the literary canon. The most influential of these developments occurred in France and gave birth to what was to be properly known as 'semiotics'. In his path-breaking work, *Mythologies*, Roland Barthes (1953) pioneered a new way of looking at popular culture. Rather than dismissing low brow cultural objects such as the new Citröen model or *steak-frites*, Barthes saw them as rich with signification. Mirroring the structuralist approach pioneered in anthropology by his colleague Claude Levi Strauss, Barthes 'decoded' these mythical objects, unmasking how they reproduced the mythological structures that served to legitimize and reinforce the dominant ideology of consumer capitalism. The semiotic tradition was continued by Jean Baudrillard (1968) and Umberto ECO (1975). Both conducted a series of analyses of popular culture, including brands, which investigated their role not as consumer goods but as cultural signifiers that underpinned or supported the ideology of capitalist modernity. Central to such early semiotics was the idea that the meaningful differentiation between objects mirrored social differences, primarily in terms of class and power.

This insight was developed by Pierre Bourdieu in his work *Distinction* (1979) in which he conducted a systematic investigation of the role of consumer practices, including brands, in constructing, maintaining and legitimizing social power relations. Although Bourdieu never recognized his debt to earlier market research, his methods built on developments within the tradition of psychographics and lifestyle segmentation, which, in turn, built on earlier, albeit less complete efforts in Bourdieu's direction on the part of American sociologists such as Rainwater (1959). Obviously, Bourdieu's theoretical perspective was different. While his main work, *Distinction*, basically replicated the empirical findings of contemporary lifestyle studies, Bourdieu's interpretation of the findings was diametrically opposed. To Bourdieu the existence of several class-specific clusters of consumer preferences showed how taste was a social construction that served to legitimize an inequitable distribution of resources and to keep people in their place through the exercise of 'soft' symbolic power.

The semiotic tradition was radicalized by Guy Debord and Jean Baudrillard, both writing in the turbulent late 1960s. Debord was a member of the situationist movement, a radical artistic *avant garde*, heir to Dadaism and Surrealism, which had emerged in the post-war years. The situationists argued that Marx's theory of commodity fetishism had now been generalized to the extent that virtually all relations between human beings had come to be mediated by artificial objects and images, among them, importantly, branded consumer goods. Debord summarized this perspective, what he understood to be a condition of total alienation – the estrangement of human beings from their real conditions of life – in his revolutionary work, the *Society of the Spectacle* (Debord, 1967). Jean Baudrillard developed the same ideas, albeit in a more sociological sense. His early work, *The System of Objects* (1968), *The Consumer Society* (1969) and *A Critique of the Political Economy of the Sign* (1972) had developed Marx's theory of commodity fetishism by engaging empirically with contemporary consumer culture. In these texts he suggested that contemporary consumerism constituted a system of objects where each element had meaning and value only in relation to the total system of objects itself, and not in relation to some underlying reality by means of which the use value of objects could be determined. In this way, Baudrillard suggested, the use value, the usefulness of objects that Marx understood to be the basis for their exchange value (or price), had now been replaced by their sign value, their symbolic value in relation to the system of consumer culture itself. To simplify: A Rolex watch is not worth its price because of its ability to keep time, but because of its position in the overall symbolic system of luxury goods, by means of which it is able to convey a particular meaning. In the 1980s, Baudrillard radicalized his position to claim that the hyper-reality of signs – now encompassing not only consumer goods but mass media in general – had replaced reality with a 'hyper-relativity of self-referential symbols', or 'simulacra', which was constitutive of everyday experience for most people. Similar to the film *Matrix* (which was in no small amount inspired by his work (Constable, 2006)), people in Baudrillard's world lived in a virtual fantasy where they were unable to 'connect' with their real conditions of existence.

Cultural Studies and brands as resources for identity

At the same time, in the UK, disciples of Hoggart and Williams founded the Centre for Cultural Studies at the University of Birmingham. The Birmingham School, as it became known, engaged directly with everyday popular culture, such as brands, television, popular fiction and youth culture. In doing so, however, they rejected what they understood to be the overly deterministic perspective of the predominantly French structuralist school of semiotics. It is true, prominent Cultural Studies scholars such as Stuart Hall (1980) argued, that commodities have sign value that can be understood to make up a self-referential system. However, that does not mean that actual people relate to them or use them that way. Instead, the empirical research that was conducted at the Centre, and later in other universities as its alumni spread across the Anglo-Saxon academic world, showed that people often appropriated consumer goods and redefined their meaning in relation to the needs of their own life and their own attempts at identity creation and meaning making. The meanings that they thus attributed to goods were often radically different from what was originally intended. Young people, Hall and Jefferson (1975) argued in their early edited work, *Resistance through Rituals*, are not simply slaves to the ideologies of mass culture. Rather they appropriate music, fashion and branded consumer goods to negotiate their own identities in a rapidly shifting post-War landscape where the old certainties of class and local tradition were quickly melting away. They used such goods in rituals of symbolic resistance by means of which they stood up against attempts on the part of overall society and its representatives, such as schools, police or social workers, to have them meekly accept their place. Similarly, young women might read women's magazines like *Jackie* that convey an ideological image of womanhood, but they do not simply adopt it, Angela McRobbie (1981) argued. Rather, they used these images in strategies to negotiate conflicting demands from family, schools, boyfriends, employers and others, and to articulate their own identity, which contained an amount of autonomy of 'resistance'. Television viewers, finally, resisted the overall ideology conveyed by television news, and instead reinterpreted the news in ways that fit into their way of making sense of the world (Hall, 1980). Overall, Stuart Hall, the head of the Birmingham Centre in the early years, argued that instead of using Marx's concept of ideology, which, at least in its French structuralist rendering, principally by Louis Althusser (1971), had become too rigid and deterministic, it would be better to adopt Italian philosopher Antonio Gramsci's concept of hegemony (Hall, 1996). As a concept, hegemony was more fluid. It signified the ability to maintain the dominance of a certain interpretation of the world on a field where, nevertheless, conflicting interpretations also existed and could sometimes affirm themselves, even to the point of threatening the established order. Accordingly, in contemporary societies, commercial culture, including brands was a prominent field on which such struggles for hegemony took place and where the dominant position did not always and everywhere prevail.

The emphasis on 'resistance' on the part of Cultural Studies could sometimes be exaggerated, as when John Fiske (1989) famously claimed that people who window shop in shopping malls exercise a form of symbolic resistance to consumer society. Over time it became the specific fetish, so to speak, of Cultural Studies, and in the 1990s this tradition began to produce findings of 'resistance' on the part of a long list of diverse subjects, often in connection to the use of consumer goods. Consumption, it seemed, remained the last space where such 'resistance' could be exercised: 'commercial cultural commodities is all that most people have', as Paul Willis observed (Willis, 1990, p. 26). While this embrace of consumer culture was criticized for its 'uncanny affinity' to contemporary Thatcherite embraces of the market as the core institution of society (McGuigan, 1992), it facilitated the incorporation of Cultural Studies within the tradition of qualitative consumer research or Consumer Culture Theory (CCT) as the tradition would be branded in retrospect (Arnould & Thompson, 2005).

The influence of Cultural Studies, along with other cultural theories from the social sciences, began as an ideologically charged postmodern turn that rebelled against what was perceived to be the hegemony of the one-dimensional view of consumers as information processors. The stage had been set in the preceding decade when a number of approaches from the social sciences, such as symbolic interactionism (Hirschman & Holbrook, 1981), anthropology (Levy, 1981; McCracken, 1986), semiotics (Mick, 1986) and phenomenology (Thompson et al., 1989) were introduced to the field. However, these remained marginal until the mid-1990s when, under headings such as 'postmodern marketing' (Brown, 1995) or 'emancipatory postmodernism' (Firat & Venkatesh, 1995), the cultural approach was firmly introduced to the field. This produced a series of studies of how consumers use consumer goods as building blocks for identity, in the form of experiences (Arnould & Price, 1993), subcultures (Schouten & McAlexander, 1995), communities (Muniz & O'Guinn, 2001), or tribes (Cova, 1997). Together these consolidated a new paradigm of consumer research, increasingly influential, and institutionalized, where the connection between consumption and 'identity-work' (Luedicke et al., 2010), the act of building and elaborating personal identity in a postmodern world of choices and possibilities, became a core assumption.

Contemporary critical approaches

Branding became more influential in the 1970s as marketing was consolidated as a business practice. At the same time new data sources such as psychographic life style research and, later on, data from bar codes and credit card scans, offered richer raw materials for the construction of brands and lifestyles. In the 1980s media market liberalization enabled a further differentiation of channels and platforms, and consumer lifestyles began to be embodied not only in brands, but in media objects like television channels and magazines. Importantly, deregulation of media markets opened up for the diffusion of a uniform global culture, made up of content brands such as *MTV, Star Wars* or *Dallas*. This became a basis for the development of global brands, which like Nike, Starbucks or Apple, aimed at constructing globally uniform consumer lifestyles able to cross over national borders and prosper in widely diverse cultural ecosystems (Levitt, 1983). In this context, branding practices expanded beyond consumption and marketing. Corporations discovered that constructing an attractive corporate brand might serve to motivate knowledge work and creativity (Maravelias, 2003; Ouchi, 1980). Cities and nations discovered branding as a way of creating the kinds of affective climates that would be conducive to developing knowledge intensive 'creative industries' or, more often, inflating real estate prices (Pike, 2011) (see also Giovanardi, Kavaratzis & Lichrou, this volume).

Increasingly the construction of such branded forms of life happened through interventions that went beyond the semiotic level. Brands began to be understood as experiential devices that, through a combination of design, taste, smell, sound and tactility would instill a similar experience in consumers (or citizens or peers) all across the world. As Pine and Gilmore pointed out in their successful book on *The Experience Economy* (1999), corporations should make use of this new plastic environment to deploy sensory, architectural and other stimuli in order to create artificial experiences around brands. Apple perfected this approach, offering an Apple experience that, while difficult to put into words, nevertheless distinguished not only Apple products but the people using those products from everyone else, to the point of providing a seemingly religious affiliation (Belk & Tumbat, 2005). Similar branded forms of artificial life constituted successful efforts in affective engineering that enabled people in a plurality of widely diverse contexts to 'feel' in similar ways about a brand. Branding took part in what Nigel Thrift (2004) identified as a new principle of social structuration, based on the organization of spatial flows of affect. Such organized affectivity would now contribute to an experientially laden 'service', which marketing scholars began to suggest as the true source of value, above and beyond the benefits of products.

Within the marketing literature there was a growing awareness that tying consumers to the brand through the creation of such artificial experiences played a part in activating them as participants to the extended process of creation of 'customer based brand equity' (Keller, 1993). That is, a conception of the value of the brand as resting not with its intrinsic qualities, but with its ability to activate consumer participation in particular ways. This development triggered new critical accounts of brands and branding. Sociologists such as Celia Lury (2004) argued that brands should be understood as something far deeper and more complex than symbols. Rather, brands were assemblages of material objects, cultural meanings, and a number of other tools – like software or affectively charged ambiences – that created self-contained artificial realties that cut deeply into the framework of everyday life. These new artificial entities were able to exercise what Scott Lash (2007) termed 'ontological power', that is, they were able to construct new relations of existence that could give direction and coherence to flows of meaning and value within the global economy, without the need for legitimizing forms of knowledge. Such manifestations of what Lury *et al.* (2012) called 'topological culture' could naturally direct the agency of subjects into the creation of new forms of intangible value. They did this by enabling their desires and (part of) their lives to unfold on the artificial plane of the brand where, like in a video game, the environment of action had been carefully engineered.

This meant that resistance and identity-work had already been anticipated by brand management. Indeed, it was such resistance, the fact that consumers did not always do what was expected of them, that constituted the true source of value on which brands fed. People's appropriation of, resistance to, or general use of brands in their own attempts at meaning making and identity construction were what generated the stylistic innovations that, through the work of cool hunters and trend scouts could feed into and give new energy to the branding process. Nike, for example, was very attentive to how their sneakers were used by young people in US inner-city 'ghettos' and draw on that usage in positing the sneaker as the component of a cool, urban (read 'black') style that could be sold also to suburban (white) kids (Goldman & Papson, 1998). Cultural Studies had, in fact, inspired a new 'administrative science' of cool hunting and trend scouting that became crucial to brand management (Arvidsson, 2008). At a more mundane level, the fact that people paid a lot of attention to brands, that brands entered into their social world as meaningful symbols that could be used to articulate everyday relations and meanings, meant that people continuously co-created the attention and affect that was the source of valuable brand equity. The presence of a branded object made a difference, a small difference as when an adult man combined a tailored suit with a pair of Nike shoes and thus made a fashion statement, or a great difference as when an adolescent boy could gain acceptance and avoid bullying by wearing a pair of Nike shoes. This was what, in the end, conferred meaning and value to brands. Ordinary consumers thus work, Arvidsson (2006) claimed, to give meaning to brands in their everyday practice, and brand management was a matter of organizing such consumer labor in ways so that it could add value to brands.

But how was such value realized? One way is through the 'premium price' that consumers were prepared to pay for a brand because of the position that it had acquired in everyday consumer practice. Apple computers, for example, retail at about double the price of technically compatible products but they are 'cooler', more people recognize them as a valuable component of their everyday social practice and this makes consumers ready to pay a higher price. Recently however, brands have come to acquire an even greater importance as financial assets.

Today, most successful companies show market values way above their book values. Such intangible values are, by definition, impossible to measure. Branding serves to establish a convention in public opinion that can justify financial valuations way in excess of book value. The spread of branding away from the field of consumer goods proper partly reflects this logic. City branding, for instance, is largely a matter of establishing a convention that justifies increasing real estate prices, or that attracts corporate investments to the city. Personal branding is, similarly, a matter of establishing a convention that gives market value to one's otherwise immeasurable assets (such as one's ability to network or to give off a positive impression). In this way, branding has evolved into a key institution in the neoliberal, finance-centered economic model. Essentially a brand puts to work and manages ever more socialized immaterial production processes in order to create cultural conventions that justify the appropriation of a share of the globally produced surplus that circulates on financial markets. This intimate connection between brands and finance explains the great investments in branding undertaken by, for example, fashion companies, at the same time as their sales revenues have declined as parts of overall profits (Arvidsson & Malossi, 2011). It is concomitant with an overall shift away from profits deriving from the production and sale of goods, toward financial rent as a source of corporate wealth (Arvidsson & Peitersen, 2013). Brands become a way to justify the appropriation of rent from the common productive processes that unfold in everyday life. This financial function of brands is particularly clear in the culture industries. Indeed, Michael Szalay's work suggests that the content and programming strategy of HBO can, to a large extent, be understood as directed at creating brand equity for financial investors, and not simply value for consumers (Szalay, 2014).

Social media and branding

The rapid diffusion of the internet and, more recently, of social media and mobile connectivity, has rendered the presence of brands and the global media culture of which they are part ever more ubiquitous in the everyday life of ordinary people. (The ordinary Facebook user, for example, spends more than 25 minutes a day on the platform (D'Onfro, 2016)). Social media also have a more capillary presence in the lives of users than older media such as television. While television, along with the older forms of fixed internet connectivity, had to be accessed in a particular place, in front of the immobile screen, mobile social media use is spread out, and social media are often accessed in short bursts that are inserted at regular intervals throughout the day. At the same time corporations have increased their spending on branding and promotion on social media, making the mobile adspend the fastest growing sector in the overall advertising market (Arvidsson & Bonini, 2015). Concomitantly, critical market research has devoted a lot of attention to how people contribute to creating brand value online, engaging in brand communities on social media and making brands part of their everyday self-expression on platforms such as Twitter or Instagram. This has been particularly important in the fashion market where the rise of fashion bloggers and Instagrammers has to some extent restructured the ways in which the fashion system operates (McQuarrie et al., 2013).

Social media also invite people to engage in self-branding practices. Platforms like Facebook and Instagram are geared toward the presentation of a public identity that needs to be updated and fashioned so as to reflect an ideal, if not actual, sense of selfhood. Some researchers have argued that these 'technical affordances' of social media platforms have rendered self-branding a new, default way of relating to self and others (Gershon, 2014; Hearn, 2008). This is particularly true for young knowledge workers entering fields such as journalism, marketing and design where self-branding is actively encouraged (Gandini, 2015). It is also the case for the (mostly) young entrepreneurs who aim at developing their own companies, whether tech start-ups or neo-artisanal 'hipster' enterprises like food trucks or vintage stores (Marwick, 2013). Like freelancers, they tend to spend more time in branding and promotion work than in actually developing the products that they wish to sell (Arvidsson et al., 2016). Some simply aim at becoming social media celebrities, cultivating a distinct Instagram profile, that they hope might acquire corporate advertising investments on the account of its consistent style and large number of followers (Marwick, 2015). The general impression of this line of research is that social media have contributed to making self-branding a ubiquitous and widespread practice. This is certainly true in some segments, notably where the need to create a personal brand is reinforced by labor market conditions. However, social media also enable researchers to have access to the hitherto hidden continent of ordinary, everyday practice. Instagram images or tweets can (relatively) easily be accessed in the millions and this gives us a view on what people actually do in their everyday life, something that previously could only be glimpsed on a limited scale by means of labor-intensive ethnographic or interview work. Building on this new availability of data, recent research has suggested that, seen as a whole, the emphasis on self-branding and on the important role that brands play in the everyday life of ordinary people might be exaggerated. Arvidsson and Caliandro (2016), as a case in point, suggest that apart from a small minority of fame seekers and fashion fans, ordinary people pay sporadic attention to luxury fashion brands in their everyday Twitter activity, tweeting about them once or twice in the course of a month.

Social media, and the integration between social media, mobile platforms and geolocalization services has also provided an additional source of data for the surveillance activities of market researchers (as well as, perhaps more uncannily, states and more or less secret police agencies). While market researchers have always been interested in surveilling consumer habits, and while their ability to do so greatly increased in the 1980s with the availability of data from bar code scans and credit card purchases, the internet and social media take this surveillance to new heights. On social media platforms such as Facebook, but also Twitter and Instagram, people routinely post information about their ordinary activities and sentiment, engaging in a continuous practice of self-surveillance, as social media visibility becomes a central component to an ongoing 'care of the (branded) self' (Marwick & Boyd, 2011). In this way, the ongoing life process in which people reproduce themselves as consumers, which remained invisible and silent, now acquires an objective reality as social media data to be mined. This makes data available on the interpersonal dynamics of consumers, and not simply their purchasing behavior. Many recent critical approaches to brand management have focused on how this 'surveillant assemblage' is constructed. With social media it seems the imaginary that people have always produced in their everyday interactions has become almost completely integrated within the value circuit of consumer capitalism (Zwick et al., 2008). People no longer suffer alienation by means of the reifying ideology of consumer capitalism, but they actively contribute to creating that alienating ideology themselves.

Perspectives for future research

In the last decade it was common for marketing and consumer researchers to have a somewhat celebratory approach to brands, emphasizing, in the style of 1970s Cultural Studies how consumers use brands in order to articulate identities and social relations. The recent trend has instead been to focus on how they are exploited by doing so (see Cova & Paranque, this volume and Fuchs, this volume). The problem with these two approaches lies with the very ubiquity of brand management. If virtually everyone is branding herself, be they the new generation of street vendors that populate the streets of Bangkok and other Asian 'creative cities' (Arvidsson & Niessen, 2015), social entrepreneurs on a quest to 'change the world' in some vague and undefined sense (Bandinelli & Arvidsson, 2012), freelance workers or social media fame seekers, then everyone can be said to be either exploited or deceived, or both. Fuchs (2010), for example, seriously suggests that everyone who uses Facebook and similar platforms should be considered 'members of a new exploited class'. Although this might be true in some abstractly theological sense, social science requires a more nuanced and productive approach.

In this context it would be interesting to see more work on how brands and brand management operate as tools for creating and maintaining productive connections within the complex industrious economy that is presently emerging at a level below that of the 'flows' of corporate capitalism. How do activist initiatives such as those found within the new food movement use brands to create and maintain alternative networks of distribution and exchange of local or organic foodstuffs? How do brands operate in the growing reality of commons-based peer production or self-organized small-scale market exchange in the information economy? How are brands used to constitute social movements)? How do brands operate in the emerging 'pirate modernity' (Sundaram, 2009) of cheap and cheerful generally low-quality 'shanzhai' electronics or fashions where mere copying has evolved into the development of pastiches of famous brands that converge into a 'generic brandedness' where any reference to 'brand identity' has been lost (Nakassis, 2013)? In short, as brands and brand management have become close to integrated aspects of normal life processes, how are these techniques used to create the kinds of links and connections that make social cooperation possible in the absence of stable organizational structures or normative integration? Drawing on accessible digital data, in combination with more traditional social research strategies, might offer new opportunities to address these questions.

References

Althusser, L. (1971). *Essays on ideology*. London, Verso.
Arnould, E.J., & Price, L.L. (1993). River magic: Extraordinary experience and the extended service encounter. *Journal of Consumer Research*, 20(1), 24–45.
Arnould, E., & Thompson, C.J. (2005). Consumer culture theory (CCT): Twenty years of research. *Journal of Consumer Research*, 31(4): 868–882.
Arvidsson, A. (2006). Brands: Meaning and value in media culture. London, Routledge.
Arvidsson, A. (2008). The function of cultural studies in marketing: A new administrative science. In M. Tadajewski and D. Brownlie (Eds.), *Critical marketing: Issues in contemporary marketing* (pp. 329–344). Chichester, Wiley.
Arvidsson, A., & Bonini, T. (2015). Valuing audience passions: From Smythe to Tarde. *European Journal of Cultural Studies*, 18(2), 158–173.
Arvidsson, A., & Caliandro, A. (2016). Brand public. *Journal of Consumer Research*, 42(5), 727–748.
Arvidsson, A., & Malossi, G. (2011). Customer co-production from social factory to brand: Learning from Italian fashion. In D. Zwick & J. Cayla (Eds.), *Inside marketing: Practices, ideologies, devices* (pp. 212–223). Oxford, Oxford University Press.
Arvidsson, A., & Niessen, B. (2015). Creative mass: Consumption, creativity and innovation on Bangkok's fashion markets. *Consumption Markets & Culture*, 18(2), 111–132.
Arvidsson, A., and Peitersen, N. (2013). *The ethical economy: Rebuilding value after the crisis*. New York, Columbia University Press.
Arvidsson, A., Gandini, A., & Bandinelli, C. (2016). Self-branding among freelance knowledge workers. In M. Crain, W. Poster & M. Cherry (Eds.), *Invisible labor: Hidden work in the contemporary economy* (pp. 239–256). Berkeley, University of California Press.
Bandinelli, C., & Arvidsson, A. (2012). Brand yourself a changemaker! *Journal of Macromarketing*, 33(1), 67–71.
Barthes, R. (1953). *Mythologies*. Paris, Éditions du Seuil.
Baudrillard, J. (1968). *Le système des objets*. Paris, Gallimard.

Baudrillard, J. (1969). *La société du consummation: Ses mythes, ses structures*. Paris, Calmann-Lévy.
Baudrillard, J. (1972). *Pour une critique de l'economie politique du signe*. Paris, Gallimard.
Belk, R.W., & Tumbat, G. (2005). The cult of Macintosh. *Consumption Markets & Culture*, 8(3), 205–217.
Benjamin, W. (1936). L'oeuvre d'art à l'époque de sa reproduction méchanisée. *Zeithschrift fur Sozialforschung*, V, pp. 40–68. Paris, Félix Alcan.
Bourdieu, P. (1979). *La distinction: Critique sociale du jugement*. Paris, Éditions de Minuit.
Brown, S. (1995). Postmodern marketing research: No representation without taxation. *Market Research Society Journal*, 37(3), 1–21.
Constable, C. (2006). Baudrillard reloaded: Interrelating philosophy and film via The Matrix Trilogy. *Screen*, 47(2), 233–249.
Cova, B. (1997). Community and consumption: Towards a definition of the 'linking value' of products and services. *European Journal of Marketing*, 31(3/4), 297–316.
Debord, G. (1967). *La société du spectacle*. Paris, Buchet-Chastel.
D'Onfro, J. (2016). Here's how much time people spend on Facebook, Instagram, and Messenger every day. *Business Insider*, April 28, 2016. Retrieved 24 July, 2018 from http://uk.businessinsider.com/how-much-time-do-people-spend-on-facebook-per-day-2016-4?r=US&IR=T
Eco, U. (1975). *Trattato di semiotica generale*. Milan, Bompiani.
Fırat, A.F., & Venkatesh, A. (1995). Liberatory postmodernism and the reenchantment of consumption. *Journal of Consumer Research*, 22(3), 239–267.
Fiske, J. (1989). *Understanding popular culture*. London, Routledge.
Fuchs, C. (2010). Labor in informational capitalism and on the internet. *The Information Society*, 26(3), 179–196.
Gandini, A. (2015). Digital work: Self-branding and social capital in the freelance knowledge economy. *Marketing Theory*, 16(1), 123–141.
Gershon, I. (2014). Selling yourself in the United States. *POLAR: Political and Legal Anthropology Review*, 37(2), 281–295.
Goldman, R., & Papson, S. (1998). *Nike culture: The sign of the swoosh*. London, Sage.
Habermas, J. (1961). *Strukturwandel der offentlishkeit. Untersuchunungen zu einer kategorie der burglichen gesellschaft*. Frankfurt am Main, Suhrkamp.
Hall, S. (1980). *Encoding and decoding television discourse*. Birmingham, Institute for Cultural Studies.
Hall, S. (1996). *Critical dialogues in cultural studies*. London, Routledge.
Hall, S., & Jefferson, T. (Eds.) (1975). *Resistance through rituals*. London, Hutchinson.
Hearn, A. (2008). Meat, mask, burden: Probing the contours of the branded self. *Journal of Consumer Culture*, 8(2), 197–217.
Hirschman, E.C., & Holbrook, M.B. (Eds.) (1981). *Symbolic consumer behavior*. Proceedings, Association for Consumer Research.
Hoggart, R. (1957). *The uses of literacy*. London, Penguin.
Horkheimer, M., & Adorno, T. (1944). *Dialektik der aufklärung: Philosopische fragmente*. Amsterdam, Querido.
Keller, K.L. (1993). Conceptualizing, measuring, and managing customer-based brand equity. *The Journal of Marketing*, 57(1), 1–22.
Lash, S. (2007). Power after hegemony: Cultural studies in mutation? *Theory, Culture & Society*, 24(3), 55–78.
Levitt, T. (1983). The globalization of markets. *Harvard Business Review*, May/June, 92–102.
Levy, S.J. (1981). Interpreting consumer mythology: A structural approach to consumer behavior. *The Journal of Marketing*, 45(3), 49–61.
Lincoln, S., & Robards, B. (2015). 10 years of Facebook. *New Media & Society*, 16(7), 1047–1050.
Luedicke, M.K., Thompson, C.J., & Giesler, M. (2010). Consumer identity work as moral protagonism: How myth and ideology animate a brand-mediated moral conflict. *Journal of Consumer Research*, 36(6): 1016–1032.
Lukács, G. (1923). *Geschichte und klassenbewusstsein. Studien über marxistische dialektik*. Berlin, Malik Verlag.
Lury, C. (2004). *Brands: The logos of the global economy*. London, Routledge.
Lury, C., Parisi, L., & Terranova, T. (2012). Introduction: The becoming topological of culture. *Theory, Culture & Society*, 29(4–5), 3–35.
Mandel, E. (1975). *Late capitalism*. London, Verso.
Maravelias, C. (2003). Post-bureaucracy: Control through professional freedom. *Journal of Organizational Change Management*, 16(5), 547–566.

Marcuse, H. (1964). *One dimensional man*. London, Abacus.
Marwick, A. (2013). *Status update: Celebrity, publicity and branding in the social media age*. New Haven, Yale University Press.
Marwick, A. (2015). Instafame: Luxury selfies in the attention economy. *Public Culture, 27*(1), 137–160.
Marwick, A., & Boyd, D. (2011). To see and be seen: Celebrity practice on Twitter. *Convergence: The International Journal of Research into New Media Technologies, 17*(2), 139–158.
Marx, K. (1973 [1867]). *Capital. Vol. I*. London, Penguin.
McCracken, G. (1986). Culture and consumption: A theoretical account of the structure and movement of the cultural meaning of consumer goods. *Journal of Consumer Research, 13*(1), 71–84.
McGuigan, J. (1992). *Cultural populism*. London, Routledge.
McLuhan, M. (1964). *Understanding media: The extensions of man*. New York, McGraw-Hill.
McQuarrie, E.F., Miller, J., & Phillips, B.J. (2013). The megaphone effect: Taste and audience in fashion blogging. *Journal of Consumer Research, 40*(1), 136–158.
McRobbie, A. (1981). Just like a Jackie story. In A. McRobbie & T. McCabe (Eds.), *Feminism for girls* (pp. 113–128). London, Routledge and Kegan Paul.
Mick, D.G. (1986). Consumer research and semiotics: Exploring the morphology of signs, symbols, and significance. *Journal of Consumer Research, 13*(2), 196–213.
Moore, P., & Robinson, A. (2015). The quantified self: What counts in the neoliberal workplace. *New Media & Society, 18*(11), 2774–2792.
Muniz, A.M., & O'Guinn, T.C. (2001). Brand community. *Journal of Consumer Research, 27*(4), 412–432.
Nakassis, C.V. (2013). Brands and their surfeits. *Cultural Anthropology, 28*(1), 111–126.
Ouchi, W. (1980). *Theory Z: Meeting the Japanese challenge*. Reading, MA, Addison.
Pike, A. (Ed.) (2011). *Brands and branding geographies*. London, Edward Elgar.
Pine, J., & Gilmore, J. (1999). *The experience economy: Work is theatre and every business a stage*. Boston, Harvard Business School Press.
Rainwater, L. (1959). *The working man's wife: Her personality, world and life style*. New York, Oceana Publications.
Schouten, J.W., & McAlexander, J.H. (1995). Subcultures of consumption: An ethnography of the new bikers. *Journal of Consumer Research, 22*(1), 43–61.
Sundaram, R. (2009). *Pirate modernity: Delhi's media urbanism*. London, Routledge.
Szalay, M. (2014). HBO's flexible gold. *Representations, 126*(1), 112–134.
Thompson, C.J., Locander, W.B., & Pollio, H.R. (1989). Putting consumer experience back into consumer research: The philosophy and method of existential-phenomenology. *Journal of Consumer Research, 16*(2), 133–146.
Thrift, N. (2004). Intensities of feeling: Towards a spatial politics of affect. *Geografiska Annaler, Series B, 86*(1), 57–78.
Williams, R. (1958). *Culture and society 1780–1940*. New York, Columbia University Press.
Willis, P. (1990). *Common culture: Symbolic work at play in the everyday cultures of the young*. Milton Keynes, Open University Press.
Zwick, D., Bonsu, S., & Darmody, A. (2008). Putting consumers to work: Co-creation and new marketing govern-mentality. *Journal of Consumer Culture, 8*(4), 163–196.

25
GENDER, MARKETING, AND EMOTIONS

A critical, feminist exploration of the ideological helix that defines our working worlds

Lorna Stevens

Introduction

This chapter offers a critical discussion of gender in marketing, arguing that binary thinking continues to reinforce traditional gender roles, despite the much anticipated 'feminization' of marketing in the 1990s. The chapter reviews the services marketing literature, specifically the role of 'feeling bodies' in the workplace, and the gender issues therein. This then leads to a review of the emotional labor literature, and a focus on the higher education sector, which increasingly draws on a services marketing paradigm to better serve its customers. The discussion then turns to the education sector, which now draws on the values and managerial practices of private industry in order to be more marketing-oriented and productive. This new managerialism or marketization, it will be argued, has reinstated more 'masculine' models of management, and has led to a reinforcement of the binary division of labor along gender lines. One of the arguments that this chapter will therefore make is that sex-typing and gender-typing are alive and well, deeply ingrained in institutional ideologies, and perhaps nowhere more tellingly than in the higher education sector, where research shows that women as 'feeling bodies' do most of the hard (emotional) labor. Finally, I will argue that by applying a more critical lens, we can sensitize ourselves to that which is assumed and taken for granted as the norm in relation to gendered marketing in the workplace. Furthermore, if we interrogate and critique the underlying ideologies and assumptions behind this binary system and its underlying ideologies and assumptions, we can challenge and begin to change our working worlds.

Gender in marketing

When we consider the evolution of marketing as a discipline it is hard to ignore the gender discourse at its heart. This was manifest in the emergence of consumer culture in the nineteenth century when the binary system of male producers and female consumers was born. The Cartesian split within marketing reflected the mind/body dichotomy in Western thought and other binaries arising from it such as men/women and culture/nature (e.g. Paglia, 1990). Embedded within these dichotomies are privilege and power (Squires, 2002), with the mind, cognition and rationality (the masculine) privileged over the body, emotions and feelings (the feminine). In marketing, the Cartesian split is visible in terms of marketing roles assigned to men and women in the workplace. This binary power equation has persisted in institutional sexism and biased work practices in education (Leathwood, 2005).

Our attention was drawn to the male/female dialectic in marketing in a number of key studies in the 1990s (Bristor & Fischer, 1991; Fischer & Bristor, 1994; Hirschman, 1991, 1993; Joy & Venkatesh, 1994; Peñaloza, 1991, 1994). The ACR conferences on gender, marketing and consumer behavior from 1991 onwards, ably led by Janeen Costa, also provided an ideal space within which to consider issues around gender, marketing and consumer behavior. In their 1994 article, Joy and Venkatesh unmasked the conflation (and trivialization) of women and consumption in marketing discourse, arguing that despite the fact that consumption was a bodily act, it was positioned as needing to be disciplined and contained, the rationale for this being that since the mind made the body consume, it was not necessary to deal directly with the body. The consequence of this was that consumer behavior and consumption itself came to be perceived as a disembodied phenomenon. This was particularly apparent in the consumer buying behavior model, which conceptualized consumer buying behavior as a logical and sequential process of problem solving. Furthermore, transcendence of the body tended to be a privilege of the male in marketing discourse, with female consumers defined as being at the mercy of their needs, wants and desires, all of which could be satisfied by careful segmentation, targeting and positioning on the part of astute marketing managers (see also Tadajewski, this volume, and Patterson, this volume). Across the Atlantic, the publication of *Marketing and Feminism: Current Issues and Research* by Catterall, Maclaran and Stevens (2000) also encouraged more critical research into the gender dichotomy in marketing theory and practice. The result of women's identification with consumption has served to devalue both women and consumption (Hollows, 2000).

The much heralded 'return to the body' across all disciplines from the 1990s reflected a growing impetus to disband dualistic thinking in recognition that the mind and body were interconnected in consumption acts (Bordo, 1993; Fırat & Venkatesh, 1995; Joy & Venkatesh, 1994). Indeed, this interest in the interconnectedness of mind and body in consumption, based on embodied theory and the premise that we experience the world through our bodies (Lakoff & Johnson, 1999), went some way to reconcile the mind/body dichotomy that previously dominated in relation to how consumption was conceptualized. The work of Scott, Cayla, and Cova (2017), Joy and Sherry (2003), Peñaloza (1999), Sherry et al. (2001), Thompson and Hirschman (1998), and Von Wallpach and Kreuzer (2013) has added to our understanding of embodied processes in marketing and consumer behavior. However, this challenge has not yet addressed gender stereotyping or affected marketing discourse, which continues to privilege the mind over the body, and, I will argue, continues to be deeply dichotomous. I point to the persistence of the military metaphor in marketing theory and practice as evidence of this.

The military metaphor invoked a mechanistic and masculine discourse that drew on military language to emphasize its 'cut and thrust' values. The military strategist model of the marketing manager intent on targeting, penetration, conquest and mastery (see Kotler & Singh, 1981) was memorably deconstructed by Desmond (1997). Likewise, most strategic models of marketing have traditionally drawn on military analogies such as 'frontal attacks', etc., to reinforce this masculinist discourse. The concept of customer service work as 'front-line' work is also consistent with this military strategy rhetoric, and reveals a gender issue: women are typically much more likely to be at that front line, in the direct line of fire, so to speak, and are more likely to have to deal directly with customer conflict (e.g. Kerfoot & Korczynski, 2005; Rutherford, 2001; Taylor & Tyler, 2000).

Throughout the 1990s and into the early 'noughties', a body of literature emerged that considered the 'feminization' of disciplines and of the workplace, and urged a more relational approach. This was characterized by teamwork, relationship building, intuition and collaboration

(Cameron & Gibson-Graham, 2003), and reflected the shift from manufacturing to service industries (Bradley, 1999; Rosener, 1990). The growing numbers of jobs based on 'serving and caring' led to a trend toward less hierarchical and more participative management styles, and a re-evaluation of "essentialised feminine attributes" that had previously been discouraged (McDowell, 1997, p. 11). However, the rise of service jobs also reflected a gender dichotomy, in that most jobs were gender-coded along traditional lines, and a "dichotomous economy of gender" (Knights & Thanem, 2005, p. 40), or sex role socialization (Claes, 1999, 2001) was implicit in this. According to Tynan (1997), the relationship marketing paradigm marked the 'feminine' turn in marketing, so that 'soft' skills, such as emotional and social skills replaced the 'hard' skills, such as rational and task oriented work, which had previously dominated. It therefore built itself upon a prior ideological binary system, rather than digging up the foundations, leveling the site, and starting afresh.

In their study of women marketing managers, Maclaran, Stevens and Catterall (1998) drew attention to the lived experiences of women marketing managers, finding that many such women felt pigeonholed and consigned to servicing roles, without any opportunity to break through the 'glass ceiling' into more strategic roles in the organizations they worked in. They felt themselves consigned to 'decorative', 'cosmetic' and 'smiling' roles, such as customer service and PR. Needless to say, these PR, sales, publicity and customer service front-line roles were considered to be of lower status, and offered less remuneration than the more strategic managerial roles performed by their male colleagues.

In 2000, Maclaran and Catterall built on their earlier study, observing that the increase of women into the marketing profession had not changed the kinds of roles they were taking, which were primarily in customer service and customer-facing roles such as market research and PR. They were hopeful that the rise of relationship management might impact on this gender coding in marketing, but the study also expressed concern about the lack of progress that had been made, and they called for greater critique of the underlying discourses that dictated men's and women's marketing roles in organizations. The continued lack of representation of women in all roles in advertising agencies illustrates the gender-typing and sex-typing that take place in the marketing workplace. Women still find themselves in account management and administration roles, rather than in more creative or strategic roles that have higher status and pay (see, for example, the body of work published in *Advertising & Society Review* under the editorship of Linda Scott; Baxter's (1990) study of women in advertising; Klein's (2000) follow-up study; and Grow and Broyles' (2011) work). So, we see little change in the gender-typing that takes place in the marketing workplace. The gender dichotomy within marketing is very apparent in the services marketing literature, and so I now turn to this body of work to explore its ideological underpinnings and gendered implications.

Services marketing and gender

Aside from the key aspects of services marketing, namely intangibility, inseparability of production and consumption aspects, perishability, heterogeneity and lack of ownership (Gabbott & Hogg, 1997, p. 137), the 7 Ps of services marketing include people and physical evidence. These aspects point to embodied elements in the service encounter, specifically the customer service qualities that the service worker 'performs'. Front-line staff are expected to be "cheerful, friendly, compassionate, sincere or even humble" (Lovelock, Wirtz & Chew, 2009, p. 281), and also need to possess empathy, courtesy and listening skills (Zeithaml, Berry & Parasuraman, 1996). Service workers are thus beholden to create positive feelings in their interaction with customers so that both short- and long-term organizational objectives are met. Other studies highlighted traits such as competence, courtesy, knowledge, reliability and communicative abilities (Parasuraman, Zeithaml & Berry, 1985). Aside from the above, there are additional expectations of employees working in the retail and hospitality industries, such as helpfulness, good humor, friendliness, positivity and playfulness (Warhurst & Nickson, 2007).

The relationship marketing paradigm put the emphasis on building long-term, meaningful relationships with customers, and much of the research in services marketing has focused on how to enhance that "personal relationship" (Gabbott & Hogg, 1997, p. 145), with the expectation that service employees are empathetic and sympathetic at the 'moment of truth' (Normann, 1984) when the encounter takes place.

Indeed, empathy is perhaps the quality most often cited in the services marketing literature. Parasuraman, Zeithaml and Berry (1985) identified eight dimensions in their service quality measurement tool (SERVQUAL), which they later refined to five: reliability, assurance, tangibles, empathy and responsiveness (RATER). These core attributes pointed to both physical and emotional aspects, a blended, embodied performance that necessitated service workers to be 'feeling bodies' and which comprised both intangible (mind) and tangible (bodily) aspects. More importantly, for my argument in this chapter, was that this also had gendered dimensions, as women were traditionally associated with bodies rather than minds, and with feelings rather than logic, and so culturally coded as being more likely to engage in such relationship building.

Aside from the requirement to be empathetic, there is also a recognition in the service literature that the service encounter has much in common with acting. Indeed, much of it has drawn on a dramaturgical metaphor (Goffman, 1959). Grove, Fisk and Bitner (1992) drew on this metaphor to explore the relationship between consumers (audience) and service workers (actors). Their study is one of many that have applied a dramaturgical metaphor to conceptualize the encounter between service organizations and customers. The performative dimensions of customer service have been explored in a number of key studies (e.g. Berry, 1981; Berry et al., 1985; Grönroos, 1985). Grove et al. (1992) referred to 'frontstage' and 'backstage' roles in this regard, with frontstage personnel carefully selected and trained to offer consistent performances with customers. They were aided by suitable props (tangibles), which helped to actualize the service quality, and prompted by 'backstage' forces to ensure their performance was consistently good and convincing, indeed being convincing and appearing to be sincere was perhaps the primary challenge of the 'frontstage worker' (Grove et al., 1992).

It was not only personality traits that were important, as this was very much an embodied performance that also required an appropriate physical appearance, such as being well-groomed and well-dressed (Grove et al., 1992). Lovelock et al.'s (2009, p. 24) book, *Essentials of Services Marketing*, has also stressed the importance of "smart outfits and a ready smile". These "ready smiles" were more often required by women, as they were more likely to be front of stage.

Knights and Thanem (2005) write that women's perceived suitability for service roles is bound up with women's cultural positioning as relational, affective, emotional bodies, which inevitably leads to gender-typing and indeed sex-typing in the workplace: women are ideally equipped to do the 'softer' work, leaving the 'hard', strategic management work to men. This is also supported by Kerfoot and Korczynski (2005), who have studied not only women's predominance in front-line service roles, but also how this reinforces traditional gender stereotypes, roles and performativities. Drawing on Butler (1990), the word performativities refers to our acts and gestures, which are "fabrications manufactured and sustained through corporeal signs and other discursive means" (p. 173). As such, our external personas are assumed by us to present a certain identity to the world, and gender, Butler argues, is a primary site where such performativities occur. The re-affirmation of traditional gender stereotypes apparent in the allocation of service roles, invariably results in the normalization of embodied, gendered performances, whereby some behaviors are deemed appropriate for women, and other behaviors are deemed appropriate for men (Butler, 1999). These behaviors invariably lead to discriminatory practices in the workplace, if men or women do not conform to the gendered expectations that are embedded in their job roles and perceived competencies as men or women.

Toynbee (2003) identifies the 6 'c's of women's work: namely catering, cashier or checkout, clerical, cleaning and caring. Obviously, a number of these skills are associated with the private or domestic realm, as James (1998) has pointed out. Women are positioned as having strengths associated with nurturing and the home, and their public roles in the workplace conflate with their domestic labor. This is particularly revealing in relation to mature women returning to the workplace. They might be much prized in front-line, 'motherly' roles, which are also of course typically poorly paid and part-time, because they are deemed to possess the nurturing skills needed. Thus, they bring their supposedly 'natural' and supposedly innate 'feminine' skills into the public sphere, and indeed this often has the effect of blurring the boundaries between the private and public spheres, indeed merging them, so that there might be little difference between their work at home and their work in the workplace (Nickson & Korczynski, 2009).

The perception that service roles are typically 'feminine' ones is evidenced by the fact that men might be very reluctant to work in emotionally driven and female-concentrated occupations, as they might perceive service work to be demeaning and servile (Nickson & Korczynski, 2009). This may vary according to education, class and age. There is a double-bind for women doing this so-called 'emotion work' in that it might be experienced as a gender trap because it is associated with the 'feminine' and thus is culturally perceived to be of less value than 'masculine' work. Indeed, the 'feminization' project, which emphasized more relational, participative and non-hierarchical forms of management, has lost its battle with the more systematized, surveillance (masculine) thrust that prevails (Nickson & Korczynski, 2009).

A normalization process of gendered roles in the workplace is "embedded within marketing, advertising and consumer offerings", argue Bettany *et al.* (2010, p. 17). They suggest that we need to adopt a stronger, poststructuralist approach. Poststructuralism defines itself in opposition to structuralism, and focuses on the multiple sources of meanings (readers, authors, texts, culture, society), and multiple interpretations. It rejects the prior focus on authors and the self, instead arguing that meaning is perceived, multiple and varied. In the context of gender, a poststructuralist approach highlights the constructed-ness of gender identity, normative forces and institutional power, and thus enables us to adopt a more nuanced and indeed critical stance in relation to the study of gender. Bettany *et al.* called for a stronger, political positioning, so that long-standing feminist concerns such as equal opportunity and parity in the workplace would be addressed rather than ignored. Such work, they argued, was on-going, and we still had some way to go before they were "fully articulated and realised" (2010, p. 17).

Maclaran *et al.* (2009, p. 719) have argued that the 'feminization' of the marketing agenda of the 1990s caused "status insecurity" among the powers that be, and that this has now led to a backlash, and a return to a more traditional 'masculine' value system. Fisher (2007) has also noted the persistence of a gendered discourse within marketing, suggesting that 'new managerialism', which extols 'masculine' values is now once again at the helm and fully in control. So, there is agreement that the feminization of marketing has failed to materialize, and indeed the ideological and institutional imperatives behind gendered marketing discourse and practices are still as pertinent now as they were twenty years ago. Furthermore, it seems we are in the grip of what Deem (2003) has referred to as a newly invigorated 'macho-masculinity' in management theory and practice. Dasu and Chase (2010) perceive this as an intensive attack on the soft side of customer management in organizations, which bears a resemblance to the zeal with which organizations have worked to redesign workflow and supply chains. This re-invigoration of the 'masculine' trivializes and relegates traditional 'feminine' activities such as nurturing and caring for others, and is made manifest in the form of a mechanistic and cynical (gendered) form of emotional labor that is simultaneously expected and denigrated in the workplace, while such labor is exploited for organizational ends (Constanti & Gibbs, 2004; Illouz, 1997).

I argue that there are strong ideological links between services marketing and emotional labor, as both engage in gendered type-casting and sex type-casting, and so I now turn to the growing literature on emotional labor in order to explore gender issues within it, and to consider where women are positioned in relation to this form of work.

Emotional labor

The term emotional labor was first coined by Hochschild in 1983 in the book *The Managed Heart: Commercialization of Human Feeling*. In it she wrote that emotional labor was the management of feeling to create a public facial and bodily display. She also refers to surface acting (one's outward behavior) and deep acting (one's inner feelings) in relation to emotional labor. The definition emphasizes that such service roles are visual performances during which employees act out an appropriate part that requires them to appear to be engaging with customers in a positive and indeed empathetic way, irrespective of how they might actually be feeling beneath the surface. This demonstrates how emotional and bodily displays work together to create a desired impression on customers (see Warhurst & Nickson (2009) for a fuller discussion of the embodied aspects of emotional labor).

Elsewhere, England and Farkas (1986, p. 91) have described emotional labor as making efforts to understand others, including empathizing with their situation, and feeling "their feelings as a part of one's own". Koster (2011, p. 68) defines emotional labor as "merging the emotions of others (spontaneous emotion and care), as well as managing one's own emotions (surface and deep acting)". It is therefore about caring about (feeling affection) and caring for (servicing other's needs). A more functional definition is offered by Ashforth and Humphrey (1993, p. 88), who define emotional labor as "the display of expected emotions by service agents during service encounters". They also observe that there are four significant factors in relation to emotional labor and the service encounter. These are that front-line service staff represent the organization to customers; that such encounters involve face-to-face interaction; that they often have a "dynamic and emergent quality" (1993, p. 90); and that there are intangible elements. The four factors place a premium on the behavior of the service agent.

The emotional labor paradigm now dominates the study of interactive service roles, and there is a significant body of work on emotional labor across numerous sectors such as nursing, hospitality, tourism and education (e.g. Ashforth & Humphrey, 1993; Hochschild, 1983; Varca, 2009; Warhurst & Nickson, 2009; Leathwood, 2005). While emotional labor has also been the subject of studies in leadership and organizational studies in the field of business and management, it has largely been ignored in the marketing field, with the exception of the work by Warhurst, Nickson, Witz and Cullen (2000a, 2000b); Warhurst, Nickson, Witz and Cullen (2000); Witz, Warhurst and Nickson (2003), Warhurst and Nickson (2007) and Warhurst and Nickson (2009) that makes reference to it, albeit that the primary focus is on aesthetic labor. There is little argument that bodies are deployed for organizational ends, but emotional labor is also an embodied 'performance', to use Hochschild's (1983) terminology. They have something else in common: both also share a pattern of discriminatory work practices, poor pay and gender stereotyping (e.g. Pettinger, 2004, 2005, 2008).

Macdonald and Sirianni (1996, p. 3) studied questions of power and governance at work and referred to the "emotional proletariat" in this regard, thereby emphasizing the exploitative nature of emotional labor. Grandey (2000, 2015) has also argued that emotional labor is above all a regulatory process aimed at meeting organizational goals. Furthermore, it creates a "simulacrum of workplace community" within service work that serves management purposes (Ezzy, 2001). In other words, the more convincing emotional laborers are, the more advantageous for the organization.

Not surprisingly, this acting out of emotions can be the cause of considerable psychological stress and emotive dissonance for service workers, notes Hochschild (1983). Indeed, there have been a considerable number of studies that focus on the adverse effects of such work on employees. Ashforth and Humphrey (1993) address the psychological challenges of emotional labor, such as pressure, dissonance and self-alienation on the part of the service agent. Varca (2009) has studied the degree of stress experienced by employees in a large communications firm call center engaged in emotional work. More recently, Hulsheger and Schew (2011) have studied the effects of surface acting on mental health, showing that such work takes its toll on employees over long periods, and often leads to ill health and job burnout. Anaza, Nowlin and Wu (2016) also discuss the negative effects of customer orientation and the imperative to have emotionally engaged employees. Ashforth and Humphrey (1993) argued that it is easier to comply with the requirements of emotional labor than to experience the horrors of dissonance. More recently Phillips, Wee Tan and Julian (2006) have also addressed emotional dissonance in their study of services marketing and the identity problems such work creates for service workers. It is also worth emphasizing that this is a gender issue, or at least an issue mostly felt by women, given that they do the lion's share of such work. A recent study by Walsh and Bartikowski (2013), for example, reflected on the cost of 'deep acting' and 'surface acting' on women and men in the workplace, finding that women engaged in surface acting were particularly negatively affected in terms of job satisfaction and stress.

It is not surprising that emotional labor takes its toll, given its performative dimensions. Unsurprisingly much of the literature on emotional labor is steeped in the language of the stage, and borrows concepts from services literature to conceptualize its requirements. Thus, the literature is replete with phrases such as 'surface acting', 'deep acting', 'feeling rules', 'display rules' and 'affective displays', as well as words such as 'actors' and 'personas' (Ashforth & Humphrey, 1993; Goffman, 1959; Hochschild, 1979, 1983). This emphasis, however, might suggest that emotional labor is always a form of acting to win over an audience, whereas emotional labor could also be genuine in some instances and thus not require acting. In fact, a service agent might be expressing an authentic self in the service encounter and indeed this constitutes a third kind of emotional labor, which is a genuine expression of expected emotion (Ashforth & Humphrey, 1993). Medler-Liraz and Seger-Guttman (2015) also allude to this third kind of emotional labor, which is for employees to show some degree of authenticity in terms of their service work, thus putting considerable pressure on emotional labor agents to be convincing and believable. They might even assume protypical characteristics that go along with the role, until their 'acting' becomes part of their authentic self-expression. That in fact is the ideal, if a recent article on the value of mindfulness in emotional labor is anything to go by. Wang, Berthon, Pitt and McCarthy (2016) write about the value of service workers *truly* empathizing with customers, thus intensifying the self-less caring skills required in this work or, as the authors put it, mindfulness enables employees "to put themselves into people's shoes and feel their feelings" (p. 658). This echoes England and Farkas' (1986) study that exhorted service workers to feel what customers felt as if they were their own feelings. If we extend the acting analogy, presumably this deep empathy would be akin to the method acting school, which we all appreciate is much more effective and impressive than simply observing an actor seemingly repeating lines from a learned script.

There has been a significant body of work that has explored feminine and female capital in the field of paid caring work, which is one of the primary domains of emotional labor. Notable among them is Skeggs' (1997) study, which considers the intersections between class and gender in relation to women's caring work, and the emotional investment of mothers in their children rather than themselves, highlighting differences between the middle-class women in the study, focused on their children's educational capital, and the working-class women she interviewed, who prioritized their children's emotional well-being, concluding that women's gender capital operates within limits. In her study of women in various roles and at various levels in nursing and social work, Huppatz (2009) found that women were unlikely to attain a higher managerial position in these professions. She makes the distinction between female (embodied) capital and feminine capital, suggesting how both are forms of capital that women may "wield in innovative ways" (Huppatz, 2009, p. 60). However, in her study she also observes that the "naturalization" of feminine capital in relation to caring work, based on the assumption that such skills and capabilities are not seen as acquired skills but as "an innate female capacity", leads to such skills being undervalued and underpaid (Huppatz, 2009, p. 55).

Huppatz (2009) draws on Bourdieu's (2001, p. 93) argument that women's symbolic capital is less culturally valued than men's: women are "separated from men by a negative symbolic co-efficient" and "a diminution of symbolic capital entailed by being a woman". Bourdieu also observes that women typically find work in "quasi-extensions of the domestic space" (p. 94), which is a concept that has much salience in this chapter. Reay (2004, p. 71), in her study on women's involvement in their children's education, suggests that Bourdieu's work does not specifically consider emotional capital, however, which is "a specifically gendered capital" that is "all about investments in others rather than the self".

Ashforth and Humphreys (1993) suggest that we need to see emotional labor in a wider, macro context that moves beyond organizational and occupational norms to consider the societal imperatives behind it, so what is the wider significance of the rise of emotional labor? Eva Illouz (1997) notes that it is laden with gender distinctions. She writes that "the communicative ethos" of managing is now aligned with "traditional female selfhood" (p. 43), and indeed the loss of self in the service of others; a feeling economy that masks "social domination" (p. 45). In her later work, *Cold Intimacies: The Making of Emotional Capitalism* (2007), she discusses how capitalism has created an emotional culture in the workplace "in which the public and private are now deeply and inextricably intertwined" (p. 3). She goes on to observe that the distinction between men and women is based on and reproduces itself through emotional cultures that comprise fixed emotional divisions, and that these underlying assumptions have found their way into the workplace and indeed have taken center stage. This is an appropriation of traditional feminine qualities to create a new, better, more communicative management style with overtly masculine traits, whereby emotions are "more closely harnessed to instrumental actions" (p. 23).

Emotional labor is clearly laced with ideological assumptions around women and 'feminine' traits attributed to them, and is not a gender-neutral phenomenon (e.g. Taylor & Tyler, 2000; Pilcher, 2007; Wolkowitz, 2006), as it is primarily undertaken by women, who are perceived to be better at performing it. Women engaged in emotional, service work are also doing gender, in the sense that they are enacting gendered roles based on stereotypical beliefs in women's social capital and interpersonal skills as women (Kerfoot & Korczynski, 2005). Such labor conflates their domestic and public roles and, needless to say, is often supervised and controlled by male emotional managers (James 1998). Their work is thus entangled with assumptions about feeling (female) bodies and rational (male) minds; what it means to be a woman, and what it means to be a man; in other words, an illustration of the binary system that continues to control us all.

Hochschild's (2012) work on the outsourced self discusses the marketization of the personal realm so that everything that had previously been part of the private and personal, such as love and child-rearing, is now available as packaged expertise. The market reaches into the heart of people's emotional lives, she argues, a realm previously shielded from market imperatives, and we are urged to see ourselves in market terms. Her earlier book, *The Managed Heart: Commercialization of Human Feelings* (1983), documented the marketization of emotions, and the gender issues embedded in it, noting that "[a]s traditionally more accomplished managers of feelings in private life, women more than men have put emotional labor on the market, and they know more about its personal costs" (p. 11). Indeed, women's traditional skills at emotion management are "more often used by women as one of the offerings they trade for economic support" (p. 20). Thus, the private, emotion management realm traditionally inhabited by women has been replicated in the public sphere in emotional labor roles that mirror those they are expected to excel at on the home front.

Given that this volume of critical work on marketing is primarily addressing the marketing academic community, it seems appropriate to now turn to one of the domains in which emotional labor is proliferating, namely that of higher education. How has the marketization of education impacted on gender roles within academe, and what can it reveal about the ideological forces at work around us?

Emotional labor in higher education

There has been a proliferation of studies in the educational field in recent years that have explored the emotional labor of teachers and lecturers in education. The significance of emotional labor in the context of higher education is obvious. Teachers and lecturers are now service providers, seeking to satisfy the demands of their customers (students), with student satisfaction the Holy Grail that must be sought (Ogbonna & Harris, 2004).

Kinman, Wray and Strange (2011) point to the clear parallels between teaching and services work in general, arguing that emotional labor within teaching has become increasingly intensive, and that this has had a detrimental effect on teachers' well-being. There have been a number of key studies on emotional labor in higher education (e.g. Berry & Cassidy, 2013; Constanti & Gibbs, 2004; Davies, 2003; Deem, 1998, 2003; Deem & Brehony, 2005; Ogbonna & Harris, 2004; Zhang & Zhu, 2008). This body of work is typically framed within the impact of new managerialism in higher education.

New managerialism "asserts the rights of managers to manage and the importance of management . . . challenging professional autonomy and discretion" (Deem, 2003, p. 242), and manifests itself as a focus on cost centers, outsourcing, performance scrutiny, surveillance, auditing, performance indicators, and league tables (Deem, 2003). Constanti and Gibbs (2004) have explored the impact of academic institutions as service providers, whereby customer/student satisfaction and profit for management have led to the exploitation of academics to satisfy both of these imperatives. The authors note that emotional labor is more "susceptible to both emotional and financial exploitation than other forms of labor" (Constanti & Gibbs, 2004, p. 246). Furthermore, they argue that the managerialist expectations of academic staff have led to "voluntary exploitation" (Constanti & Gibbs, 2004, p. 248). Berry and Cassidy (2013) also express concern at the intensification of emotional labor in higher education. Findings from their study showed that lecturers performed high levels of emotional labor compared to other professions that were more often associated with it, such as nursing, and they highlighted the fact that high levels of emotional labor were linked to dysfunctional factors such as problems in relation to well-being, job satisfaction and job performance. Ogbonna and Harris (2004) have also studied the effect of the marketization of higher education and the toll it has taken on academic staff in relation to the emotional labor expected of them. Their study identified significant gender differences, with female lecturers feeling particularly vulnerable to the managerial control exerted on them in relation to their emotional labor performance.

Turning to gender issues within emotional labor in higher education, there is a growing body of literature that explores its gendered implications. The 'feminization' across many disciplines was marked by a growing interest in the social and relational aspects of such public service work. Ahmed's study of 'affective economics' (2004) and Leathwood and Hey's (2009) article discuss how emotions work in certain ways to do certain things. Both studies unpick the gendered assumptions within higher education, showing how such emotional skills are coded as feminine (see also Leathwood & Read, 2009).

In addition, the 'new managerialism' in higher education has been the subject of a significant body of feminist critique (e.g. Davies, 2003; Deem, 2003; Leathwood, 2005; Morley, 2005). In her 2005 study, Leathwood writes that despite the circulation of optimistic discourses about the long-awaited revalidation of the 'feminine' in management, this has not materialized due to the powerful force of the "masculinist new managerialism" (p. 388) sweeping through further and higher education. Private sector management practices, she argues, now apply, whereby middle management positions are feminized as the (female) neo-liberal subject of "emotionality, caring and introspection" (Walkerdine, 2003, p. 242). Drawing on Nancy Chodorow's (1978) work, Leathwood (2005) notes that idealized feminized identities, such as caring and nurturing, are constructed in relation to others, whereas their masculine counterparts are constituted as "standing alone, independent and autonomous" (p. 401).

Chowdhry's (2014) study showed that female lecturers were strongly identified with nurturing requirements in regard to students, including "spoon feeding" (p. 566), which was also demonstrated in Larson's (2008) study of the caring performance of women lecturers in higher education (their "pink collar duties", as she describes it), with both studies suggesting that much of this work was invisible and unrecognized. Leathwood and Read's (2009) study also focused on the particular pressures faced by women lecturers in relation to the emotional labor expected of them. Finally, Morley (2005) offers a particularly scathing insight into "hegemonic masculinities and gendered power relations" (p. 411) within the new managerialist paradigm in higher education, with its emphasis on competition, auditing, performance, control and measurement. She focuses in particular on the teaching quality movement, demonstrating how "women's socialized patterns of caring" are appropriated by it, thus creating a "psychic economy", such as quality assessment exercises in teaching and learning, which is in fact "a gendered care chain" (Morley, 2005, p. 413). Women typically find themselves inextricably immersed and enmeshed in such work, while their male colleagues often manage to evade them in order to pursue research productivity and competitive individualism!

Koster (2011) offers a more personal account of emotional labor in higher education, discussing her own "extraordinary emotional labor" (p. 69) in her role as a lecturer on gender in a higher education institution. She emphasizes that this was indeed a gender issue, as she sought to create boundaries and impose limitations on the exhausting and boundary-less expectations placed on her by her students. Koster (2011) concurs with other studies, previously mentioned, that women not only provide more emotional labor than men in higher education, but are also subject to societal expectations that they will do so. This emotional 'housework' or 'pink-collar' work is both stressful and time consuming. It blurs the boundaries between the public and private sphere, offers no professional or monetary remuneration and, above all, is taken for granted. Deem's (2003) study has also shown that gendered expectations and constraints are as firmly in place as ever, with what she terms a "macho-masculinity" (p. 243) deeply embedded in management, which is based on tacit understandings that disadvantage women.

To return to Leathwood's (2005) study, she observes that women are in fact often hybrids between academic autonomy and traditional femininity, struggling to manage these dual expectations, a double-edged sword one might say. At the time of writing this chapter, there is little to suggest that the tide is likely to turn away from the gender-typing and sex-typing in higher education that seems to have gathered fresh momentum in recent years. In fact, the macho-managerialist grip on education is likely to tighten as, post-Brexit, we brace ourselves for the storms to come in terms of falling student numbers, greater competition, reduced budgets, less research-funding, and even greater accountability for our students' and managers' satisfaction.

Conclusion

This chapter has taken us on a journey that began with the gender dichotomy in marketing, a discussion of the much anticipated 'feminization' of disciplines and, specifically, how this has impacted (or not) in marketing in the academy and in the workplace. This led into a review of services marketing and the gender issues therein, showing that women are positioned as the 'feeling bodies' of much marketing work, reinforcing gender-typing and sex-typing in the workplace. The emotional labor literature tells a similar story, and is equally revealing in terms of the gendered issues within it. Finally, I focused on emotional labor within the higher education sector, particularly the growing body of feminist work in this fertile field, which has critiqued emotional labor and its implications for women. A review of this literature shows how the current masculinist new managerialism has impacted on all of us, but particularly on female academics, who are expected to be adept at managing the 'caring' demands of this newly marketized domain. Once again, ideologies around women's 'nature' and their cultural conditioning to nurture others (Chodorow 1978) conspire to reinforce gender stereotypes.

One of the key objectives of this chapter has been to draw together two domains: services marketing and emotional labor, and show their underlying ideologies from a gendered perspective. It is apparent that when underlying ideological biases are not sufficiently challenged at their foundations they can be reinvigorated by market forces, as has clearly been the case with the stalled 'feminization' of disciplines and workplaces. One might equally argue that a re-appropriation (and exploitation) of the 'feminine' for organizations' own ends is more accurate. A greater awareness of that which is considered the norm, and a more critical approach generally, can enable us to challenge what is expected from us, and the gendered assumptions upon which these expectations are based. Continuing to cast a critical eye on that which is normalized, while potentially dangerous in terms of our professional careers, and to find outlets for our work that challenge the dominant paradigm, is important, as it is only by unpicking the underlying ideologies that shape our experiences that we can begin to discuss them, problematize them and ultimately change them.

References

Ahmed, S. (2004). Affective economics. *Social Text*, 22(2), 117–139.
Anaza, N.A., Nowlin, E.L., & Wu, G.J. (2016). Staying engaged on the job: The role of emotional labor, job resources, and customer orientation. *European Journal of Marketing*, 50(7/8), 1470–1492.
Ashforth, B.E., & Humphrey, R.H. (1993). Emotional labor in service roles: The influence of identity. *Academy of Management Review*, 18(1), 88–115.
Baxter, M. (1990). *Women in advertising*. London, Institute of Practitioners in Advertising.
Berry, K., & Cassidy, S. (2013). Emotional labour in university lecturers: Considerations for higher education institutions. *Journal of Curriculum and Teaching*, 2(2), 22–36.
Berry, L.L. (1981). The employee as customer. *Journal of Retail Banking*, 3(March), 33–40.
Berry, L.L., Zeithaml, V.A., & Parasuraman, A. (1985). Quality counts in services too. *Business Horizons*, 28(3), 44–52.

Bettany, S., Dobscha, S., O'Malley, L., & Prothero, A. (2010). Moving beyond binary oppositions: Exploring the tapestry of gender in consumer research and marketing. *Marketing Theory*, *10*(1), 3–28.

Bordo, S. (1993). *Unbearable weight: Feminism, western culture, and the body*. Berkeley, University of California Press.

Bourdieu, P. (2001). *Masculine domination*. Cambridge, Polity Press.

Bradley, H. (1999). *Gender and power in the workplace: Analysing the impact of economic change*. Basingstoke, Macmillan Press.

Bristor, J., & Fischer, E. (1991). Feminist thought: Implications for consumer research. *Journal of Consumer Research*, *19*(4), 518–536.

Butler, J.P. (1999). *Gender trouble: Feminism and the subversion of identity*. London, Routledge.

Cameron, J., & Gibson-Graham, J.K. (2003). Feminising the economy: Metaphors, strategies, politics. *Gender, Place & Culture*, *10*(2), 145–157.

Catterall, M., Maclaran, P., & Stevens, L. (Eds.) (2000). *Marketing and feminism: Current issues and research*. London, Routledge.

Chodorow, N.J. (1978). *The reproduction of mothering: Psychoanalysis and the sociology of gender*. Berkeley, University of California Press.

Chowdhry, S. (2014). The caring performance and the 'blooming student': Exploring the emotional labour of further education lecturers in Scotland. *Journal of Vocational Education and Training*, *66*(4), 554–571.

Claes, M.-T. (1999). What is equality and how do we get there? *International Labour Review*, *138*(4), 431–446.

Claes, M.-T. (2001). Women, men and management styles. In M. Loutfi (Ed.), *Women, gender & work* (pp. 385–404). Washington, International Labour Office.

Constanti, P., & Gibbs, P. (2004). Higher education teachers and emotional labour. *International Journal of Educational Management*, *18*(4), 243–249.

Costa, J.A. (1991). *Proceedings of 1st conference on gender and consumer behavior*. June, Salt Lake City, UT, University of Utah.

Dasu, S., & Chase, R.B. (2010). Designing the soft side of customer service. *MIT Sloan Management Review*, *52*(1), 33–39.

Davies, B. (2003). Death to critique and dissent: The policies and practices of new managerialism and of 'evidence-based practice'. *Gender & Education*, *1*(10), 91–103.

Deem, R. (1998). New managerialism and higher education: The management of performances and cultures in universities in the UK. *International Studies in Sociology of Education*, *8*(1), 47–70.

Deem, R. (2003). Gender, organizational cultures and the practices of manager-academics in UK universities. *Gender, Work & Organizations*, *10*(2), 239–259.

Deem, R., & Brehony, K.J. (2005). Management as ideology: The case of 'new managerialism' in higher education. *Oxford Review of Education*, *31*(2), 217–235.

Desmond, J. (1997). Marketing and the war machine. *Marketing Intelligence and Planning*, *15*(7), 338–351.

England, P., & Farkas, G. (1986). *Households, employment and gender: A social, economic, and demographic view*. Hawthorne, NY, Aldine Publishing Co.

Ezzy, D. (2001). A simulacrum of workplace community: Individualism and engineered culture that service work and management encourage. *Sociology*, *35*(3), 631–650.

Fırat, A.F., & Venkatesh, A. (1995). Liberatory postmodernism and the reenchantment of consumption. *Journal of Consumer Research*, *22*(3), 239–267.

Fischer, E., & Bristor, J. (1994). A feminist poststructuralist analysis of the rhetoric of marketing relationships. *International Journal of Research in Marketing*, *11*(4), 317–331.

Fisher, G. (2007). 'You need tits to get on round here': Gender and sexuality in the entrepreneurial university of the 21st century. *Ethnography*, *8*(4), 503–517.

Gabbott, M., & Hogg, G.C. (1997). *Contemporary services marketing management: A reader*. London, The Dryden Press.

Goffman, E. (1959). *The presentation of self in everyday life*. New York, Anchor Books.

Grandey, A.A. (2000). Emotional regulation in the workplace: A new way to conceptualize emotional labour. *Journal of Occupational Health Psychology*, *5*(1), 95–110.

Grandey, A.A. (2015). Smiling for a wage: What emotional labor teaches us about emotion regulation. *Psychological Inquiry*, *26*(1), 54–60.

Grönroos, C. (1985). Internal marketing: Theory and practice. *American Marketing Association's Services Conference Proceedings* (pp. 41–47). Chicago, IL, American Marketing Association.

Grove, S.J., Fisk, R.P., & Bitner, M.J. (1992). The service experience as theater. Retrieved January 2017 from www.acrwebsite.org/volumes/7341/volumes/v19/NA-19

Grow, J., & Broyles, S.J. (2011). Unspoken rules of the creative game: Insights to shape the next generation from top advertising creative women. *Advertising & Society Review, 12*(1). Available online https://muse.jhu.edu/article/423610.

Hirschman, E.C. (1991). A feminist critique of marketing theory: Toward agentic-communal balance. Retrieved January 2017 from www.acrwebsite.org/volumes/gender/v01/SD%20Gender%20Conference%202%20-%20A%20Feminist%20Critique%20of%20Marketing%20Theory.pdf

Hirschman, E.C. (1993). Ideology in consumer research, 1980 and 1990: A Marxist and feminist critique. *Journal of Consumer Research, 19*(4), 537–555.

Hochschild, A.R. (1979). Emotion work, feeling rules, and social structure. *American Journal of Sociology, 85*(3), 551–575.

Hochschild, A.R. (1983). *The managed heart: Commercialization of human feelings*. Berkeley, University of California Press.

Hochschild, A.R. (2012). *The outsourced self: Intimate life in market times*. New York, Metropolitan Books.

Hollows, J. (2000). *Feminism, femininity & popular culture*. Manchester, Manchester University Press.

Hulsheger, U.R., & Schewe, A.F. (2011). On the costs and benefits of emotional labor: A meta-analysis of three decades of research. *Journal of Occupational Health Psychology, 16*(3), 361–389.

Huppatz, K. (2009). Reworking Bourdieu's capital: Feminine and female capitals in the field of paid caring work. *Sociology, 43*(1), 45–66.

Illouz, E. (1997). Who cares for the caretaker's daughter? Towards a sociology of happiness in the era of reflexive modernity. *Theory, Culture & Society, 14*(4), 31–66.

Illouz, E. (2007). *Cold intimacies: The making of emotional capitalism*. Cambridge, Polity Press.

James, N. (1998). Emotional labour: Skill & work in the social regulation of feelings. In L. Mackay, K. Soothill & K. Melia (Eds.), *Classic texts in health care* (pp. 219–225). Oxford: Butterworth-Heinemann.

Joy, A., & Sherry, J.F. (2003). Speaking of art as embodied imagination: A multisensory approach to understanding aesthetic experience. *Journal of Consumer Research, 30*(September), 259–282.

Joy, A., & Venkatesh, A. (1994). Postmodernism, feminism, and the body: The visible and the invisible in consumer research. *International Journal of Research in Marketing, 11*(4), 333–357.

Kerfoot, D., & Korczynski, M. (2005). Gender and service: New directions for the study of 'front-line' service work. *Gender, Work & Organization, 12*(5), 387–399.

Kinman, G., Wray, S., & Strange, C. (2011). Emotional labour, burnout and job satisfaction in UK teachers: The role of workplace social support. *Educational Psychology, 31*(7), 843–856.

Klein, D. (2000). *Women in advertising, 10 years on: Findings and recommendations of a study commissioned by the Institute of Practitioners in Advertising*. London, IPA.

Knights, D., & Thanem, T. (2005). Embodying emotional labour. In D. Morgan, B. Brandth & E. Kvande (Eds.), *Gender bodies & work* (pp. 31–43). London, Ashgate Publishing.

Koster, S. (2011). The self-managed heart: Teaching gender and doing emotional labour in a higher education institution. *Pedagogy, Culture & Society, 19*(1), 61–77.

Kotler, P., & Singh, R. (1981). Marketing warfare in the 1980s. *The Journal of Business Strategy, 3*(Winter), 30–41.

Lakoff, G., & Johnson, M. (1999). *Philosophy in the flesh: The embodied mind and its challenge to western thought*. New York, Basic.

Larson, H.A. (2008). Emotional labor: The pink collar duties of teaching, currents in teaching and learning. *Teaching and Learning, 1*(1), 45–56.

Leathwood, C. (2005). Treat me as a human being – don't look at me as a woman: Femininities and professional identities in further education. *Gender & Education, 17*(4), 387–409.

Leathwood, C., & Hey, V. (2009). Gender(ed) discourses and emotional sub-texts: Theorising emotion in higher education. *Teaching in Higher Education, 14*(4), 429–440.

Leathwood, C., & Read, B. (2009). *Gender and the changing face of higher education: A feminised future?* London, SRHE & Open University Press.

Lovelock, C.H., Wirtz, J., & Chew, P.Y.P. (2009). *Essentials of services marketing*. Singapore, Pearson Education.

Macdonald, C.L., & Sirianni, C. (1996). *Working in the service society*. Philadelphia, Temple University Press.

Maclaran, P., & Catterall, M. (2000). Bridging the knowledge divide: Issues on the feminisation of marketing practice. *Journal of Marketing Management, 16*(6), 635–646.

Maclaran, P., Miller, C., Parsons, E., & Surman, E. (2009). Praxis or performance: Does critical marketing have a gender blind-spot? *Journal of Marketing Management, 25*(7–8), 713–728.

Maclaran, P., Stevens, L., & Catterall, M. (1998). The 'glasshouse effect': Women in marketing management. *Marketing Intelligence & Planning, 15*(7), 309–317.

McDowell, L. (1997). *Capital culture: Gender at work in the city*. Oxford, Blackwell.

Medler-Liraz, H., & Seger-Guttman, T. (2015). The relationship between emotional labor strategies, service provider hostility, and service quality. *Services Marketing Quarterly, 36*(3), 210–225.

Morley, L. (2005). Opportunity or exploitation? Women and quality assurance in higher education. *Gender & Education, 17*(4), 411–429.

Nickson, D., & Korczynski, M. (2009). Editorial: Aesthetic labour, emotional labour and masculinity. *Gender, Work and Organization, 16*(3), 291–299.

Normann, R. (1984). *Service management strategy and leadership in service businesses*. New York, Wiley.

Ogbonna, E., & Harris, L.C. (2004). Work intensification and emotional labour among UK university lecturers: An exploratory study. *Organization Studies, 25*(7), 1185–1203.

Paglia, C. (1990). *Sexual personae: Art and decadence from Nefertiti to Emily Dickinson*. London, Penguin Books.

Parasuraman, A., Zeithaml, V.A., & Berry, L.L. (1985). A conceptual model of service quality and its implications for future research. *Journal of Marketing, 49*(4), 41–50.

Peñaloza, L. (1991). Boundary construction, feminism & consumer research. In J.A. Costa (Ed.), *Proceedings of 1st Conference on Gender and Consumer Behavior*. June, Salt Lake City, UT, University of Utah.

Peñaloza, L. (1994). Crossing boundaries/drawing lines: A look at the nature of gender boundaries and their impact on marketing research. *International Journal of Research in Marketing, 11*(4), 359–379.

Peñaloza, L. (1999). Just doing it: A visual ethnographic study of spectacular consumption at Niketown. *Consumption, Markets & Culture, 2*(4), 337–400.

Pettinger, L. (2004). Brand culture and branded workers: Service work and aesthetic labor in fashion retail. *Consumption, Markets & Culture, 7*(2), 165–184.

Pettinger, L. (2005). Gendered work meets gendered goods: Selling and service in clothing retail. *Gender, Work & Organization, 12*(5), 460–478.

Pettinger, L. (2008). Developing aesthetic labor: The importance of consumption. *International Journal of Work Organization & Emotion, 2*(4), 327–343.

Phillips, B., Wee Tan, T.T., & Julian, C. (2006). The theoretical underpinnings of emotional dissonance: A framework and analysis of propositions. *Journal of Services Marketing, 20*(7), 471–478.

Pilcher, K. (2007). A gendered 'managed heart'? An exploration of the gendering of emotional labor, aesthetic labor, and body work in service sector employment. *Reinvention: A Journal of Undergraduate Research*. Retrieved January 2017 from www.warwick.ac.uk/go/reinventionjournal/pastissues/launchissue

Reay, D. (2004). Gendering Bourdieu's concepts of capitals? Emotional capital, women and social class. *The Sociological Review, 52*(2), 57–74.

Rosener, J.B. (1990). Ways women lead. *Harvard Business Review, 68*(6), 119–125.

Rutherford, S. (2001). Any difference? An analysis of gender and divisional management styles in a large airline. *Gender, Work & Organization, 8*(3), 326–345.

Scott, R., Cayla, J., & Cova, B. (2017). Selling pain to the saturated self. *Journal of Consumer Research, 44*(1), 22–43.

Sherry, J.F., Kozinets, R.V., Storm, D., Duhachek, A., Nuttavuthisit, K., & Deberry-Spence, B. (2001). Being in the zone: Staging retail theater at ESPN Zone Chicago. *Journal of Consumer Psychology, 14*(1–2), 151–158.

Skeggs, B. (1997). *Formations of class and gender: Becoming respectable*. London, Sage.

Squires, J. (2002). *Gender in political theory*. Cambridge, Polity Press.

Taylor, S., & Tyler, M. (2000). Emotional labour and sexual difference in the airline industry. *Work, Employment and Society, 14*(1), 77–95.

Thompson, C.J., & Hirschman, E.C. (1998). An existential analysis of the embodied self in postmodern consumer culture. *Consumption, Markets & Culture, 2*(4), 401–447.

Toynbee, P. (2003). *Hard work: Life in low-pay Britain*. London, Bloomsbury.

Tynan, C. (1997). A review of the marriage analogy in relationship marketing. *Journal of Marketing Management, 13*(7), 695–704.

Varca, P.E. (2009). Emotional empathy and front line employees: Does it make sense to care about the customer? *Journal of Services Marketing, 23*(1), 51–56.

Von Wallpach, S., & Kreuzer, M. (2013). Multi-sensory sculpting (MSS): Eliciting embodied brand knowledge via multi-sensory metaphors. *Journal of Business Research*, *66*(9), 1325–1331.

Walkerdine, V. (2003). Neoliberalism, working-class subjects and higher education. *Contemporary Social Science*, *6*(2) (June), 255–271.

Walsh, G., & Bartikowski, B. (2013). Employee emotional labor and quitting intentions: Moderating effects of gender and age. *European Journal of Marketing*, *47*(8), 1213–1237.

Wang, E.J., Berthon, P., Pitt, L., & McCarthy, I.P. (2016). Service, emotional labor, and mindfulness. *Business Horizons*, *59*(6), 655–661.

Warhurst, C., & Nickson, D.P. (2007). Employee experience of aesthetic labor in retail and hospitality. *Work, Employment & Society*, *21*(1), 103–120.

Warhurst, C., & Nickson, D.P. (2009). 'Who's got the look?' Emotional, aesthetic and sexualized labour in interactive services. *Gender, Work and Organization*, *16*(3), 385–404.

Warhurst, C., Nickson, D.P., Witz, A., & Cullen, A.M. (2000a). Aesthetic labour in interactive service work: Some case study evidence from the 'new' Glasgow. *Service Industries Journal*, *20*(3), 1–18.

Warhurst, C., Nickson, D., Witz, A., & Cullen, A.M. (2000b). Aesthetic labour: An unforeseen future of work and employment. *Management Research News*, *23*(9–1), 154–155.

Witz, A., Warhurst, C., & Nickson, D. (2003). The labour of aesthetics and the aesthetics of organization. *Organization*, *10*(1), 33–54.

Wolkowitz, C. (2006). *Bodies at work*. London, Sage.

Zeithaml, V.A., Berry, L.L., & Parasuraman, A. (1996). The behavioral consequences of service quality. *Journal of Marketing*, *60*(April), 31–46.

Zhang, Q., & Zhu, W. (2008). Exploring emotion in teaching: Emotional labor, burnout, and satisfaction in Chinese higher education. *Communication Education*, *57*(1), 105–122.

26
BIOPOLITICAL MARKETING AND THE COMMODIFICATION OF SOCIAL CONTEXTS

Detlev Zwick and Alan Bradshaw

Introduction

Digital marketers like to talk about the consumer empowerment generated by new information and communication technologies. Marketing experts agree that we have more choice, more information, more entertainment, more transparency, and lower prices thanks to Amazon, Facebook, Youtube, and all the rest. The Empowerment-through-Technology chorus is so loud and cohesive that we might easily take its message for granted. And in some limited respect, consumers might feel empowered when shopping on Amazon.com or in the malls comparing prices across many stores with their iPhones on hand. But let us be very clear about the idea of empowerment that is promoted by the cheerleaders of what Jodi Dean (2009) calls 'communicative capitalism'. Real empowerment, so much should be clear, can never be 'granted' to consumers by those in economic (and thus political) power. In the final analysis – and putting aside for a moment the fact that even empowered consumers are still constructed first and foremost as subjects of consumption – the ideal of the empowered consumer (rational, enlightened, informed, restrained, un-manipulable) is completely antithetical to any needs of capital. Therefore, any call for actual consumer empowerment would automatically be a radical demand and an insurgent claim aimed at undermining and replacing capital's power to dominate labor totally. In the end, it is important to recognize that any technology employed by marketing today aims to become a technology of consumer control (even if never completely successful), which permits empowerment only in a version sanctioned by capital. That is why marketing (and capital more generally [see Lazzarato, 2004]) today is biopolitical. It wants to govern life completely while appearing to not govern at all. So, how does marketing do this?

In this chapter, we introduce our theory of biopolitical marketing and argue that biopolitical marketing wishes to supersede hitherto dominant corporate modes of marketing management based on customer manipulation and control. Biopolitical marketing is a mode of governing consumers that aims at finding (or actively creating) opportunities for consumer participation (e.g., in the process of new product innovation [see Dujarier, 2016; von Hippel, 2005] and brand communication [see Arvidsson, 2008]) for the purpose of creating value for the company. Put differently, biopolitical marketing aims to mobilize and extract value from the production of consumer creativity, communication, lifestyles, and subjectivities. It is a vision of marketing that wants to replace the conventional ethos of consumer discipline and control with an ethos of the internet, which emphasizes open non-hierarchical collaboration, autonomy, and harmonious social production. Biopolitical marketing rejects any clear distinction between marketer and consumer and sees marketing as entangled with, and increasingly indistinguishable from, the fabric of everyday life. Biopolitical marketing is, in the words of Ashton Kutcher, 'un-marketing'. Our goal in presenting our theory that marketing is changing by becoming biopolitical is to explain why everything we do, even our acts of resistance, appears to always end up reproducing capital (Wernick, 1991, Aronczyk & Powers, 2010).

Biopolitics

Biopolitics is a concept mostly associated with Michel Foucault and his 'Birth of Biopolitics' lectures (2004) that describe how, in the reprogramming of classic liberalism, a political ideology that sought to confine the influence of markets and put the economy in the service of the state, to neoliberalism, an ideology that considers the state as a handmaiden of the economy, a new normative order of reason, or governmentality, emerges that disseminates economistic logic of cost and benefits across a wide range of sites, from workplaces to prisons, schools, families, gyms and crèches (Brown, 2015). Biopolitics, therefore, is the process through which all our bodily, social, and intellectual capacities are qualified in terms of productive capacities; how, in other words, life itself is put to work. Foucault's example of the proto biopolitical subject is *Homo oeconomicus*, a figure wholly configured within the normative order of reason that submits every sphere and every activity to economization, self-interest, and logics of cost/benefit analysis, competition, investment, etc. Biopolitics, in other words, represents the making of a world where all activities of life, including questions like who to marry and how to optimize the value of time spent with one's children, are to be evaluated by their economic benefits.

A prominent contemporary example of biopolitics is the rise of the so-called 'happiness industry' (Davies, 2016) or 'Wellness Syndrome' (Cederstrom & Spicer, 2015); a conjunction of positive psychology, employability, personal banking, weight loss, personal grooming, meditation, in such a way that life becomes a constant exercise of human optimization. It is important to emphasize the moralistic character of biopolitics; those who fail to optimize their lives are demonized, and inasmuch as biopolitics is a regime of personal responsibility, it also is an ideology of disavowing responsibility for those who fail to successfully self-optimize.

In the context of marketing, we define the biopolitical as a governing rationality capable of generating new productive relations and social contexts then making them available for commodification. In other words, biopolitical marketing attempts to manage life to emerge in a way that permits complete economization of life while at the same time maintaining the belief in the autonomy of the individual actor in the market.

Biopolitical marketing and participatory media (Web 2.0)

Social media marketing is a practice in which we see biopolitical management of autonomous and 'anarchic' consumer life, where lives that are unrestrained are the source of innovative and productive communicative 'work' valued by marketers (see Arvidsson, 2007; Fisher & Smith, 2011; Zwick, Bonsu, & Darmody, 2008). In participatory media, marketing's goal is to monitor and nurture what, drawing from Halberstam (2013), should be referred to as 'wild' social production. Halberstam's wild is about "shifting, changing and morphing extemporising political positions quickly and effectively to keep up with the multimedia environment in which we all live to stay apace" (Halberstam, 2013, p. 29). Marketers have come to recognize the value of wild (meaning uncontrolled, ungoverned, and anarchic) consumer behavior and communication that some online spaces foster because it is in the wild where radically different ideas, trends, and lifestyles are being created.

We argue that it is the collision of the wild space of consumerist production with the task of marketers to extract value from that space that gives rise to *biopolitical marketing*. Marketing becomes biopolitical because it wants to valorize and absorb the productivity of life itself rather than merely *sell stuff* (cf. Rose, 2001; Virno, 2004; see also Arvidsson, 2005). This is to recognize that the most potent forms of innovation and value are not going to be produced within direct waged labor, but in the ungoverned collective activities of the crowd. While this tendency remains as true now as it was in Marx's day, the rise of social media platforms allows marketers to initiate certain forms of production and capture the value of that production.

Perhaps unsurprisingly we see much attention within marketing scholarship given to communities, particularly in those where unmanaged groups gather online, of their own volition, and whose activities are valuable to marketers (see e.g. Fournier & Lee, 2009; Schau, Muniz, & Arnould, 2009; Weinberg, 2009). Meanwhile, popular press social media consultants and entrepreneurs also fixate on online customer communities (see e.g. Qualman, 2009; Weinberg, 2009; Solis, 2010; Kerpen, 2011). In this convergence, we observe how community is being actively imagined as a social media marketing 'tool' with tremendous potential for corporate profit generation.

In this emphasis on community, we see a resonance with O'Dwyer's vision of the web as a 'virtual communism': an "immaterial space that trades in knowledge and culture, at once free from commercial subjugation and conversely capable of exerting influence on the material substrate of capital" (O'Dwyer, 2013, p. 498). Accordingly, we see throughout the literature on social media brand communities recurring emphases on cooperation, egalitarianism, and a flourishing of creative minds and practices. However despite its notional communism, the participatory spaces of Web 2.0 remains a site in which new content is created in order to be immediately privatized. For this reason Fuchs (2017) argues against using the term 'social media' because we are mostly referring to privately owned organizations that actively privatize user-generated content. Hence, as Kleiner and Wyrick (2007) argue, what is offered by companies are spaces of content creation, however the content created in these spaces is privately owned, which would be the equivalent of Royal Mail deciding that it should own the copyright to all of the content that it delivers. So, while at first glance Web 2.0 might appear as revolutionary and communistic, it is in fact an extraordinary process of value appropriation by companies because not just content is to be privatized and ordered for the purpose of profit extraction, but also increasingly the frames in which we are to communicate and maintain our relationships are to be commercially structured. Just as the new owner is now able to financially exploit the resource for private profit, the actual producer of value will have no means of exploiting the resource and might come to depend on the new owner.

In conceptualizing biopolitical marketing, we owe a great debt to Jodi Dean's (2009) theory of *communicative capitalism* which analyzes the exploitation and management of communication, feelings, emotions, and social relations that are found in ideals of inclusion and participation in information, entertainment, and communication technologies. Communicative capitalism, then, is a particular process that captures resistance and intensifies global capitalism precisely through ideals of inclusion and participation in our information, entertainment, and communication technologies. Communicative capitalism might be regarded as a capitalism grounded in capturing value from all activities people engage in as they try to make a life together. In doing so, communicative capitalism turns what appears to be a process of inclusion and participation that strengthens community into a process of micro targeting and hyper-personalized selling (Turow, 2011).

Just like communicative capitalism, biopolitical marketing is grounded in the affective and cultural lives of consumers and therefore it is important that the illusion prevails that they are autonomous and voluntary agents. It is therefore immediately distinct from any notion of marketing as a top-down mechanism in which marketers seek to control consumers. Instead biopolitical marketing wants to insert their commodities and brands into the social lives of their consumer. What matters, then, is that this commodity and brand, in its incorporation into consumer subjectivity, produces continuous dynamic value (see e.g. Arvidsson, 2005, 2007). Therefore, it is no less than the art of marshaling the creative, entrepreneurial, and cooperative capacities of consumers into production (Arvidsson, 2007; Zwick et al., 2008). For example, the astonishing value of the company Facebook Inc., approaching 1 trillion dollars, is largely based on the 'work' of its over 2 billion users. Facebook provides the ways and means for its users to participate in the making of Facebook as a media and consumption platform. As these users post, share, comment, and consume content on Facebook, the company is able to improve its ability to transform and package these users into valuable audiences that can be sold to businesses looking to disseminate highly targeted marketing messages. Another example of a business that makes money by enabling users to participate is the music streaming application Shazam. In addition to streaming songs, Shazam can be used to identify names of songs and artists heard in an ad or on the radio. As users around the world call on Shazam to help identify artists and songs, the company receives extremely valuable data about just emerging music trends and possible hits days and even weeks before any competitor. Just as with Facebook, it is, in effect, the aggregate action of hundreds of millions of users of the app that made Shazam worth around 400 million dollars for Apple Inc.

We identify two points of direct correspondence between biopolitical marketing and communicative capitalism. One, capital no longer monopolizes production, innovation, or value creation and must consequentially learn how to capture productive energies elsewhere. Two, while participatory media demonstrate that their users are entrepreneurial, collaborative, productive, and creative, we also see that this kind of collective participation and production often wishes to remain outside the commercialization efforts of marketers, brands, and companies.

This contradiction between marketers' wish to always commodify the autonomous productivity of the crowds and the crowds' often anti-commercial and communal agency, defines the complexity and 'queerness' of biopolitical marketing. In other words, what makes the crowds of participatory media so commercially interesting to marketers is precisely the fact that these crowds are not limited by company rules and management structures. Marketers often realize that the more autonomous and free these communities are the more innovative and creative (and therefore valuable) they might become. To paraphrase Halberstam, 'there are no marketers *in the wild*' (cf. Halberstam, 2013). We might say, then, that biopolitical marketing is tasked with extracting value from people whose creativity is valuable because it is not governed by marketing interests and who do not want marketing and commercial interests to infiltrate their activities.

The customer community in marketing

Since the rise of Web 2.0 around 2005, online communities having increasingly attracted marketing attention. Of particular interest to us is the large volume of business discourse (such as blogs, popular consulting books, business conferences, and workshops) that address the question of how to both generate but also manage online customer communities. Particularly influential within these debates are Li and Bernoff, authors of *Groundswell* (2008), Tamar Weinberg, author of *The New Community Rules* (2009), and Brian Solis, author of *Engage!* (2010; with a foreword by comedic actor and co-founder of the social media marketing consultancy *Katalyst* Ashton Kutcher). These authors and gurus address large audiences on the topic of generating value from communal consumers.

Of particular interest to us is how marketers mobilize online communities to resolve key contradictions; namely, can they do marketing while appearing not to do *any* marketing, how can the corporate profit motive co-exist with the fantasy of the internet as a place for gifting and sharing, how can marketers turn the creativity of consumers into private capital, and how can the anarchy of the 'wild' survive the marketer's desire for control? From this perspective biopolitical marketing is a process of commodifying all communication without antagonizing the communicators. Thus, the way marketing resolves this key contradiction of contemporary capitalism is by becoming biopolitical and it is precisely when marketing learns to become biopolitical that communities and other forms of collective participation and collaboration become of interest to marketing professionals. Indeed, online communities are a perfect example of a novel gathering of consumers that apparently stand outside capitalist commodity relations and, for that precise reason, becomes an object of great curiosity and interest for professional social media marketing managers. For Tamar Weinberg (2009), the task of the social media marketer is to make a community. The vision is to bring together consumers and marketers and watch them innovate, improve brand value, and simply have a great time hanging out with other consumers and the marketer (Weinberg, 2009). We argue that customer community allow us to see the contradictions playing out in three primary and distinctive ways, discussed below.

1. The community reconfigures marketing as un-marketing

As Gabriel and Lang (1995) attest, there is widespread cynicism and mistrust among consumers about marketing messages and intention. In this context, marketers, perhaps self-conscious about how they are negatively represented as sleazy agents of persuasion, are developing practices that bypass these perceptions. The narratives of digital social media managers, therefore, typically positions itself as the solution to marketing's crisis of legitimacy which they see as nefarious long-standing marketing methods designed to discipline and control consumers. For these young and tech-savvy marketers, participatory media marketing shall bring about a paradigm shift in marketing itself. For example, in texts by prominent social media marketing experts such as Solis (2010) and Stratten (2010), we see propagated the idea that marketing has to be *'un'-done* and we see the rise of the term *'un-marketing'* throughout the consulting literature. 'Un-marketing' refers to a reimagining of marketing and a reaction to a corporate-controlled top-down technique. In its place, we see enthusiastic commitments to participatory consumer engagement in forums that are collaborative and non-hierarchical (for example, see Kutcher in Solis, 2010; Stratten, 2010, 2014). Marketers, we are told, are to be born again as partners in consumer-producer co-creation activities based on principles of equality and shared power.

However, despite the great enthusiasm of social media 'un-marketers' as they modernize disciplinary models of marketing and demand that the subject be reinvented according to principles of communitarian self-governance and collaboration, nonetheless new contradictions continue to emerge that are characteristic of communicative capitalism. This should hardly surprise us because the corporate profit motive prevails and demands that even communities of autonomous and 'wild' participants must still be commercially exploited. This is to say that as marketing evolves to un-marketing, it retains its *raison d'être*. The challenge for social media managers is therefore to achieve a level of sensitivity to this practical challenge of commodifying social relations that themselves do not want to be commodified. This paradoxical challenge is to be met by adopting the 'correct marketing mindset' in which marketers can show empathy and respect toward the opinions, creations, and cultural idiosyncrasies of the community while still nonetheless continuing to pursue profit. The guru Tamar Weinberg (2009, pp. 52–53) nicely captures the strangeness of the task:

> Later, your "ulterior motive" can be communicated (just as long as you continue giving back to the community and its members look up to you as a respected contributor), but it's more important to establish yourself as a reputable member who wants to give back to the community first. Once you do, you can begin to take, as long as the community is receptive and wants to know more about you as a community participant, but you should always keep giving.

Weinberg, therefore, understands that marketing must take, but that it must do so without appearing to take – by giving back! In this sense the communist sensibility invoked relies on a double exhortation to keep giving but always as a precursor to 'taking'. As Kutcher (in Solis, 2010, p. ix) puts it: "Marketers, don't control us, support us; don't talk to us, listen!", or more directly, marketers are expected to market without 'doing' marketing overtly.

2. The community controls consumers by empowering consumers

Throughout the texts of Kutcher, Solis, and others a libertarian impulse prevails that promotes a notion of personal freedom and autonomy as freedom from any state authority or coercive social institutions (see e.g. Rubel in Downes and Mui, 2000; Miller, 2008). From this perspective, consumer communities are no more than the logical extension of cyber-utopian projects in which horizontality and anti-authoritarian discourses that favour bottom-up power will work to facilitate entrepreneurialism, self-ownership, value creation, and innovation. At this moment we might say that marketing shakes hands with so-called 'Californian ideology' (see Dyer-Witheford, 2015), that weds seemingly contradictory imaginations of the internet as, on the one hand, an autonomous and ungoverned space owned by all and controlled by no one[1] and, on the other, a space for unrestrained corporate empire building and commercial exploitation. Californian ideology is the combination of these positions in examples of entrepreneurs describing themselves as social innovators making the world a better place, despite the carnage they bring to certain professions (for example, Uber's impact on taxi drivers). In direct correspondence with this Californian ideology, in biopolitical marketing we encounter a discourse of empowerment, sharing, and networked collaboration that champions technological capitalism and individual self-reliance as the basis for its collective ethic. For example, consider Kevin Kelly's (2009) feverish announcement of a "global collectivist society" which, he argued, amounts to a "New Socialism." This socialism is "not class warfare. It is not anti-American; indeed digital socialism may be the newest American innovation." Biopolitical marketing is replete with such neo-libertarian narratives that celebrate individual freedom, digital collectivism, and decentralized self-organization and reject state control. Strange conjunctures therefore arise which appear to, at least in the short term, overcome their contradictory nature, such as the commercialization of self-organizing, and collectivized entrepreneurialism.

Marketing is now re-cast as a digital capitalist socialism which is a fun party of self-determined collaboration, a celebration of personal autonomy, and a flourishing of unrestricted sharing. We can immediately recognize that these discourses stand as an alternative to marketing's conventional undesirability grounded in bureaucratic top-down control. Marketing is hence transformed into a communal ethos of digital socialism based on consensual partnership with consumers who are certainly not controlled but rather are *invited* by the corporation as equals in the joint task of joyous co-creation. From this perspective, practices that once sought to control consumers, or absorb them into centralized, technocratic, and rationalized structures appear at best anachronistic, and at worst crude and abusive. Of course, while no longer repressing consumers, biopolitical marketing does not actually free consumers from marketing control. Instead, the delicate task is one of sensitively withdrawing the phenomena of marketing control and doing so by designing platforms in which creative consumer behavior will function productively and in a format nonetheless pre-prepared for surplus value extraction.

3. The community creates marketing value while marketing does not

How can marketers extract surplus value from the affective and communicative labor of communities? This is the challenge that faces biopolitical marketing because these forms of value production are not the express purpose of these communities, and indeed would go against the general ethos of many. At a basic level, marketing remains the same as it ever was: a social technology and a mode of valorization that works for consumers to perceive offers as valuable. As authors such as Ritzer (2009) and Ritzer and Jurgenson (2010) argue, the mechanism through which communities are encouraged to labor with and for corporations is now called value co-creation and this is increasingly considered to be at the center of a firm's value. Co-creation of value is not itself a new concept (see Ritzer, 2009), however recent business discourses draw on Web 2.0 as a rich opportunity to reconfigure production as increasingly dependent upon the active participation of formerly passive(ized) consumers (see e.g. Lagace, 2004; Donaton, 2006).

For advocates of co-creation, value production is an outcome of marketers and consumers collaborating in the manufacturing of products, services, and, increasingly, communication and therefore consumers ought to be regarded as a stock of unimaginable creative and innovative potential that awaits development and exploitation by smart managers. Mainstream business scholars such as Prahalad and Ramaswamy (2000, 2002, 2004a, 2004b) and Vargo and Lusch (2004) fundamentally challenge traditional conceptions of marketing by claiming that the locus of economic value creation is moving toward interactions with consumers, and away from classical production-orientations. In this shift, the role of biopolitical marketers, then, is no longer about controlling the production of value but rather about appropriating the value produced from the cultural, technological, social, and affective labor of consumers.

Conclusion

The biopolitical marketing paradigm is one in which customer communities are held as harbingers of new engagements between marketers and consumers. For the newly emergent profession of social media marketing managers, the idea of online customer communities is highly exciting because it is an idea of social technology charged with the transformation of how marketing governs consumers. Biopolitical marketing, therefore, breaks with 20th-century marketing assumptions because digital and social media marketers are no longer concerned with determining how consumers consume. Instead their task is to integrate marketing right into the DNA of how communities function, how and where communication exists and then to unify these as the general task of our existence. At such a point, marketing is not an external process witnessed in advertisements and promotional cultures, but rather marketing is immanent in our sense of selves, our sense of creativity, and our sense of community. Marketing that is biopolitical dissolves the separation between what the marketer wants and what the consumer wants. Biopolitical marketing, therefore, is a fantasy of a world of total capitalist enclosure in which consumers' activities and desires and that of marketers and brand managers *all become one*. In a world where biopolitical marketing rules, marketers are no longer the other of consumers.

But this fantasy remains a fantasy and the contradictions that exist will not be willed out of existence, despite the great enthusiasm of the community and social media proselytizers whose books can be found in an airport bookshop near you. Despite the fanfare, consumers will always be the 'other' of marketing and therefore marketing remains a process of constant and incessant identification and appropriation of an as yet non-commodified 'other'. From a critical marketing perspective, biopolitical marketing therefore represents marketing's latest attempt to resolve the fundamental contradiction of contemporary capitalism.

Note

1 This radically libertarian idea is perhaps best characterized by hacking culture and Wikipedia as well as the utopian vision of the internet such as former Grateful Dead John Perry Barlow's famous Manifesto of the Independence of Cyberspace (Electronic Frontier Foundation, 1996).

References

Aronczyk, M., & Powers, D. (2010). *Blowing up the brand: Critical perspectives on promotional culture*. New York, Peter Lang.
Arvidsson, A. (2005). Brands: A critical perspective. *Journal of Consumer Culture, 5*(2), 235–258.
Arvidsson, A. (2007). Creative class or administrative class? On advertising and the 'underground'. *ephemera: theory & politics in organization, 7*(1), 8–23.
Arvidsson, A. (2008). The ethical economy of customer coproduction. *Journal of Macromarketing, 28*(4), 326–338.
Brown, W. (2015). *Undoing the demos: Neoliberalism's stealth revolution*. Brooklyn, NY, Zone Books.
Cederstrom, C., & Spicer, A. (2015). *The wellness syndrome*. London, Pluto.
Davies, W. (2016). *The happiness industry: How the government and big business sold us well-being*. London, Verso.
Dean, J. (2009). *Democracy and other neoliberal fantasies: Communicative capitalism and left politics*. Durham, NC, Duke University Press.
Donaton, S. (2006). How to thrive in the new world of user-created content: Let go. *Advertising Age*. Retrieved 2014 from http://adage.com/columns/article?article_id=108884
Downes, L., & Mui, C. (2000). *Unleashing the killer app: Digital strategies for market dominance*. Boston, MA, Harvard Business School Press.
Dujarier, M.-A. (2016). The three sociological types of consumer work. *Journal of Consumer Culture, 16*(2), 1–17.
Dyer-Witheford, N. (2015). *Cyber-proletariat: Global labour in the digital vortex*. London, Pluto.
Fisher, D., & Smith, S. (2011). Cocreation is chaotic: What it means for marketing when no one has control. *Marketing Theory, 11*(3), 325–350.
Foucault, M. (2004). *The birth of biopolitics: Lectures at the Collège de France 1978–1979*. London, Palgrave Macmillan.
Fournier, S., & Lee, L. (2009). Getting brand communities right. *Harvard Business Review*, April, 105–111.
Fuchs, C. (2017). Marx's *Capital* in the information age. *Capital & Class, 41*(1), 51–67.
Gabriel, Y., & Lang, T. (1995). *The unmanageable consumer: Contemporary consumption and its fragmentations*. Thousand Oaks, Sage.
Halberstam, J. (2013). Charming for the revolution: A gaga manifesto. *e-flux, 44*(4). Retrieved 2014 from www.e-flux.com/journal/charming-for-the-revolution-a-gaga-manifesto/
Kelly, K. (2009). The new socialism: Global collectivist society is coming online. *Wired* (May 22). Retrieved May 23, 2009 from www.wired.com/2009/05/nep-newsocialism/
Kerpen, D. (2011). *Likeable social media: How to delight your customers, create an irresistible brand, and be generally amazing on Facebook (& other social networks)*. New York, McGraw-Hill.
Kleiner, D., & Wyrick, B. (2007). Infoenclosure 2.0. *Mute, 2*(4). Available at www.metamute.org/editorial/articles/infoenclosure-2.0

Lagace, M. (2004). Your customers: Use them or lose them. Available at http://hbswk.hbs.edu/item/4267.html

Lazzarato, M. (2004). From capital-labour to capital-life. *ephemera: theory & politics in organization, 4*(3), 187–208.

Li, C., & Bernoff, J. (2008). *Groundswell: Winning in a world transformed by social technologies.* Boston, MA, Harvard Business Press.

Miller, M. (2008). *Online marketing heroes: Interviews with 25 successful online marketing gurus.* Indianapolis, Wiley.

O'Dwyer, R. (2013). Spectre of the commons: Spectrum regulation in the communism of capital. *ephemera: theory & politics in organisation, 13*(3), 497–526.

Prahalad, C.K., & Ramaswamy, V. (2000). Co-opting customer competence. *Harvard Business Review, 78*(January–February), 79–87.

Prahalad, C.K., & Ramaswamy, V. (2002). The cocreation connection. *Strategy and Business, 27*(2), 51–60.

Prahalad, C.K., & Ramaswamy, V. (2004a). Co-creation experiences: The next practice in value creation. *Journal of Interactive Marketing, 18*(3), 5–14.

Prahalad, C.K., & Ramaswamy, V. (2004b). *The future of competition: Co-creating unique value with customers.* Boston, Harvard Business School Publishing.

Qualman, E. (2009). *Socialnomics: How social media transforms the way we live and do business.* Hoboken, Wiley.

Ritzer, G. (2009). Correcting an historical error. *Keynote Address. Conference on Prosumption.* Frankfurt, Germany, March, 2009.

Ritzer, G., & Jurgenson, N. (2010). Production, consumption, prosumption: The nature of capitalism in the age of the digital 'prosumer'. *Journal of Consumer Culture, 10*(1), 13–36.

Rose, N. (2001). The politics of life itself. *Theory, Culture & Society, 18*(6), 1–30.

Schau, H.J., Muniz, A.M., & Arnould, E. (2009). How brand community practices create value. *Journal of Marketing, 73*(5), 30–51.

Solis, B. (2010). *Engage! The complete guide for brands and businesses to build, cultivate, and measure success in the new web.* Hoboken, John Wiley.

Stratten, S. (2010). *Unmarketing: Stop marketing. Start engaging.* Hoboken, John Wiley.

Turow, J. (2011). *The daily you: How the new advertising industry is defining your identity and your worth.* New Haven, Yale University Press.

Vargo, S., & Lusch, R. (2004). Evolving to a new dominant logic for marketing. *Journal of Marketing, 68*(1), 1–17.

Virno, P. (2004). *A grammar of the multitude for an analysis of contemporary forms of life.* Cambridge, MA, Semiotext(e) and MIT Press.

Von Hippel, E. (2005). *Democratizing innovation.* Cambridge, MA, MIT Press.

Weinberg, T. (2009). *The new community rules: Marketing on the social web.* Sebastopol, CA, O'Reilly.

Wernick, A. (1991). *Promotional culture.* London, Sage.

Zwick, D., Bonsu, S.K., & Darmody, A. (2008). Putting consumers to work: 'Co-creation' and new marketing govern-mentality. *Journal of Consumer Culture, 8*(2), 163–196.

27
EXPLOITATION AND EMANCIPATION

Bernard Cova and Bernard Paranque

Introduction

Critical inquiry has emerged in recent years as a practice in the marketing discipline. The theoretical and conceptual foundations of critical thinking are largely to be found in Marxist philosophy. Marketing practices are accordingly interpreted through the dual exploitation/emancipation concept. These are two sides of the same coin and at the edge is alienation. Initially conceived in relation to production activities, this dual concept has been used in consumer research in a somewhat disconnected way. Emancipation was first mobilized to study resistance and escape from the consumption society in the wake of the Frankfurt School. Exploitation was later used – at the beginning of the 21st century – to discuss the blurriness of boundaries between consumption and production. Today, we question the relevance of this dual concept to rethink marketing.

The concept of exploitation as the cornerstone of Marxist social theory

The concept of exploitation is the cornerstone of Marxist social theory and is defined as the unequal exchange of labor for goods (Roemer, 1985). Workers are exploited if, and only if, they work more time than is embodied in the goods they can purchase with their income. The notion of exploitation assumes two types of actors: the exploiters and the exploited. The concept of exploitation is central in social and political theory and in a number of debates ranging from analyses of labor relations to gender discrimination and the debate on modern slavery.

The term exploitation is both simple and complex. Simple, because it refers to the use of something (a resource or time) and complex because it also means domination over another person. In this sense, it is linked to another term, namely, alienation, but through a specific relationship in the way in which exploitation is practiced.

The concept of exploitation takes various forms ranging from a technical definition to one with an ethical dimension (Roemer, 1985). Labor exploitation can be considered as the use, extraction and acquisition of labor understood as a resource, as in the case of oil, for example. However, exploitation can also refer to one person's domination over another, owing to certain positions in trade power relations in the labor market or inequality in access to or use of a resource or a means of production owing to private ownership that affects such access or use. Under these conditions, exploitation can lead to the expropriation of the product of a person's work.

In a capitalist sense, exploitation is therefore characterized as the use of labor power to produce surplus value (Bensussan & Labica, 1999) and therefore profit, and more specifically, "the appropriation of a part of the output of producers by a non-producer" (Weeks, 2010, p. 23). Marx measured exploitation as the rate of surplus-value determined by the proportion of unpaid labor: "The rate of surplus-value is therefore an exact expression for the degree of exploitation of labor-power by capital, or of the labourer by the capitalist" (Marx, 1887/1999).

Therefore, by excluding the technical exploitation of a natural resource, exploitation covers a broad concept of domination starting with slavery and its modern forms, such as organized labor immigration as seen in the Emirates, Saudi Arabia and cities such as Paris, or organized prostitution. In all cases, exploitation is defined as free work carried out for others who profit from it and implies an underlying trading relationship.

Exploitation can be defined along two dimensions. The first corresponds to unpaid work, as in the case of slavery, but also volunteering and user communities. The second is work for which only a partial payment is made corresponding to labor power, which coincides with the status of an employee and the contract associated with this relationship (Weeks, 2010). This latter dimension expresses both an economic relationship – the appropriation of the surplus product – and a social relationship – the division into social classes (Bensussan & Labica, 1999). However, this is not a question of theft, since the work is carried out under a contract that specifies the terms and corresponding payment.

Alienation

The concept of alienation reinforces that of exploitation and describes a social relationship characterized by a person's lack of control over the conditions of their activity. This leads to a distinction between subjective alienation, understood as the feeling of not having control over one's life in psychological terms, and objective alienation, which refers to the very conditions in which the activity is carried out and the impossibility of controlling or deciding these working conditions.

- Subjectively speaking, alienation corresponds to a more psychological feeling of divestment and becoming estranged and disconnected from other people, institutions or one's natural state of being (Bensussan & Labica, 1999). Alienation is characterized as a state in which the subjects pursue goals or follow practices that, on one hand, no external actor or factor obliges them to follow and, on the other hand, they do not truly desire or approve of (Rosa, 2010).
- Objectively speaking – in law – alienation is considered an act through which a person relinquishes, by gift or sale, a good that they own (Bensussan & Labica, 1999). More generally, alienation is a state where social activity such as work has goals imposed on it that are not consistent with the individual's motives (Sève, 2012).

Only when freedom of contract for everyone is legally (and perhaps paradoxically) recognized, can objective alienation in economics become identifiable:

> The alienation of the worker in his product means not only that his labor becomes an object, an external existence, but that it exists outside him, independently, as something alien to him, and that it becomes a power on its own confronting him. It means that the life which he has conferred on the object confronts him as something hostile and alien.
> Marx, 1932/1959, p. 58

Exploitation can exist without objective alienation (merely a perception) and refers to the tangible conditions in which the activity is deployed. In the wake of Marx, we can argue that

> [i]f the workers related to their product as an expression of their own essence and recognised themselves in their product and were recognised by others in their work, then this was not the basis for alienation; on the contrary, this was the only genuinely human relation.
>
> Marxists Internet Archive Encyclopedia, 1999–2008,
> www.marxists.org/glossary/terms/a/l.htm#alienation

The two concepts of exploitation and alienation are therefore connected by certain types of social relationships characterized by the private ownership of the means of production and contractual formalization of the working relationship by law. "Presupposing private property, my work is an alienation of life, for I work in order to live, in order to obtain for myself the means of life. My work is not my life" (Marx & Engels, 1932, section 3). Consequently, the issue of capitalist exploitation can only be addressed if two dimensions are considered. On the one hand, the possibility of carrying out freely chosen work, on the other hand, the possibility of acknowledging that not all, but only part, of the work is paid for. Specifically, the work required to allow the worker to provide for his or her needs (basic needs such as food, but also those recognized as necessary for a given state of society, its economic and social reproduction). This raises questions about unpaid work (and therefore exploitation) and surplus work likely to reintegrate the value chain via the business (and therefore alienation) (Böhm & Land, 2012).

Emancipation

The concept of alienation is closely intertwined with the concept of exploitation, like the specific conditions of its practice, but also defines the conditions in which emancipation is possible. Thus, "alienation can be overcome by restoring the truly human relationship to the labor process, by people working in order to meet people's needs, working as an expression of their own human nature, not just to earn a living" (Marxists Internet Archive Encyclopedia, 1999–2008, www.marxists.org/glossary/terms/a/l.htm#alienation).

Emancipation is defined as the process of being set free from constraints, deliverance from physical, intellectual, moral or spiritual fetters. Marxist emancipation entails overcoming the capitalist ethos and is fully realized "with the suppression of the capitalist mode of production" and the removal of obstacles imposed by the conditions of wage labor. People are capable of fighting back against life-destructive and unsatisfying forms of exploitation. For all exploited people, the goal of struggle is the same – comprehensive, universal access to the means of life-support, development and enjoyment – but articulated through different concrete histories, anchored in different tangible experiences of structurally identical barriers (Alvesson & Willmott, 1992).

Emancipation from exploitation and forms of alienation, objective and subjective, can therefore only occur in the canonical form of collective appropriation of the means of production, that is, the abolition of private ownership of these means, by promoting other forms of collective appropriation. This can take the form of new methods of organizing and collectively managing material and/or immaterial resources as 'commons' through more or less formalized rules and specific governance (Ostrom, 2011; Hardt & Negri, 2009). However, it is not actually sufficient to modify the rules of ownership to challenge the exploitation and alienation of a social system. Indeed, literature on cooperatives clearly demonstrates that this remains a central question, given that they operate in a context of dominant trade relations. For example, cooperatives such as Mondragon or trusts such as the John Lewis Partnership Limited, where employees have ownership of the company, do not need trade unions, assuming the capital/labor relation has no specific meaning. While objective alienation is challenged, exploitation in the sense of a social production relationship is maintained or at the very least questionable (Parker et al., 2014; Paranque & Willmott, 2014).

From production to consumption

Production is not the only possible locus of both objective and subjective alienation as Veblen (1899/1944) and Marcuse (1964) demonstrated in relation to the role of consumption in constructing social differentiations between social classes and categories. In fact, in the 1960s, the debate on this subject widened with the publication of *La Société de Consommation* (Baudrillard, 1970) which argued that alienation was not based on the act of production, but rather on the fact that consumers will be caught in a form of alienation associated with their mode of consumption. The idea is that the capitalist mode of consumption reinforces the alienation of the mode of production by making us captives of social relationships through the consumption practices and in the name of consumer freedom. This consumption is directly linked to the development of leisure time, a new sphere of consumption. However, Marcuse (1969/1971) underlines how much this consumption as leisure is dependent on each person's social position, because workers, employees or managers approach their leisure with the qualities, attitudes, values and behaviors in line with their position in society. According to Marcuse (1967), beyond simply leisure, the world, i.e., the society in which we live, has itself become a 'company'. The objects we find in it are things we must use to occupy or fill a life that would be empty without them. In other words, consumption strengthens, if not exploitation then both objective and subjective alienation, in that it reinforces not only the mode of production, but also our degree of satisfaction as citizens and consumers:

> Under the rule of a repressive whole, liberty can be made into a powerful instrument of domination. The range of choice open to the individual is not the decisive factor in determining the degree of human freedom, but what can be chosen and what is chosen by the individual. The criterion for free choice can never be an absolute one, but neither is it entirely relative. Free election of masters does not abolish the masters or the slaves. Free choice among a wide variety of goods and services does not signify freedom if these goods and services sustain social controls over a life of toil and fear-that is, if they sustain alienation. And the spontaneous reproduction of superimposed needs by the individual does not establish autonomy; it only testifies to the efficacy of the controls.
>
> Marcuse, 1964, pp. 9–10

As such, the idea that the market offers liberation is deemed completely illusionary by Marxist and critical researchers. However, worth recalling is that Marx himself underlined the power of capitalism and the market to foster social development and innovation compared to feudalism and monarchy (Meiksins-Wood, 2002).

Today, people as seemingly free consumers expressing their innermost desires through buying a pair of Nike trainers are, of course, not really free and nor do they express their true selves.

What they believe to be their own desires, emanating from their autonomous will as unique individuals, are, unbeknown to them, the product of a manipulation whereby the suppliers of goods enslave their imagination. They desire what they are led to desire. Supply subordinates and determines demand.

Boltanski & Chiapello, 2006, p. 427

The concept of alienation has thus followed the paths of the society, transitioning from worker alienation in a world driven by production to consumer alienation in a world driven by consumption.

Consumer emancipation?

The possibility of consumer emancipation from alienation has been debated since the 1990s in consumer research. Emancipation has particularly focused on freedom from the totalizing constraints of the marketplace and its illusory freedom of choice. Theory and research have taken to addressing the questions of whether and under what conditions consumers can be emancipated from subjective alienation:

- A first variant of emancipation (Ozanne & Murray, 1995) calls for the development of critical reflexivity and resistance. Consumers resist and potentially become emancipated from the market to the extent that their consumption practices sidestep the market authority (Holt, 2001).
- A second variant (Fırat & Venkatesh, 1995) envisions consumers engaging in fragmented self-production in spaces apart from the market in that "to escape from dominant meanings is to construct our own subjectivity" (Elliott, 1997, p. 290).

Resistance

Post-Marxian approaches inspired by the Frankfurt School and critical sociology assign a dominant and oppressive role to the market. Consumer resistance is seen as both combative and necessary. According to Ozanne and Murray (1995), consumer emancipation requires the "reflexively defiant consumer". Emancipation is possible if one develops a reflexive distance from the marketing code (i.e., becoming code conscious), acknowledging its structuring effects and disentangling marketer's artifice from the value in use of marketer-supplied resources (Arnould, 2007a). Through resistance, consumers form a different relationship with the marketplace in which they identify unquestioned assumptions and challenge the status of existing structures as natural. Through reflection, consumers might choose to defy or resist traditional notions of consumption, become more independent from acquisition and disposition systems or define their own needs independent from the marketplace (Holt, 2001). Consumer resistance focuses on consumers opposing or eluding a dominant force exerted by certain actors and especially companies (Lee *et al.*, 2011):

- Individuals can feel saturated and repelled by the manipulative, if ineffective, advances of companies. Selling tactics are resisted in the name of autonomy and ethics. Complaining behavior, boycotts and 'culture jamming' are all expressions of dissatisfaction, feelings of harassment and moral sanction applied against hegemonic practices and propaganda.

- Individuals question whether certain companies are acceptable as trading partners and as responsible actors for future generations. Whereas companies urge consumers to trust them and to rely on their business skills, individuals can choose to ignore or avoid them and instead pursue alternative distribution channels, such as second-hand markets and consumer-to-consumer exchanges.

Resistance to consumption is often twinned with anti-consumption in the search for consumer emancipation. Anti-consumption can be classified into three non-exclusive phenomena: rejection, restriction and reclaiming. In rejection, individuals intentionally and meaningfully exclude particular goods from their consumption cycle, for example, rejecting Nike for functional, symbolic or ethical reasons. The idea of restriction incorporates cutting, lowering and limiting consumption when complete anti-consumption is not possible, for example, restricting electricity or water use. While rejection is about avoiding the consumption of some goods and restriction is about the reduction of some goods, reclaiming represents an ideological shift of the acquisition, use and dispossession processes. For example, voluntary simplifiers reclaim their identity via production instead of consumption when they choose to grow their own vegetables rather than acquire them through conventional markets. Similarly, dumpster divers and ecological artists reclaim 'trash' from the dispossession process and imbue 'waste' with new meaning/value (Lee et al., 2011). In some cases, consumer resistance is 'voiced' (Hirschman, 1970) through acts of anti-consumption directed against a domineering corporation, leading to boycotting its products. At other times, resistance might also be expressed through certain consumption choices, for instance, opposing the dominant retail channel through the formation of consumer collectives that fulfill consumption needs (Kates & Belk, 2001).

Beyond the 'reflexively defiant consumer', individuals can bypass the market by attempting to construct their own everyday patterns with their peers, those who belong to their 'tribe' (Cova, 1997) without any external impositions; their position is that of defectors (i.e. Hirschman's (1970) 'exit'). Far from being submissive, individuals take an openly rebellious stand. The market is by no means the center of their lives, since they have rejected its power and the pre-set schemas it seeks to impose in favor of edifying their own set of experiences, strongly characterized by solidarity links and reliant on the strength of local networks. Their daily lives and consumption patterns are self-structured. This is precisely the case with 'LETS' (Local Exchange Trading System) in the UK or 'SEL' (the French equivalent), which propose an alternative economy based on the community sense that arises in local associations. Bartering, social networking, community services and so forth, all contribute to the self-structuring of these local systems. These are neo-hegemonic movements of resistance and withdrawal aimed at building and separating off communities, to establish sub-culturally protected communities supportive of the search for personal and collective identity in the face of the market (Kozinets & Handelman, 2004). At the farthest ends of the spectrum of these movements that completely withdraw, we find groups such as the Branch Davidians in the US or certain groups within radical/cultural feminism (Bounds, 1997).

Individuals can also divert the market by using human resistance tactics in the face of the market totalizing logic. This is not achieved through active resistance (such as consumer boycotts) or by refusing to buy products and brands, but by using them in ways that are foreign or antagonistic to those intended by the producers.

> The powerful define and construct places like shopping streets and malls, houses, cars, schools and factories, which they seek to control and rule, using strategies and plans. The weak, for their part, are forced to operate in these places, but are constantly seeking

to convert them into their own "spaces", using ruse, guile and deception and relying on suddenness and surprise.

Gabriel & Lang, 1995, p. 140

Consumers invent their own everyday uses and meanings thanks to ingenuity, clever insights and the subversive tactics employed to re-arrange objects and instructions imposed on them in order to re-appropriate the marketing system as their own (de Certeau, 1984). Consumers divert the marketing system to conquer it and intervene on a local scale to refuse having uses and meanings imposed on them (Aubert-Gamet, 1997). This consumer guerrilla position is akin to 'twisting' (Cova & Cova, 2000). "Unorthodox uses of standardized objects are not seen merely as semiotic games, but genuine acts of rebellion against the authority of the producer" (Gabriel & Lang, 1995, p. 139). At a collective level, consumers can twist marketplaces by transforming transactional spaces, as in the case of tailgating (Bradford & Sherry, 2015, p. 147), in which

[e]mpty, vacant, anonymous, or transactional space used primarily for mundane purposes, is transformed into vibrant, personalized, interactional place enjoyed by groups for extraordinary purposes. The former space is merely occupied, whereas the latter place is vivified, colonized and shared by a community of co-creators.

All these resistance attempts may be deemed illusory by critical researchers. Boltanski and Chiapello (2006) argue in quite some detail that capital and market systems are also dependent on the expression of such critiques to commodify new spheres as well as incorporate new modes of legitimation. Resistance can thus be seen as the creative brain behind capitalism.

Escape

Postmodern research suggests that consumers can be emancipated by escaping the totalizing logic of the marketplace (Fırat & Venkatesh, 1995). The postmodern consumer, living in a fragmented society, enjoys more potential maneuvering choices than under the realm of modernism. Fırat and Venkatesh (1995, p. 258) claim that, "much consumption does take place outside the market system", citing as examples flea markets and swap meets typically, albeit not exclusively, organized in terms of a market logic. They argue that to be emancipated, the "way forward" is to seek a space beyond the market, which requires identifying a social space beyond the reach of the market by positioning the consumer in the "lifeworld" and outside the market system (Fırat & Venkatesh, 1995, p. 258). Consumer emancipation can materialize if they are able to move in these social spaces "without the perennial panopticon of the market" (Fırat & Venkatesh, 1995, p. 258).

In his ethnography of the Burning Man Festival, Kozinets (2002) describes a process in which consumers engage in a hyperreal temporally constrained event to achieve emancipation. He posits that by removing the totalizing elements of the marketplace and creating an environment that is free from urban constraints, consumers are able to free themselves from the totalizing marketplace logic. Practices used at Burning Man to distance consumers from the market include discourses supporting communality and disparaging market logics, alternative exchange practices and positioning consumption as self-expressive art. Although Burning Man's participants materially support the market, they successfully construct a temporary hyper-community to practice divergent social logics. Escape from the market, if at all possible, must be conceived as similarly temporary and local. Escapes into the American West such as the Mountain Man rendezvous (Belk & Costa, 1998) or river rafting (Arnould, Price, & Tierney, 1998) are a fascination in consumer research where extraordinary experiences emancipate individuals from the harmful effects of over-civilization, extracting them from the "urban 9 to 5 lifestyle" (Arnould et al., 1998, p. 103). Contact with the elements, such as a surfer's "union with the wave" (Canniford & Shankar, 2013, p. 1055) or feeling the force of the river in rafting (Arnould et al., 1998) seem to compensate for the exploitive conditions at work. Research highlights the return to the primitive, the communal and the natural as allowing a regenerative escape from the constraints of tedious and tepid everyday life. Indeed, everyday life in a civilized world is construed as what people try to escape through extraordinary experiences. Generally, most studies on various forms of extraordinary consumption experiences are framed as an escape from structure (Tumbat & Belk, 2011). Research has largely adopted the Turnerian structure/antistructure analytical dichotomy (Turner, 1969) to describe experiential settings: structure is the organization of society and the mundane social cosmos that alienates the individual; antistructure is something potentially positive with regenerative qualities such as pilgrimages. Antistructure liberates individuals from the obligatory everyday constraints of their normal statuses and roles (Turner, 1969). This romantic ideology of consumption construes the (re)connection with the primitive, sublime and sacred during extraordinary experiences (Canniford & Shankar, 2013) as a break with civilized, mundane and profane everyday life.

To satisfy the logic of modern progress and all that goes with it, which is associated with the perpetual maximization of profit ideology, the world has become increasingly normed, rationalized to the extreme, down to the slightest detail and minutely programmed in its functionality and symbolic aspects (Gottdiener, 1997). Recent research pushes the notion of escape beyond antistructure to consider, "how do people deal with the constant pressure of policing and representation, undo their fixed positions and enter into processes of dis-identification?" (Papadopoulos, Stephenson, & Tsianos, 2008, p. 80). Scott, Cayla and Cova (2017) find an answer to this question in the pain that participants feel when they take part in extraordinary experiences such as the Tough Mudder obstacle race that knocks their minds and bodies alike. This pain causes them to escape into themselves, something that Le Breton (2015) refers to as 'blackouts'. This escaping into oneself affects those finding themselves in professional situations where they face daily pressure to perform (Costas & Kärreman, 2016). This escape into oneself might be construed as a new escape route in the sense of Papadopoulos et al. (2008) in their treatise on 'imperceptible politics', namely, the everyday escape practices that represent daily acts of subversion. The only person who sees the escape into him or herself is the individual, that is, the escape is imperceptible to everyone else (also within a professional context), and makes it impossible to determine exactly when people are engaging in such escapes. Engaging in dis-identification moments of this type can therefore be analyzed as betrayals that are enacted and performed through the secret of the extraordinary experience.

Critical thinking, as in the case of Arnould (2007a), could argue that an escape from the marketplace is illusory and impossible, and consider consumers as trapped within the alienating market logic. All the moves to reclaim personal 'authenticity', the quasi-orgiastic ecstasies of anti-consumerist festivals, the nostalgia of retroscapes and carnivals, the socially engaged projection of utopia or politically motivated ecotourism are "forms of Romantic consumerism. Thus, the utopian spirit, however progressively motivated, is colonized by market logic" (Arnould, 2007a, p. 104).

Consumer exploitation?

While Marxist theory considers consumption as wasteful, postmodern research introduces the idea that consumption could be a positive social activity (Lyotard, 1984). For postmodernists, consumption could be an emancipatory force if consumers were allowed to pursue their consumptive goals as part of their everyday life experiences (Fırat & Venkatesh, 1995). Consumers increasingly perceive and understand "the benefits of participation in self-service processes, including the emancipatory benefits of being 'producers'" (Manolis et al., 2001, p. 236). This consumer takes an active role, casting aside the passive role to become a protagonist:

> Whether one chooses protagonist, consum'actor, prosumer or some other neologism of choice, the point of these awkward verbal gestures is that the co-creative producer of genuine, political, less commercial experiences is far removed from the passive mass market consumer of the post-war consumerist boom.
>
> Arnould, 2007b, p. 192

Researchers holding this and similar views laud consumer involvement in branding and production since it empowers them to create their own lives and contribute positively to companies. This elimination of the boundary between consumers and producers is a key proposition of the proponents of value co-creation (Prahalad & Ramaswamy, 2004; Vargo & Lusch, 2004). A generic idea in value co-creation marketing discourses is that. thanks to the Internet, consumers have become more powerful and creative as subjects and this new way of being has a knock-on effect on their consumption and on the way they use the market, with the consumption act itself turning into an area where they can exercise creativity and power (Berthon et al., 2007).

The idea that we have moved from a producer-driven mode of value creation to a harmonious, exploitation-free mode of value co-creation has now begun to receive critical scrutiny from academics in the fields of marketing, anthropology and sociology. Value co-creation has spurred debates among marketing researchers. The intensity of these debates "demonstrates how much is at stake – conceptually and politically – when the roles of consumer and producer become blurred" (Cova, Dalli, & Zwick, 2011, p. 231).

Humphreys and Grayson (2008, p. 976) ask:

> Is consumer input into the production process a net positive; does it reconnect the laborer with the products of his or her labor? Or, is it exploitation twice over, once when the object is produced and twice when it is sold back for a profit?

From a post-Marxian perspective, co-creation as understood by Prahalad and Ramaswamy (2004) potentially signifies consumer exploitation because the producers of surplus labor value (consumers in this scheme) are not compensated for their work by the appropriator of such value. Exploitation might even be present when co-productive activities are undertaken voluntarily and, at times, with a significant degree of enjoyment. According to some critics, consumer exploitation under the rubric of value co-creation takes place on two related but different levels:

- First, consumers are not generally paid for the know-how, enthusiasm and social cooperation they contribute to the design, development and manufacturing processes of goods and services.
- Second, customers typically pay a price premium for the fruits of their own labor as the use value provided by co-created commodities is likely higher than that accomplished through rationalized systems of standardized production. In other words, the customer labor that goes into customizing goods and services ends up increasing the price these same customers have to pay for their creations.

According to this post-Marxian view, the power of consumers and freedom to create are merely superficial, as companies actually shape consumer agency (Zwick, Bonsu, & Darmody, 2008). Corporations create a new class of customers, the consumer proletariat (Arvidsson, 2006), to exploit them in a new form of capitalism without any contractual agreement. This exploitation does not stop with consumers expressing a subversive approach; on the contrary, companies would embed consumer resistance as a further creative force integrating conventional forms of collaboration (Zwick et al., 2008).

Value co-creation discourses participate in consumer governmentality (Foucault, 1978) through the new faces they produce and promote. These discourses create a type of consumer who is emancipated thanks to her/his own competencies. As Shankar, Cherrier and Canniford (2006) demonstrate, this type of discourse is simultaneously liberating and disciplining. Researchers who argue for marketing's consumer governmentality use it to stigmatize the liberating discourses of consumer power alongside the consumer agency discourses (Arnould, 2007b) and the service dominant logic (Vargo & Lusch, 2004) that accompanies them, the argument being that they are only superficially liberating. In this view, the specter of competent, empowered and emancipated consumers haunts today's marketers (Zwick et al., 2008). This specter does not at all liberate consumers but instead establishes a form of governmentality with the purpose of summoning a specific form of life where consumers participate voluntarily in the co-creation of value. Indeed, to be able to act as creative consumers, individuals must have been shaped, guided and molded into this competent consumer personage, which reproduces the frame of objective alienation within specific capitalist relationships.

Rethinking exploitation and emancipation in consumer research

In considering the evolution towards co-creation and prosumption, Humphreys and Grayson (2008, p. 977) state, "it is in this empirical context that the academic constructions of consumers as dupes or heroes as well as previous theories of false consciousness can be tested and perhaps rethought". In addition, Ritzer (2014, p. 20) argues that post-Marxian theorists position prosumers as

> suffering from false consciousness and that, in fact, they are deluding themselves in thinking they are not being exploited. However, it is also possible that they are not exploited in a classic Marxian sense and that the concept needs to be revised to take into account the new realities. It is also possible that an entirely new concept is needed.

The notion of compromise between different orders of worth put forward by Boltanski and Thévenot (2006) stands as a potential response to these calls for the theoretical rethinking of exploitation and emancipation. In a compromise, people are neither dupes nor heroes, they cooperate to act in a relevant way in different orders of worth, without trying to clarify the principle upon which their agreement is based. Emerging from the Alfisti case that Cova, Pace and Skålén (2015) study is a particular form of compromise. The Alfisti (Alfa Romeo enthusiasts) collaborate with the company without settling the conflict between the brand they love (Alfa Romeo) and the company that according to them has destroyed it (Fiat Group). They make an agreement with themselves and fellow Alfisti to set aside a dispute between two orders of worth that overlap but do not fit together perfectly: the inspired order of the brand community and the market order of the company. According to Boltanski and Thévenot (2006, p. 279), compromises lead to situations in which people are made uncomfortable as circumstances bring together elements from different orders of worth. One way of solidifying a compromise is to develop objects composed of elements from different orders at the service of the common interest, i.e., composite objects. The composite object in the case here presented is the Alfisti. com collaborative platform (Cova *et al.*, 2015). The problem of composite objects such as the Alfisti.com platform is that by being equivocal, their existence depends on the goodwill of the actors – the Fiat Group and the Alfisti – to create and maintain the compromise between the two orders (Boltanski & Thévenot, 2006). In the Alfisti case, consumers temporarily put aside possible sources of conflict to maintain the composite object. They understand that Fiat used its Alfa Romeo brand to involve them in a collaboration that would eventually benefit the company, but despite this, continue to take part in the branding program because they want to help the Alfa Romeo brand. Interpreting these consumers as engaging in compromises makes more sense than interpreting them as being exploited or emancipated. Consumers who make compromises do not have a naive or romantic view of their involvement in value co-creation processes as sometimes stated (Shankar *et al.*, 2006). Aware that they are being manipulated, they freely choose the extent of their 'dupery' and involve themselves to maximize individual and collective enjoyment.

Another response to the calls for the rethinking of exploitation in consumer research is to be found in the development of digital labor on social media. In the same vein as that described with respect to the Alfisti.com platform, participation in social media is voluntary and not coerced via economic exchange (Rey, 2012). Digital work might lead to commercial gain but this is not the motivation behind consumer engagement in social networks. Anderson, Hamilton and Tonner (2016, p. 397) argue,

> consumer participation in social media is more social than digital as it is characterized by sharing. This obligation to share is driven by observational vigilance and conspicuous presence, thus making the practice of social networking a form of social labor.

As consumers are generally paid little or nothing in return for the value they create for social media platforms, the rate of exploitation approaches infinity with digital labor, since the structural conditions of the digital/sharing economy require only the expression of self-motivated consumers, the rate of alienation is reduced. Digital labor is embedded in everyday sociality: work processes have shifted from the workshop to society. Consumers are willing to participate in activities that profit companies so long as nothing interferes with their ability to do whatever it is they want to do. In the absence of alienation,

> exploitation has been adapted to the new conditions of immaterial production. Rather than keeping most of the exchange value of the commodities produced and returning a small amount in the form of wages, the capitalist keeps all of the exchange value from the lease or sale of information commodities, whereas the user, simultaneously derives use value from the very same commodities.
>
> *Rey, 2012, pp. 415–416*

Nevertheless, the present questioning in marketing (Humphreys & Grayson, 2008; Ritzer, 2014), far from rendering Marxian concepts obsolete, highlights their relevance, particularly to understanding new forms of social relationships that tend to cover exploitation. This is the case of alienation, which is covered up by new forms of exploitation without any type of formal labor relationship. Indeed, collaborative experiences today make consumers work without any contractual agreement.

Conclusion

The general trend in consumer research questions how consumers might resist and escape market alienation. In addition, scholars have recently focused on the exploitation of co-creative consumers. All this has produced a rich corpus of critical approaches mobilizing the Marxian concepts of exploitation, emancipation and alienation. However, by reifying consumption, scholars overlook that this activity is embedded in production relations and hence power relations, and that it cannot be emancipatory in itself. As Weeks (2010) points out, value theory, which underlies exploitation in our societies, reflects class/power relations in a commodity-producing society, focusing on production-oriented relations between human beings rather than on human relations per se (Roubine, 1972). The arguments of marketing researchers are backed by neo-liberal ideological precepts (Fitchett, Patsiaouras, & Davies, 2014) and are situated within the capitalist system that seeks exchange value to create more value. In a certain sense, what our journey through exploitation/emancipation in consumer research shows is that the free laborer has been replaced by the free consumer in a type of postmodern translation of the maxim 'the freedom of a free fox among free chickens'.

Further research needs to explore sharing and collaborative economies that stand as paradigmatic examples of this replacement. On the one hand, collaboration and sharing are experiences of escape from 'the reign of value'; on the other hand, it is a new way to seek value and organize new forms of exploitation. It could be interesting to understand how these economies, while promoting consumer emancipation from the market, develop new forms of worker exploitation as shown by the Uber case. Research must therefore envision the development of social innovations that keep the 'fox' outside the community.

References

Alvesson, M., & Willmott, H. (1992). On the idea of emancipation in management and organization studies. *Academy of Management Review*, 17(3), 432–464.
Anderson, S., Hamilton, K., & Tonner, A. (2016). Social labor: Exploring work in consumption. *Marketing Theory*, 16(3), 383–400.
Arnould, E.J. (2007a). Should consumer citizens escape the market? *Annals of the American Academy of Political and Social Science*, 611(1), 96–111.
Arnould, E.J. (2007b). Consuming experience: Retrospects and prospects. In A. Carù & B. Cova (Eds.), *Consuming experience* (pp. 185–194). Oxon, Routledge.
Arnould, E.J., Price, L.L., & Tierney, P. (1998). Communicative staging of the wilderness servicescape. *Service Industries Journal*, 18(3), 90–115.
Arvidsson, A. (2006). *Brands: Meaning and value in media culture*. London, Routledge.
Aubert-Gamet, V. (1997). Twisting servicescapes: Diversion of the physical environment in a re-appropriation process. *International Journal of Service Industry Management*, 8(1), 26–41.
Baudrillard, J. (1970). *La société de consommation*. Paris, Denoël.
Belk, R.W., & Costa, J.A. (1998). The mountain man myth: A contemporary consuming fantasy. *Journal of Consumer Research*, 25(3), 218–240.
Bensussan, G., & Labica, G. (Eds.) (1999). *Le dictionnaire critique du Marxisme*. Paris, PUF Quadrige.
Berthon, P.R., Pitt, L.F., McCarthy, I., & Kates, S.M. (2007). When customers get clever: Managerial approaches to dealing with creative consumers. *Business Horizons*, 50(1), 39–47.
Böhm, S., & Land, C. (2012). The new 'hidden abode': Reflections on value and labor in the new economy. *The Sociological Review*, 60(2), 217–240.
Boltanski, L., & Chiapello, E. (2006). *The new spirit of capitalism*. New York, Verso.
Boltanski, L., & Thévenot, L. (2006). *On justification: Economies of worth*. Princeton, Princeton University Press.
Bounds, E.M. (1997). *Coming together/coming apart: Religion, community, and modernity*. New York, Routledge.

Bradford, T.W., & Sherry, J.F. (2015). Domesticating public space through ritual: Tailgating as festival. *Journal of Consumer Research*, *42*(1), 130–151.
Canniford, R., & Shankar, A. (2013). Purifying practices: How consumers assemble romantic experiences of nature. *Journal of Consumer Research*, *39*(5), 1051–1069.
Costas, J., & Kärreman, D. (2016). The bored self in knowledge work. *Human Relations*, *69*(1), 61–83.
Cova, B. (1997). Community and consumption: Towards a definition of the 'linking value' of product or services. *European Journal of Marketing*, *31*(3/4), 297–316.
Cova, B., & Cova, V. (2000). Exit, voice, loyalty and . . . twist: Consumer research in search of the subject. In S. Beckmann & R. Elliott (Eds.), *Interpretive consumer research* (pp. 25–46). Copenhagen, Copenhagen Business School Press.
Cova, B., Dalli, D., & Zwick, D. (2011). Critical perspectives on consumers' role as 'producers': Broadening the debate on value co-creation in marketing processes. *Marketing Theory*, *11*(3), 231–241.
Cova, B., Pace, S., & Skålén, P. (2015). Brand volunteering: Value co-creation with unpaid consumers. *Marketing Theory*, *15*(4), 465–485.
de Certeau, M. (1984). *The practice of everyday life*. Berkeley, University of California Press.
Elliott, R. (1997). Existential consumption and irrational desire. *European Journal of Marketing*, *31*(3/4), 285–296.
Fırat, A.F., & Venkatesh, A. (1995). Liberatory modernism and the re-enchantment of consumption. *Journal of Consumer Research*, *22*(3), 239–267.
Fitchett, J.A., Patsiaouras, G., & Davies, A. (2014). Myth and ideology in consumer culture theory. *Marketing Theory*, *14*(4), 495–506.
Foucault, M. (1978). La gouvernementalité, cours du 1/2/1978. In M. Foucault (Ed.), *Dits et ecrits, Tome III* (pp. 635–657). Paris, Gallimard.
Gabriel, Y., & Lang, T. (1995). *The unmanageable consumer: Contemporary consumption and its fragmentation*. London, Sage.
Gottdiener, M. (1997). *The theming of America: Dreams, visions, and commercial spaces*. New York, Westview Press.
Hardt, M., & Negri, A. (2009). *Commonwealth*. Cambridge, MA, Harvard University Press.
Hirschman, A. (1970). *Exit, voice, and loyalty*. Cambridge, MA, Harvard University Press.
Holt, D.B. (2001). Deconstructing consumer resistance: How the reification of commodified cultural sovereignty is entailed in the parasitic postmodern market. *Advances in Consumer Research*, *28*(1), 123–124.
Humphreys, A., & Grayson, K. (2008). The intersecting roles of consumer and producer: A critical perspective on co-production, co-creation and prosumption. *Sociology Compass*, *2*(3), 963–980.
Kates, S.M., & Belk, R.W. (2001). The meanings of lesbian and gay pride day resistance through consumption and resistance to consumption. *Journal of Contemporary Ethnography*, *30*(4), 392–429.
Kozinets, R.V. (2002). Can consumers escape the market? Emancipatory illuminations from Burning Man. *Journal of Consumer Research*, *29*(1), 20–38.
Kozinets, R.V., & Handelman, J.M. (2004). Adversaries of consumption: Consumer movements, activism, and ideology. *Journal of Consumer Research*, *31*(3), 691–704.
Le Breton, D. (2015). *Disparaître de soi: Une tentation contemporaine*. Paris, Métailié.
Lee, M.S., Cherrier, H., Roux, D., & Cova, B. (2011). Anti-consumption and consumer resistance: Concepts, concerns, conflicts, and convergence. *European Journal of Marketing*, *45*(11/12), 1680–1687.
Lyotard, J.F. (1984). *The postmodern condition: A report on knowledge*. Minneapolis, University of Minnesota Press.
Manolis, C., Meamber, L.A., Winsor, R.D., & Brooks, C.M. (2001). Partial employees and consumers: A postmodern, meta-theoretical perspective for services marketing. *Marketing Theory*, *1*(2), 225–243.
Marcuse, H. (1964). *One-dimensional man studies in the ideology of advanced industrial society*. New York, Routledge and Kegan Paul.
Marcuse, H. (1967). *Philosophy and revolution* [Philosophie und Revolution]. Berlin, Verlag.
Marcuse, H. (1969/1971). *Ideen zu einer kritischen theorie der gesellschaft*. Frankfurt, Suhrkamp.
Marx, K. (1887/1999). *Capital*. Volume 1. Retrieved July 5, 2018 from www.marxists.org/archive/marx/works/1867-c1/index.htm
Marx, K. (1972/1959). *Manuscrits de 1844*. Moscow, Progress Publishers. Retrieved from www.marxists.org/archive/marx/works/1844/manuscripts/labour.htm
Marx, K., & Engels, F. (1932). Comments on James Mill. Retrieved July 5, 2018 from www.marxists.org/archive/marx/works/1844/james-mill/index.htm

Marxists Internet Archive Encyclopedia (1999–2008). Retrieved July 5, 2018 from www.marxists.org/glossary/terms/a/l.htm#alienation

Meiksins-Wood, E. (2002). *The origin of capitalism: A longer view*. New York, Verso.

Ostrom, E. (2011). *Governing the commons*. New York, Cambridge University Press.

Ozanne, J.L., & Murray, J.B. (1995). Uniting critical theory and public policy to create the reflexively defiant consumer. *American Behavioral Scientist, 38*(4), 516–525.

Papadopoulos, D., Stephenson, N., & Tsianos, V. (2008) *Escape routes: Control and subversion in the twenty-first century*. London, Pluto Press.

Paranque, B., & Willmott, H. (2014). Cooperatives – saviours or gravediggers of capitalism? The ambivalent case of the John Lewis Partnership. *Organization, 21*(5), 604–625.

Parker, M., Cheney, G., Fournier, V., & Land, C. (Eds.) (2014). *The Routledge companion to alternative organisation*. London, Routledge.

Prahalad, C.K., & Ramaswamy, V. (2004). Co-creation experiences: The next practice in value creation. *Journal of Interactive Marketing, 18*(3), 5–14.

Rey, P.J. (2012). Alienation, exploitation, and social media. *American Behavioral Scientist, 56*(4), 399–420.

Ritzer, G. (2014). Prosumption: Evolution, revolution, or eternal return of the same? *Journal of Consumer Culture, 14*(1), 3–24.

Roemer, J.E. (1985). Should Marxists be interested in exploitation? *Philosophy and Public Affairs, 14*(1), 30–65.

Rosa, H. (2010). *Alienation and acceleration: Towards a critical theory of late-modern temporality*. Aarhus, Aarhus University Press.

Roubine, I. (1972). *Essay on Marx's theory of value*. Detroit, Black and Red.

Scott, R., Cayla, J., & Cova, B. (2017). Selling pain to the saturated self. *Journal of Consumer Research, 44*(1), 22–43.

Sève, L. (2012). *Aliénation et émancipation*. Paris, La Dispute.

Shankar, A., Cherrier, H., & Canniford, R. (2006). Consumer empowerment: A Foucauldian interpretation. *European Journal of Marketing, 40*(9/10), 1013–1030.

Tumbat, G., & Belk, R.W. (2011). Marketplace tensions in extraordinary experiences. *Journal of Consumer Research, 38*(1), 42–61.

Turner, V.W. (1969). *The ritual process: Structure and antistructure*. Ithaca, NY, Cornell University Press.

Vargo, S.L., & Lusch, R.F. (2004). Evolving to a new dominant logic for marketing. *Journal of Marketing, 68*(1), 1–17.

Veblen, T. (1899/1994). *The theory of the leisure class: An economic study of institutions*. New York, Penguin.

Weeks, J. (2010). *Capital, exploitation and economic crisis*. London, Routledge.

Zwick, D., Bonsu, S.K., & Darmody, A. (2008). Putting consumers to work: Co-creation and new marketing governmentality. *Journal of Consumer Culture, 8*(2), 163–196.

28
POLITICAL ECONOMY APPROACHES TO TRANSNATIONAL COMMODITY MARKETS

An application to the case of the global palm oil market

Martin Fougère

Introduction

Mainstream academic marketing has rarely explicitly engaged with political economy approaches. This might seem rather odd since the interest in markets could be expected to warrant a broader political-economic understanding, that is, one that would take into account questions of production, trade, regulation and government, with an emphasis on the power of different associated institutions and its consequences in terms of distribution of income and wealth. The most visible applications of a political economy perspective in mainstream marketing journals were published in the 1980s. Arndt's (1981, 1983) articles on a suggested 'political economy paradigm' for (both micro- and macro-) marketing, stand out, as do the works by Dwyer and colleagues (Dwyer & Welsh, 1985; Dwyer & Oh, 1987) on the political economy of marketing channels. In relation to micromarketing, a key characteristic of the political economy approach is claimed to be that it "views the business firm (or organizations in general) as a political coalition of internal and external stakeholder groups" (Arndt, 1981, p. 40). When moving to the macro level, Arndt argues that a political economy lens leads us to focus on "the structure and functioning of the social and economic control system", with particular interest in "the interplay of the three sets of institutions, markets, politics, and hierarchies" (ibid.).

Three decades later, mainstream marketing seems to remain largely uninformed by political economy perspectives. First, at the micro level, in what some authors have labeled a 'new marketing myopia', marketing tends to be characterized by a "single-minded focus on the customer to the exclusion of other stakeholders", "an overly narrow definition of the customer and her/his needs" and "a failure to recognize the changed societal context of business that necessitates addressing multiple stakeholders" (Smith et al., 2010, p. 4). Second, the political imagination of marketing (to the extent that there is one) still seems to give most agency to "the consumer as voter, judge and jury" (Schwarzkopf, 2011, p. 8), overlooking or downplaying the role of other political agents (cf. Denegri-Knott, this volume). Third, the standard responses that marketing offers in relation to transnational political-economic challenges (related to e.g., development and/or sustainability) place a great deal of faith in consumption and 'free' markets (including, free from politics as it were) as forces for good (Witkowski, 2005). A broader political consciousness is largely marginalized in marketing scholarship, outside of authors such as Fırat and Dholakia (2003), Bradshaw et al. (2006) or Varman (2008), and of more societally minded outlets such as *Journal of Macromarketing, Journal of Public Policy & Marketing, Consumption, Markets & Culture*, or, more occasionally, *Journal of Marketing Management* and *Marketing Theory*.

In a world where marketing has massive impacts not just on economies but on politics, organizations and lived experiences of people around the world, it is critical to both (1) give extensive consideration to other stakeholders than customers/consumers, and (2) bring back an international political economy (IPE; combining insights from economics and international relations) perspective to marketing, especially to transnational markets, in order to shed light on "the interplay of power, the goals of the power-wielders, and the productive economic exchange systems" (Zald, 1970, p. 223). While many marketing studies have already acknowledged the importance of multiple stakeholders, IPE approaches to the study of transnational markets remain scarce within marketing outlets. That said, critical marketing scholars might wish to contribute to neighboring, multi-disciplinary academic fields which are drawing more significantly on political economy, such as 'business and society' and 'development studies'.

Global sustainable development issues constitute a particularly interesting domain in relation to which a political economy perspective can help deliver a more thorough (and critical) understanding of transnational commodity markets. In relation to these issues, a marketing assumption could be that consumer power is the main way to address these issues through a form of market-based governance relying on standards and certification. A political economy approach, on the other hand, leads us to pay attention to how these standards are the result of interactions among multiple stakeholders, how different stakeholders are included in and excluded from these processes, what resistance and alternative governance possibilities there might be and so forth.

After this introduction, the chapter provides suggestions of IPE approaches that could be relevant for critical studies of transnational commodity markets: (1) a problematization from a sustainability perspective (emphasizing not only economic but also social and environmental impacts of the commodity markets); (2) inspired by Polanyi (1944), a critical study of the three factors of production ('fictitious commodities') land, labor and money; (3) Marxist approaches to IPE (dependency theory and world-systems theory); (4) analyses of Global Commodity Chains (Gereffi, 1994, 1995), Global Value Chains (Gibbon et al., 2008) and Global Production Networks (Coe et al., 2008); (5) neo-Gramscian approaches to IPE, emphasizing hegemonic struggles; and finally (6) Laclau and Mouffe's (1985) post-foundational discourse theory, which can be seen as both a departure from and a complement to neo-Gramscian approaches to IPE. The chapter then moves on to a review of (1) studies of certification markets (Foley, 2012; Mutersbaugh, 2002; Ponte, 2008, 2012; Taylor, 2005) which notably illuminate the impacts of the certifications from the perspectives of developing-country producers; and (2) studies of multistakeholder initiatives (Busch, 2014; Levy et al., 2010, 2016; Moog et al., 2015) which draw on neo-Gramscian IPE to problematize how standards are designed to protect the interests of big industry actors. As an illustration of what an IPE perspective on transnational markets can bring, the case of the global palm oil market is then discussed through the six approaches to IPE introduced earlier. Finally, the conclusion suggests from what angles the critical marketing studies drawing on IPE approaches may relate to various contemporary marketing topics.

IPE approaches relevant to critical studies of transnational commodity markets

The approaches listed below are by no means meant to be comprehensive of the realm of IPE possibilities, but they are, each in its own way (some are more empirical and/or descriptive, others more theoretical and/or normative), those that come to mind when thinking about transnational commodity markets studied from a critical perspective.

The first suggested approach is light on theory; it simply consists in problematizing transnational markets from a sustainability perspective, which entails thinking in terms of the three pillars of sustainability: economic, environmental and social impacts. Going beyond mainstream marketing discussions of value (co-)creation and thinking about impacts in these broader sustainability terms provides a path to political economy, in the sense that the question of impacts helps understand who might win and who might lose from, for example, the growth in the production of a specific commodity – which is itself often driven by a growth in the demand, and thus closely relates to questions of sustainable consumption, which are dear to critical marketers. Thus, an empirical study in terms of economic, environmental and social impacts can lead to deeper political insights, which may then be illuminated through various critical theories – for example those introduced below. Here, economic impacts are about more than just macro-economic growth, and they include questions related to sustainable livelihoods at micro and meso levels. There is typically a range of environmental and social impacts, which are often – though not always – related to the key factors of production of land and labor.

The question of the factors of production leads us to Polanyi's (1944) discussion of the three fictitious commodities land, labor and money. As a way to frame a critical analysis, starting with a study of these three factors of production might help in generating IPE insights. To Polanyi (1944, p. 178), land is a fictitious commodity because its "economic function is but one of the many vital functions of land". Thinking in terms of land (central especially in relation to resource commodities) thus leads the researcher to political-economic questions, such as issues of property rights and access to resources. In most cases, both land and labor issues relate to the regulatory and enforcement power of the state. This means that an IPE understanding typically involves a study of how various states directly or indirectly help the private sector in getting access to both land and labor. The question of money, or capital, might sound more straightforwardly economic, but here too the role of the public sector is often the key in supporting investment through loans and subsidies or through direct investment by state-owned businesses. Thus, systematically investigating the questions of land, labor and capital can be a way of delivering a critical IPE perspective on a transnational commodity market. For example, exploitative patterns (of developing-country resources by developed countries, of cheap labor by capitalist elites, etc.) may be uncovered.

These types of exploitative patterns can be illuminated through Marxist IPE studies of transnational commodity markets. In particular, dependency theory and world-systems theory come to mind here. Especially primary commodities have long been presented as problems if they are to be the sole bases for development strategies of developing countries. In particular, Prebisch (1950) argued that exporting only these types of commodities leads to a decline in the terms of trade, making the gap worse between the rich and poor countries, and reinforcing an exploitative relationship later studied in a more global way by scholars of the dependency school (e.g., Amin, 1976), and elaborated upon in a more holistic way in world-systems theory (e.g., Chase-Dunn & Grimes, 1995; Wallerstein, 2004), with its description of the 'world-economy' characterized by uneven, exploitative interrelationships between 'core' countries and 'periphery' or 'semi-periphery' countries. In parallel with these macro-analyses of exploitation, Hymer (1976, 1979) showed how the market power enjoyed by multinational corporations in oligopolistic industries translates into political power, and indeed extreme relations of exploitation between rich and poor countries.

World-systems theory, in turn, has had a direct influence on the literature on Global Commodity Chains (GCC). The GCC approach focuses on three (Gereffi, 1994) and later four (Gereffi, 1995) key dimensions to be analyzed as characterizing GCCs: the input-output dimension, the geographical dimension of territoriality, the dimension of governance, and, added later, the institutional framework. The GCC framework has been criticized among other things for its too simplistic 'ideal types' of governance (buyer-driven vs. producer-driven), which were largely in line with the world-systems theory research agenda: explaining the differences in the power relations between the more capital-intensive (buyer-driven) industries and the more labor-intensive (producer-driven) industries. Partly for empirical reasons, this distinction in terms of the two ideal types was dropped in the later literature on Global Value Chains (GVC), thereby providing a more intricate understanding of power relations, albeit with a somewhat less critical edge. That said, the GVC literature has been characterized by lively debates around how governance of complex inter-organizational networks should be understood, including through the critical discursive notion of governance as 'normalization' (see Gibbon et al., 2008), drawing on convention theory to explain the re-alignments of practices toward norms and standards. With the multiplication of, for example, certification standards mobilized in the transnational governance of commodities and their value chains, this understanding is particularly relevant to critical marketers, and more broadly to those marketers interested in debates on labeling and product disclosure norms (e.g., Arnould et al., 2009; Ingenbleek & Immink, 2010). In order to include in the analysis not only the governance of inter-firms' transactions but also all the relevant other actors and relationships, the more holistic framework of Global Production Networks (GPN) has been developed (Henderson et al., 2002). It is an attempt to integrate into the analysis: (1) the macro-structures of the global economy (the institutions and conventions of the capitalist market system); (2) the networks of interaction between a multiplicity of actors, including states, firms, labor, but also consumers and certifiers, among many others; and (3) the uneven distribution of benefits and negative impacts (see Coe et al., 2008). Thus, it is explicitly concerned with who wins and loses, for example, in areas where the production of a commodity is expanding, while at the same time integrating the important role of the consumers in having an impact on this expansion. The GPN approach is thus explicitly about IPE, and its descriptive framework can be combined with other critical approaches.

One such approach is the neo-Gramscian perspective on IPE – 'neo' because it takes Gramsci's (1971) understanding of national class conflict to international arenas and considerations of 'world order' (see Cox, 1987). Levy (2008) notes that the move from GCC to GPN has marked a gradual shift toward conventional perspectives on competitiveness, diluting the original critical edge of the GCC approach (see also Bair, 2005). It is thus important to inform GPNs through a neo-Gramscian approach, which helps us understand the dialectical way in which GPNs are both shaped by and constitutive of the broader context, including neoliberal ideology and its related institutions, inter-state structures, etc. (Levy, 2008). Gramsci's (1971) concept of hegemony stands for what brings relative stability to society, through the influence of a dominant alliance, or 'historical bloc'. As Levy (2008, pp. 951–952) puts it, "hegemony in capitalist democracies relies primarily on consensual processes that accommodate subordinate groups to some degree, through a measure of political and material compromise and by the dissemination of ideologies that convey a mutuality of interests". For example, Cox (1987) shows how international institutions such as the World Trade Organization (WTO) have contributed to delivering this relative alignment of interests through the normalization of neoliberal and consumerist ideologies. Thus, when applied to the context of GPNs, the neo-Gramscian perspective leads us to see why weaker actors and groups might consent to be involved in a GPN despite their lack of power in affecting its governance and rules: through the hegemonic ideology, their identities and interests have been constructed as somewhat aligned with those of the dominant group, i.e., capitalist elites from both the public and private sectors. Ultimately, however, the objective of a neo-Gramscian approach to transnational commodity markets is also to assess "the potential and limitations of strategies for challenging and changing GPNs, and the intertwined political and economic character of these challenges" (Levy, 2008, p. 945). Since hegemonies are contingent, it is possible for subordinate groups to engage in hegemonic struggles through wars of position which can be deployed in multiple terrains – e.g., at different regulatory levels (transnational, national or local), and through different types of institutions and actions.

Building on, and in some ways going beyond, the neo-Gramscian perspective, Laclau and Mouffe's (1985) post-foundational discourse theory is also centered around the concept of hegemony. It invites us to pay particular attention to how a hegemonic project is discursively articulated through certain dominant signifiers called nodal points, which give meaning to a range of floating signifiers, i.e., terms whose meaning might be different from one discourse to another. Laclau and Mouffe (1985) take the notion of radical contingency of all discourses seriously and call for counter-hegemonic discourse articulation that would target the nodal point and other key signifiers of hegemonic discourses, as well as establish other powerful nodal points and key signifiers in order to give alternative meanings to floating signifiers. For example, 'sustainability' might be defined as a matter of sustaining economic growth in a hegemonic discourse, but it could be defined through an entirely different priority in a counter-hegemonic discourse. For this counter-hegemonic discourse to gain sufficient traction, however, it needs to get various struggles on board and thus it needs to be articulated around a nodal point that can sustain a 'chain of equivalence', a sort of rallying point that the different struggles can all adhere to. Compared with neo-Gramscian approaches, the post-foundational approach does away more firmly with Marxist economic determinism – the primacy of economic class relations and the economic base are argued not to be universal since social relations are radically contingent. This makes the approach suspect from a traditional Marxist perspective – it is accused of downplaying the accumulation of economic wealth of the elites as the overwhelmingly most important factor in establishing and maintaining hegemonic power – but it also opens up possibilities of taking the hegemonic struggle to domains that might not be chiefly economic. These possibilities will be illustrated in the section where the six approaches will be applied to the case of the global palm oil market.

Review of IPE studies of certification markets and standards

Far from a comprehensive review in a field that is eminently cross-disciplinary, this section is meant to provide some examples of IPE studies of transnational commodity markets and standards that are relevant to critical marketing – until now (and to my knowledge), studies explicitly positioned in critical marketing have not dealt with these types of issues, but it is my contention that critical marketers would gain by paying more attention to them.

A great deal of attention has been put on certification, labeling and standards in marketing scholarship, but rarely from an IPE perspective. IPE perspectives are sometimes implicitly present, however. For example, Arnould *et al.* (2009) investigate the effects of Fair Trade scheme participation on income, educational attainment and health in three countries, and indeed find positive economic impacts, as well as overall (though uneven) impacts on education and health. While this is not a critical IPE perspective, in the sense that it is chiefly concerned with the effectiveness of institutions – in this case, whether the institution of Fair Trade labeling delivers on its promises or not – it does touch upon important sustainability issues so can be construed as corresponding to the first category of critical engagement with transnational commodity markets described in the previous section. For another example, Ingenbleek and Immink (2010) problematize some power issues in the formulation of Corporate Social Responsibility standards in the Netherlands. They do so by relying on two largely 'depoliticized' theories, stakeholder theory and institutional theory (see Levy (2008) on why institutional theory gains by being complemented with the concept of hegemony, which emphasizes the economic base and the political nature of the struggles to shape institutional fields). Thus, while there are political economy elements in their analyses, they are not explicitly critical, at least not in the terms suggested in the previous section.

The absence of explicit critical IPE studies of transnational commodity markets within marketing leads me to turn to studies of markets from outlets that are not formally associated with the marketing discipline in the remainder of the review in this section. First, let us look into some critical IPE studies of certification markets. These types of studies are particularly relevant to critical marketing scholars, not least because they tend to see certification as 'market-based' instruments of governance, in which market power and political power get intertwined. Mutersbaugh's (2002) study of organic coffee certification in Oaxaca, Mexico starts from a position that is somewhat reminiscent of Arnould et al. (2009): a will to investigate whether this type of certification empowers smallholders (in various ways) and promotes sustainable agriculture. However, the study is designed in a very different way, as a field study where the interests of labor and producer unions are central and where possible social and economic tensions caused by the certification process itself are problematized from the outset, since the focus is on the disruption caused by the change process. Mutersbaugh's (2002) findings, about a different kind of certification, in a different context and with a different research design, are not as encouraging as Arnould et al.'s (2009). In particular, he finds that: (1) local leaders become burdened by new heavy responsibilities related to certification; (2) all households find themselves tied to a new logic of 'market-price interdependence' whereby they must be concerned with the production practices of other households, since some neighboring non-organic practices could lead to decertification; and (3) producer unions have to help those who attempt to get certified while their ability to defend producer interests is constrained by certification norms. Also partly in relation to coffee, but with different kinds of certification, Taylor's (2005) comparative study of Fair Trade coffee and Forest Stewardship Council (FSC) certification is an example of a GCC analysis, informed by the theory of embeddedness from economic sociology. A key insight is that both types of certification struggle with the tension between the need to be connected to mainstream markets and the vision to create alternative markets. Taylor (2005, pp. 136–137) develops an IPE framework meant to cover three main aspects: "how the benefits of certified commodity chains are being distributed; the extent to which conventional market practices and logics are questioned; and how internal governance mechanisms manage the diverse interests and influence of their participants".

Associated with the GVC literature and notably the idea of governance as 'normalization' (for example, through certifications), Ponte's (2008, 2012) studies of the Marine Stewardship Council (MSC) show that there is strong institutional and normative pressure (for example, through the Food and Agriculture Organization of the UN (FAO), and through the promotion of sustainability goals) for developing countries to aim for MSC fishery certification. However, MSC certification does not seem to deliver on its promises of environmental benefits and even development. In particular, especially small-scale developing-country fisheries have clearly been marginalized in

MSC processes (Ponte, 2008). Complementing Ponte's findings, Foley (2012) also studies MSC certification but in what appear to be more 'developed' regions in Newfoundland and Labrador. He finds that far from being a neutral tool for sustainability or market access, MSC certification has power effects for the certification holders to control resource access and relations of production, noting that this power was used to expel a community-based fishing co-operative from the certified group in 2010 (Foley, 2012). Thus, these IPE studies of MSC certification provide insights on the marginalization of weaker actors at macro (developing countries), meso (lower income communities within countries) and micro levels (specific small organizations within certified groups), all while describing the dynamics between the different levels.

Second, somewhat similar to Ingenbleek and Immink's (2010) focus, a number of studies in the business and society literature take an interest in how different stakeholders are involved in the design of various certifications and standards, especially within multistakeholder initiatives (MSIs). A handful of these studies qualify as critical IPE, mostly following Levy's (2008) suggestion of adopting a neo-Gramscian IPE approach. From this perspective MSIs can be seen as "evidence of both the continuing hegemony of neoliberalism as well as various responses to it" (Busch, 2014, p. 513). The neo-Gramscian approach leads us to understand an MSI as "a negotiated arrangement . . . which primarily serves the interests of a dominant coalition . . . but is portrayed as representing the general interest" (Levy et al., 2010, p. 93). Thus, the issues 'governed' by MSIs can be seen as contested fields of 'hegemonic struggle' that involve counter-hegemonic movements. This means that what is important is not only to look into how well represented the various stakeholders are in the decision-making process for the standards (e.g., Ingenbleek & Immink 2010), but also to seek to understand the broader institutional political-economic context (see Moog et al., 2015). This broader context is characterized by, among other things, neoliberal trade policies, well entrenched structures of capitalism through financial markets and corporate governance norms, and the preference of the most influential international organizations (e.g., the United Nations) for soft law initiatives over binding multilateral treaties (Busch, 2014; Levy et al., 2010; Moog et al., 2015). Thus, private authority keeps growing in global governance, which makes it far easier for NGOs to join soft law arrangements than to obtain stronger binding regulation. That said, many NGOs do engage in a 'war of position' in a multiplicity of terrains – in MSIs, but also in relation to governments at various levels, in the media, through networked social movements, etc.

Recent neo-Gramscian studies of the development of the Global Reporting Initiative (GRI) (Levy et al., 2010) and the FSC (Moog et al., 2015) display dynamics of gradually taming the more radical initial objectives of the two initiatives. In both cases, this has led a number of NGOs to reconsider whether participating in the MSIs – even if engaging in a sort of 'war of position' from within – is an effective way to spend their limited resources. There is a risk for the NGOs to be co-opted and to contribute to sustaining the hegemonic bloc. One alternative for NGOs can certainly be to engage with the MSIs from the outside. In a recent study of the evolution of coffee sustainability standards (Levy et al., 2016), it is clear that some of those NGOs that started from a radical stance opposed to the development of standards together with the industry, eventually contributed to stronger standards, as a result of an incremental process of mutual accommodation which re-aligned 'value regimes' over time.

Illustration: the global palm oil market

The global palm oil market has attracted much public and academic attention in recent years, both because it represents an impressive 'commodity boom', with a very fast growth in demand and production, and because this oil palm expansion on the macro level leads to massive macro- and micro-economic, social and environmental impacts, including a range of alarming negative externalities. Around 85% of the world's palm oil is produced in Indonesia and Malaysia, with over 50% in Indonesia alone. In the biggest producing countries, the annual growth rate is estimated to be about or more than 10%, and palm oil production is also growing fast in various subtropical parts of the world, notably in South America, West Africa, and other parts of South-East Asia. Everywhere it expands, palm oil production leads to controversies related to questions of land rights, labor and environmental impacts.

It thus makes sense to begin exploring the global palm oil market from a sustainability perspective, thinking about economic, social and environmental impacts. In terms of economic impacts, palm oil has no doubt been the most important growth engine of Indonesia in the past decade, but this has raised many issues locally, such as the need for balancing trade-offs between subsistence and commercial agriculture, between monoculture and diversification, between smallholders and large plantations, and between the investments from the public and private sectors (e.g., Cramb & McCarthy, 2016a). Within Indonesia and Malaysia, the boom has also affected many livelihoods, as it has required the migration of labor, thereby disrupting rural poor communities. In macro-economic terms, the demand has been growing at the fastest pace in China and India (by far the two biggest markets by now), while growth has been slowing down in Europe and the US partly as a result of sustainability and health concerns of consumers and regulators – for example, the EU regulatory framework on renewable fuels will most likely make palm oil-based biodiesel deemed not sustainable by 2020.

When it comes to social impacts, the most salient issues relate to processes of land allocation and the social injustice associated with these processes. A small number of large agribusiness firms have benefited from the benevolence of the bureaucratic elites in Indonesia and Malaysia, getting access to land and thereby taking it away from local and indigenous communities (Cramb & McCarthy, 2016a). This – and other changes such as the growth of migrant labor – have led to local conflicts which have sometimes been very violent. In addition, the labor conditions at the plantations have been highly precarious, especially for the migrant workers. Finally, environmental impacts have been the most controversial: forest destruction and conversion of peatlands lead to massive biodiversity loss and an extreme growth in greenhouse gas (GHG) emissions, notably due to the methane gas released when peatlands are drained. Many endemic species of Borneo and Sumatra – the most symbolic of which, the orangutan, has become 'the flagship species' of activism against oil palm expansion – are endangered as they lose their habitat and are beaten or killed when they are found on oil palm plantations. In addition, the almost systematic use of fire in land clearing often causes larger forest fires and leads to air pollution and haze which have negative health impacts on populations and cause international tensions as other countries such as Singapore are strongly affected too. Water pollution, due to the need to establish plantations on steeper and steeper land and the waste caused by palm oil production, is also observed in many producing areas. These alarming environmental impacts have led regulators (notably in Indonesia) to establish moratoria, first on the conversion of peatlands and primary forest, and then on any new oil palm plantation, but the inability to enforce existing regulation in the remote areas of Borneo and Sumatra has been a problem too.

Going beyond a neutral listing of impacts, Polanyi (1944) invites us to look into the three factors of production of land, labor and capital. Cramb and McCarthy (2016b) have done this systematically in Indonesia and Malaysia. Drawing on Hall et al. (2011), they find that all four 'powers' that can provide access to land to large commercial interests – regulation, the market, force, and legitimation – have been deployed to favor the expansion of palm oil production: "in particular, the regulatory power of the state has been used to redefine land rights, reclassify land types, and facilitate the consolidation, privatization, and commodification of all types of land"

(Cramb & McCarthy, 2016b, p. 39). Vast state lands which overlap with claims of customary lands have been allocated to the private sector for oil palm development, thereby often clashing with traditional local governance of customary lands – although the picture is complex as land governance varies tremendously from one local community to another. In addition, a number of joint ventures between public or private sector and customary landholders have had contentious consequences, involving many court cases. Beyond the question of land tenure is the issue of land-use planning and land-use change: the lack of effective land-use planning is obvious in both Indonesia and Malaysia, as much of the land freed up for 'agriculture' has been devoted to the very export-oriented oil palm monoculture.

When it comes to labor, it is estimated that about 4 million people work in oil palm production in Indonesia and Malaysia (Cramb & McCarthy, 2016b). The key distinction is between the smallholders, who can devote some of their labor to other livelihood activities than palm oil, and the fully employed labor on estates, whether local or migrant – the latter allegedly represent about two-thirds of the oil palm workers in Indonesia and Malaysia, mostly internal migrants in Indonesia but also international migrants from Bangladesh, Indonesia, Myanmar and other South-East Asian countries in Malaysia (Cramb & McCarthy, 2016b). Allegations of violations of international labor norms in the plantations abound, as a number of watchdog reports have uncovered very poor working conditions (Finnwatch, 2014). The question of whether oil palm plantation labor improves local livelihoods in a significant way is quite contested, and varies depending on the labor regime (smallholder vs. employee) and area. Casual wages and other opportunities in the vicinity of the big estates often do improve livelihoods but due to relatively low labor-intensiveness (in comparison with land) on oil palm plantations, "only a limited number of local households can find casual employment on the estates" (Cramb & McCarthy, 2016b, p. 45). Another problem is that the shift to monoculture has deprived women of the status they had under mixed agricultural livelihoods models: they now become fully dependent on poorly paid oil palm work, while their husbands often migrate elsewhere.

Finally, the sources of capital in the oil palm production complex have seen very significant shifts over time. While the key investments originally came from foreign-owned plantation companies, the public sector and international development institutions such as the World Bank and the Asian Development Bank, the Malaysian and Indonesian private sectors have now become the biggest investors, often supported by international investment banks and funds. These private companies have been the key drivers of oil palm expansion, and they have grown to be some of the most important publicly listed corporations in the Malaysian, Singaporean and Indonesian stock exchanges. These investors are now "interested primarily in maximising the marginal returns to capital and will seek . . . to access extensive areas of cheap, unencumbered land . . . and a stable (i.e., 'tied'), low-wage labor force, regardless of political boundaries" (Cramb & McCarthy, 2016b, p. 48). Thus, they are now investing beyond the already overexploited Peninsula of Malaysia and Sumatra, in Borneo, Sulawesi, Papua, but also on other continents, notably West Africa and Central America.

The capitalist logic driving the political dynamics of the global palm oil market was already clearly visible in the above description of land, labor and capital, but it can be further illuminated through additional theories. For example, the resource curse caused by excessive exploitation of primary resources as a basis for the economy of a country (notably discussed in dependency theory) probably can be claimed to characterize Indonesia (more than Malaysia). Indonesia on the whole is a poorer country (at least in terms of income per capita) where a large 'reserve army' of cheap labor is present and can be exploited in the large oil palm estates, in both Indonesia and Malaysia. In world-systems theory terms, Malaysia could be considered a part of the 'semi-periphery' and Indonesia (especially Borneo, Sumatra, Sulawesi and Papua, i.e., the main oil palm areas) a part of the 'periphery'.

The GCC, GVC and GPN lenses might lead to a number of additional insights into palm oil political economy. For example, the GCC perspective makes us pay attention to the power of the big transnational buyers of palm oil, such as Unilever or Nestlé. To a large extent, it is the legitimacy needs of these large transnational corporations that drove the need for a market-based governance of palm oil sustainability, in the shape of the MSI Roundtable for Sustainable Palm Oil (RSPO). A GVC perspective à la Ponte (2008, 2012) would then look into which of the stakeholders tend to be marginalized in the MSI. Cheyns (2014), for instance, shows how local communities and smallholders do not really have a voice in RSPO, unless they receive support from NGOs (such as critical RSPO member Sawit Watch in this case). Interestingly, the large Malaysian plantation company IOI, a founding member and board member of RSPO, was suspended from the certification in spring 2016 following watchdog reports about mainly labor conditions at the plantations (Finnwatch, 2014) and an RSPO investigation. This suggested stricter governance and enforcement principles, but IOI was later reinstated in RSPO, to the dismay of some key members such as Unilever, which reiterated its will not to "resume sourcing palm oil products from IOI until we see tangible progress" (see Unilever, 2016). Thus, Unilever, possibly the largest palm oil buyer in the world, exerts its market power while attempting to retain the legitimacy of its claim that it buys only 'sustainable palm oil'. A GPN approach would examine the importance of such global actors and their commitments (for example, the overall driving role of Unilever, in partnership with WWF and the UN Global Compact, in setting up MSIs), and link it to both the networks of interaction between key actors on global and regional levels (including, but not only, through RSPO), and the patterns of winners and losers 'on the ground', in the areas around the plantations.

Still, in relation with RSPO, neo-Gramscian approaches might look more specifically into, for example, how the hegemonic bloc is represented in, and its interests are served by, RSPO. As Pye (2016, p. 430) notes (drawing on Poulantzas, who can be seen as a neo- or post-Gramscian too), RSPO does not mark a disappearing state power on the part of Malaysia and Indonesia, because "the dominant palm oil corporations are closely linked to state power, particularly to the Malaysian national state" (including the aforementioned IOI). Economic growth through palm oil production has for a long time been a central part of the Malaysian and Indonesian developmental states, and thus the 'private' Malaysian and Indonesian companies that have a strong say in RSPO all have strong ties to their respective states. A neo-Gramscian approach might also investigate how a possible war of position is played out in a multiplicity of terrains. For example, Sawit Watch, the NGO that supports minority voices in Cheyns' (2014) article is both a member of RSPO and a strong critical voice within it, and it is closely linked with other NGOs such as Friends of the Earth Indonesia/Walhi, which does not engage much with RSPO (discarded as 'greenwash' by Walhi West Kalimantan Director Anton Widjaya (Widjaya, 2013)) but instead provides legal and practical support to local communities in areas around oil palm plantations (or projects thereof). Meanwhile, global NGOs such as Greenpeace or Friends of the Earth International discuss the palm oil sustainability challenges with the aim to affect regulation at various levels (for example, Indonesian regulation or EU renewable energy directive, relevant in relation to biofuels). Interesting outcomes of this war of position relate to (1) a likely 'success' on the biofuel front, as palm oil biodiesel will probably be deemed unsustainable in the next step of EU renewable energy policy in 2020, and (2) a sort of 'co-optation' of Greenpeace and the Rainforest Action Network (RAN) when they joined the Palm Oil Innovation Group (POIG) with WWF and a number of progressive plantation companies. This could be interpreted as a move on Greenpeace and RAN's part from a radical position to a reformist position, since POIG's explicit "intention" is "to build on the RSPO's standards and commitments" (RAN, 2013) and POIG is thus more or less aligned with RSPO as a hegemonic project. Following

Levy et al. (2016), this can be analyzed as a re-alignment of value regimes, which somewhat reinforces the hegemonic bloc.

Finally, a post-foundational discourse perspective could indeed look at RSPO as a hegemonic project since it is an organization that claims to be broadly representative of the stakeholders of palm oil production and governs palm oil sustainability standards through consensus – in this sense, its aspiration is clearly to be hegemonic. Analyzing how the hegemonic discourse of RSPO and its key members is articulated is what I am trying to do in ongoing research (e.g., Fougère, 2015). It entails identifying the hegemonic discourse's nodal point and its other key open signifiers, as well as the meanings given to some key floating signifiers such as 'sustainability', 'regulation', and (market) 'demand'. The next step is to unpack how the initially rather well aligned counter-hegemonic movement articulated its discourse around a completely different nodal point ('land-use change'), thereby creating a chain of equivalence that was well sustained until success was reached in relation to the biofuels question at EU level in 2013. From 2013 on, however, the counter-hegemonic discourse can be said to have become 'disarticulated' as a result of complex dynamics which, notably, led to the founding of POIG, where hegemony-related (WWF, some companies) and counter-hegemony-related (Greenpeace, RAN) actors joined forces. What could a post-foundational perspective bring beyond a more traditional neo-Gramscian perspective? In this case, taking radical contingency seriously (and thus not subscribing to Marxist economic determinism) might help us to understand the relative success of the counter-hegemonic movement when it comes to the EU regulation on biofuels: when powerful signifiers attached to key global governance agendas – in particular the climate and biodiversity agendas – are available, they can be discursively leveraged. In this case, the 'land-use change' signifier is tied to the United Nations Framework Convention on Climate Change (UNFCC) and the 'indirect land-use change' signifier is directly operationalized in EU policy on biofuels; they were both very prevalent in the articulation of the counter-hegemonic discourse, which has led some industry actors (biofuels producers, members of RSPO) to be at least partially on the losing side of this battle in the war of position, despite their economic weight.

Conclusion

From what angles might critical marketing studies drawing on IPE approaches relate to various marketing topics, besides the obvious, more thorough understanding of transnational commodity markets? Based on the six somewhat overlapping approaches introduced in this chapter, I suggest four avenues for an engagement with various marketing topics through IPE. First, the simple problematization of sustainability relates to questions of (un)sustainable consumption of commodities. An engagement with transnational political-economic aspects not only helps to understand what is not sustainable with particular transnational markets but also gives ideas of where the problem might foremost lie, and what might be done about it, including (though not only) through the power of consumers. One associated research question could be: How can the consumption of [commodity X] be made (more) sustainable?

Second, Marxist IPE and the GCC approach provide us with insights into how the governance of commodity chains or networks has been increasingly 'buyer-driven' – although this is a contentious 'ideal type', in the broadest sense it problematizes the power of large transnational (often Western) buyers. In an equally dichotomous ideal type distinction, it can be argued that these buyers are more on the 'marketing' (as opposed to 'production') side of the equation: they are often large retailers or transnational corporations with valuable brands, which typically enjoy strong market power in their respective industries. Increasingly, the big brands of an industry are targeted for governance solutions to problems in GPNs – this is the case, for example, in the clothing industry, where the famous fashion brands are those giving strong legitimacy and power to initiatives such as the Bangladesh Accord on Fire and Building Safety. This trend is particularly relevant for critical marketing scholars, and IPE approaches help in studying what is going on. One associated research question could be: What is the role of leading brands in the regulation of GPNs?

Third, the GPN perspective and the neo-Gramscian studies of MSIs invite considering consumers and other consumption-related actors (e.g., certifiers) as important actors in understanding transnational commodity markets. These actors, however, are always networked with other types of actors, not usually in the forefront in marketing scholarship but directly affecting markets through their actions: states, NGOs, trade unions, people not just as consumers but as workers and/or active citizens, etc. This is thus once again an invitation for marketers to broaden their understanding of transnational commodity markets and understand better how marketing actors are networked with other stakeholders. One associated research question could be: How are the political impacts of consumption choices complemented by other political impacts in the regulation of transnational commodity markets?

Fourth, and finally, the post-foundational approach potentially provides important takeaways for social marketing. The palm oil case, with online activism directed toward Western consumers using orangutans as the flagship species of the palm oil sustainability issue, is a case in point of counter-hegemonic social movements eventually failing to sustain a robust chain of equivalence between their different struggles. The orangutan, as a sort of nodal point, is even proving something of a divisive figure as its suffering is often blamed on the local communities in Indonesia, whose struggles would need to be aligned with the species protection struggle in order for the movement to be stronger (see Fougère, 2016). Understanding the need for establishing and sustaining a discursive chain of equivalence could be an important insight for social marketing theory and practice, but it requires an IPE imagination where the different struggles that could possibly be aligned need to be understood. One associated research question, in cases in which social marketing seeks to advance a counter-hegemony, could be: How successful is social marketing in articulating a counter-hegemonic discourse leading to a strong chain of equivalence?

References

Amin, S. (1976). *Unequal development*. Hassocks, Harvester Press.
Arndt, J. (1981). The political economy of marketing systems: Reviving the institutional approach. *Journal of Macromarketing*, *1*(2), 36–47.
Arndt, J. (1983). The political economy paradigm: Foundation for theory building in marketing. *Journal of Marketing*, *47*(4), 44–54.
Arnould, E.J., Plastina, A., & Ball, D. (2009). Does fair trade deliver on its core value proposition? Effects on income, educational attainment, and health in three countries. *Journal of Public Policy & Marketing*, *28*(2), 186–201.
Bair, J. (2005). Global capitalism and commodity chains: Looking back, going forward. *Competition and Change*, *9*(2), 153–180.
Bradshaw, A., McDonagh, P., & Marshall, D. (2006). The alienated artist and the political economy of organised art. *Consumption, Markets and Culture*, *9*(2), 111–117.
Busch, L. (2014). Governance in the age of global markets: Challenges, limits, and consequences. *Agriculture and Human Values*, *31*(3), 513–523.
Chase-Dunn, C., & Grimes, P. (1995). World-systems analysis. *Annual Review of Sociology*, *21*(1), 387–417.
Cheyns, E. (2014). Making 'minority voices' heard in transnational roundtables: The role of local NGOs in reintroducing justice and attachments. *Agriculture and Human Values*, *31*(3), 439–453.
Coe, N.M., Dicken, P., & Hess, M. (2008). Global production networks: Realizing the potential. *Journal of Economic Geography*, *8*(3), 271–295.

Cox, R.W. (1987). *Production, power, and world order*. New York, Columbia University Press.

Cramb, R., & McCarthy, J.F. (2016a). Introduction. In R. Cramb & J.F. McCarthy (Eds.), *The oil palm complex: Smallholders, agribusiness and the state in Indonesia and Malaysia* (pp. 1–26). Singapore, NUS Press.

Cramb, R., & McCarthy, J.F. (2016b). Characterising oil palm production. In R. Cramb & J.F. McCarthy (Eds.), *The oil palm complex: Smallholders, agribusiness and the state in Indonesia and Malaysia* (pp. 27–77). Singapore, NUS Press.

Dwyer, F.R., & Oh, S. (1987). Output sector munificence effects on the internal political economy of marketing channels. *Journal of Marketing Research*, *24*(4), 347–358.

Dwyer, F.R., & Welsh, M.A. (1985). Environmental relationships of the internal political economy of marketing channels. *Journal of Marketing Research*, *22*(4), 397–414.

Finnwatch, 2014. The law of the jungle: Corporate responsibility of Finnish palm oil purchases. Retrieved July 10, 2018 from www.finnwatch.org/images/palmoil.pdf

Firat, A.F., & Dholakia, N. (2003). *Consuming people: From political economy to theatres of consumption*. London, Routledge.

Foley, P. (2012). The political economy of Marine Stewardship Council certification: Processors and access in Newfoundland and Labrador's inshore shrimp industry. *Journal of Agrarian Change*, *12*(2–3), 436–457.

Fougère, M. (2015). Palm oil sustainability through the lens of agonistic pluralism: Hegemonic and counter-hegemonic discourses. Conference paper, CR3+ conference. Retrieved July 10, 2018 from www.isaebrasil.com.br/cr3/docs/Anais-CR3.pdf

Fougère, M. (2016). The construction of animal moral superiority: Representations of orangutans in relation to the palm oil sustainability issue. Conference paper, SCOS conference in Uppsala, Sweden. Retrieved July 10, 2016from https://scos2016.wordpress.com/program/book-of-spoors/

Gereffi, G. (1994). The organization of buyer-driven global commodity chains: How US retailers shape overseas production networks. In G. Gereffi & M. Korzeniewicz (Eds.), *Commodity chains and global capitalism*. Westport, CT, Praeger Publishers.

Gereffi, G. (1995). Global production systems and Third World development. In B. Stallings (Ed.), *Global change, regional response: The new international context of development* (pp. 100–142). Cambridge, Cambridge University Press.

Gibbon, P., Bair, J., & Ponte, S. (2008). Governing global value chains: An introduction. *Economy and Society*, *37*(3), 315–338.

Gramsci, A. (1971). *Selections from the prison notebooks*. New York, International Publishers.

Hall, D., Hirsch, P., & Li, T.M. (2011). *Powers of exclusion: Land dilemmas in Southeast Asia*. Singapore, NUS Press.

Henderson, J., Dicken, P., Hess, M., Coe, N., & Yeung, H.W.-C. (2002). Global production networks and the analysis of economic development. *Review of International Political Economy*, *9*(3), 4436–4464.

Hymer, S. (1976). *The international operations of national firms*. Cambridge, MA, MIT Press.

Hymer, S. (1979). The multinational corporation and the international division of labor. In R.B. Cohen, N. Felton, J. van Liere, & M. Nkosi (Eds.), *The multinational corporation: A radical approach* (pp. 140–164). Cambridge, Cambridge University Press.

Ingenbleek, P.T., & Immink, V.M. (2010). Managing conflicting stakeholder interests: An exploratory case analysis of the formulation of corporate social responsibility standards in the Netherlands. *Journal of Public Policy & Marketing*, *29*(1), 52–65.

Laclau, E., & Mouffe, C. (1985). *Hegemony and socialist strategy: Toward a radical democratic politics*. New York, Verso.

Levy, D.L. (2008). Political contestation in global production networks. *Academy of Management Review*, *33*(4), 943–963.

Levy, D.L., Brown, H.S., & De Jong, M. (2010). The contested politics of corporate governance: The case of the global reporting initiative. *Business & Society*, *49*(1), 88–115.

Levy, D., Reinecke, J., & Manning, S. (2016). The political dynamics of sustainable coffee: Contested value regimes and the transformation of sustainability. *Journal of Management Studies*, *53*(3), 364–401.

Moog, S., Spicer, A., & Böhm, S. (2015). The politics of multi-stakeholder initiatives: The crisis of the Forest Stewardship Council. *Journal of Business Ethics*, *128*(3), 469–493.

Mutersbaugh, T. (2002). The number is the beast: A political economy of organic-coffee certification and producer unionism. *Environment and Planning A*, *34*(7), 1165–1184.

Polanyi, K. (1944). *The great transformation: The political and economic logics of our time*. Boston, Beacon Press.

Ponte, S. (2008). Greener than thou: The political economy of fish ecolabelling and its local manifestations in South Africa. *World Development*, *36*(1), 159–175.

Ponte, S. (2012). The Marine Stewardship Council (MSC) and the making of a market for 'sustainable fish'. *Journal of Agrarian Change, 12*(2–3), 300–315.

Prebisch, R. (1950). *The development of Latin America and its principal problems.* Lake Success, NY, United Nations.

Pye, O. (2016). Deconstructing the roundtable on sustainable palm oil. In R. Cramb & J.F. McCarthy (Eds.), *The oil palm complex: Smallholders, agribusiness and the state in Indonesia and Malaysia* (pp. 409–441). Singapore, NUS Press.

RAN (2013). Palm oil producers, NGOs launch responsible palm oil initiative at RSPO AGM. Retrieved July 10, 2018 from www.ran.org/palm-oil-producers-ngos-launch-responsible-palm-oil-initiative-rspo-agm

Schwarzkopf, S. (2011). The consumer as 'voter,' 'judge,' and 'jury': Historical origins and political consequences of a marketing myth. *Journal of Macromarketing, 31*(1), 8–18.

Smith, N.C., Drumwright, M.E., & Gentile, M.C. (2010). The new marketing myopia. *Journal of Public Policy & Marketing, 29*(1), 4–11.

Taylor, P.L. (2005). In the market but not of it: Fair trade coffee and forest stewardship council certification as market-based social change. *World development, 33*(1), 129–147.

Unilever (2016). Unilever responds to the RSPO decision to lift the suspension of the IOI Group. Retrieved July 10, 2018 from www.unilever.com/news/press-releases/2016/Unilever-reacts-to-palm-oil-suppliers-suspension-from-RSPO.html

Varman, R. (2008). The political economy of markets and development: A case study of health care consumption in the State of Kerala, India. *Critical Sociology, 34*(1), 81–98.

Wallerstein, I. (2004). *World-systems analysis: An introduction.* Durham, NC, Duke University Press.

Widjaya, A.P. (2013). The politics of palm oil expansion and tropical deforestation in Indonesia. Presentation at Helsinki University Social Forum Dialogues series, November 29.

Witkowski, T.H. (2005). Antiglobal challenges to marketing in developing countries: Exploring the ideological divide. *Journal of Public Policy & Marketing, 24*(1), 7–23.

Zald, M.N. (1970). Political economy: A framework for comparative analysis. In M.N. Zald (Ed.), *Power in organizations* (pp. 221–261). Nashville, Vanderbilt University Press.

29
SOCIAL MEDIA, BIG DATA, AND CRITICAL MARKETING

Christian Fuchs

Introduction

Social media and big data have become ubiquitous keywords in everyday life. The term social media is commonly used for social networking sites (e.g. Facebook, Weibo), blogs (e.g. WordPress, Tumblr), micro-blogs (e.g. Twitter), user-generated content-sharing sites (e.g. YouTube, Flickr, Instagram), or wikis (e.g. Wikipedia) (Fuchs, 2017b, chapter 2). Big data refers to the collection and analysis of data in such vast quantities that humans are incapable of processing them – only algorithms can (Fuchs, 2017b, chapter 2). There are diverse sources of big data, one example being credit and debit card transactions. So, the term big data is not limited to social media. At the same time, given that Facebook has about 1.8 million monthly active users[1] and Google processes more than 100 billion searches per year on average,[2] these two U.S. Internet companies are probably the largest data processors in the world. This tells of an inherent link between big data and social media. While social media characterize the techno-social systems enabling human interaction on the Internet, big data are the digital results of human activities. Google, Facebook and other online platforms tend to store all data and meta-data for long periods of time and therefore require huge server farms consisting of numerous supercomputers.

Google and Facebook are two of the world's largest companies. In the 2016 Forbes ranking of the world's 2,000 largest transnational corporations, Google (the holding company Alphabet Inc. is now the parent company of Google) occupied rank 27 with its annual profits of US$ 17 billion. Facebook was on rank 188 with annual profits of US$ 3.7 billion. One should not be mistaken: Google and Facebook are not communications companies. They do not sell the ability to communicate. Rather, they are the world's largest advertising agencies. Their profits almost exclusively derive from targeted advertising. Understanding social media and big data therefore requires that we contextualize these phenomena through the critical study of marketing and advertising.

Critical marketing studies are based on the insight that "marketing has devoted too much attention to refining itself as an instrumental science, with the corollary emphasis on the production of knowledge for the 'marketing organization', not for wider stakeholders" (Tadajewski, 2010, p. 776). Further, it is a "systematic critique of marketing theory and practice" that uses "some form of critical social theory . . . whether this is drawn from the neo-Marxist critical theory tradition, some variant of humanism, feminism" or other approaches (Tadajewski, 2010, p. 774). As a consequence, critical marketing does not mean conducting marketing critically or studying how to make marketing critical. Rather, critique and marketing are polar, dialectical opposites, just like socialism and capitalism. Critical marketing is a critique of marketing that aims at creating knowledge that helps us overcome both capitalism and marketing. Critical marketing studies as a discipline understands itself as being part of an emancipatory social science (Tadajewski & Brownlie, 2008). Taking a critical marketing perspective on social media means to apply critical social theory for understanding social media's power structures.

The task of this chapter is to critically understand social media and big data's political economy. It outlines key classical texts (second section), contemporary texts (third section), and future research directions (fourth section) that can help us achieve this goal.

Key theoretical approaches

There are many critical approaches that matter for critically understanding the Internet and social media. In a text like this chapter, one is necessarily limited to the number of key texts and thinkers one can introduce. I will here focus on four classical thinkers and one text by each of them: Dallas Smythe, Karl Marx, Raymond Williams, and Sut Jhally.

Dallas Smythe: 'Communications: Blindspot of Western Marxism'

Dallas Smythe's (1977) article *Communications: Blindspot of Western Marxism* has become a key text in the political economy of communication and when it comes to understanding advertising's political economy. Smythe's starting point is a critique of many Marxists' understanding of communications as transmitters of ideology, and of advertising as belonging to an unproductive sphere of capital circulation. "The mass media of communications and related institutions concerned with advertising, market research, public relations and product and package design represent a blindspot in Marxist theory in the European and Atlantic basin cultures" (Smythe, 1977, p. 1). Smythe criticized that a lot of critical and administration scholars analyze commercial media in terms of messages, information, images, meaning, entertainment, orientation, education, manipulation, and ideology. He argues for a perspective that gives a stronger role to the category of labor in the critical study of communication and culture.

Smythe bases his analysis on Karl Marx's (1867) insight that the commodity is capitalism's elementary form and that abstract labor produces the commodity's value. Smythe asks in the *Blindspot* essay: What is the advertising-based commercial media's commodity? Who produces the commercial media's commodity? Given that advertising-based media tend to provide their content gratis as a gift, the information cannot be the commodity.

Smythe gave the following answer:

> I submit that the materialist answer to the question – What is the commodity form of mass-produced, advertiser-supported communications under monopoly capitalism? – is audiences and readerships (hereafter referred to for simplicity as audiences). [. . .] Of the off-the-job work time, the largest single block is time of the audiences which is sold to advertisers.
>
> Smythe, 1977, p. 3

Audiences would work to create the demand for monopoly capital's commodities (Smythe, 1977, p. 6).

Audiences produce attention that is sold as audience commodity to advertisers. Therefore, according to Smythe, audiences conduct unpaid audience labor that produces the audience commodity and are exploited by advertisers. Smythe stressed that in capitalism, also unpaid labor is exploited and produces value. This focus was in line with developments in Autonomous Marxism and Marxist Feminism in the 1970s: Autonomous Marxists such as Antonio Negri (1988) stressed that there is a collective social worker who creates value inside and outside the factory and the office. They argued that society in capitalism is a social factory. Marxist Feminists stressed that housework (re)produces labor-power as a commodity and is therefore exploited by capital (e.g. Dalla Costa & James, 1973). Smythe's work, Autonomous Marxism, and Marxist Feminism have in common that they stress the importance of the exploitation of unpaid labor for capitalism's existence (see also Cova & Paranque, this volume and Arvidsson & Giordano, this volume).

In the age of digital media, there has been a resurgence of interest in Smythe's works. My contribution in this respect has been the linking of the notions of audience labor and the audience commodity to targeted online advertising (Fuchs, 2012). How does Smythe's work matter for understanding social media? On social media, we are partly audiences watching, reading and listening and partly producing consumers (prosumers) creating content ourselves. So, for example on YouTube, most of us tend to predominantly watch videos. Many of these videos have in-video advertisements. So, we not only consume the free content, but also provide attention to advertisements. And Google sells this attention to advertisers as a commodity. One difference to television is that on YouTube, users can produce and publish videos. So some users upload their own videos from time to time. And a smaller group of professional YouTubers tries to earn a living from creating YouTube content. By browsing videos on YouTube, searching on Google, and visiting websites, we produce a lot of meta-data that reveals a lot about our personal interests and tastes.

Google stores all of this data on its servers and identifies it with the IP address with which we access the Internet. Google also gains access to various other online data sources and thereby builds personal profiles of interests. Therefore, we do not simply find an audience commodity on social media, but also a big data commodity. In order to find out more about consumers' tastes and interests, advertisers and media organizations no longer need to conduct consumer surveys. The constant real-time surveillance of online behavior and long-time storage of personal data allow for targeting advertisements based on individual profiles. The big data commodity allows an advertiser to, for example, target an ad for a soft drink to all users in London in the age group 16–30 who have, at some point in time, googled the soft drink's name. The creation of big data commodity is a sophisticated form of surveillance and exploitation of user labor.

Karl Marx: 'The fetishism of the commodity and its secret'

'The Fetishism of the Commodity and its Secret' forms the fourth section of the first chapter in Karl Marx's main work *Capital Volume I* (Marx, 1867, pp. 163–177). In *Capital Volume I*'s first chapter, Marx shows that in capitalism both economic and ideological dimensions play an important role: A commodity has an economic dimension because it is produced by labor within class relations. The section on the commodity fetishism adds to the analysis that a commodity also has an ideological and aesthetic dimension that tries to deceive and manipulate humans. Marx here returns to the analysis of ideology that he advanced in an earlier work, *The German Ideology*, where he defined ideology as a *camera obscura* that makes humans and their social relations "appear upside-down" (Marx & Engels, 1845, p. 42).

The social relations between workers' labor appear not "as direct social relations between persons in their work, but rather as material relations between persons and social relations between things" (Marx, 1867, p. 166). Marx calls this phenomenon "the fetishism which attaches itself to the products of labor as soon as they are produced as commodities" (p. 165). He summarizes the causes of the commodity's fetish character in the following words:

> Objects of utility become commodities only because they are the products of the labor of private individuals who work independently of each other . . . Since the producers do not come into social contact until they exchange the products of their labor, the specific social characteristics of their private labors appear only within this exchange.
>
> *p. 165*

The notion of commodity fetishism points out that phenomena such as commodities and money are ubiquitous in our everyday lives in capitalist society. Given their thing-like status, we cannot directly see where they are coming from and how they have been produced. Therefore capitalism, commodity exchange, and money appear to be natural forms of the organization of society, to which no alternatives exist. Fetishism de-historicizes society. Fetishism is, on the one hand, a particular aesthetic of the commodity. On the other hand, all ideology is fetishistic in character as it attempts to legitimate, naturalize, and justify specific forms of domination and exploitation.

The most influential theoretical take-up of Marx's notion of commodity fetishism can be found in Georg Lukács' 1971 book *History and Class Consciousness*. Commodity logic conceals "every trace of its fundamental nature: the relation between people" so that "a relation between people takes on the character of a thing and thus acquires a 'phantom objectivity'" (Lukács, 1971, p. 83). Lukács coined the notion of reification. Generally speaking, reification (another term for it is alienation) means conditions under which humans are not able to control and determine the structures that shape their lives. Reification therefore can exist in all realms of life (Fuchs, 2016, chapter 5). Lukács was particularly interested in economic and cultural reification. "Reification requires that a society should learn to satisfy all its needs in terms of commodity exchange" (Lukács, 1971, p. 91), which includes "the separation of the producer from his means of production" (Lukács, 1971, p. 91). Lukács added another important dimension to the theory of commodity fetishism: His notion of reified consciousness stressed the subjective dimension of ideology and fetishism. Ideology and fetishism are not just objective structures and strategies; they are also experienced and lived. Ideology aims at influencing human consciousness. Lukács' works have had major influence on Marxist ideology critique, including the approach of the Frankfurt School.

We can learn from Chapter 1 of Marx's *Capital* that when analyzing capitalist phenomena such as advertising and targeted advertising on social media, there is always an economic and a cultural dimension, as well as aspects of labor and ideology. Dallas Smythe's notions of audience labor stress advertising's labor dimension. Given that, as Marx shows, any commodity also has a fetishistic and ideological dimension, one also needs to look at the ideological dimension of the audience commodity. The works of Sut Jhally and Raymond Williams can help us better understand commodity fetishism in the context of advertising.

Sut Jhally's 'Advertising as Religion' and Raymond Williams's 'Advertising: The Magic System'

Sut Jhally's (2006) essay 'Advertising as Religion: The Dialectic of Technology and Magic' analyzes advertising's fetishistic and ideological structure. Jhally points out that in capitalism, the division of labor ensures that people only work on one part of a product. Because of the division between mental and physical labor, and the fact that goods come to us through markets, we do not understand their origins. "The social relations of production embedded in goods are systematically hidden from our eyes. The real meaning of goods, in fact, is *emptied* out in capitalist production and consumption" (Jhally, 2006, p. 88). Advertising taps into this void: Commodity fetishism empties commodities of human meaning. We cannot understand the meanings of life and experiences of commodity producers, as these are all removed from the equation. In an artificial way, advertising creates ideological meanings that it bestows on commodities. "Into the void left by the transition from traditional to industrial society comes advertising . . . The function of advertising is to refill the emptied commodity with meaning . . . Production empties. Advertising fills. The real is hidden by the imaginary" (Jhally, 2006, pp. 88–89). He adds that the "most important functions that advertising performs is to provide meaning for the world of goods in a context in which true meaning has been stolen" (Jhally, 2006, p. 93).

Advertising is tremendously powerful because it tells stories and provides meanings about goods and the economy that are not presented in other forms. It uses various strategies for doing so, e.g. the strategy of black magic (Jhally, 2006, p. 91): Humans suddenly transform in supernatural ways through commodity use. Advertising is a secular form of religion. Advertising is a system of commodity fetishism: It promises satisfaction and happiness through the consumption of things (Jhally, 2006, p. 102). For Jhally, advertising is propaganda that promotes the ideology of human happiness through the consumption of commodities. By analyzing advertising as ideological commodity propaganda and commodity consumption ideology, Jhally defies positivist definitions of advertising that describe it as useful information for consumers that helps them navigate commercial options in complex markets. A typical example of such an uncritical definition of advertising defines it as "a channel of information from manufacturers to Consumers" that merely "tells where to find what you want" (Kaptan, 2002, p. 28).

In his essay 'Advertising: The Magic System' (2000), Raymond Williams analyzes the history of advertising. He shows that in the early stages of capitalism, advertising was seen as harmful and was therefore limited by an advertising tax. The emergence of advertising, as we know it today, can – in the main – be traced back to the emergence of monopoly capitalism in the late 19th century (see Harbor, 2017).

> Advertising was developed to sell goods, in a particular kind of economy. Publicity has been developed to sell persons, in a particular kind of culture. The methods are often basically similar: the arranged incident, the "mention", the advice on branding, packaging and a good "selling line".
>
> *Williams, 2000, p. 183*

Comparable to Jhally, who sees advertising as capitalism's secular religion, Williams analyzes advertising as capitalism's commodity magic: Advertising is capitalism's system of "organized magic" (Williams, 2000, p. 186) and "organized fantasy" (p. 193).

> You do not only buy an object: you buy social respect, admiration, health, beauty, success, power to control your environment. The magic obscures the real sources of general satisfaction because their discovery would involve radical change in the whole common way of life.
>
> *p. 189*

Jhally and Williams's analyses of advertising as capitalism's religion and magic system correspond to Marx's analysis of commodity fetishism in general. Marx (1867) argued that a commodity is a peculiar thing; it is "strange" (p. 163), "metaphysical" (p. 163), "'mystical'" (p. 164), and "'mysterious'" (p. 164). As a consequence, the commodity "stands on its head", and "grotesque ideas" (p. 163) about the commodity's nature emerge.

Marx's notion of the commodity fetishism and Jhally and Williams's applications of this concept to the critical analysis of advertising also matter in respect to social media; first, in the context of social media advertisement's general structure, and second in respect to social media's inverse commodity fetishism. McDonald's is one of the biggest advertisers on Facebook. One example posting shows a "Mexican burger" and says: "Get in the mood for Mexico with spicy Habanero chilli mayo in this week's #GreatTastesoftheWorld: the Mexican Stack!"

The ad presents a particular image of a burger as being tasty, multicultural, international, spicy, etc. McDonald's presents itself as fostering an international lifestyle and eating culture by adopting culinary influences from all over the world. This image is, however, fetishistic, illusionary, magic, and religious. It is a belief system that might not correspond to the actual reality of the production of the burger that is advertised. The consumer does not know where the meat and ingredients come from and under what conditions they are produced. The advertisement distracts attention from common criticisms of McDonald's relating to working conditions, possible health and environmental impacts, the McDonaldization of the world, etc. The advert is fetishistic because it tries to create a brand image that only presents the burger and the company in a positive light and disregards the actual social conditions of production. What is specific for commodity fetishism on social media? Advertising's commodity fetishism in print publications and broadcast media (radio, television) is standardized and unified, every consumer of these media receives the same advertising messages. In contrast, we find personalized and targeted commodity fetishism on social media. Advertisers such as McDonald's can target its ads at users who, based on their previous online activity, for example, appear to be fond of fast food.

Targeted commodity fetishism is a first feature of advertising on social media. A second feature is what I in various publications have termed the inverse commodity fetishism (Fuchs, 2014, chapter 11; Fuchs, 2015, chapter 5). In conventional commodity fetishism, one cannot experience the social context of commodity production but is directly confronted with the logic of money and the commodity. On Facebook and other targeted-advertising-based social media platforms, the commodity fetishism is inverted: Because access to the platform is free and the sale of the big data commodity is hidden, one does not experience monetary exchange or commodity purchase on Facebook. Instead, the social dimension of communication, sharing, and community is what is foregrounded and experienced. As an effect, the commodity form is hidden behind the social form so that commodity fetishism tends to take on an inverted form. For Facebook users, it is not directly experienceable that users produce a commodity for Facebook; that they actually work for Facebook; and that they are the ones generating the company's profits. The inverse commodity fetishism makes it more difficult for users to perceive themselves as workers who are creating value and are being exploited (see also Arvidsson & Giordano, this volume and Cova & Paranque, this volume).

The ideological effects of commodity fetishism are an immanent manipulative feature of online advertising. Social media also enable an algorithmically engineered form of manipulation, namely the manipulation of emotions and attention. This became evident when researchers from Princeton University conducted a large-scale experiment on Facebook (Kramer *et al.*, 2014): The emotional tone of postings shown on the Newsfeed of 689,003 users was manipulated.

Two parallel experiments were conducted for positive and negative emotion: One in which exposure to friends' positive emotional content in their News Feed was reduced, and one in which exposure to negative emotional content in their News Feed was reduced.
[...]
[The] results suggest that the emotions expressed by friends, via online social networks, influence our own moods, constituting, to our knowledge, the first experimental evidence for massive-scale emotional contagion via social networks ... and providing support for previously contested claims that emotions spread via contagion through a network.

Kramer et al., 2014, pp. 8788–8789

Such research has implications for advertising and marketing: If negative messages are kept from the News Feed, then users are more likely to positively engage with content, including advertisements and the company's postings. The experiment that was supported by Facebook also shows that technically it is easy to manipulate what is seen and not seen on the News Feed. It is just a small step from research about manipulating emotions to practically conducting such manipulation. The effect would be that social media platforms would become purely positivist, suppressing attention to critical content, possibly also including the critique of politics and corporations. Facebook is a targeted-advertising machine and one of the world's largest advertising corporations. Manipulation for the sake of keeping users and advertising clients happy can easily result in the filtering out of critical postings. The result is then a platform that is an instrument of capitalist interests and censors everything that does not adhere to the logic of commodities.

Engineering and manipulating emotions and sociality on social media can easily result in one-dimensional social media. The Princeton researchers and Facebook were criticized for not obtaining the users' informed consent for the online experiment they participated in. Facebook apologized to its users.[3] The Electronic Privacy Information Centre demanded that Facebook makes its News Feed algorithm public because the secrecy of algorithms enables and supports possible manipulation.[4]

Current key areas of research

This section focuses on two key areas of current critical research about social media: digital labor and digital alienation.

Digital labor

The notion of digital labor emerged in the context of the 2009 conference The Internet as Playground and Factory organized by Trebor Scholz at The New School in New York (see http://digitallabor.org). Later, also a collected volume of some of the presented contributions was published (Scholz, 2013). The basic idea is that user activity on commercial digital media is unpaid labor that creates value and a digital commodity. Therefore, social media companies such as Facebook and Google exploit users. My own contribution to the digital labor literature has been the combination of the digital labor concept with critical and Marxist theory (see Fuchs, 2010, 2012, 2014, 2015).

If one wants to understand a particular aspect of capitalism, then one needs to look at how commodity production is organized. Marx has provided a framework for such an analysis (see Fuchs, 2010):

$$M - C\ (c, v) .. P .. C' - M'$$

A capitalist corporation invests monetary capital M for purchasing specific commodities C as means of production. This includes labor-power (variable capital v) as well as resources and instruments (constant capital c). Labor-power is the subjective dimension of the means of production. Resources and instruments form the means of production's objective dimension. In the production process P workers transform the objects in order to create a new commodity C', in which labor-time and a surplus-product is objectified. The new product is more than the sum of its elements. When the commodity C' is successfully sold then an increased capital sum M' is created. A part of C' is reinvested so that a new cycle of accumulation starts, while other parts are paid out as interest, dividends, bonuses, and rent. The point of capitalism is the accumulation of capital, production with a monetary profit. The commodity C' is sold at a price that is higher than the investment costs. The commodity C' and its value are created by labor. But the workers do not own the products they create. They are only remunerated for part of their work in the form of wages. The surplus-value and surplus-product they create remain unremunerated. The key aspect of capitalism is that capital accumulation can only work by exploiting workers, which means that part of their labor is unpaid and that capitalists own the products that workers create.

The question that arises in the context of social media is how Marx's framework can be used. The access to Facebook, Google, YouTube, Twitter, etc. is not a commodity. This also implies that these companies' paid employees do not create a commodity, but rather a gift. But all of these companies are for-profit. So, there must be a different commodity and a different kind of value-generating activity. Marx's framework can be modified for social media capitalism as follows (Fuchs, 2010, 2012, 2014 [chapter 11], 2015 [chapter 5]):

$$M - C\ (c, v1) .. P1\ (\text{social media platform}), v2 .. P2 .. C' - M'$$

v1 is the paid employees who create and maintain the social media platform. Access to the platform is a gift, a 'free lunch' for the users, who form the unpaid labor force v2. Their online activities create in the second production process P2 the big data commodity C' that is sold to advertisers so that an increased sum of monetary capital M' can be accumulated. All labor-producing commodities for capitalists involve unpaid labor that creates surplus-value.

The difference between regular wage-labor and unpaid digital labor is that in the latter case there is no wage, which means that all labor-time is surplus labor-time. This circumstance is a feature that social media's digital labor shares with housework (Fuchs, 2010, 2017a). Kylie Jarrett (2016) uses the notion of the digital housewife for pointing out parallels between unpaid online labor and houseworkers' domestic, reproductive labor.

> Consumer labor is akin to domestic labor . . . because it is a site of social reproduction: a site for the making and re-making of the social, affective, ideological and psychological states of being that (may) accord with appropriate capitalist subjectivities.
> *Jarrett, 2016, p. 71*

The implication of the notion of digital labor is that Google, Facebook, Twitter and other online corporations that use the targeted-advertising capital accumulation model exploit users;

that usage of these platforms is labor-time; that digital workers are part of the contemporary proletariat; that value-production is not limited to factories and offices; and that activities that might feel pleasurable and personal can nonetheless be forms of economic exploitation.

The Marxist notion of digital labor results in a theoretical discussion (e.g. Fisher & Fuchs, 2015; Proffitt, Ekbia & McDowell, 2015). The main criticisms can be summarized in the following ideal-type arguments:

1   "Marx is a 19th-century theorist. A 19th-century theory is not fit for explaining 21st-century phenomena. Marx's theory is outdated."
2   "Only wage workers are productive workers who are exploited by capital. Facebook users do not work and are not exploited because they do not earn a wage."
3   "Facebook users are not producers, but media consumers. Consumption does not create any value."
4   "Social media is part of the advertising economy that is situated in capitalism's sphere of circulation, in which commodities are not produced, but sold. Circulation labor is not productive, but rather unproductive. Facebook therefore is a rent-seeking corporation that consumes the profits and value created by wage workers in other parts of the economy."
5   "The focus on the exploitation of users as unpaid trivializes much worse forms of exploitation, such as Taylorist labor and slave work."

Such arguments tend to imply that there is no problem with Facebook and Google. Their logic is: "They do not exploit us and therefore nothing needs to be done against them". Counter-arguments can be summarized as follows (see Fuchs, 2015, chapter 5; see also Fuchs, 2017a):

1   The 2008 crisis of capitalism and its consequences show that Marx was right and remains important. Marx was a historical and dialectical thinker. Just like capitalism remains the same by constantly changing, also the categories used for analyzing capitalism undergo a dialectic of continuity and change. The transformation of the Marxian formula of capital accumulation from $M - C (c, v) .. P .. C' - M'$ into $M - C (c, v1) .. P1, v2 .. P2 .. C' - M'$ on social media shows that the online targeted-advertising economy is based on such a dialectic of continuity and change.
2   If you assume that only wage workers are exploited in capitalism and that only a wage worker can be a productive worker, then the implication is that house workers, who are still predominantly female, and the world's estimated 30 million slaves are also not exploited. Your assumption is politically problematic. Marx saw productive labor as value-generating labor. One can produce value for capital without being paid.
3   There is in general a dialectic of production and consumption. Production involves the consumption of the means of production. Consumption produces meanings, effects, and the need for more production. Social media are different from traditional communication technologies. On social media, there is not a clear differentiation between producers and consumers of content or between production, circulation and consumption technologies. The computer is a convergence technology. Consumption on social media is better termed 'usage'. And usage is also the production of data, meta-data, and often user-generated content. Social media users are prosumers.
4   The reason why a commodity produced by a brand company is much more expensive than a standard commodity has to do with the fact that branding involves advertising and marketing labor. In the contemporary economy, advertising forms an important industry in itself. It is therefore unrealistic to dismiss this part of the economy as unproductive. One can charge rent

on a persistent product that was only created once but does not need constant labor input for being re-produced. But the big data commodity is frequently updated and renewed, so there is an actual labor input and a renewal of the commodity. It is therefore not feasible to argue that Facebook is a rentier. A rentier is a monopolist who controls a specific resource (usually land or real estate) and charges money to tenants, users or leasers. Marx argued that transport labor is a form of productive circulation labor. Transport labor is the labor that is needed for transporting a commodity from the place where it is produced to the places where it is sold and consumed. Audience labor and social media users' digital labor is ideological transport labor that helps transporting advertisements that are commodity ideologies and product propaganda to users.

5 The logic of the argument 'A is not exploited because the exploitation of B is more violent' disregards how different forms of exploitation are united in an international division of labor, from which transnational corporations benefit. They exploit a diverse range of workers in order to accumulate capital. The production of digital media and data is based on an international division of digital labor, in which we find slave workers extracting minerals, Tayloristic assemblage workers, low-paid software engineers and call center agents, highly paid and highly stressed software engineers, precarious freelancers, user labor, etc. The notion of the international division of digital labor stresses that digital capital exploits all of these digital workers and that they therefore have a common interest to struggle against capital and to organize across national boundaries in the form of a digital labor union. The notion of digital labor is not limited to the users of targeted-advertising-based social media platforms. Marx stressed the connectedness of diverse forms of labor with the notion of the collective worker. In the international division of digital labor, there is collective digital labor.

Not all digital labor is unpaid and based on advertising. YouTube has introduced YouTube Red in the USA and is also rolling out the same program in other countries: Members of YouTube Red pay a subscription fee for access to ad-free premium videos (including music, series and vloggers' content).

> Our new paid membership, YouTube Red, lets members enjoy any video on YouTube without ads while still supporting creators . . . New revenue from YouTube Red membership fees will be distributed to video creators based on how much members watch your content.[5]

YouTube celeb vloggers such as Lilly Singh (who had 11 million followers on her YouTube Channel in January 2017), PewDiePie (53 million), MatPat (8 million), Toby Turner (2 million), Joey Graceffa (7.5 million)[6] have produced series and movies for YouTube Red. YouTube stars are a labor aristocracy, who can earn some money from their profiles because they managed to accumulate a large number of subscribers. While there is a small number of labor-aristocratic YouTube-Vloggers, the vast number are proletarianized digital workers, working precariously and struggling to earn a living online. YouTube only enables this YouTube aristocracy to produce premium content that is paid for by YouTube Red subscribers. In this model, YouTube can be seen as a temporary employer of these YouTube celebs that pays them a wage for the creation of specific content. YouTube Red subscribers are consuming audiences paying for access to premium content. With the introduction of YouTube Red, Google has diversified its capital accumulation model. It continues to use targeted advertising as a main revenue source and has in addition introduced a subscription service. YouTube is therefore based on two forms of digital labor: (a) users' digital labor of watching and creating in the case of advertising sponsored part of the platform; (b) the YouTube labor aristocracy's paid labor that creates premium content for YouTube Red.

Digital alienation

Alienation (*Entfremdung*) is a term that Marx used for characterizing conditions that humans are not in control of and under which they live. Alienation signifies not only an objective structural condition, but also a subjective feeling of dissatisfaction. In discussions about digital labor, there have been different approaches about how to think of alienation in the context of social media.

Mark Andrejevic argues that commercial social media only have an appearance of being non-alienating because they foster play and sociality. But in reality, using them means a form of digital alienation, "a form of the enclosure of the digital commons" (Andrejevic, 2012, p. 84). "Users have little choice over whether this [surveillance] data is generated and little say in how it is used" (Andrejevic, 2012, p. 85). Such "external, storable, and sortable collection of data about" users' "social lives" is "separated from us and stored in servers owned and controlled by, for example, Facebook" (Andrejevic, 2011, p. 88). "Algorithmic alienation" (Andrejevic, 2014, p. 189) determines users' lives by data mining, big data analysis and statistical correlations (see also Tadajewski, this volume).

Eran Fisher (2012) understands digital alienation in a different way. For him, it "signals an existential state of not being in control over something (the labor process, the product, etc.)" (Fisher, 2012, p. 173).

> [Less] alienation refers to a greater possibility to express oneself, to control one's production process, to objectify one's essence and connect and communicate with others. Thus, for example, working on one's Facebook page can be thought of as less alienating than working watching a television program.
>
> *Fisher, 2012, p. 173*

Social media

> establish new relations of production that are based on a dialectical link between exploitation and alienation: in order to be de-alienated, users must communicate and socialize: they must establish social networks, share information, talk to their friends and read their posts, follow and be followed. By thus doing they also exacerbate their exploitation.
>
> *Fisher, 2012, p. 179*

Fisher's conclusion is that on social media, low alienation creates high exploitation.

Andrejevic and Fisher have two different understandings of digital alienation. For Andrejevic, it is an objective condition, while for Fisher it is a subjective feeling. We do, however, not have to categorically separate subjective and objective alienation. Alienation is both an objective condition and something that is or is not felt. In the book *Critical Theory of Communication* (Fuchs, 2016), I have suggested a matrix of alienation that distinguishes three types and three dimensions of alienation. We can discern between economic, political and cultural alienation. Each of these types is organized on the subjective level (attitudes and feelings), the intersubjective level (social agency and interaction), and the objective level (structures and products of activity). Combining these types and levels results in a matrix with nine forms of alienation (Fuchs, 2016, p. 167). The alienation matrix can be applied to Facebook and other commercial social media platforms (see Table 29.1).

Table 29.1 The matrix of digital alienation

Forms of alienation/reification	Subjects' attitudes and feelings		Intersubjectivity (social agency and interaction)	Object (structures, products)
Economic reification	Feeling of alienation: "Facebook exploits me!"	Feeling of non-alienation: "Facebook is fun and voluntary and gives me social advantages. Therefore I do not feel exploited."	Exploitation of users' digital labor; users' non-ownership of platforms	Users' lack of control over the use of personal data
Political reification	Feeling of alienation: "The surveillance-industrial complex that Facebook is part of threatens freedom."	Feeling of non-alienation: "For greater security, we have to give up some privacy. I therefore don't mind state surveillance of social media."	Political control and surveillance of citizens' communication	Citizens' lack of control over how political institutions regulate the Internet, establishment of a surveillance-industrial complex
Cultural reification	Feeling of alienation: "Facebook is mindless babble, narcissistic self-presentation and showing off."	Feeling of non-alienation: "Facebook is a great form of socializing with other people."	Asymmetric visibility of users that favors celebrities, corporations and powerful institutions	Asymmetric influence on public meaning making, centralized online attention structures and online visibility

Source: Fuchs (2016, p. 171)

One important aspect of the matrix of digital alienation is that it goes beyond the economic realm. It also covers forms of political control and cultural disrespect. Social media is also a realm of the accumulation of political and cultural power that produces winners and losers. Another important aspect of the matrix is that objective digital alienation does not automatically imply subjective digital alienation. Although Facebook users are objectively exploited, they do not necessarily feel exploited, seeing that there is inverse commodity fetishism on corporate social media platforms. We therefore have to distinguish between feelings of digital alienation and non-alienation. In general, there is only an opportunity for societal change when conditions and the collective structure of feelings of alienation coincide. There is, however, also no guarantee that such change will automatically or necessarily be politically progressive in character.

Directions for future research

Studying social media and big data from a critical marketing perspective is interesting but also complex. It involves multiple dimensions, topics, questions, and approaches. This section identifies possible research questions that remain fairly unexplored and could be taken up by PhD students and other scholars. The list that follows is not complete, rather, it provides some examples.

- What are commonalities and differences between users' attitudes toward targeted advertising in Western countries and non-Western countries in Asia, Africa and Latin America?
- How do traditional trade unions use social media and what do they think of the possibility of the creation of digital labor unions?
- What have workers' and users' experiences been in the digital sharing economy (including Airbnb, Uber, and online freelancing platforms such as Amazon Mechanical Turk and Upwork)?
- What are the experiences and political attitudes of digital workers in the international division of digital labor? What do they think of the perspective of the world's digital workers uniting in a global movement or union?
- What have been the experiences of people who have tried to establish alternatives to Facebook, Google, YouTube, Twitter, etc.? What problems have they faced? What challenges, limits and problems do platform co-operatives face? Are there ways for such limits to be overcome?
- What kind of class are professional YouTubers? What kind of class consciousness do they have? How do they think about capitalism, entrepreneurship, neo-liberalism, freelancing, and precarious labor?
- How has marketing and advertising based on big data and social media changed the film and music industries? What do artists think about these changes? What is the role of precarious labor among artists in the social media age?
- How do right-wing parties and social movements (Trumpism, pro-Brexit movement, Front National, nationalists, racists, xenophobes, etc.) use targeted advertising, big data and social media to advance their ideologies? How do they use social media as forms for political communication? What do everyday users think about such advertisements and right-wing online communication?
- How does marketing and targeted advertising change with the rise of the Internet of Things? What dangers do such forms of advertising entail? What do actual or potential users think about these dangers?
- What are the limits and problems of big data? How do users think about big data-based advertising and targeted advertising? How do they think about non-commercial, commons-based, non-profit alternatives?

- How can an alternative paradigm to big data positivism and computational social science be established? What critiques can be leveled at these largely quantitative approaches? What alternative critically oriented social media research methods do we need to develop and how can they be applied to ideology critique?
- How are specific forms of ideologies expressed on social media?
- What policies are needed for advancing non-commercial, non-profit, commons-based social media?
- How can the logic of social media and online communication be decelerated and the political public sphere thereby be best advanced? What are slow media 2.0? What are the potentials of slow media 2.0?
- What are the dangers of branded online content and native online advertising? How do branded online content and native online advertising make use of big data? What do users think of branded online content?
- What problems does the labor face in the context of crowdfunding? What power asymmetries and ideologies can we find in the world of crowdfunding? What have been the experiences of actual project coordinators on crowdfunding platforms such as Kickstarter? How does crowdfunding relate to neo-liberalism and the ideology of entrepreneurship?
- What controversies develop when digital advertising gurus meet digital labor activists in focus groups to debate digital capitalism?

Conclusion

Social media and big data are relatively new phenomena. At the same time, they reflect old power structures, but in new ways. This chapter focused on the analysis of social media's political economy based on various critical theory approaches. It used classical concepts such as the audience commodity, audience labor, and commodity fetishism to show that critical analysis of advertising and targeted advertising needs to look at both economic and ideological dimensions. Facebook and Google are not communications corporations but the world's largest advertising agencies. Current research in critical social media studies focuses on issues such as digital labor and digital alienation. Given that social media and big data will not disappear overnight, the critical study of these phenomena remains an important task.

Notes

1 Data source: Facebook, SEC Form 10-Q, November 2016
2 Data source: www.internetlivestats.com/google-search-statistics/, accessed on November 10, 2016.
3 www.theguardian.com/technology/2014/jul/02/facebook-apologises-psychological-experiments-on-users
4 www.theguardian.com/technology/2014/jul/04/privacy-watchdog-files-complaint-over-facebook-emotion-experiment
5 https://support.google.com/youtube/answer/6306276?hl=en-GB
6 http://uk.businessinsider.com/youtube-red-original-movies-and-shows-2015-10?r=US&IR=T/#youtuber-joey-graceffa-will-star-in-a-new-youtube-murder-mystery-series-10

References

Andrejevic, M. (2011). Social network exploitation. In Z. Papacharissi (Ed.), *A networked self* (pp. 82–102). New York, Routledge.
Andrejevic, M. (2012). Exploitation in the data mine. In C. Fuchs, K. Boersma, A. Albrechtslund & M. Sandoval (Eds.), *Internet and surveillance: The challenges of Web 2.0 and social media* (pp. 71–88). New York, Routledge.

Andrejevic, M. (2014). Alienation's returns. In C. Fuchs & M. Sandoval (Eds.), *Critique, social media and the information society* (pp. 179–190). New York, Routledge.

Dalla Costa, M., & James, S. (1973). *The power of women and the subversion of the community*, second edition. Bristol, Falling Wall Press.

Fisher, E. (2012). How less alienation creates more exploitation? Audience labor on social network sites. *tripleC: Communication, Capitalism & Critique, 10*(2), 171–183.

Fisher, E., & Fuchs, C. (Eds.) (2015). *Reconsidering value and labor in the digital age*. Basingstoke, Palgrave Macmillan.

Fuchs, C. (2010). Labor in informational capitalism and on the Internet. *The Information Society, 26*(3), 179–196.

Fuchs, C. (2012). Dallas Smythe today – the audience commodity, the digital labor debate, Marxist political economy and critical theory: Prolegomena to a digital labor theory of value. *tripleC: Communication, Capitalism & Critique, 10*(2), 692–740.

Fuchs, C. (2014). *Digital labor and Karl Marx*. New York, Routledge.

Fuchs, C. (2015). *Culture and economy in the age of social media*. New York, Routledge.

Fuchs, C. (2016). *Critical theory of communication: New readings of Lukács, Adorno, Marcuse, Honneth and Habermas in the age of the Internet*. London, University of Westminster Press.

Fuchs, C. (2017a). Capitalism, patriarchy, slavery, and racism in the age of digital capitalism and digital labor. *Critical Sociology, 43*. doi: 10.1177/0896920517691108.

Fuchs, C. (2017b). *Social media: A critical introduction*, second edition. London, Sage.

Harbor, K. (2017). 'At the desire of several persons of quality and lovers of musick': Pervasive and persuasive advertising for public commercial concerts in London 1672–1749. *Journal of Marketing Management, 33*(13–14), 1170–1203.

Jarrett, K. (2016). *Feminism, labor and digital media: The digital housewife*. New York, Routledge.

Jhally, S. (2006). Advertising as religion: The dialectic of technology and magic. In S. Jhally, *The spectacle of accumulation: Essays in culture, media, & politics* (pp. 85–97). New York, Peter Lang.

Kaptan, S.S. (2002). *Advertising: New concepts*. New Delhi, Sarup & Sons.

Kramer, A.D.I., et al. (2014). Experimental evidence of massive-scale emotional contagion through social networks. *Proceedings of the National Academy of the Sciences of the United States of America, 111*(24), 8788–8790. Retrieved July 4, 2018 from www.pnas.org/content/111/24/8788

Lukács, G. (1971 [1923]). *History and class consciousness*. London, Merlin.

Marx, K. (1867). *Capital volume I*. London, Penguin.

Marx, K., & Engels, F. (1845). *German ideology*. Amherst, NY, Prometheus.

Negri, A. (1988). *Revolution retrieved: Selected writings on Marx, Keynes, capitalist crisis & new social subjects 1967–83*. London, Red Notes.

Proffitt, J.M., Ekbia, H.R., & McDowell, S.D. (Eds.) (2015). Special forum on monetization of user-generated content: Marx revisited. *The Information Society, 31*(1), 1–67.

Scholz, T. (Ed.) (2013). *Digital labor: The Internet as playground and factory*. New York, Routledge.

Smythe, D.W. (1977). Communications: Blindspot of western Marxism. *Canadian Journal of Political and Social Theory, 1*(3), 1–27.

Tadajewski, M. (2010). Towards a history of critical marketing studies. *Journal of Marketing Management, 26*(9–10), 773–824.

Tadajewski, M., & Brownlie, D. (2008). Critical marketing: A limit attitude. In M. Tadajewski & D. Brownlie (Eds.), *Critical marketing: Issues in contemporary marketing* (pp. 1–28). Chichester, John Wiley.

Williams, R. (2000). Advertising: The magic system. In R. Williams, *Culture and materialism* (pp. 170–195). London, Verso.

30
MARKETING AND THE PRODUCTION OF CONSUMERS' OBJECTIVE VIOLENCE

Eduardo André Teixeira Ayrosa and Renata Couto de Azevedo de Oliveira

Introduction

On May 19, 2015, a cardiologist named Jaime Gold, 56 years old, was attacked by a group of boys in Rio de Janeiro. He was stabbed in the abdomen, and died the next morning. His death triggered a wave of emotional reactions among the residents of Rio de Janeiro's Zona Sul, a large and affluent part of the city, where the feeling of insecurity, already high, literally skyrocketed. He was riding his bicycle around the Lagoa Rodrigo de Freitas, a lagoon linked to Ipanema beach by a 140-meter channel. Today, three years later, a shrine marks the spot of the attack: a bike is tied to the low metal railings that are supposed to protect passersby from falling into the lagoon (see Figure 30.1). The boys, all minors, wanted his expensive bike to sell on the black market. This alone, however, does not explain the extreme brutality of the attack.

Jaime Gold's tragic story, in all its gory simplicity, tells us a lot about violence, social inequality, social recognition, and consumption. Urban violence has been present in the life of the residents of many cities like Rio de Janeiro for generations. Nevertheless, Jaime Gold's attack was still very shocking. The attacker could have been anyone fitting a certain set of characteristics, a stereotype that Rio residents, or Cariocas as they like to be known as, know all too well. The better off residents feel fragilized and victimized by such social situations, but have difficulty understanding that this sort of violence might not, in fact, be a one-way phenomenon. They cannot conceive the idea that excluded people might also feel disrespected, and even violated by public displays of wealth. Yet, any act of violence like this can be interpreted as a response to lifelong daily oppression.

Relation with the Other is an important topic within the field of consumer culture. While such relations are at the very core of consumer culture theories (Arnould & Thompson, 2005; Slater, 1997), they are also neglected in situations where the Other is excluded from the market (Eckstrom & Hjort, 2009; Hill, 2002), disrespected (Bouchet, 2014) or simply dehumanized (Hill & Martin, 2014). In this chapter, we propose that consumer culture naturalizes violent relations with the Other. By focusing on objective forms of violence (Balibar, 2002; Žižek, 2014), we contend that consumer culture plays an important role in the establishment of what we call a *plateau of indifference*, a level of objective violence below which any act becomes invisible, or concealed behind a veil of naturalization. In this chapter, we present a review of different violence theories that help us understand violent relations with a human and sometimes invisible

Figure 30.1 Improvised memorial to violence victims in Lagoa Rodrigo de Freitas, Rio de Janeiro, at the spot where Jaime Gold was murdered. Picture by Eduardo Ayrosa.

Other, and build propositions that summarize the role of consumer culture in the production of objective violence.

Violence: from Hobbes to Freud

Violence is present in the founding myth of the State itself and indeed appears to be inherent in the human condition as a whole. The well-known maxim *Homo homini lupus* – "Man is a wolf to another man" – figures both in Hobbesian State theory as well as in Freudian thought and leads us to believe that without the presence of a State (for Hobbes) or Culture (for Freud), a natural (Hobbesian) or barbarian (Freudian) State would ultimately prevail.

Hobbesian political theory on the origins of society and the basis of political power is centered on a contract, and sees a disproportion between limitless human desires (appetites) and the means of satisfying them, which are always limited. A natural state is thus configured as a war "and not war, but a war of every man against every man" (Hobbes, 1998, p. 29). The Hobbesian man, endowed with reason, is both a God and a wolf to another man (Hobbes, 1998, p. 3). He is a God within the context of his city, among its citizens, who are ruled in justice and in charity, and a wolf to other cities, when defending his domains, using "the virtues of war, which are violence and fraud" (Hobbes, 1998, p. 4), and acting as a voracious beast.

The famous phrase "*Homo homini lupus*" is not actually Hobbesian, but Greek. It is present in the adaptation by the Roman playwright Plautus known as *Asinaria*, or *The Comedy of Donkeys*:

"*Lupus est homo homini, non homo, quom qualis sit non novit*".[1] A possible translation is: a man is not a man but a wolf to a stranger. Reason and self-knowledge are, for Hobbes, tools that prevent man from making use of violence and lies. By knowing himself, he is also able to know his Other, provided that this Other is a citizen of the same State. The respectful recognition of alterity is, therefore, limited by the State.

Freud, in turn, offers a more comprehensive view of human nature. In his concept, aggressiveness, hostility and cruelty, inherent in human beings, are jointly the source and representation of what he called the "principle of pleasure". Due to mutually imposed limitations in the name of security, men enter into a cultural or communal life, and, if on the one hand, they are thus able to maintain their gains and improve their lives, on the other, they end up suffering from the frustrations and limitations imposed upon them by the "principle of reality".

Reason also appears in Freud when he recognizes the will of man to "improve his lot on earth through work" (Freud, 1961, p. 46) and through the "power of love which made man unwilling to be deprived of his sexual object – woman – and made the woman unwilling to be deprived of the part of herself which had been separated from her – her child" (Freud, 1961, p. 48). Another point he has in common with Hobbes is his recognition that it is only the primeval head of the family that enjoys instinctive freedom. This creates an extreme contrast "between a minority who enjoyed the advantages of civilization and a majority who were robbed of those advantages" (Freud, 1961, p. 62).

Hobbes views citizens' behavior within the same society as charitable and fair while the citizens from other societies are seen as ferocious beasts. Freud, meanwhile, is rather adamant about the absence of the dual character proposed by Hobbes, which he makes quite clear in the fifth part of his *Civilization and its Discontents*. He views all men as each other's wolves:

> Men are not gentle creatures who want to be loved, and who at the most can defend themselves if they are attacked; they are, on the contrary, creatures among whose instinctual endowments is to be reckoned a powerful share of aggressiveness. As a result, their neighbour is for them not only a potential helper or sexual object, but also someone who tempts them to satisfy their aggressiveness on him, to exploit his capacity for work without compensation, to use him sexually without consent, to seize his possessions, to humiliate him, to cause him pain, to torture him, to kill him. *Homo homini lupus*.
>
> Freud, 1961, p. 58

Such aggressiveness, according to Freud, is not related to property. He states that communism views humans as inherently good, and that through the elimination of private property, such aggressiveness can be mitigated, while it is property that provides the power that corrupts humans' passive nature. Freud disagrees with this position, since in his view, such aggressiveness lies "in the field of sexual relationships" (Freud, 1961, p. 60). The Other, in his opinion, may become a recipient of such aggressiveness simply by being different: "It is always possible to bind together a considerable number of people in love, so long as there are other people left over to receive the manifestations of their aggressiveness" (Freud, 1961, p. 61).

While it is easy, based on such a concept, to understand the conflicting relationships that exist between national groups (this is Freud's remark), it is necessary to extend this concept of the Other to a consumer society. Bearing in mind the debacle of national identity and its substitution by other forms of identity formation based on work and consumption (Bauman, 2004), this Other becomes the "different" within the same society, but on different social strata.

Thus, not only Latinos, but people with scarce resources (Ekström & Hjort, 2009) might well become recipients of such aggressiveness, in whatever form it might manifest itself, ranging from personal acts of violence to refusing recognition. To some extent, therefore, Freud and Hobbes come to a common concluding proposition: the Other is the main recipient of social violence. Freud calls such a phenomenon "the narcissism of minor differences" (Freud, 1961, p. 61).

The Other and Otherness

Both Hobbes and Freud put the Other at the heart of the violence debate. If in their times the Other was more closely related to a foreigner or someone from another society, such a scenario has become that much more complex in the consumer society and consumer culture of today. In a short abstract, Bouchet (2014, p. 964) wrote that violence "proceeds from the denial of the boundary of the other", and its expression lies in the "lack of respect for others precisely because they are someone else". Consequently, Bouchet implies that it is impossible to recognize alterities located in different contexts, and this applies to the social, financial, economic and cultural abyss between the citizens of the same State. Is it possible to recognize or refer to the excluded from the market as being the Other? Is there something that leads us to overlook the Other, always relegating them to the position of invisible strangers?

We should also perhaps consider that the greatest violence that we, ourselves, commit without even realizing it, is to refuse to recognize others. Although we are sometimes situated in very different contexts, despite our preferences, we are essentially all human beings with the same fundamental feelings. Žižek gives an account (Žižek, 1994, pp. 1–2) in which he claims to have been criticized for giving a lecture on Hitchcock while his former country was on fire. If he had behaved like a victim to the watching audience, he would then have aroused compassion and a false sense of guilt, which must be understood as the opposite of narcissistic satisfaction (that the people in the audience were alive and well while so many "others" died brutally). However, Žižek behaves like someone in the audience, and breaks with what he calls a "silent ban". He finally understands what it is that is intolerable to Western eyes about the war in Sarajevo: not the lacerated bodies, raped women, or starving prisoners, but the tragedy that is synthesized in the fact of the people in Sarajevo, simple human beings, in spite of the war being a part of their lives, make their way to work just like they do every day. "The moment we take full note of this fact, the frontier that separates 'us' from 'them' is exposed in all its arbitrariness and we are forced to renounce the safe distance of external observers" (Žižek, 1994, p. 2). When that frontier falls and we identify with the Other, then we realize that we live in a "peaceful fiction". For Žižek, violence, which manifests itself in wars, for instance, is not an acceptable interruption of a daily peaceful routine. On the contrary, this same daily peaceful routine is in fact a fiction within a permanent state of war. There is no such thing as non-violence.

In the construct of the Other as a stranger within the context of post-political biopolitics[2] (Žižek, 2014, p. 45) we are faced with a contradiction: on the one hand, we have an extreme respect for the Other, which in fact translates into a desire to avoid harassment; and on the other, we have the human being reduced to a figure described by Agamben as *Homo sacer* (defined and discussed below) (Agamben, 1998). When cast to appear as different from us, "Others" – in war-affected countries, or in a condition of poverty and social exclusion – might be the target of our compassion as passive spectators and of our false sense of guilt (bourgeois guilt?). Alternatively – and this is an important outcome – they might simply be ignored and treated with a frightening *indifference* when, for instance, we apparently tolerate thousands of anonymous deaths in the case of war, or turn our attention away from poverty.

When these "Others" are cast by post-political biopolitics as strangers, they gain our compassion, provided they are kept at a safe distance. However, they can just as easily be carelessly sacrificed. After all, they are strangers, we do not empathize with them and hence we do not necessarily identify with them. They are not humans like us, but rather belong to the species *Homo sacer*.

Benjamin and the critique of violence

The relativization of violence recognition proposed by Žižek (2014) and the conception of the idea of *Homo sacer* by Agamben (1998) are both influenced by Walter Benjamin's thoughts on violence present in his 1921 work entitled *A Critique of Violence* (Benjamin, 1996). Its original German title, *Zur Kritik der Gewalt*, is of particular interest, as the word *Gewalt* is ambiguous, meaning both violence and power (and such ambiguity also applies to the English version). Benjamin constantly plays with these two concepts in his text. A footnote to the Brazilian translation stresses that the semantics of the word oscillate throughout the text of Benjamin, sometimes being able to assume both meanings, which are marked in the text translation with an asterisk. Benjamin explores the relationship among violence, law and justice: "When the consciousness of the latent presence of violence in a legal institution disappears, the institution falls into decay" (Benjamin, 1996, p. 288). In this work, Benjamin associates two important concepts with what Žižek calls "objective violence": *mythical* and *divine violence*.

Freud points out (1961, p. 48) law is the first precept of the taboo that creates the totemic culture, whose purpose is to conserve communal life. On the one hand, Benjamin understands that it is through violence that existing law is established and maintained (as *Macht*, or Power), thereby assuring social order and the state of things as they are, through the use of what Benjamin calls *mythic violence*. On the other hand, there is the violence that Benjamin calls *divine*, one that does not establish the law but instead annihilates it, since it does not privilege one group to the detriment of another when it is present. In other words, everyone is equally affected by it.

Divine violence frees individuals from the bonds of that which is considered Right, demanding no sacrifices. One could even say that divine violence establishes equality among people, rather than differentiating between them, as happens in the case of mythic violence. In Žižek's (2014, p. 155) interpretation, Benjamin's concept of divine violence introduces us to the figure of the *Homo sacer* (Agamben, 1998). In the different spheres of divine violence, killing is neither a crime nor a sacrifice, but it is rather a violence that purifies the guilty (of living a natural life) not of their guilt, but of the law: "Mythical violence is bloody power over mere life for its own sake, divine violence pure power over all life for the sake of the living. The first demands sacrifice, the second accepts it" (Benjamin, 1996, p. 297).

One should perhaps pay particular attention at this point to the concept of *Homo sacer*. This is a figure that is present in works that will be explored in this chapter, including those by Agamben (1998) and Banerjee (2011). To define *Homo sacer* in his book, Agamben (1998, p. 71) resorts to Pompeius Festius:

> The sacred man is the one whom the people have judged on account of a crime. It is not permitted to sacrifice this man, yet he who kills him will not be condemned for homicide; in the first tribunitian law, in fact, it is noted that "if someone kills the one who is sacred according to the plebiscite, it will not be considered homicide." This is why it is customary for a bad or impure man to be called sacred.
>
> *Agamben, 1998, p. 71*

The life of the *Homo sacer* is a "bare life" or "mere life", the life that supports the link between violence and law. Not liable to sacrifice but exposed to death, and excluded from divine right (hence cannot be sacrificed) and from the right of men (whoever kills him cannot be punished) suggest that we have here an "exclusive inclusion", which is translated by Agamben as the subjection of life to the power of death (Castro, 2012, pp. 74–75).

According to Benjamin, each of us is a *Homo sacer* except for our sovereigns (political leaders, nobles, clergymen and so forth). The law is the same for everyone, all are equal, and all are subject to mythical power/violence. Archetypically, mythic violence is described by Benjamin as a form of self-assertion of gods, as fate and a manifestation of their existence. There would be no such thing as punishment, as in established political power, and it would only be translated into the definition of the frontier between men and gods. Punishment is associated with the act of judging, which in turn consists of the manifestation of a judgment of value, in determining what is good and what is bad. It is this characteristic of judgment that is marked in the law, whereas in the case of punishment by gods, the guilt transfigures itself into a threat and keeps men away from transgression. It can be atoned for, which is not the same as punishment.

In a consumer culture, the position of gods can be interpreted as that of the dominant class. The market, in its own way, builds new and unwritten forms of distinction, which can be compared to social capital and its corresponding habitus (i.e. our socialized ensemble of values, views and perspectives that orient us to our lifeworld), as in, for example, Bourdieu's (1984) concepts. Consumption-related narratives and discourses – and their corresponding habitus – gradually create forms of life that define people as insiders or outsiders. Outsiders are the "excluded" in such a system. An interesting way of instantiating *Homo sacer* in our current time would be to look at the story of Jaime Gold, the doctor who was murdered in Rio de Janeiro, as mentioned in the introduction. While a newspaper, *O Globo*, carefully described Jaime's life, his work, his family, his friends and the football team he supported, the murderer's life was described on the following day in the same newspaper merely in terms of his police record (his name was concealed as he was a minor). As one of the excluded, and at that moment, a murderer, he was denied a life story. Such a refusal to grant him a past might not, however, have been a consequence of the second contingency (his crime), but rather of the first, in other words, his status of exclusion. This is not to say that his crime could, in any sense, be forgiven. Recurring to the concept of the banality of evil (Arendt, 2006), taking someone's life could be as banal to the killer as using an expensive bike is to an ordinary consumer. Despite not being equal in act, citizen/consumer and killer are, in a way, equal in (lack of) conscience of their acts.

Another example of this can be seen in the horror manifested by middle-class consumers over the so-called "rolezinhos", events organized through the social media, whereby lower-class people gather in large groups to go to middle- and upper-class shopping centers. Few "rolezinhos" occurred in 2013 and 2014. The most noticeable ones took place in São Paulo and Rio de Janeiro. On some of these occasions, despite there being few or no cases of theft registered, the police were nevertheless called in. In many of these cases, the shopping centers in question closed their doors earlier than usual. Fearing a drop in sales, the Associação Brasileira de Lojistas de Shopping (ALSHOP – Brazilian Association of Shopping Center Retailers) called for special security mandates[3] to be imposed. Despite the large number of people involved in these "rolezinhos", their market-exclusion from an inclusive marketplace might be deemed, at best, as somewhat threatening. A reader's comment submitted in response to the article on "rolezinhos" on *O Globo*'s website described the people taking part in such "rolezinhos" as "having no culture, no education, being drug users, having no life expectations, and listening to funk music". Another comment suggested that the police should not hit, but rather kill them at once. Taking part in a "rolezinho" is like a Hubris – an act of defiance against the "wrath of gods", in this case, the logic of the dominant upper classes.

Balibar and Žižek

Any definition of violence runs the risk of being reductionist, reflecting and privileging only violent acts. In this sense, Catley and Jones (2002, pp. 29–30) warn us that a reductionist approach primarily seeks to find an essential core meaning for the term "violence", even though it recognizes the existence of what they call "conflicting representations" of it. This usually ends up providing definitions that can be found in dictionaries and in the law, and which might determine our understanding of what violence essentially means. On the other hand, as Catley and Jones (2002) also note, to fall into the temptation to view violence as indeterminable due to our inability to condense into one single concept all those acts considered as violent leads us to understand violence solely according to a dominant perspective that, in turn, can be considered reductionist. In order to avoid such "temptation", we intend to rely on the theoretical support of Balibar (2002) and Žižek (2014), authors who provide us with a suitable typology of violence. Žižek (2014) proposes what he calls a "triumvirate" of violence, composed of (i) subjective violence and objective violence, which is subdivided into (ii) systemic and (iii) symbolic. Žižek was inspired, however, by Balibar's concepts of ultra-objective violence, or faceless cruelty, and ultra-subjective violence, or cruelty in the face of Medusa (Balibar, 2002, p. 143). The choice of these authors as a theoretical support for the present work is based on the understanding that to try to understand violence as "crime and terror, civil confrontations and international conflicts" (Žižek, 2014, p. 17) is to deliberately limit violence to acts and events that rise above a "zero degree of violence" and disrupt the natural order of things (Žižek, 2014, pp. 17–18). To do that would be to confirm those perspectives already contemplated in dictionaries and the Law, as well as in studies relating to Politics, Law, Political Sociology and so many other disciplines, all in detriment to the presence of violence in our world view.

The theoretical approach adopted by Žižek is similar to the exercise of ontological defatalization and denaturation present in the work entitled Critical Marketing Studies (Tadajewski, 2016, p. 3). Defatalization is a concept that, according to Bourdieu (1998), and in association with the historical analysis conceived by Paul Ricœur, takes into account the space of experience and perspectives as "mutually causal, creating a perpetual 'generational transmission of meaning' and constructing a new understanding of historical time." (Trubnikova, 2016). In general terms, a view inspired by defatalization aims to rethink events in order to avoid simple causal logic (cause and effect), considering the project of the future as "always open and clear . . . influenced by many random factors and a certain 'horizon of expectations' on the part of living generations" (Trubnikova, 2016, p. 2). This makes it possible to "think beyond the existing economic structures in society and imagine and promote social change" (Tadajewski, 2016, p. 4).

On the other hand, ontological denaturalization in the field of marketing studies has its roots in Critical Management Studies (CMS) (Tadajewski, 2016). It aims to "deconstruct the reality of organizational life or the 'veracity' of organizational knowledge by exposing its 'unnaturality' or irrationality" (Fournier & Grey, 2000, p. 181). This implies the denaturalization of categories and assumptions given as certain and that inform mainstream analyses (Alvesson & Willmott, 2012, p. 121). For example, in marketing studies, denaturalization forces us to face the formation of consumer identity, a prerogative rooted in Consumer Culture Theory (CCT), as something not so natural (Tadajewski, 2016, p. 3).

Since naturalized violence has not been an object of investigation in marketing or consumer studies thus far, we have resorted to organization studies, believing that some considerations can easily be expanded to marketing and consumption phenomena. For Bicalho, naturalization can be defined as "a sociohistorical process of rationalization and justification of the occurrence of violence, as well as to the corresponding individual and collective passivity" (Bicalho, 2008, p. 30). Passivization of violence refers to the historical failure of resistance movements, as well as to the individual and social consent in force (Faria & Meneghetti, 2002). Banalization, in turn, "alludes to disregard for the instauration of violence that has become an imperative in everyday life, possibly due to the mitigation of critical awareness" (Bicalho, 2008, p. 30).

Justified, rationalized and taken as part of the natural order of things, violence becomes part not only of economic and political systems, but also of diverse institutions, masking itself in the habituality of social and interpersonal relations (Sá, 1999, p. 55). In Sá's opinion, violence can be established through the absolutization of one point of view, the disregard of the Other and the legitimation of agency. In a consumer society, the difference based on conspicuous consumption becomes the norm, "exclusivity" is something available to anyone who is an "insider" in the consumer society, and as we mentioned previously, the excluded from the market (the outsiders) oscillate between invisibility and "*sacer*" status. This leads us to Balibar's and Žižek's concept of objective violence.

As we noted earlier, Žižek (2014) splits objective violence into two subcategories: systemic and symbolic violence. He describes systemic objective violence as "that which is typical of the social conditions of global capitalism, which implies the 'automatic' creation of excluded and disposable individuals (from the homeless to the unemployed)" (Žižek, 2014, p. 26). Balibar makes no distinction between systemic and symbolic violence in his typology, referring only to *ultra-objective* violence, the "cruelty without a face" (Balibar, 2002, p. 143), which produces "disposable people". These are parts of humanity that are excluded from the scope of work, understood here as economic activity, but are maintained within the margins of the market, since this is an absolute that knows no external limits. In Balibar's words: "The Market is the World. When it excludes you, you cannot leave it in search of another America, settle there and start again" (2002, p. 142). Accordingly, disposable human beings are

> a social phenomenon, but it tends to look, at least in some cases, like a "natural" phenomenon, or a violent phenomenon in which the boundaries between what is human and what is natural, or what is post-human and what is post-natural, tend to become blurred.
>
> *Balibar, 2002, p. 143*

Symbolic objective violence is associated with language and "the imposition of a certain universe of meaning" (Žižek, 2014, p. 17) in addition to the forms normally reproduced discursively. And how does this relationship between language and violence take place? Žižek (2014) considers language as the most important factor of division among people, forcing us to live in completely different worlds even though we live on the same street. The Slovene philosopher is categorical in stating that "verbal violence is not a secondary distortion, but the ultimate resort of every specifically human violence" (Žižek, 2014, p. 63). To paraphrase Bourdieu (1991, p. 40), there are no innocent words.

We are dealing here with an idea of language that goes beyond human capacity to communicate messages. The language that is present in the idea of symbolic objective violence serves as a shelter to the human essence (Duarte, 2005, p. 13). Language is, according to Duarte (2005), a saying that shows something, not to be confused with the ability to enunciate any particular message. Language does not reveal essences. On the contrary, its function is to create essences, according to Heidegger's guidance, which uses the word "essence" (*wesen*, in German) as a verb, that is, "to essentiate" (Žižek, 2014, p. 64). Language thus reduces the thing it tries to convey.

Žižek (2014) resorts to Hegel to say that symbolization is a violent act per se. It mortifies the thing being symbolized by inserting it in a field exterior to the thing itself. This process of simplification and reduction is complemented by another, that of naturalization or normalization of certain ideas, attitudes and norms, which lose their characterization as being ideological. They seem natural, neutral and spontaneous. This is translated as ideology in its purest and most effective form according to Žižek (2014, p. 41), making any idea, such as symbolic violence, for example, manifest itself as something natural, like the air that we breathe, queueing to buy the latest version of the iPhone, visiting slums in Rio de Janeiro in a military-looking Jeep, or even as non-violence.

At this point, it is important to review some ideas related to symbolic violence present in a number of works by Bourdieu and Wacquant. Symbolic violence is that which is applied to the person himself, exercised by a social agent with his own complicity (Bourdieu, 2001; Bourdieu & Wacquant, 2004). Symbolic violence can also be described as "gentle violence, imperceptible and invisible even to its victims, exerted for the most part through the purely symbolic channels of communication and cognition (more precisely, misrecognition), recognition, or even feeling" (Bourdieu, 2001, pp. 1–2). Not only is it not recognized as violence by its agents, or indeed by its victims, it does not seem to be recognized by academics either, especially in marketing studies, since it is usually relegated to the periphery as an object of research.

After exposing objective violence, subjective violence seems to be a rather simple concept. Subjective violence is apparent, brutal, and a frightening aspect of our lives as citizens and members of humanity. It is exercised by a clearly identifiable agent (Žižek, 2014). If we consider that every citizen is "familiar" with (or should one say "numbed by") a certain level of everyday naturalized violence (objective violence), and if we call this level a *plateau of indifference*, subjective violence is experienced when an act or event exceeds that plateau that separates what is tolerable and normal from what is outrageous and unacceptable in the social sphere. What is deemed as violent in one context is seen as "natural" in another. It might be a normal everyday event in a slum in Rio de Janeiro to hear gun shots, or to see a dead body on the way home (like in a war), but it is very uncommon to see a white European-looking man riding an expensive motorbike in the same region. Such a biker would offend the local way of life by doing something that might be commonplace in his original milieu but which is clearly alien in a favela or slum neighborhood.

Urban violence is a classic example of subjective violence, which breaks through the plateau of indifference that establishes a zero degree of noticeable violence. It is conceived as a set of "forms of behavior that can be classified as crimes by the established legal statutes, promoted by certain social agents against the physical and patrimonial integrity of residents or people in transit in urban areas" (Paiva, 2014, p. 19). Homicide, drug dealing, physical assaults and terrorism are just some examples of urban and subjective violence. This is the most important, if not the only form of violence that is academically researched within the marketing area. Its effect on people is staggering. Balibar calls it "violence with a Medusa face" for it can metaphorically turn anyone who faces it eye to eye into stone. It mesmerizes and is spectacular in its own cruel way. Descriptions of the way Dr. Jaime Gold was butchered in Rio de Janeiro abounded during the days that followed the brutal attack. Everyone became aware of this horror, but no one realized the abysmal social divide that separated Dr. Gold from his murderer, which was only briefly substantialized in the form of a US $2,000 bicycle. Consumption is the right of every citizen after all, but the conscience of such a right is not enough to deter a policeman from stopping a black boy riding a US $2,000 bike. Subjective and objective violence are, then, intrinsically linked: subjective violence is a symptom of objective violence (systemic or symbolic) (Žižek, 2014).

The concept of violence in marketing research

A search for papers published in 17 selected international marketing journals[4] containing the word "violence" produced 21 titles. A simple analysis of the complete list of keywords in each of these papers indicated that subjective violence still prevailed. Violent media content (e.g. Martin & Collins, 2002; Söderlund & Dahlén, 2010; Zlatevska & Spence, 2012), urban violence (e.g. Pieterse, 2009), sexual violence (e.g. Bourke, 2012; Davis & McGinnis, 2016), gender violence (e.g. Gurrieri & Cherrier, 2016; Martam, 2016), family violence (e.g. Venturini, 2016), domestic violence (e.g. Keller & Otjen, 2007), violence in the markets (e.g. Martin & Collins, 2002; Smith & Raymen, 2015), symbolic violence (e.g. Couldry, 2001; Hazir, 2016), publicity violence (e.g. Zlatevska & Spence, 2012), bullying (e.g. Bishop & Phillips, 2006), violence against women (e.g. Terman, 2016), suicide (e.g. Tosini, 2009) and epistemic violence (Varman & Saha, 2009) were some of the manifestations of violence when the papers were analyzed a priori. Looking carefully at the keywords listed, we can conclude that most of them contemplate definitions related to Žižekian subjective violence, although some lead to objective manifestations of violence in their womb (e.g. domestic violence, commonly associated physical aggression, threat, rape and even death, can also be manifested in conjunction with acts of symbolic violence, such as psychological abuse, blame and emotional blackmail, among others).

Forms of representing violence associated with disciplinary power are favored, and there is a visible effort to define exactly what violence is, which is perfectly understandable given the necessity to clearly describe the object of research in an academic work submitted to a peer-reviewed journal. This confronts what Catley and Jones (2002) call the undecidability of the concept of violence: by defining what violence is, they introduce a particular concept of the word associated with a particular program, matrix or premise, present in the popular, legal and managerialist discourses on the subject in question (Catley & Jones, 2002, pp. 30–31). Our position is that this hampers the possibility of acknowledging the constitutive role of violence in the formation of subjectivities, thus rejecting the existence of epistemic violence.

This approach is traditionally associated with the seizure of power as being sovereign[5] (Foucault, 1977) and is, therefore, translated into a not only powerful but also hegemonic view. We also note that this approach is present in periodicals with high H indexes, gatekeepers within the area. Thus, it is possible to infer that the production and reproduction of knowledge in marketing privileges an approach that is identified with the mainstream of violence, in other words, with its subjective understanding.

One might argue that the almost absolute dominant focus on subjective violence can be determined by a world view typical of more homogeneous societies, where the plateau of indifference is more widely established and where any act of violence is seen as such in all ways of life. Thus, in a more heterogeneous society, where the State does not have the monopoly on violence – such as in the Brazilian case – the scenario might be different. An analysis of Brazilian journals, nevertheless, confirms the dominance of a focus on subjective violence. It is important to note, however, that in addition to the majority contemplating violence in its subjective form, many articles also highlight an association between violence and poverty (e.g. Bovo, 2004), urban and social inequality (e.g. Sobrinho & Inojosa, 2005), social exclusion (e.g. Madeira & Rodrigues, 2014) and territories of poverty (e.g. Oliveira, 2005), to use expressions contained in these papers. It is believed that such associations could lead to a study of violence that uses a systemic objective approach, but considerations regarding violence as being a direct consequence of the capitalist system are not made in any of the theoretical references used. It is important to raise a cautionary note: these Brazilian papers are published in the field of business and public administration, but none of them is dedicated primarily to marketing. From this we can conclude that although marketing studies are carried out under the umbrella of administration, violence does not seem to be deemed a relevant topic to marketing, but rather to studies of organizations, such as those by Alcadipani (2010); Carrieri, Aguiar & Diniz (2013), and Carrieri, Souza & Aguiar (2014).

Why is violence not an object of study in marketing,[6] or indeed in consumer studies, an area of knowledge that has gained great prominence and adherence among scholars both in Brazil and abroad in recent decades, as part of the internationally aligned movement of CCT? Why do those studies, both Brazilian and international, that look at the question of violence, if only objectively, limit themselves to characterizing it as symbolic, and almost never as systemic? Some considerations about these issues will be made in the next section, in which we address the *near* silence of marketing and consumer studies on the subject of violence, and how studies aligned with macromarketing view marketing as a technique and discipline as dehumanizing (Hill & Martin, 2014). We believe that these are central questions in exploring the violence associated with consumption and the production of subjectivities alien to it.

Marketing, dehumanization and violence

Marketing can be considered as violent in its essence precisely because it does not respect otherness.

Bouchet, 2014, p. 964

The disregard academic researchers in marketing show toward naturalized forms of violence is such that Bouchet's brief summary of work presented at the 39th Macromarketing Conference acts as a beacon. The definition of violence presented by the author addresses the denial of the "other's" borders, and the lack of respect for "others" precisely because they are other people. Bouchet is, to some extent in line with Bourdieu and Wacquant's approach to showing violence as a fundamental expression of inequality in the relationship between two people. From this, the victim of violence is not exempted by his own authority, since his will and his desire are alienated, thanks to relations of power that not only reduce the freedom of others, but also violate the subjectivity of others. Assuming that human desires are limitless, and human free will is limited by power (Hobbes, 1998) or culture (Freud, 1961), violence emerges as both a constitutive and a menacing force within this order of things. In Bouchet's (2014, p. 964) words, "violence threatens human relationships as long as men face limits – individually or collectively – and, since it is precisely the symbolic organization of relations to the limits that characterizes humanity, violence will always be among men". Therefore, we cannot think of a non-violent society since violence is essentially the wire on which any human enterprise balances (Bouchet, 2014). Instead, we should strive to understand how violence becomes so deep-rooted in society. Returning to Balibar (2002) and Catley and Jones (2002), there is simply no use in trying to design a non-violent instrument or structure, since this would be violent in itself.

Marketing is reductionist in dealing with political issues, says Bouchet (2014 p. 964), ignoring fundamental issues facing humanity such as desire, anxiety, and violence. The imposition of marketing logic on any alternative logic, individual or collective (a characteristic of a consumer culture), ends up transforming every human question into something that can be bought and sold, that is, it disregards alterities and, therefore, configures itself as violent. (Bouchet, 2014).

Bouchet's argument can be best illustrated using the work of Hill and Martin (2014). They do not directly address the issue of violence, but instead focus on broadening the marketing paradigm. These authors raise three topics and their consequences, and refer to the disregard mentioned by Bouchet in generally seeing marketing practices and theories as a logic that ignores "people's heterogeneity in favor of simplistic ways of operationalizing success" (Hill & Martin, 2014, p. 18). These topics are:

(1) theoretical disregard of the majority of people in favor of a narrow, affluent socio-economic subset; (2) languages of research and practice that dehumanize people with whom marketers engage and exchange; and (3) paradigmatic constructs that eliminate systemic realities and challenges from consideration.

Hill & Martin, 2014, p. 17

Hill and Martin approach marketing as a synonym of exchange and point out that despite previous attempts to extend the conceptual domain of the discipline (Kotler, 1969, 1972), the focus has been more on understanding what it involves and how the exchange occurs than on who might or might not participate in such a process. This includes a variety of different views, "from the service dominant logic of Vargo and Lusch (2004) (for practitioners) to Belk's concept of the extended self (1988) (for consumers)" (Hill & Martin, 2014, p. 17). One way of illustrating the authors' point of view is to quote the work of Hemais and Faria (2015) on studies that address the issue of consumption at the Bottom of the Pyramid (or BoP). In their work, these Brazilian authors point out that initial studies on BoP, conducted between the late 1960s and the late 1970s, reflected a concern over the power asymmetry between low-income consumers and large companies. Such considerations were dissipated with the rise of neoliberalism and marketing fundamentals in the academic and business communities. Even in the 2000s, in a post-cold war globalization context, such studies have assumed a new characteristic. This involves low-income consumers, around four billion people in all who are considered "economically disadvantaged" (Hemais & Faria, 2015) and live on less than two dollars a day, but who represent mathematically an aggregate power of consumption that translates into a "fortune" for companies willing to adapt their offerings (Hemais & Faria, 2015; Prahalad & Hart, 2002; Prahalad & Hammond, 2002). Thus, the equation "US$ 2.00 × 365 days × 4,000,000,000" (Hill & Martin, 2014, p. 19) translates into a homogeneous segment without a face, without a name and without the diversities and challenges that those at the BoP face as part of their reality.

Bearing in mind that marketing oscillates between utility and utilitarianism (Moura, Rossi & Pinto, 2009), we would like to highlight the fragility of the utilitarian doctrine. Canto-Sperber (2007, p. 737) points out that this doctrine is concerned with the consequences that actions have on the happiness of the individuals involved, not on the happiness of the social collective, resulting in their classification being between good and bad. As a result, utilitarianism is taken as "the moral par excellence of the modern *homo economicus*, liberated from traditional religious and moral taboos and chiefly concerned with maximizing his personal gains" (Canto-Sperber, 2007, p. 737). In this context, it is possible to better understand Bouchet's (2014) position on the reductionist nature of marketing and its characterization as violent and a discipline that imposes its logic of individualism and maximization of self-interest. Marketing, considered exclusively as a utility, promotes dehumanization, exclusion, and the reification of people. Tadajewski (2016) argues that marketing seduces individuals through its organizations and agents, imposing a logic that promises full satisfaction and fulfillment through consumption, but does not take into account the costs of such a positioning. Individual rational choices, aimed at hedonic satisfaction and the avoidance of pain and frustration (Moura *et al.*, 2009, p. 42), as well as maximizing advantage – characteristics that permeate marketing discourse – are related not only to liberalism, but also to a project of Western modernity that has existed for more than 300 years. This involves values, practices and institutions, and has the market as a mediator of relations that occur in the geo-temporal space of globalized nation-states.

Conclusion

Consumer culture, which translates into "a social agreement in which the relationship between lived culture and social resources, between meaningful lifestyles and the material and symbolic resources on which they depend, are mediated by markets" (Slater, 1997, p. 17), was already part of the very construction of the modern world and of the universalizing project of Western modernity from as early as the eighteenth century. This was a characteristic that distinguished it from the rest of the world, "as a modern, progressive, free, rational culture" (Slater, 1997, p. 18). Slater stated that in the bosom of consumer culture "there was an assumption of domination and infamy, in which the West saw itself as civilized and rich by law, possessing universal values". This characterization evokes the considerations made by Dussel & Ibarra-Colado (2006), Ibarra-Colado (2008) and Bouchet (2014) in their respective works about disregarding the Other and, consequently, about violence. Consumer culture is therefore the "flagship for the advancement of Western enterprise, Western markets and the Western way of life", with "global pretensions and reach" (Slater, 2001, p. 18). In his book, he outlines consumer culture using seven aspects, five of which are of special importance here:

i "The culture of consumption is *a priori* universal and impersonal" (Slater, 2001, p. 34), that is, production is carried out on a large scale to serve a generic public. Everything can become a commodity, at least for part of its existence. In addition, all must be consumers since social relations, identities and everyday life are ultimately sustained and reproduced through commodities.
ii "Consumer culture identifies freedom as private choice and private life" (Slater, 2001, p. 35), that is, choices are made privately, and aim to increase private pleasures and comforts, not to build a better society.
iii "Needs are *a priori* insatiable and unlimited" (Slater, 2001, p. 36), a characteristic considered normal and essential for order and for socio-economic progress.
iv "Consumer culture is a privileged means of negotiating identity and status in a post-traditional society" (Slater, 2001, p. 37), that is, nothing is given to the individual, who must instead construct his own identity within a context in which access to goods is regulated exclusively by money, indicating, therefore, social standing.
v "The culture of consumption represents the growing importance of culture in the modern-day exercising of power" (Slater 2001, p. 38), that is, the affinity of the culture of consumption with signs, images and publicity aesthetizes the goods consumed and their environment, creating flexible, unstable, and highly negotiable status and generating a value-in-use image by the producer so that the potential buyer can recognize himself.

The way Slater presents these aspects reveals some of the central points that enable us to establish a relationship between consumer culture and violence in a critical way. We conclude with a summary of the review that has been conducted in this work, followed by a brief discussion of contradictions that can be explored in future empirical research on the subject.

First of all, we should recall that violence can appear in objective and subjective forms, but only subjective acts of violence are visible to a person. Violent acts are deemed as naturalized if they occur below what we called the *plateau of indifference*, a given level of violence in society below which violent acts are considered as "normal", things that happen in everyday life and, as such, do not deserve special attention. This relates to what Žižek called "objective violence". Anything that crosses the threshold represented by the plateau of indifference affects our subjectivity in some way, and thus can be considered as *subjective violence*. The level at which the plateau of indifference lies is dependent on socio-historic as well as contextual conditions, including the historical level of violence in the area in question.

The idea of the plateau of indifference is corroborated by Balibar's statement that "there are certainly degrees in the amount of violence which goes along with civilizing ideals, but nothing like a zero degree" (2002, p. 145). Violence is therefore the very reality in which we find ourselves. There is no such thing as non-violence and so there is nothing constituting our reality that could possibly escape this logic. When we refer to a plateau of indifference, we reject, therefore, the idea of non-violence. Instead we choose to work with the idea of a level below which violence is tolerated or simply not perceived.

Given the centrality of consumer culture in everyday life as the dominant form of production and reproduction of meaning and identity management (Arnould & Thompson, 2005, 2007; Dittmar, 2007; Slater, 2001, it is difficult – if not impossible – to *completely* escape the market (Holt, 2002; Kozinets, 2002). Thus, one might argue that consumer culture, as the dominant logic that organizes our daily experience and existence, *is* objectively violent since it provides no way out. In considering comments made by Bishop and Phillips (2006), based on Hegel, about the role of "Love" as "the only possible solution to several kinds of violence produced by discord" (p. 383), Hill's (2002) work on the role of love to support excluded persons provides support to our contention that violence is, in a way, inherent in consumer culture.

As Balibar (2002, p. 142) puts it, "the Market is the World", it is "an absolute" that is closely aligned with the consumption logic, and is objectively violent. This idea is reinforced by the so-called "marketization" or "consumerization" of the substrates of daily life, as Eckhardt, Dholakia and Varman (2012) suggest. Indeed, these movements are based on neoliberal values that aim to discipline, destroy, dehumanize and destabilize, as Conway and Heynen (2006, p. 17) allege, but in a way that such "outcomes are rationalized as social inevitabilities".

Since objective violence is naturalized, it is present in a silent and private relationship with the Other that defines the self. This appears in the world in the form of identity and status management (Slater's aspect (iv)) and in an intersubjectively negotiated aestheticscape (Slater's aspect (v) above). The excluded from the market, a human Other, is also excluded from this self-defining equation. Since in a consumer culture "freedom" is strongly related to freedom of choice (Slater's aspect (ii)), this human Other, the excluded, unable to make choices in the market, relies on the State or, borrowing Tennessee Williams' expression, on the "kindness of strangers", which Hill (2002) calls "expressions of other-centered love". The excluded is frequently sacrificed (Agamben, 1998) or dehumanized (Hill & Martin, 2014). Such disdain is present in Hill's (2002) description of the way his key informants are treated by State social workers and doctors.

Reactions to exclusion are frequently seen as subjective violence. We are not considering here thefts carried out to minimize an immediate state of necessity, which are sometimes considered as lawful by the Brazilian judiciary. Having consumption as the dominant and organizing logic of our society also implies having it as the central point of reference for "personal, social, economic and cultural life" (Fitchett et al., 2014). The consumer is seen as an active agent and the market as the (most) legitimate provider of contexts "through which individuals should seek to explore, identify and experience the world around them" (Fitchett, Patsiaouras & Davies, p. 3), even though a good part of the population is excluded from any such economic activity. How does this equation work? We cannot answer this question, but we can argue that the consumption logic also shows those who are excluded from the market, but are still maintained within its boundaries. After all, as stated in item (iii) above, it is difficult, if not impossible, to escape the market. Indeed, the excluded want exactly what the included want, the very same (possibly unrestricted) access to commodities, even though they cannot afford them. The consumption culture, as such, affects us all.

A variety of objects can be observed considering our reflections concerning objective consumer violence and the way plateaux of indifference affect human life. Fashion, for instance, as a powerful signifier of social difference, opens many research opportunities. On the very first line of his seminal 1904 paper, Simmel (1957) stresses an important contradiction:

> Fashion is a form of imitation and so of social equalization, but, paradoxically, in changing incessantly, it differentiates one time from another and one social stratum from another. It unites those of a social stratum and segregates them from others.
>
> *Simmel, 1957, p. 541*

Such form of social distinction, which is something that has happened since Elizabethan times (McKendrick, Brewer & Plumb, 1982), shows an ugly face in the arena of fast fashion. Overconsumption, ephemerity, and disregard for a whole human and environmental tragedy that an H&M US$ 34.99 fitted jacket allegedly fetishistically hides are objects that can be investigated through an objective violence frame. The same applies to consumer education and socialization practices. Nevertheless, as the form of violence we are describing here is naturalized, its nature becomes a major challenge to empirical investigation since it is not only usually non-ostensive but also unconscious to the actor, their peers, and everyone who is immersed below a given plateau of indifference. The researcher interested in investigating objective violence empirically should: (a) take a perspective external to the plateau of indifference, and actively try to understand ostensibly "natural" and harmless acts as potential acts of violence in the eyes of the Other; and (b) consider the use of critical discourse analysis as it might help uncover objective violence as speech acts.

Concerning a commitment with practical issues, we suggest that the only way one can devise a less-violent form of consumption is by implementing more inclusive forms of consumer socialization. The objective violence concept might be useful to produce an Other-aware citizen, conscious of their position in a violent system. Hill's (2002) work offers a good example of such attempts. Nevertheless, we should bear in mind that the other-centered love Hill proposes can be criticized since it produces a narcissistic gain, a sort of "jouissance" in helping the Other, a gain that only the included in the market have access to. Thus, it seems that we are essentially faced with two aporias. First, although we recognize some acts as being more violent than others, everything runs the risk of being considered violent, which definitely hampers any attempt at investigating violent phenomena. Second, although we academics are desperately seeking to help build a better world through critical thinking, it is perhaps somewhat naive to think about a non-violent consumer culture. Bearing all this in mind, we seem to have very objective reasons, in every single act, to try to do more good than harm.

Notes

1 The Latin Library <www.thelatinlibrary.com/plautus/asinaria.shtml>. Accessed on Sept. 1, 2017.
2 Post-political biopolitics (Žižek, 2014, p. 45) is a combination of Foucauldian biopolitics with specialized managerial and administrative principles regarded as neutral in the sense that they are not ideologically supported, nor do they carry the banner of some ideological belief. In general, biopolitics "is what causes life and its mechanisms to enter into the domain of explicit calculations, and makes power-knowledge an agent of transformation of human life" (Foucault, 1988, p. 134). On the other hand, the feeling that we are not faced with "old ideological conflicts" (Žižek, 2014, p. 45) is ensured precisely by an ideology,

that is, of the capital or neoliberal, which translates into actions, discourses and beliefs of the group which Žižek calls "neoliberal communists" (Žižek, 2014, p. 29). Tired of the old doctrines and positioning themselves as pragmatists facing what they consider to be concrete problems, neoliberal communists seek to act in order to solve such problems by, for example, creatively approaching crises, mobilizing people, governments and companies, irrespective of any labels. Its exponents, for the Slovenian philosopher, are Bill Gates, Thomas Friedman and George Soros. Ironically Žižek nicknamed them "Men of Porto Davos" (Žižek, 2014, p. 27).

3 Conheça a história dos 'rolezinhos' em São Paulo – notícias em São Paulo. (Jan. 14, 2014). *O Globo – G1*. Taken from http://g1.globo.com/sao-paulo/noticia/2014/01/conheca-historia-dos-rolezinhos-em-sao-paulo.html (accessed February 14, 2017).

4 *Journal of Marketing, Journal of Marketing Research, Journal of Consumer Research, Theory, Culture & Society, Psychology & Marketing, Journal of International Marketing, International Marketing Review, European Journal of Marketing, Journal of Public Policy & Marketing, Journal of Consumer Culture, Journal of Macromarketing, Journal of Consumer Policy, Journal of Marketing Education, Marketing Theory, Journal of Marketing Management, Journal of Consumer Behavior, Consumption, Markets & Culture* (CMC).

5 The classification between sovereign and disciplinary power is found in Foucault, especially in *Discipline and Punish* (Foucault, 1977), when the French philosopher describes the transfiguration of sovereign power exercised through public and wild spectacles of torture into a discrete power, in which punishment is configured as an administrative mechanism based on the economy of punishment and on political technologies, understood here as a conjunction between knowledge and power (Rabinow, 1984, p. 17). Thus, it is by employing disciplinary power that one can produce "docile bodies that may be subjected, used, transformed and improved" (Foucault, 1977, p. 136) through disciplinary institutions such as military barracks, hospitals, schools and factories.

6 This is, of course, starting to change. The *Journal of Marketing Management* is about to publish a special issue devoted to violence, the market and marketing. This is being edited by Rohit Varman and will appear sometime in 2018.

References

Agamben, G. (1998). *Homo sacer: Sovereign power and bare life*. Stanford, Stanford University Press.
Alcadipani, R. (2010). Violencia e masculinidade nas relações de trabalho: Imagens do campo em pesquisa etnográfica. *Cadernos EBAPE.BR, 8*(1). Retrieved July 5, 2018 from www.scielo.br/scielo.php?pid=S1679-39512010000100007&script=sci_abstract&tlng=pt
Alvesson, M., & Willmott, H. (2012). *Making sense of management: A critical introduction*. London, Sage.
Arendt, H. (2006). *Eichmann in Jerusalem: A report on the banality of evil*. London, Penguin Publishing Group.
Arnould, E.J., & Thompson, C.J. (2005). Consumer culture theory (CCT): Twenty years of research. *Journal of Consumer Research, 31*(4), 868–882.
Arnould, E.J., & Thompson, C.J. (2007). Consumer culture theory (and we really mean theoretics): Dilemmas and opportunities posed by an academic branding strategy. In R.W. Belk & J.F. Sherry (Eds.), *Consumer Culture Theory, Vol. 11* (pp. 3–22). Amsterdam, Elsevier.
Balibar, É. (2002). *Politics and the other scene*. London, Verso.
Banerjee, S.B. (2011). Voices of the governed: Towards a theory of the translocal. *Organization, 18*(3), 323–344.
Bauman, Z. (2004). *Identidade: Entrevista a benedetto vecchi*. Rio de Janeiro, Zahar.
Benjamin, W. (1996). Critique of violence. In M.P. Bullock, M.W. Jennings & H. Eiland (Eds.), *Selected writings: 1913–1926* (pp. 277–300). Cambridge, MA, Belknap Press.
Bicalho, R.D.A. (2008). *Categorias frankefurteanas para uma tipologia da violência nas Organizações*. Paper presented at the V Encontro de Estudos Organizacionais da ANPAD, Belo Horizonte.
Bishop, R., & Phillips, J. (2006). Violence. *Theory, Culture & Society, 23*(2–3), 377–385.
Bouchet, D. (2014). *What is violence?* Paper presented at the 39th Annual Macromarketing Conference, London, UK.
Bourdieu, P. (1984). *Distinction: A social critique of the judgement of taste*. Cambridge, MA, Harvard University Press.
Bourdieu, P. (1991). *Language and symbolic power*. Cambridge, MA, Harvard University Press.
Bourdieu, P. (1998). *Acts of resistance: Against the tyranny of the market*. New York, The New Press.
Bourdieu, P. (2001). *Masculine domination*. Stanford, Stanford University Press.

Bourdieu, P., & Wacquant, L. (2004). Symbolic violence. In N. Scheper-Hughes & P. Bourgois (Eds.), *Violence in war and peace: An anthology* (pp. 272–274). Malden, MA, Blackwell.

Bourke, J. (2012). Sexual violence, bodily pain, and trauma: A history. *Theory, Culture & Society, 29*(3), 25–51.

Bovo, C.R.M. (2004). Pobreza, direitos e vidas: algumas evidências. *Pensamento & Realidade. Revista do Programa de Estudos Pós-Graduados em Administração-FEA, 14.*

Canto-Sperber, M. (2007). *Dicionário de Ética e Filosofia Moral*. São Leopoldo, UNISINOS.

Carrieri, A.D.P.A., Aguiar, A.R.C., & Diniz, A.P.R. (2013). Reflexões sobre o indivíduo desejante e o sofrimento no trabalho: O assédio moral, a violência simbólica e o movimento homossexual. *Cadernos EBAPE, 11*(1), 165–180.

Carrieri, A. de P., Souza, E.M., & Aguiar, A.R.C. (2014). Trabalho, violência e sexualidade: Estudo de lésbicas, travestis e transsexuais. *RAC, 18*(1), 78–95.

Castro, E. (2012). *Introdução a Giorgio Agamben: Uma arqueologia da potência*. Belo Horizonte, Autêntica Editora.

Catley, B., & Jones, C. (2002). Deciding on violence. *Philosophy of Management, 2*(1), 23–32.

Conway, D., & Heynen, N. (2006). The ascendancy of neoliberalism and emergence of contemporary globalization. In D. Conway & N. Heynen (Eds.), *Globalization's contradictions: Geographies of discipline, destruction and transformation* (pp. 17–33). New York, Routledge.

Couldry, N. (2001). The hidden injuries of media power. *Journal of Consumer Culture, 1*(2), 155–177.

Davis, R., & McGinnis, L.P. (2016). Conceptualizing excessive fan consumption behavior. *Journal of Retailing & Consumer Services, 28*(January), 252–262.

Dittmar, H. (2007). *Consumer culture, identity and well-being: The search for the 'good life' and the 'body perfect'*. New York, Psychology Press.

Duarte, A. (2005). Heidegger e a linguagem: Do acolhimento do ser ao acolhimento do outro. *Natureza humana, 7*(1), 129–158.

Dussel, E., & Ibarra-Colado, E. (2006). Globalization, organization and the ethics of liberation. *Organization, 13*(4), 489–508.

Eckhardt, G.M., Dholakia, N., & Varman, R. (2012). Ideology for the 10 billion: Introduction to globalization of marketing ideology. *Journal of Macromarketing, 33*(1), 7–12.

Ekström, K.M., & Hjort, T. (2009). Hidden consumers in marketing: The neglect of consumers with scarce resources in affluent societies. *Journal of Marketing Management, 25*(7/8), 697–712.

Faria, J.H.D., & Meneghetti, F.K. (2002). *A instituição da violência nas relações de trabalho*. Paper presented at the XXVI ENANPAD, Salvador.

Fitchett, J.A., Patsiaouras, G., & Davies, A. (2014). Myth and ideology in consumer culture theory. *Marketing Theory, 14*(4), 495–506.

Foucault, M. (1977). *Discipline and punish: The birth of the prison*. New York, Vintage Books.

Foucault, M. (1988). *História da sexualidade I: A vontade de saber*. Rio de Janeiro, Graal.

Fournier, V., & Grey, C. (2000). At the critical moment: Conditions and prospects for critical management studies. *Human Relations, 53*(1), 7–32.

Freud, S. (1961). *Civilization and its discontents*. New York, W.W. Norton Company.

Gurrieri, L., & Cherrier, H. (2016). Controversial advertising: Transgressing the taboo of gender-based violence. *European Journal of Marketing, 50*(7–8), 1448–1469.

Hazir, I.K. (2016). Wearing class: A study on clothes, bodies and emotions in Turkey. *Journal of Consumer Culture, 17*(2), 413–442.

Hemais, M.W., & Faria, A. (2015). *O surpreendente (ou estranho) apogeu dos consumidores de baixa renda em marketing: Uma análise geo-histórica*. Paper presented at the VI Congresso Nacional de Administração e Contabilidade – AdCont, Rio de Janeiro.

Hill, R.P. (2002). Compassionate love, agape and altruism: A new framework for understanding and supporting impoverished consumers. *Journal of Macromarketing, 22*(1), 19–31.

Hill, R.P., & Martin, K.D. (2014). Broadening the paradigm of marketing as exchange: A public policy and marketing perspective. *Journal of Public Policy & Marketing, 33*(1), 17–31.

Hobbes, T. (1998). *On the citizen*. Cambridge, Cambridge University Press.

Holt, D.B. (2002). Why do brands cause trouble? A dialectical theory of consumer culture and branding. *Journal of Consumer Research, 29*(June), 70–90.

Ibarra-Colado, E. (2008). Is there any future for critical management studies in Latin America? Moving from epistemic coloniality to 'trans-discipline'. *Organization, 15*(6), 932–935.

Keller, S.N., & Otjen, A.J. (2007). Creating and executing an applied interdisciplinary campaign for domestic violence prevention. *Journal of Marketing Education, 29*(3), 234–244.

Kotler, P. (1972). A generic concept of marketing. *Journal of Marketing, 36*(April), 46–54.

Kotler, P., & Levy, S.J. (1969). Broadening the concept of marketing. *Journal of Marketing, 33*, 10–15.

Kozinets, R.V. (2002). Can consumers escape the market? Emancipatory illuminations from Burning Man. *Journal of Consumer Research, 29*(1), 20–38.

Madeira, L.M., & Rodrigues, A.B. (2014). Novas bases para políticas públicas de segurança no Brasil a partir das práticas do governo federal no período 2003–2011. *RAP, 49*(1), 3–21.

Martam, I. (2016). Strategic social marketing to foster gender equality in Indonesia. *Journal of Marketing Management, 32*(11–12), 1174–1182.

Martin, B.A.S., & Collins, B.A. (2002). Violence and consumption imagery in music videos. *European Journal of Marketing, 36*(7/8), 855–873.

McKendrick, N., Brewer, J., & Plumb, J. H. (1982). *The birth of a consumer society: The commercialization of eighteenth-century England*. London, Europa Publications.

Moura, L.S.C.S.S.D., Rossi, C.A.V., & Pinto, D.C. (2009). Marketing cínico: Reflexões sobre utiludade e utilitarismo. *Pretexto, 10*(3), 37–46.

Oliveira, A.S. (2005). O policiamento e a democracia. *Organizações & Sociedade, 12*(33), 129–148.

Paiva, L.F.S. (2014). A violência como evento de ressignificação e construção da realidade social. In C.R. Barreira & Paiva, L.F.S. (Eds.), *Violência como campo de pesquisa e orientação* (pp. 19–36). Campinas, Potes Editores.

Pieterse, E. (2009). African reverberations of the Mumbai attack. *Theory, Culture & Society, 26*(7–8), 289–300.

Prahalad, C.K., & Hammond, A. (2002). Serving the world's poor, profitably. *Harvard Business Review*. Retrieved February 5, 2014 from https://hbr.org/2002/09/serving-the-worlds-poor-profitably

Prahalad, C.K., & Hart, S.L. (2002). O pote de ouro na base da pirâmide. *HSM Management, 32*, 14–27.

Rabinow, P. (1984). *The Foucault reader*. New York, Pantheon Books.

Sá, A.A. (1999). Algumas questões polêmicas relativas à psicologia da violência. *Psicologia: teoria e prática, 1*(2), 53–63.

Simmel, G. (1957). Fashion. *American Journal of Sociology, LXII*(6), 541–558.

Slater, D. (2001). *Cultura do Consumo & Modernidade*. São Paulo: Nobel.

Slater, S.F., & Narver, J.C. (1994). Does competitive environment moderate the market orientation-performance relationship? *Journal of Marketing, 58*(January), 46–55.

Smith, O., & Raymen, T. (2015). Shopping with violence: Black Friday sales in the British context. *Journal of Consumer Culture, 17*(3), 677–694.

Sobrinho, E.J.M.A., & Inojosa, R.M. (2005). Gestão social nos municípios: A violência e a cultura de paz. *RAP, 39*(2), 279–295.

Söderlund, M., & Dahlén, M. (2010). The 'killer' ad: An assessment of advertising violence. *European Journal of Marketing, 44*(11/12), 1811–1838.

Tadajewski, M. (2016). Critical marketing studies and critical marketing education: Key ideas, concepts and materials. *RIMAR – Revista Interdisciplinar de Marketing, 6*(2), 3–24.

Terman, R. (2016). Islamophobia, feminism and the politics of critique. *Theory, Culture & Society, 33*(2), 77–102.

Tosini, D. (2009). A sociological understanding of suicide attacks. *Theory, Culture & Society, 26*(4), 67–96.

Trubnikova, N. (2016). Modern historical epistemology through the prism of Paul Ricoeur' transactions. Retrieved February 16, 2017 from www.shs-conferences.org/articles/shsconf/abs/2016/06/shsconf_rptss2016_01140/shsconf_rptss2016_01140.html

Varman, R., & Saha, B. (2009). Disciplining the discipline: Understanding postcolonial epistemic ideology in marketing. *Journal of Marketing Management, 25*(7–8), 811–824.

Venturini, R. (2016). Social marketing and big social change: Personal social marketing insights from a complex system obesity prevention intervention. *Journal of Marketing Management, 32*(11–12), 1190–1199.

Žižek, S. (1994). *The metastases of enjoyment: Six essays on woman and causality*. London, Verso.

Žižek, S. (2014). *Violência: seis reflexões laterais*. São Paulo: Boitempo.

Zlatevska, N., & Spence, M.T. (2012). Do violent social cause advertisements promote social change? An examination of implicit associations. *Psychology & Marketing, 29*(5), 322–333.

INDEX

Locators in *italics* refer to figures and those in **bold** to tables.

Achrol, R. 232, 233
action research 372–375, 378
activities, interests, and opinions (AIO) 173
addiction, consumer sovereignty 214–215
Adorno, T. W.: arts marketing 138; critical perspectives 203, 204; critical theory 159, 160; ideology 308
advertising 22–23, 185; capitalism 470–472; changing forms 190–191; critical sociology 161–162; information processing perspectives 186–187; production 164, 188–190; research trajectories 185–192; socio-cultural perspectives 185–186; transmission theory of communication 186–188
aesthetics, arts marketing 141
Agamben, G. 485–487
agency: the body 385–386, 393–395; and consumer sovereignty 212–213; lifestyle research 180; *see also* choice; consumer sovereignty
aggressiveness 484–485; *see also* violence
alcohol addiction 214–215
Alderson, Wroe 310–311
Alfisti case 448–449
algorithm-generated discrimination 213
algorithmic alienation 477
alienation: digital 477–479, **478**; exploitation and emancipation 440–441, 442, 443, 449, 450
alternative hedonism 260
alternative markets: arts marketing 144–146; ethical consumption 258; international political economy 258
Althusser, Louis 307, 407
Alvesson, M. 165, 166
Amazon's Alexa 77–78

Andrejevic, Mark 477
anthropocentrism 279–280
anti-consumption: ideology 309; nationalist ideology 327; neo-colonialism 56; resistance 444–445; visual approaches 376
anti-social behaviors, critical social marketing 89
Apple, experience economy 408–409
Aristotle 3, 4
Arnold, D. 50–51
Arnould, E. J. 237, 324–325, 368, 446–447, 457–458
Artificial Intelligence (AI) 77–78
arts marketing 22, 135–138; alternative markets 144–146; arts vs. markets debate 135, 140–142; creative methods of enquiry 146–147; creativity in marketing practice 142–143; cultural practice and theory of branding 137, 143–144; definition 136; development of theory and practice 138–140; future directions 147–148; research context 140–148
Arvidsson, A. 27
Ashworth, G. J. 116, 117
Atkinson, Paul 157
attitude-behavior gap 257, 266; *see also* ethical consumption gap
audience labor 468–469
Austro-Marxism 15
authenticity: escape 446; place marketing 125; *see also* credibility; legitimation
Ayrosa, E. A. T. 30–31

Balibar, E. 488–490
banking, historical context 10
Baratz, M. S. 296–297
Bardhi, F. 313, 315

Index

Barthes, Roland 406
Bartky, Sandra 73
Batia lifestyle research 178
Baudrillard, Jean 406–407
Bauman, Z. 262
bell hooks (Gloria Jean Watkins) 68
Bellamy, Edward 4–7, 8–9
Benjamin, Walter: arts marketing 138; brand management 405; violence 486–488
Benton, Ray 7
bereavement 23, 370
Bernays, Edward 9–10
between-domains distance 245, 246
Bhabha, H. 54, 57–58
big data: critical performativity 13–14; home and quantified life 76–78; social media 30, 467–468, 469, 473, 479–480
biopolitical marketing 28, 430–431, 436–437; customer community 433–436; participatory media 431–433
biopolitics 216–218, 431, 485–486
bioviolence 30–31, 215–216
Black racial stigma in consumer culture: consumption and racial inequality 355–356; middle class 354; research study 356–363
blurry boundaries 356, 360, 361
bodies 385–386; agency of 393–395; body project 391–393; gender in marketing 416; mind-body distinction 384, 386–387; representation 389–391; technologized body 73–74; *see also* embodiment
Boltanski, L. 445, 448–449
Borch, Fred 2
Bottom of the Pyramid 493
Bouchet, D. 485, 492–493, 494
boundary transcendence/transition 356, 360–362
boundary work, racial stigma 356, 358–363
Bourdieu, Pierre: arts marketing 139, 140; brand management 406; embodiment 384, 388–389, 392, 393; gender in marketing 422; lifestyle research 173, 175, 178; violence 490, 492
Bradshaw, A. 28, 137, 141, 217
brand communities 217
brand facilitation 129
brand management 27, 403–404; contemporary critical approaches 408–410; Cultural Studies 407–408; future directions 411–412; identity 407–408, 409; ideologies 404–405; post-war years and the rise of semiotics 405–407; social media 403, 410–411
branding: arts marketing 143–144; Eurocentrism 51–52; marketing organizations 166; place marketing 118–119, 125–126, 128–129; symbolism 187–188
bright boundaries 356
Brown, S. 235–236
Brundtland Report 105

Buddhism, religious critiques of the market 276, 277, 278
Burning Man Festival 445
business schools 169
Butler, Judith 68
buyers *see* consumption; seller-buyer relationship

Californian ideology 435
Canniford, R. 147, 371
capabilities approach 110
capital: embodiment 388, 389; global palm oil market 461; technologized body 74–75
capitalism: advertising 470–472; brand management 405–406; communicative 432–433; conflict 11; consumption 202–205; customer orientation 201; emotional labor 422; ethical consumption 256–257, 260–262, 264–265; exploitation 439–440; global palm oil market 461; historical context 4–5, 9; ideology 307–308, 309, 314; Marxist theory 157–158; perception of marketing 16–17; place marketing 122–124; postcolonial theory 56; power studies 296; religious critiques of the market 271, 272–273, 275–276, 277–281; subalternity 59–60; violence 30, 489, 491–492
caring work 421–422
Carrington, M. 24, 260–261, 265–266
cartels 208
Cartesianism: gender in marketing 415–416; mind-body distinction 384, 386–387
Catholic Social Teaching 90
Catley, B. 488, 491
cellulite example 209
certification, international political economy 457–458
Chakrabarty, D. 58
Chalmers, L. V. 167
Changkhwanyuen, P. 276, 277, 278
Chatterjee, P. 51
Chatzidakis, A. 24, 260, 265
Chiapello, E. 445
China: arts marketing 140–141; consumer sovereignty 208; global brands 327; power studies 296
choice 25–26, 337–339; compromise 209–210; and consumer sovereignty 206–208, 212–215, 340–341; discursive power model 299; female hormones 217; hegemonic power model 293–296; merits of 341; meso/macro levels 343–345; micro levels 341–343; as moral pinnacle 339–340; reflections and way forward 346–348; religious critiques of the market 275–276; sovereign power model 290–292; *see also* consumer sovereignty
choicelessness 25–26, 337, 346–348
Christianity, religious critiques of the market 276, 277, 279–280

Index

Cicero 4
citizens: ethical consumption lexicons 262–263; ideology 313
city marketing 115, 118–119; *see also* place marketing
civil rights movement 354–355
class *see* social class
Classical economics era, service-dominant logic 227
Clough, R. 373
Coca-Cola, postcolonial theory 51–52, 56
co-creation: anti-consumption 445; biopolitical marketing 433–436; choice 344; exploitation 447–448; power studies 292, 298, 300; service-dominant logic 230–231, 236, 237; social media 189
Cohen, Lizbeth 354–355
Cold War, international marketing 321
colonialism, racial stereotypes 54–55; *see also* postcolonial theory
commercial marketing 86
commodification: biopolitical marketing 430, 431; decommodification 258–259; land 460–461; religious critiques of the market 280–281
commodities, transnational markets 455–463
commodity fetishism 404, 406, 469–472
commodity value 468–469
communications 30; advertising production 189–191; social media 468–469; transmission theory 186–188
communicative capitalism 432–433
communities: action research 375; biopolitical marketing 433–436; critical social marketing 89–90
competition: consumer sovereignty 207, 208; marketplace dynamics 212; place marketing 123–124
competitive advantage: ethical consumption 256; place marketing 118, 124; service-dominant logic 227, 230
compromise: choice 209–210; exploitation and emancipation 448–449
conflict, marketing 11; *see also* violence
conspicuous waste 8, 9
consumer choice *see* choice
consumer culture: brand management 408–409; embodiment 391–393; ethical consumption 259–262; non-Western context 324–325; Other and Otherness 482–483, 487; power studies 298–299; violence 30–31, 482–483, 487, 494; *see also* racial stigma in consumer culture
consumer culture theory (CCT): consumer sovereignty 210–211, 212–213; consumer vulnerability 367, 368–369; Eurocentrism 50, 51–52; ideology 313–314; non-Western cultures 319, 324–325; violence 488
consumer lifestyle 22

consumer sovereignty: and choice 206–208, 212–215, 340–341; Critical Marketing Studies 205–215; ethical consumption 257, 263–266; ideology 308; marketing as exchange 211–212; marketplace reality 210–211; power studies 290–292, 301
consumer vulnerability 26, 366–367, 378–379; action research 372–375; context 367–369; definition 366; future directions 377–378; stories 369–372, 378; visual culture 375–377, 378
consumer-driven innovation 28–29
consumers: Critical Marketing Studies 24–26; emancipation 443, 448–449; embodiment 26, 383–384, 389–395; ethical consumption lexicons 262–263; exploitation 446–449; ideology 313; lifestyle research 172–173, 175–179, 180–181; 'lock-in' 214; responsibilizing 257, 263–265
consumption: arts marketing 144–145; boundary work 356; capitalism 202–205; consumer sovereignty 207–208; critical theory 159–160; emancipation 442–443; feminism 69; modernity 42–43; non-Western context 325–326, 328–329; power studies 296; and racial inequality 355–356; religious critiques of the market 277–278; structuring of 26, 174; subalternity 59–60; *see also* ethical consumption
container theory of society 108
conventional place marketing 117–119
cool hunting 258
co-optation, ethical consumption 258–259
co-production, service-dominant logic 230–231, 236
core-periphery relations 455–456, 461
corporate social marketing 93
corporate social responsibility (CSR) 257, 263–264, 458
corporeal schema 387
Coskuner-Balli, G. 22, 180
cosmetic surgery 74–75, 393
cosmopolitanism 359–360
costs, power studies 292–293
costs of marketing 2–3, 7
country-of-origin (COO), postcolonial theory 55
Cova, B. 28–29
Cowie, J. 311
Cox, Reavis 310–311
creativity: arts marketing 142–143, 146–147; metaphors 245
credibility, market intelligence/knowledge 164–165; *see also* authenticity; legitimation
credit cards: lifestyle research 180–181
credit cards, lifestyle research 180–181
Critical Discourse Analysis (CDA) 126
critical macromarketing 99–100
Critical Marketing Studies 1; choice 212–215; consumer sovereignty 205–215; consumers and markets 24–26; definition 3; exploring 17–22; international marketing 320; marketing

as exchange 211–212; marketing concepts 196–205, 216–219; non-Western cultures 324; practices 22–24, 27–31; violence 488–489
critical performativity 13–17
critical social marketing: contemporary context 86–91; emergence 85–86; future directions 91–93
critical sociology 161–162
critical studies of marketing work 155–156; classical sources of inspiration 157–162; critical interpretation 157; critical sociology 161–162; critical theory 159–160; Foucauldian theory 160–161; future directions 167–169; market intelligence and knowledge 164–165; marketing organizations 165–167; marketing work meaning 156–157; Marxist theory 157–159; plans and strategies 163–164; products 162–167; seller-buyer relationship 163
critical theory 159–160, 168; ideology 307–308; market intelligence/knowledge 164
Crockett, D. 26
Crossley, N. 394
cultivated growth **261**
cultural alienation 477, **478**
cultural appropriation 127–128
cultural capital: arts marketing 139, 140, 143, 144; place marketing 122; social class 139
cultural codes 59, 140, 144, 274
cultural context: advertising 185–186, 188, 191–192; arts marketing 137, 143–144; brand management 405–407; critical performativity 14–15; globalization 109–110; ideology 309; international marketing 323; media and selfies 71–73; modernity 39–40, 43; place marketing 121–122; postcolonial theory 55; *see also* consumer culture; customer lifestyle research; non-Western cultures
Cultural Studies, brand management 407–408
cultural turn 64, 172–175
culture industries 201–202, 204
customer as king/queen 206, 213; *see also* consumer sovereignty
customer community 433–436
customer orientation: historical context 198, 199–201, 204–205; marketing organizations 166; service-dominant logic 231
customer relationship management (CRM) 246–247, 299
customers: 'making customers' 9–10; place marketing 116; *see also* consumption
cyborgs 70–71

Dahl, R. 287, 291, 292–293
dance metaphor 249
dark marketing 215–216
data: biopolitical marketing 218; stories 369–370; *see also* big data

de Beauvoir, Simone 67
de Certeau, M. 294, 295, 302
Dean, Jodi 432
Debord, Guy 406
decommodification 258–259
defatalization 15, 488
degrowth agenda 259, **261**, 261–262
dehumanization, and violence 492–493
Deleuze, G. 138
democratization 108–109
demographics, lifestyle research 172–3
denaturalization 488–489
Denegri-Knott, J. 24, 287, 298, 299, 300, 301
depoliticization 104, 108–109
deterritorialization 138
developmental macromarketing 98, 99–100, 108
Dholakia, Nik 17–18, 24–26, 348
Dholakia, Ruby Roy 25–26, 348
digital alienation 477–479, **478**
digital labor 449
digital technology *see* technology
discourse analysis 126–127
discursive constructionism 385
discursive power model 297–301, *299*
dispositives 301
dissatisfaction in marketing 209
distributive justice 12
divine violence 486
division of labor: capitalism 470–471; digital labor 476; gender 415; postcolonial theory 51; service-dominant logic 229, 236; Smith, Adam 3
Dixon, D. F. 3
domestic labor 419
domesticated capital 180
dominant social paradigm (DSP): globalization 111, 112; macromarketing 21, 98–99, 100, 102, 104–105
Dove soap campaign 190–191, 192
Downey, Hilary 370–371
downshifting 259–260
Drucker, Peter 156, 198–199
drugs addiction 214–215
DuBois, W. E. B. 358
Dunnett, Susan 26
Durkheim, Emile 273, 356

Eagleton, T. 307, 308
Eckhardt, G. M. 24–25, 313, 315
ecological degradation, religious critiques of the market 279–280; *see also* sustainability
ecological footprint 106
economic alienation 477, **478**
economic context: arts vs. markets debate 135, 140–142; globalization 108; macromarketing 102; religious critiques of the market 279–280; *see also* international political economy
Edison, S. 240

education, gender in marketing 423–425
elitism, place marketing 122–123
emancipation 439, 441–442, 450; consumers 443, 448–449; escape 445–446; production and consumption 442–443; resistance 443–445
embodiment 26, 383–384; agency of bodies 393–395; the body 385–386; body project 391–393; Bourdieu, Pierre 384, 388–389, 392, 393; consumer research 389–395; future directions 395; Merleau-Ponty, Maurice 384, 386–387, 394; representation 389–391
emerging markets (EMs) 330
emotional labor 27–28, 420–425
emotions, consumer vulnerability 376–377
empathy, services marketing 418
empowerment: biopolitical marketing 430, 435–436; consumer sovereignty 340–341; consumer vulnerability 366–367, 373; feminism 20, 66–68, 69–70; lifestyle research **177**; non-Western cultures 328; place marketing 129; service-dominant logic 302; sovereign power model 291, 292; subalternity 59–60
energy use, social marketing 91
Enlightenment: critical theory 159; historical context 53; ideology 313
enterprising self, feminism 73–75
entertainment, arts marketing 139
entrepreneurialism: arts marketing 141–142; place marketing 120, 124
environmentalism 105–106; *see also* sustainability
epistemological reflexivity 11–13
epistemologies of the south 330–331
ethical consumption 24, 256–257, 266–267; embeddedness within consumer culture 259–262; lexicons 262–263; mainstreaming and co-optation 258–259; methodological traditions 265–266; power studies 296; responsibilizing the consumer 257, 263–265
ethical consumption gap 257, 264–265, 266
ethics: action research 374; critical social marketing 85, 93; exploitation 439–440
ethnocentrism, social marketing 90
ethnoconsumerism 325–326
ethnography: advertising 190–191, 192; lifestyle research 180; place marketing 128; poetry 371; seller-buyer relationship 163
Eurocentrism, postcolonial theory 49, 50–52
Ewen, S. 9–10, 162
exchange: ethical consumption 258; hegemonic power model 295–296; marketing as 211–212; role performance 249; service-dominant logic 226–227; social exchange theory 246, 248
exit options 339
experience economy 408–409
experiential consumption 384

exploitation 439, 450; alienation 440–441; consumers 446–449; Marxist social theory 439–440

Facebook: advertising 190–191, 472–473; big data 467; communicative capitalism 433; digital labor 475–476; feminism 72; self-branding 410–411
Fair Trade: ethical consumption 258–259, 262; international political economy 458, 459
false consciousness 308
Fanon, F. 49, 54, 55
fashion: dissatisfaction 209; embodiment 392; lifestyle research 179–180
female hormones, and choice 217
feminine in management 424
feminine turn in marketing 417, 419–420; *see also* gender in marketing
feminism 19–20, 64, 78; consumer sovereignty 211–212; first wave 66–67; fourth wave 69–70; future research 70–71; home and quantified life 75–78; meaning of 64–65; media 67, 71–73; second wave 67–68; selfie culture 71–73; technologized body and enterprising self 73–75; third wave 68–69; Veblen, Thorstein 8
fertility-regulated desire 217
field, embodiment 388, 389
films, visual culture 376–377
financial systems: globalization 107; historical context 10
first wave feminism 66–67
Fisher, Eran 477
Fisk, George M. 320
Fiske, John 407–408
flexible accumulation 122–123, 124
food consumption, power studies 301
forcefields, marketing as 204
Forest Stewardship Council (FSC) 459, 460
Foucauldian theory: critical studies of marketing work 160–161; market intelligence/knowledge 164
Foucault, Michael: biopolitics 431; discursive power model 297, 299, 301; postcolonial theory 50–51
Fougère, M. 29
fourth wave feminism 69–70
fragmentation, lifestyle research 179
framing effect, service-dominant logic 232–234
Frankfurt School: arts marketing 138, 140; brand management 404–405; critical social marketing 85–86; critical theory 159–160, 168; ideology 307–308; power studies 294, 297; resistance 443
Frazier, E. Franklin 362
freedom: and choice 339–340; exploitation 440–441; globalization 110; from the marketplace 29; neoliberalism 344–345; *see also* choice

freeganism 180
French Theory 160–161
Freud, Sigmund 483–485, 486
Friedman, Milton 339
Fromm, E. 110, 202, 203, 204
Fuat Fırat. A 17–18, 25–26; lifestyle research 179; marketplace dynamics 212; postmodernism 41
Fuchs, Christian 30

Gandhi, L. 52
Gandhi, Mahatma 348
Gassenheimer, J. B. 211, 212
gender: bodies 73–75, 390–391, 393; critical social marketing 88; feminism 65; lifestyle research 180; marketing organizations 167
gender identity: feminism 68, 70; virtual reality 71–72
gender in marketing 27–28, 415–417; emotional labor 420–425; higher education 423–425; services 417–420
geographical context 115–116, 125; *see also* place marketing
geopolitics of knowledge 329–331
German Historical School: epistemological reflexivity 11–13; international marketing 320; positivism 13
Gibson, Katherine 46
Giordano, A. 27
Giovanardi, M. 21
global brands, non-Western cultures 327
Global Commodity Chains (GCC) 456, 462
global footprint 106
Global North: ethical consumption 262; postcolonial theory 49, 50–60
global palm oil market 459–463
Global Production Networks (GPN) 456–457, 462
Global Reporting Initiative (GRI) 459
Global South: postcolonial theory 49, 50–60; theories of south 330–331; *see also* non-Western cultures
Global Value Chains (GVC) 456, 458–459, 462
globalization: cultural context 109–110; definition 107; dominant social paradigm 111, 112; economic context 108; international marketing 322–323; macromarketing 98–99, 105–108, 111–112; non-Western cultures 327–331; political context 108–109; power studies 296; technological context 110–111; transnational commodity markets 455–463
Gold, Jaime case 482, *483*, 487, 490
Goldberg, Marvin 85–86
Golden Rule 7
good life 260
Goods-Dominant (G-D) logic 228–230, 234, 236–238

Google: big data 467, 469; digital labor 475–476
Gordon, Ross 20–21, 85–86
Gould, S. 370
Goulding, C. 327
government: consumer sovereignty 208–209; globalization 107; macromarketing 102; power studies 292–293; social marketing 87
government intervention: consumer sovereignty 208–209; religious critiques of the market 277–278
governmentality: co-creation 448; social marketing 91
Graham, Julie 46
Gramsci, Antonio: Global Production Networks 456–457; ideology 307, 308; power studies 294, 295, 297; subalternity 58
greening, and sustainability 105–106
Greenpeace 462–463
groupie identity 146–147
Guattari, F. 138
guilt fetishism 258

Habermas, Jurgen: colonization of the life world 405; ideology 308
habitual behavior 214
habitus: critical social marketing 91; embodiment 388–389; lifestyle research 173, 175
Hackley, C. 22–23, 156
Hall, Stuart 407
Hamilton, Kathy 26
happiness industry, biopolitics 431
Haraway, D. 70–71, 73, 75, 77–78
Harvey, David 120, 122–123, 124
Haugaard, M. 288
Hayek, F. 230, 340
health: consumer sovereignty 213–215; consumer vulnerability 376; critical social marketing 85; political context 108–109
health insurance 338
hedonism: ethical consumption 260; religious critiques of the market 274
hegemonic commodity markets 456–457
hegemonic power model 293–297, *299*
hermeneutic of suspicion 157
Herodotus 4
high cultural consumers (HCC) 178, 181
higher education, gender in marketing 423–425
Hill, R. P. 492–493
historical context 1–3; Bellamy, Edward 4–7; brand management 404–407; conflict 11; customer orientation 198, 199–201, 204–205; epistemological reflexivity 11–13; feminism 66–70; international marketing 320–323; lifestyle research 172–173; modernity 37–41, 53; place marketing 116–117; postmodernism 37; power studies 299–300; profit orientation

199–201; racial stigma in consumer culture 354–355; Roman and medieval reflections 3–4; social marketing 20–21, 83–85; subalternity 58–59; Veblen, Thorstein 8–10
HIV/AIDS film 376
Hobbes, Thomas 290, 483–485
Hochschild, A. R. 27, 163, 420, 421, 422–423
Hofstede, G. 323
Holt, D. B. 174, 175–178, 179
home: feminism and the quantified life 75–78; social marketing 91
Homo sacer 485–487
Horkheimer, M.: advertising 202, 204; arts marketing 138; critical theory 159, 160; ideology 308
Houston, F. S. 211, 212
human dignity, religious critiques of the market 280–281
human trafficking 215–216
humanism 7
Hunt, S. 228, 230, 232, 233, 240
Hutt, William: consumer sovereignty 206, 207; government intervention 208; habitual behavior 214
hybridity, postcolonial theory 56–58
hypermodernity **42**

identity: aggressiveness 484–485; arts marketing 145–146, 147; body project 391–392; brand management 407–408, 409; lifestyle research 173, 179–180, 181; organizational 118; *see also* gender identity
ideology 24–25, 306–309; brand management 404–405; Californian ideology 435; choice 344–348, **347**; and marketing 310–316; marketing as a blunt instrument of 314; marketing as bereft of 310–312; marketing as innately ideological 312–314
ill-being, religious critiques of the market 278–279
image marketing 116
image of the marketplace 19
immigration *see* migrants
in situ research 22, 155, 157
India, global brands 327
individualism, macromarketing 101
Indonesia, global palm oil market 459–463
inequalities: algorithm-generated discrimination 213; consumer sovereignty 208–209; racial stigma in consumer culture 355–356
influencers, consumer sovereignty 210–211
information *see* market intelligence/knowledge
innovation: consumer-driven 28–29; market driving 200; place marketing 128–129
Instagram 73, 410–411
institutions: advertising 188–189; consumer sovereignty 208–209; corporate social responsibility 257, 263–264; critical studies of marketing work 169; customer orientation 199–201; lifestyle research **177**, 180–181, 182; marketing concept 198–199; organizational identity 118; power studies 292
intangible values 410
intelligence *see* market intelligence/knowledge
intentional arc 387
international commodity markets 455–463
international marketing 25, 320–323; *see also* non-Western cultures
international political economy 29, 453–454, 463–464; global palm oil market 459–463; studies of certification markets and standards 457–459; transnational commodity markets 455–457
Internet, biopolitical marketing 431–433; *see also* social media
interpersonal/marriage metaphor 245–247, 248–249
intersectionality 68, 69
intertextuality 191–192
interviews: critical studies of marketing work 155; racial stigma in consumer culture study 356–363
Islam, religious critiques of the market 274, 275, 276

Jafari, A. 24, 274, 326–327
Jhally, Sut 470–473
Jones, C. 488, 491
Jones, Edward David 324
Judaism, religious critiques of the market 276, 279–280

Kant, Immanuel 140
Kärreman, D. 165, 166
Kavaratzis, M. 21
Kearns, G. 120, 122
Keith, R. J. 198–200, 201, 207, 209
Kelley, Eugene 20, 84, 85
Kerrigan, F. 22, 137, 143–144
Kiel, D. 236, 239
Kilbourne, W. 21, 100, 105–106
Kinley, David 11, 12–13
knowledge *see* geopolitics of knowledge; market intelligence/knowledge
knowledge-discovery process 230
Korczynski, M. 340–341
Koster, S. 420, 424
Kotler, Philip: critical social marketing 84–85; ideology 311–312; place marketing 116, 117; service-dominant logic 232, 233; social marketing 87
Kravets, O. 19–20
Kubacki, K. 136–137
Kuhn, T. S. 226, 227–228, 230, 239
Kuran, T. 277

labelling: ethical consumption 262; international political economy 457–458; power studies 301
Laclau, E. 457
land: commodification 460–461; international political economy 455–456
language: ethical consumption lexicons 262–263; metaphor 245–249; place marketing research 126–127; service-dominant logic 228–231, 234, 235–236; violence 489–490
Larsen, G. 22, 136–137
late modernity **42**
Lazer, William 20, 84, 85, 173
Leathwood, C. 424–425
Lefebvre, Henri 294, 295
legitimation: globalization 109; lifestyle research **176–177**, 179–180, 182; marketing in society 196, 199–205; service-dominant logic 232–233; *see also* authenticity; credibility
Leidner, R. 163
leisure class 7, 8
Levitt, T.: international marketing 322–323; marriage metaphor 245, 246; sales and marketing 2
Levy, S.: critical social marketing 84; ideology 311–312; place marketing 116; service-dominant logic 232–233; social marketing 87
Lewin, K. 372–373
Lichrou, M. 21
Lien, M. E. 164
lifestyle research 22; cultural turn 172, 174–175; history of 172–173; institutions **177**, 180–181, 182; legitimation 182; legitimation and transformation **176–177**, 179–180; research context **177**, 181–182; symbolic boundaries 175–179, **176**, 181
Lights in Darkest England (LIDE) 83–84
liquid modernity **42**
List of Values (LOV) 173
Litman, Simon 320
lived body 386
living standards, critical perspectives 202–203
Locke, J. 101–102
'lock-in' 214
low cultural consumers (LCC) 178, 181
Lukács, Georg 404–405, 470
Lukes, Stephen 296–297
Lusch, R. F.: foundational premises 226, 228–231; framing effect 232–234; historical narrative 226–228; logic or rhetoric 235–236; O'Shaughnessy affair 234–235; revisions and extensions 236–239; service-dominant logic 23, 225–226

McDonalds: advertising 472; non-Western cultures 327; power studies 293
Maclaran, P. 19–20
McRobbie, Angela 407

macromarketing 21; critical 99–100; critical social marketing 91–92; cultural context 109–110; definition 99; dominant social paradigm 98–99, 100, 102, 104–105; economic context 102, 108; Pareto Optimality 104–105; political context 100–102, 108–109; sustainability and globalization 98–99, 105–108, 111–112; technological context 102–104, 110–111
mainstream marketing studies 1, 197
majority principle 202
'making customers' 9–10
Malaysia, global palm oil market 459–463
managerial marketing 98
managerial research 15, 185–187, 190
managerialism 415, 419, 424
Marcuse, Herbert: critical theory 160; ideology 308; production and consumption 442; technology 103–104
Marine Stewardship Council (MSC) 458–459
market driving 200
market intelligence/knowledge: critical studies 164–165; service-dominant logic 230, 240
market shaping 200
marketing: Bellamy, Edward 4–7; conflict 11; critical performativity 13–17; epistemological reflexivity 11–13; historical context 1–3; ideologies 310–316; non-Western context 325–326; perception of 2; positivism 13; Roman and medieval reflections 3–4; Veblen, Thorstein 8–10
Marketing as a Social and Economic Process era 227
marketing as art 141
marketing concepts, Critical Marketing Studies 23, 196–205, 216–219; *see also* religious critiques of the market
marketing control 198–199
marketing education 2
marketing management: biopolitical marketing 430; power studies 291; relationship marketing 243, 244, 246, 250; service-dominant logic 227
marketing organizations, critical studies 165–167
marketing professionals: consumer sovereignty 205, 209; exploitation 28; marketing concept 199; marketing work meaning 156–157; power of 209; seller-buyer relationship 163
marketing revolution 200
marketing theory, political context 196–197, 216–218
marketing work 156–157; *see also* critical studies of marketing work
markets: alternative markets 144–146; vs. arts debate 135, 140–142; consumer sovereignty 210–211; Critical Marketing Studies 24–26
marriage metaphor 245–247, 248–249
Martin, K. D. 492–493

Marxism: brand management 404; critical studies of marketing work 157–159; digital alienation 477; digital labor 473–476; emancipation 441, 442; ethical consumption 262; exploitation 439–440, 446–447; hegemonic power model 294; ideology 307; religious critiques of the market 273; social media 468–470; superstructural forces 202; transnational commodity markets 457
masculine values in marketing 419–420; *see also* gender in marketing
masculinist new managerialism 424
mass media *see* media
materialism, religious critiques of the market 278
media: advertising 187, 189–191; biopolitical marketing 431–433; critical performativity 14–15; feminism 67, 71–73; representation 390–391; visual culture 375–377; *see also* social media
Medicare 338
medieval perspectives 3–4
medium theory 405–406
Merleau-Ponty, Maurice 384, 386–387, 394
metamodernism **42**
metaphor: gender in marketing 416–417; relationship marketing 244–249
methodologies: action research 372–375, 378; arts marketing 146–147; critical studies of marketing work 167–168; ethical consumption 265–266; place marketing research 126–127; stories 369–372, 378; visual culture 375–377, 378
middle class: Other and Otherness 487; racial stigma in consumer culture 354–355, 357–358, 361, 362
migrants, lifestyle research 175–178
Mikes, Chris 23
military metaphor 416
mind-body distinction 384, 386–387, 415–416
mindfulness, emotional labor 421
modernity 17–18; binaries **39**; conditions of 41; consumption 42–43; cultural context 39–40, 43; domains **40–41**; historical context 38–41; postcolonial theory 53–56; and postmodernism 43–44
Moeran, B. 163, 164, 167
monetary capital, Marxist theory 158–159
Moniruzzaman, M. 215–216
Moor, L. 87
morality: choice 339–340; religious critiques of the market 280–281
more-than-representational methods 147
Morgan, A. E. 8–9
motivations: capitalism 205; power studies 292–293
Mouffe, C. 457
multistakeholder initiatives (MSIs) 459, 462
Mumby, D. M. 162, 166

Murray, J. B. 205
museums, critical performativity 14–15
music subcultures 145–146
mythic violence 486

narrative *see* stories
nation branding 119
national identity 484–485
nationalist ideology 309
natural body 385
necrocapitalism 56, 314, 315
Neoclassical economics era 227
neo-colonialism, anti-consumption 56
neo-Gramscian approaches 456–457, 459, 462
neoliberalism: choice 344–345, 346; critical social marketing 86–87, 88, 92; ethical consumption 263, 264, 267; ideology 311, 312–314; place marketing 120–121, 122–123; postcolonial theory 56; religious critiques of the market 281; subalternity 59–60
neo-Marxism, ethical consumption 262
Nestlé 462
Neurath, Otto 13, 14–15
new emerging logic 236; *see also* service-dominant logic
new managerialism 415, 419, 424
NGOs 459, 462–463
Nike, criticisms of 16–17
Nippert-Eng, C. 362
nonprofit organizations, place marketing 116
non-representational methods 147
non-Western cultures 319; culture, markets and marketing 323–325; international marketing 320–323; potential of critical marketing 329–331; re-thinking consumption and marketing 325–329
Normann, R. 230

O'Donohoe, S. 369–370
Oliveira, R. de 30–31
O'Malley, L. 23–24
one-dimensional encounters 163
ontological denaturalization 197
O'Reilly, D. T. 136–137, 143–144, 145
organizational identity 118; *see also* marketing organizations
organizations *see* institutions
organs trade 215–216
O'Shaughnessy, John 234–235
O'Shaughnessy, Nicholas 234–235
Otago Forums 238
Other/Otherness 482–483, 485–486, 487
outcome matrix, relationship marketing 245–246
over-interpretations 168
ovulatory effect 217
ownership, emancipation 441–442
Ozanne, J. L. 205

Pace, S. 28–29
Packard, Vance 162
Palm Oil Innovation Group (POIG) 462–463
palm oil market 459–463
paradigm shifts 226–227, 234
Pareto Optimality 104–105
participation, social marketing 87, 89–90, 92
participatory media, biopolitical marketing 431–433; *see also* social media
patriarchy 65
Patterson, Maurice 26
perception of marketing: criticisms 16–17; historical context 2; image of the marketplace 19
performativity, critical 13–17
periphery-core relations 455–456, 461
personality traits: lifestyle research 173; services marketing 418–419
perverts 216–218
petit bourgeoisie, racial stigma 354–355
pharmaceutical industry: choice 340; price fixing 200
Philo, C. 120, 122
Piacentini, Maria 26
Pillsbury 198, 199–200
place marketing 21, 115–116; conventional marketing perspectives 117–119; critiques 119–128; future directions 128–129; historical development 116–117
place-product 117–118
planning, place marketing 115
plans (marketing), critical studies 163–164
plateau of indifference 490, 491, 494, 496
Plato 3, 4, 6
Plummer, J. T. 173
poetry, consumer vulnerability 370–372
Polanyi, K.: religious critiques of the market 273, 274; sharing economy 313; transnational commodity markets 455, 460
political alienation 477, **478**
political context: arts marketing 145; choice 346–348, **347**; globalization 108–109; macromarketing 100–102; marketing theory 196–197, 216–218; power studies 292–293; social marketing 87
political economy: marketing research 453–454; social media 468, 480; *see also* international political economy
political theory, power studies 288
positivism, historical context 12–13
possessive individualism 101
postcolonial theory 18–19, 49–50, 52–53, 60; ambivalence and hybridity 56–58; Eurocentrism 49, 50–52; modernity 53–56; non-Western cultures 330; subalternity 58–60
post-Marxism, exploitation 447–448
postmodernism 17–18, 21, 37–38; consumer sovereignty 213; Cultural Studies 408; escape 445; exploitation 447–448; fragmentation 44;

and modernity 43–44; overview 41–44; research context 45–46
poststructuralism: the body 385; feminism 68–69; lifestyle research 174
post-truth 37
Potter, J. 165
poverty: religious critiques of the market 276–277; subalternity 59–60; visual culture 375–377
power relations: biopolitical marketing 217–218; consumer sovereignty 211–212; critical perspectives 197; critical social marketing 88, 89–90; emotional labor 420–421; Foucauldian theory 160–161; freedom 29; marketing organizations 167; profit orientation 201; silent power 168; social marketing 87
power studies 24, 287–288, 301–302; discursive power model 297–301, *299*; hegemonic power model 293–297, *299*; new research directions 292–301; reading the map 288, *289*; sovereign power model 290–293, *299*
practice theory 90–91
Prakash, G. 51, 53–54
price, brand management 409–410
price fixing 199–200
private property, macromarketing 101–102
production: advertising 164, 188–190; arts marketing 144–145; emancipation 442–443; ethical consumption 256–257; ethical consumption lexicons 262–263
productive capital, Marxism 158–159
products of marketing, critical studies 162–167
profit orientation: historical context 199–201; religious critiques of the market 277–278
Prus, R. C. 163
psychology, reactance theory 341
public services, place marketing 120–121
Puchta, C. 165
pursuit of profit 201

quantified life, feminism 75–78

racial context: advertising example 190–191; consumer sovereignty 213; ideology 309; postcolonial theory 54–55; skin-bleaching 75
racial stigma in consumer culture 353–354; Black consumption 355–356; Black middle class 354; boundary transcendence/transition 356, 360–362; boundary work 356, 358–363; from petit bourgeoisie to middle class 354–355; research study 356–363
Rainforest Action Network (RAN) 462–463
Ramirez, R. 230
rationality, and technology 103–104
reactance theory 341
Reconstruction, USA 354
reflexivity: anti-consumption 444–445; critical social marketing 89; epistemological 11–13

regional marketing 115; *see also* place marketing
relationship marketing 23–24, 243–244, 249–250; customer relationship management 246–247, 299; future directions 248–249; gender 418; interpersonal/marriage metaphor 245–247, 248–249; metaphor 244–249; *see also* seller-buyer relationship
reliability, assurance, tangibles, empathy and responsiveness (RATER) 418
religious critiques of the market 271–275; future directions 281; human dignity 280–281; ill-being 278–279; poverty and social injustice 276–277; social solidarity 275–276; state intervention 277–278; sustainability and ecological degradation 279–280
representation: arts marketing 147; bodies 389–391; self-branding 410–411; Social Representations Theory 375–377; technologized body 73–75
research context: advertising 185–192; arts marketing 140–148; brand management 411–412; choice 346–348; consumer vulnerability 367–369, 377–378; critical studies of marketing work 157, 167–169; embodiment 389–395; feminism 66–67; international marketing 320–323; lifestyle research 22, **177**, 181–182; postmodernism 45–46; power studies 287–288, 292–302; relationship marketing 248–249; religious critiques of the market 271–275, 281; in situ 22, 155, 157; social media 473–476, 479–480; violence 491; *see also* historical context
research into market *see* market intelligence/knowledge
resistance: brand management 407–408, 409; emancipation 443–445
Resource-Advantage (R-A) theory 232
responsibility: lifestyle research 180–181; responsibilizing the consumer 257, 263–265; *see also* ethical consumption
rhetoric: ethical consumption 261–262; service-dominant logic 228–231, 234, 235–236
Ricoeur, P. 157, 488
Rokeach Values Survey (RVS) 173, 174–175
role performance 248–249
rolezinhos 487
Roman perspectives 3–4
Rook, Dennis 384
Rorty, James 201
Roundtable for Sustainable Palm Oil (RSPO) 462–463

sales: distinction from marketing 2; marketing work 156; seller-buyer relationship 163
sameness, place marketing 125
Sandıkcı, Ö. 25, 275
Sassen, Saskia 56
Saudi Arabia, feminist selfie campaign 72

savoir 45
scandal effect 17
Schor, Juliet 340, 343–344
Schroeder, J. 287
science, and technology 103
second wave feminism 67–68
self-branding 403, 410–411, 412
selfie culture, feminism 71–73
self-objectification 73
seller-buyer relationship: critical studies of marketing work 163; relationship marketing 246–250
semiotics: advertising 186, 188–189; brand management 405–407
Sen, Amartya 110
sensor-based technology 76
service marketing: emotional labor 420–425; and gender 417–420
service quality measurement tool (SERVQUAL) 58, 418
service-dominant logic 23, 225–226, 239–240; foundational premises 226, 228–231; framing effect 232–234; historical narrative 226–228; logic or rhetoric 235–236; O'Shaughnessy affair 234–235; power studies 292, 298, 300–301; revisions and extensions 236–239
SERVQUAL scale 58, 418
sex trade 215–216
Shankar, A. 12–13
sharing economy 313–314
Shibley, Fred 10
silent power 168
Skålén, P. 28–29, 156, 166
skin-bleaching 75
slavery 440
slavery abolition 83–84
Sloterdijk, P. 308
Smith, Adam: consumer sovereignty 206; division of labor 3; macromarketing 102; service-dominant logic 230
Smith, T. M. 106
Smythe, Dallas 468–469
social capital: arts marketing 139; consumer culture 487; embodiment 389; gender 422; lifestyle research 175, 180; social marketing 91
social class: consumer sovereignty 212–213; consumer vulnerability 369; gender 421–422; hegemonic power model 294–295; leisure class 7, 8; lifestyle research 172–173, 175–178; Other and Otherness 487; racial stigma in consumer culture 354–355, 357–358, 361, 362
social context, place marketing 122–123
social exchange theory 246, 248
social justice, religious critiques of the market 276–277
social marketing 20–21; critical 85–93; definition 84; historical context 83–85; place marketing 116; United Kingdom 87

social media 480; advertising 189, 190–191, 472–473; big data 30, 467–468, 469, 473, 479–480; biopolitical marketing 431–433; brand management 403, 410–411, 412; current areas of research 473–476; digital alienation 477–479, **478**; exploitation and emancipation 449; feminism 69–70; future directions 479–480; gender identity 72; selfie campaigns 72–73; theoretical approaches 468–473; un-marketing 434–435
social practice theory 90–91
Social Representations Theory (SRT) 375–377
social solidarity 180, 273, 275–276
social theory: exploitation 439–440; ideology 307; power studies 288
socialism, historical context 4–5, 10
socially constructed body 385
soft skills 417–418
Soper, Kate 259–260
sovereign power model 290–293, *299*
sovereignty *see* consumer sovereignty
spectacularization 18
standards of living, critical perspectives 202–203
Starbucks, non-Western cultures 327
state *see* government; government intervention
status-oriented consumption 26
stay-at-home fathers study 180
stereotypes, postcolonial theory 55; *see also* racial stigma in consumer culture
Stevens, L. 27–28
Stiegler, Bernard 45
stigma 353; *see also* racial stigma in consumer culture
Stone, T. 370
stories: consumer vulnerability 369–372, 378; place marketing research 127
strategies, critical studies of marketing work 163–164
stress, emotional labor 421
structural adjustment programs 56
structuring of consumption 26, 174
style of life 175; *see also* lifestyle research
subalternity 58–60
subculture 145–146
subjective violence 490, 491
Süerdem, A. 274, 275
suffragette movement 66
superstructural forces 202
sustainability: definition 105; ethical consumption 256, 259–262, **261**; global palm oil market 460; macromarketing 98–99, 105–108, 111–112; religious critiques of the market 279–280; transnational commodity markets 455
Svensson, P. 22, 164–165
symbolic boundaries, lifestyle research 175–179, **176**, 181

symbolic capital: arts marketing 139; embodiment 389, 392; gender 73, 422; lifestyle research 173, 175
symbolic violence 488, 489–490
symbolism, advertising 187–188
systemic violence 488, 489
systems theory, service-dominant logic 239

Tadajewski, M.: German Historical School 12, 13; marketing theory 2, 23; power studies 296, 298, 299, 301
Target data collection 218
tattooing 393
Taylor, Frederick 10
Taylor, Henry Charles 324
teaching, emotional labor 423–425
technologized body, feminism 73–75
technology: advertising 190–191; arts marketing 146; biopolitical marketing 430–431, 431–433; brand management 403; branding 410–411; exploitation and emancipation 449; feminist research 70–71; globalization 110–111; home and quantified life 76–78; macromarketing 102–104; power studies 301; *see also* social media
Tesco data collection 218
theories of south 330–331
Thévenot, L. 448–449
third wave feminism 68–69
Third World, postcolonial theory 52–60
Thompson, C. J. 174–175, 180, 324–325
time-space compression, place marketing 124
Tosdal, Harry 1, 209
totalitarian ideology 314
tourism destinations, place marketing 117
Toynbee, P. 419
traditions, lifestyle research 174
Transformative Consumer Research (TCR) 372–374, 377
transmission theory of communication 186–188
transnational commodity markets 455–463
transnational spaces 108
Troester, M. 174–175
Trump presidency, postmodernism 37, 45
trustworthiness *see* authenticity; credibility; legitimation
Turkey: feminist selfie campaign 72–73; non-Western cultures 326–327
Turley, D. 369–370

Unilever 462
United Kingdom, social marketing 87
United States: health insurance 338; international marketing 321–322; racial stigma in consumer culture 354–355, 356–363
universal marketing rhetoric 225, 229, 239; *see also* service-dominant logic

un-marketing 434–435
urban violence 490
User Generated Content (UGC) 189
Üstüner, T. 178
utilitarianism 493

value propositions 231
values: biopolitical marketing 436; brand management 404; commodities 468–469; intangible 410; lifestyle research 173, 174; power studies 300–301; service-dominant logic 231, 237
values and lifestyle systems (VALS) 173, 174
Vargo, S. L.: foundational premises 226, 228–231; framing effect 232–234; historical narrative 226–228; logic or rhetoric 235–236; O'Shaughnessy affair 234–235; revisions and extensions 236–239; service-dominant logic 23, 225–226
Varman, R. 18–19, 24–25
Veblen, Thorstein: capitalism 4; historical context 8–10; legitimation 201; marketplace dynamics 212
vegetarianism 7
Venkatesh, A.: ethnoconsumerism 325–326; lifestyle research 179; modernity 17–18; postmodernism 17–18, 41
vested interests 208
videography 377
Vienna Circle 13
violence 482–483, 494–496; Balibar and Žižek 488–490; Benjamin, Walter 486–488; bioviolence 30–31, 215–216; capitalism 30, 489, 491–492; dehumanization and marketing 492–493; from Hobbes to Freud 483–485; ideology 314; marketing research 491–492; modernity 53–56; Other and Otherness 482–483, 485–486; postcolonial theory 51
virtual communism 432
virtual reality, gender identity 71–72
Visconti, L. 371–372
visual culture, consumer vulnerability 375–377, 378; *see also* image marketing

voluntary simplicity 259–260
Voogd, H. 116, 117
vulnerability *see* bereavement; consumer vulnerability

Wacquant, L. 388, 490, 492
wages, digital labor 474–475
Wallerstein, I. 330
Warhol, Andy 141
wealth: consumer sovereignty 208; religious critiques of the market 276–277
Weber, Max: boundary work 356; lifestyle research 175; religious critiques of the market 272–273, 274
Weinberg, Tamar 434, 435
welfare: historical context 4–5; place marketing 120–121
well-being: consumer sovereignty 213–215; religious critiques of the market 278–279
wellness, biopolitics 431
Wells, D. W. 173
Western world *see* Eurocentrism; Global North
White, L. 110
White, Percival 1–2, 10
Whorfian hypothesis 106
Wiebe, G. D. 84
Williams, J. 237
Williams, Raymond: critical sociology 161–162; ideology 308; social media 470–473
Williamson, Judith 186
within-domain similarity 245, 246
women's movement 67–68; *see also* feminism
working consumer thesis 28–29
world systems theory 456
World Trade Organization (WTO) 456–457
World War II: international marketing 321; non-Western cultures 324

YouTube: big data 469; digital labor 476

Zaltman, G. 84–85
Žižek, S. 314, 485, 486, 488–490
Zwick, D. 28, 217, 287